HALF THE HUMAN EXPERIENCE

HALF THE HUMAN EXPERIENCE

THE PSYCHOLOGY OF WOMEN

THIRD EDITION

Janet Shibley Hyde   ◆
Denison University

D. C. Heath and Company

Lexington, Massachusetts

Toronto

To three important role models in my life:
my mother, Dorothy Reavy Shibley
and Professors Celeste McCullough and Marion Diamond

ACKNOWLEDGMENTS

Page 2   From Dorothy L. Sayers "The Human Not-Quite Human" in *Unpopular Opinions* (Victor Gollancz, 1946), p. 116.

Page 39   From Daniel Goleman "Jason and Medea's Love Story." Reprinted from *Psychology Today Magazine* Copyright © 1976, American Psychological Association, p. 84.

Page 44   From Sigmund Freud "Some Psychichal Consequences of the Anatomical Distinction Between the Sexes" in *Collected Papers of Sigmund Freud*, Vol. 5, ed. by Ernest Jones, M.D. Copyright 1959 by Basic Books, Inc., Publishers. Also in *The Standard Edition of the Complete Works of Sigmund Freud*, translated by James Strachey, Vol. 19 (Hogarth Press Ltd.), p. 252. Copyright Sigmund Freud Copyrights Ltd. The Institute of Psycho-Analysis. Reprinted by permission of the publishers.

Page 49   Abridged from R. Moulton, "A Survey and Re-evaluation of the Concept of Penis Envy." Contemporary Psychoanalysis, 7 (1970): 84–104. Used with permission.

Page 73   From *In a Different Voice* by Carol Gilligan. (Cambridge, Mass.: Harvard University Press, 1982). Reprinted by permission.

Page 90   From *A Room of One's Own* by Virginia Woolf (1929), p. 108. Reprinted by permission of Harcourt Brace Jovanovich, Inc., The Hogarth Press, and The Literary Estate of Virginia Woolf.

Page 106   Reprinted with permission of Macmillan Publishing Company from *Social Psychology* by Roger Brown. Copyright © 1965 by The Free Press.

Page 154   From *Our Bodies, Ourselves*. Copyright © 1971, 1973, 1976 by the Boston Women's Health Book Collective, Inc. Reprinted by permission of Simon & Schuster, Inc.

Page 204   From "Fail: Bright Women" by Matina Horner. Reprinted from *Psychology Today Magazine* Copyright © 1969 American Psychological Association.

Page 246   From *Our Bodies, Ourselves*. Copyright © 1971, 1973, 1976 by the Boston Women's Health Book Collective, Inc. Reprinted by permission of Simon & Schuster, Inc.

Page 252   Reprinted by permission of G. P. Putnam's Sons from *No More Menstrual Cramps and Other Good News* by Penny Wise Budoff, M. D. Copyright © 1980 by Penny Wise Budoff, M. D.

Page 274   From *The Female Orgasm* by Seymour Fisher. Copyright © 1973 by Basic Books, Inc.

Page 291   Excerpt from Barbara Hariton, "The Sexual Fantasies of Women." *Psychology Today* (March 1973), vol. 6, pp. 39–44. Reprinted by permission of Barbara Hariton, Private Practice, Jericho, L. I., N.Y. 11753.

Page 300   From *The Second Sex* by Simone de Beauvoir, translated and edited by H. M. Parshley, Alfred A. Knopf, 1952.

Page 320   Excerpt from *Women and Madness* by Phyllis Chesler. Copyright © 1972 by Phyllis Chesler. Reprinted by permission of Doubleday & Company, Inc.

Page 350   From Deena Metzger "It Is Always the Woman Who Is Raped" in *The Rape Victim* ed. by D. R. Nass (Kendall/Hunt Publishing, 1977) p. 6.

Page 380   From *In Love and Trouble* by Alice Walker (New York: Harcourt Brace Jovanovich, 1973), p. 48. Reprinted by permission.

Page 394   Nikki Giovanni. Last two lines of the first stanza and the last two lines of the third stanza of "My House (26 feb 72)" from *My House* by Nikki Giovanni. Copyright © 1972 by Nikki Giovanni. By permission of William Morrow & Company.

Page 402   From John Stuart Mill, "The Subjection of Women" (1869), reprinted in *Three Essays by J. S. Mill* (Oxford University Press, 1912).

Preface

My basic goal in preparing a third edition of *Half the Human Experience* is to provide a text on the psychology of women for undergraduates who have little or no background in psychology — perhaps only an introductory course. Although the book is designed as a core text for psychology of women courses, it may also serve appropriately as one of several texts in a women's studies course or as a supplementary text in a variety of psychology courses.

Three characteristics of this book — its readability, comprehensiveness, and scholarship — were well received in previous editions, and I have worked to retain and improve these. I have come to believe that the readability of texts is a feminist principle. Feminists, as one of their goals, have attempted to demystify science, and as part of that effort we must demystify psychology, including the psychology of women. My goal therefore has been to provide a text with solid and up-to-date scholarship, clearly explained so that students can readily understand it. As a psychologist, a scientist, and a feminist, I also believe it is important to foster students' critical-thinking skills. Accordingly, I introduce feminist critiques of traditional research methods in psychology in Chapter 1 and then carry through this critical perspective in succeeding chapters. As in the previous editions, the feminist perspective is presented and clearly labeled so that readers can decide for themselves whether they find that perspective persuasive.

There are some major additions in this revision, including a wholly new chapter on the psychology of men. Depending on the instructor's approach, this chapter may be introduced at several different points in the course. I have placed it early in the text as Chapter 5, following the chapter on androgyny. This sequence will work well for those who approach the course as a psychology of gender and who want to introduce men's issues early. The chapter as it now stands previews many of the topics that will be covered in more detail in the succeeding chapters on women. For those whose perspective is more explicitly focused on women, this chapter might be used at the end of the course where it will serve to recapitulate many themes presented earlier.

Other major changes include some additions to already existing chapters. Chapter 3, Theoretical Perspectives, has been expanded to include sociobiology and the feminist critique of it, Chodorow's neo-analytic theory, Bem's gender schema theory, Gilligan's critique and reformulation of moral development theory, and the feminist theoretical perspective. Chapter 7, the lifespan chapter, has been expanded to include more recent work on women's major adult roles as worker, mother, wife, and housewife. Chapter 14 on problems of adjustment and psychotherapy now contains a major section on the eating disorders of anorexia and bulimia, including a personal history of an anorexic. Chapter 15, formerly on violence against women, was changed to a chapter on victimization; and sexual harassment and incest were added as major topics. In the last chapter I have added a section titled "Paradigms, Science, and Feminism," in which I explain Kuhn's concept of paradigm in science and then argue that feminism represents a new paradigm in the science of psychology.

I have added a new appendix, Psychology of Women Resource Directory, listing names and addresses of some important organizations related to issues in the psychology of women. I hope that these will be useful to readers. Throughout, I have made many minor revisions and updates — too numerous to mention.

I realized, in preparing this new edition, that I was intensively revising it exactly ten years after I did the intensive research and writing on the first edition. Psychology of women as an academic field has changed a great deal in those ten years. As an author, I found that I faced different problems in 1983 from those I faced in 1973. Ten years ago the problem was that the field was too new and the research was therefore too thin. Often I would come to a major point that needed to be addressed and find little data, perhaps not even a single study. In 1983, the problem was the opposite: there is almost too much research — not that there can ever be too much research, but rather that there is more than can possibly be included in a single undergraduate text. Our field of psychology of women is filling the pages of two major journals — *Psychology of Women Quarterly* and *Sex Roles* — at astounding rates, and other major psychology journals regularly include articles on the psychology of women. This abundance of research is a marvelous state for our field to be in, but it also means that I had to pick and choose and could not include all studies.

To compensate for all of the additions, I needed to make some deletions. The chapter on cross-cultural perspectives on gender roles was deleted, partly because I see that women's studies outside psychology has grown and differentiated enormously in the last ten years. In most colleges and universities, there are now many women's studies courses, and many of you are doubtless on campuses where there is a sociology or anthropology course that covers the cross-cultural perspective in great detail; therefore, this topic now seemed less appropriate for inclusion in a current text on the psychology of women.

Many reviewers made valuable contributions with their critical comments on the manuscript. Special, heartfelt thanks go to L. Anne Peplau and Michele Wittig for carefully reviewing the entire manuscript. Reviewers of individual chapters also provided great help and deserve thanks: Joseph Pleck, Annette Brodsky, and Marjorie Whittaker Leidig. Of course, many positive contributions remain in this edition from reviewers of previous editions, and I continue to extend my gratitude to them.

Finally, a special bouquet of thanks goes to the Psychology Editor at D. C. Heath, Nancy Osman. She treated this book as one who loves the topic. She has a profound understanding, better than many psychologists, of the value of encouragement (positive reinforcement) in keeping an author going through the demanding process of revising a text. Her contributions have shaped and improved this text.

I owe thanks to many people at Denison University for their help and support: Kathy Russell of the Philosophy Department for consultations on paradigms and the history of science; Ann Fitzgerald, Director of Women's Studies, who had the vision to create Women's Studies at Denison over ten years ago and rode herd cheerfully over a headstrong group of faculty; President Bob Good and Provost Lou Brakeman, for their enthusiastic support of and appreciation for Women's Studies; Roger Blaine, Reference Librarian, who never seems to tire of filling my interlibrary loan requests for obscure articles. And I owe thanks to the students over the years in the senior seminar on Psychology of Women: their insights have found their way into this book in many places.

My hope is that this book will help all of us — students and professors (who are really just long-term students) — gain a deeper, richer, more growth-promoting understanding of the psychology of women.

Janet Shibley Hyde

Contents

5
Psychology of Men   105

6
Gender Differences in Personality
and Behavior   137

7
From Infancy to Old Age:
Development Across the Lifespan   153

8
Abilities, Achievement, and Motivation   185

9
Women and Language   211

1
Introduction

> *The first thing that strikes the careless observer is that women*
> *are unlike men. They are "the opposite sex" — (though why*
> *"opposite" I do not know; what is the "neighboring sex"?).*
> *But the fundamental thing is that women are more like men*
> *than anything else in the world.*
>
> DOROTHY SAYERS, Unpopular Opinions

Yesterday my daughter Margaret, age four and a half (the half is very important to her), was telling me about the games she had been playing at her preschool. She played with her boy friend, Dimitrios. He says he's going to marry her when they grow up. They played "Superfriends." She told me that Dimitrios chose a character he wanted to be, such as Superman, and then she played the female counterpart, Supergirl. Or they played "Dukes of Hazzard," and she was Daisy. I had to sit down for a minute while processing the significance of all she was saying. She hasn't even started kindergarten yet, and her femaleness and its requirements are so clear to her. She understands that the male chooses what he wants to be and then she follows, picking up the female counterpart role. She has learned that he is Super*man* while she is Super*girl*. I tried to talk her out of it. I said if he is Superman, she could be Super*woman*. She said there is no Superwoman. I asked her why Dimitrios always got to choose what they played. Why couldn't she pick Wonderwoman and he could be Wonderman? or Wonderboy? She said it couldn't be played that way. I asked why. She said it just couldn't. After a while I gave up (partly for theoretical reasons that will be discussed in Chapter 4). But the point of the story is that gender, and specifically femaleness, are important qualities in our society. Even preschoolers understand the social significance of these attributes. Margaret and her friends have already learned (and believe me, I didn't tell her all this) that males choose and lead and females follow. They understand heterosexuality and marriage as important parts of their role requirements.

This book is about being female, what it means in our society, what it means biologically, and how all of this is incorporated into the behavior, thoughts, and feelings of girls and women.

SEX, GENDER, AND SEXISM

Before proceeding, some terms need to be defined. First, it is worth noting that in our language the term "sex" is sometimes used ambiguously. That is, sometimes it is used to refer to sexual behaviors such as sexual intercourse, while other times it is used to refer to males and females. Usually, of course, the meaning is clear from the context. For example, if an employment application says "Sex: ——," you don't write "As often as possible." It is clear here that the question is about whether you are a female or a male. On the other hand, what is the topic of a book entitled *Sex and Temperament in Three Primitive Societies?* Is it about female roles and male roles in those societies, or is it about the sexual behavior of primitive people?

To reduce this ambiguity, I am going to use the term "sex" to refer to sexual behaviors and the term "gender" to refer to males and females (Hyde, 1979). "Gender differences," then, refers to differences between females and males. Other scholars have adopted other conventions in this regard. For example, some scholars prefer to use the term "sex differences" to refer to innate or biologically produced differences between females and males, and "gender differences" to refer to male-female differences that result from learning and the social roles of females and males (e.g., Unger, 1979). The problem with this terminology is that studies often document a female-male difference without providing any evidence as to what causes it — biology, society, or both. Therefore, I am simply going to use the term "gender differences" for male-female psychological differences, and leave their causation as a separate question.

Sexism is another term that will be relevant to some of the discussions in this book. Sexism can be defined as discrimination or bias against people based on their gender. Some people use the term "reverse sexism" for discrimination against males, although it would seem preferable to use the term "sexism" for discrimination against either females or males on the basis of their gender. (Actually, using my terminology, the term should probably be "genderism," but it will not be used because sexism and sex bias are the standard terms.) Here we will be concerned with sexism as

FIGURE 1.1

DOONESBURY   by Garry Trudeau

Source: Copyright, 1974 G. B. Trudeau/Distributed by Universal Press Syndicate.

discrimination against women. Some people feel uncomfortable using the term "sexism," because they think of it as a nasty label to hurl at someone or something. Actually, however, it is a good, legitimate term that describes a particular phenomenon, namely discrimination on the basis of gender, particularly discrimination against women. It will be used in that spirit in this book, not as a form of name-calling. Finally, it is important to recognize that not only men, but women as well, can be sexist.

One final term that needs to be defined in this context is *feminist*. A feminist is a person who favors political, economic, and social equality of women and men, and therefore favors the legal and social changes that will be necessary to achieve that equality. Feminists generally consider this term preferable to others such as "women's libber" or "libber," which are often used in a derogatory manner.

Let us turn now to the topic at hand.

IS THERE A PSYCHOLOGY OF WOMEN?

Depending on the inflection, the above question has different meanings, and therefore requires different answers. Is there a *psychology* of women? Thus emphasized, the question refers to whether a psychological approach to understanding women, as compared with, say, a political or economic one, is valuable. I will leave this question unanswered for the present, but I hope to demonstrate in the course of this book that the psychological approach is both interesting and important, and that attempts to remedy women's political status, by themselves, may leave a host of psychological ills still present and in need of attention.

Is there a psychology of women? The second variation of inflection raises the issue of whether the psychology of women actually exists, whether it is a legitimate area of specialization within the field of psychology. Does the area contain sufficient content, research, and theory to be considered a subdiscipline of psychology? Or is it just a fad, another kind of "pop psych" (as some of my colleagues have suggested) that will produce a few paperbacks and then be forgotten, a field with which no "respectable" psychologist would want to be associated?

In fact, the psychology of women has quite respectable ancestry in a traditional field of psychology known as *differential psychology*. That people differ, one from another, in their behavior has probably been obvious ever since humans have been capable of self-awareness. For the last century these individual differences in behavior have been the subject of scientific study. One particular dimension of individual differences is the differences between males and females, and these have received their due — perhaps more than their due — attention, both in research and in theories. Developmental theorists, from Freud to the modern role theorists, have given considerable attention to the observed gender differences in behavior. Generally their theories have had the problem (to which we will return later) of viewing the male as normative and the female as a deviation from this norm.

In the last 15 years, the psychology of women has emerged as a distinct area, which already has to its credit the discovery of some phenomena — androgyny, menstrual-cycle changes in mood, and, largely through the research of Masters and Johnson, a better understanding of female sexuality. There is no doubt, then, that there *is* a psychology of women, with a long history of theory and research and with a current life of new and important discoveries. Recognizing this, there is a division of the American Psychological Association on the psychology of women.

Finally: is there a psychology of *women?* This inflection raises the question of whether women have a special psychology different from that of men. Certainly there are abundant stereotypes implying that women differ psychologically from men — they are reputed to be less rational and logical, and to have different attitudes toward and motivations for sex. Psychological research indicates that some of these stereotypes have a basis in reality, and that some simply do not. It is this research — showing when men and women differ psychologically and when they don't, and what this tells us about women's psychology — that is the topic of this book.

There is a paradox inherent in trying to understand the psychology of women, a paradox that is captured in the quote at the beginning of this chapter. Women are at once different from men and very similar to men. While gender differences are important in defining women's psychology, gender similarities are also important. Both scientific and nonscientific views of women have concentrated on how they differ from men; I hope to pay attention to the similarities. This paradoxical tension between gender differences and gender similarities will be a continuing theme throughout the book.

WHY STUDY THE PSYCHOLOGY OF WOMEN?

Most textbooks include an introductory section on why people should study that particular topic; the idea is, presumably, to motivate people to continue with the course and with reading the book. Such a section does not seem quite so necessary in a book on the psychology of women. The main reason for studying it is obvious: it is interesting. Many women, for example, take such a course because they want to understand themselves better, a goal they may feel was not met by their other psychology courses. Men may take such a course wanting to understand women better. Therefore, many good personal reasons exist for wanting to study the psychology of women.

There are also some good academic reasons for studying the psychology of women. Many of the traditional psychological theories have literally been theories about man. They have treated women, at best, as a variation from the norm. Perhaps the best example is psychoanalytic theory, to be discussed in Chapter 3. Similarly, a sex bias has existed in many aspects of psychological research, a point to be discussed later in this chapter. As a result, traditional psychology has often been about men, and it has often operated from very traditional assumptions about gender roles. One way of correcting these biases is by developing a psychology of women. Psychology of women thus provides information about a group that has often been overlooked in research and theory, and it opens up new perspectives on gender roles and ways they might be changed.

Finally, one other reason for studying the psychology of women is that the female experience differs *qualitatively* from the male experience in some ways. Only women experience menstruation, pregnancy, childbirth, and breastfeeding. In addition to these biologically produced experiences, there are culturally produced uniquenesses to women's experience

FIGURE 1.2

Dustin Hoffman was looking for a script that would let him explore the questions "What makes someone a man?" and "What makes someone a woman?" and he found it in *Tootsie.*

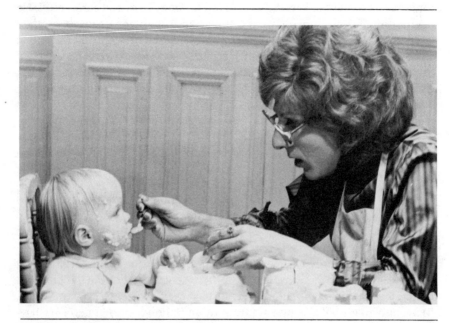

Source: Copyright © 1982, Columbia Pictures Industries, Inc. Photograph courtesy, Museum of Modern Art Film Stills Archive.

produced by the gender roles in our culture. For example, walking down the street and being whistled at is an experience nearly unique to women in our culture. One of the points of the feminist movement, and particularly of consciousness-raising groups, is that women need to communicate more with each other about these female experiences. It is therefore worthwhile to have a course that provides information on these topics, and that also gives people a chance to express their feelings about their experiences. Such communication should help women cope better with the female experience, or change the aspects of it that need to be changed.

SHOULD MEN STUDY THE PSYCHOLOGY OF WOMEN?

Some men express a hesitancy about studying the psychology of women, as if somehow the secrets of women's psychology should be known only to women or women's psychology were unimportant. Yet it would seem to be of the utmost interest, not to mention practical value, to be able to understand one's spouse, girl friend, boss, or co-worker better. It is a rare male who never interacts with females, and certainly there is value in having a better understanding of such a large part of humanity.

In addition, research suggests that some of the phenomena discovered in women's psychology may also, in this time of social change, be in the process of becoming common for men. For example, in 1946, the sociologist Mirra Komarovsky documented the stresses of conflicting role expectations for college women — academic competence and career orientation are expected, yet these are in conflict with traditional femininity, which is also expected. More recently, Komarovsky (1973) documented the appearance of a similar phenomenon for college men, who now seem to be caught in a conflict between the norms of intellectual superiority for men versus intellectual equality of women and men. With the current upheaval in gender roles, the psychology of women has much to say about the psychology of men. Recognizing this, Chapter 5 in this book is on the psychology of men.

SOURCES OF SEXIST BIAS IN PSYCHOLOGICAL RESEARCH

Although research in psychology of women is really in its infancy, it is progressing at a rapid pace. Certainly I will be able to provide you with much important information about the psychology of women in this book, but there are still more questions yet to be answered than have been already answered. With research on psychology of women expanding so rapidly, many important discoveries will be made in the next 10 or 20 years. Therefore, someone who takes a course on the psychology of women should do more than just learn what is currently known about women. It is probably even more profitable to gain some skills so as to become a "sophisticated consumer" of psychological research. That is, it is very important that you be able to read intelligently and to evaluate future studies of women that you may find in newspapers, magazines, or scholarly journals. To do this, you need to develop at least three skills: (1) know how psychologists go about doing research; (2) be aware of ways in which sexist bias may affect research; and (3) be aware of problems that may exist in research on gender roles or psychology of women. The following discussion is designed to help you develop these skills.

How psychologists do research   Figure 1.3 is a diagram of the process that psychologists go through in doing research, shown in rectangles. The diagram also shows some of the points at which bias may enter (to be discussed in more detail below), shown in circles.

(4)   The process, in brief, is generally this: the scientist starts with some theoretical model, whether a formal model such as psychoanalytic theory, or merely a set of personal assumptions. Based on the model or assumptions, the scientist then formulates a question. The purpose of the research is to answer that question. Next, she or he designs the research, which involves several substeps: a behavior must be chosen; a way to measure the behavior must be devised; a group of appropriate subjects must be chosen; and a research design must be developed. One of these substeps — finding a way to *measure* the behavior — is probably the most fundamental aspect of psychological research. Two interesting examples of measuring behavior relevant to psychology of women are the tests to measure androgyny (to be discussed further in Chapter 4) and the motive to avoid success (to be discussed further in Chapter 8).

The next step is for the scientist to collect the data. The data are then analyzed statistically and the results are interpreted. Next, the scientist publishes the results, which are read by other scientists and incorporated into the body of scientific knowledge (and also are put into textbooks). Finally, the system comes full circle, because the results are fed into the theoretical models that other scientists will use in formulating new research.

Now let us consider some of the ways in which sexist bias — bias that may affect our understanding of the psychology of women or of gender roles — may enter into this process (Grady, 1981).

Biased theoretical model   The theoretical model or set of assumptions the scientist begins with has a profound effect on the outcome of the research. Sexist bias may enter if the scientist begins with a biased theoretical model. Perhaps the best example of a biased theoretical model is psychoanalytic theory as formulated by Freud. A person with a psycho-

FIGURE 1.3

The process of psychological research (rectangles), and ways in which sexist bias may enter (circles).

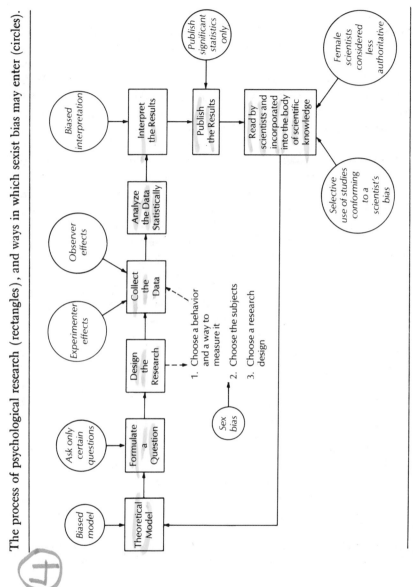

analytic orientation might design research to document the presence of penis envy, or masochism, or immature superego in women; someone with a different theoretical orientation wouldn't even think to ask such questions. It is very important for you to become sensitive to the theoretical orientation of a scientist reporting a piece of research — and sometimes the theoretical orientation isn't stated, it just has to be inferred — because that orientation affects the rest of the research and the conclusions that are drawn.

What questions are asked   The questions a scientist asks are shaped not only by a theoretical model but also by gender-role stereotypes. Bias may enter when only certain questions are asked and others ignored, partly as a result of stereotypes. For example, there are many studies of fluctuations in women's moods over monthly cycles. However, until quite recently no one has thought to ask whether men also might experience monthly mood fluctuations. Reading the research, one might get the impression that women are moody and men are not; but the research appears to indicate this only because no one has investigated men's mood shifts. Stereotypes about women and men have thus influenced the kinds of questions that have been investigated scientifically.

Sexist bias in choice of subjects   There is good evidence that bias exists in choosing subjects for psychological research. In particular, males are used more frequently as subjects than females are. Not only is this true in research with humans (Carlson, 1971a; Dan and Beekman, 1972) but it is also true in research with animals. In a survey of studies of animal behavior, we found that 62 percent of the studies used one gender only, and of those, 75 percent used males only (Hyde and Rosenberg, 1976). Therefore, nearly half of all studies were based on male subjects only.

In research with humans, some entire areas of research have been conducted using male subjects only. A good example is the classic research on achievement motivation, which was based on males only (McClelland et al., 1953).

It seems likely that the choice of subjects is influenced in part by the kind of behavior the psychologist is studying, as well as by gender-role stereotypes. For example, in social psychologists' research on aggression — a "masculine" behavior — nearly 50 percent of the studies were done using male subjects only as compared with about 10 percent using females only and 40 percent using both genders. This 50 percent is higher than the percentage of male-only research in psychology in general (McKenna and Kessler, 1977). Therefore, it seems that when psychologists study a stereotyped "masculine" behavior — aggression — they are not likely to include female subjects.

The problem with this kind of bias is that it leads us to have not a psychology of human behavior, but rather a psychology of male behavior.

Experimenter effects   In the step of research in which the data are collected, two important kinds of bias may enter: experimenter effects and observer effects.

Experimenter effects occur when some characteristic of the experimenter affects the way subjects behave, and thus affects the outcome of the experiment (Rosenthal, 1966). In particular, it has been demonstrated that the gender of the experimenter may affect subjects' behavior. For example, in sex research, subjects report more sexual feelings to an experimenter of the same gender than to one of the opposite gender (Walters et al., 1962). The evidence indicates that with children, female experimenters get better performance, while with adult subjects, male experimenters get better performance (Rumenik et al., 1977; see also Harris, 1971).

It is rather disturbing to realize that an experiment might have different outcomes, depending on whether the experimenter was a man or a woman. Moreover, since the majority of psychological research, at least until recently, has been conducted by men, it seems possible that the results might have been quite different had it been conducted by women.

Incidentally, the problem of sexist bias from experimenter effects is not an unsolvable one. The situation can be handled by having several experimenters — half of them female, half of them male — collect the data. This should balance out any effects due to the gender of the experimenter, and demonstrate whether the gender of the experimenter did have an effect on the subjects' behavior. Unfortunately this procedure is seldom used, mostly because it is rather inconvenient.

Observer effects   Another important bias that may enter at the stage of data collection is observer effects.

Observer effects occur when the experimenter's expectations for the outcome of the research influence his or her observations and recording of the data. For example, in one study observers (really the subjects) were to count the number of turning movements by planaria (flatworms); half of the observers had been led to expect a great deal of turning, the other half very little. The observers who expected a great deal of turning reported twice as many turns as the observers who expected little (Cordaro and Ison, 1963). To paraphrase Flip Wilson, what you expect is what you get.

Observer effects may be a source of bias in gender role research and psychology of women research. In particular, scientists are no more immune than lay people are to having stereotyped expectations for the behavior of females and males. These stereotyped expectations might lead scientists to find stereotyped gender differences in behavior where there are none. As an example, consider research on gender differences in aggression of nursery school children. If observers expect more aggression from boys, that may be just what they get, even though the boys and girls behaved identically. This is analogous to the observers who expected more turns from the planaria and found just that.

The technical procedure that is generally used to guard against observer effects is the "double-blind." It simply means that observers are kept unaware of (blind to) which experimental group subjects are in, so that the observers' expectations cannot affect the outcome. Unfortunately, the double-blind method is virtually impossible in gender differences research, as the gender of a subject is almost always obvious from appearance, and therefore the observer cannot be "blind" to it or unaware of it.

One exception is infants and small children, whose gender is notoriously difficult to determine, at least when clothed. This fact was used in a clever study that provides some information on whether observer effects do influence gender roles research. Adults rated the behavior of 17-month-old children on videotape (Meyer and Sobieszek, 1972). For a given child, half the observers were told it was a male, and half were told it was a female. Although the results were not conclusive, there was some suggestion that observers rated the behavior of a child differently depending on what gender they thought the child was.

Unfortunately, there are no other studies available documenting whether observer effects influence the outcomes of gender-role research. It remains to be demonstrated, for example, whether trained scientists would have the same bias as the adults in the study described above. Therefore we cannot make any firm statements about how much of a problem observer effects are. At the very least, though, we should be aware of them, and certainly they deserve further research.

Bias in interpretations   Once the scientist has collected the data and analyzed them statistically, the results must be interpreted. Often the interpretation a scientist makes is at best a large leap of faith away from the results. Therefore this is also a stage at which bias may enter.

As an example, let us consider a fairly well-documented phenomenon of psychological gender differences. A class of students takes its first exam in Introductory Psychology. Immediately after taking the exam, but before getting the results back, the students are asked to estimate how many points (out of a possible 100 points) they got on the exam. On the average, males will estimate that they got higher scores than females will estimate they got (see Chapter 8). At this point, the data have been collected and analyzed statistically. It can be stated (neutrally) that there are statistically significant gender differences, with men estimating more points than women. The next question is, how do we interpret that result? The standard interpretation is that it indicates that women lack self-confidence or have low confidence in their abilities. The interpretation that is not made, although it is just as logical, is that men have unrealistically high expectations for their own performance.

The point is that, given a statistically significant gender difference, it can often be interpreted in two opposite ways, one of which is favorable to men, one of which is favorable to women. Sometimes there is no way of verifying which interpretation is right. As it happens in the example above, there is a way, since we can find out how the students actually did on the exam. Those results indicate that women estimate their scores fairly accurately, while men make fairly large overestimates. Thus the second interpretation is probably more accurate than the first.

It is important to become sensitive to the point at which scientists go beyond their data to interpret them, and to become aware of when those interpretations may be biased. Other good examples of bias in interpretations are the research on gender differences in rod-and-frame test performance (to be discussed in Chapter 8) and gender differences in language (Chapter 9).

Publishing significant results only Once the data have been analyzed and interpreted, the next step is to publish the results. There is a tendency in psychological research to publish "significant" results only. This does not mean significant in the sense of "important" necessarily; it means significant in the sense of being the result of a statistical test that reaches the .05 level of significance.

What are the implications of this tendency for our understanding of gender roles and psychology of women? It means that there is a tendency to report statistically significant gender differences and to omit mention of nonsignificant gender differences. That is, we tend to hear about it when males and females differ, but we tend not to hear about it when males and females are the same. Thus there would be a bias toward emphasizing gender differences, and ignoring *gender similarities*.

This bias may also enter into psychology of women research such as menstrual cycle studies (a point to be discussed in detail in Chapter 11).

Other biases The final two biases shown in Figure 1.3 are fairly self-explanatory and require little discussion here. If there is a tendency for reports by female scientists to be considered less authoritative than reports by male scientists, this would introduce bias, particularly when combined with bias due to experimenter effects as discussed previously. Also, another kind of bias is introduced if scientists have a tendency to remember and use in their work studies that conform to their own biases or ideas, and to ignore those that do not.

Conclusion We have discussed a number of problems with research that may affect our understanding of women — and men. Of course, they probably are not present in every study in the area, and certainly I don't mean to suggest that all psychological research is worthless. The point is to become sensitive to biases that may — or may not — be present when one is reading reports of research. It is particularly important for you to become sensitive to the theoretical orientation of a writer and to biased interpretations of results.

Feminist alternatives   All of the preceding criticisms are important and you should be aware of them, but we need to go beyond those criticisms to offer some constructive alternatives. In doing so, we can think about *gender-fair research* and *feminist research*.

Gender-fair research is research that is not guilty of any of the biases discussed in the previous sections (Grady, 1981). Some characteristics of gender-fair research are as follows: (1) Single-gender research is never or almost never done. Even in situations where a single-gender design might seem to be justified — for example, examining women's fluctuations in mood over the menstrual cycle — the demand for gender-fairness and inclusion of the other gender might lead to better understandings — for example, a discovery of fluctuations in men's moods. (2) Theoretical models, underlying assumptions, and the kinds of questions asked should always be examined for gender-fairness. For example, the minute someone proposes to do research on the effects of mothers' depression on their children, it should be asked whether fathers' depression also has an effect on children. Otherwise, we assume that only mothers influence children and that fathers have no influence, which is fair to neither mothers nor fathers. (3) Both male and female researchers should collect data in order to avoid experimenter effects. (4) Interpretations of data should always be examined carefully for gender-fairness, and possibly several interpretations should be offered. For example, if there is a significant gender difference in the number of points students estimate they will get on an exam, two interpretations should be offered: that women underestimate and lack self-confidence, and that men overestimate and have unrealistic expectations for their performance. In a sense, then, gender-fair research proposes that we continue to play the research game by the same set of rules it has always had — tight controls, careful interpretations, and so on — but that we improve things so that the rules are observed fairly.

Feminist researchers might argue that we need to go even further in reforming psychological research. There really is no comprehensive, definitive statement of the principles of feminist research, but some people have articulated thoughts in that direction (e.g., Carlson, 1972; Wallston, 1981; Parlee, 1981; Wittig, 1983, 1984) and I will present some of those ideas here. Feminist researchers might argue that the classic form of psychological research — the tightly controlled laboratory experiment — needs to be revised. It is manipulative, intended to determine how manipulations of the independent variable cause changes in the dependent variable. It objectifies and dehumanizes the people it studies, calling them "subjects." It emphasizes differentiation, taking people out of their natural environments in order to control all of those things the experimenter considers irrelevant. In all these senses — the manipulativeness, the objectification, the differentiation — traditional psychological experimentation might be accused of being masculine or patriarchal. The feminist alternatives are several: (1) Do not manipulate people, but rather observe them in their natural environment and try to determine how they experience their natural lives and worlds, thus emphasizing relatedness rather than differentiation. (2) Do not call the people who are studied "subjects," but rather "participants." (3) Do not think in simple terms of variable A causing effects on variable B, but rather in terms of complex, interactive relationships in which A and B mutually influence each other. Again, relatedness is emphasized. (4) Devote specific research attention to the special concerns of women. (5) Do not assume that scientific research and political activism are contradictory activities (Wittig, 1984). Good research — by documenting current conditions — can facilitate social change. And the psychologist who has political activism and social change as goals can still do good research; such researchers are obligated to articulate their values, but that is a good rule for all scientists. All of these principles open up new vistas for researchers and you to think about.

Personally, I think that we ought to integrate and respect both approaches, gender-fair and feminist. The traditional psychological experiment needs reform, but I would hate to throw it out entirely. It functions best when combined with naturalistic research looking at complex mutual influences. Gender-fair research and feminist research might diverge on some issues, though. For example, feminist researchers would value investigation of battered wives as an issue of special concern to women. Gender-fair researchers would point out that there are some battered husbands and that they should be researched as well. Feminist researchers might reply that there are far more battered wives than battered husbands and that feminist research need not necessarily concern itself with battered husbands. I cannot easily resolve this issue, and so I encourage you to think about it yourself.

LOOKING AHEAD

In the next chapter we shall consider the antecedents to the psychology of women by looking at the images of women in mythology and religion — at the "pre-scientific" view of women. These images are an expression both of reality and of the superstitions regarding women among primitive, less "civilized" people. They are also a source of many of the stereotypes and unquestioned assumptions held about women in this "scientific" age. In Chapter 3 we shall look at the contributions to the understanding of female development by some of the major theoretical systems of psychology — psychoanalytic theory, social learning theory, and cognitive-developmental theory. A controversial new theory, sociobiology, is examined, as is another interesting new theory, gender schema theory.

Following these theoretical views, later chapters will focus on research about what women are actually like psychologically. Chapter 4 is about the traditional personality characteristics called femininity and masculinity, and a more contemporary concept, androgyny. Chapter 5 examines the "new research" on the psychology of men, done from a feminist perspective. Chapter 6 reviews evidence on gender differences in personality to see the ways in which women and men differ and the ways in which they are similar. In Chapter 7 we shall discuss female experiences, adjustment, and roles across the lifespan, from birth to old age. We discuss women and achievement in Chapter 8, by considering research on gender differences in intellectual abilities, research on achievement in women, and several psychological factors (achievement motivation, motive to avoid success, and attribution patterns) that may contribute to women's success or lack of it. Chapter 9 is about women and language — whether there are gender differences in language use, how the structure of the English language treats women, and how women and men communicate nonverbally.

Chapters 10 to 13 are about women in relation to their bodies. Chapter 10 considers the evidence on whether there are biological influences — such as hormone effects — on gender differences and female behavior. Chapter 11 is about psychological research on several women's health issues — menstruation, menopause, pregnancy and childbirth, abortion, and mastectomy. Chapter 12 explores female sexuality, including Masters and Johnson's research on the physiology of female sexual response, research on the psychology of female sexuality, and sexual dysfunction and therapy for women. Chapter 13 is about lesbianism — a variation in female sexuality that has been prominent in the women's movement debate — and bisexuality. Chapter 14 considers various problems that may occur in female adjustment, what happens to women when they seek psychotherapy for their problems, and what new therapies are being developed for women. Chapter 15 is about the victimization of women as seen in rape, wife-battering, sexual harassment on the job, and incest.

An attempt is made in Chapter 16 to widen our perspective beyond the psychology of middle-class white women, by considering what is known about the psychology of black women. In the final chapter, I summarize some of the major themes of the book and suggest important questions for the future.

A number of important themes will recur throughout the book. One is *gender similarities*, the phenomenon that females and males are psychologically more similar than they are different. Another is the difference between *theory* and *empirical evidence*. Many theories of women's behavior have been proposed. Some have solid data (empirical evidence) backing them, while others do not. Not every theory is true, nor is every one a good description or explanation of behavior. Just because Freud said something does not make it true (or false). Readers need to become sensitive to the difference between statements based on theory and statements based on empirical evidence. Another important distinction is *traits* versus *situational determinants* of behavior. A continuing controversy in psychology is whether behavior is determined more by a person's enduring traits (such as a personality trait), or whether behavior is determined more by the particular situation the person is in. Advocates of the latter position point out how inconsistent people's behavior can be from one situation to another — for example, a man may be aggressive toward a business competitor, but passive or nurturant toward his wife. This suggests that his behavior is not determined by an enduring personality trait (aggressiveness), but rather by the particular situation he is in. Later in the book we will also refer to this issue as a distinction between intrapsychic or internal factors (traits) and external (situational) factors. Applied to the psychology of women, the question becomes whether women are more influenced by personality traits that distinguish them from men, or whether their behavior is more determined by the situations they find themselves in. For example, is the lack of professional accomplishments by women due to some trait such as the motive to avoid success (Chapter 8), or to situational factors such as job discrimination? This distinction also has practical implications. In trying to improve women's lives, if we decide that the problem is personality traits, then we would try to change the early experiences or childrearing practices that create those personality traits. If we decide, on the other hand, that situational factors are more important, we would want to change the situations women are in, such as ending job discrimination. Finally, one other important theme is the importance of *values* in a scientific understanding of women. Values affect the scientific theories that are proposed and the way research is done. In particular, they affect the way research is interpreted, a point discussed earlier in the chapter. Readers need to become sensitive to the values expressed by a particular scientific position.

PSYCHOLOGY'S FOREMOTHERS

One emphasis of the feminist movement has been recognizing and valuing the accomplishments of women. In part, that involves rediscovering some important contributions that women have made. Here is a short self-quiz about some important achievements by eminent psychologists. Take the quiz before turning to the answers on the next page.

Q1. Who did the research on black children that was critical in the United States Supreme Court decision to desegregate the nation's schools (*Brown v. Board of Education*)?

Q2. Who established that babies can swim?

Q3. Who conducted the famous social psychology study "The Robbers' Cave Experiment"?

Q4. Who authored the famous study "Albert and the White Rat"?

Q5. Who produced the widely used Stanford-Binet IQ Test?

Q6. Who developed the Cattell Infant Intelligence Test Scale?

Q7. What do the following books have in common: *The Growth of Logical Thinking of the Child*, *The Child's Conception of Space*, *The Child's Conception of Geometry*, and *The Early Growth of Logic in the Child*?

Q8. Who did the landmark research on the authoritarian personality?

Q9. Who wrote "Learning to Love," the classic report of research on the development of bonds of affection in monkeys?

FIGURE 1.4

Dr. Mamie Phipps Clark who, with her husband, Dr. Kenneth Clark, did the research on black children that was critical in the 1954 Supreme Court decision to desegregate the nation's schools.

Source: Courtesy Dr. Kenneth B. Clark.

Here are the answers to the questions on the previous page:

A1. Kenneth Clark and *Mamie Phipps Clark.*
A2. *Myrtle McGraw.*
A3. Muzafer Sherif, O. J. Harvey, W. E. Hood, and *Carolyn Sherif.*
A4. John B. Watson and *Rosalie Raynor.*
A5. Lewis Terman and *Maud Merrill.*
A6. *Psyche Cattell.*
A7. You are partially correct if you said that they were all authored by the famous male psychologist Jean Piaget; but they were all coauthored by his long-time female collaborator, *Barbel Inhelder.*
A8. *Else Frenkel-Brunswick.*
A9. Harry Harlow and *Margaret Harlow.*

Source: Nancy F. Russo and Agnes N. O'Connell. "Models from Our Past: Psychology's Foremothers." *Psychology of Women Quarterly,* 1980, 5, 11–54.

2

Images of Women in Mythology and Religion

*So the Lord God caused a deep sleep to fall upon the man,
and while he slept took one of his ribs and closed up its place
with flesh; and the rib which the Lord God had taken from
the man he made into a woman and brought her to the man.
Then the man said,*
> *"This at last is bone of my bones
> and flesh of my flesh;
> she shall be called Woman,
> because she was taken out of Man."*

GENESIS 2:21–23

Eve, the first woman, responsible for the fall of humanity; Pandora, the first woman in Greek mythology, who released all the evils besetting humanity when she opened the forbidden box; Ishtar, the Babylonian earth mother and fertility goddess, but also goddess of war and destruction; Marilyn Monroe, a myth in her own time — how have women been represented in mythology, and what insight does this give us into the psychology of women? What does this tell us about attitudes toward women, how men view women, and how women view themselves?

JUNG'S THEORY

It may seem strange to begin a scientific book by looking at mythology, which is hardly amenable to study in the laboratory, to evaluation on the basis of numbers of bar presses or correct answers to true-false questions. Yet, according to some psychologists, myths do represent an important source of information about human psychology, and particularly about its unconscious aspects.

The psychologist Carl Jung and his followers have argued most strongly for analyzing mythology, together with dream contents, for a better understanding of the unconscious; the unconscious, according to Jung, has an important influence on the total personality. According to this theory, the personality of any given individual has its roots in history. (For a brief review of Jung's theory of personality, see Hall and Lindzey, 1970.) The part of the psyche that contains these ancient memory traces is called the *collective unconscious*. It is a storehouse of memory traces inherited from all previous generations, and from animal ancestors as well — what Jung calls one's "racial" memory. Jung, of course, does not mean that these memories are inherited in the sense of being passed by genes and chromosomes, but rather that they represent universal inherited ten-

FIGURE 2.1

Adam and Eve by Albrecht Dürer (Germany, 1471–1528).

dencies for people to think and to perceive in certain ways. The collective unconscious contains these universal symbols and interpretations that are shared by all people, ancient and modern. These symbols appear both in dreams and in myths.

The collective unconscious contains numerous *archetypes,* which are universal "inherited" ideas containing a large emotional component. For example, there is a mother archetype, which is the image of what a mother is, formed through all the centuries of human interaction with mothers. Thus, an infant interacts with its mother not only on the basis of what the mother does, but also on the basis of the baby's archetype of mother, possessed at birth and shared with all other people.

Therefore, following Jung's theory, one must look at history and mythology for a better understanding of modern attitudes toward women. Current attitudes not only may result from interactions with women in the current social structure, but also may contain a component carried over from previous generations, according to Jung, in the collective unconscious. Thus, in looking at mythological views of women, we may actually be seeing our own unconscious views, free of the cover of rationalization.

Two important archetypes contained in the collective unconscious are particularly helpful in understanding the psychology of women. Like Freud, Jung recognized the inherent *androgyny* of all people — that any person, whether male or female, has both a masculine side and a feminine side. Jung used the term "anima" to refer to the feminine archetype in men, and "animus" to refer to the masculine archetype in women. Thus, the anima is a personification of the feminine psychological tendencies in a man, such as moods, hunches, receptiveness to the irrational, capacity for personal love, a feeling for nature, and a relation to the unconscious or spiritual (von Franz, 1964). The animus personifies the masculine psychological tendencies in a woman, including rationality, strong convictions, courage, and truthfulness. The anima, like the animus, may be either a positive or a negative force in the personality. For example, the negative part of a man's anima can be revealed in depressed moods, insecurity, unrealistic romanticism, or nasty, destructive remarks. The negative part of a woman's animus may be expressed as brutality, destructiveness, and a numbing of the emotions. But the anima and the animus, in their positive aspects, allow people to relate to and to understand members of the other gender. Thus, men understand women by virtue of their own feminine component, the anima, as women understand men through their animus.

A casual reading of Jungian views of psychology of women (for example, de Castillejo, 1973) may leave one with the feeling that his theory is very sexist in its orientation, with references to "feminine" tendencies, a woman with too strong a masculine component, or the need for women to get in touch with their own feminine natures. However, when referring to the "feminine principle," the Jungian analyst does not mean the feminine role as defined by a particular culture, but rather a principle or law that transcends any particular time, much like the law of gravity (Harding, 1971). The feminine principle represents the nonrational, the spiritual, and is the basis for human relationships. Further, the feminine principle is not possessed by women only, but is also part of men, although it is generally expressed more strongly in women. In addition, in the Jungian approach a differential valuing is not attached to the masculine as compared with the feminine — it is recognized that the masculine as well as the feminine can be either good or evil, and that both components must be in balance in a well-developed personality. Indeed, Jungian analysts contend that many of our contemporary problems, including the low status of women, may be attributed to the fact that ours is a masculine era, relying on science and rationality for solving problems, with a concomitant neglect of the feminine principle (Harding, 1971). Their suggestion is that we need to regain a sense of the feminine — of emotion, intuition, relatedness.

In summary, mythology can provide important information about psychology, in particular about the psychology of women. The importance of mythology is especially apparent from the theoretical perspectives of Jungian psychology, although scientific support for Jungian interpretations is lacking. Jung also provides some concepts useful in understanding the psychology of women, for example the anima and animus, which are the opposite-gender components in an individual's personality.

In the next chapter, we shall consider Freudian theory, a theory that is clearly male-centered. In evaluating Jung's theory, it is important to appreciate that, although Jung was a contemporary of Freud, his theory is not male-centered. One scholar contrasted Freud and Jung as follows:

> They served different gods, Freud's was sexual, Jung's mercurial — more nearly bisexual. They were imprinted by different archetypes, Freud by the Father, Jung by the Son of the Mother. Freud's way was patriarchal (based on reason, logic, and the attempt to master the unconscious), whereas Jung's way was matriarchal (open to the irrational and imaginal, he believed in letting the unconscious live and even submitting to it). (von Franz, 1975, cited in Hall, 1980)

Let us proceed now to see how women have been portrayed in mythology.

FEMININE EVIL

One of the clearest images of women in mythology is their portrayal as the source of evil (Hays, 1964). In the Judeo-Christian tradition, Eve disobeyed God's orders and ate from the fruit of the tree of knowledge. As a result, Adam and Eve were forced to leave the Garden of Eden and

Eve, the woman, became the source of original sin, responsible for the fall of humanity. In a more ancient myth, the Greek god Zeus created the lovely maiden Pandora to bring misery to earth in revenge for the theft of fire by Prometheus. Pandora was given a box or jar containing all the evils of the world, which she was told not to open. But Pandora opened the box, and thus all the evils it contained spread over the world. In Chinese mythology the two forces Yin and Yang correspond to feminine and masculine, and Yin, the feminine, is seen as the dark, or evil, side of nature. In the story of Cleopatra, which is on the borderline between mythology and history, the Egyptian queen is seen as destroying Mark Antony through the powers of her sexuality.

Historically, perhaps the most frightening manifestation of the belief in feminine evil was the persecution of witches beginning in the Middle Ages and persisting into Puritan America. Guided by the Church in a Papal Bull of 1484, the *Malleus Maleficarum*, the Inquisition tortured or put to death unknown numbers of witches. The objective fact appears to be that the vast majority of those accused and tried were women (Hays, 1964). Thus, it is woman who is seen as being in collaboration with the devil, visiting evil upon humans.

In major myths from diverse cultures, then, as well as in historical occurrences, women are seen as being evil, and further as being morally weak, unable to resist temptation, false, and deceitful. How can such a negative view of women be explained? One possibility is that these negative views are simply a result of male chauvinism. Men think women are inferior and express this in myth, or create such myths to "keep women down." However, there is also a psychological explanation: that socially organized attitudes toward women, such as those expressed in mythology, arise from basic tensions and anxieties experienced by men (Hays, 1964). That is, because men are in power in most societies, they will be the ones who shape the intellectual thought, including the myths. Men experience tension and anxiety that will be reflected in mythology. In particular, men experience tensions and anxiety about women, because women are unknown and mysterious — that is, they are different from men. The tendency to fear the strange or the unknown seems to be a strong human tendency (Hays, 1964; de Beauvoir, 1952). Hence, men construct myths in which women are portrayed as the source of evil because men feel anxiety and fears about women.

In yet another interpretation, the Jungian analyst might view myths of feminine evil as resulting not from actual experience with women, but rather from the man's own anima, the feminine principle in his own personality. Thus, the myths of feminine evil result from man's inner, subjective conflicts with his own feminine nature (Harding, 1971).

In summary, a frequent image of women in mythology is that they are the source of evil. It seems likely that this view is an expression of the anxieties men feel about women. This dynamic may also help to explain the other mythical images of women, which will be explored in the following sections.

FERTILITY GODDESS/EARTH MOTHER

The procreative functions of women have been celebrated in myth with the worship of fertility goddesses and earth mothers. In Palestinian and Egyptian mythology, Astarte — like her Babylonian version, Ishtar — is the queen of heaven, the mother of all, who gives the power of reproduction and fertility in the fields, to animals, and to humans. By extension, she also becomes the goddess of sexual love and desire. In Egyptian mythology, Isis is the great mother and fertility goddess; in Greek mythology Aphrodite and Cybele are worshiped for their fertility. Even today we acknowledge the goddesses of creativity, the Muses.

Women in myth, then, have been worshiped for their creativity or fertility and thus valued and revered. But there is another side to the fertility goddess. Ishtar is the goddess of fertility, but she is also the goddess of bloodshed, war, and destruction. The Fates, three goddesses in Greek mythology, control the course of life, but also the time of death. The mother who has the power to give life also has the power to take it away (Lederer, 1968).

The earth mother/fertility goddess image of women in mythology, then, is at best an *ambivalent* image. ("Ambivalence" means having mixed feelings — positive and negative — about something.) Goddesses are worshiped for their powers of control: revered for their powers of fertility, yet feared for their ability to destroy life. This ambivalent attitude not only characterizes the images of women found in mythology but is also a continuing theme in psychology of women generally, as we shall see in later chapters.

WOMEN AS SEXUAL BEINGS

In addition to the fertility goddess image, the sexuality of women has been a prominent theme in myths and in history, an example being Aphrodite, the Greek goddess of love and sexuality, or modern sex goddesses, such as Marilyn Monroe and Bo Derek.

But here, once again, the image of woman is an ambivalent one. Woman's sexuality is attractive and arousing, but also threatening, a source of fear (Lederer, 1968). The sex goddess can also be the castrating woman. The Pomo Indians of California have a myth in which the young girl has thorns about her vagina that the young man breaks off before marrying her. Twenty-two versions of the myth have been found in North

America alone, and it also occurs in the mythology of Siberian tribes, as well as in that of India and New Guinea (Hays, 1964). Certainly the prevalence of this symbol of the castrating vagina attests to its importance in representing psychological functioning, as the notion of Jungian archetypes would suggest. In related myths, the female reproductive organs are seen as being a wound, a theme continued in Freudian theory (see Chapter 3).

At times in history, the ambivalence toward female sexuality has been exaggerated to the point of absurdity. An example is during the Victorian era, when women were categorized as one of two types, the virgin or the whore. The two aspects of female sexuality were transformed into two separate persons, the good woman and the bad woman.

How can this negative view of female sexuality be explained? Some feminist authors argue that it arises from the concept of the woman as *chattel* (Millett, 1969). In many cultures, the woman has been viewed as a piece of property owned by her husband, or as chattel. (A good example of this attitude was the use of the chastity belt, which was popular in the Middle Ages and which still can, I am told, be purchased from mail-order houses. With this device, the man could lock away his property while he was gone.) Men fear the woman's sexuality because they fear her unfaithfulness; because the woman is viewed as chattel, or property, unfaithfulness means that a possession has been stolen, that there has been trespassing on the man's property. Fears of female sexuality, then, are related to the notion that women are property which can be stolen. Further, men's anxiety may result from the fact that maternity can be determined absolutely, but paternity cannot. Perhaps the fear of female unfaithfulness is also related to men's fears about their own sexual skills and inadequacies — will she find that other men are better lovers?

Expanding the explanation given for the myths of feminine evil, it seems possible that the taboos and myths surrounding female sexuality arise from male fear of female sexual processes because they are alien and mysterious (Hays, 1964). Menstruation and childbirth are processes never experienced by men, and they set women apart from men. Men fear these unknown, alien processes, and they create taboos to help control their fears. Mythology reflects the fantasies and anxieties men experience about female sexuality, as, for example, in the myth that female sexual organs are a result of castration.

Certainly attitudes toward sexuality and attitudes toward women are closely intertwined (Woudenberg, 1977). When sexuality is feared, women are feared. Those cultures which have positive sexual attitudes also tend to view women positively. Apparently the association arises at least in part because the one continuing source of interaction between men and women, and thus the way men "know" women, is through sex. Hence, it is not surprising that attitudes toward women and attitudes toward sexuality are related.

The question arises as to the direction of causation: do fears of sexuality cause negative attitudes toward women, or do negative attitudes toward women cause men to fear sex? Observations of the many sanctions against male homosexuality and masturbation suggest that sex is feared even when women are not involved. This, in turn, suggests that fears of sexuality are primary, and that these contribute to shaping attitudes toward women. With men's striving to be rational, sexuality remains elusive and poorly understood, a powerful source of pleasure, and yet a fearful challenge to their personal sense of adequacy. Does man project upon woman whaat he poorly understands in himself?

In summary, female sexuality is viewed ambivalently in mythology; it is seen as alluring, yet threatening. This ambivalence may arise from the anxieties men experience about female sexual processes, which are alien and mysterious to them.

THE MOON

From primitive times, the moon has been one of the symbols most closely associated with women (Harding, 1971; Briffiault, 1927). All the Near Eastern fertility goddesses — Ishtar, Astarte, Cybele — are moon goddesses.

The association between women and the moon probably arose in the minds of early peoples in several ways. First, from primitive times, the moon, like woman, was thought to be a source of fertility. Indeed, some tribes that had not yet discovered the sexual basis of reproduction believed that a woman could become pregnant if moonlight fell on her. In some communities the moon is called the Lord of Women. In such communities women have charge of matters concerned with the food supply, for they are believed to have the power of the moon to make things grow. Moon goddesses are mother goddesses and fertility goddesses.

A second source of the primitive association between woman and the moon was probably the common phenomenon of cyclicity. Early people probably noted that both the moon and women have a monthly cycle, and therefore must be associated. Indeed, the word "menstruation" means "moon change" (*mens-* refers to both "moon" and "month").

The waxing and waning phases of the moon symbolize the good/evil ambivalence that seems to be so characteristically a part of the view of woman. Thus, the moon symbolizes not only the fertility of its waxing phase, but also death, storms, and destruction in its waning. It is also thought to be the source of inner storms and conflict, and thus to influence lunacy. These two aspects of the moon — and of women — have sometimes even been represented by two separate goddesss. For example, in Greek mythology Aphrodite represents the Bright Moon and Hecate the Dark Moon (Harding, 1971).

Women were also thought to derive magical powers from their association with the moon. The moon was thought to control rain, and the functions of rainmaking and of controlling the weather were almost invariably in the hands of women (Harding, 1971). Closely related to the notion that women possess magical powers is the idea that women are filled with *mana* (Hays, 1964). Mana — a powerful force that infuses, particularly, the alien or mysterious — is an important concept among primitive peoples. Women are thought to be filled with this force because they also are unknown, mysterious to men. The mana notion is another expression of ambivalence toward women — the power of mana is at once attractive and frightening.

Interestingly, the moon goddess generally has a son who dies and is reborn, but she is regarded as being a virgin (Harding, 1971) — note the parallels with the Virgin Mary. The virginity is surprising in view of the goddess's chief function of being a mother, the source of fertility. Apparently the term "virgin" is best interpreted here as meaning "unmarried" and thus not controlled by man; the moon goddess is the goddess of sexual love, but not of marriage. As such, she is a person unto herself. This is one of the few exceptions to the male as normative principle (to be discussed below) — the moon goddess is not defined in terms of her marriage or her relationship to a male god. She is depicted as the feminine principle itself, not a variation on the male.

In sum, woman is associated with the symbol of the moon, representing fertility but also the ambivalent forces of life and death.

THE MALE AS NORMATIVE

Throughout mythology the male is seen as normative, the female as a variant or deviation. That is, the male is the important one, the major representative of the species, the "normal" one, and the female is a variation on him. As Simone de Beauvoir expresses it, man is the Subject, woman is the Other (1952). Or, as another writer put it, woman is little more than a tail wagged by the male ego (Hays, 1964).

In the biblical creation myth (Genesis 2), Adam, the man, is created first; Eve, the woman, is later fashioned out of his rib, almost as an afterthought. In this and many other creation myths, man is created first; he is the major, important part of the species. Woman comes second and is only a variant on the male, the normative. There are even myths in which a woman is created by castrating a man.

Perhaps the best example of the male-as-normative theme is in our language. The word "man" is used to refer not only to a male, but to people in general. When the gender of a person is unknown, the pronoun "he" is used to refer to "him." (Would we dare have said "to refer to her"?) The species as a whole is man; woman is merely a subset. This topic will be discussed in detail in Chapter 9.

To explain the concept of "normativeness," an analogy can be made to handedness. In our society, right handedness is normative, and left handedness is considered unusual or deviant. The world is basically set

FIGURE 2.2

The male as normative is a theme from mythology that has continued to the present. Here the male is normative in sports.

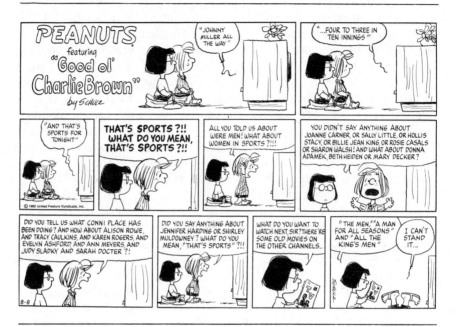

Source: © 1982 United Feature Syndicate, Inc.

up for right-handed people, and lefties have difficulty adjusting in everything from finding scissors that fit them to finding a satisfactory place at the dinner table. Just as left-handed people live in a world made for the right-handed, so women live in a world made for men, in which the male is normative.

Throughout mythology and history, then, a dominant theme is that the male is normative. He is the chief member of the species and woman is a variation or deviation. It seems likely that psychological effects result from this view, particularly as it is expressed in language, although we are lacking empirical research to document such effects.

WOMEN IN THE JUDEO-CHRISTIAN TRADITION [1]

As people formed by Western culture, even in what is often termed the post-Christian age, our views have been profoundly shaped by the Judeo-

---

[1] The author is indebted to the Rev. Clark Hyde for his assistance in preparing this section.

Christian tradition. Therefore, it will help us to comprehend the traditional Western understanding of women if we look at its religious basis, a basis that is so pervasive that it affects even those who claim no part of that religious tradition.

The basic source of "data" for this understanding is the Bible, which is the normative expression of the Judeo-Christian tradition. It is, whatever various theories of its inspiration might say, a very human book. It is the product of nearly 2000 years of human experience and reflection, and it contains a rich diversity of views on life and the human condition. It is therefore an extremely complex body of literature and cannot be oversimplified without doing violence to its integrity. Thus, while much of the biblical tradition is, in the strict sense, sexist, as we shall see, it also has great liberating insights into the relationship between women and men. The Judeo-Christian tradition runs the gamut, from the view of women expressed in the Eighteen Benedictions, in which the Rabbinic Jew thanked God that he was born neither a Gentile, nor a slave, nor a woman, to St. Paul's affirmation of the spiritual equality of women and men — "there is neither Jew nor Greek, there is neither slave nor free, there is neither male or fmale, for you are all one in Christ Jesus" (Galatians 3:28).

Judaism   We begin by looking at the Old Testament and the religion of the people known collectively as Israel. This religious tradition must be understood in light of the attitudes of the people of the ancient Near East — Babylon, Egypt, Assyria — attitudes that the Israelites at once shared and transcended. In the Old Testament there is a kind of tension between various understandings of women. Women are seen as subservient to men, with an assumption that this is an intrinsic part of the natural order. Yet at the same time, many aspects of womanhood are valued highly in the religion of Israel, and it is safe to say that the status of women in the Jewish tradition was decidedly superior to that of women in all other civilizations of the Near Eastern or Mediterranean worlds.

Two experiences in the history of Israel were crucial to that people's formation of religious self-understanding and of their view of woman. These were: (1) the patriarchal and Exodus periods, a time of nomadic wanderings, and (2) the invasion and settlement of Canaan — now known as Palestine or the Holy Land — and the evolution of Israel into a settled agricultural and commercial nation. During both these times, extremely important religious revolutions took place for Israel that tied cultural views of women to the religious tradition.

During the period of the patriarchs and of the Exodus, roughly 2000 to 1200 B.C., the Israelites were a group of nomadic tribes, constantly on the move seeking food for their herds, always ready to fight off marauding animals or other tribes competing for scarce grazing land. The tribes were closely knit bodies based on patriarchal kinship in which procreation was highly valued and carefully regulated. The functions of hunter, herder, and warrior became exceptionally important, indeed necessary, to survival. Contemporary cross-cultural research indicates that in such societies differences between women and men are emphasized (Barry et al., 1957), masculine strength is highly valued, and males have higher status than females. Procreativity, continuing the tribe, also becomes important, as does the need for order, in particular the need to regulate sexual relationships. Given these conditions, it is not surprising that we find Old Testament women viewed as the property or *chattel* of males, defined almost exclusively in procreative terms, their purpose being to produce children, preferably male children. Many institutions reflected this, such as the bride-price, in which a young man bought his wife from her father; the levirate marriage, in which a man was obliged to marry his brother's widow if she were childless so that his line would continue; and the nonreciprocal nature of divorce, possible at a man's whim, impossible for a woman. Thus, probably owing to cultural context, *male dominance* is a prominent theme in Judaism and the Old Testament.

The second important cultural period, the crossing of the Jordan and the settlement in Palestine, which occurred roughly between 1200 and 1000 B.C., brought Israel into contact with a settled agricultural people, the Canaanites. The Canaanites were concerned in their religious practices chiefly with fertility of the crops, an urgent matter for a struggling agricultural economy, and with human fertility. The Canaanites believed that they could promote fertility by imitative magic; that is, by performing the sexual act in religious ceremonies, they re-enacted the relationship between Asherah (Astarte), the earth mother, and Baal, the sky king, and thus, they believed, stimulated the crops to fertility. The most notable feature of this imitative magic was cultic prostitution in the temples, involving both male and female prostitutes as ministers of the religion. Women were highly involved, both as priestesses and as participants, because they symbolized the mother earth whose fertility was so valued.

The religious practices of the Canaanites had a great impact on the religion of Israel because of Israel's violent reaction against the perceived idolatry and immorality of the Canaanites. From roughly 1000 to 587 B.C., the champions of the orthodox Hebrew religion fought continually against both the abandonment of Hebrew religion for the none-too-subtle attractions of the fertility cult, and the attempt to introduce Canaanite practices and ideas into Judaism (or Yahwism, so named because Yahweh was God's name).

One of the results of this conflict between the religion of Israel and that of the indigenous Canaanites was further negativism about the nature of women. Women were seen, in their sexuality, to be dangerous to pure Yahwism and, indeed, as agents of evil. The Old Testament expressions of the myth of *feminine evil* were fortified by the situation that Israel found upon settlement in Palestine. As Yahwism developed, it became more concerned with creation and the earth; but the creation myths that were added were attributed to Yahweh's male image and not to any female deity, as in other Near Eastern religions. This served to reinforce the twin motifs of male dominance and feminine evil that are found throughout the Old Testament.

The prime example of the feminine evil theme is the figure of Eve. According to the myth of the Fall (Genesis 2, 3), Eve is the author of sin and the cause of man's expulsion from Paradise. Yet, Eve has her other side as well. Her name is said to mean "mother of all living," and her feminine creativity is given a great deal of prominence. Further, there is in both Old Testament creation myths (Genesis 2, the more ancient, and Genesis 1, the product of a later time), a recognition of the interdependence of women and men. According to Genesis 2, woman was created because God saw that "it is not good for man to be alone," and in Genesis 1, we find that "God created man . . . male and female he created them." Thus, even while woman is seen as the author of evil and the subject of man, she is yet seen as an indispensable part of God's creation.

This brings us to a third theme that runs through the Old Testament view of women: the *high valuation placed on woman as mother and wife.* Hebrew literature and mythology paid high tribute to the great mothers of the nation, such as Sarah, Rachel, and Miriam. The home was declared to be the woman's sphere, but the home was much more productive than it is in our post-industrial age, for it was the center of commercial and mercantile life. Thus, the woman's role was seen as vital to the health and strength of the nation.

In its public form, the religion of the Old Testament is a masculine prerogative; yet its central observances such as the Sabbath and the Passover take place in the home and include women as an integral part. There is no clearer expression of this understanding of woman as the mistress of the home than the thirty-first chapter of Proverbs:

> A good wife who can find?
> > She is far more precious than jewels.
> The heart of her husband trusts in her,
> > and he will have no lack of gain.
> She does him good, and not harm,
> > all the days of her life.
> She seeks wool and flax,
> > and works with willing hands.
> She is like the ships of the merchant,
> > she brings her food from afar.
> She rises while it is yet night and
> > provides food for her household and tasks for her maidens.
> She considers a field and buys it;
> > with the fruit of her hands she plants a vineyard.

. . .

She opens her hand to the poor,
and reaches out her hands to the needy.

. . .

She opens her mouth with wisdom,
and the teaching of kindness is on her tongue.
She looks well to the ways of her household,
and does not eat the bread of idleness.
Her children rise up and call her blessed;
her husband also, and he praises her.
"Many women have done excellently,
but you surpass them all."
Charm is deceitful, and beauty is vain,
but a woman who fears the Lord is to be praised.
Give her of the fruit of her hands,
and let her works praise her in the city gates.

Throughout Jewish tradition, these three themes continue to exist in tension. The male is dominant, and woman is the subject of man according to the design of a masculine God. Women are the source of evil; through Eve, mankind fell from grace, and her sexuality is seen as a threat and a temptation. Yet, in the home the woman is highly regarded and, on occasion, called to perform acts of heroism on behalf of the nation.

Christianity   Christianity took over the traditional Jewish view of women, and that view was then magnified by the cultural context in which the Christian faith was formed. The Roman Empire of the first century A.D. was marked by decadence and sexual immorality that shocked the Jews (as the television series, *I, Claudius* illustrated vividly). Further, during its first two centuries, the Christian Church believed that Christ would return at any moment, bringing the end of time, and so family life was considered to be of limited importance. Therefore, at the beginning, Christian theology heavily stressed the concepts of masculine dominance and feminine evil.

In addition to the three themes discussed above, there is a fourth, present in Jewish tradition but reaching its fruition in Christianity — that of the *spiritual equality of women and men.* Women were included in the ministry of Jesus in a way unknown in first-century society, Jewish and Gentile alike. Women were important actors in the most significant events of Jesus' life — from Mary who bore him, to the women who were the first to discover the empty tomb. Jesus, who taught by homely examples and cultural commonplaces, *never* used the concept of feminine frailty or evil to make a point (Sayers, 1946). Indeed, in his preaching, he made it quite clear that mutuality was to prevail in the relationship between men and women. For example, in his teaching on divorce (Mark 10:2–12), he applied to men criteria previously applied only to women and thus destroyed the double standard. There is no evidence that Jesus assigned women an inferior position, and every suggestion that he regarded women and men as spiritually equal.

Much of the Church's teaching downgrading women is attributed to St. Paul, the great apostle of early Christianity, and much of it deservedly so. Yet, at the same time, in Paul's churches women were accorded positions of trust and leadership. Paul also expanded on Jesus' teaching about divorce, and he said that marital relations must be based on absolute equality: "For the wife does not rule over her own body, but the husband does; likewise the husband does not rule over his own body, but the wife does" (I Corinthians 7:4). St. Paul is also responsible for the definitive statement of spiritual equality of women and men noted on page 32.

In the later Church the revolutionary impact of this teaching of the spiritual equality of women and men was blunted by the cultural context, but it remained a vital part of Christian tradition. In the early Church, ministers were expected to be married (I Timothy 2:1–5), and it was not until the fourth and fifth centuries that clerical celibacy became normative. In New Testament literature, pride and lack of faith are seen as the central sins. Only later, under the impact of conflict with Roman culture, did sexual sins (and the revived theme of feminine evil) take the prominence that characterizes much of Christian theology. In early Christian thought, Mary is seen primarily as the bearer of God, the mother of redeemed humanity, who by her "yes" to God reversed the effects of Eve's "yes" to the serpent. Only in later Christian theology is her virginity stressed, thus removing the threat of sexuality from the virtue of her motherhood.

In summary, three themes emerge from a study of the images of women in the Jewish tradition: male dominance, feminine evil, and the valued role of the woman as mistress of the home. Christianity incorporates these three themes and adds a fourth theme, the spiritual equality of women and men. These themes appear to have arisen through an interaction of the religions themselves with the cultures in which they developed (for example, the early Hebrew reaction to the Canaanite fertility cults). Although patriarchal notions of male dominance prevailed, women were accorded a valued, if limited, status, finally brought to fruition in the Christian notion of spiritual equality of women and men, yet a 2000-year history of Christian practice has substantially ignored this theme.

WHEN WOMEN WERE IN POWER . . .

The mythical images of women discussed up to this point have generally been negative, or at best ambivalent. I have attempted to explain these negative images in terms of anxieties experienced by men, who are in power and thus create the myths of the culture. Negative images of women occur in *patriarchal* societies — societies in which men have most of the political, legal, and economic power, and in which women have fewer privileges and rights, and lower status. The assumption is that images of women in mythology are so predominantly negative because virtually all societies, past and present, have been patriarchal.

In a provocative book, *Mothers and Amazons*, originally published in Germany in 1930, Helen Diner explored the nature of mythology and society in a time when women were in power — during *matriarchal* times. She relied on a theory developed by the Swiss anthropologist Bachofen in his *Das Mutterrecht* (Mother-right) in 1861. Bachofen argued that at the dawn of human history, human social organization passed through three successive stages. The first was one of general sexual promiscuity, with little social organization. In the second stage, social organization increased and a true matriarchy emerged. Apparently during this stage people had not discovered the nature of sexual reproduction, and instead believed in parthenogenesis, reproduction by the female alone through the development of an unfertilized egg. Women were thus viewed as extremely powerful, and they assumed control of the society. Not until the third stage, with the revolutionary discovery of paternity, did a patriarchy emerge. It should be noted that this theory is in disrepute among scholars (see, for example, Bamberger, 1974), who question whether matriarchies ever really existed. Nonetheless, conclusive proof for either side of the argument is lacking, and Diner's speculations are provocative enough to be worth considering.

If, at some early time, women were in power, if matriarchy did actually precede patriarchy, the myths emerging from such a period might be expected to present quite different views of women from those of a patriarchal society. According to Diner, in the earliest creation myths the female is the original life force, from which is then created the male. This would seem the logical mythical account to arise in a society that believed in parthenogenesis. For example, in Babylonian lore the original being, Thalat, gave birth to a divine couple from which the world was created. In the earliest Greek creation myth, the female earth emerges first and then creates the sky and elements. Thus, in the earliest myths, the female is the original, the male the derivative. Creation myths in which the female is derived from the male, for example that of Adam and Eve, occurred later. This corresponds in time to a matriarchal society occurring first, followed by a patriarchal society. And in matriarchal society, the female is normative.

The Amazons, a legendary race of warrior women ruled by a queen, are perhaps the best known example of mythical matriarchy. Diner also argued that matriarchy was characteristic of the Spartans of Greece, of China through the Dynasty, among the common people of Japan, and in Tibet. The widespread belief that the female is the primal life force is attested to by myths of the virgin birth of Christ, Buddha, Quetzalcoatl, Montezuma, and Genghis Khan.

Thus, if early matriarchies did exist, they appear to have produced a much different view of women in mythology, for women were seen as the primary life force, the normative. Future research may yet discover matriarchal cultures, with a correspondingly more positive view of the female in myth.

NONCONSCIOUS IDEOLOGIES

Psychologists Sandra and Daryl Bem (1970) have argued that there is a nonconscious ideology influencing women's psychology. A *nonconscious ideology* is an ideology (set of ideas) to which we are exposed without being aware of it, either because (1) the ideas are so common and widely accepted that they are not noticed, much as a fish is not aware that it lives in a wet environment, or (2) the ideas are in a form that is subtle and not likely to be noticed or attacked. The myths and religious views discussed above are all good examples. A further example of a nonconscious ideology are the jokes in which women are portrayed as foolish, stupid, or incompetent (Zimbardo and Meadow, 1974). No one would argue against the content of a joke — that would be acting like a poor sport. And so such jokes became part of a nonconscious ideology that teaches that women are inferior, an ideology that is all the more dangerous because it is neither conscious nor overt, and therefore cannot effectively be attacked.

Here, we consider two more examples of nonconscious ideologies.

Example I: Jason and Medea revisited   Daniel Goleman (1976) analyzed the content of stories in adventure magazines for teen-age boys such as *Action for Men* and *Saga*, and romance magazines for teen-age girls such as *True Story* and *Real Romance*. He noticed that many of the plots in these magazines were simply modernized versions of the plots of ancient myths. As an example, here is a summary of the Greek myth of Jason and Medea:

> Jason had to retrieve the Golden Fleece to earn the right to the royal throne. The Fleece was the skin of a divine ram that was essential to his country's spiritual well-being; it was held by the king of a distant and hostile land. Jason set off with the Argonauts, an able-bodied band dedicated to helping him capture it. Each Argonaut had a special ability; Jason's was seduction, and he was unscrupulous in using women for his own ends.
>
> After many hardships, the Argonauts reached the country where the Fleece was held, only to find themselves hopelessly outnumbered. Medea, a young princess whose father had the Fleece under guard, saved the day. Bored with her home and boyfriends, she fell in love with Jason. Although her family warned her against this stranger, Medea betrayed her family ties, revealed her father's secrets for guarding the Fleece, and

fled with Jason. Totally devoted to Jason, Medea even slew her half-brother to help her lover escape with the Fleece.

Jason returned home triumphant and made Medea queen. But he cared more for ambition than for her. When she learned that Jason planned to divorce her and marry another princess to expand his kingdom, her love for him turned to hate. Enraged, Medea killed the would-be bride and her father, as well as her own sons by Jason.

Ashamed and repentant, Medea returned home to a forgiving family and a dull but safe marriage to the prince of a nearby kingdom. Jason died, heartbroken by the murder of his sons. (Goleman, 1976, p. 84)

Compare that plot with this one from a 1975 issue of *True Romance.*

Sixteen-year-old Becky hitch-hiked home to Portland after a year's absence, four months pregnant and unwed. Becky's odyssey began at a rock concert where she met Guy, a "gorgeous" school drop-out and wanderer, to whom she was immediately attracted. Her parents disapproved, and argued that there were "a lot of nice guys right in this neighborhood" she should date. In defiance, she met Guy in secret. When Guy decided to leave for a commune in Sacramento, Becky packed some clothes, left a note to her parents, and went with him.

With no one to tell her what to do, Becky found a new liberation in eating, sleeping, and making love as she pleased. But the bubble burst one day when Colette, a sexy readhead, moved into the commune. Guy was openly attracted to her and indifferent to Becky's hurt feelings. On top of this, Becky found she was pregnant and when she told Guy, he angrily blamed her for being careless. Becky, shaken, realized Guy had stopped loving her, if he ever had.

Becky returned home, where she learned that her rash departure had tragic effects on her family. Her mother, heartbroken and depressed, was in a mental hospital; her father was hardpressed to pay for her treatment. Even so, her father welcomed Becky back, and stood by her through the ordeal of giving her baby up for adoption. As her father assured her, "Families help one another when there's trouble." A chastened Becky wishes she could somehow undo all the damage she's caused, and resolves to build a better, more worthwhile life. (Goleman, 1976, p. 84)

What messages do such stories convey to the young people reading them? Girls reading the story are implicitly being told: (1) Beware of men — their seductiveness will lead to your downfall; (2) beware of sexuality — it, too, can be your downfall; (3) stay with your family, obey your parents, and don't be adventurous; (4) other women are the enemy (e.g., Colette); and (5) women are dangerous — they are capable of murdering their own children (Medea) or causing their mother's mental breakdown (Becky); in short, the myth of feminine evil is retold.

The more general point is that such stories are sources of nonconscious ideologies, and the ideologies of gender roles they present are quite similar to those found in age-old myths.

Example II: Genderisms in advertising   Anthropologist Erving Goffman (1977) analyzed the composition of photographs used in popular advertising. He noticed that the composition of the photographs often contained "genderisms," that is, subtle stereotyped themes. As an example, men were almost always shown with their heads higher in the photograph than women's, even when both the man and the woman were seated or in some other situation in which height should make little difference. According to Goffman's analysis, this positioning reflects a ritualized subordination of women. Typically one lowers one's head when in the presence of a person of superior authority and power, as when bowing to a king. Thus the lower position of women may reflect their subordinate status to men.

Once again we have a nonconscious ideology; the stereotyped idea is presented subtly. Nonetheless, it probably reflects widespread themes of male dominance and female subordination in our society, and indeed the composition of the photographs may help to perpetuate these themes.

FEMINISM AND RELIGION

During the last two decades, the women's movement has had a significant impact on the religious community. The effect varies among different religious traditions, with more liberal groups being more affected by feminism. At the same time, there has been some opposite impact; that is, the women's movement has made some conservative groups more militant in opposition to feminism. Effects have occurred in at least four areas.

Religious leadership   Women have demanded, and in many cases gained, a much more central role in various religious groups. Women are typically to be found serving on governing boards and congregational committees and as delegates to national conventions. A key issue has been the ordination of women to the professional ministry, frequently a cause for significant debate and even division. Women are now ordained in all "mainline" Protestant groups, with the Episcopal Church's 1976 decision in favor being the most recent. Women are not ordained in most conservative Protestant churches, the Southern Baptist Convention being the notable example. Neither the Roman Catholic Church nor the Eastern orthodox churches allow women to be priests. Women have been ordained as rabbis in reform and reconstructionist Judaism for some time. The first woman to study for the rabbinate at the conservative Jewish Theological Seminary was admitted in 1983; orthodox Judaism does not permit women to be rabbis.

Women's issues   The religious community finds itself in the thick of the debate over several items on the feminist agenda. Many liberal and moderate Protestant groups take a pro-choice position on abortion and are represented by the Religious Coalition for Abortion Rights. These same churches tend to favor the Equal Rights Amendment. On the other hand, much of the organized opposition to abortion comes from the Roman Catholic Church and various conservative Protestant groups. The so-called New Religious Right, which includes many of the latter groups, has played a major role in lobbying against the Equal Rights Amendment and similar legislation.

Feminist theology   A new generation of feminist theologians and biblical scholars challenges the assumptions and methods of generations of theological study. They regard the Judeo-Christian tradition as based on a male-dominant patriarchal foundation, and seek to revise religious scholarship in nonsexist terms. This concern has led some feminists to reject all or most of the Western religious tradition, while others maintain that the tradition can be reformed along fully inclusive lines. In this effort, the term "inclusive" is used to include women and to affirm the equality and worth of women, and to deny patriarchy and male-dominance. Feminist scholarship, as practiced by, for example, Mary Daly, Rosemary Radford Ruether, Phyllis Tribble, and Elizabeth Schüssler Fiorenza, is increasingly commanding the serious attenion of American religious scholars.

Inclusive language   The work of feminist theologians and the increasing number of women in positions of religious leadership have led to a searching examination of the language of worship and even of scripture. (See Chapter 9 for a discussion of psychologists' research on the language issue.) Service books and hymnals have been revised to eliminate sexist language, and new liturgies are being developed to reflect a feminist religious consciousness. Two types of revision have been made. First, many groups have sought to use inclusive language for all references to people in their worship. No longer can "man," "men," or "brothers" serve to designate humanity in the language of worship for most moderate and liberal religious bodies. However, an even more radical concern has appeared — the language used for the deity. At present, most American Christians and Jews are reluctant to revise their "God-talk," but some revisions are occurring. Perhaps the most notable example is the recently published *Inclusive Language Lectionary,* a project of the National Council of Churches that renders the portions of the Bible read in many churches into inclusive language. A comparison of its version of John 1:14–18 with the fairly traditional *Revised Standard Version* is instructive.

Revised Standard Version:

And the Word became flesh and dwelt among us, full of grace and truth; we have beheld his glory, glory as of the only Son from the Father. (John bore witness to him, and cried, "This is he of whom I said, 'He who comes after me ranks before me, for he was before me.' "). . . . No one has ever seen God; the only Son, who is in the bosom of the Father, he has made him known.

Inclusive Language Lectionary (1983):

And the Word became flesh and dwelt among us, full of grace and truth; we have beheld the Word's glory, glory as of the only child from [God] the Father [and Mother]. (John bore witness to the Child, and cried, "This was the one of whom I said, 'The one who comes after me ranks before me, for that one was before me.' "). . . . No one has even seen God; the only Child, who is in the bosom of [God] the [Mother and] Father, that one has made God known.

IN CONCLUSION

I have suggested that mythology provides a way of increasing our understanding — although not the scientific way we will attempt in the remaining chapters — of the psychology of women, and particularly of the attitudes men hold toward women. Two persisting themes have been the ambivalence of attitudes toward women and the view that the male is normative. Strikingly, these two themes are also found in scientific theory and research on women.

A final speculation is that mythology may be another source of a nonconscious ideology acting upon women. In earliest childhood, the little girl learns that she, Eve, was created from Adam's rib, and that God is male. Mythical creation stories, like jokes, are not subject to rational argument and debate. They are not, after all, supposed to represent actual historical fact. But will the little girl know that these stories represent the experience of a patriarchal society? Or will she simply believe that God is male, and that women are the source of evil in the world? Feminists seek to revise some of these aspects of religion.

SUGGESTIONS FOR FURTHER READING

Hall, N. (1980). *The moon and the virgin*. New York: Harper & Row. This book elaborates a Jungian psychology of women.

Nunnally-Cox, Janice (1981). *Foremothers: Women of the bible*. New York: Seabury. Nunnally-Cox attempts to reconstruct the positive contributions of the Jewish and Christian women in the Bible.

3
Theoretical Perspectives

[Girls] notice the penis of a brother or playmate, strikingly visible and of large proportions, at once recognize it as the superior counterpart of their own small and inconspicuous organ, and from that time forward fall a victim to envy for the penis.

SIGMUND FREUD, *Collected Papers*

Understanding the nature of the differences between males and females has fascinated people probably since the dawn of the human species. In the last chapter we saw how men have attempted to understand and explain women by constructing myths about them. In the past century, science has come to dominate intellectual thought. And so it is not surprising that men (and sometimes also women) have more recently attempted scientific understandings of women. In the present chapter we will examine some major psychological theories, having their roots in science, that have been formulated to explain women and the differences between women and men.

In later chapters we shall look at empirical data for a further understanding of women and gender roles. The reader can then contrast these theoretical views with what is known based on scientific data.

PSYCHOANALYTIC THEORY

Psychoanalytic theory was formulated by Sigmund Freud. Despite the advent of new models of human psychological development, few can doubt the influence of psychoanalytic theory in psychology, not to mention its penetration into the language and thinking of most lay people. Psychoanalytic theory not only describes human behavior, but it has also acted to shape human behavior. For example, Freud's theory of female sexuality (see Chapter 12) held that women could have two kinds of orgasm — vaginal or clitoral — and that the vaginal orgasm was the more "mature," that is, the better, of the two. Some women have spent hours trying to achieve the elusive vaginal orgasm, and have sought psychotherapy when they were unable to attain it, all as a result of Freud's theory. Certainly the theory has had an impact on human life, and in particular on women.

Freud viewed humans as being dominated by instincts. These instincts are focused in different regions of the body collectively referred to as the *erogenous zones*. Each zone is a part of the skin or mucous membrane highly endowed with blood supply and nerve endings that are very sensitive to stimulation. The lips and mouth constitute one such region, the anal region another, and the genitals a third. Thus Freud noted that sucking produces pleasure, as does elimination, and rubbing the genitals.

Stages of development One of Freud's greatest contributions was to view human personality as being the result of *development*. That is, he saw the personality of an adult as the result of previous experiences, and he believed that early childhood experiences were most critical. He proposed a stage theory of psychosexual development, each stage being characterized by a focus on one of the erogenous zones. According to his view, all humans pass through the stages in a fixed, chronological sequence — first the oral, then the anal, and then the phallic stage — during the first five or six years of life. Thus during the first stage, the oral, the infant derives pleasure from sucking and eating and experiences the world mainly through the mouth. Following this is the anal stage, in which pleasure is focused on defecating.

In attempting to explain the development of gender identity and differences between males and females, Freud postulated that boys and girls pass through the first two stages of psychosexual development, the oral and the anal, in a similar manner. For both genders at this time, the mother is the chief object of love. It is during the *phallic stage*, around the ages of four to six, that the development of the genders diverges. As one might suspect from the name for this stage, females will be at somewhat of a disadvantage in passing through it.

During the phallic stage, the boy becomes fascinated with his own penis. It is a rich source of pleasure and interest for him. A critical occurrence during the phallic stage is the formation of the *Oedipal complex*, named for the Greek myth of Oedipus, who killed his father and married his mother. In the Oedipal complex, the boy sexually desires his mother. His attachment to her is strong and intense. He also wishes to rid himself of the father, who is a rival for the mother's affection. But the father is too powerful an opponent, and the boy fears that the father will retaliate. He fears that the father will do him bodily harm, particularly to his beloved penis, so that the boy comes to feel *castration anxiety*. Through a complicated series of maneuvers the boy resolves the problem. He admits to an inability to possess the mother and do away with the father, the potential dangers being too great. He represses his libidinal impulses toward the mother, and makes the critical shift to identifying with the father. In the process of *identification* with the father, the boy introjects (takes into himself as his own) the values, the "thou-shalt-nots," of society as represented by the father and thus comes to have a conscience or superego. But more important for our purposes is that, in identifying with the father, he comes to acquire his gender identity, taking on the qualities the father supposedly possesses — strength, power, and so on.

The sequence of events in the phallic stage is considerably different for the girl. According to Freud, the first critical event is the girl's stark realization that she has no penis. Because children are so interested in their own and others' genitals during this stage, Freud believed that the girl will inevitably notice the boy's protrusion and her own cavity. Presumably she recognizes that the penis is superior to her own anatomy. She feels cheated and envious of males, and thus comes to feel *penis envy*. She also feels mutilated, believing that at one time she possessed a penis, but that it had been cut off — indeed Freud believed that the fires of the boy's castration anxiety are fed by the boy's observation of the girl's anatomy, which he sees as living proof of the reality of castration. Her desire for a penis, her penis envy, can never be satisfied directly, and instead becomes transformed into a desire to be impregnated by her father. Holding her mother responsible for her lack of a penis, she renounces her love for her mother and becomes intensely attachd to her father, thus forming her own version of the Oedipal complex, sometimes called the Electra complex. Thus the sequence of events is reversed: for the boy, the Oedipal complex leads to castration anxiety, whereas for the girl, the parallel to castration anxiety — penis envy — occurs first and leads to the formation of the Oedipal complex. The desire to be impregnated by the father is a strong one, and persists in the more general form of maternal urges, according to Freud.

Passivity, masochism, and narcissism   Freud believed that there are three key female personality traits: passivity, masochism, and narcissism. Here I shall focus on passivity and masochism.

In the outcomes of the Electra complex Freud saw the origins of the two well-known — at least to Victorians — feminine qualities, *passivity* and *masochism*. In choosing the strategy for obtaining the desired penis by being impregnated by the father, the girl adopts a passive approach — to be impregnated, to be done to, not to do — and this passive strategy persists throughout life. The desire to be impregnated is also masochistic, in that intercourse (in which, in Freudian terminology, the woman is "penetrated") and childbirth are painful. The female, therefore, in desiring to be impregnated, seeks to bring pain to herself.

Lest the foregoing strains your credulity, perhaps some quotations from Marie Bonaparte, an early follower of Freud, will indicate the strength of these convictions.

> Throughout the whole range of living creatures, animal or vegetable, passivity is characteristic of the female cell, the ovum whose mission is to *await* the male cell, the active mobile spermatozoan to come and *penetrate* it. Such penetration, however, implies infraction of its tissue, but infraction of a living creature's tissue may entail destruction: death as much as life. Thus, the fecundation of the female cell is initiated by a kind of wound; in its way, the female cell is primordially "masochistic." (1953, p. 79)

All forms of masochism are related, and in essence, more or less female, from the wish to be eaten by the father in the cannibalistic oral phase, through that of being whipped or beaten by him in the sadistic-anal stage, and of being castrated in the phallic stage, to the wish, in the adult feminine stage, to be pierced. (1953, p. 83)

Vaginal sensitivity in coitus for the adult female, in my opinion, is thus largely based on the existence, and more or less unconscious, acceptation of the child's immense masochistic beating fantasies. In coitus, the woman, in effect, is subjected to a sort of beating by the man's penis. She receives its blows and often, even, loves their violence. (1953, p. 87)

As we saw, the resolution of the Oedipal complex is critical for the boy's development, being necessary for the formation of his gender identity and superego. Unfortunately, for the girl the resolution of the Oedipal complex is neither as direct nor as complete. She was led to the Oedipal complex by her desire for a penis, a desire that can never truly be satisfied. More importantly, the prime motivation in the boy's resolving his Oedipal complex was his overpowering fear of castration. For the girl, castration is an already accomplished fact, and thus her motivation for resolution of the Oedipal complex is not so strong, being motivated only by the comparatively abstract realization that her desires for her father cannot be gratified.

Immature superego For the female the Oedipal complex is never as fully resolved as it is for the male. It is not surprising, then, that related personality processes should differ for females and males. According to Freud, the girl's unsuccessful resolution of the Oedipal complex leads the female to lifelong feelings of inferiority, a predisposition to jealousy, and to intense maternal desires. Further, it leads females to be characterized by an *immature superego*. For the boy, one of the positive outcomes of resolving the Oedipal complex is the internalization, or introjection, of society's standards, thereby forming a superego. But the girl's attachment to the parents is never "smashed" as is the boy's, and she continues to be dependent on the parents for her values. She never internalizes her own values as completely as does the boy; continuing to rely on others, she thus is characterized by a less mature sense of morality, or an immature superego. In Freud's own words,

Their [girl's] superego is never so inexorable, so impersonal, so independent of its emotional origins as we require it to be in men . . . That they show less sense of justice than men, that they are less ready to submit to the great necessities of life, that they are more often influenced in their judgments by feelings of affection or hostility — all these would be amply accounted for by the modification in the formation of their superego which we have already inferred. (1948, pp. 196–197)

> . . . Girls remain in it [the Oedipal conflict] for an indeterminate length of time; they demolish it last, and even so incompletely. In these circumstances the formation of the superego must suffer; it cannot attain the strength and independence which give it its cultural significance. (1933, p. 129)

In summary, Freud postulated a basic model for the acquisition of gender identity in the male, with a parallel model for the female. A basic assumption is the importance and superiority of the male phallus. It is so important to the boy that, in the throes of love for his mother, he fears that his father will harm the penis and he thus gives up his love for his mother and comes to identify with his father, thereby acquiring his own gender identity and introjecting the values of society. For the girl, on the other hand, penis envy, an instant recognition of the superiority of the penis and a sense of envy over not having one, is primary. She turns her love away from her mother and toward her father in an attempt to regain the penis, but is unsuccessful. Her Oedipal complex is never completely resolved, and as a result her moral development is less adequate.

Criticisms of psychoanalytic theory   Numerous general criticisms and feminist criticisms of Freudian theory have been made.

From a scientific point of view, a major problem with psychoanalytic theory is that most of its concepts cannot be evaluated scientifically to see whether they are accurate. Freud believed that many of the most important forces in human behavior are unconscious, and thus they cannot be studied by any of the usual scientific techniques.

Another criticism that is often raised is that Freud derived his ideas almost exclusively from work with patients who sought therapy. Thus his theory may describe not so much human behavior as disturbed human behavior. In particular, his views on women may contain some truth about women who have problems of adjustment, but may have little to do with women who function well psychologically.

Many modern psychologists feel that Freud overemphasized biological determinants of human behavior and did not give sufficient attention to the influence of society and learning in shaping behavior. In particular, his views on the origin of differences between males and females, and on the nature of female personality, are heavily biological, relying mostly on anatomical differences — as the famous phrase has it, "Anatomy is destiny." In relying on anatomy as an explanation, Freud ignored the enormous forces of culture acting to create differences between females and males.

Feminists have raised numerous criticisms of Freudian theory, including those noted above (e.g., Weisstein, 1971; Sherman, 1971). They are particularly critical of Freud's assumption that the clitoris and vagina are inferior to the penis. Freud's views have been termed "phallocentric."

The superiority of the penis may have seemed a reasonable concept in the Victorian era in which Freud wrote, but it is difficult to believe today, and certainly has no scientific documentation backing it.

A related question is whether little girls would, in fact, instantly recognize the superiority of the penis. While case histories are available to document the existence of penis envy among women seeking therapy (see case history), it remains to be demonstrated that penis envy is common among women, or that it has a large impact on their development. Indeed, empirical research indicates that in psychiatric studies the penis-envy theme is not nearly so common among women as is castration anxiety among men (Bosselman, 1960). This suggests that Freud, in writing from a male point of view, accurately observed the castration anxiety of the male, but was less accurate when constructing a parallel —penis envy — for the female.

A CASE HISTORY ILLUSTRATING PENIS ENVY

The following is an example of the sort of case history that a psycho-analyst would see as demonstrating penis envy.

> An unsuccessful artist who had always resented being a woman came to treatment very depressed and anxious at having allowed herself to become pregnant. Her husband had recently become extremely successful, and her envy of and competition with him were enormous, especially since she was blocked in her own professional development. She felt that the best way to "show up" her husband was to do the one thing he could not do — bear a child.

> She expressed only hatred and contempt for her mother, who had been a dependent, ineffectual housebound woman. This resentment seemed to have started at the birth of her sister, three years younger, at which time the patient hid herself and refused to talk for days. The mother was hospitalized for depression when the patient was twelve. The father was an unsuccessful artist, an exciting, talented person whom the patient adored. She turned away from her mother and spent the next ten years of her life trying to be her father's son. He encouraged her painting and took her to exhibitions. However, he was very inconsistent and bitter, given to terrifying rages; he would alternate between leading her on and slapping her down. Her fantasy of being like a boy was brutally crushed at a time when she was preparing for a bas mitzvah; she thought she would be allowed to have one "as good as a boy's" but was suddenly humiliated publicly at puberty and sent home from the synagogue on the Sabbath because it was decided that she was now a woman and could no longer stay and compete with the men and boys. Menarche intensified her resentment of female functions, but she compensated with fantasies of having a son and traveling around the world with him — self-sufficient, no longer needing her family or her father. While in Europe on a scholar-ship, she fell in love and, while petting with the boy, had the only orgasm

she has ever experienced. She feared his increasing power over her, experienced a resurgence of dependency needs and fled home. She felt she had spent her life trying to win her father's approval. But when she finally had a one-man show, he taunted her, "Why not give it up, go home, and make babies?"

After his death and her professional failure, she became increasingly depressed. At the age of thirty, she decided to get pregnant — after having been married four years. (She had previously been phobic about pregnancy and remained a virgin until her marriage.) She felt that her baby was conceived out of emptiness, not fullness, and then feared that the child would take her life from her. Having a baby trapped her, she felt; she could no longer try to be like a man. It was as though she had had a fantasy penis which she finally had to relinquish.

There was plenty of evidence of typical penis envy in this case. As a girl, the patient even tried to compete with boys in urinary contests, and was furious because she always lost. She first associated her bedwetting with rage at not having a penis, but finally viewed it as a way to punish [her] mother for turning to [the] sister, and as an effort to recover the maternal solicitude she had lost. She envied, and was attracted to, men who had powerful drives for achievement and were free to pursue them. The penis was for her a symbol of such drives; to possess it would also save her from being like her mother. In one sense, she wanted a baby as a substitute for not having a penis; but she also had a burning wish to be a good mother — to prove her own validity as well as to "undo" her past. Her difficulty in achieving this wish forced her to work through her relationship with her mother, which she had contemptuously shelved, finding competition with men more exciting and less anxiety-provoking.

Source: Abridged from R. Moulton, "A Survey and Re-evaluation of the Concept of Penis Envy," *Contemporary Psychoanalysis*, 7 (1970):84–104. Used with permission of the author and publisher.

Feminists also note the similarities between psychoanalytic theory and some of the myths about women discussed in the previous chapter. In this context, Freud seems simply to be articulating age-old myths and images about women in "scientific" language. The mythical image of the female genitals as a wound is transformed into a theory in which females believe themselves to have been castrated. The image of women as sinful and the source of evil is translated into the scientific-sounding "immature superego." Certainly Freud's phallocentrism is a good example of a male-as-normative model. Basically, for Freud, a female is a castrated male. His model of development describes male development, female development being an inadequate variation on it.

Finally, feminists object to Freud's distinction between clitoral and vaginal orgasm and his belief that the vaginal orgasm is the more mature (better) one. This point will be discussed in detail in Chapter 12.

Nonetheless, it is important to recognize Freud's important contributions in his recognition of the importance of development in shaping human personality, and particularly in shaping gender identity.

VARIATIONS ON A FREUDIAN THEME

There have been various attempts within the psychoanalytic school to reform Freud's theory. Here we shall look briefly at some of the proposed variants that are relevant to women.

Karen Horney Several of the most prominent psychoanalytic theorists were women, and, not surprisingly, they made some modifications on Freud's theory. Horney's theoretical papers show an evolution over time in her own thinking. Originally she accepted Freud's ideas wholeheartedly; in a 1924 paper she eagerly documented the origins of penis envy and of the castration complex in women. However, she soon became critical of these notions, and in a 1926 paper she pointed out that Freudian notions really articulate the childish views boys have of girls (much as I have pointed out that they represent age-old myths), and that Freud's psychological theory of women had been phallocentric.

Her chief disagreement with Freud was over his notion that penis envy was the critical factor in female development. Horney used the master's tricks against him and postulated that the critical factor was male envy of the female, particularly of her reproductive potential (*womb envy*), and suggested that male achievement really represents an overcompensation for feelings of anatomical inferiority (a femininity complex). Bettelheim (1962) elaborated upon this notion with observations on puberty rites of primitive tribes, from which he concluded that womb envy is a very real force and that penis envy has been greatly exaggerated.

Helene Deutsch In 1944, Helene Deutsch published a weighty two-volume work entitled *Psychology of Women*, the major attempt within the psychoanalytic school for a complete understanding of the psychological dynamics of women. In many ways, Deutsch is more of an observer and analyst than she is a theorist; her book contains numerous excerpts from case histories to illustrate major tenets of the psychoanalytic view of women.

Deutsch's major contribution was to extend Freud's analysis of female development, which essentially ended with the phallic stage and Oedipal complex, to later stages of development. She began in the prepuberty period because she saw the critical processes in woman's psychological development revolving around the transition from being a girl to being a woman. She then continued to describe female development and personality in adolescence and adulthood.

Deutsch largely retained a Freudian orthodoxy in her thinking. For example, she believed that to be a woman one must develop a "feminine core" in the personality, including the traits of narcissism, masochism, and passivity. She also held that instinct and intuition were very important to a feminine personality.

She elaborated on Freud's distinction between the function of the clitoris and the function of the vagina. She saw the switch from clitoral eroticism to a focus on the vagina as being an important task during prepuberty and adolescence. This switch represented a shift from activity to passivity, the clitoris representing the active, masculine component that the woman must give up to be truly feminine (Deutsch, 1924). Deutsch viewed this as the hardest task of libidinal development — a task further complicated by the beginning of menstruation, which revived feelings of castration.

Deutsch coined the term "masculinity complex" to refer to certain instances of women's failure to adjust. Such women are characterized by a predominance of masculine active and aggressive tendencies, which brings them into conflict with both their surrounding environment and their own feminine tendencies.

Deutsch viewed motherhood as the most critical feature in woman's psychological development. Indeed, the whole second volume of *Psychology of Women* was devoted exclusively to this topic, and she saw prepuberty and adolescence as mainly an anticipation of motherhood.

> Thus woman acquires a tendency to passivity that intensifies the passive nature inherent in her biology and anatomy. She passively awaits fecundation: her life is fully active and rooted in reality only when she becomes a mother. Until then everything that is feminine in the woman, physiology and psychology, is passive, receptive. (1944, Vol. I, p. 140)

Deutsch's view of the psychology of women is at once insightful and laden with the confusion of cultural and biological forces typical of psychoanalytic theory. For example, she believed that female passivity is a result of anatomy and biological functioning and failed to recognize that it is a culturally assigned part of the female role.

Erik Erikson Erikson's reformulation and extension of psychoanalytic theory provides a more sophisticated view of social influences on development. Here we will concentrate on his major contribution to the psychology of women, his concept of inner space.

Erikson theorized that the key factor in female personality was not the reactive penis envy but rather a constructive, creative sense of a vital *inner space*. As he put it,

> But how, then, does a woman's identity formation differ by dint of the fact that her somatic design harbors an "inner space" destined to bear the offspring of chosen men and, with it, a biological, psychological, and ethical commitment to take care of human infancy? Is not the disposition for this commitment (whether to be realized in actual motherhood or not) the core problem of female *fidelity?* (1964, p. 5)

His major empirical evidence that this phenomenon exists comes from the play constructions of children. Children were asked to pretend to be motion picture directors, and to construct an exciting scene from a movie with a variety of miniature figures (people, animals, furniture, blocks). The girls generally produced an interior scene, with a configuration of furniture or an enclosure built with blocks. The people were inside, primarily in static positions, and the scene was generally peaceful. Occasionally there were portrayals of elaborate doorways. Boys, on the other hand, portrayed exterior scenes, sometimes with high walls with protrusions such as towers. The scenes depicted exciting action, often with downfall and ruin, such as automobile accidents. In sum, then, the girls portrayed inner, and the boys, outer space. Interestingly, the girls occasionally showed intrusions into their interior scenes by animals or dangerous men; their reaction was not fear or anger, but rather, pleasurable excitement and humor.

Certainly such observations could be criticized as the sole empirical basis for Erikson's assertions, although there is some independent supporting evidence (Franck and Rosen, 1949). His study has been criticized on the basis that it was poorly controlled and that the subjects were too old (they were 10-, 11-, and 12-year-olds) to rule out cultural factors as causes of the gender differences.

Erikson contrasted his understanding of women with the Freudian one as follows:

> . . . a shift of theoretical emphasis from the loss of an external organ to a sense of vital inner potential; from a hateful contempt of the mother to a solidarity with her and other women; from a "passive" renunciation of male activity to the purposeful and competent activity of one endowed with ovaries and a uterus; and from a masochistic pleasure in pain to an ability to stand (and to understand) pain as a meaningful aspect of human experience in general, and of the feminine role in particular. (1964, p. 13)

Another important contribution of Erikson was that he saw personal and gender identity as continuously subject to change and differentiation throughout the life of the individual, and that he did not concentrate exclusively on the infant/child period. That is, his developmental theory extends across the entire lifespan. As we shall see, this is particularly relevant in describing the developmental processes involved in identity acquisition in women.

FIGURE 3.1

Chodorow argues that mothering (most childcare being done by women) produces vastly different experiences for boys and girls, resulting in girls who want to mother and boys who dominate and devalue women.

Source: Jerry Howard / Positive Images.

Nancy Chodorow   Nancy Chodorow's book *The Reproduction of Mothering* (1978) is a controversial new addition to the psychoanalytic literature. In her book Chodorow fuses psychoanalytic theory, sociological theory, and the feminist perspective (strange bedfellows, indeed!) in an attempt to answer the question "Why do women mother?" That is, why is it that in all cultures it is the women who do almost all of the care of children? Her thesis, in brief, is that childcare done by women produces vastly different experiences for daughters than for sons. Childcare done by mothers produces daughters who want to mother, and thus mothering reproduces itself. Women's mothering also produces sons who dominate and devalue women.

Infants start life in a state of total dependency, and, given the current division of labor, those dependency needs are satisfied almost exclusively by the mother. In addition, infants are narcissistic or self-centered, and have trouble distinguishing between the primary caretaker — the mother — and themselves. Because mothers do such a good job of meeting their every need, infants blissfully assume that mothers have no other interests besides themselves. As babies grow, perhaps as younger siblings are born, unpleasant reality eventually becomes clear as they come to understand that mothers do have other interests.

Chodorow contends that the early, intensely close relationship with the mother affects the sense of self and general attitudes toward women, for both boys and girls. Both males and females continue to expect women to be caring and sacrificing, and that forever shapes their attitudes toward women. The girl's sense of self is profoundly influenced because her intense relationship to her mother is never entirely broken. Therefore, girls never see themselves as separate in the way boys do, and girls and women continue to define themselves more in *relational* terms.

Boys, on the other hand, begin with the same intense attachment to the mother. But in order to develop a masculine identity, they must smash or repress the relationship to the mother. Thus masculinity comes to be defined negatively, as nonfemininity. Masculinity involves denying feminine maternal attachment. And thus all women come to be devalued as part of the male's need to separate himself from his mother (and all women) and define a masculine identity for himself. Fathers are essentially absent, and therefore their masculine qualities become idealized, and the notion of masculine superiority emerges. Simultaneously, men's capacity for parenting is reduced by their denial of relatedness.

In adulthood, men's relational needs are less than women's, and men's needs are satisfied by a relationship with a woman, in which they recapture the warmth of the infant relationship with their mother. Adult women have greater relational needs that cannot entirely be satisfied by a man. So women have babies, their relational needs are satisfied, and the cycle repeats itself.

According to Chodorow's analysis, her question "Why do women mother?" is not so small as it might appear. Women's mothering perpetuates the whole division of labor by gender, for once women are committed to be the exclusive childrearers, men must do the other jobs necessary for society to continue. Further, women's mothering creates the devaluation of women. Thus exclusive childrearing by women is a central issue.

How can Chodorow claim to have integrated feminism into her theory when her theory so clearly smacks of Freud? First, Chodorow makes feminist reconstructions of some of Freud's ideas. For example, she argues that girls' penis envy results not from a girl's recognition of the inherent superiority of the penis (as Freud said), but rather because the penis symbolizes the power men have in our society. Second, Chodorow does not stop with her analysis of the family dynamics that produce the whole situation. She continues to say that the only way for the cycle to be broken is for men to begin participating equally in childcare. She believes that, unless men do so, women will perpetually be devalued. As she concludes,

> Any strategy for change whose goal includes liberation from the constraints of an unequal social organization of gender must take account

of the need for a fundamental reorganization of parenting, so that primary parenting is shared between men and women. (Chodorow, 1978, p. 215)

Chodorow's theory is so new, and so few studies have been done to test its hypotheses, that it is difficult to evaluate it. Most of the evidence Chodorow cites in her book is clinical — that is, it comes from individual histories of people seeking psychotherapy. As such, Chodorow's theory is open to the same criticism that was made of Freud's, namely that it is based on disturbed personality and experience. On occasion, Chodorow does mention more solid scientific findings, but then proceeds to ignore them. For example, she mentions an important finding that parents tend to treat children quite similarly, regardless of gender, but that finding is not consistent with her theory, so she dismisses it (Chodorow, 1978, p. 98). Her belief that personality, and even the division of labor by gender, is determined by the time children are four or five years old would be disputed by many developmental psychologists. Finally, she eventually advocates social change by having fathers participate equally in childcare, but her theory indicates that present-day fathers, who are the products of the last generation of mothering, should be incapable of childrearing. How can change ever be made, then? (Personally, I think that men right now are perfectly capable of being good childrearers, but that idea does not follow logically from her theory.) Many feminists would agree that men should participate more equally in childcare, but not for the reasons Chodorow gives.

SOCIOBIOLOGY

Sociobiology is a controversial new theory initially proposed by Harvard biologist E. O. Wilson in his book *Sociobiology: The New Synthesis* (1975), a massive, 700-page work filled with countless examples from insect life. He followed this with a popularized version, *On Human Nature* (1978). David P. Barash has also provided a readable and thoughtful text in his *Sociobiology and Behavior* (1982).

Wilson originally defined sociobiology as "the systematic study of the biological basis of all social behavior" (1975, p. 4). But I think a better definition is provided by Barash (1982): "sociobiology is the application of evolutionary theory to understanding the social behavior of animals, including humans." That is, sociobiologists are specifically concerned with understanding how social behaviors — such as aggression or caring for the young — are the product of evolution. In fact, a better term for this discipline would probably be "socioevolution," but I will stick to "sociobiology" because it is the standard term.

To understand what sociobiology has to say about women and gender roles, we must first discuss evolutionary theory. Evolution, as modern biologists understand it, is a product of *natural selection*, a mechanism first proposed by Charles Darwin. His basic observation was that living things overreproduce — that is, they produce far more young than would be needed simply to replace themselves. Yet population sizes remain relatively constant. Therefore, many individuals must not survive. There must be differential survival, with the fittest organisms surviving and others not. In popular conceptions the "fittest" animal is the most aggressive, but evolutionary theory defines fitness differently. *Fitness* is defined in this theory as the relative number of genes an animal contributes to the next generation. The bottom line is producing lots of offspring, specifically healthy, viable offspring. Thus a man who jogs 10 miles a day, lifts weights, and has a 50-inch chest, but whose sperm count is zero, would be considered to have zero fitness according to sociobiologists. Over generations, there is differential reproduction, the fittest individuals producing the most offspring. Genes that produce fitness characteristics become more frequent, and fitness characteristics ("adaptive" characteristics) become more frequent; genes and associated characteristics that produce poor fitness become less frequent.

The basic idea of the sociobiologists is that the evolutionary theory of natural selection can be applied to social behaviors. That is, a particular form of social behavior — let's say caring for one's young — would be adaptive, in the sense of increasing one's reproductive fitness. Other social behaviors — it seems to me female infanticide would be one of them — would be maladaptive, decreasing one's reproductive fitness. Over the many generations of natural selection that have occurred, the maladaptive behaviors should have been weeded out, and we should be left with social behaviors that are adaptive because they are the product of evolutionary selection. From this logic flows the *central theorem of sociobiology*: when a social behavior is genetically influenced, the animal should behave so as to maximize fitness (Barash, 1982).

With this as background, let us now consider some specific arguments of sociobiologists that are of special relevance to women.

Parental investment   One of the things sociobiologists have attempted to explain is why it is typically the female of the species that does most of the care of offspring. Remember that this phenomenon was also central to Chodorow's theory, but the sociobiologist offers a very different explanation for it. The sociobiologist's explanation rests on the concept of parental investment (Trivers, 1972). *Parental investment* refers to behaviors or other investments of the parent with respect to the offspring that increase the offspring's chance of survival, but also cost the parent something. This all becomes relevant to gender because females generally have a much larger parental investment in their offspring than males do. At the moment of conception, the female has the greater parental investment — she has just contributed one of her precious eggs. The male has contributed merely a sperm. Eggs are precious because they are large cells, and the female produces only one per month (at least in humans, and perhaps only one or several in a year in other species of mammals). Sperm are "cheap" because they are small cells and are produced in enormous numbers. For example, there are 300 million sperm in the average human male ejaculate, and a man can produce that number again in 24 to 48 hours. So at the moment of conception the female has invested much with her precious egg, but the male has invested little with a single sperm. In mammals, the female then proceeds to gestate the young (for a period of nine months in humans). Here again she makes an enormous investment of her body's resources, which otherwise could have been invested in doing something else. Then the offspring are born, and the female, at least among mammals, nurses them, once again investing time and energy.

The next step in the logic is this: it is most adaptive for whichever parent has the greater parental investment to continue to care for the off-spring. Here we have the female, who has invested her precious egg, her gestation, and her nursing; it would be evolutionary insanity for her to abandon the offspring when they still need more care in order to survive. In contrast, the male has invested relatively little and his best reproductive strategy is to "sleep around" and impregnate as many females as possible, producing more offspring carrying his genes. This works particularly well if he can count on the female to take care of the offspring so that they survive.

In short, the sociobiologist says that women are the ones who do the childcare for two reasons. The first is that the female has a greater parental investment and therefore it is adaptive for her to continue to care for her offspring. The second reason arises from a basic fact: maternity is always certain, whereas paternity is not. The female is sure that the offspring are hers. The sociobiologist would say that she knows that those young carry her genes. The male cannot be sure that they are his offspring, carrying his genes. It is thus adaptive for the female — it increases her fitness — to care for the offspring to make sure that they, and her genes, survive. It does not increase the male's fitness to care for offspring that may not carry his genes. Therefore, females take care of the offspring.

There are exceptions to this pattern, and they are worth considering. One is songbirds, who are notable because the male and female participate quite equally and cooperatively in care of their young (Barash, 1982). But sociobiologists believe that they can explain the exception as well as the general rule. Songbirds have a monogamous mating system that makes paternity a near certainty. Thus it is adaptive for the male to care for the young because he can be sure that they carry his genes. In addition, young birds require an enormous amount of food per day. It is doubtful that they could survive on the amount of food brought to them by a single parent. Thus it is highly adaptive for both parents to participate in care of the offspring, and would be highly maladaptive for fathers or mothers to ne-glect them.

Sociobiologists extend the logic of evolution to explain why female orgasm evolved in humans. The background is that female orgasm is thought to exist in few, if any, other species. Why, then, does it exist in humans?

Sociobiologists say that human female orgasm has evolved because human babies are born particularly helpless, dependent, and in need of parental care (Barash, 1982). Essentially, they need two parents in order to survive. A monogamous mating system, with permanent pairing of mother and father, would be adaptive and favored in evolution. The female orgasm (and the human female's continuous interest in sex at all phases of the menstrual cycle) thus evolved in order to hold together that permanent pair.

Sociobiologists also extend their theorizing to explain the *double standard* — that is, that among humans the male is allowed, even encouraged, to be promiscuous, whereas the female is punished for engaging in promiscuous sex and instead is very careful and selective about whom she has sex with (Barash, 1982). The explanation has to do with that precious egg and those cheap sperm. It is adaptive for her to be careful of what happens to the egg, whereas it is adaptive for him to distribute sperm to as many females as possible. Anticipating her greater parental investment, the female also must be careful about whose genes she mixes with her own. (This line of thinking gives a whole new meaning to the expression "choosy mothers.")

Sexual selection   Sexual selection is an evolutionary mechanism originally proposed by Darwin as acting in parallel to natural selection and as producing gender differences. Essentially, sexual selection means that different selection pressures act on males and females, and thus males and females become different. *Sexual selection* consists of two processes: (1) one gender (usually males) competes among themselves, in order to gain mating privileges with members of the other gender (usually females); and (2) members of the other gender (usually females) have preferences for certain members of the first gender (usually males) and decide which of them they are willing to mate with. In short, males fight and females choose. Process (1) neatly explains why the males of most species are larger and more aggressive than the females — aggression is adaptive for males in competition, and they are the product of sexual selection. Sexual selection explains, for example, why among many species of birds it is the male that has the gorgeous plumage while the female is rather dowdy. Plumage is a way that males compete among themselves, and females are attracted to the most gorgeous males. Females, on the other hand, in their roles as choosers, need not be gorgeous and have not been selected to be so. Perhaps they have been selected for wisdom (I said that, not a sociobiologist!).

Sexual selection, then, is a mechanism that generally can be used to explain gender differences. It is particularly useful in explaining the greater size, strength, and aggressiveness of males.

Many more examples could be given, but you have seen the main ones

FIGURE 3.2

Sociobiologists argue that gender differences in aggression in humans and other species are a result of sexual selection in evolution.

Source: Miriam Austerman / Animals, Animals.

dealing with women's issues. The thrust of the argument is clear: the sociobiologist argues that the social behaviors we see in animals and humans today evolved because they were adaptive.

Feminist criticism   Feminists are not exactly delighted with sociobiology (for feminist critiques, see Weisstein, 1982; Janson-Smith, 1980; Hrdy, 1981). Two basic criticisms have been raised. First, many feminists are generally wary of biological explanations of anything. The reason is that biology always seems to end up being a convenient rationalization for perpetuating the status quo. For example, the sociobiologist's belief is that the greater aggression and dominance of males is a result of sexual selection and is controlled by genes. Therefore, men are genetically dominant, and women are genetically subordinate, and the subordinate status of women will have to continue because it is genetic. That kind of logic is a red flag to a feminist. Sociobiologists are not so naive that they ignore environmental influences entirely, so the argument becomes a question of emphasis, sociobiologists emphasizing biology and feminists emphasizing environment.

Second, feminists object that sociobiologists do a highly selective reading of both data and theories. Sociologists tend to view data from an androcentric (male-centered) perspective and to talk selectively about those studies that confirm their androcentric theory, ignoring those studies that contradict it. For example, the female chimpanzee — the chimpanzee is our nearest evolutionary relative — is notoriously promiscuous (Janson-Smith, 1980). When she is in estrus, she mates indiscriminately with many males. That does not fit into sociobiology, which says that she should be choosy about the male with whom she mates and that the most aggressive, dominant male should be the only one to have the privilege of inseminating her. The sociobiologists tend to ignore chimpanzees.

As another instance of androcentric bias, consider the case of a famous young female macaque (monkey) named Imo, living with her troop on an island off Japan.

> Scientists provisioned the troop there with sweet potatoes. Imo discovered that washing sweet potatoes got the sand off. Her discovery quickly spread among the other juniors in the troop, who then taught their mothers, who in turn, taught their infants. Adult males never learned it. Next, scientists flung grains of wheat in the sand to see what the troop would do. Rather than laboriously picking the wheat out of the sand grain by grain, Imo discovered how to separate the wheat from the sand in one operation. Again this spread from Imo's peers to mothers and infants, and, again, adult males never learned it. The fact that these Japanese macaques had a rudimentary culture has been widely heralded. (Weisstein, 1982, p. 46).

Had the genders been reversed, with Imo being a male and the females being unable to learn, one can imagine the attention these facts would have been given by sociobiologists. They would have made much of the genius of the male and the lack of intelligence of females. As it is, Imo's gender is not discussed, and the learning failure of the males is similarly ignored.[1] Sociobiologists, then, seem to ignore many animal examples that contradict human stereotypes.

From a feminist perspective, even the sociobiologists' attention to theory is selective and androcentric. For example, sexual selection, as noted above, contains two parts. The part that produces competition and aggression in males has received much attention from sociobiologists. But they have ignored the second part, in which females make choices among males. The second part could be used as an explanation for human females' being more intelligent, more perceptive, or more powerful and controlling than human males, but that avenue of thought is never explored by sociobiologists.

Sociobiologists also rely heavily on data from nonindustrial societies, specifically hunter-gatherer societies that are supposed to be like those that existed at the dawn of the human species, millions of years ago. Once

---

[1] In case you are not sufficiently impressed with Imo, have you figured out a good way to separate the wheat from the sand? Imo did it by throwing both into the water, where the wheat floated and the sand sunk to the bottom.

again, the emphasis is androcentrically selective. The sociobiologist emphasizes "man the hunter" and how he evolved to be aggressive and have great physical prowess. In discussing this, Wilson (1978, p. 127) makes much of how natural selection for these traits is reflected in men's current superiority in Olympic track events. Later on the same page, he mentions that women are superior in precision archery and small-bore rifle shooting in the Olympics, but does not seem to see this as inconsistent with the evolution of only man as the hunter. "Woman the gatherer" is ignored, although she may have formed the foundation for early human social organization (Janson-Smith, 1980).

The feminist criticisms, then, are that sociobiology can rationalize and perpetuate the subordination of women, and that its evidence rests on a selective, androcentric citing of the data, ignoring many contradictions.

SOCIAL LEARNING THEORY

A popular explanation for gender differences in behavior is "conditioning." That is, boys and girls act appropriately for their gender because they have been rewarded for doing some things and punished for doing others. The notion is that principles of operant conditioning explain the acquisition of gender roles. Thus, some behaviors are rewarded for girls while others either are not rewarded or are even punished, so that the girl comes to perform the rewarded behaviors more frequently, the unrewarded ones less frequently or not at all. For example, little girls are rewarded for being quiet and obedient, while little boys are rewarded for athletics and achievement. Consequently, children acquire gender-typed behaviors because they are rewarded or approved. This is thought to be the essential process creating gender-typing.

Social learning theory is a major theoretical system in psychology, designed to describe the process involved in human development (see Bandura and Walters, 1963). In particular, it has been used to explain the development of gender differences (Mischel, 1966). In explaining the shaping of children's behavior, social learning theory uses the notion of *direct reinforcement* described above — that is, the idea that rewards and punishments are given differentially to boys and girls for gender-typed behaviors, and that children therefore come to perform the rewarded, gender-appropriate behaviors more frequently and the punished, gender-inappropriate behaviors less frequently. But social learning theory also emphasizes the importance of two additional processes: *imitation* and *observational learning*. Imitation means simply that children do what they see others doing. Observational learning refers to situations in which children learn by observing the behavior of others, even though they may not actually perform the behavior at the time, perhaps not using the information until months or years later. These three mechanisms, then — direct reinforcement, imitation, and observational learning — are thought to underlie the process of gender-typing, that is, the acquisition of gender-typed behaviors, according to social learning theory.

Acquiring gender roles   Given the way roles are divided in our culture, infants of both genders are biologically and psychologically dependent on the mother. According to the social learning approach, because the mother is the source of attention and care, the association of the mother's presence with comfort leads the child to value mother-presence and to experience anxiety or discomfort in her absence. Thus, as mother-presence comes to be equated with pleasure and mother-absence with discomfort, the mother takes on important meaning to the infant — she becomes an effective reinforcer of the child's behavior. In the course of development, the mother's demands and expectations for the child's behavior increase and the child learns to perform those acts that will bring about approval. The child's behavior comes to be keyed to the mother's approval or disapproval.

Applying the theory to the process of gender-role learning, the mother presumably reacts differently to gender-typed behaviors in her child. For example, she may react positively when her daughter displays feminine behaviors, such as nurturance, and negatively when she displays masculine behaviors, such as aggressiveness. In effect, she rewards feminine behaviors and may punish masculine behaviors. Social learning theory asserts that these reinforcements will be effective in shaping the child's behavior.

Later, stimulus generalization occurs. That is, stimuli similar to the mother, for example, the father and other adults, also become effective reinforcers of behavior. These other adults also presumably react differentially to gender-appropriate behavior in the child, and apply reinforcements similar to those the mother has used. Thus male and female children are treated differently, the rewards being given in accordance with cultural prescriptions regarding appropriate behavior for males and females.

According to social learning theory, gender-typing involves another process, imitation. The child imitates the behavior of other people. The child's imitation is motivated partly by the power of authority figures, so that he or she is particularly likely to imitate parents or other adults. Behaving like a particular person gives the child the sense that she or he possesses that person's power. With regard to gender-role learning, the theory assumes that children tend to imitate the same-gender parent and other same-gender adults more than opposite-gender adults. That is, the little girl imitates her mother and other women more than she does men. This mechanism of imitation helps to explain the acquisition of the complex and subtle aspects of gender roles that probably have not been the object of direct reinforcements. Further, imitation and direct reinforcement may interact. For example, the girl may imitate a behavior of her mother's and then be rewarded for it, once again furthering the process of gender-typing.

FIGURE 3.3

Children learn gender roles in part by imitation of adults.

Source: Photo by Misha Erwitt / Magnum.

The child does not actually have to perform a behavior in order to learn it. A behavior may become part of the child's repertoire through observational learning. Such information may be stored up for use perhaps ten or fifteen years later, when a situation in adolescence or adulthood calls for a knowledge of gender-appropriate behaviors. For example, a young girl may observe her mother caring for an infant brother or sister. Although the little girl may not perform any infant-care behaviors at the time, much less be rewarded for them, she nonetheless may store up the information about infant care for use when she herself is a mother. Once again, gender-typing occurs through mechanisms other than direct reinforcement.

In more advanced learning, children also learn to anticipate the consequences of their actions. Here also, an action need not be performed for the child to understand the reinforcements or punishments that will result.

The little girl knows in advance that her attempts to join Little League will be met with opposition, and perhaps even with direct punishments. Higher-order conditioning also occurs so that, for example, verbal cues may serve as strong reinforcements or punishments. The words "sissy" and "mannish" acquire a punishing quality all their own.

According to social learning theory, then, gender-typing results from differential rewards and punishments as well as learning in the absence of direct reinforcement, by imitation of same-gender models and observational learning.

Evidence for social learning theory   Social learning theory has stimulated a great deal of research aimed at documenting the existence — or nonexistence — of the mechanisms it proposes. The research makes it possible to begin to assess the adequacy of the social learning model for the development of gender differences.

There have been numerous demonstrations of the effectiveness of imitation and reinforcements in shaping children's behavior, in particular gender-typed behaviors such as aggression. A good example is a study by the phychologist Albert Bandura (1965). In the first phase of this experiment, children were divided into three groups and shown one of three films. In all the films, an adult model was performing aggressive behavior, but in one film the model was rewarded; in another, punished; and in the third, left alone without consequences. The children's aggressive behavior was then observed. As the social learning approach would predict, children who had viewed the model being punished performed the least aggressive behavior. Further, and consistent with the findings of many other investigators (see Chapter 6), boys performed more aggressive behavior than girls. In the second phase of the experiment, the children were offered attractive reinforcements (pretty sticker pictures and juice treats) for performing as many of the model's aggressive responses as they could remember. Gender differences nearly disappeared in this phase, and girls performed nearly as many aggressive behaviors as boys.

This experiment illustrated several important points. The first phase demonstrated that children do imitate, and that they do so differentially depending on the perceived consequences of the behavior. Notice that in this phase the children themselves were not actually reinforced, but simply observed the model being reinforced. The second phase illustrated how gender differences in aggressive behavior can be influenced by reinforcements. When girls were given equal direct reinforcement for aggression, they were nearly as aggressive as boys. Certainly the experiment is evidence of the power of imitation and reinforcement in shaping children's behavior. However, even though these effects have been demonstrated in the laboratory, this does not necessarily imply that they are the mechanisms underlying the natural acquisition of gender differences (Baldwin, 1967).

Criticisms of social learning theory   The mechanisms postulated by social learning theory — differential reinforcement, imitation, and observational learning — intuitively appear to be reasonable explanations for why gender differences develop. Nonetheless, it is important to remember that these ideas must be tested scientifically. The study by Bandura discussed above is one kind of test of social learning theory. But we still need to know some other things, namely (1) do parents and others actually reinforce the behavior of boys and girls differentially; and (2) do children really imitate parents and others of their own gender more than people of the other gender? The available evidence seems to support point (1), but not point (2).

There is evidence that parents treat boys and girls differently, and that they differentially reward some — though certainly not all — behaviors in boys and girls (Block, 1978; Sherman, 1978). In particular, parents emphasize different values for boys and girls (Block, 1973). Achievement and assertion are encouraged in boys, while girls are taught to control these characteristics; a sense of relatedness (concern for relationships with other people) is emphasized for girls.

The evidence does not support, however, the notion that children tend to imitate people of their own gender more than people of the opposite gender (Maccoby and Jacklin, 1974). When offered an opportunity to imitate either a male or a female model, young children do not tend to behave more like the model whose gender is the same as their own; indeed, their behavior appears to be fairly random with respect to the gender of the model. This raises the distinction between *learning* and *performance*. It is possible that children learn equally from models of both genders, but that they differentially perform what they have learned, depending on the perceived consequences of their behavior and the gender-appropriateness of the behavior. This point is illustrated in the study by Bandura mentioned above. Although the girls were less aggressive than the boys in the first phase of the experiment, they were almost equally aggressive in the second phase. The results from the second phase suggest that the girls had learned as much as the boys about the model's aggressive behavior, but that in the first phase they did not perform what they had learned, and did so only in the second phase when encouraged by reinforcements.

In summary, social learning theory postulates that three important mechanisms are involved in the development of gender differences: differential reinforcement, imitation, and observational learning. The power of reinforcements and imitation in influencing children's behavior has been demonstrated in numerous experiments. It also seems that parents do differentially reinforce some gender-typed behaviors. However, research calls into question whether children do imitate same-gender models more than opposite-gender ones. These latter results suggest that other, more complex processes must be involved, in addition to those postulated by social learning theory, in the development of gender differences.

THE COGNITIVE-
DEVELOPMENTAL MODEL

In terms of impact, perhaps the closest equivalent in the second half of this century to Freud's work in the first half is the developmental theory founded by Jean Piaget. Kohlberg (1966) has extended Piaget's cognitive principles to the realm of gender roles.

Much of Piaget's thinking arose from his observations of the errors children made in answering questions such as those asked on intelligence tests. He concluded that these errors did not indicate that the children were stupid or ignorant, but rather that they had a different world view, or *cognitive organization* from that of adults. He discovered that the cognitive organizations of children change systematically over time, and he constructed a stage theory of cognitive (intellectual) development to describe the progression of these changes. Interestingly, concepts of gender and gender identity undergo developmental changes parallel to the development of other concepts.

Gender roles and gender constancy If you ask a three-year-old girl whether she is a boy or a girl, she will answer correctly that she is a girl. But if you ask her whether she can grow up to be a daddy, she will incorrectly answer yes. A six- or seven-year-old girl will not make this error. The three-year-old understands the concept of gender, but does not yet have the concept of *gender constancy* — the knowledge that gender is a permanent part of the self or identity. The development of these concepts is amusingly illustrated by Kohlberg (1966, p. 95):

> (Jimmy has just turned four, his friend Johnny is four and a half)
> Johnny: I'm going to be an airplane builder when I grow up.
> Jimmy: When I grow up, I'll be a mommy.
> Johnny: No, you can't be a mommy. You have to be a daddy.
> Jimmy: No, I'm going to be a mommy.
> Johnny: No, you're not a girl, you can't be a mommy.
> Jimmy: Yes, I can.

Apparently Johnny has acquired the concept of gender constancy, whereas Jimmy hasn't.

According to Kohlberg, the acquisition of these basic concepts of gender constancy and gender identity (around the ages of four to six) is the crucial basis for the acquisition of gender role. Once the little girl knows she is a girl and will always be a female, this gender identity becomes an important part of personal identity. Gender identity then determines basic valuations (whether a person or behavior is believed to be "good" or "bad"). Motivated to have a positive sense of self, the girl comes to see femaleness as good. She then associates this valuation with cultural stereotypes, so that the female role becomes attractive to her. And finally she identifies with her mother, who is a readily available example of the female role the girl wishes to acquire. Thus children are motivated to adopt gender roles as part of their attempt to understand reality and to develop a stable and positive self-concept.

Cognitive-developmental theory essentially views gender-role learning as one aspect of cognitive development. The child learns a set of rules regarding what males do and what females do, and behaves accordingly. Gender-role learning is thus viewed not as externally imposed, but rather as largely self-motivated. The child essentially engages in self-socialization and self-selects the behaviors to be learned and performed on the basis of rules regarding the gender-appropriateness of the behavior.

Cognitive-developmental theory points up an important potential problem in female development. It asserts, quite reasonably, that normal, healthy children tend to value the self, and therefore their own gender. Therefore little girls grow up thinking "female is good." Unfortunately, this does not correspond to cultural valuations of gender roles, in which the male role is valued more highly. Thus the girl is placed in a conflict situation in which her human need is to value the female role, yet culture informs her that it is not a valued role. We shall discuss the implications of this situation further in the next chapters.

Criticisms of cognitive-developmental theory   Kohlberg's basic argument is that the acquisition of the concept of gender constancy and, with it, the concept of gender identity is the important first step in gender-typing. Once these concepts have been formed, say around five to seven years of age, the child essentially "self-socializes." What evidence is there supporting these ideas?

First, it is clear that there is a concept of gender constancy that develops in children around the ages of five to seven. Evidence comes from children's comments such as those quoted earlier in this chapter, and from their responses to direct questioning by psychologists (e.g., Marcus and Overton, 1978). There is also some evidence that kindergarteners who have acquired gender constancy prefer to observe same-gender models, as compared with opposite-gender models, whereas children who do not yet have a concept of gender constancy have no such preference (Slaby, 1974, cited in Maccoby and Jacklin, 1974, p. 365). Preschoolers who have acquired gender constancy are more stereotyped in their views of adult occupations than are preschoolers who do not have gender constancy (O'Keefe and Hyde, 1983).

However, it is also clear that children's gender-typed interests appear when they are far too young to have acquired the concept of gender constancy (Maccoby and Jacklin, 1974; O'Keefe and Hyde, 1983). That is, gender-typed toy and game preferences appear when children are two or three, yet children do not develop gender constancy until they are between the ages of five and seven. This is inconsistent with Kohlberg's theory, which would say that gender-typed interests should not appear until after gender constancy develops.

It seems reasonable to conclude that Kohlberg's notion of gender constancy and "self-socialization" explains some aspects of gender-role development, but that other mechanisms — such as those in social learning theory — are also functioning.

I should also note that Kohlberg has presented his model of the development of gender identity for the male only; thus, much of what I have said is based on my inferences of what the model would be for the female. In fact, the model may break down in attempting to explain the acquisition of female gender identity. According to the theory, one of the child's main motives for adopting a gender role is the power and value the child sees in that role; yet the female role has less power and value. Is the girl therefore less motivated to adopt her role than is the boy? Kohlberg (1966, pp. 121–122) attempts to avoid this problem by saying that girls are motivated by the competency and "niceness" they perceive the female role to represent. Certainly it would be desirable to have a more complete explication of the process of female gender-role development from the cognitive-developmental point of view.

Kohlberg on moral development   Kohlberg's other major contribution to psychology has been his analysis of moral development, that is, children's changing cognitions or understandings about morality (Kohlberg, 1969; Colby et al., 1983). Although the analysis is not directly about women, it has important implications for women. First, you need to know how Kohlberg has studied children's moral development and how he has determined that there are stages in children's moral reasoning.

Kohlberg has studied children's moral thought by presenting them with a moral dilemma, of which the following is an example:

> In Europe, a woman was near death from a special kind of cancer. There was one drug that the doctors thought might save her. It was a form of radium that a druggist in the same town had recently discovered. The drug was expensive to make, but the druggist was charging 10 times what the drug cost him to make. He paid $200 for the radium and charged $2,000 for a small dose of the drug. The sick woman's husband, Heinz, went to everyone he knew to borrow the money, but he could only get together about $1,000, which is half of what it cost. He told the druggist that his wife was dying and asked him to sell it cheaper or let him pay later. But the druggist said, "No, I discovered the drug and I'm going to make money from it." So Heinz gets desperate and considers breaking into the man's store to steal the drug for his wife.

A child is asked if Heinz should steal the drug and why. The important part is not whether or not the child says Heinz should steal, but rather the child's answer to the question "why," which reflects the child's stage of development of moral reasoning.

TABLE 3.1. **Kohlberg's versus Gilligan's understanding of moral development**

Kohlberg's Levels and Stages	Kohlberg's Definition	Gilligan's Levels
Level I. Preconventional morality		Level I. Preconventional morality
Stage 1. Punishment orientation	Obey rules to avoid punishment	Concern for the self and survival
Stage 2. Naive reward orientation	Obey rules to get rewards, share in order to get returns	
Level II. Conventional morality		Level II. Conventional morality
Stage 3. Good-boy/ good-girl orientation	Conform to rules that are defined by others' approval/disapproval	Concern for being responsible, caring for others
Stage 4. Authority orientation	Rigid conformity to society's rules, law-and-order mentality, avoid censure for rule-breaking	
Level III. Postconventional morality		Level III. Postconventional morality
Stage 5. Social-contract orientation	More flexible understanding that we obey rules because they are necessary for social order, but the rules could be changed if there were better alternatives	Concern for self and others as interdependent
Stage 6. Morality of individual principles and conscience	Behavior conforms to internal principles (justice, equality) to avoid self-condemnation, and sometimes may violate society's rules	

Based on his research, Kohlberg has concluded that people go through a series of three levels in their moral reasoning as they mature, and that each level is divided into two stages, for a total of six stages. These stages are defined on the left side of Table 3.1. In Level I, preconventional morality, children (usually preschoolers) have little sense of rules, and obey simply to avoid punishments or obtain rewards. For example, Heinz should not steal because he might get caught and put in jail. In Level II, conventional morality, children (usually beginning in elementary school) are well aware of society's rules and laws and conform to them rigidly; there is a law-and-order mentality and a desire to look good in front of others. For example, Heinz should not steal because stealing is against the law. Finally, in Level III, postconventional morality, a person transcends the rules and laws of society and instead behaves in accordance with an internal, self-defined set of ethical principles. For example, it is acceptable for Heinz to steal because human life is more important than property. In Level III, it might be judged acceptable to violate laws in some instances in which they were unjust. The perfect example of Level III morality is the life of Mahatma Gandhi as shown so clearly in the recent movie *Gandhi*. For him, equality and freedom were self-accepted, internalized values that allowed him to violate the laws of his country, and he persisted in following his own principles despite the disapproval of authorities, which was sometimes so severe that he was beaten.

According to Kohlberg's research, most adults never reach Level III, and instead persist in Stages 3 and 4 of Level II, stoutly believing in law and order and conforming to rules in order to avoid the disapproval of their neighbors.

Kohlberg has also found evidence of gender differences in moral development, and here the interest for the psychology of women begins. Kohlberg found that most males eventually reach Stage 4, whereas most females only reach Stage 3. From this it might be concluded that females have a less well-developed sense of morality. Freud's immature superego returns dressed up in a modern, scientific costume.

In evaluating Kohlberg's theory, there is evidence that children pass through the early stages he specified, in the order in which he specified them (e.g., Kuhn, 1976). On the other hand, there are certain value judgments involved in setting up the hierarchy of stages in the way he did; in particular, it seems odd to have a Level III that few adults ever reach (someone once joked that the only people who reach Level III are Kohlberg and his graduate students). In my opinion, though, one of the most insightful critiques of Kohlberg's works is the feminist analysis by Gilligan (1982).

Gilligan: A new perspective on moral development   Harvard psychologist Carol Gilligan has provided a feminist critique of Kohlberg's work on moral development in her book *In a Different Voice* (1982). She also provides a reformulation of moral development from the woman's point of view.

Several of her criticisms follow from our earlier discussion of sexist bias in research. The main character of Kohlberg's dilemma is Heinz, a man. Perhaps females have trouble identifying with him. Some of the other moral dilemmas Kohlberg uses are more gender-neutral, but one is about the captain of a company of Marines. Once again, women may find this a bit hard to relate to. Gilligan (1982, p. 18) also points out that the subjects who form the basis for Kohlberg's theorizing are a group of 84 *males*, whom he has followed for 20 years, beginning in their childhood. When a theory is based on evidence from males, it is not surprising that it does not apply well to females. Finally, Gilligan points out a bias in Kohlberg's interpretation: the phenomenon that women only reach Stage 3 is interpreted as a deficiency in female development, whereas it might just as easily be interpreted as being a deficiency in Kohlberg's theory, which may not adequately describe female development.

Gilligan does not stop with a critique of Kohlberg. She extends her analysis to provide a feminist reformulation of moral development. Her reformulation is based on the belief that women are reasoning differently about the moral dilemmas — that is, they are speaking in a different voice (hence the title of her book) — and that their voices have not been listened to. In order to understand her ideas, listen to the voices of 11-year-old Jake and 11-year-old Amy responding to the Heinz dilemma. First Jake:

> For one thing, human life is worth more than money, and if the druggist only makes $1,000, he is still going to live, but if Heinz doesn't steal the drug, his wife is going to die. (*Why is life worth more than money?*) Because the druggist can get a thousand dollars later from rich people with cancer, but Heinz can't get his wife again. (Gilligan, 1982, p. 26)

Now Amy, asked if Heinz should steal the drug,

> Well, I don't think so. I think there might be other ways besides stealing it, like if he could borrow the money or make a loan or something, but he really shouldn't steal the drug — but his wife shouldn't die either. (*Why shouldn't he steal the drug?*) If he stole the drug, he might save his wife then, but if he did, he might have to go to jail, and then his wife might get sicker again, and he couldn't get more of the drug, and it might not be good. So, they should really just talk it out and find some other way to make the money. (Gilligan, 1982, p. 28)

Jake would be scored as showing a mixture of Stages 3 and 4, but also as reaching some elements of mature Level III mortality (Gilligan, 1982, p. 27). Amy, on the other hand, just doesn't fit very well into the scoring system. Jake, like Kohlberg, sees the issue as one of rules and balancing the rights of individuals: the right of the druggist to profit, and the right of Heinz's wife (who remains nameless) to life. In contrast, Amy sees the issue as one of relationships: the problem that the druggist fails to live up to a relationship to the needy woman, the need to preserve the relationship between Heinz and his wife, and the need to avoid a bad relationship between Heinz and the druggist. Her solution similarly does not involve rules, but rather relationships — they should "talk it out" and mend the relationships.

Gilligan contrasts these two approaches to moral reasoning in several ways. The *justice perspective* views people as differentiated and standing alone and focuses on the rights of the individual; the *care perspective* emphasizes relatedness between people and communication. Males tend to stress justice; females tend to stress caring. Males focus on agreements and contracts between people; females focus on attachments between people. In essence, women tend to think differently about moral questions. Kohlberg devised his stages of moral reasoning with the male as norm; thus women's answers appear immature, when in fact they are simply based on different concerns.

What evidence is there for Gilligan's theorizing? Two studies, one with college students and one with adolescents, demonstrated that women's moral judgments, compared with men's, are more tied to feelings of empathy and compassion (Haan, 1975; Holstein, 1976). Gilligan herself also presented several studies in support of her views. Here I will consider one of these, the abortion decision study. She interviewed 29 women, between the ages of 15 and 33, all of whom were in the first trimester of pregnancy and were considering abortion. They were interviewed a second time one year later. Notice how she shifted the moral dilemma from a male stranger named Heinz to an issue that is far more central to women. Just as Kohlberg saw three major levels of moral reasoning, so Gilligan found three levels among these women, but the focus for the levels was different (see the right side of Table 3.1). In Level I, preconventional morality, the woman making the abortion decision is concerned only for herself and her survival. An example is Susan, an eighteen-year-old, who was asked what she thought when she found out that she was pregnant:

> I really didn't think anything except that I didn't want it. (*Why was that?*) I didn't want it, I wasn't ready for it, and next year will be my last year and I want to go to school. (Gilligan, 1982, p. 75)

Women who have reached Level II have shifted their focus to being responsible and to caring for others, specifically for a potential child. Women in Level II see their previous, less mature, Level I responses as selfish. These themes are articulated by Josie, a seventeen-year-old, in discussing her reaction to being pregnant:

> I started feeling really good about being pregnant instead of feeling really bad, because I wasn't looking at the situation realistically. I was looking at it from my own sort of selfish needs, because I was lonely. Things weren't really going good for me, so I was looking at it that I could have a baby that I could take care of or something that was part of me, and that made me feel good. But I wasn't looking at the realistic side, at the responsibility I would have to take on. I came to this decision that I was going to have an abortion because I realized how much responsibility goes with having a child. Like you have to be there; you can't go out of the house all the time, which is one thing I like to do. And I decided

that I have to take on responsibility for myself and I have to work out a lot of things. (Gilligan, 1982, p. 77)

Typical of Level II thinking, she sees Level I thinking as selfish, and shifts her concern to being responsible to the child. Notice that deciding to have an abortion or not to have an abortion is not what differentiates Level I from Level II. Either decision can be reached at either level. For example, in Level I the concern for self and survival can lead to having an abortion so that a baby does not interfere with one's life. However, the Level I concern for self and survival can also lead one not to have an abortion in order to have a baby for fun, giving and receiving love, and so on.

Finally, in Level III moral reasoning, the self and others are seen as interdependent, and there is a focus on balancing caring for others (the fetus, the father, parents) with caring for oneself. A woman must have reasonably high self-esteem to reach this level, for without it the "caring for self" aspect looks like a return to the selfishness of earlier levels, rather than a complex balancing of care extended to all, including herself. In this stage, caring is not the crude product of female socialization, but is rather a universal ethical principle that all should follow. A recapitulation of her earlier moral reasoning and her current balancing of caring is articulated by Sarah, who is faced with a second abortion:

> Well, the pros for having the baby are all the admiration that you would get from being a single woman, alone, martyr, struggling, having the adoring love of this beautiful Gerber baby. Just more of a home life than I have had in a long time, and that basically was it, which is pretty fantasyland. It is not very realistic. Cons against having the baby: it was going to hasten what is looking to be the inevitable end of the relationship with the man I am presently with. I was going to have to go on welfare. My parents were going to have me for the rest of my life. I was going to lose a really good job that I have. I would lose a lot of independence. Solitude. And I would have to be put in a position of asking help from a lot of people a lot of the time. Con against having the abortion is having to face up to the guilt. And pros for having the abortion are I would be able to handle my deteriorating relation with (the father) with a lot more capability and a lot more responsibility for myself. I would not have to go through the realization that for the next twenty-five years of my life I would be punishing myself for being foolish enough to get pregnant again and forcing myself to bring up a kid just because I did this. Having to face the guilt of a second abortion seemed like not exactly — well, exactly the lesser of two evils, but also the one that would pay off for me personally in the long run because, by looking at why I am pregnant again and subsequently have decided to have a second abortion, I have to face up to some things about myself. (Gilligan, 1982, p. 92)

Gilligan summarizes the differences between men's and women's moral reasoning as follows:

> The moral imperative that emerges repeatedly in interviews with women is an injunction to care, a responsibility to discern and alleviate the "real and recognizable trouble" of this world. For men, the moral imperative appears rather as an injunction to respect the rights of others and thus to protect from interference the rights to life and self-fulfillment. . . . Development for both sexes would therefore seem to entail an integration of rights and responsibilities through the discovery of the complementarity of these disparate views. (Gilligan, 1982, p. 100)

How good is Gilligan's theory? First, I think it is an excellent example of the "new feminist scholarship." She detected the male-centeredness of Kohlberg's analysis of moral reasoning. She then reconstructed the theory after listening to what females said and shaped a developmental model from it. The theory is new so there are few studies providing evidence for or against it — Gilligan conducted three studies herself, all supporting it, and the studies by Haan and by Holstein, mentioned earlier, are also in agreement. Another study demonstrated that the gender of the main character in Kohlberg's moral dilemmas can affect the level of subjects' moral reasoning (Bussey and Maughan, 1982). But basically it is too early to evaluate Gilligan's theory. My intuitive reservation about it comes from my own firm belief in gender similarities. Much of Gilligan's writing sounds as though men display one kind of moral thinking and women display a totally different kind. I suspect that there are some men who show "female" moral reasoning of the kind quoted earlier, and some women who display "male" moral reasoning. What is demonstrated is average differences. But that does not negate the importance of Gilligan's discovery of a much different side of moral reasoning, a side that is probably more common among females. Her work is a beautiful example of the feminist reconstruction of psychology.

GENDER SCHEMA THEORY

This brain teaser has been popular for the last few years:

> A father and his son were involved in a car accident in which the father was killed and the son was seriously injured. The father was pronounced dead at the scene of the accident and his body was taken to a local mortuary. The son was taken by ambulance to a hospital and was immediately wheeled into an operating room. A surgeon was called. Upon seeing the patient, the attending surgeon exclaimed, "Oh my God, it's my son!"
>
> Can you explain this? (Keep in mind that the father who was killed in the accident is not a stepfather, nor is the attending physician the boy's stepfather.)

If you have not heard this before, give yourself some time to solve it before reading the next paragraph, which contains the solution.

The solution is that the surgeon is the boy's *mother*. But why is it so difficult for most people to think of this solution? It is exactly this sort of question that is addressed by psychologist Sandra Bem's gender schema theory (1981).

First, you need to understand what a schema is. Schema is a concept from cognitive psychology, the branch of psychology that investigates how we think, perceive, process, and remember information (for a good summary of schema theory, not applied to gender, see Alba and Hasher, 1983). A *schema* is a general knowledge framework that a person has about a particular topic. A schema organizes and guides perception. To gain a more specific understanding of what a schema is, read the following description carefully and then, without looking back at it, answer the questions that follow.

> You decide to go to your favorite restaurant for dinner. You enter the restaurant and are seated at a table with a white tablecloth. You study the menu. You tell the waiter that you want prime rib, medium rare, a baked potato with sour cream, and a salad with blue cheese dressing on it. You also order red wine. A few minutes later the waiter returns with your salad. Later he brings the rest of the meal, all of which you enjoy, except the prime rib is a bit overdone.

Now answer the following questions:

1. What kind of salad dressing did you order?
2. Was the tablecloth red-checked?
3. What did you order to drink?
4. Did the waiter give you a menu?

You probably found the questions easy to answer. The important point is, what was your answer for question 4? The correct answer is "no," because there is no mention in the story of the waiter handing you a menu. Many people incorrectly answer "yes" to this question. The reason is that most of us have a restaurant schema in our stored knowledge. This schema contains certain characteristics that are common to most restaurants, as well as events that generally occur in most restaurants. A schema generally helps us process and remember information, and your restaurant schema may have helped you answer questions 1, 2, and 3. But schemas also act to *filter and interpret* information, and they can therefore cause errors in memory. A common part of a restaurant schema is that a waiter hands you a menu. Therefore, your restaurant schema probably filled in this piece of information that really was not described in the story and caused you to make an error. An individual's perception and memory of information, then, is a result of the interaction of the incoming information with the individual's preexisting schema.

Psychologist Sandra Bem (1981) has applied schema theory to understanding the gender-typing process in her gender schema theory (see also Martin and Halverson, 1983). Her proposal is that each one of us has as part of our knowledge structure a *gender schema,* a set of gender-linked associations. Further, the gender schema represents a basic predisposition to process information on the basis of gender. That is, it represents our tendency to see many things as gender-related and to want to dichotomize things on the basis of gender. The gender schema processses new, incoming information, filtering and interpreting it. Thus the gender schema theory provides a ready answer for why the brain teaser at the beginning of this section is so difficult. Most of us have a gender schema that contains a link between man and surgeon. Therefore, making an association from surgeon to woman or mother is difficult, if not impossible.

Bem says that the developmental process of gender-typing or gender-role acquisition in children is a result of the child's gradual learning of the content of society's gender schema. The gender-linked associations that form the schema are many: girls wear dresses and boys don't; boys are strong and tough, girls are pretty (perhaps learned simply from the adjectives adults apply to children, rarely or never calling boys pretty, rarely or never calling girls tough); girls grow up to be mommies, boys don't.

There is a further process. The gender schema becomes closely linked to the self-concept. Thus five-year-old Amanda knows she is a girl and also has a girl schema that she attaches to her own sense of girlhood. Amanda's self-esteem then begins to be dependent on how well she measures up to her girl schema. At that point, she becomes internally motivated to conform to society's female gender role (a point much like Kohlberg's). Society does not have to force her into the role. She gladly does it herself and feels good about herself in the process. Finally, Bem postulates that different individuals have different gender schemas. The content of the schema varies from one person to the next, perhaps as a result of the kinds of gender information to which one is exposed in one's family throughout childhood. And the gender schema is more central to self-concept for some people, those who are highly gender-typed (masculine males and feminine females).

Evidence for gender schema theory   Because gender schema theory is so new, there have not been enough studies to evaluate it. But let us look at three studies that illustrate how the theory can be tested and that all support the theory.

In one study, Bem (1981) gave a list of 61 words, in random order, to subjects who were college students. Some of the words were proper names, some were animals, some verbs, and some articles of clothing. Half of the names were masculine and half were feminine. One-third of the animals were masculine (gorilla), one-third were feminine (butterfly), and one-third were neutral (ant). Similarly, one-third of the verbs and the articles of clothing were each masculine, feminine, and neutral. The subjects' task was to recall as many of the 61 words as they could, in any order. It is known from many previous studies that subjects in memory tasks as these tend to cluster words into categories based on similar meaning; this is indicated by the order in which they recall the words. For example, if the subject organized the words according to gender, the recall order might be gorilla, bull, trousers; but if the organization was according to animals, the recall order might be gorilla, butterfly, ant. If gender-typed subjects (masculine males and feminine females, as measured by the Bem Sex Role Inventory, a test to be discussed in Chapter 4) do possess a gender schema that they use to organize information, then they should cluster their recalled words into gender groupings. That is exactly what occurred. Gender-typed subjects tended to cluster words according to gender, a result that supports gender schema theory.

In another experiment, five- and six-year-old children were shown pictures of males and females performing gender-consistent activities (such as a boy playing with a train) and gender-inconsistent activities (such as a girl sawing wood) (Martin and Halverson, 1983). One week later the children were tested for their recall of the pictures. The results indicated that the children distorted information by changing the gender of the people in the gender-inconsistent pictures, while not making such changes for the gender-consistent pictures. That is, children tended to remember

FIGURE 3.4

Pictures used in the Martin and Halverson research on gender schemas and children's memory. (Left) A girl engaged in a gender-consistent activity. (Right) Girls engaged in a gender-inconsistent activity. In a test of recall a week later, children tended to distort the gender-inconsistent pictures to make them gender-consistent; for example, they remembered that they had seen boys boxing.

Source: National Institute of Mental Health.

the picture of the girl sawing wood as having been a picture of a boy sawing wood. That result is just what would be predicted by gender schema theory: incoming information that is inconsistent with the gender schema if *filtered out* and *reinterpreted* as being consistent with the gender schema. This study also indicates that the gender schema is present even in five-year-olds.

In a third study, Bem (1981) measured the reaction times of college students to gender-linked adjectives, such as "independent," "feminine," "competitive," and "loves children." The words were projected, one at a time, on a screen. The subject's task was to press one of two buttons, "me" or "not me," according to whether or not the adjective was character-istic of him or her. The reaction time is the amount of time from pre-sentation of the word until the subject presses either button. If there is a gender schema that processes incoming information, then information that is consistent with one's gender schema, particularly as it relates to the self, should be processed faster than information that is not consistent with the gender self-schema. As an example, if I asked you "Is a robin a bird?" you would probably respond quickly. If I asked you "Is a penguin a bird?" you would probably respond more slowly. Robins fit your bird schema so you can process that question quickly. Penguins do not fit your bird schema as well, and so that question is processed more slowly — essentially you have to think about it longer. The results were that gender-typed subjects did indeed make schema-consistent judgments faster than they made schema-inconsistent judgments, a result that supports gender schema theory.

Criticisms of gender schema theory   Psychologists Janet Spence (president of the American Psychological Association in 1983) and Robert Helmreich (1981) have provided a critique of Bem's gender schema theory. Un-fortunately, most of their points are meant for a professional audience and are too technical to be included here. One point is that Bem's measuring of gender-typing includes only a narrow part of the masculinity and the femininity in people's personalities. Thus her measuring of individual differences in the gender schema may lose much of the complexity of people's masculinity and femininity. And Bem's focus on the gender-typing of personality as measured on paper-and-pencil checklists says nothing about gender-typing in actual behavior, or about how actual be-haviors are affected by the gender schema.

THE FEMINIST PERSPECTIVE

Many people view the feminist movement as a political group with a par-ticular set of goals to work for, a lobbying group trying to serve its own ends, like the National Rifle Association does. What is less recognized is that feminism has an articulated philosophical, theoretical basis. Thus it seems appropriate to include the feminist perspective as one of the theoretical approaches in this chapter. This viewpoint spans many areas besides psychology, but it certainly fits well in any psychological approach to understanding women.

Most of the other perspectives in this chapter had only one or perhaps two authors who articulated the theory: Freud for psychoanalysis, Bandura and Mischel for social learning theory, Kohlberg for cognitive-developmental theory. The feminist perspective is different because it was created by no single person. Instead, numerous writers have contributed their ideas. This is quite consistent with the desire of feminists to avoid power hierarchies and not to have a single person become the authority. But it also means that the feminist perspective as I have crystallized it here, has been drawn from many sources. Some of the central concepts and issues of the feminist perspective follow.

Gender as status and power   Feminists view gender as similar to a *class* variable in our society. That is, males and females are unequal just as the lower class, the working class, the middle class, and the upper class are unequal. Men and women are of unequal *status*, women having the lower status.

After reviewing studies of people's interactions in small groups, two sociologists concluded that the best explanation for the results was the gender-as-a-status-variable hypothesis proposed by feminists (Meeker and Weitzel-O'Neill, 1977). When a small group of people are brought together to work on a task, sharp gender differences sometimes emerge: the men are highly task-oriented, making lots of comments to "get things done," whereas the women are more oriented toward the social relationships among the group members. Yet other studies do not find this pattern of gender differences. The authors concluded that these contradictory results can best be explained by the hypothesis that men have higher status than women. Thus in small group interactions men are expected to be more competent than women, and competitive and dominating behavior is therefore seen as legitimate for men but not for women. However, in certain special circumstances these effects can be reversed, and assertive, competitive behavior becomes legitimate for women; examples of such situations are (1) when a woman has been appointed to be the leader of the group by an outsider such as the experimenter, and (2) when the content of the task is seen as an area of competence for women rather than for men, such as evaluating the quality of daycare centers. Thus these authors concluded that the evidence — at least from studies of small group interactions — supports the hypothesis that gender is a basic status variable.

From the observation of the lesser status of women comes another basic feminist argument, that sexism is pervasive. Women are discriminated against in diverse ways, from the failure of the passage of the Equal Rights

Amendment (which must mean that it is still legal to discriminate on the basis of gender), to the male-centeredness of psychological theories, from the different pay scales for women and men, to the boss pinching his secretary. Thus sexism exists in many spheres: political, academic, economic, and interpersonal.

A closely related concept is the inequality of *power* between men and women, men having more power than women. One of the classic works of the feminist movement is Kate Millett's *Sexual Politics* (1969); she defined "politics" as the study of power, and thus in analyzing sexual politics she focused on power relationships between women and men. Once again, the areas of greater male power are diverse. Most political leaders are men, and thus have the power to pass laws that affect women's lives. That is an obvious example of male power. But feminist analysis has extended the power concept to many other areas, for example, to seeing rape not as a sexual act but as an expression of men's power over women (e.g., Brownmiller, 1975).

One saying of the feminist movement has been "the personal is political" (MacKinnon, 1982). Once again, "political" refers to expressions of power. Feminists have reconceptualized many acts that were traditionally viewed as personal, as simple interactions between individuals, into acts that are seen as political, or expressions of power. As examples, Mr. Executive pats the fanny of Miss Secretary, or John rapes Mary. Traditionally, these have been thought of as personal, individual acts. They were understood to be the product of an obnoxious individual such as Mr. Executive, or of a rare, disturbed individual such as John, or of the inappropriately seductive behavior of Miss Secretary or Mary. The feminist recasts these, not as personal acts, but as political expressions of men's power over women.

FIGURE 3.5

A key point of the feminist perspective is that women have less power than men do in many areas: political, interpersonal, economic.

Source: © 1983 King Features Syndicate, Inc.

Sexuality One of the central issues in the feminist perspective is sexuality (MacKinnon, 1982). There have been many specific feminist issues: rape, incest, abortion, birth control, sexual harassment on the job, pornography. Although these issues are diverse, note that all have the common link of sexuality. Female sexuality has been repressed and depressed, but rarely expressed. The problem, according to feminist analysis, is that women's sexuality is controlled by men. The issue, again, is power: men have the power to control women's sexuality, for example, the power to deny abortion. As Stanford Law Professor Catharine MacKinnon put it, "Sexuality is to feminism what work is to marxism: that which is most one's own, yet most taken away" (1982, p. 1).

Two other central issues in the feminist perspective are *the family* and *work*. Unfortunately, space does not permit a discussion of those issues here (for extended discussions, see Deckard, 1983; Jaggar and Struhl, 1978).

Gender roles and socialization Feminists have also highlighted the importance of gender roles and socialization in our culture. American society has well-defined roles for males and for females. From their earliest years, children are socialized to conform to these roles. In this regard, the feminist perspective is in close agreement with social learning theory. The feminist sees these roles as constricting to individuals. Essentially, gender roles tell children that there are certain things they may not do, whether telling a girl she cannot be a doctor or a boy that he cannot be a nurse. Because gender roles shut off individual potentials and aspirations, feminists believe that we would be better off without them, or at least that they need to be radically revised.

Interestingly, cross-cultural evidence indicates that American society is not unique in its emphasis on gender roles and socialization. Anthropologists such as Margaret Mead (1935, 1949) have discovered that other cultures have gender roles considerably different from our own; for example, in some other cultures men are reputed to be the gossips, and women are thought to be the appropriate ones to carry heavy loads. Despite all the cross-cultural diversity in gender roles, two universal principles seem to hold. First, every known society recognizes and elaborates gender differences (Rosaldo, 1974), a point that is consistent with feminists' emphasis on the power and pervasiveness of gender roles. Second, the male role, whatever it is, is always valued more (Mead, 1935; Rosaldo, 1974). For example, in some parts of New Guinea the women grow sweet potatoes and the men grow yams; but yams are the prestige food, the food used in important ceremonies. Even in this case where the labor of females and males is virtually identical, what the male does is valued more. This finding is consistent with the feminist concept of gender as a class variable.

External versus internal sources of problems Kim is a victim of rape. Suzanne is a victim of depression. Traditional psychological analyses focus on the internal nature and causes of their problems. Kim might be viewed as bringing on the rape by "teasing" a man. Suzanne might be viewed as having personal problems of adjustment. Feminists are critical of analyses that assume that women's problems are caused by internal or personal factors. Feminists instead view the *sources of women's problems as being external*. Kim's problem is recast as having its roots in a society that condones, indeed encourages, male aggression. Suzanne's problem is recast as having its roots in a society that attaches little value and recognition to being a housewife and mother. This theme of external factors will recur in Chapter 14 in the discussion of the theoretical basis of feminist therapy.

Consciousness-raising In the late 1960s and early 1970s, as the modern feminist movement gained momentum, consciousness-raising (C-R) groups were popular. Ideally, such groups begin with a small group of women sharing their personal feelings and experiences; they then move to a feminist theoretical analysis of these feelings and experiences, and from this should flow action, whether it involves an individual woman restructuring her relationship with her partner, or a group of women lobbying for a new law to be passed. Although consciousness-raising groups are not as common as they were a decade ago, the process of consciousness-raising remains central to feminism.

There is a temptation to see C-R groups as merely a fun sort of activity that some feminists engage in. However, consciousness-raising occupies a far more fundamental and serious position within feminism. As one theorist put it,

> Consciousness raising is the major technique of analysis, structure of organization, method of practice, and theory of social change of the women's movement. (MacKinnon, 1982, p. 5)

Thus consciousness-raising is central to the feminist perspective for a number of reasons. First, it is a means for women to get in touch with their experiences and understand themselves. Previously, the only tools women had for understanding themselves were various psychological theories, such as psychoanalytic theory, that were male-centered and defined women from a male point of view. Through the sharing of personal feelings and experiences, women in C-R groups can come to know and understand women from a female point of view. But consciousness-raising does not stop with sharing. It proceeds to theoretical analysis. Women come to see that what they had perceived as individual problems are actually common and are rooted in external causes. For example, Linda has been beaten by her husband. In the C-R group, she discovers that three of the other women have also been beaten by husbands or lovers. In so doing, she comes to recognize two central points: that the personal is political (the individual beating by her husband is part of a larger pattern of power in society), and that the sources of her problems are external, rooted in the structure of society, rather than a result of her own internal deficiencies. Finally, the C-R group becomes the power base for political action. Linda and the other three women might decide to found a shelter for battered women.

Varieties of feminism   One of the difficulties in writing this section on the feminist perspective is that there are actually several different kinds of feminism, differing in everything from their theoretical analysis to their model for social change to their vision of the ideal society. One method of categorization is to conceptualize three major types of feminism: (1) liberal or moderate feminism, (2) Marxist or socialist feminism, and (3) radical feminism (e.g., Deckard, 1983; Jaggar and Struhl, 1978; Jaggar, 1977).

Liberal feminism holds that women should have opportunities and rights equal to those of men. Basically, liberal feminists believe in working within the system for reform. The liberal feminist position is exemplified by organizations such as NOW (National Organization for Women), which is the major group lobbying for the Equal Rights Amendment. The notion here is that American society is founded on basically good ideals, such as justice and freedom for all, but the justice and freedom need to be extended to women.

Marxist or *socialist feminism* argues that the liberal feminist analysis of the problem is superficial and does not get to the deeper roots of the problem. Marxist feminism views the oppression of women as just one instance of oppression based on class, oppression that is rooted in capitalism. Marxist feminists, for example, point out the extent to which the capitalist system benefits from oppressing women in ways such as wage discrimination. What would happen to the average American corporation if it had to start paying all of its secretaries as much as plumbers earn (both jobs require a high school education and a certain amount of manual dexterity and specific skills)? The answer is that most corporations would find their economic structure ruined. Women's situation will not improve, according to this point of view, without a drastic reform of American society, including a complete overhaul of the capitalist economic system and the concept of private property.

Radical feminists such as Shulamith Firestone (1970) find the Marxist feminist analysis too superficial. Radical feminists argue that the oppression of women can occur in any economic system. Ironically, radical feminists return the focus to biology. They argue that the oppression of women is rooted in biology, specifically in the biological differences between genders, and particularly in the fact that only women can bear children. They believe that the latter fact explains the prehistoric origins of the lower status of women: women were physically incapacitated by pregnancy and the care of infants, women became dependent on men, and men thus gained power over women. Radical feminists look hopefully to technology — such as test-tube babies, artificial insemination of surrogate mothers, perhaps even cloning — to free women from the biological functions that oppress them. For radical feminists, women's situation will not improve substantially until all gender distinctions are eliminated, both socially and biologically.

The point here is that all feminists and all feminist viewpoints are not alike. There is a wide spectrum of belief. Probably most of the academic feminist psychologists who have contributed to the psychology of women would be classified as liberal feminists, working for reform within institutions. But Marxist feminists or radical feminists might also be found within the field of psychology, and certainly they are common in some other academic disciplines, such as sociology and philosophy.

Evaluation of the feminist perspective   One criticism of the feminist perspective comes from the New Right and other conservative groups (see, for example, Eisenstein, 1982). They believe that women's roles and status are rooted in biology, perhaps ordained by God, and certainly "natural." They therefore find the feminist viewpoint just plain wrong. These arguments involve basic questions of value that are difficult to deal with scientifically.

The feminist perspective spans many disciplines, and was not specifically proposed as a scientific theory. That means that some of its propositions are difficult to evaluate scientifically. The notion of men as a class having power over women will recur in several studies mentioned later in this book; an example is Henley's research on touch as an expression of power in male-female interactions (see Chapter 9). Also, the data on issues of sexuality for women are the focus in several later chapters (11, 12, 13, and 14). Feminists' concepts about gender roles and socialization are supported by anthropologists' evidence, as discussed earlier. I don't mean to evade the question, but it seems to me that the issues raised by feminists are so broad that it is best to wait until you have read the rest of this book before attempting an evaluation.

IN CONCLUSION

In this chapter I have presented six major theoretical perspectives: psychoanalytic theory, sociobiology, social learning theory, cognitive-developmental theory, gender schema theory, and the feminist perspective. They operate from vastly different underlying assumptions and provide considerably different views of women. Psychoanalytic theory and sociobiology both see the nature of women and gender differences as rooted in biology: evolution, genes, and anatomy. Social learning theory falls at the other end of the nature-nurture continuum, seeing gender differences and gender roles as products of the social environment. Feminist theory, too, emphasizes society as the producer of gender roles. Cognitive-developmental theory is an interactionist theory, emphasizing the interaction between the state of the organism (stage of cognitive development) and the information available from the culture. Gender schema theory also emphasizes the cognitive aspects of gender-typing and the interaction between the knowledge structures in the individual and the incoming information from the environment.

With regard to scientific evidence for the various theories, certainly there are far more studies supporting social learning theory and cognitive-developmental theory than there are supporting psychoanalytic theory. The evidence concerning the tenets of sociobiology is quite mixed. Gender schema theory has some supporting evidence, but is too new to have been tested enough. The same is true of the feminist perspective.

The three developmental theories postulate different sequences of processes in role acquisition (see Figure 3.6). In psychoanalytic and social learning theory, parental attachment comes first and leads to identification, which leads to the acquisition of gender identity. But in cognitive-developmental theory, the process is reversed — gender identity is formed first, and it leads to modeling and attachment.

FIGURE 3.6

Theoretical sequences in the girl's gender identification.

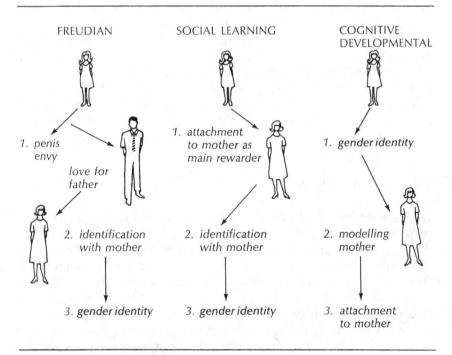

Source: After Kohlberg, 1966.

Because our basic purpose is to understand women and gender-role development, what insights do these theories give us? No one theory by itself is adequate for understanding women — there is no "right" theory. Yet no theory is completely wrong. Each contributes something to our understanding. Freudian theory was important historically in emphasizing the notion of psychosexual development, highlighting the notion that an individual's gender identity and behavior have their roots in previous experiences. To understand an individual's gender identity as an adult, or at any age, for that matter, one must look at the person's life history. A second important contribution from psychoanalytic theory is the concept of *identification*. Though one might dispute the factors Freud postulated as creating identification, the fact remains that children usually do identify strongly with the same-gender parent, and this identification is an important force in gender-role development.

Social learning theory is important in its emphasis on the social and cultural components of gender-role development — the importance of society in shaping gender-typed behaviors. It points out, quite correctly, that boys and girls are treated differently. Social learning investigators have contributed some very impressive laboratory demonstrations of the power of reinforcements in shaping children's behavior, in particular gender-typed behaviors. Social learning theory also highlights the importance of imitation in the acquisition of gender role. Modern mothers who are concerned about freeing their children from gender-role restrictions might do well to keep these forces in mind. It is axiomatic that children do as you do (they imitate), not as you say. If a mother wants to avoid restrictive gender-role stereotypes for her daughter, it may help to encourage her to be a doctor or a lawyer; but in the end, the mother's own behavior may have a much greater impact than her verbal encouragements. I found myself assembling a child's bentwood rocker one Christmas Eve for these very reasons. My four-year-old daughter Margaret was watching, and the rocker needed to be put together in order to be her little brother Luke's present the next morning. I started to call my husband to do "his" job. But then I realized the consequences of such an action. I stiffened my upper lip, got the screwdriver, and started following the instructions. A half-hour later, the rocker was in one beautiful piece, I felt triumphant, and Margaret was impressed. I don't know what the long-term consequences for her may be, but I do know that I don't want her to imitate helplessness.

The feminist perspective shares with social learning theory an emphasis on external, social, environmental shaping of gender roles. Ironically, it shares with psychoanalytic theory an emphasis on sexuality as a critical issue in the lives of humans. Feminism adds the concepts of power, status, and class in male-female relations.

Finally, cognitive-developmental theory emphasizes that gender-role learning is a part of the rational learning processes of childhood (as contrasted with the libidinal motivations postulated by psychoanalytic theory).

Gender schema theory shares the emphasis on cognition, or the intellectual processes underlying gender-typing. It points out the extent to which we process information in terms of gender and distort information that is not consistent with our gender-typed expectations. Further, cognitive-developmental theory emphasizes that gender-role learning does not result solely from externally imposed forces of society, but arises at least in part from intrinsic motivation. Children actively seek to acquire gender roles, sometimes to the dismay of parents who want their children to be untouched by gender-role stereotypes. Gender roles seem to be helpful to children in structuring and understanding the reality of the world about them.

SUGGESTIONS FOR FURTHER READING

Bem, Sandra L. (1983). Gender schema theory and its implications for child development: Raising gender-aschematic children in a gender-schematic society. *Signs, 8,* 598–616. In this provocative article, Bem discusses the implications of her gender schema theory for parents who wish to do feminist childrearing.

Gilligan, Carol (1982). *In a different voice.* Cambridge, MA: Harvard University Press. Gilligan's reconstruction of moral development from a female point of view is wonderful, and quite readable.

Hrdy, Sarah B. (1981). *The woman that never evolved.* Cambridge, MA: Harvard University Press. Hrdy is a feminist sociobiologist at Harvard and she has provided a readable, lively, feminist critique and reformulation of sociobiology.

Weisstein, Naomi (1982, November). Tired of arguing about biological inferiority? *Ms.,* pp. 41–46. This critique of sociobiology makes fascinating reading.

4

Femininity, Masculinity, and Androgyny

It is fatal to be a man or woman pure and simple; one must be woman-manly or man-womanly.

VIRGINIA WOOLF

The concepts of masculinity and femininity are intuitively appealing and meaningful to the average person. Most of us have a sense — perhaps not well thought out — of what characteristics make a man "masculine" or a woman "feminine." Traditionally, of course, it was thought desirable for men to be masculine and women to be feminine. Such an assumption was made not only by lay people; it also underlies several of the theories in the previous chapter, and much of the traditional psychological research. In the last few years, however, a new ideal for both genders has been emerging — androgyny. In this chapter we shall see how psychologists have studied femininity, masculinity, and androgyny, and what the results of those studies have been.

THE CONCEPT OF MASCULINITY-FEMININITY

There are several different ways of conceptualizing masculinity-femininity (M-F), and they vary in their complexity. These are illustrated in Figure 4.1.

The M-F typology   The simplest view of M-F is that there are two types (hence the term "typology") of people, masculine ones and feminine ones. The notion is that we could categorize all human beings by placing each one into one or the other of these "boxes." It is then assumed that these two categories correspond very closely to a person's biological gender — that is, that virtually all females are in the feminine category and virtually all males are in the masculine category.

There are a number of problems with this conceptualization of M-F. Basically, it commits the *typological error,* which occurs any time we try to put people into simple categories or types (Rosenberg and Sutton-Smith, 1972). People are just not that simple, and a model that tries to put them into one of two categories — feminine or masculine — is guilty of oversimplification. It is a rather naive — not to mention conservative — model in its assumption that all or most women are feminine and all or most men are masculine. Its assumption that a female will consistently demonstrate nothing but feminine personality characteristics is certainly questionable.

FIGURE 4.1

Progressive conceptualizations of masculinity-femininity.

1. The typological categorization

2. The unidimensional, bipolar continuum

masculinity ◄—┴——┴——┴——┴——┴——┴——┴——┴——► femininity

3. The two-dimensional scheme

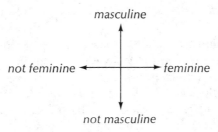

4. The multidimensional scheme

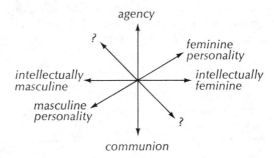

Finally, this model ignores all the variability from one woman to the next, not to mention the potentially great similarities between the genders. Nonetheless, this conceptualization is widespread and persisting.

The M-F continuum   A somewhat more sophisticated conceptualization is that masculinity-femininity can be represented by various gradations on a continuum (the second section of Figure 4.1). This, like the previous model, is intuitively appealing. The notion is that we can go beyond saying that a person is "masculine" and instead say that some people are very masculine, others moderately masculine, and others not very masculine, and similarly for femininity. Thus, for example, we might say that Burt Reynolds is more masculine than Ted Kennedy, who in turn is more masculine than Woody Allen. These people would presumably fall at varying points along a continuum or scale.

The continuum or scale is unidimensional and bipolar. "Unidimensional" means simply one-dimensional, that is, that we can represent all the varieties of masculinity and femininity on a single scale. This is quite a different model from that used in discussing androgyny, which requires two dimensions, as we shall discuss later in this chapter. The term "bipolar" simply means "two poles." The notion is that masculinity falls at one end or pole of this scale, femininity at the other end or pole. The idea, then, is that masculinity and femininity are opposites.

I shall postpone criticisms of this model until I have discussed the various psychological tests that have been constructed using it as a basis.

Measuring masculinity-femininity   One of the first things that psychologists must do when they want to study a particular phenomenon of human behavior is devise a way to *measure it*. Often this takes the form of constructing a psychological test. Research on masculinity-femininity is no exception. Numerous psychological tests have been developed to measure it. Virtually all of them are based on the unidimensional, bipolar continuum model of M-F.

One example of a standard test of masculinity-femininity is the FE (for femininity) scale of the California Psychological Inventory (Gough, 1957). Some items from it are shown in Figure 4.2. It is a simple, paper-and-pencil test, with a person responding true or false to items, depending on whether

FIGURE 4.2

Some sample items that differentiate males from females and are therefore used to measure masculinity-femininity.

Item	Response indicating femininity
Sometimes I have the same dream over and over.	True
I am somewhat afraid of the dark.	True
I think I could do better than most of the present politicians if I were in office.	False
I would like to be a soldier.	False
I think I would like the work of a librarian.	True
I want to be an important person in the community.	False

Source: Reproduced by special permission from California Psychological Inventory by Harrison G. Gough, Ph.D. Copyright 1956 by Consulting Psychologists Press, Inc.

the items describe the person or not. Then a score is computed that places the person at some point along the bipolar continuum.

How are items chosen for such tests? They are chosen in a rather simple way — the criterion being that they must differentiate biological males from biological females. That is, an item is chosen if it shows marked gender differences, meaning that a much different proportion of males as compared with females will respond affirmatively to it. Therefore, an item such as "I prefer a tub bath to a shower" can appear on such tests, not because it reflects anything profound about the essence of masculinity or femininity, but simply because males tend to prefer showers and females tend to prefer tub baths. The implicit assumption, then, is that "femininity" is the quality of women that differentiates them from men.

What is the purpose of such tests? Many psychological tests are designed to differentiate one group from another. For example, a scale might be devised to measure the degree of a person's paranoia. Using this scale, a psychologist could tell whether a person was so disturbed as to need psychiatric care. By analogy, one might think that the purpose of M-F tests was to separate males from females. That is, of course, not the case, and there are certainly more efficient ways of telling who is male and who is female. Neither are M-F tests designed for use in applied settings such as deciding which of several candidates should be hired for a job. M-F tests have instead been designed to be used for research purposes. For example, they can be used in research designed to find out whether the degree of one's masculinity-femininity (or the extent of gender-typing) is related to certain other psychological characteristics. As an example of such research, it has been found that creativity and intelligence tend to be associated with cross-gender-typing (Maccoby, 1966). That is, boys who score more toward the feminine end of an M-F scale than the average for boys, and girls who score more toward the masculine end than the average for girls, tend to be more creative and intelligent than average. In other words, gender-role nonconformity seems to have some benefits associated with it. This is an interesting result, and such research would not have been possible without some method of measuring M-F, such as an M-F test.

Criticisms of M-F tests   Perhaps the most important criticism of M-F tests is that they are based on the assumption that masculinity-femininity is unidimensional and bipolar (Constantinople, 1973). There is some question as to whether M-F is so simple that it can be scored on a single scale, or whether, instead, it might require several scales to capture its complexity. There is also a serious question as to whether M-F is bipolar. The bipolarity assumption means that masculinity and femininity are opposites of each other. Further, it means that the more masculine one is, the fewer feminine traits one exhibits. But is that necessarily true? For example, if a man cultivates a "feminine" hobby such as cooking, that may increase his femininity, but does it necessarily decrease his masculinity — does it take away from the fact that he is a championship boxer? The more recent research on androgyny, to be discussed in the next section, provides an alternative model that is not subject to these criticisms.

Some other criticisms also deserve mention (Constantinople, 1973). One is that the psychologists who construct M-F tests never really get around to defining precisely what they mean by "femininity" or "masculinity." They typically settle for the meaning of gender differences when they choose items, with an implicit definition that femininity is whatever women are that men aren't. This may be very practical, but it does not give us much insight into what femininity or masculinity really is. Further, some tests emphasize gender-role preference (what I would like to be), whereas other measures emphasize gender-role adoption (what I actually do); it is not clear which of these tests measures true femininity or masculinity. For example, a girl might express rather masculine gender-role preferences, but might be very feminine in what she actually does, perhaps because she fears rejection from her peers if she does what she really wants to do. There is a contradiction between her gender-role preferences, which are masculine, and her gender-role adoption, which is feminine. Which is she, then, feminine or masculine? One M-F test might say feminine, and another might say masculine. Finally, there is a confusion between the masculinity-femininity of personality versus the masculinity-femininity of behavior (Spence and Helmreich, 1978). Should one be scored for femininity on the basis of one's personality traits (e.g., nurturance, sensitivity), or on the basis of behavior (e.g., cooking, child-rearing)? Generally, then, there is a problem in this area of research because of an ambiguity about exactly what is meant by "masculinity" and "femininity."

THE CONCEPT OF ANDROGYNY

The question that needs to be raised is, why can't a person be both feminine and masculine? In fact, most of us know people who are both. An example would be a woman who has strong achievement drives, is very successful at her career, plays tennis very well, and likes to wear jeans, and who at the same time likes to cook and sew, wear long dresses, and is very sensitive and caring. The problem is that traditional M-F tests can't handle her. The research on androgyny was designed to study such people.

Androgyny means having both masculine and feminine psychological characteristics. It is derived from the Greek roots *andro*, meaning man (as in androgens) and *gyn*, meaning woman (as in gynecologist). An androgynous person, then, is a person who has both masculine and feminine psychological characteristics.

FIGURE 4.3

The androgynous nature of humans is shown in this illustration from a sixteenth-century alchemy manuscript.

As shown in Figure 4.1, the concept of androgyny is based on a two-dimensional model of masculinity-femininity. The idea is that instead of masculinity and femininity being opposite ends of a single scale, they are two separate dimensions, one running from not feminine to very feminine, and the other from not masculine to very masculine. This would allow for androgynous people, that is, people who are high on both femininity and masculinity. It also would allow for feminine people, and for masculine people. In the third diagram of Figure 4.1, the androgynous people would be the ones falling in the upper right-hand quadrant. The two-dimensional model — unlike the unidimensional, bipolar model — allows for people who are both highly masculine and highly feminine, that is, androgynous.

Measuring androgyny Psychologist Sandra Bem (1974) has constructed a test to measure androgyny (see also Spence and Helmreich, 1978) that is shown in Table 4.1. It consists of 60 adjectives or descriptive phrases. Subjects are asked to indicate, for each, how well it describes them on a scale from 1 (never or almost never true) to 7 (always or almost always true). Of the 60 adjectives, 20 are stereotypically feminine,[1] 20 are stereotypically masculine, and 20 are neutral, that is, not gender-typed. Items 1. 4, 7, etc. in Table 4.1 are masculine; items 2, 5, 8, etc., are feminine; and 3, 6, 9, etc. are neutral. Therefore "self-reliant" is a masculine characteristic, "yielding" is feminine, and "helpful" is neutral

Once the test has been taken, subjects are given two scores: a masculinity score and a femininity score. The masculinity score is the average of their self-ratings of the masculinity items, and their femininity score is the average of their self-ratings of the femininity items. This will give each person a score on each of the two scales shown in the two-dimensional diagram in Figure 4.1. The androgynous people should be in the upper right-hand part, which means they should be high on masculinity and high on femininity. Bem (1977) defines "high" as being above the median (the median is a kind of average). Therefore people are androgynous if they are above the median on masculinity and above the median on femininity (the median on each of these scales is generally about 4.9). A feminine person who scores high (above the median) on femininity but low (below the median) on masculinity would fall in the lower right-hand quadrant in Figure 4.1. Similarly, a masculine person who scores high on the masculinity scale but low on the femininity scale would fall in the upper left-hand quadrant. Finally, people who score low on both scales fall in the lower left-hand quadrant and are called "undifferentiated" because they don't rate themselves very highly on any of the adjectives, masculine or

---

[1] Unlike the constructors of the M-F tests, Bem did not avoid defining M and F by simply relying on gender differences. Instead, femininity was defined as those characteristics that are considered socially desirable for women in our culture, and similarly for masculinity.

matt: 4.75
4.45

Mas Fem

fen
4.55   4.55 masculine
5.20   5.05 fem

TABLE 4.1. Are you androgynous?

The following items are the Bem Sex Role Inventory. To find out whether you score as androgynous on it, first rate yourself on each item, on a scale from 1 (never or almost never true) to 7 (always or almost always true).

1. self-reliant 5
2. yielding 4
3. helpful 6
4. defends own beliefs 5
5. cheerful 6
6. moody 5
7. independent 6
8. shy 4
9. conscientious 6
10. athletic 2
11. affectionate 6
12. theatrical 6
13. assertive 5
14. flatterable 5
15. happy 5
16. strong personality 5
17. loyal 5
18. unpredictable 5
19. forceful 5
20. feminine 6
21. reliable 6
22. analytical 4

23. sympathetic 5
24. jealous 5
25. has leadership abilities 6
26. sensitive to the needs of others 5
27. truthful 5
28. willing to take risks 3
29. understanding 5
30. secretive 4
31. makes decisions easily 7
32. compassionate 5
33. sincere 5
34. self-sufficient 6
35. eager to soothe hurt feelings 5
36. conceited 4
37. dominant 5
38. soft-spoken 4
39. likable 5
40. masculine 3
41. warm 5

42. solemn 4
43. willing to take a stand 5
44. tender 5
45. friendly 6
46. aggressive 4
47. gullible 4
48. inefficient 4
49. acts as a leader 6
50. childlike 5
51. adaptable 5
52. individualistic 5
53. does not use harsh language 6
54. unsystematic 4
55. competitive 5
56. loves children 6
57. tactful 5
58. ambitious 6
59. gentle 5
60. conventional 5

SCORING:

(a) Add up your ratings for items 1, 4, 7, 10, 13, 16, 19, 22, 25, 28, 31, 34, 37, 40, 43, 46, 49, 55, and 58. Divide the total by 20. That is your masculinity score.

(b) Add up your ratings for items 2, 5, 8, 11, 14, 17, 20, 23, 26, 29, 32, 35, 38, 41, 44, 47, 50, 53, 56, and 59. Divide the total by 20. That is your femininity score.

(c) If your masculinity score is above 4.9 (the approximate median for the masculinity scale) and your femininity score is above 4.9 (the approximate femininity median) then you would be classified as androgynous on Bem's scale.

Sources: Bem (1974), Bem (1977), Hyde and Phillis (1979).

feminine. Therefore, having taken the Bem Sex Role Inventory, an individual can be placed in one of four categories: masculine, feminine, androgynous, or undifferentiated.

In her work with college students, Bem typically finds that about one-third of them are androgynous, according to her scale (see Table 4.2).

TABLE 4.2.   Percentages of college students classified as androgynous, masculine, feminine, or undifferentiated

	Androgynous	Masculine	Feminine	Undifferentiated
Females	27	14	32	28
Males	32	34	8	25

Based on a sample of 715 students at the University of Texas.

Source: From *Masculinity and Femininity: Their Psychological Dimensions, Correlates, and Antecedents* by J. Spence and R. Helmreich. Copyright 1978, University of Texas Press. Used by permission.

IS IT BETTER TO BE ANDROGYNOUS?

As an ideal, androgyny sounds good. It permits freedom from gender-role stereotypes and allows people to express their opposite-gender tendencies. But what are androgynous people like in reality? Do they function well psychologically; do they behave adaptively in society? Or do they suffer from problems of confused gender identity? Does society view them suspiciously because of their gender-role nonconformity? There are a number of studies that give us some answers to these questions.

Pressure-to-conform study   Bem has done several studies to find out how androgynous people, as compared with stereotyped people, actually behave in various demanding situations (Bem, 1975; Bem and Lenney, 1976; Bem et al., 1976). Her general prediction in these studies is that androgynous people should do better in a wider variety of situations, because they are capable of being feminine or masculine when the situation calls for it. Stereotyped people, on the other hand, may do well when stereotyped behavior is required, but in situations demanding cross-gender behavior, they will do poorly.

The "pressure-to-conform study" was one such experiment (Bem, 1975). Subjects were brought to the laboratory in groups of 4 males and 4 females. They were then placed in individual booths equipped with microphones and earphones. Their task was to judge how funny some cartoons were; they thought that they were participating in an experiment on humor. The cartoons had previously been rated by an independent set of judges and half of them had been judged very funny, half of them not at all funny.

Subjects were asked to rate how funny each cartoon was. Before giving their rating, however, they heard what they thought were the others in their group giving their ratings. In fact what they were hearing was a tape recording, with voices saying that a particular cartoon was funny when it wasn't and vice versa.

The idea was that subjects who stuck to their guns and gave their opinions of the cartoons honestly, refusing to be influenced by the others, would be displaying the "masculine" trait of independence. Those whose opinions were swayed by the others and gave ratings similar to them, rather than really telling how funny the cartoons were, would be showing the "feminine" characteristic of compliance or conformity.

Her prediction for the outcome of the study was that those subjects who had been classified as masculine by the Bem Sex Role Inventory would be independent or nonconforming. Feminine subjects, on the other hand, would be more likely to conform. Androgynous subjects should be able to be masculine or feminine. In this situation, Bem believes that independence is the most desirable behavior, and therefore she predicted that androgynous subjects would be independent. The results turned out exactly as predicted — masculine and androgynous subjects did not differ significantly from each other, and both groups were significantly more independent than the feminine subjects.[2]

Good-listener study In another study, the subject listened as a lonely transfer student poured out a list of troubles in adjusting to college life (Bem, 1976). The interaction was watched from behind a one-way mirror and subjects were scored for their responsiveness and sympathy for the talker, as a measure of their nurturance.

The idea is that the "feminine" quality of nurturance is what is called for in this situation. Bem predicted that feminine subjects would be more nurturant than masculine subjects. Androgynous people, able to be either masculine or feminine, should do what is appropriate, namely, be nurturant. The results turned out as predicted: feminine subjects and androgynous subjects of both genders did not differ from each other, and both groups were significantly more nurturant than masculine subjects.

In sum, these two studies, when taken together, indicate that androgynous people probably function better in a wider variety of situations than do gender-typed people. Because they have both masculine and feminine characteristics in their repertoire, they are capable of being masculine when that is appropriate (as in the pressure-to-conform study when independence is appropriate) and they are capable of being feminine when that is appropriate (as in the good-listener study, where nurturance is most appropriate). In short, androgynous people have an advantage because they are flexible.

Self-esteem The traditional assumption in psychology was that gender-typing was a good thing in terms of personal adjustment. That is, it was thought that the well-adjusted person would be appropriately gender-typed

---

[2] If you are a psychology student, you might want to notice that this and the next study are means by which Bem can establish the *validity* of the Bem Sex Role Inventory. That is, to be valid, the scale should be able to differentiate various groups of people, based on theoretical predictions. That is precisely what this study does.

(feminine if a female, masculine if a male), and that people who were not so gender-typed would be poorly adjusted. But even some of the traditional research, based on the unidimensional, bipolar model of M-F, contradicted these assumptions. For example, high femininity in females has been shown to be correlated with high anxiety and low self-esteem (e.g., Cosentino and Heilbrun, 1964; Gall, 1969; Gray, 1957; Sears, 1970; Webb, 1963). High masculinity in adult men has been correlated with high anxiety, high neuroticism, and low self-acceptance (Harford et al., 1967; Mussen, 1962).

With a test to measure androgyny now available, we are in a position to see how well-adjusted androgynous people are, and how their adjustment compares with that of gender-typed people. Research indicates that androgynous people and masculine people tend to be high in self-esteem, in comparison with feminine people and undifferentiated people who tend to be lower in self-esteem (Bem, 1977; Spence et al., 1975). The ordering of groups, from highest to lowest in self-esteem, has been found consistently to be: androgynous, masculine, feminine, undifferentiated (Spence and Helmreich, 1978). These results, then, give no evidence that androgynous people are poorly adjusted, suffering from confusions of gender-role identity. Instead they indicate that androgynous people have high self-esteem, an important psychological characteristic. The point that masculine people tend to have higher self-esteem than feminine people is certainly worth noting. The implications of this finding will be discussed further in Chapter 14.

Two conclusions emerged in a major review of the dozens of studies of the psychological implications of androgyny (Taylor and Hall, 1982). First, there is no support for psychologists' traditional assumption that masculinity is best for men and femininity is best for women. For example, masculinity is highly correlated with self-esteem for men, but masculinity is also highly correlated with self-esteem for women. Thus the purely gender-typed feminine woman is at a disadvantage in terms of psychological health. Second, although both masculinity and femininity are positively correlated with self-esteem, masculinity shows a consistently higher correlation. In short, whether one is a man or a woman, one's masculine characteristics seem most related to self-esteem and other measures of psychological health.

These findings have important implications in the area of mental health and psychotherapy. This will also be discussed in Chapter 14. Briefly, it has been suggested that the old model of gender-typing as part of mental health be replaced with new visions of mental health such as androgyny (Kaplan, 1976).

Androgyny as an ideal   *Psychology Today* magazine asked its readers for their ideas about masculinity (Tavris, 1977). When the women respondents described their notion of the ideal man, they basically described someone who was androgynous. Ideally, they wanted someone who was self-confident, successful, and willing to fight for his family and his beliefs ("masculine" characteristics), but who was also warm, gentle, and willing to lose ("feminine" characteristics). In describing their ideal woman, men respondents also chose an androgynous combination of characteristics — intelligent and self-confident, yet warm, gentle, and able to love. This suggests the possibility that androgyny has emerged as an ideal in our society.

Of course, *Psychology Today* readers are scarcely a random sample of the American population; they tend to be more educated and more liberal than the average American. It would be a mistake to conclude that blue-collar workers yearn for androgyny. This study does suggest an important area needing research — namely, how do people react to androgynous people in comparison with gender-typed people?

Problems?   Androgyny sounds so wonderful, but are there any problems with it? Basically, the concept has become popular so recently, and the research is so new and relatively small in quantity, that it is probably too early to tell. But at least two possible problems can be raised. (For a summary of feminist criticisms of androgyny, see Lott, 1981.)

First, androgyny is advantageous in freeing people from the restrictions of rigid gender-role stereotypes. In so doing, however, it may be setting up an extraordinarily demanding, perhaps impossible, ideal. For example, in the good old days, a woman could be considered reasonably competent ("successful") if she could bake bread well. To meet new standards and be androgynous, she not only has to bake bread well, but also has to repair cars. That is, androgyny demands that people be good at more diverse things, and that may be difficult. Indeed, the characteristics required to be androgynous sometimes seem almost mutually contradictory. For example, on the Bem Sex Role Inventory, in order to be androgynous, one needs to be forceful and dominant ("masculine" items) and also shy and soft-spoken ("feminine" items). It is hard to see how a person could be all of those at once. Of course, the ideal androgyn would be expected to display different characteristics in different situations, depending on what was most appropriate; but knowing what is most appropriate is also rather difficult.

Some feminist scholars have also raised a second criticism of androgyny (Orloff, 1978). They regard it as essentially a "sell-out" to men. That is, to become androgynous, women need to add masculine traits to their personalities, or become more like men. The argument has been made that what we should do, rather than to encourage women to become more like men, is to concentrate on valuing those things that women do and are. To these scholars, rediscovering and cherishing womanhood would be preferable to encouraging androgyny. This, of course, is a matter of personal values.

Other scholars have pointed out that we need to be careful about generalizing from androgyny in *personality* traits (as measured by the Bem Sex Role Inventory) to expecting androgyny in actual *behavior* or in *attitudes* about gender roles (Spence and Helmreich, 1980). That is, just because a person is rated as androgynous on the Bem Sex Role Inventory does not mean he or she will necessarily behave flexibly in all situations, nor that he or she will have liberal attitudes about women's roles.

STAGES OF GENDER-ROLE DEVELOPMENT

A friend of mine recently recounted the following story. Both she and her husband hold Ph.D.'s and are professors of political science. Both are feminists, and they try to have an egalitarian marriage and run an egalitarian household. Yet one day their little son came home from kindergarten, glibly telling them how women could be nurses and not doctors, and men could be doctors and not nurses. To say the least, our friend was quite dismayed by this. She had certainly never told her son such things, and in fact had told him quite the opposite. Probably some of you have had similar experiences, or know of people who have, and can appreciate the frustration parents feel when, after all of their efforts to teach their children about gender-role equality and freedom, the children still keep coming up with the same tired, old stereotypes that people have traditionally held. However, some recent research and theory in psychology provide an explanation for this phenomenon, not to mention a ray of hope for parents.

Psychologist Joseph Pleck (1975) has proposed that children go through stages in their understanding of gender roles. Basically, he has applied cognitive-developmental theory to children's understanding of gender roles, much as Kohlberg did (as discussed in Chapter 3). Kohlberg, however, stopped his theoretical descriptions when children were five or six; Pleck has extended the theory to describe older children and adults (for other, similar theorizing, see Block, 1973; Rebecca et al., 1976; Ullian, 1976).

According to Pleck's theory, there are three stages of gender-role development, and these stages parallel the stages of moral development in children. In the first stage of moral development in children, the premoral or preconventional phase, children are dominated by their desire to gratify their own impulses, and seek to be good only to avoid punishment. In the corresponding *first stage of gender-role development*, the child's gender-role concepts are disorganized. The child may not even know her or his own gender yet, and has not yet learned that only men are supposed to do certain things, only women others. (In Kohlberg's terms, such children have not yet acquired the concepts of gender identity or gender constancy.) In the second stage of moral development, conventional role conformity, children conform to rules mostly to get approval from others, particularly authorities. In the corresponding *second stage of gender-role development*, children know the rules of gender roles and are highly motivated to conform to them themselves, and also to make others conform to them. This stage begins in childhood and probably reaches its peak in adolescence when gender-role conformity is strongest. In the third stage of moral development, the postconventional phase, moral judgments are made on the basis of internalized, self-accepted principles rather than on the basis of external forces. In the corresponding *third stage of gender-role development*, people manage to go beyond (transcend) the limitations of gender roles imposed by society; such individuals develop psychological androgyny in response to their own inner needs and values. Pleck, then, views androgyny as a stage of development.

Of course, many adults never make it out of the second stage of moral development to move on to the third stage. An example would be the man who donates a lot of money to a charity because it will get him respect and approval from important people, rather than because of an internalized belief that the charity is a good cause and he should support it. So, too, some people never go beyond the second stage of gender-role development and move on to androgyny; they remain for their entire lives restricted by rather tight limitations of gender roles.

Pleck's theory is informative in answering the question originally posed, namely, why do children who should have very flexible ideas about gender roles instead have rigid — sometimes absurdly rigid — ideas? This theory suggests that children, as part of their cognitive development and their attempts to understand how the world works, must go through a stage of gender-role restrictiveness. Essentially, they must first learn the common preconception that only men can be doctors and only women can be nurses. Then they can learn that there are exceptions to that rule and that girls can become doctors. Feminist parents probably cannot realistically expect that their children will skip stage two of gender-role development. What they can hope for, and provide the stimulus for, is their children eventually reaching stage three and androgyny.

What evidence is there concerning Pleck's theory? Eileen O'Keefe and I did a study to test some of the predictions of Pleck's model (O'Keefe and Hyde, 1983). We studied the occupational gender-role stereotypes (e.g., only men can be doctors, only women can be nurses) of preschoolers, kindergarteners, third-graders, and sixth-graders. If Pleck is correct, preschoolers should show relatively less stereotyping, being in the preconventional or first stage. Kindergarteners, third-graders, and sixth-graders should all be highly stereotyped because they are in the conventional or second stage. Stereotyping would decline in late adolescence and adulthood, although we did not interview people in those age groups. In agreement with Pleck's predictions, stereotyping did increase somewhat from the preschool group to the kindergarten group. However, in contradiction to Pleck's model, stereotyping of adult occupations declined sharply among the third-graders and sixth-graders. Sixth-graders seemed convinced that all jobs could be done by men or by women. Thus it seems that the decline in stereotyping occurs earlier than Pleck says it should, so that his theory did not receive much support in our study. On the other hand, as Pleck noted, the theory helps to make sense out of some apparently conflicting studies. For example, some studies show that daughters of working mothers have quite traditional gender-role concepts when they are young (Hartley, 1959, 1960); but another study showed that maternal employment is associated with daughters' high achievement and androgyny later in life (Siegel et al., 1963). Perhaps the kind of roles parents model make little difference in childhood, when all children are in a conforming stage, but by late adolescence or adulthood these people are able to benefit from the liberated models their parents provided.

IN CONCLUSION

Psychologists have spent a good deal of time trying to understand the nature of femininity and masculinity. Much of that effort has gone into constructing masculinity-femininity tests and then using them in research. More recently, androgyny has emerged as an alternative way of understanding and transcending masculinity and femininity. Tests to measure androgyny have also been devised. It should be emphasized that masculinity-femininity tests and androgyny tests should be used for research purposes only; they should *not* be used in applied situations such as selecting persons to fill jobs or assigning students to particular classes in an educational setting.

Ten years after its introduction into psychology, I think we can say two things about the concept of androgyny. First, it challenges our traditional notions of masculinity-femininity and suggests new ways of behaving that may be more adaptive and satisfying. That is good. Second, androgyny is not a surefire remedy for all of the gender-related evils in society. Although it is an interesting and important concept, we cannot expect too much of it. Research and theorizing must move on.

SUGGESTION FOR FURTHER READING

Bem, Sandra. (1975). Androgyny vs. the tight little lives of fluffy women and chesty men. *Psychology Today*, 9(4), 58. This is an easy-to-read introduction to Bem's research on androgyny.

5

Psychology of Men

In the United States a real boy climbs trees, disdains girls, dirties his knees, plays with soldiers, and takes blue for his favorite color. . . . In college the boys smoke pipes, drink beer, and major in engineering or physics. . . . The real boy matures into a "man's man" who plays poker, goes hunting, drinks brandy, and dies in the war.

ROGER BROWN, Social Psychology

Perhaps it seems odd to you to have a chapter on the psychology of men in a book on the psychology of women, particularly when I have argued earlier that much of traditional psychology has been a psychology of men, one that has, for example, ignored women's issues (menstruation, woman battering) and done research with male subjects only. But, even though that is true, traditional psychology was not purposeful in or conscious of being a psychology of men. Emerging from the feminist movement and feminist scholarship of the 1970s, there is now a self-aware psychology of men. It is rooted in feminism and aware of the power of gender roles, and particularly of how the male role influences the lives of men. It is this emerging psychology of men that we will consider in this chapter. It will also serve as a preview of many of the issues for women, to be taken up in more detail in later chapters.

A milestone in this new field was the publication of psychologist Joseph Pleck's *The Myth of Masculinity* (1981). It provides a summary and critique of both traditional and emerging research on the psychology of men. It will form the basis for many of the concepts of this chapter.

THE MALE ROLE

Just as there are gender-role stereotypes about women, there are such stereotypes about men. In Chapter 6 (see Table 6.1) we will see what those are. Socially desirable masculine characteristics include aggressiveness, independence, hiding emotions, and being logical (Rosenkrantz et al., 1968).

Several methods have been suggested for organizing the long list of masculine traits. For example, research suggests that there are four major factors in stereotypes about males (Brannon and David, 1976):

1. No sissy stuff — Masculinity involves the avoidance of anything feminine (such as eating quiche). Note that in this aspect of masculine stereotypes, masculinity is defined negatively; it means avoiding femininity.

2. The big wheel — The masculine person is a "big wheel." He is successful, is looked up to, and makes a lot of money, thereby being a good breadwinner.
3. The sturdy oak — Masculinity involves exuding confidence, strength, and self-reliance.
4. Give 'em hell — The masculine person is aggressive (perhaps to the point of violence) and daring.

Recent history: Changes in the male role Today there are ambiguities and strains in the male role. For example, men are supposed to be aggressive, yet it is increasingly unacceptable for them to rape or beat their wives. They are expected to be aggressive lions at work in the corporation or on the athletic field, yet they are expected to magically transform themselves into tender, loving pussycats as they walk through the door to their own homes. Men are supposed to possess great physical strength and be active, yet what is adaptive in today's society is to be able to interact intelligently with a computer while sitting quietly at the keyboard.

Pleck (1981) argues that the sources of these ambiguities and strains become clear if we look at the recent history of changes in the male role. Whenever roles change, ambiguities are created because of contradictions between the old role and the new one. The individual feels a personal sense of strain in the tension between these roles, perhaps having been raised by the standards of the old role and then needing to function as an adult in the new role, and perhaps not even being aware that there is an old role and a new role.

In the late 1800s, the Victorian era in the United States and England, differences between men and women were controlled externally, and very

FIGURE 5.1

Are modern men caught in the shift from traditional roles to modern roles?

strictly, by institutions (Pleck, 1981). Men went to all-male colleges, lived in fraternities, and drank at the all-male saloon. Later they functioned in the corporate boardroom, where no woman ever entered. Indeed, in those days my own alma mater, Oberlin College, although amazingly progressive in being coeducational, required men to walk on the sidewalk on one side of the street and women to walk on the sidewalk on the opposite side. In those days it was clear — though oppressive to those involved — what a man should do, and no one questioned the meaning of masculinity.

But somehow, in less than a century, we jolted from men and women walking on separate sidewalks to men actually becoming women through transsexual surgery. All-male colleges became coeducational, all-male saloons became singles' bars, and some women even entered the corporate boardroom. In short, external, institutional definition and control of masculinity declined.

Pleck argues that as society loses one kind of control over people's lives, it increases control over other aspects of their lives. Thus, as external, institutional control of masculinity declined, emphasis shifted to internal, psychological masculinity and gender identity. And at that point the psychologists stepped in. Pleck believes it was no accident that the first major work on psychological masculinity-femininity, Terman and Miles' *Sex and Personality* (1936), was published at the height of the Great Depression, just when traditional definitions of masculinity — having a job and being a breadwinner — were threatened most seriously. Thus the shift was from externally defined masculinity to internally defined masculinity — or from what side of the street you were supposed to walk on, to what end of a masculinity-femininity scale you score on and what your gender identity is. As Pleck put it, "If holding a job to support a family could no longer be counted on to define manhood, a masculinity-femininity test could" (1981, p. 159).

Paralleling these historical changes from external to internal definitions of masculinity, there was a shift in the traits and behaviors expected of men. That is, there was a shift from the traditional male role to the modern male role.

The *traditional male role* has been found in the nineteenth century in all social classes in the United States, in nonindustrial societies studied by anthropologists, and in working class communities today. In the traditional male role, physical strength and aggression are of primary importance. Tender emotions are not to be expressed, although anger is permitted. The traditional male likes to spend his time with other men and defines his masculinity in the male group. Although he is married, he regards himself as superior to women, and does not value an egalitarian, emotionally close relationship with women.

By contrast, in the *modern male role*, primary importance is given to success on the job and earning a lot of money. Thus working well in the corporation (which requires interpersonal skills and intelligence) and gaining power over others are far more important than physical strength. The modern male prefers the company of women and validates his masculinity through them. A high-quality intimate relationship with one woman, rather than numerous anonymous conquests, is his goal. Emotional sensitivity may — indeed, should — be expressed with women, but self-control is still the name of the game on the job.

Some men, of course, find even the modern male role to be oppressive and seek new options and liberation from it. Many others are caught in historical change, in the conflicts and strains between the traditional male role and the modern male role.

Violations of the traditional male role   In the preceding discussion we have focused on the content of the male role and some of the complexities involved in it. But if we are concerned about liberating people from gender roles, we must wonder what happens when a male violates the role.

A pair of interesting experiments provide information on this question (O'Leary and Donoghue, 1978). In the first, college students read a biographical sketch of a man and his ratings on the Bem Sex Role Inventory (see Chapter 4 for an explanation of the BSRI). The biographies and ratings were fictitious. Half of the subjects received information describing a traditional male — he was committed to a career in business and had very masculine ratings on the BSRI. The other half of the subjects received information describing a nontraditional male — he wanted to be a kindergarten teacher and had very feminine ratings on the BSRI. Subjects then rated the man on a number of scales, such as competence and social attractiveness. The results indicated that there were no significant differences between the traditional and nontraditional males in the ratings of their competence and social attractiveness. Indeed, subjects expressed a slight preference for the nontraditional male as a work partner.

The second experiment explored people's reactions to a real male, instead of to the printed descriptions presented in the first experiment (O'Leary and Donoghue, 1978). Subjects interacted with a male who was actually a confederate of the experimenters. The task was for the subjects and the confederate to make a decision about how best to resolve a conflict between eight-year-old Johnny and a classmate who hit him in the stomach and called him a sissy for being a teacher's pet. For half of the subjects, the confederate behaved like a traditional male and advocated that Johnny stand up for his rights and fight back. For the other half of the subjects, the confederate behaved in a nontraditional manner and recommended that Johnny be picked up from school each day in order to avoid confrontation. Later the subjects rated the confederate on scales such as liking for him and confidence in his decision-making ability. The results indicated that there were no significant differences between the traditional and nontraditional males in how much they were liked, confidence in their decision-making ability, and their independence.

The results of these two studies, taken together, suggest that people (or at least college students) do not react negatively to men who violate the traditional male role, contrary to what we might have expected.

Other studies, however, do not always produce such optimistic outcomes. Among children, sex-role violations are punished more severely when committed by boys than when committed by girls (Fling and Manosevitz, 1972; Hartley, 1959; Lansky, 1967). Other studies of adults indicate that male-role violators are viewed negatively (Costrich et al., 1975; Seyfried and Hendrick, 1973). And people react very negatively to men who show signs of incompetence or failure (e.g., Deaux and Taynor, 1973). I should also note that, in the two experiments by O'Leary and Donoghue, the violation of the male role was only moderate (being a kindergarten teacher); it seems likely that more extreme violations of the male role (being a househusband) would be viewed more negatively.

What can we conclude, then, about what happens to men who violate the male role? Probably the best answer is that things are complex and it depends. It seems likely that male-role violation is viewed more negatively in children, perhaps because of people's underlying concern with "correct" development of gender identity. People may feel more lenient about role violations in adult men, whose gender identities are presumably already securely formed. It also may depend on what aspects of the male role are violated. For example, people may be fairly tolerant of nontraditional occupations, but intolerant of traits such as incompetence, dependence, or submissiveness, or of anything carrying connotations of homosexuality.

PSYCHOLOGY'S VIEW OF MEN AND MASCULINITY

Traditional psychology has been greatly concerned with gender-role identity in males. As noted above, beginning in the 1930s the notions of masculinity and masculine identity were considered critical, and a large body of research, continuing to the present, was spawned. Pleck (1981) sees this body of research as based on the belief in the critical importance of masculine identity, or as based on the male sex-role identity (MSRI) paradigm. He has analyzed the set of assumptions involved in this traditional view, as well as whether or not the data support these assumptions. Some of the most critical assumptions are reviewed below.

One critical assumption of the MSRI paradigm is that *gender-role identity results from identification/modeling and, to a lesser extent, reinforcement and cognitive learning, and that cognitive learning is more important in males than in females.*[1] This assumption appears to be quite reasonable

---

[1] *Gender-role identity* is defined as the hypothetical psychological structure representing the individual's identification with his or her own gender group; it demonstrates itself in the individual's gender-appropriate behavior, attitudes, and feelings.

and certainly is consistent with traditional psychological theories (see Chapter 3). On reviewing the evidence, however, Pleck (1981) concludes that research does not support any of the several parts of this assumption. Let us consider why in a bit more detail.

Both psychoanalytic theory and social learning theory view identification/modeling as the cause of gender-role identity in children. The idea is that children identify with and model the same-gender parent (see Chapter 3). But psychoanalytic theory and social learning theory contradict each other as to which traits of the father encourage identification. Psychoanalytic theory says the boy identifies with his father out of fear of the father's wrath. Therefore, a punishing father should encourage identification. Social learning theory says it is the warm, nurturant, reinforcing father who encourages identification. Research does not support the punishing father idea from psychoanalytic theory. There is some support for the notion that warm fathers foster masculine identification in their sons, but the evidence is mixed and, at best, correlational (e.g., see Mussen, 1961; Sears et al., 1965). The identification/modeling assumption also predicts that sons should be more like their fathers than they are like their mothers, because boys should be identifying with and modeling their fathers. For example, if a boy has a talkative, outgoing father and a quiet, shy mother, the theories say that he should be talkative and outgoing because he identifies with his father and tries to be like him. But the data don't support this idea either — boys are not very similar to either parent on gender-typed traits (Maccoby and Jacklin, 1974).

The other part of this first assumption is that cognitive learning of gender roles should be more important for boys than it is for girls. The reasoning is something like this. In their formative, preschool years, boys spend most of their time with their mothers and little time with their fathers, because mothers are at home and fathers are off at work. This makes it rather difficult to identify with the father, because he is not there. Thus identification with the father does not work well as a source of masculine identity. The boy must then resort to other means for gaining a masculine identity, specifically, cognitive learning of masculinity (cognitive-developmental theory — see Chapter 3) from general cultural sources such as TV, books, and so on. Although there is one pair of studies supporting this whole idea (McArthur and Eisen, 1976a, 1976b) far more research on the issue is needed.

In short, we do not really know how males develop a masculine identity. The research is often contradictory or inadequate, and much of it was based on unidimensional measures of masculinity-femininity (see Chapter 4) which do not recognize the possibility of androgyny.

A second assumption of the MSRI paradigm is that *the development of gender identity is risky and prone to errors, particularly in males.* The belief that errors are more likely in development of a masculine identity is based in part on the point noted above, namely that fathers are not around often enough for boys to identify with them. Data on transsexuals are also often presented as evidence. Transsexuals are persons who feel they are trapped in the body of the wrong gender; they are the people who seek sex-change operations. The person who has a male body but believes he is truly a woman is called a male-female transsexual. Data indicate that, among those people seeking sex-change operations, male-female transsexuals outnumber female-male transsexuals by a ratio of 3 to 1 (Green, 1975). That is, it is more common to have a person with a male body who has failed to form a (correct) masculine identity and instead has a feminine identity. This would be evidence that masculine identity development is more prone to error. The problem is that these data are only for reported cases, and may ignore many female-male transsexuals who never seek a sex-change operation in part because the operation in that direction is far more difficult. There is other evidence on the second assumption, but it turns out to be weak, too. Overall, then, the evidence is poor that males are more vulnerable than females are to problems in the development of their gender identities (Pleck, 1981).

A third assumption of the MSRI paradigm is that *appropriate gender-role identity is necessary for good psychological adjustment*. Applying this to the psychology of men, the assumption would be that masculinity is necessary for good adjustment in a male. Once again, this assumption fails the test of the data. I reviewed one highly relevant line of research in Chapter 4 — namely, the androgyny research, which indicates that it is not the gender-typed person who shows the best adjustment, but rather the androgynous person. Research shows that, both in adolescence and adulthood, high masculinity in males is actually associated with poor adjustment (Mussen, 1961, 1962; Pleck, 1981). The third assumption thus doesn't have much evidence supporting it, and in fact has strong evidence against it.

A fourth assumption of the MSRI paradigm is that *men's negative attitudes and behaviors toward women are a result of problems of gender-role identity that are caused by mothers*. Three possible ideas have been proposed about exactly what feature of the mother-son relationship causes problems; all three include an assumption that fathers do not participate much in rearing their sons. One possibility is that the little boy experiences the power his mother has over him as overwhelming and threatening. In adulthood, then, men try to control and subordinate women in order to defend against their fear of women's (mother's) control of them (this is the idea of Karen Horney, whose theories were discussed in Chapter 3). A second possibility is that the issue is not power, but rather identification. The idea is that the little boy mistakenly identifies with his mother because his father is not around, but he later realizes that he must get rid of this identification and become masculine. Thus men fear the feminine part of their identity and react to this fear by dominating and controlling those who are feminine — namely, women (this is the idea of Nancy Chodorow, whose theory was also discussed in Chapter 3). A third possibility considers mothers as agents of socialization. Socialization of boys frequently consists of punishing feminine behaviors, and mothers, who do most of the socialization, therefore punish boys for femininity. As a result, boys come to dislike their mothers and to generalize this dislike to all women. Actually, the second and third possibilities contradict each other — in the second the problem is that mothers make boys feminine, whereas in the third the problem is that mothers make boys masculine.

Any or all of these possibilities, then, could be used to explain why men have negative attitudes toward women. In extreme cases, they might be used as explanations of rape or wife-battering. What the feminist would note, though, is that in all cases the mother is being blamed.

There really is not enough definitive research on this fourth assumption to decide whether it is accurate or not. But perhaps the more important point is that there are two much simpler explanations about why men hold negative attitudes toward women: (1) men do so because it is to their advantage (negative attitudes about women justify and perpetuate men's privileged position in society; and (2) such attitudes are widespread in our culture and it is not surprising that each new generation of little boys picks them up.

A fifth assumption of the MSRI paradigm is the school feminization hypothesis: *boys have academic and adjustment problems in school because schools are feminine* (most teachers are female, teachers encourage femininity, and schools have a feminine "image") *and that only makes boys' identity problems worse.* Once again, the data do not support this assumption (Pleck, 1981). For example, research on academic performance shows that there is no difference between boys who have female teachers and those who have male teachers (e.g., Asher and Gottman, 1973; see review by Gold and Reis, 1982).

In summary, none of the assumptions of the MSRI paradigm, which has been psychology's traditional view of men, have much evidence backing them.

Perhaps you are wondering why I have told you all of these things and then told you each of them is wrong. There are two reasons. First, it is important to understand the assumptions underlying traditional psychology's view of men and to understand that those assumptions are questionable at best. Second, an important conclusion comes out of this discussion, namely that psychology's obsessive concern with masculine identity is simply not useful and not validated by data. If we let go of the concept of masculine identity — as an important thing and a goal of development — we are in turn freed from some worries, for example, about boys in father-absent families and whether they will "turn out all right" (which often means developing a masculine identity).

Although the conclusion here is that the male sex-role identity paradigm is not a very good one, there is an alternative approach for the future, the sex-role strain paradigm, which is discussed in the next section.

A NEW VIEW: SEX-ROLE STRAIN

Current feminist research on both the female role and the male role is often based on a new set of assumptions, called collectively the sex-role strain (SRS) paradigm (Pleck, 1981). Here are some of the assumptions of the SRS paradigm.

The first assumption is that *gender roles are contradictory and inconsistent*. There are multiple aspects of these inconsistencies in gender roles. For example, research indicates that today's college men are caught in tension between the traditional norm that men should be intellectually superior to women and the modern norm that men and women should be intellectual equals (Komarovsky, 1973). As we noted earlier in this chapter, some of these inconsistencies are created because gender roles have changed over time. The more general point is that these contradictions in gender-role norms are sources of stress to men, because men may be uncertain as to which role they are to follow, or because in following one they violate another — for example, by establishing an intellectually egalitarian relationship with a woman, a man fails the male superiority test. Note that the SRS paradigm focuses on gender roles as a source of strain to individuals, compared with the MSRI paradigm, which viewed gender roles and masculine identity as goals to be achieved.

A second assumption of the SRS paradigm is that *a large proportion of individuals violate gender roles*. The idea here is that gender roles often become so idealized, so difficult, and so unrealistic that most people cannot live up to them, at least not on all occasions. Therefore, only a few people are actually perfect examples of their gender role, and the rest bumble along in various degrees of failure to live up to it. For example, a survey of readers of *Psychology Today* magazine showed that large numbers of men felt they lacked certain male traits that are considered socially desirable, such as self-confidence, independence, and competitiveness (Tavris, 1977). That gap between what men think they actually are and what they think is expected of them causes strain.

A third assumption of the SRS paradigm is that *violating gender roles has worse consequences for males than it does for females*. The evidence on this point is actually rather mixed. Earlier in this chapter we reviewed some of those studies, and they show that male-role violators are sometimes viewed negatively, but in other cases they are accepted.

A fourth assumption of the SRS paradigm is that *some characteristics that are prescribed by gender roles are actually maladaptive.* That is, some gender-role characteristics do not help a person function well psychologically. The aggressive component of the male role is a prime instance (Pleck, 1981). For example, men's liberationist Marc Fasteau (1974) analyzed the Pentagon Papers and showed how expansion of the Vietnam War was linked to concerns about power, strength, and dominance in the writings of influential male leaders. If socialization of males for aggressiveness plays a role in creating wars, it seems reasonable to call it maladaptive. It also leads to a whole series of interesting questions about what things would be like if socialization practices were different. If men were not socialized for aggressiveness, would there still be wars?

In this section we have considered the sex-role strain paradigm. It shifts emphasis away from traditional psychology's concern with masculine identity. Instead, it views gender roles as sources of strain for people: gender roles are contradictory, many individuals violate them, some aspects of gender roles are maladaptive, and males pay a particularly high price for violation of their role. Because this model is new, there are not yet enough data to test it critically, as has been done with the male sex-role identity paradigm. Until more evidence accumulates, the sex-role strain paradigm will provide new perspectives on gender roles, and particularly on the male role.

LIFESPAN DEVELOPMENT

In this section we will adopt the developmental perspective, tracing issues for males as they arise from infancy to adulthood.

Infancy Most of the evidence indicates that *gender similarities* are the rule in infancy (see Chapter 7). Yet there is evidence that newborn boys have a higher activity level than newborn girls (Block, 1976). The question is, what does that mean in terms of later behavior? Does it predict the higher rate of hyperactivity in boys in the elementary school years? Does it create the higher level of aggressiveness in boys? And what causes the higher activity level in boys? Unfortunately, we do not yet know the answers to these questions.

One experience of male infants that is worth noting and investigating more is circumcision. Circumcision (surgical removal of the foreskin of the penis usually done within a few days of birth) is routinely done to most male infants born in hospitals in the United States, although the procedure is increasingly being questioned. There are several reasons for circumcision. One is religious — it is part of Jewish religious practice, symbolizing the covenant between God and His people. There are also health reasons. Removal of the foreskin permits better cleaning of the penis. Some argue that circumcision reduces the risk of cancer of the penis, as well as the risk of cancer of the cervix among wives of circumcised men (see Hyde, 1982). The evidence on these points is not very strong, however.

The more interesting question for us, though, is what the psychological effects of this early trauma might be on the male infant. Research actually indicates there is no effect (Brackbill, 1981). That is, there appear to be no differences in behavior between circumcised and uncircumcised boy babies.

Childhood   As the boy moves from infancy to childhood, the peer group becomes increasingly important as an influence. School-aged children spend considerably more time with their peers than with their parents (Bronfen-brenner, 1970). Further, children care a great deal about the approval of their peers, so that the peer group is a powerful shaper of behavior through modeling, positive reinforcers, or punishments.

Children tend to be gender-segregated in their play — that is, boys play with boys and girls play with girls. In an interesting study, naturalistic observations were made of preschoolers' play (Fagot and Patterson, 1969). When teachers suggested that boys switch to some "feminine" activities, the boys resisted. The teachers' views appeared to mean little to them; what they wanted was the company and approval of the other boys.

Gender-segregated play and the gender-typing of toys and activities seem to have mutually facilitating effects. That is, the more the boy plays in the all-male group, the more he plays with trucks; the more he plays with trucks, the more playing house seems alien; thus he avoids playing with girls and shows an even stronger preference for the company of boys, which means more play with trucks, which means more play with boys; and so the pattern spirals.

Boys have more problems in school — in the sense that they are more frequently put in remedial classes and more frequently referred to psychologists than girls are (see Chapter 7). One possible explanation comes from the well-established finding that the incidence of *hyperactivity* is far higher in boys than in girls. The most common estimate is that among hyperactive children the ratio of males to females is about 6 to 1, or about 86 percent of hyperactive children are male and only 14 percent are female (Wright et al., 1979; Kenny et al., 1971). Hyperactive children are characterized by an extremely high activity level in situations — such as the school classroom — where it is clearly inappropriate. Hyperactive children characteristically also have problems of attention; that is, their attention span tends to be short. The greater incidence of hyperactivity in boys may help to explain their school difficulties. The attentional problems are likely to create learning problems and referral to remedial classes. The hyperactivity itself is irritating to teachers and probably leads them to refer children to psychologists. This line of reasoning raises two further questions. First, how would schools change if there were more male elementary school teachers who themselves had been hyperactive as children? Would they be more sympathetic as well as more skillful as teachers of hyperactive boys? Second, why are there so many more hyperactive boys than girls? No one really has an answer to this question. One speculation is that hyperactivity is a result of a developmental or maturational lag; that is, children gain more control of their activity level with age, and the hyperactive child may simply be a very slow maturer (Wright et al., 1979). If boys generally are slower to mature than girls, perhaps their greater rate of hyperactivity is a result of their slower maturation.

Adolescence   An increase in the intensity of peer demands for conformity to gender roles occurs in adolescence (see Chapter 7). Here we will concentrate on one aspect of the male role that is highly demanding in adolescence: athleticism. As the popular song put it, "You've got to be a football hero to get the love of a beautiful girl." In one survey of ten high schools, students said that being an athletic star was the most important factor in popularity for a boy (Coleman, 1976).

FIGURE 5.2
Some have argued that boys have more problems in school than girls do because most teachers are women, with whom boys have trouble identifying. The research, however, does not support this claim; there are no differences between boys with male teachers and boys with female teachers.

Source: J. Berndt / The Picture Cube.

Consider the athlete role from the perspective of the sex-role strain paradigm. In one study, 24 men in their twenties were interviewed. Half of them had been varsity athletes, and the others had not been involved in athletics (Stein and Hoffman, 1978). The study was aimed at identifying sources of male-role strain, based on the sex-role strain paradigm. The sources of strain, of course, varied between the athletes and the nonathletes. The athletes reported a strain resulting from ambiguity as to whether it was most important to succeed as an individual or as a team. A second source of strain resulted from a changing value attached to athletics at different times in the lifespan. In high school, athletics is a supreme, unquestioned value. In college, it continues to be important for some but is less important for most. At age 30, no one cares a bit about your high school varsity letter in football, nor about the thousand hours that went in to earning it. Another source of strain for the athletes was the obsession with winning, expressed so eloquently by Vince Lombardi: "Winning isn't everything. It's the only thing." The problem is that in a contest between two teams, only one can win, and that means that half the players go home losers. Sports, of course, do not have to be structured competitively. Feminists have emphasized "new games" and noncompetitive sports. But the dominant reality in American athletics has been competition, and that produces losers. In focusing on the psychological strains created by the athlete role, we should not forget that actual physical damage is also part of the reality. For example, I knew one boy who continued to play as quarterback on the high school football team despite the fact that he had broken several ribs in a previous game.

The athlete role also creates strain for the male nonathlete (Stein and Hoffman, 1978). The boy who is a nonathlete is essentially flunking part of the masculinity test. Remember how children choose others one by one when forming teams? The uncoordinated or unskilled boy is chosen last. The message can be devastating — not only are you a poor athlete, but your peers don't want you on their team. My husband, who spent his high school years being an intellectual, recounts a story about himself that is a perfect illustration of the way the male nonathlete is treated. He was in a football scrimmage in a gym class. The teacher was giving instructions to members of the team as to what to do in the next play. After all the others had been given specific things to do, he looked at the last poor fellow and said, "Hyde, when the ball is snapped, you fall down and we'll hope that someone on the other team trips over you." The message to the nonathlete is clear: "You're a failure."

In sum, the competitive, success-oriented emphasis on athletics, particularly in high school, seems to create problems both for the athlete and the nonathlete. We need a new, noncompetitive, health-oriented vision of athletics. You may get shin problems from jogging or sore muscles from jazzercising, but you won't get a bruised ego.

Adulthood In this section on the period of adulthood for men, we will first consider two traditional roles for men: that of provider and that of soldier. Next, we will discuss a role of emerging concern, fatherhood. Finally, we consider whether there is a male mid-life crisis perhaps analogous to the menopause experience for women.

The provider role: Several centuries ago, before the Industrial Revolution, men and women shared the provider role (for a review of these concepts, see Doyle, 1983). Men were respensible for providing food, either by hunting or by farming, and shelter, perhaps by building it themselves. But women, too, were expected to be providers. They provided food, in such activities as growing a garden, milling flour, and cooking. They were responsible for other kinds of providing as well, such as producing clothing by spinning, weaving, and sewing it. In short, men and women shared the provider role. In an agricultural society, they shared time and space as well, for men were not off in factories while women remained at home.

Then came the Industrial Revolution. Men went out to work in factories, and women stayed home. Thus their roles became far more divided. The work men did became less intrinsically satisfying — for example, forging a particular part for a particular machine is likely to be less satisfying than growing and harvesting one's own grain to became food on the table. Often the only good thing about the work was the money that was earned. Simultaneously, there was a shift for men from the provider role to the *good provider role.* That is, with the shift to an emphasis on earning money, the man was expected to be a good provider for his family — to earn a lot of money. The more money he earned, the more successful and manly he was.

It is an understatement to say that the good provider role is a high-pressure one. Once again, the sex-role strain paradigm is applicable: the good provider role for men is a source of strain. There is the pressure of being the sole provider, with a great deal of money needed to support the modern family and the wife not earning any. Further, the good provider role is a highly competitive role; a man is in competition with other men to provide for his family better than those other men provide for theirs. Finally, it is a role that is destroyed by unemployment, which may occur through no fault of one's own but rather as a result of economic conditions. It is no wonder that the Great Depression shook the foundations of manhood. Nor is it a wonder that one of the slogans of the men's liberation movement is "We're not just success objects."

Current conditions may ease some of the strains of the good provider role for men. Most notably, the majority of wives now hold paying jobs, and the two-paycheck marriage is becoming the norm. This reduces the pressure on the man of being the sole provider. But other trends may be working in the opposite direction. In contrast to the social activism of the 1960s and 1970s, the decade of the 1980s gives every sign of a return to concern over success on the job and making money. With that the pressure of the good provider role increases. Recent best-selling self-help books offer ample testimony to the current trend, with titles such as *Winning Through Intimidation* and *Looking Out for Number One*. Rather than offering alternatives to the good provider role, they show men how to go about it more intensely.

The military: The military experience has been a standard one for American men. There are approximately 23.7 million veterans, and approximately half of the employed male population has served an average of 27 months in active duty (Arkin and Dobrofsky, 1978). All have in common having experienced the rite of passage known as basic training. Most go through the experience when they are between the ages of 17 and 20, a critical junction between adolescence and adulthood and an important time in identity development.

What is the result of the military experience for the individual male? It makes a man out of him, of course. Slogans such as "The Army will make a man out of you" and "The Marines take only a few good men" provide ample testimony to the cultural notion that the military experience turns boys into men.

To gain a better view of what actually transpires as men go through the military experience, consider one man's recollections of his training.

> I went into the Army like a lot of people do — a young scared kid of 17 told he should join the Army to get off probation for minor crimes. At the time the Army sounded real fine: three meals, rent-free home, adventure and *you would come out a man*. (It's amazing how many parents put this trip on their kids.)
>
> In basic training I met the dregs of the Army. (Who else would be given such an unimportant job as training "dumb shit kids"?) These instructors were constantly making jokes such as "don't bend over in the shower" and encouraging the supermasculine image of "so horny he'll fuck anything." People talked about fucking sheep and cows and women with about the same respect for them all.
>
> Not many 17-year-olds could conform to such hard core experience. You're told the cooks were gay (pieces of ass for your benefit). The "hard core" sergeants with all these young "feminine" bodies (everyone appears very meek, i.e., feminine, when constantly humiliated, by having his head shaved and being harassed with no legitimate way of fighting back) were always dunghole talking ("your ass is grass and Jim's the lawnmower").
>
> These "leaders" are the *men*; that pretty much makes you the "pussy's" — at the very most "boys." You have to conform to a hard core, tough image or you're a punk. And I began to believe it because of my insecure state of mind, which was so encouraged in training. I was real insecure, so I wanted to be a superman and went Airborne, which, unlike most of the Army, is more intense and worse than basic training. The pressures of assuming manhood are very heavy.

Not only are you hard, you're Airborne hard — sharp, mean, ruthless. You have to be having an impressive sexual life or a quick tongue to talk one up. You've got to be ready to fight a lot because you're tough and don't take shit from anyone. All these fronts were very hard for me to keep up because they contradicted everything I felt. I didn't feel tougher than anyone. I was very insecure about my dick size and ability to satisfy women.

All I had was my male birthright ego. I stayed drunk to be able to struggle through the barroom tests of strength and the bedroom obstacle courses. The pressures became heavier and stronger, requiring more of a facade to cover up the greater insecurity. To prove I was tougher I went looking for fights and people to fuck over. To prove I was "cock strong" I fucked over more women and talked more about it. I began to do all the things I was most insecure about doing, hoping that doing them would make me that "real man."

Having survived the initial shock of such a culture I became very capable in such required role-playing as toughest, meanest, and most virile — the last meaning a cold unreproachable lover (irresistible to women and un-approachable by other men).

(Anonymous, "When a Woman Is Attacked," 1975, pp. 127–128)

The military's operational definition of manhood is clear: the real man is hyperaggressive, has no emotions, and treats women as objects. Some scholars have referred to this process, particularly combat training, as "military socialization" (Arkin and Dobrofsky, 1978), a socialization into the male role (at least as defined by the military) at the beginning of adulthood.

Two recent changes in the military need to be considered: the shift from a draft to an all-volunteer Army in 1973, and the increased entry of women into the military, including basic training. With the shift to a volunteer Army, advertising promotions for recruits have become "modern." Instead of selling the macho Marine image, the emphasis is now on pre-senting military enlistment as a chance to acquire job skills. It has been argued, though, that the male socialization is still powerfully present. The content is no longer toughness, but rather being successful as a bread-winner, and here the good provider role surfaces once more.

The entry of women into the military is a scene set for conflict. As the above excerpt testifies, basic training is not designed to have women be a part of it. Which side of the conflict will emerge triumphant? Will women change the military, making it more humane and androgynous? Or will the military change women recruits, producing platoons of macho women? Only time and research will tell.

Fatherhood: The father role is one of the major adult roles for men. In considering this role, there are two interesting topics for the psychol-ogist to investigate. One is to examine the effects of the father on his children, technically called *paternal influence*. The other is to consider the father role and its meaning for the man himself — what are the satisfactions of being a father, what are the frustrations, and so on. Because there is so much more research on the first topic, it will be discussed first (for reviews, see Lamb, 1976, 1979; Lynn, 1974; Biller, 1971, 1974).

What kinds of effects do fathers have on their children, or do they have much influence at all given the limited number of hours of father-child contact? Studies indicate that fathers can be as competent in caring for infants and as responsive to them as mothers are (Parke, 1979). It is also clear that, from the earliest interactions, mothers and fathers give different kinds of attention to their children. Specifically, mothers are more likely to engage in caregiving activities, while fathers engage in play, particularly rough, stimulating play (Parke and O'Leary, 1976). In short, mothers exchange dirty diapers for clean ones, and fathers give horseback rides. Research also shows that, once children pass their first birthday, fathers begin directing more attention to their sons and less to their daughters (Lamb, 1979). Thus children's interest is drawn to the same-gender parent, and children develop a preference for the same-gender parent. This, of course, may be the heart of the whole gender-typing process.

Much of the evidence on the effects of fathers on their children has been based on studies of *father absence*. The logic is that if we compare children in intact (both parents present) families with those in father-absent (usually through divorce) families, any differences between children in the two situations must be indicative of the effects of fathers on children. Such studies typically find that boys in father-absent homes are "deficient" in their gender-role development, usually defined as scoring low on a masculinity-femininity test (e.g., Biller and Bahm, 1971). The flaw in these studies is that there are all kinds of problems involved in father-absent families besides the father not being there (Lamb, 1979). The father-absent family typically has financial worries, and the mother is often under severe emotional stress due to divorce or widowhood. Thus it is not clear whether boys' problems in father-absent families are due to the father's absence or to the variety of other difficulties that occur.

Notice that this line of research is rooted in the male sex-role identity paradigm discussed earlier in this chapter. It is based on the notion that gender identity is essential for development and that males get their gender identity from their fathers. Thus father absence is expected to be dangerous, particularly to sons. However, as Pleck (1981) concluded, the MSRI paradigm is not a particularly good one and is not supported by research evidence. Specifically, researchers fail to find much of a correlaiton between fathers and sons in masculinity.

Thus the evidence coming from the father-absence studies is flawed, both because of faulty design and because of rooting in the MSRI paradigm. What would be more useful is to conceptualize fathers' influence as part of a more complex system of influence on children. For example, sons are probably more likely to identify with and to be like their fathers if father and son have a warm, nurturant relationship (Lamb, 1979). Thus only some fathers and sons would be expected to be similar — namely, those with warm, nurturant relationships. Further, the father's influence doubtless depends not only on the father-son relationship but also on other relationships, such as the father-mother relationship and the mother-son relationship. I would love to tell you the results of research considering fathers' influence in this complex way, but there isn't any, at least not yet.

When fathers are present, how much time do they spend with their children? In one widely cited study, Rebelsky and Hanks (1971) attached tape recorder microphones to newborn infants. They found that fathers spend only an average of 38 seconds per day talking with their infants. This low level of paternal involvement seemed scandalous. However, there is reason to think that the results of the study may have been idiosyncratic — for example, only ten fathers were sampled. More recent, better-sampled research indicates that fathers spend more than 38 seconds per day on their children. One way to approach questions of how time is spent is the *time budget* or *time diary method*, in which individuals keep a careful record of all their activities for a 24-hour day, usually on a detailed diary form. The results of one such study are shown in Table 5.1 (Pleck, 1983). As you can see in the table, fathers spend only about a quarter of an hour per day, on the average, on childcare. But childcare was defined very narrowly in this study, including only direct interaction with children; thus a father who sits and reads the newspaper but is available to his children while his wife is off shopping would not count the time as childcare. Another important result can also be seen in the table — husbands of employed wives do not spend any more time in housework or childcare than do husbands of nonemployed wives. This points up the important problem that men's roles have not changed in ways necessary to complement the changes in women's roles as women have increasingly entered the labor force.

The other side of the father role is the way the father perceives and responds to that role. Is it a source of satisfaction, or of inadequacy and frustration? Research indicates that men shift in their sources of satisfaction at different times in the life cycle. Specifically, when a man is a father

TABLE 5.1. Time use for housework and childcare (in hours/day) of employed husbands and of wives

	Housework		Childcare	
	Husband	*Wife*	*Husband*	*Wife*
Wife Employed	1.63	3.37	0.24	0.64
Wife Not Employed	1.59	5.60	0.25	1.16

Source: In H. Lopata & J. Pleck, eds., *Research in the Interweave of Social Roles*, Vol. 3: *Families and Jobs*. Greenwich, CT: J.A.I. Press, 1983. Used by permission.

of young or school-aged children, he tends to define his happiness in terms of family life (Harry, 1976). At earlier times and later times, his happiness is found outside the family, in activities such as sports or hobbies. Thus fatherhood does seem to have a major impact, becoming a focus of attention and a source of happiness. There is a stereotype that men get most of their satisfaction from work, whereas women get most of their satisfaction from their families. However, well-sampled studies find that both men and women rate marriage and the family as more satisfying than work (Campbell et al., 1975).

Male mid-life crisis? One author summed up the mid-life period (I will define this roughly as the decade between the ages of 40 and 50) as follows:

> The hormone production levels are dropping, the head is balding, the sexual vigor is diminishing, the stress is unending, the children are leaving, the parents dying, the job horizons are narrowing, the friends are having their first heart attacks; the past floats by in a fog of hopes not realized, opportunities not grasped, women not bedded (sic!), potentials not fulfilled, and the future is a confrontation with one's own mortality. (Lear, 1973)

This points to the complex forces, biological, personal, and social, that converge on the middle-aged man.

Traditional psychology, as well as the general public, have viewed personality as changing and developing only in childhood and adolescence, and then remaining stable and unchanging throughout adulthood. Perhaps this represents a need many of us have to see adults as stable and predictable. For example, it may be difficult for many college students to comprehend that their parents are currently going through as much development and change as a college student is. Nonetheless, there is considerable evidence that substantial personality changes occur throughout adulthood (Brim, 1976).

Let us consider in more detail the nature of the changes that were summarized in the above quotation. First, testosterone levels begin to decline around age 40. One consequence is that erections may occur more slowly. If a man understands this as a normal developmental change, it will not be traumatic, but if there is a lack of such understanding, the changes may become traumatic and be interpreted as a sign of loss of virility. Beyond this change in sexual response, little is known about the effects of declines in levels of testosterone and other hormones.

Several extensive research programs have investigated various psychological and social factors that are important to the mid-life male (Levinson, 1978; Lowenthal et al., 1975; see also review by Brim, 1976). These are discussed below.

Most human beings have a desire to feel good about themselves based on their achievements. For men, this positive sense of self comes mainly from the job or career. Around age 40 many men recognize that there is an *aspiration-achievement gap*, that is, that their actual achievements have not matched the high aspirations they had in their twenties. The question is, how does a man resolve this aspiration-achievement gap for himself? For many men, perhaps the majority, there is a gradual reconciliation, with a downward shift in aspirations until they are at a realistic level, and the man emerges feeling good about himself. For others, the reconciliation is not easy, and there is a crisis and depression.

Erik Erikson (1950) considers one of the major tasks of adult development to be a resolution of the issue of *stagnation versus generativity*. Most people seem to have a deep-seated desire to feel a sense of growth, or generativity, in their lives. At age 40, with a receding hairline, it is difficult to see oneself as continually growing, and a sense of stagnation may set in. It is possible to resolve this issue in adulthood by finding a sense of growth in other sources, such as the growth of one's children or grandchildren, and that represents a positive resolution of this issue. The question arises as to how single men, or gay men, with no children can gain a continual sense of generativity. There are, however, many other ways to maintain that sense, such as taking an interest in fostering the careers of one's younger coworkers.

Confrontation with death is another theme of the mid-life period. Signs of aging are apparent on the man's own body, and it is likely that one of his close friends will die of a heart attack or other causes. Once again, this experience may lead to negative outcomes such as depression. Or it may lead to a positive outcome in which the man comes to terms with the idea of his own death, reorders the priorities of his life, perhaps in some wonderful ways, and recognizes that happiness is not always to be found in the future, but must be sought in the present.

Relationships within the family also shift (Brim, 1976). The children grow up and leave home, leaving the husband and wife alone together. Although it is a popular stereotype that this is a difficult time in marriage, producing many divorces, in fact the data indicate that married couples on the average rate the post-parental period as one of the happiest in their lives (Brim, 1976). The man's own parents may become increasingly dependent on him, requiring a transformation of that relationship. And the man's wife, freed from childcare responsibilities, may seek an education, a new career, or a more active involvement in a career she already has, requiring a renegotiation of the marital relationship.

Systematic, well-sampled research indicates that men in their forties, compared with men aged 25–39 and 50–69, do show significantly higher depression scores and more alcohol and drug use; on the other hand, their levels of anxiety are no higher, nor do they report any less life satisfaction or happiness (Tamir, 1982). Thus it seems that men in their forties have some problems, but the problems are probably not much worse than those men face at other ages.

This section began with an implied question: is there a male mid-life crisis? The answer must be that things are a bit too complicated to give a yes or no answer. First, it is important to question the notion that there are fixed stages of adult development, meaning there is a "crisis stage" at age 40 or some other age. Popularized books such as Gail Sheehy's *Passages* have given the public the impression that there are specific crises that predictably happen to people at certain ages. The actual research does not support that idea at all (Brim, 1976). In part, things are not so predictable because different things happen to different people at different times. For instance, if in the twelve months after his 40th birthday a man fails to get a promotion, has his best friend die of a heart attack, has to move his parents to a nursing home, and has frequent episodes of erection problems, he probably will have a crisis. But another man may not experience these things, or they may happen in a different order, or they may be spread out over a period of five or ten years. The changes for such a person will be much more gradual, never reaching a crisis. Rather than talking about "stages" and "crises," it is preferable to talk about "transitions" (Brim, 1976). This last term expresses the notion that there are changes in adult personality, but that they do not occur at fixed times, they do not have to be of crisis proportions, and they often lead to positive, growth-promoting outcomes.

HEALTH ISSUES

A baby boy born in the United States in 1979 can expect to live 69.9 years; a baby girl can expect to live 77.8 years (U.S. Bureau of the Census, 1981). In short, men live about 8 fewer years than women do. The argument rages as to whether the difference in life expectancy is due to biological factors or environmental factors. That is, are men more biologically vulnerable, more susceptible to disease, genetic defects, and so on; or are men the victims of their environment, specifically of the male role — the "lethal aspects of the male role" as one psychologist put it? In this section we will examine the evidence on both sides of the issue (for more extended discussions, see Harrison, 1978; Turner, 1982).

On the biological side of the argument, it has been found that males have a higher death rate than females even prenatally. At conception, the ratio of males to females is probably about 110 to 100.[2] At birth the male to female ratio is down to about 105 to 100 (Harrison, 1978). That is, even before birth males have a higher death rate (Stevenson, 1966). One

---

[2] You may be wondering why males and females are not conceived in equal numbers. The answer seems to be that sperm that bear the Y chromosome (Y-bearing sperm), and therefore produce a male at conception, are lighter than X-bearing sperm. This in turn is because the Y chromosome is smaller than the X chromosome. This may allow the Y-bearing sperm to swim better or faster and make them likelier to reach the egg.

can scarcely attribute this to socialization into the male role. The higher prenatal mortality rate for males is probably due to sex-linked recessive genetic defects or diseases, such as hemophilia (see Chapter 10). It has also been found that females have more resistance to infectious diseases than males because there are genes on the X chromosome that increase one's immune resistance (Goble and Konopka, 1973).

A study by Madigan (1957) is often cited as evidence for the biological determination of higher mortality rates in males. It was designed to test the hypothesis that higher male mortality rates are due to the greater stresses of the male role — the competitiveness of male jobs, the pressure for success and high earnings — compared with the "easy life" of the housewife/mother. Cleverly, Madigan thought of one situation in which the roles and stresses on males and females would be identical, or nearly so — nuns and monks. The results were that the nuns lived longer than the monks, and both had life expectancies essentially the same as the rest of the population. Because environment was equalized for the two groups, the conclusion must be that biological factors determined the shorter lives of the monks. There have been serious criticisms of the Madigan study, however. Specifically, the monks smoked more than the nuns did, and, as we shall see, smoking is a critical factor. Thus the nuns and monks did not have truly equal experiences.

There is evidence on the environmental side of the argument. A thorough analysis of the causes of deaths in males and females indicates that about one-third of the male-female difference is due to smoking (Waldron, 1976; Waldron and Johnston, 1976). Of the leading causes of death in which males outnumber females, two are lung cancer and heart attacks, and cigarette smoking is implicated in both. Another leading cause of death in which males outnumber females is cirrhosis of the liver, and that is related to excessive drinking, a behavior pattern that is considered more appropriate for males than females. Accidents — specifically, car and truck accidents and shooting accidents during hunting — are another cause of death in which males outnumber females; again they can clearly be linked to patterns of socializing males for such traits as aggressiveness and risk-taking. Thus some specific behaviors associated with the male role — smoking, drinking, aggression, and risk-taking — can be linked to higher death rates in males. It doesn't stretch the data to call these "lethal aspects of the male role."

There has been a great deal of publicity recently about the Type A, or coronary-prone, behavior pattern (Friedman and Rosenman, 1974; Matthews, 1982). Type A behaviors include extremes of aggressiveness and hostility, competitiveness, difficulty in relaxing, impatience, and a chronic sense of urgency about time, or "hurry sickness." Type A behaviors have been linked significantly to coronary heart disease (Matthews, 1982), and, as mentioned earlier, that is a leading cause of the greater number of male deaths. It is hard to avoid noticing that the list of Type A traits reads like a litany of the male role. Thus, insofar as males are socialized into such traits, it seems likely that they will become Type A individuals and will have a greater risk of developing heart disease. From a feminist point of view, it should be noted that most of the research on Type A has been conducted with male subjects only, and it is important that such research be extended to females.

An important related question is, what will happen to women as they become increasingly liberated and able to do things formerly reserved for males? If the liberation of women means liberating them to smoke, drink, and be aggressive, competitive, and hurried, will the ultimate reward be an earlier death? The available data indicate that this is not likely. For example, from 1940 to 1977 women's participation in paid jobs and careers increased substantially, yet deaths from coronary heart disease among women fell rapidly during this period (Siegel, 1978) — indeed, the rates for women declined faster than did the rates for men, both declines being due to greatly improved medical techniques. There is also evidence that Type A women who have been in the work force for more than half of their lives are no more likely to have heart disease than Type A home-makers (Haynes et al., 1978). Thus it may be that women can take on some aspects of the male role without too much risk. Nonetheless, I would not want to be part of the group of women who tests whether the female body can survive three packs of cigarettes and four martinis a day.

In conclusion, it seems that neither biological factors nor environmental factors alone can explain the higher mortality rates of males. Male deaths from heart disease and cirrhosis of the liver seem linked to environmental factors, specifically, the male role and smoking and drinking behaviors. But these can scarcely explain the higher rate of male deaths prenatally. Thus the higher male mortality rate is most likely due to a combination of biological factors (sex-linked genetic defects, immune factors) and environmental factors (the male role, which encourages smoking, drinking, and Type A behaviors).

MALE SEXUALITY

The research of Masters and Johnson (1966) indicates that men go through the same biological stages in sexual arousal as women do: excitement, plateau, orgasm, and resolution (see Chapter 12). A major process during both male and female arousal is vasocongestion, or increased blood flow into the genitals. In men, the vasocongestion produces erection of the penis. In males past puberty, orgasm is accompanied by ejaculation, the penis emitting a milky fluid containing sperm. But it has been theorized that some women, too, may ejaculate during orgasm (see Chapter 12). One difference between males and females is that males have a refractory period following orgasm. A refractory period is a period of time during which one cannot be restimulated to orgasm. Women have no such refractory period, and thus can have multiple orgasms, whereas men are generally limited to single ones. The length of the refractory period in men varies, depending on a number of factors, including age. In young men, the refractory period may be as short as a few minutes, whereas in men over the age of 65, it might be 24 hours.

What is more intriguing than biology is the psychology of male sexuality. An important first point is that, according to traditional definitions, sexuality — specifically, heterosexuality — is a central aspect of male identity (Gross, 1978). Males are supposed to be very interested in sex and good at it. The increasing recognition of women's interest in sex does not diminish its centrality for men — in fact, it may heighten it.

Psychologist and sex therapist Bernie Zilbergeld has provided a superb analysis of male sexuality — and how to cope with it — in his book *Male Sexuality* (1978). His central thesis is that men in our culture are taught a "fantasy model of sex," an unrealistic, idealistic set of expectations that put intense performance pressures on them. He captures the message of the fantasy model of sex in the title of one of his chapters: "It's Two Feet Long, Hard as Steel, and Can Go All Night," referring to the fantasy model of the enormous, ever-erect, aroused penis. He details the various aspects of the fantasy model in ten cultural myths about male sexuality, discussed below.

Myth 1: Men should not have, or at least not express, certain feelings. A central part of the male role is being unemotional. That means that feelings of love, tenderness, and perhaps even vulnerability are inappropriate and unmasculine. Unfortunately, those are precisely the emotions that are essential in developing intimate relationships. They are the emotions that enrich the sexual experience. Is it any wonder that males — particularly adolescent males for whom masculine identity is a key concern — focus mainly on the physical aspects of sexuality and neglect the emotional aspects? It is as though the culture had handicapped them from birth, crippling their tenderness, intimacy, and sensuality. Zilbergeld urges women to understand this problem as a handicap and, rather than resenting men's lack of emotional expressiveness, to help them to overcome their handicap and discover their tender, intimate selves.

Zilbergeld argues that it is this myth that leads men to mislabel their feelings and to think that what they are feeling is a sexual need for intercourse, when in fact what they are experiencing is love, or tenderness, or just a need for a good cuddle. Growing up thinking that they experience only lust, men mislabel other feelings. They think they want intercourse when what they really are experiencing is a need for a hug or for someone to say "I love you."

Myth 2: In sex, as elsewhere, it's performance that counts. Our culture is highly achievement-oriented, and we tend to turn sex into just one more achievement situation (Slater, 1973; Albee, 1977). We express this in language such as "achieving" orgasm, and in setting up achievement goals in sex, such as simultaneous orgasms for the man and woman. In addition, achievement is a key feature of the male role.

Myth 3: The man must take charge of and orchestrate sex. Put this myth together with the preceding one, and you have a situation in which sex becomes, for the man, an achievement situation in which he is expected to perform masterful tricks. However, the work of Masters and Johnson (1970) and others indicates that achievement-orientation and performance-orientation contribute importantly to sexual dysfunctions such as erection problems. When one sets up an achievement goal, one is also setting up the possibility of failure. Fear of failure creates anxiety, and anxiety quickly ruins the pleasure of sexual expression and produces sexual dysfunction.

The extent of performance pressures on men is strikingly illustrated in this account by two sex therapists:

> We'll never forget the man who called himself a premature ejaculator even though fairly regularly he lasted for forty-five minutes of vigorous thrusting. We know he lasted this long because his partner confirmed it. Actually, she had never been orgasmic in intercourse and had no desire to become so. She much preferred shorter intercourse because she some-times became so sore through almost an hour of thrusting that she could barely sit down the next day. That had little influence on the thinking of our client, who was convinced that she would have orgasms if only he could last an hour. (Zilbergeld, 1978, p. 257)

Myth 4: A man always wants and is always ready to have sex. Men are portrayed as always interested in sex and easily arousable. But that is not always true. Men need to learn to acknowledge that sometimes, in certain situations, or when they are tired, or with a certain partner, they are just not in the mood. Men need to learn to say "No," something women received more than adequate training for, but men learned was not part of their script.

Myth 5: All physical contact must lead to sex.

Myth 6: Sex equals intercourse.

Myth 7: Sex requires an erection. These three myths go together. In our culture we have learned a script for sexual interactions. The script specifies what should occur and in what order. Kissing, hugging, and touching progress to heavy petting, which progresses to intercourse, at least if everything goes well. As a result, we do not know how to relax and enjoy sex that consists only of kissing and touching. I once gave a talk on sex to a group of adolescent girls whom a social worker considered predelinquents. I was supposed to convey some information or inspiration that would keep them from getting pregnant. I suggested oral-genital sex as a way of having enjoyable sex with no risk of pregnancy. One girl raised her hand and said, with a penetrating honesty of the adolescent, "But that isn't *real* sex." She expressed perfectly the sentiment in our culture. Anything other than intercourse is not "real" sex, or is merely a ritualistic prelude to the real thing. The problem with all of this, from the male point of view, is that an erection is absolutely essential if intercourse is to take place. Erections are nice if they happen on their own; when they are an entrance requirement, things are not such fun. Once again, the stage is set for anxiety, fear of failure, and failure. Part of the remedy is to learn that there are many enjoyable aspects of sex that require no erection — in fact, the only thing that requires an erection is intercourse.

Myth 8: Good sex is a linear progression of increasing excitement terminated only by orgasm. The idea here is that in good sex one should get more and more and more aroused until it all ends in orgasm. This notion is so thoroughly engrained in our sexual scripts that we never pause to consider alternatives — for example, letting arousal subside for a few minutes of conversation, or resting, or whatever. And what happens if it becomes apparent that one or the other partner will not have the climactic orgasm? Does that mean that everything else was a waste of time? Only if orgasm has been set as a performance goal. But if one shifts to considering all aspects of sex as pleasurable in themselves, and decreases or lulls in arousal as acceptable, then occurrences such as lack of orgasm or loss of erection are not disasters. Rather they are things that sometimes happen during sex. This myth is particularly hard on men because of the myth that they must be in charge of the sexual sequence.

Myth 9: Sex should be natural and spontaneous. Of course, spontaneous sex can be nice, but all good sex does not have to be that way. The problem with the emphasis on spontaneity is that it discourages some important things from happening. For example, some people fail to plan for birth control because they say it interferes with the spontaneity of sex. That logic has a high chance of producing an unwanted pregnancy. The spontaneity/naturalness myth is also responsible for many men neglecting to educate themselves about sex. It is better to recognize that good sex sometimes does take planning and learning, which is in contradiction to beliefs that sex is just natural and that men are born sex experts.

Myth 10: In this enlightened age, the preceding myths no longer have any influence on us. Most people are aware that a sexual revolution has been going on for more than a decade. Many therefore think that the old norms and stereotypes no longer have an influence on us. That idea is incorrect for two reasons. First, many adults today were raised on the old scripts and have not managed to shed them completely or even partly. You may find yourslf interacting with people who believe all of the myths. Second, the sexual revolution did not do away with myths and norms; rather, it created new ones. Men used to be the only ones required to be sexual performers; now women are also supposed to be. It used to count as successful sex if the man had an orgasm; now the man and woman must have a simultaneous orgasm. The old myth of the man as sexual expert has not died, but has become even more demanding.

Zilbergeld recommends that men try to shed the sexual scripts that they have learned and to spend some time discovering what is truly pleasing to them sexually, expressing those ideas, and then trying to have sex that way, rather than the way society dictates.

Recent sex research has turned up many unexpected findings about male sexuality. For example, men sometimes fake orgasm. They want more emotional involvement in sex. And they feel under great performance pressure (e.g., Shanor, 1978). What is happening is that we are beginning to appreciate the complexity of male sexuality, in part by adopting the feminist perspective of examining the influence of gender roles on male sexuality, and then considering ways in which men can be liberated from some of the restrictions and demands of those roles.

BLACK MEN

Traditional psychology's view   Both theories and research in the social sciences have traditionally viewed the black man as downtrodden, having a poor self-concept, and being psychologically castrated. There are several reasons why this view is neither very realistic nor very useful. First, the traditional view is based on historical tracing of the black male role back to the days of slavery. This historical analysis has ignored the strong contributions of black men to their families, even within the confines of slavery (Staples, 1978). For example, Alex Haley's *Roots* portrayed many male characters who were responsible, strong, and had a good sense of themselves.

A second problem with the notion of the castrated black male is that it rests on the concept of black matriarchy. Black matriarchy is an interpretation of the fact that the percentage of female-headed households is larger among blacks than it is among whites (see Chapter 16). But this ignores the fact that the *majority* of black households are headed by men. Once again, the black man's contributions have not been sufficiently recognized. From a feminist point of view, it is interesting that the relatively egalitarian black family, when viewed by white male social scientists, has appeared matriarchal (Staples, 1978).

The view of black men as having a poor self-concept ignores the various ways in which people learn to cope with their situations in life. The results of oppression may seem less severe, depending on the context in which one is making judgments. For example, unemployment is often a terribly depressing experience for white men. The black man may be better able to cope with unemployment if many of his friends are also unemployed, although that scarcely makes unemployment pleasant. Yet black men have a reference group within their own culture by which they judge themselves, and against which they may come out quite well (Staples, 1978). Attribution theory (see Chapter 8) points out that it is important what attributions people make for their successes and failures. The civil rights movement has made blacks aware of discrimination as a force in their lives. Thus a black man who fails to get a promotion on the job may make the external attribution that the failure was due to discrimination, rather than the internal attribution that the failure was due to his own lack of ability. The former attribution keeps one's self-concept well intact.

Developmental issues   In a 1968 best-seller, *Black Rage*, psychiatrists William Greer and Price Cobbs said, "Whereas the white man regards his manhood as an ordained right, the black man is engaged in a never-ending struggle for its possession." There has been concern within traditional psychology about the development of adequate male identity in blacks, particularly black youths, given the high percentage of female-headed black households (e.g., Pettigrew, 1964). Such a view ignores the time fathers may spend with their sons, even though they are not part of the same household, and the contributions of older brothers, uncles, and grandfathers. Further, there are many black American culture heroes with whom the black youth can identify. Depending on his concerns at the time, the young black male identifies with different culture heroes (Taylor, 1976)

FIGURE 5.3
Dr. Martin Luther King, Jr. Black boys, even in father-absent homes, have other men to serve as role models.

Source: Leonard Freed / Magnum Photos, Inc.

— for instance, if his passion is sports, his idol may be Reggie Jackson, or if his interest is in politics and civil rights, it may be Martin Luther King, Jr. Thus there are many sources of identification for a black youth besides his own father.

Earlier in this chapter the sex-role identity paradigm was discussed. The concern over black male identity is clearly part of this paradigm. Having concluded that the sex-role identity paradigm is not a very good one and that concerns over gender identity are overblown, we must conclude that there has been too much emphasis on black male identity. If we shift to the sex-role strain paradigm, we see sex roles as sources of psychological strain for black men, which is probably a more productive approach.

Roles: Breadwinner, husband, father   A basic fact is that there is a high unemployment rate among black men. For example, in July, 1982, the unemployment rate for whites (both men and women) was 8.7 percent and 7.9 percent for adult white males. For adult black males, it was 15.7 percent (*The World Almanac*, 1983), double the rate for whites. The high unemployment rate creates a gender-role problem because the role of breadwinner or good provider is an important part of the male role in the United States. Thus black men, and particularly black male teenagers, may feel that they are not fulfilling this part of their role. From the perspective of the sex-role strain paradigm, we again see gender roles as a source of strain.

Not being able to fulfill this part of the male role may express itself in a number of ways. It may turn into antisocial behavior, violence, and crime, accounting for the high crime rate among black male teenagers. It has also been suggested that volunteering for the Army becomes an alternative means of fulfilling the male role — one-third of Army recruits are black men (Staples, 1978).

The role of husband is closely tied to the breadwinner role. Black men are understandably reluctant to take on the responsibility of marriage when unemployment is such a justified fear. Research shows, though, that black men have egalitarian attitudes toward marriage. Even black male adolescents expect egalitarian roles for men and women in marriage, in areas such as authority, housekeeping, and childcare (Rooks and King, 1973).

The father role, too, is closely tied to the breadwinner role, and the responsibility of supporting children is a source of stress to the unemployed black man. On the other hand, fathering children can be a means of fulfilling the male role for the lower-class black man who is denied much success in the breadwinner role. Interestingly, middle-class black men father fewer children than any other group in our society and, in particular, father fewer than lower-class black men do (McKay, 1978). It seems that the middle-class black man, who is successful in the breadwinner role, has less of a need to fulfill the male role by producing offspring. Research shows that middle-class black men are very child-oriented and participate more in child-rearing than do white men (Daneal, 1975).

In sum, the sex-role strain paradigm seems to be most useful in understanding the experience of the black male. We can examine, for instance, how the breadwinner role is a source of strain to a group that has such a high unemployment rate. Data are scarce, but the sex-role strain paradigm suggests many interesting and productive approaches for future research: — for example, what is the impact of the "no sissy stuff" part of the male role on black men? Does it contribute to their devaluing of women, or does it help them find satisfaction in their role, or is it not relevant in black culture?

IN CONCLUSION

An important point in this chapter was the distinction between the male sex-role identity paradigm and the sex-role strain paradigm. The MSRI paradigm was part of traditional psychology and was based on the assumption that a man must have a masculine identity in order to be psychologically healthy. As we saw, the MSRI paradigm is just not borne out by the evidence — boys' masculinity is not correlated with their fathers' masculinity, father absence does not necessarily produce inadequate masculinity, and so on. The alternative model is the SRS paradigm, which views gender roles as sources of strain in our culture. Although this paradigm is too new to have much evidence backing or contradicting it, it is useful in understanding some of the topics covered later in the chapter. For instance, it is useful in understanding the problems created by the emphasis on athletic prowess for males creating strains both for the athlete and the nonathlete; and it is useful in understanding the problem of unemployment for the black male in a culture that stresses the breadwinner, or good provider, role as a definition of manhood.

SUGGESTIONS FOR FURTHER READING

Doyle, James A. (1983). *The male experience.* Dubuque, IA: Wm. C. Brown. This is a nicely written, modern account of the psychology of men.

Pleck, Joseph H. (1981). Prisoners of manliness. *Psychology Today*, September, 69–83. This is a highly readable account of Pleck's critique of traditional psychology's view of men and masculinity.

6

Gender Differences in Personality and Behavior

Man should be trained for war and woman for the recreation of the warrior.

NIETZSCHE

All of you have probably heard dialogues such as the following:

MCP*:   "Of course she did that, because she's so emotional. Women are just more emotional than men."

AF**:   "Women *are not* more emotional than men. How can you say that?"

MCP: "Yes they are."

AF: "No they're not."

et cetera, et cetera.

Debates such as these are often not productive because they essentially end up setting one person's opinion against another's. The more productive approach is to realize that MCP's statement, "Women are just more emotional than men," is scientifically testable. That is, one can collect actual data on men and women to see if it is true. In this chapter we shall consider research that has done just that — looked at gender differences in various personality characteristics and behaviors — to see how different the personalities of women and men are. Research on gender differences in abilities will be discussed in Chapter 8.

STEREOTYPES, REAL DIFFERENCES, AND THE NATURE–NURTURE ISSUE

Before we look at the various personality characteristics and behaviors that have been investigated, it is important to make a distinction among the following: gender-role stereotypes, psychological gender differences that have been empirically determined to exist ("real" differences), and the causes of gender differences, whether biological or environmental.

Gender-role stereotypes are simply the things (behaviors, personality traits) that people expect from males and females. Research shows that, even in modern American society, and even among college students, there is a consensus that males and females do differ psychologically in many ways (Ruble, 1983; Rosenkrantz et al., 1968). A list of these stereotyped traits is given in Table 6.1.

---

* MCP = male chauvinist pig
** AF = ardent feminist

TABLE 6.1.   Stereotyped personality characteristics

There is a consensus among Americans that the following are characteristics of men and women.

Masculine Characteristics Considered Socially Desirable

Very aggressive
Very independent
Not at all emotional
Not at all easily influenced
Very dominant
Likes math and science very much
Not at all excitable in a minor crisis
Very active
Very competitive
Very skilled in business
Knows the ways of the world
Very adventurous
Can make decisions easily
Almost always acts as a leader
Very self-confident
Not at all uncomfortable about being aggressive
Very ambitious

Feminine Characteristics Considered Socially Desirable

Very tactful
Very gentle
Very aware of feelings of others
Very religious
Very neat in habits
Very strong need for security
Enjoys art and literature very much
Easily expresses tender feelings

Source: Rosenkrantz et al., 1968; Ruble, 1983.

When data are collected on the actual behavior and personality of females and males, the stereotypes turn out to be true in some cases ("real" differences), but not in others. For example, there is a stereotype that males are more aggressive than females; this turns out to be a real difference, as we will see later in this chapter. On the other hand, there is a stereotype that women are less intelligent than men, although actual research shows this not to be true; there are no gender differences in IQ. In this case, the stereotype is false. A *real difference*, then, is a gender difference that has been found to exist based on data collected on the personality or behavior of males and females.

Finally, if a gender difference (a real difference) is found, it requires one more step of analysis — and a very difficult one — to determine *whether the difference is biologically or environmentally caused.* For example, because there is a well-documented gender difference in aggression, we cannot automatically infer that it is biologically caused (e.g., by sex hormones), nor can we automatically decide that it is produced by environmental factors (e.g., socialization). Gender differences may be caused by environmental factors, biological factors, or both. Sophisticated research is necessary to uncover the complex interplay of biological and environmental forces at work.

GENDER DIFFERENCES VERSUS INDIVIDUAL DIFFERENCES

Suppose we say that a particular study of kindergarten children showed boys to be more aggressive than girls. Just what exactly does that mean?

Such a statement generally means that there were average differences between males and females, and that these differences were statistically significant. It most certainly does not mean, however, that all the males were more aggressive than all of the females. With data on gender differences, the distributions, while showing average differences, generally overlap to a great extent (see Figure 6.1). Typically there is a great deal of

FIGURE 6.1

Examples of distributions of scores for males and females that might lead to statistically significant gender differences in the trait.

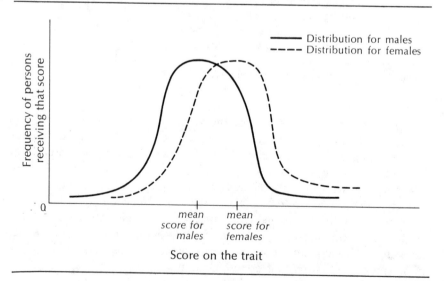

variability among members of one gender (individual differences). Therefore one should not be surprised to find an aggressive little girl in the kindergarten in our imaginary study. There may be some very aggressive little girls, but the boys, on the average are more aggressive. And, particularly if the number of subjects is large, a statistically significant gender difference may be found even though the average scores of males and females are fairly close.

The point is that even when there are average gender differences in a particular trait, there are almost always still large individual differences — differences from one female to the next and from one male to the next. Often these individual differences are more important than the average gender differences. A finding that females are less aggressive than males should certainly not lead one to expect that all females are unaggressive.

Often in this book I will make a statement such as "males are more aggressive than females" as a kind of shorthand for the more precise — but awkward — "males, on the average, are more aggressive than females." Individual differences and the great overlap of distributions should always be kept in mind, however.

MACCOBY AND JACKLIN: THE PSYCHOLOGY OF SEX DIFFERENCES

At this point, there are literally thousands of studies investigating psychological gender differences. These studies have attempted to document the "real differences," using the terminology introduced above. This should mean that we have a thorough understanding of which behaviors show gender differences and which do not. Unfortunately, things are a bit more complicated than that. Often the results of different studies contradict each other. For example, some studies of gender differences in infants' activity levels find that boys are more active, whereas others find no differences. In such cases, what should we conclude? Are boys more active than girls?

Another problem is that sometimes a single study that finds a gender difference will be widely cited and included in textbooks, and the five other studies of the same behavior that found no gender difference will be ignored. It seems likely that this occurs particularly when a finding of gender differences confirms the stereotypes held by authors and the general public. As an example, many child psychology texts cite the finding that boys are more active than girls, and further argue that this may be a source of later gender differences and of the active assertiveness of the adult male role. However, in the actual studies of infants' activity levels, two of the reports found gender differences that were not statistically significant (Knop, 1946; Lewis et al., 1963). According to the rules of science, a gender difference should be statistically significant before it is worth talking about. A third study that is cited as evidence, in fact, used male infants only as subjects (Bell, 1960). It is difficult to see how such a study could be evidence for gender differences.

To bring some order out of this chaos, Stanford psychologists Eleanor Maccoby and Carol Jacklin attempted to review systematically the huge number of studies of psychological gender differences, publishing their findings in a book entitled *The Psychology of Sex Differences* (1974). In all, they reviewed over 2000 articles and books, most of them published after 1966. They made particular efforts to find studies that had tested for gender differences in psychological characteristics but had found none. They concluded that some widely held beliefs about gender differences have little or no scientific evidence backing them. They also found that there are some gender differences that are very solidly documented. Maccoby and Jacklin's conclusions will be mentioned frequently in this chapter in the discussion of gender differences in personality, and also in Chapter 8 in the discussion of gender differences in abilities.

Maccoby and Jacklin's book instantly became a classic in the field, in part because the authors are highly respected psychologists, and in part because there was a great need for such a book. Later, however, the book was criticized — perhaps the most serious criticisms coming from Berkeley psychologist Jeanne Block (1976). She argued that Maccoby and Jacklin had a bias toward finding no gender differences. She found some clerical errors in their tallying of studies and felt that their categorizing of studies was sometimes arbitrary. Finally, young subjects were overrepresented in the studies surveyed by Maccoby and Jacklin; 75 percent were based on subjects 12 years old or younger, and nearly 40 percent were based on pre-schoolers. This, of course, is not Maccoby and Jacklin's fault; it simply reflects the way psychologists have chosen to do their research. Nonetheless, it means that we know very little about gender differences in adults, and most of that is based on data from college students — still scarcely a broad age range. Block pointed out that many gender differences do not appear until adolescence, and so findings of no gender differences with young children may be misleading.

In the sections that follow, I will cite Maccoby and Jacklin's conclusions when they seem to be accurate and will refer to other sources if they have provided convincing evidence that Maccoby and Jacklin's conclusions are not accurate.

We shouldn't leave this discussion, however, without noting a moral that emerges. Often a very interesting gender difference will be found in a study, and the study will be given a great deal of publicity, including being discussed in textbooks and professors' lectures. Students need to develop a critical attitude in such cases. The first question one should ask when hearing such a report is, has this finding been replicated? *Replicated* means that the study has been repeated independently by other scientists and the same results obtained. A single study that finds a gender difference is not very convincing. Are there other studies of the same behavior that find no difference? Or have many different scientists all found this difference consistently? One study doth not a gender difference make.

Now let us proceed to see whether there is evidence for gender differences in a variety of personality characteristics and behaviors. I have put them in roughly the following order: those for which there is good evidence of a gender difference come first, those where the evidence is somewhat mixed come next, and, finally, those in which there appears to be no gender difference are last.

AGGRESSIVENESS

Gender differences Perhaps the most consistently documented psychological gender difference is in aggressiveness, with males being more aggressive than females (Maccoby and Jacklin, 1974). This difference holds up for every one of the many different kinds of aggression that have been studied, including physical aggression, verbal aggression, and fantasy aggression. Further, this gender difference has been found in all cultures in which the appropriate data have been collected.

Developmentally, this difference appears about as early as children begin playing with each other, around the age of two or two and a half. The difference continues consistently throughout the school years. Of course, as people get older, they become less aggressive, at least in the physical sense. It is rare to see adults rolling around on the floor as they punch each other, compared with the frequency with which that occurs on an elementary school playground. We have less information available on gender differences in adult aggression, but we do know that the vast majority of crimes of violence are committed by men (although female crime is on the increase). According to the results of social psychologists' research on aggression (most of it done in the laboratory with college students), there are some situations in which there are no gender differences; but it is rare for women to be more aggressive than men (Frodi et al., 1977). In particular, women are likely to be as aggressive as men when it appears that it would be justified or even prosocial to be aggressive. It also seems that men and women react differently to provocation: what angers a man (and leads him to be aggressive) tends to make a woman anxious, not angry or aggressive.

I was interested in finding out how large are individual differences in aggression relative to average gender differences, so I reviewed a large number of studies (143, to be exact) of gender differences in aggression, looking at the statistical analyses they reported (Hyde, 1984). I found that, although gender differences in aggression do appear consistently, the difference is not large relative to the individual differences — in fact, the size of the difference is approximately as large as that shown in Figure 6.1.[1] The analysis also showed that gender differences in aggression are largest among preschoolers; gender differences become smaller with age and are quite small among college-aged subjects.

What causes the gender difference?   The causes of the gender difference in aggressiveness have been hotly debated, with the nature and nurture teams battling against each other. The nurture team attributes gender differences in aggressiveness to the greater size and musculature of males and/or differences in the levels of the sex hormone testosterone. These factors will be discussed in detail in Chapter 10.

On the nurture side, a number of environmental forces might produce the observed gender difference: (1) Aggressiveness is a key part of the male role in our society, and unaggressiveness or passivity a key part of the female role. Following the logic of cognitive-developmental theory, as soon as children become aware of gender roles, girls realize that they are not supposed to be aggressive and boys know that they should be. As I noted in Chapter 3, this logic does not work very well in explaining how gender differences develop so early, but it may be helpful in explaining gender differences among older children. (2) Children imitate same-gender adults more than opposite-gender adults, and they see far more aggression in men than in women, particularly on TV and in movies. Hence boys imitate men, who are aggressive, and girls imitate women, who are unaggressive. However, as noted in Chapter 3, the evidence indicates that there is not much of a tendency for children to imitate same-gender adults more than they imitate opposite-gender adults. (3) Boys receive more rewards for aggression and less punishment for it than girls do. These reinforcements and punishments might be in a physical form, such as spanking, or in a verbal form such as comments from adults like "Boys will be boys" in response to a boy's aggression, and "Nice young ladies don't do that" to a girl's aggression. Boys also may be rewarded in the form of status or respect from their peers for being aggressive, whereas girls receive no such reward. Actual studies, however, indicate that boys are punished more for aggression than girls are by both parents and teachers (Maccoby and Jacklin, 1974; Serbin et al., 1973; Hyde and Schuck, 1977). This poses a problem for this explanation. However, psychologists believe that some kinds of punishments for aggression may actually increase a child's aggression rather than decrease it. Therefore the punishments that boys receive may actually make them more aggressive. (4) A somewhat more complex cultural argument takes into account the fact that, simply because of the way our culture organizes child care, the major disciplinarians of small children are women

---

[1] If you have studied statistics, it will be meaningful to you to know that the male and female means are about 0.5 standard deviation apart, and that gender differences account for about 5 percent of the variation in aggression scores ($\omega^2 = .05$).

— mothers and teachers. Research indicates that children's identification with a punishing adult is important in what kind of effects the punishment will have. If the child is highly identified with the adult, punishment will decrease aggression, whereas if the child is not identified with the adult, punishment increases aggression (Eron et al., 1974). Little girls are more

FIGURE 6.2

Gender differences in aggressiveness appear early.

Source: Photo by Cary Wolinsky/Stock Boston.

highly identified with their mothers and female teachers than boys are. Hence punishment by mothers and female teachers would decrease the aggression of girls and increase the aggression of boys. There are some empirical data to support this explanation (Hyde and Schuck, 1977). One implication of this line of reasoning is that if we want to reduce the aggressiveness of boys, or increase the aggressiveness of girls, or minimize gender differences, we will need to get fathers more involved in caring for their children and get more men to be nursery school and elementary school teachers.

The question of what causes gender differences in aggressiveness is a complex one that has not been completely resolved by scientific data. Perhaps the best conclusion to make at this point, and the one that seems to agree best with the existing data, is that there are probably rather small biologically based gender differences in aggressiveness, and that cultural forces act to magnify these differences considerably (Hyde and Schuck, 1977).

Dominance   The majority of studies show that males are more dominant than females (Block, 1976). Dominance behaviors may involve things like getting one's own way, or having a reputation for toughness in a kind of human pecking order. Such behaviors may be a bit more subtle to get at than the kinds of physical aggression discussed in previous sections. Nonetheless, they are important for two reasons: First, they are more important in adult interactions than are behaviors such as punching and kicking. Thus they may be important in how women function in the world of work or in other adult interactions. Second, dominance is an important reflection of a person's *status*. Dominant individuals have higher status than subordinate individuals. Feminist theorists have noted that gender is an important status variable, with men having higher status than women (e.g., Henley, 1973). Thus gender differences in dominance behaviors may reflect the differential status of women and men, or may even contribute to that differential status.

To illustrate the way psychologists measure dominance and find gender differences, let us consider in detail a study by Kathrynn Adams and Audrey Landers (1978). Copies of paintings were shown to pairs of college student subjects; however, one member of each pair was really a confederate of the experimenters. The subjects saw pairs of paintings, and their initial task was to write down which one of each of the twenty pairs they thought was more attractive. The pairs had previously been rated as being equal in attractiveness by other subjects. After subjects had made their individual decisions, the experimenter told them that they must come to a joint decision on which of each pair was more attractive. On six of the pairs, the confederate voiced his or her opinion second and disagreed with the subject. If the subject stuck to her or his guns, the confederate would offer a challenge, and the process continued up to a possible twenty challenges.

The number of challenges that the subject withstood was a measure of the subject's dominance.

In this study, there was a significant gender difference. Males withstood an average of about nine challenges, whereas females withstood an average of about six. Based on this finding, Adams and Landers concluded that males were more dominant than females.

Dominance was essentially defined by Adams and Landers as resistance to another's attempts at influence. Some people would dispute this definition. They might say that this study does not demonstrate gender differences in dominance, but rather demonstrates gender differences in influenceability or conformity or cooperativeness. Maccoby and Jacklin (1974) included in their category of behaviors classified as dominance such things as attempts to influence another child's behavior, attempts to influence an adult's behavior, reputation (ranked by peers) for "toughness" among children, and leadership. The point is that "dominance" is defined by different researchers in different ways, and at best it is a complex concept. Thus it is not surprising that it is a complex matter to determine whether there are gender differences in dominance.

SELF-CONFIDENCE

Suppose a group of students take their first exam in Introductory Psychology. Immediately after they complete the exam and before they receive their grades, we ask them to estimate how many points (out of a possible 100 points) they think they got on the exam. Most studies indicate that we will find a gender difference, with females estimating that they will get fewer points than males estimate (Block, 1976; Berg and Hyde, 1976; McMahan, 1982). Psychologists interpret this as indicating that females have lower self-confidence than males do.

This difference between males and females has been found consistently in many studies. Even in a study involving a group of preschoolers, with an average age of four-and-a-half years, girls had lower expectancies for their performance on various tasks than boys did (Crandall, 1978). This was also found to be true of elementary school children (Crandall, 1969).

The gender difference in self-confidence is an important one. There is evidence that people with low expectations for success avoid engaging in challenging tasks. Thus this gender difference may have important effects on women's careers and accomplishments, a point to be discussed further in Chapter 8.

Although there is a fairly consistent gender difference in self-confidence, we need to place some qualifications on the general result (Lenney, 1977, 1981). First, whether females give lower estimates of their expectancies depends on the kind of tasks involved. For example, females do not give lower estimates if they are made to think a task is gender-appropriate for them. Second, the gender difference depends on the kind of feedback given to people about their performance. If females are given clear and unambiguous feedback about how well they are doing, or how good their abilities are, then their estimates are not lower than males'. Finally, the gender difference depends on the presence or absence of social comparisons or social evaluations. If other people are present and everyone is being compared with one another, then women give low estimates; but if they work alone or in situations where they do not expect their performance to be compared with others, then their estimates are not lower. Therefore it seems that women have lower self-confidence than men in some situations, but not in others.

Before leaving the topic of self-confidence, I need to note one further complication, namely interpretation of the results. The objective, statistical result in the studies we have been discussing is that males estimate they will get more points on the exam or some other task. To use the terminology of Chapter 1, the *interpretation* of this result is that males have more self-confidence than females, or that *females are lacking in self-confidence.* This interpretation carries with it the implication that females have a kind of psychological deficit. Would it be possible to make a different interpretation that would still be consistent with the data? An alternative interpretation is that males' estimates are too high (rather than females' being too low) and that males are unrealistically confident. This alternative is just as reasonable an interpretation of the gender difference, but this interpretation implies a problem for males. As it turns out, with tasks such as these it is possible to decide which interpretation is more accurate, because we can find out how students actually did on the exam. As it turns out, males tend to overestimate their performance by about as much as females underestimate theirs, although some studies find girls' estimates to be accurate and boys' to be inflated (Crandall, 1969; Berg and Hyde, 1976). Therefore, there is some truth in each interpretation — men are probably a bit overconfident and women a bit underconfident.

ACTIVITY

There has been quite a bit of debate among psychologists as to whether there are gender differences in activity level. Certainly if you ask the average parent or teacher, they will tell you that boys are more active. Most child psychology texts have maintained that this is true. Maccoby and Jacklin (1974), however, concluded that the data were ambiguous — some studies showed no differences, some showed males to be more active, and a few showed that females were more active. Then Block (1976), in her critique of Maccoby and Jacklin, concluded that the evidence does show that boys are more active than girls; of the 59 relevant studies, 24 found boys significantly higher, 3 found girls significantly higher, and the rest found no difference.

Where does that leave us? It seems reasonable to conclude that boys are more active than girls, although the difference is probably not quite so marked as the difference in aggressiveness. It is also well-established that the great majority — about 80 to 85 percent — of hyperactive children are boys (Stewart et al., 1966; Chess, 1960).

What causes this gender difference? The arguments are similar to those made about aggressiveness, and the issue has not been resolved in either case. What we do not know is how much the developmental precocity of girls contributes to this difference. Stated briefly, girls are ahead of boys in development. As children grow older, they learn to control their activity more. It might be, then, that the lower activity of girls represents simply a greater ability to control activity because of their being somewhat more mature than boys.

INFLUENCEABILITY

Most social psychology texts state that women are more influenceable than men. Women are said to be more easily persuaded, more suggestible, and more conforming. As one text put it:

> The most consistent and strongest factor that differentiates people in the amount they conform is their sex. Women conform more than men. . . . (Freedman et al., 1970, p. 239)

Psychologists Alice Eagly and Linda Carli (1981) reviewed the available studies on influenceability. They concluded that there are significant gender differences in influenceability, with men being less influenceable; but they also found that the size of this gender difference is small — about half the size of the gender difference in aggression. In studies in a somewhat different area, group pressure to conform (e.g., Asch, 1956), gender differences are also significant, with females showing more conforming responses; however, that may simply reflect the tendency of females to try to preserve harmony in a group. We can conclude, then, that females are somewhat more influenceable than males and somewhat more conforming, but that the difference is a small one.

Another fascinating result emerged from Eagly and Carli's analysis. They looked at the relationship between the gender of the researcher and the results of the study. They found that there was a significant relationship, with male researchers finding larger gender differences and greater persuasibility and conformity among women than female researchers found. This is an excellent example of the sorts of experimenter effects and observer effects discussed in Chapter 1. The researcher's gender might influence the outcome of the study in several ways. Perhaps researchers choose topics that favor the interests or expertise of members of their own gender. Perhaps researchers design settings for their research that make members of their own gender feel more comfortable and therefore less likely to be influenced. Or perhaps there is a bias in publishing or reporting gender differences, with female researchers more likely to report nonsignificant gender differences, perhaps because they are delighted to find that women are not so influenceable. A sobering finding, keeping in mind that men found larger gender differences, was that 79 percent of the authors of the influenceability studies were men. Thus the portrayal of women has likely been profoundly affected by the fact that most of the researchers have been men. Our understanding of both men and women would have been far better had men and women been equally represented as researchers.

ANXIETY

Most studies show that girls are more fearful, timid, and anxious than boys (Block, 1976). Once again, though, the difference is not simple. Most of the studies that find differences are based on self-reports, but studies based on direct observations often find no gender difference (Maccoby and Jacklin, 1974). To illustrate the difference between self-reports and direct observations, suppose a psychologist is trying to determine whether girls are more fearful of dogs than boys are. If the psychologist is using the self-report method, he or she would interview children and ask them if they are afraid of dogs. Using the method of direct observation, the psychologist would bring a dog into the room and see whether the children behave fearfully.

What we know, then, is that girls and women are more willing to admit that they have anxieties and fears. It is possible that these self-reports reflect that females actually are more fearful and anxious than males. But it is also possible that males and females experience the same levels of fear and anxiety and that females are only more willing to admit them. This might be a result of gender-role stereotypes, which portray women as fearful and timid and men as fearless and brave. This would encourage women to admit their feelings and men to pretend not to have them. At this point, however, studies have not been able to resolve this issue.

EMPATHY

Empathy means feeling the emotion another person is feeling. It essentially involves putting yourself in another's place emotionally. According to stereotypes, females are more empathic than males, as part of the general stereotype of emotional expressivity in females and emotional inexpressivity in males. Is this stereotype a real difference?

Psychologists Nancy Eisenberg and Randy Lennon (1983) reviewed studies of empathy and found that the results on gender differences were rather mixed. Gender differences in empathy seem to depend on the way in which they are measured. When people respond to self-report questionnaires containing items like "Seeing people cry upsets me," the gender difference is large, with females showing more empathy. Using a different measure, designed to measure "empathy" in newborn infants, girl infants are more likely to cry when they hear a tape recording of another infant crying, but the size of this gender difference is only moderate. Finally, when actual psychological measures of emotional responding are used, or when researchers unobtrusively observe actual behavior (facial expressions, tone of voice), gender differences are small. Perhaps gender differences are largest with the questionnaires because the questions tap gender-stereotyped responses. For example, the item mentioned earlier, "Seeing people cry upsets me," sounds a lot like the stereotypes of women as being emotional and aware of the feelings of others, discussed in the first section of this chapter. The items may measure stereotypes more than reality. Thus, although the evidence does indicate that females are somewhat more empathic than males are, the difference is a small one.

SOCIABILITY

It is also part of conventional wisdom that females are more "social" than males. Maccoby and Jacklin (1974), however, have concluded that this belief is unfounded and that there are actually no gender differences in sociability.

To measure sociability in infants, psychologists showed them various pictures, some of human faces, some of geometric forms. The idea was that if the female infants spent more time gazing at human faces, this would indicate that they were more interested in social stimuli. There were a few scattered reports that this was the case, but when Maccoby and Jacklin reviewed all the research, they concluded that there was no evidence of a gender difference.

In childhood, it seems that boys and girls are equally responsive to social reinforcement. There does not seem to be a gender difference in the amount of time spent interacting with playmates. In fact, at some ages it appears that boys actually spend more time with friends. The pattern of social interaction, however, does tend to be somewhat different — boys tend to congregate in large groups or gangs, whereas girls are more likely to interact in pairs or small groups.

The evidence, then, does not support the notion that females are more social or dependent on social reinforcements.

IN CONCLUSION

In this chapter I have tried to assess the evidence for gender differences in some important personality characteristics and behaviors. For some of these — particularly for aggression and self-confidence — there was good evidence of a difference. For others — activity, anxiety, influenceability, and empathy — there seemed to be a gender difference, but a smaller one. Finally, for one — sociability — there was no good evidence of a gender difference.

The danger in focusing so much on gender differences is that we will start to think that males and females have entirely different personalities. Although there are some differences, as we have seen, what is perhaps more impressive are the similarities. For a stereotyped trait such as sociability, there appear to be no gender differences. Even for aggression, the gender difference is not large. And we have not even begun to discuss a long list of characteristics that have probably never shown a gender difference in anyone's research and have, therefore, been omitted from mention — for example, honesty, conscientiousness, sincerity. It is important to remember that *gender similarities* are probably more the rule than gender differences.

7

From Infancy to Old Age: Development across the Lifespan

At age twelve I was among the first of my friends to begin to menstruate and to wear a bra. I felt a mixture of pride and embarrassment. For all of my life I had been a chubby, introspective child, but a growth spurt of a few inches, along with my developing breasts, transformed me one summer into a surprisingly slim and shapely child-woman. The funny thing was that on one level I had always known this would happen. Yet it was as if a fairy godmother had visited me. I felt turned on, but I was mostly turned on to myself and the narcissistic pleasure of finding I was attractive to boys.

FROM Our Bodies, Ourselves

My daughter loves to look at the family photograph albums. She begs to see the pictures of herself as a baby or a two-year-old and to hear the stories of the funny things she did or said at that age. She nags to see the pictures of me dressed in my cowgirl outfit at age five and to hear how I wanted to be Dale Evans (Roy Rogers' other half) when I grew up. Then she triumphantly announces, "But you didn't, you're a professor." She sees the picture of me as an awkward-looking eight-year-old, dressed in a ballet costume for my first dance recital, and we laugh together at how I still don't dance very well. She is fascinated, as most people are, with the process of psychological development — how different she is at five from the way she was at two, how different adults are from what they thought they would be when they were children, how predictable some things are from childhood to adulthood. In this chapter we shall consider the development of female personality and roles across the lifespan.

INFANCY

As noted above, psychologists have spent an extraordinary amount of time studying children, particularly preschoolers and infants. The study of gender differences has been no exception. Investigations of infant gender differences have had two primary motives. First, it has been thought that if gender differences were found in newborns — say when they are only one day old — they must surely be due to biological factors, because gender-role socialization can scarcely have had time to have an effect. The idea, then, was to try to discover the biological causes of gender differences by studying newborns. Second, many investigators think it is important to study the way parents and other adults treat infants, in order to discover the subtle (and perhaps not so subtle) differences in the way adults treat boy babies and girl babies, beginning the process of socialization at a tender age. I shall review research in these two areas below.

Infant gender differences Establishing what behaviors in infants show gender differences has the same complications as does establishing any gender difference (as discussed in Chapter 6). To this is added the further complication of trying to establish whether these differences really mean anything in terms of later behavior, in childhood or adulthood. As in Chapter 6, many of our conclusions will be based on the reviews by Maccoby and Jacklin (1974) and Block (1976).

First, it should be noted that most infant behaviors do not show gender differences. That is, *gender similarities* are the rule for most behaviors. For example, in a study of infants at three weeks of age and again at three months, twelve behaviors were measured (Moss, 1967). At three weeks, only six of the twelve showed significant gender differences, and at three months, only four of the six still showed gender differences (males fussed more, were more irritable [cried and fussed], and were more often awake and passive, while females slept more). Only four of twelve variables, then, showed stable gender differences at three weeks and three months. The majority of behaviors showed gender similarities.

Nonetheless, there are some behaviors for which there is evidence of gender differences. Newborn girls seem to have greater *tactile sensitivity* (sensitivity to touch) than newborn boys (Block, 1976). This may be measured, for example, by blowing air on the baby's cheek or stomach and seeing whether she or he responds.

There are probably differences in *activity level*, with boys having the higher activity (Block, 1976). In small infants, this may be measured by counting the amount of swinging arms or kicking legs. In older babies, it might be measured by counting the number of squares the baby crawls across on a playroom floor. The differences here, however, are small and rather inconsistent; Maccoby and Jacklin concluded there were no differences, but Block, in re-reviewing the evidence, concluded that there were.

One widely cited study found evidence of greater separation distress in female infants (Goldberg and Lewis, 1969; Messer and Lewis, 1972). This refers to the distress an infant feels when separated from the mother, in this case by placing a barrier between the two. This might indicate greater attachment or dependency in girls. However, more recent research has shown that minor manipulations of the experimental procedure could eliminate or even reverse the gender difference (Jacklin et al., 1973; Maccoby and Jacklin, 1974). Thus there is not good evidence to support the notion of greater separation distress or dependency of female infants.

Some evidence does exist, then, for very early gender differences in at least two behaviors, tactile sensitivity and activity level. The next question is, what does this mean? The results by themselves are of little interest, except perhaps to a trivia expert. They become important if they predict later behavior, in childhood or adulthood. For example, if people high in tactile sensitivity in infancy turn out to be high in empathy in adulthood, then the greater tactile sensitivity of girl infants may explain the greater empathy of girls and women (discussed in Chapter 6). To get evidence for this supposition, however, requires *longitudinal developmental research.* This means starting out with a group of infants and following them through their lives until they are adults. The research for a project of this type is very time-consuming and costly, so not much of it has been done. There are some suggestions of the kind of results that may occur. For example, tactile sensitivity has been related to vigor, assertiveness, and persistence in the late preschool years (Bell et al., 1971). Ironically, this would predict that girls should be more vigorous and assertive than boys. Further research in this area should be extremely informative.

Adults' treatment of infants   The other area of interest in infant research concerns whether, even at this early age, parents and other adults treat males and females differently.

Once again, *gender similarities* seem to be the rule; for the most part parents treat male and female babies similarly (Maccoby and Jacklin, 1974). Nonetheless, there do seem to be some differences. Boys are handled more roughly (Maccoby and Jacklin, 1974), and boys generally receive more responses from adults, such as being held by the mother (Lewis, 1972).

Some of these studies are based on direct observations of parent-child interactions, whereas others are based on parents' self-reports of their behavior toward their babies. The problem with this is that not only do parents influence infants, but infants also influence parents. Therefore, if there are differences in the behavior of boys and girls, these may cause the differences in parental treatment rather than the reverse. For example, if boys cry more, that may explain why they are held more.

A well-designed experiment, the *Baby X Study,* controlled these factors (Seavey et al., 1975). The adult subjects (all nonparents) were told they were participating in a study on infants' responses to strangers. They were brought into an observation room and a three-month-old infant (actually a female) in a yellow jumpsuit was put on the floor in the room with them. One-third of the subjects were told the baby was a boy, one-third were told she was a girl, and the other third were given no gender information. Three toys were near the baby — a small rubber football (a "masculine'" toy), a Raggedy Ann doll (a "feminine" toy), and a plastic ring (a "neutral" toy). The interactions between the subject and the baby were observed from behind a one-way mirror for three minutes. The frequency of using each of the toys was recorded, and ratings were made of the behavior of the adults toward the infant. Afterward, the subjects also rated their own impressions of the infant.

A number of interesting results emerged. With regard to choice of toy, there was an interaction between gender of the subject and gender-label of the baby. The results are shown in Table 7.1. The football was not really very popular in any condition, probably because it does not seem to be a very appropriate toy for such a small baby. This suggests the interesting speculation that the age of the child is more important than the gender in determining toy choice, although this would have to be investigated in a separate experiment. As expected, the doll was used most frequently when the baby was introduced as a girl. On the ratings of the interactions, and on the subjects' ratings of the babies, however, there were no significant differences depending on the label given to the baby. Some of the most

TABLE 7.1. Mean frequency of toy choices for babies by the adults in the Baby X Study

		Toy		
Gender of Subject	*Baby Labeled*	*Football*	*Doll*	*Teething Ring*
Male	Boy	.33	.72	.61
	Girl	.50	1.61	.94
	No label	.85	.71	1.42
Female	Boy	.57	.71	1.00
	Girl	.50	1.27	1.05
	No label	.40	1.23	.70

Source: From "Baby X: the effects of gender labels on adult responses to infants" by Carol Seavey et al., 1975, *Sex Roles, 1.* Published by Plenum Publishing Corporation. Reprinted by permission.

interesting results came from the neutral label group. Many of them inquired what the baby's gender was. Most of them had formed an opinion of what the baby's gender was by the end of the session (57 percent of male subjects and 70 percent of female subjects thought that it was a boy) and had stereotyped rationales for their beliefs. Those who thought it was a boy noted the strength of the grasp or lack of hair, while those who thought it was a female remarked on the baby's roundness, softness, and fragility.

What can we conclude from this study? It would seem that gender is important in adults' interactions with children, something that is particularly evident when the adults are not told a child's gender. However, the effects are not simple, and they may not be large. None of the ratings of the interactions showed gender-label effects. For example, the adults did not automatically give a football to the "boy." Further, the effects depended not only on the gender-label given the baby, but also on the gender of the adult subject. Future research will have to untangle the complexities of adults' treatment of boy babies compared with girl babies.

CHILDHOOD

Gender differences.   Already by the early preschool years, several reliable gender differences have appeared. One is in *toy and game preference*. By two or three years of age, girls sew, string beads, and play at housekeeping, while boys play with guns, toy trucks, tractors, and fire engines, and do carpentry (Maccoby and Jacklin, 1974). What we don't know is what causes this early gender-typing of activities or interests. It may be that it has some biological basis, since it appears so early. But it is also true that there has been a chance for several years of socialization to take place.

Another difference that appears early is in *aggressiveness*. About as soon as aggressive behavior appears in children, around the age of two, there are gender differences; boys are more aggressive than girls. This difference persists throughout the school years (see Chapter 6).

Socialization   The forces of gender-role socialization become more prominent in childhood. *Socialization* refers to the ways in which society conveys to the individual its expectations for his or her behavior. The child's own immediate family may begin to have different expectations for her or him. For example, girls may be expected to help with the dinner dishes, boys to take out the garbage. The culture at large also has a tremendous impact. The schools, whether purposely or unwittingly, often transmit the information of gender-role stereotypes (Chafetz, 1974, p. 88ff.). I recently heard the story of a second-grade teacher urging on a little girl balking at doing a mathematics problem by saying "you must learn to do your arithmetic so you'll be able to do the marketing for your husband when you grow up." Children's readers still depict girls and women in restrictive, boring, passive, supportive, or downright stupid roles (Weitzman et al., 1972). Television is also a major transmitter of stereotyped information to the growing girl, depicting women as chiefly preoccupied with the shininess of their floors, the whiteness of their wash, and their own beauty (McArthur and Resko, 1975; Mamay and Simpson, 1981). Indeed, much of the absurdity of gender-role stereotypes may arise not from the actual roles of men and women, but rather from the caricatures of these roles portrayed on television, which the young girl may see as an important source of information about the nature of the adult world.

Further, the stereotyping of television messages has been demonstrated to have an actual effect on children's behavior. In one study, four-to-six-year-old children viewed a film similar to *Sesame Street* shows in which Muppet-like characters said that a set of toys belong to a boy; another group of children saw the same film, except that the characters said the toys were a girl's, and a third group of children saw a version of the film in which the characters said the toys could be for either boys or girls (Cobb et al., 1982). After viewing the film, children played more with the toys that had been described as gender-appropriate for them. In the condition in which the toys were described as being appropriate for both boys and girls, the children preferred those toys (compared to toys not shown in the film). This result suggests that children can respond positively to non-stereotypical messages on television.

It is also true that there is considerable variation from one family to the next in the way children are socialized to gender roles. Very "liberated" parents may take great pains to give trucks to their daughters and dolls to their sons and to make sure that the mother and father share equally in childcare duties. A more traditional family will probably encourage more traditional roles.

One factor that creates variation both between and within families in socialization forces is the size of the family and the child's ordinal position among siblings (Sutton-Smith and Rosenberg, 1970). For example, girls with sisters, as compared with girls with brothers, are significantly more interested in "feminine" activities.

School It seems that girls make the adjustment to school with much greater ease than boys do. Boys are referred for psychological evaluation and are found in remedial classes considerably more frequently than girls are (Andrews and Cappon, 1957; Dreger et al., 1964; Spivack and Spotts, 1965; Werry and Quay, 1971). (Note how this contrasts with adjustment problems in adulthood, see Chapter 14.) Girls' interactions with teachers seem to be more pleasant and less full of conflict. In one study, kindergarten girls related to adults twice as frequently as boys did (Lott, 1978).

Tomboys Despite the results on gender differences and socialization, not every girl conforms. One study found that 63 percent of a group of junior high girls said they were tomboys, and 51 percent of a sample of adult women recalled having been tomboys in childhood (Hyde et al., 1977). Not every girl, then, is staying at home playing with dolls. In fact, probably the majority are engaging in the active games that have traditionally been called "masculine." Perhaps tomboyism is simply childhood's version of androgyny (Hemmer and Kleiber, 1981).

Although many social critics emphasize the restrictiveness of girls' socialization, it is probably true that opposite-gender behavior is far less tolerated for boys than it is for girls. Many parents tolerate their daughters climbing trees and playing baseball, but get very upset at a son playing with dolls. It is, after all, far worse to be a sissy than to be a tomboy. As one investigator commented,

> . . . demands that boys conform to social notions of what is manly come much earlier and are enforced with much more vigor than similar attitudes with respect to girls. (Hartley, 1959, p. 458)

It seems, then, that particular areas exist in which there are gender differences in childhood, and that socialization does occur to some extent. It is also true, however, that gender similarities are the rule, and that many girls are allowed a great deal of freedom and are encouraged to achieve in school. Severe gender-role pressures probably do not come until later in adolescence. But in a sense, this may be even more difficult for the girl than would be consistent gender-role restrictions. Throughout most of her childhood she is free to pursue achievements, and only later is she told that these achievements are not appropriate.

ADOLESCENCE

If the behavior and development of males and females are so similar for about the first ten years of life, how do the gender differences in adult personality and roles arise? In the early years, females do better in school and have fewer adjustment problems than boys. Yet in adulthood females have low-status jobs and contribute less than men in the professions (Chapter 8) as well as having a higher incidence of mental illness (Chapter 14). Although the groundwork for these differences is prepared in childhood, the real precipitating factors most likely occur in adolescence. These will be discussed below.

The femininity-achievement incompatibility   In adolescence, a cultural rule starts to be enforced on the girl: achievement and femininity are incompatible — that is, to achieve is gender-inappropriate. If the girl continues to achieve she will be unfeminine, and to be feminine is not to achieve. The girl is caught in a situation in which two equally important systems of values are in conflict. One is the desire for a positive sense of self, the sense that one is a worthwhile, productive person. Achieving, getting good grades, and excelling have been encouraged and rewarded so far, providing a major avenue for establishing the self as having worth and value. But the reward system changes abruptly at adolescence. The competing system is the desire to be a good female, to conform to gender-role expectations, and to be feminine, with whatever rewards that carries. The desire to be a competent, worthwhile person is now incompatible with the desire to be good in the female role; society at large does not value the female role (Broverman et al., 1972).

The reward system may change in adolescence for either or both of two reasons. One is that heterosexual relationships, popularity, and dating rise to importance; thus the peer group may begin enforcing the rules of the femininity-achievement incompatibility. Parents, too, may change their teachings as they begin to see popularity and marriageability as important for their daughter. The timing of the change in the parents' emphasis, of course, varies greatly from one family to the next. In one, the girl may be urged to stop studying and to start having boyfriends when she is in sixth grade, while in another, achieving a college education will be viewed as far more important than dating, and the parents do not begin asking about marriage prospects until the young woman announces that she is going to go to graduate school and get a Ph.D.

Data on the changing social emphases at adolescence and their impact on the girl are rather slim. One study compared preadolescent (fifth-grade) girls and adolescent (tenth-grade) girls on a measure of gender-role stereotyping. The tenth-grade girls had significantly higher stereotyping scores, indicating that the tenth-grade girls rated women significantly lower than men on socially valued traits related to competence (Baruch, 1975).

FIGURE 7.1

In early adolescence, the girl learns that her status will be determined by her attractiveness, not her achievements.

Source: Photo by Eve Arnold/Magnum.

Another study found that 26 percent of the college women studied experienced conflict over the contradictory role expectations ("masculine" and achievement-oriented versus "feminine" and family-oriented) that their families had for them (Komarovsky, 1946).

Perhaps most relevant is a study of the self-concept of students in the third through twelfth grades (Rosenberg and Simmons, 1975). The results indicated that gender differences were small among the younger children and that striking gender differences emerged during adolescence. At that time, girls became more self-conscious than boys; the adolescent girls were increasingly people-oriented, whereas adolescent boys stressed achievement and competence. In another study, high school juniors and seniors were asked whether they would most like to be independent, successful, or well-liked (Rosenberg, 1965). Adolescent girls emphasized being well-liked (60 percent compared with 35 percent of the boys), whereas boys were much more likely to stress success (46 percent compared with 29 percent).

Certainly the origin of the *double-bind* for females, a most important influence on female personality, lies in the conflict between achievement and femininity (Horner, 1970a, 1972). The adolescent girl is caught in a classic double-bind situation in which she wants both of two alternatives, but the two alternatives are incompatible. She wants both to be feminine and to achieve, but the two are perceived as being incompatible. Certainly here would appear to be the origins of much of the ambivalence and conflict in female personality — the adolescent girl finding it difficult to combine, because of imposed cultural contingencies, being a worthwhile individual and a proper female (Broverman et al., 1972). In this we see one source of the adjustment problems some adult women have.

Dating and friendship   The rituals of dating are also an important force influencing adolescent female personality development. Competition against other girls for the attention of boys becomes essential to success; other females become the enemy. The competition is in itself somewhat frustrating because the competitor must remain passive in such an important battle; the girl cannot directly choose the boy and call him for a date. On the other hand, the passive aspects of this social interaction for the female should not be overemphasized. The antics displayed by many teenage girls in their attempts to attract male attention are about as passive as a three-ring circus complete with wild animals and neon lights.

A fairly common phenomenon of adolescent female dating is the date with an "older man," which is not only common, but encouraged. This phenomenon is probably related to the differences in developmental levels of females and males. Puberty and the accompanying growth spurt occur about two years earlier in girls than boys (Hyde, 1979). The teenage girl with a discerning eye can tell that many of the males of her own age are less mature than she is, and that to relate to someone of her own maturity, she must date an older male. The unfortunate result is that the female is in the position of being naive and inexperienced, the male wise, worldly, and knowing. This might be seen as a force pushing the female into the subordinate role in adulthood.

One rule that becomes quickly apparent in the dating game is that females are valued for their appearance, males for their achievements. This phenomenon has been documented in a number of social psychology studies. For example, in one study snapshots were taken of college women and men (Berscheid et al., 1971). A dating history of each subject was also obtained. Judges then rated the attractiveness of the women and men in the photographs. For the women there was a fairly strong relationship between attractiveness and popularity; the women judged more attractive had had more dates in the last year than the less attractive women. There was some relationship between appearance and popularity for men, but it was not so marked as it was for women. In another long-term study, begun in the 1930s, fifth- and sixth-grade girls were rated as to the attractiveness of their appearance (Elder, 1969). Years later they were tracked down. As it turned out, the more attractive the preadolescent, the more "successful" she had been in getting a husband. The most beautiful girls had married well-to-do, successful men. It seems that a woman's status is determined by her appearance, a man's by his achievements.

Another noticeable phenonemon among adolescent females is the formation of girl-groups or cliques, tight-knit groups of girls engaging in mutual sharing and often more than a little plotting. The student of behavior wishing to identify such phenomena can generally spot these cliques by the immense amount of giggling that emanates from them. It has been suggested that these groups are important in learning social definitions of femininity and in learning about sexual impulses (Douvan and Adelson, 1966). Unfortunately, the latter function at least is not as well served for girls, who are less likely than boys to exchange sexual information (Kinsey et al., 1953).

Women's friendship patterns in adulthood have attracted quite a bit of research attention recently, and some of the results will be discussed later in this chapter.

The search for identity   According to Erik Erikson (1950) adolescence is the stage in which the primary developmental crisis is a quest for identity. For the male, adult identity will be defined largely in occupational terms (Angrist, 1969) — "I am a doctor." Adolescence and the growing identity then become a preparation for this adult identity — "I must start to take science courses and become a responsible student in order to become a doctor."

For the adolescent girl, however, this process seems to be considerably different (Psathas, 1968). She does not anticipate that work outside the home will be a major source of identity for her (Douvan, 1970). College women often say they are preparing themselves to be teachers or social workers, not because they want to educate the minds of youth or do good works for humanity, but rather so that they "will have something to fall back on" (in case of unexpected widowhood or divorce). Job or occupation is simply not seen as a major source of identity. Instead, the main priority is still family (Greenglass and Devins, 1982) and the major source of identity is the husband and later the children — that is the wife-mother role. The man sees himself as a doctor; the woman sees herself as a doctor's wife. On the most glorious day of her life, her wedding day, a portrait is taken that soon appears in the newspaper. The caption says "Mrs. Robert Jones," not Susan Jones or Susan Smith-Jones, leaving not a trace of her former name (identity) and giving all-too-clear evidence that from that time on, her identity is defined in terms of her husband.

Therefore, in the late adolescent period, when the male is actively striving to develop an adult identity, we see the female postponing identity formation in an attempt to maintain a flexible identity that can adapt itself to the as-yet-unknown husband (Angrist, 1969). Forming a distinctive identity might make the girl unmarriageable. For example, a girl may decide to become the best nuclear physicist in the world. But if she later meets the man of her dreams, with the one exception that he has no plans to be married to the world's best nuclear physicist, she may have eliminated a good marriage prospect for herself. Shirley Angrist (1969) uses the term *contingency training* to describe this phenomenon. Flexibility is built into women's personality in the socialization process by contingency training. Woman lives by adjusting to and preparing for anticipated and unanticipated contingencies: the unknown qualities of the future husband, lack of guarantee of marriage, possible economic necessity of work, possible childlessness, children leaving home, and divorce or widowhood. For the adolescent female, the marriage/unknown-husband contingency is certainly the most salient (Psathas, 1968). Although a flexible personality may be a detriment to professional achievement (Chapter 8), in other areas it may be very valuable. If contingencies are truly beyond one's control, the ability to adapt is very functional.

Another way of looking at female identity formation is to recognize the distinction between *personal identity* and *vested identity*.[1] Personal identity refers to the person's identity as a unique individual, and in particular to those behaviors and activities that are intrinsically rewarding to the individual. Vested identity, on the other hand, refers to those behaviors and activities for which the person receives extrinsic rewards (for example, a paycheck), those behaviors that are expected by society, perhaps because of the gender of the individual. For example, a twelve-year-old girl may very much enjoy (derive intrinsic gratification from) active sports and the thrill of scientific discovery. These are important components of

---

[1] The author thanks Lois Ventura and Sherry Ziegler for suggesting the distinction between these concepts, although in somewhat different terms.

her personal identity. In contrast, her vested identity, particularly in the future, will consist of being a housewife and mother and conforming in other ways to the expected female role. She will receive extrinsic rewards for performing these behaviors, and will be viewed negatively if she does not carry these out — for example, if she chooses not to have children or chooses not to marry. A critical process of adolescence and early adulthood is to match personal identity with vested identity as an adult. This is accomplished particularly through the process of occupational choice. For example, a boy who experiences the intrinsic gratification of the thrill of scientific discovery may begin studying hard and preparing himself for a career as a physicist or an experimental psychologist. Or, if he enjoys working on cars, he may prepare himself to be a mechanic. For him, vested adult identity, the things that are extrinsically rewarding, are likely to be congruent with personal identity, those things that are intrinsically rewarding. For females, however, the adult vested identity of housewife/mother is normative, it is expected. Hence the wide variations that exist in the personal identities of growing girls often cannot be reflected through occupational choice in their adult vested identities. The girl who would enjoy being an athlete or a scientist has her role aspirations channeled into being a housewife and mother. She is often not encouraged to choose a vested identity that will be congruent with her personal identity.

Of course, today not every young woman makes marriage her major goal (Komarovsky, 1982). Particularly among college woman, a career may be the foremost concern, with marriage and children seeming at most a remote occurrence in the future. Today, then, it seems that three alternative female identity patterns have emerged (Dellas and Gaier, 1975):

1. Traditional role and stereotype: Awaiting marriage
2. Achievement and role success: Achievement in valued areas of our androcentric society
3. Bimodal identity: Commitment to family and career

Unfortunately, none of these three alternatives escapes the double-bind (Denmark and Goodfield, 1978) that will remain as long as there is an incompatibility between femininity and achievement. The adolescent girl who chooses the traditional role today may find herself and others wondering why she didn't accomplish more in the world of work (Luria, 1974). The girl who chooses the achievement-oriented identity will be questioned for her lack of husband and children. And the girl who chooses the bimodal identity will suffer the pulls between the conflicting areas of her life (Hodgson and Fischer, 1981).

A study of women graduating from college in the years 1967 to 1970 provides some information on the life expectations of women in late adolescence (Luria, 1974). Similar studies of women a generation ago indicated that their typical expectation was not to hold a paying job, but rather to devote their lives to being housewives, mothers, and volunteer workers.

In contrast, the majority of college women in this recent study expected to hold paying jobs at least during some periods in their lives. However, the transformation is not radical — most of them still did not anticipate holding jobs while their children were preschoolers, but did plan to work once their children entered school. As the investigator concluded,

> Thus, while motivation to work is not low on the average . . . the conditions under which these women say they will work are still highly constrained by their prospective view of their job as mothers of preschoolers and infants. (Luria, 1974, p. 316)

In sum, while I have suggested that personality development may be quite similar in females and males during infancy and childhood, adolescence represents a major divergence. The expectations for the girl suddenly change and become conflicting: achievement is not rewarded as it was formerly, femininity is demanded, and achievement and femininity are seen as being incompatible, creating a double-bind, or ambivalence, in female personality. Later in adolescence, identity formation becomes a key process, but the contingencies are such that it may not occur at this stage and may instead be postponed.

EARLY ADULTHOOD

Wife, housewife, mother   Most adult women define their identity almost completely in terms of their wife-mother role. Therefore it is important to consider the merits and disadvantages of this traditional course of action.

Young wives typically enjoy the intimacy and sharing of their marital relationship, and generally find the early years of marriage to be rewarding (Campbell et al., 1975). Achievement urges are often suppressed at this time, in favor of "accomplishing" the wife-mother role. Some authors have suggested that wives experience "vicarious achievement" through their husband's job, making the husband's job a "two-person career" (Lipman-Blumen, 1972; Papanek, 1973).

Overall, however, marriage seems to favor men rather than women. Married women report more depression than married men do; married men are less depressed than never-married men, but married women do not have a similar advantage over never-married women (Radloff, 1975). Single men report less life satisfaction than married men, but for women the difference is reversed — single women report more satisfaction than married women (Gurin et al., 1960; Bradburn and Caplovitz, 1965).

Sociologist Ann Oakley (1974) did a major study on housewives and their feelings about housework. The basic assumption of her study — that housework could be thought of and analyzed as work — is an unusual one because the general public, as well as social scientists, have tended to think that housework is not really work. The traditional logic goes like this:

1. Women belong in the family, while men belong "at work."
2. Therefore men work, while women do not work.
3. Therefore housework is not a form of work. (Oakley, 1974, p. 25)

Oakley believes that housework is a form of work just like any other job, except that it is not paid. She found that housewives are sensitive to the categorization of their work as nonwork. As an ex-typist put it:

> I think housewives work just as hard. I can't stand husbands who come home and say "Oh look you've done nothing all day, only a bit of housework and looked after the child." But I reckon that's tiring myself, well, not tiring, it's just as hard as doing a job — I don't care what any man says. . . . My husband says this — that's why I feel so strongly about it. (Oakley, 1974, p. 45)

In general, Oakley found that housework evokes a mixture of feelings, but dissatisfaction predominates: 70 percent of the London housewives she interviewed were dissatisfied with housework. The common reasons for dissatisfaction were monotony, loneliness, lack of structure, and long hours. The average woman spent 77 hours per week on housework. The smallest number of hours spent on housework by any woman in Oakley's sample was 48 hours per week, and that was reported by one of the women who was employed full-time outside the home. Some women also commented on the unconstructive nature of housework — for example, every morning the housewife makes the beds, which will only be unmade that evening and have to be made again the next morning.

Autonomy — being one's own boss — was the most valued part of the housewife role. An ex-computer programmer put it this way:

> To an extent you're your own master . . . you can decide what you want to do and when you want to do it . . . it's not like being at work when somebody rings you up and you've got to go down and see them or you've got to do this and that within half an hour. (Oakley, 1974, p. 42)

The women's previous experiences with jobs outside the home were related to their satisfactions or dissatisfactions with housework. Specifically, women who had previously had high-status jobs (computer programmer, fashion model) were all dissatisfied with housework.

The women differed from one another in the extent of their personal identification with the housewife role. Those who were highly identified with it tended to structure the job by establishing routines (Monday is the day we wash our clothes, Tuesday we iron them . . .) and by setting high standards for the work. A critical factor in shaping high or low identification with housework was the identification with that role modeled by the woman's own mother. Many women have told me of the guilt they experience as they walk out the door, leaving a messy kitchen; the guilt is related to an almost tangible ghost of one's own mother sitting on one's shoulder saying "Bad, bad, bad." Women need to analyze their own identification with the housewife role and how this was shaped by their mothers. They can then begin to analyze how they can experience more satisfaction — or at least less guilt — in regard to housework. Personally, I am very grateful that my own mother was a feminist long before it was fashionable. She saw housework as something to be gotten done as quickly as possible, through using one's wits, so that one could do more satisfying things like playing the piano. As a result, I think, I rarely experience the housework "guilt ghost." Right on, Mom!

The mother role is probably the most satisfying part of the traditional complex of female roles. Even here, however, there may be problems. The feeding demands of small infants leave many mothers constantly exhausted, and it is not until infants are several months old that they can respond with one of their heartwarming smiles. Interactions with young children are stimulating in their own way, but many women feel a need for some interactions with other adults during the day.

Motherhood is so basic an assumption of the female role that it is easy to forget that society pressures women to be mothers; indeed, the pressure is so strong that the situation has been called the *motherhood mandate* (Russo, 1979). Consistent with the idea of a motherhood mandate, research indicates that people who choose to be childless tend to be viewed as poorly adjusted and misguided (Peterson, 1983; but see Shields and Cooper, 1983, for contradictory evidence). Interestingly, however, married couples without children report greater happiness than do married couples with children (Campbell et al., 1975).

Whether or not a woman wants children and how many children she wants can be predicted by a number of factors; her memory of her mother's love in early childhood, a feminine gender-role identification, and anti-feminist attitudes are all related to a desire to have children (Gerson, 1980). Also, women from large families — having three or more siblings — express more desire for children than do women from smaller families (Gerson, 1980).

One option that is being recognized increasingly is *voluntary childlessness*. Terminology makes a difference here. Some reject the term *childless*, which may seem to imply some sort of deficit, in favor of *child-free*. Research shows that women arrive at the decision to remain childless through different paths. Some women arrive at the decision fairly early in life, perhaps even before marriage; they are called "early articulators" (Houseknecht, 1979). Others marry and postpone the decision many times, finally deciding for childlessness relatively late; these are called "postponers." Both of these groups of voluntarily childless women tend to be high in autonomy and achievement orientation (Houseknecht, 1979). A high level of autonomy or independence would be expected from these women because they have been able to make a decision that goes against a great deal of societal pressure. The high levels of achievement orientation also make sense: these women tend to want high levels of achievement in their careers, which may seem incompatible with having children. Early articulators differed from postponers in some ways. In particular, early articulators tended to report less warmth in their families when growing up, and less compatibility of attitudes with their parents. Perhaps they have no desire to recreate a family situation that was not particularly pleasant for them, and thus they make the decision to remain childless early. Research also shows that a supportive reference group is extremely important to women making the decision to remain childless (Houseknecht, 1979). For example, a young woman in her second year of medical school may begin to think that it would be impossible to maintain a medical practice and rear children. If she has many women friends who are also medical students and are also reaching similar conclusions, and who offer her positive support for her decision, she is more likely to decide to be childfree.

Women and work   The fact that the majority of American women hold jobs outside the home is one of the best kept secrets in our country. Among women between the ages of 18 and 64, 57 percent hold jobs (U.S. Department of Labor, 1978). The working woman, then, is not a variation from the norm, she *is* the norm.

FIGURE 7.2

The fact that the majority of American women (57 percent) hold jobs outside of the home is one of the best kept secrets in our country.

Source: Photo by Steven Lewis/The Picture Cube.

A distinction can be made between the process of *career choice* (discussed in the section on adolescence) and the *decision to work*. Career choice probably involves mostly psychological variables, matching interests and abilities with the requirements of a particular job. In contrast, an adult woman's decision as to whether or not she will work is more a product of situational factors (Nieva and Gutek, 1981). One type of these is economic factors. If the woman is single, she must usually work to support herself; if she is married, her decision to work will be influenced by how adequate her husband's income is as support for the family. The husband's attitudes toward his wife's working have a powerful influence. One study found that the levels of wives' careers in 1974 could be predicted by their husbands' power motivation measured in 1960 (Winter et al., 1977). Specifically, a high level of career involvement in a wife was associated with low power motivation in her husband. Children are another important factor influencing a woman's decision to work. The more children a woman has, the less likely she is to work (Nieva and Gutek, 1981). However, this is a correlational result, and causality should not be inferred from it. In fact, there is evidence that the influence works in the opposite direction: participating in the labor force appears to reduce the number of children that women want and have (Nieva and Gutek, 1981).

There are many stereotypes about women and work. Below I shall consider some of them, and what the actual data say.

Stereotype 1: Women are working only for pin money. The idea behind this stereotype is that most women are only providing a second income, that the husband supports the family, and the wife is working only to provide a few frills. In fact, however, most women work because of stark economic necessity. In 1977 nearly two-thirds of all women in the labor force were single, widowed, divorced, separated, or had husbands whose earnings were less than $10,000 (U. S. Department of Labor, 1978). The majority of women workers were the sole supporters of their families, or were married to men whose incomes would have put them below the poverty line.

Stereotype 2: Women shouldn't be hired for jobs requiring training, because they will just quit when they get married or pregnant. The assumption here is that women are more likely to quit their jobs than men are. Overall, that is true. However, when occupational level and income are controlled, males and females do not differ significantly in turnover rates (Mead and Kaplan, 1965, p. 52). This simply means that women are found disproportionately in dull, dead-end jobs, and there is a high turnover rate in those jobs, whether men or women are in them. Given the same job and the same pay, females and males have about the same turnover rate. Today, most women are in the labor force for more than just a few years. In 1970, the average woman could expect to spend 22.9 years of her life in the labor force (U. S. Department of Labor, 1978).

Stereotype 3: Women are often sick, and thus miss too many days of work. In fact, in 1974 women averaged 5.1 sick days per year and males averaged 4.8, scarcely a difference worth talking about (U. S. Bureau of the Census, 1976, p. 88).

Stereotype 4: A woman who is really ambitious and qualified can get ahead anyway. It is true that some women get ahead, but they are relatively few in number. All other factors aside, what the woman worker must often face is simple job discrimination. For example, the average woman worker is as well-educated as the average man worker — both have a median of 12.6 years of schooling — but she makes only three-fifths as much as he does, when both work full-time year around (U. S. Department of Labor,

FIGURE 7.3

Women aspiring to nontraditional careers must often face various forms of psychological discrimination; for example, many people do not want to work for a woman boss and have difficulty recognizing a woman in a leadership role.

Source: Photo by Abigail Heyman/Magnum.

1978). In 1977 women were 79 percent of clerical workers, but only 22 percent of managers and administrators (U. S. Department of Labor, 1978). Most investigators agree that women are discriminated against in employment. Given the same education, job, experience, and so on, they are given less pay and are promoted more slowly (see review by Almquist, 1977).

Aside from these statistical analyses, there are several interesting studies that have documented the psychological aspects of job discrimination against women. A classic study demonstrated that, even when the work of a female is identical to that of a male, it is judged as inferior (Goldberg, 1968; replicated by Peterson et al., 1971). Female college students were given scholarly essays in a number of academic fields to evaluate. All of the subjects rated the same essays, but half of them rated essays bearing the names of male authors (for example John T. McKay), while the other half rated the same essays with the names of female authors (Joan T. McKay). The essays were identical except for the names of the authors. The results were that the essays were rated higher when the author was male, even when the essay was in a traditionally feminine field such as dietetics. It appears that the work of males is valued more even if it is identical to that of females. It is interesting to note that the raters in this study, those who gave lower value to female work, were themselves females.

In another study of gender and discrimination in the evaluation of work, the opposite effect was found; it was called the "talking platypus effect" (Abramson et al., 1977). Undergraduates read a one-page biography of a stimulus person. Half of them read about a male and half about a female; further, in half of the biographies the person was a lawyer, and in the other half the person was a paralegal worker. Interestingly, the female attorney was rated as *more* competent than the male attorney. The authors believe that, with public awareness of the obstacles to achievement that women face, people actually overvalue a woman who has demonstrated a high level of achievement. If you hear a platypus talking, it doesn't much matter what it says, it is simply a wonder that it can say anything at all.

How can we resolve these two apparently contradictory studies, one showing discrimination against women and one showing discrimination against men? The answer, I think, lies in the extent to which there is external evidence that the person's work is excellent. When there is ample evidence that the person is exceptionally competent — such as the female lawyer in the Abramson et al. study — women are not underrated and may actually be overrated. However, when the quality of the work is more ambiguous and there is no outside demonstration of its excellence — as was the case with the essays in the Goldberg study — then discrimination against women by underrating them is likely to occur. What are the practical implications of these findings? The problem is that in many real-world situations, such as when being hired for a first job just out of college or graduate school, the quality of a woman's work is ambiguous. And that is exactly when discrimination against women is most likely to occur.

Surveys show that many people do not want to work for a woman boss (Kanter, 1977). Social psychology studies have documented that it is difficult for a woman to assume and be recognized in a leadership role. For example, one study investigated this by using the phenomenon that the person seated at the head of a table is usually recognized as being the leader of a group (Porter et al., 1978). Subjects were shown photographs of groups seated around a table and were asked to rate the leadership attributes of each member of the group. A man seated at the head of the table in a mixed-gender group was clearly seen as the group's leader, but a woman occupying that position was ignored. Women at the head of the table were recognized as leaders only when the group was all-female.

When women occupy positions of leadership — for example, as a supervisor on a job — the evidence, then, indicates that they tend to be stereotyped as not having the right characteristics to be successful leaders. In real-world job situations, there are two possible reasons why women leaders might be viewed in this way. One is that they are truly lacking in personality traits, interpersonal skills, and so on, that are necessary in the supervisory role. For example, research shows that women are less aggressive than men (Chapter 6), and effective corporate managers need to be aggressive. A second reason is that women supervisors, as part of the complex network in a corporation, have less power than their male counterparts do (Nieva and Gutek, 1981). Power involves such things as being able to grant pay raises or promotions to subordinates or being able to influence the decisions of those higher up the corporate ladder. If workers perceive women supervisors as having less power, it should be no surprise if they are unenthusiastic about working for them.

One interesting study investigated the first hypothesis above — namely, that when women are placed in supervisory roles they behave differently, perhaps less skillfully, than men do. In a simulation of an organizational setting, a male or female undergraduate was placed in the role of supervisor of either a three-man or three-woman work group in the adjacent room (Instone et al., 1983). The workers did some rather trivial clerical tasks and were in fact confederates of the experimenters. In some cases the workers were compliant, continuing to produce work at a high rate. In other cases the workers were noncompliant — their productivity dropped sharply, and they expressed negative attitudes such as "I'm bored, this is a pain." Supervisors were permitted to do a number of things in dealing with the workers: they could do positive things, such as give pay increases or give positive talks; or they could do negative things, such as give pay decreases or fire the workers. (Notice that in this cleverly controlled laboratory study, the second hypothesis discussed above — that females have less access to power in corporations — is ruled out because male and female supervisors were given identical power in the experiment.) The question was, do females behave differently as supervisors than males do? The results did show some gender differences consistent with stereotypes. Compared with males, females made fewer attempts to influence their workers. Females were also less likely to use rewarding strategies, particularly promises of pay increases, and were more likely to use negative, coercive strategies, such as pay deductions. However, these differences were small, supporting the notion that gender similarities are the rule.

An additional finding of the Instone et al. study is important. The female subjects reported strikingly less confidence in their ability to supervise their workers than did male subjects. This gender difference in self-confidence has been found in other research (Chapter 6). Previous research has shown that men in leadership positions who have low self-confidence are less likely to exert influence and more likely to use coercive techniques than are men who have high self-confidence. The leadership behaviors of the women in this study, then, may be more a result of their lack of self-confidence than of any kind of innate lack of leadership ability. Their lack of self-confidence is odd given that the female subjects actually reported as much prior experience in supervisory roles as the male subjects did. On the other hand, the authors noted a positive correlation between amount of supervisory experience and self-confidence in women — the more experience a woman had, the more self-confidence she had. Therefore, the authors concluded on a hopeful note: the more supervisory experience women are given, the more their self-confidence will increase, which in turn will improve their supervisory behaviors, so that they will make more influence attempts and use more positive strategies in dealing with their workers.

The second hypothesis above — that women as leaders have less power in organizations — implies that women also need to find ways to increase their power (for an excellent summary and analysis, see Smith and Grenier, 1982). Some of this will involve women getting specific instruction, for example, assertiveness training or instruction on how to plan careers. But women also need to learn how to use the structural bases of power that exist within organizations. Power can come from any of three sources (Smith and Grenier, 1982): (1) participating in activities critical to the organization's survival or its current pressing problems; (2) participating in activities that control uncertainty (if the computer breaks down frequently at inopportune moments, then the computer repairperson has power); and (3) participating in activities controlling resources such as money, people, or information. Women can learn to use any or all of these strategies for gaining power.

Working mothers Of all mothers with children under 18 years of age, 59 percent were in the labor force in 1982 (U. S. Department of Labor, 1982). Even among mothers with preschool children, 50 percent work outside the home (U. S. Department of Labor, 1982). Thus there are a lot of working mothers — 18.7 million, to be exact (U. S. Department of Labor, 1982). What do we know about how being a mother and holding a job interact psychologically?

In adulthood, it seems that the femininity-achievement incompatibility of adolescence is rerun under a new format, the work-mother incompatibility (Epstein, 1970; Hoffman, 1974b; Chafetz, 1974). That is, many people believe that women with children should stay at home and take care of them and should not hold jobs. The belief is that a working mother cannot be a good mother.

Psychologist Lois Hoffman (1974b) has done a detailed review of research on the effects of maternal employment on children. She concluded that there was no evidence that school-age children suffer either emotional or intellectual deprivation as a result of their mothers being employed. Indeed, working mothers seem to encourage more independence in their children, something that would generally be considered a good idea. Some evidence also exists that working mothers provide different role models for their children and that, at least for daughters, this may be beneficial. It also appears that the effects of the mother's employment depend on her psychological state — for example, her attitude toward working.

The conflicts experienced by working mothers have been extensively documented (Paloma and Garland, 1971; Barilyn, 1970; Holmstrom, 1972; Fogarty et al., 1971; Hartley, 1960). The woman may be caught working two full-time jobs, and feeling that she is doing neither adequately. She may experience feelings of guilt that she is neglecting her children in order to work. Because of the complex demands on her time, there may also be conflicts with her wife role, with less time remaining for her husband. Children must still be fed and taken to the doctor, even with an eight-hour workday. If the working mother has an understanding husband, he may help out with the cooking, cleaning, or babysitting, but the clear understanding remains that these are all her responsibilities, and he is being a "nice guy" to help her. Even highly liberated professional women are not free from the restrictions and conflicts of roles. Such women tend to demand that their husbands be even brighter than they, and speak of their husbands as being exceptionally talented (Birnbaum, 1975). This represents a subtle kind of role conformity, in which the exceptionally talented woman still ensures that her husband is brighter than she. As one feminist put it, "We won't be really liberated until we are free to marry men who are dumber and shorter than we are."

Dual-career couples With careers for women emerging as an important social trend, there has been increasing interest in dual-career couples, that is, married couples in which both partners are committed to careers.

In one intensive study of ten dual-career couples, the participants reported extreme problems of work overload, but nonetheless said that the intellectual and psychological benefits of their lifestyle far outweighed the disadvantages (St. John-Parsons, 1978). The economic advantages of the pattern allowed the couples to reduce their work overload in some ways. For example, nine of the ten couples hired domestic help, so they did not have to do housecleaning. In the area of family responsibilties, however, traditional roles persisted. For example, the decision about hiring domestic help was left to the wives for the most part. Care of sick children also tended to fall to the wives. On the other hand, disciplining of the children was viewed as a shared responsibility by all of the couples. All of the families appeared to be healthy and active, and the children did not seem to have problems resulting from their parents' dual-career pattern.

One possible explanation for the traditional division of labor in household and family tasks in these otherwise nontraditional couples is that the couple negotiates. The wife gets more childcare, allowing her to compensate for the time she spends away from the children (and perhaps reducing her guilt?); the husband gets a set of tasks consistent with the male role and therefore not threatening to his sense of masculinity (Weingarten, 1978).

Recent research, based on large, well-sampled groups of subjects, indicates that both husbands and wives from couples in which the wife works express as much satisfaction with their marriages as do husbands and wives from couples in which the wife is exclusively a homemaker (Booth, 1977; Yogev, 1982; Staines, 1978). One study even found no differences between the two groups of husbands on biochemical measures of stress (Booth, 1977). In short, the participation of women in work or careers does not seem to produce miserable marriages.

Divorce   The Census Bureau has estimated that, if present trends continue, one-fourth of women born between 1935 and 1939 will have seen their first marriages end in divorce by the time they reach age 50 in the 1980s (U.S. Bureau of the Census, 1972). Divorce rates are high, but remarriage rates are also high. However, remarriage rates for women are lower than those for men. In 1969, 221 out of every 1000 divorced men remarried, whereas 135 out of every 1000 divorced women remarried (Scanzoni and Scanzoni, 1976). Accordingly, of the 6.5 million Americans who are currently divorced, 4 million are women (O'Leary, 1977).

The psychological processes involved in divorce and the period following it have been studied extensively (e.g., Bohannon, 1970; Brown et al., 1976; Weiss, 1976). Divorce is a period of transition and grief, and many have likened it to the process of bereavement following the death of a spouse. Divorce counselor Mel Krantzler speaks of divorce as "the death of a relationship" and believes that a time of grieving is essential to emotional healing. The change in status and roles may be stressful. A woman has to shift from the role of wife to that of divorcée, which may be particularly difficult for the woman who has defined much of her identity by the wife role.

In interviews, divorced and separated mothers note a number of added stresses in their lives (Brown et al., 1976). Their financial burdens are increased, as are their responsibilities. The divorced mother generally not only has to rear her children, but support them as well. Then, on top of that, she has to see to it that the car is repaired, in addition to many other tasks that her husband might have done formerly. Conflicts between work and children, which I have noted earlier, seem to intensify. Nonetheless, many women noted some advantages to their single parent status, such as an increased sense of autonomy and independence.

The single woman   It is difficult to remember how radical the concept of the *Mary Tyler Moore Show* — now in reruns — was when it began in the late 1960s. It was about an attractive, bright woman in her thirties who was *happily single*, and who never, in the course of the series, got married. The concept of a woman being purposely single and being happy was a new one.

The number of high school and college women who do not intend to marry is about 5 to 6 percent (Douvan and Adelson, 1966); even in data collected in 1973 and 1975, the percentage has not increased (Donelson, 1977).

Nonetheless, being a single woman is increasingly being viewed as a valid alternative lifestyle for women. In 1974, nearly one-quarter (23.4 percent) of women aged 24 were in the "never married" category; the comparable figure in 1960 was 16 percent (*Current Population Reports,* 1974). Census experts are not entirely sure whether these statistics indicate a trend toward not marrying, or a trend toward marrying later.

Two advantages are typically mentioned in discussions of being a single woman (Donelson, 1977). One is freedom. There is no necessity to agree with someone else on what to have for dinner, what TV program to watch, or how to spend money. There is the freedom to move when it is advantageous to one's career — or to stay put and not to move to follow a husband's career. The other advantage is a sense of self-sufficiency and competence. The single woman has to deal with the irritation of fixing the leaky faucet herself, but having done so, she gains a sense that she is competent to do such things. As noted earlier, single women have higher reported life-satisfaction than married women. Among single women, life-satisfaction is correlated with having good health, not being lonely, living with a female housemate, having many casual friends, and being highly involved with work (Loewenstein et al., 1981).

In a society as marriage-oriented as ours, it is not surprising that there are disadvantages to being a single woman. Most of the social structures for adults involve couples' activities, and the single person is often excluded. Loneliness is another disadvantage that is mentioned frequently.

In one study, one-quarter of childless single women expressed regret at not having had children — but that means that three-quarters expressed no such regret (Loewenstein et al., 1981).

Sociological studies indicate that higher levels of intelligence, education, and occupation are associated with singleness among women (Spreitzer and Riley, 1974). Single women tend to value achievement and personal growth, whereas married women tend to value personal relationships (Gigy, 1980). One sociologist concluded that high-achieving women may consider marriage too confining and therefore choose not to marry (Havens, 1973). Note that this is a much different matter from saying that such women are not likely to be chosen. The decision is apparently theirs. For most women, however, being single is not a result of an early, explicit decision, but rather is a result of many small choices, many not made deliberately (McGinnis, 1974). These women may essentially drift into singleness and, once there, discover that they like it.

Friendship   Lucia and Eva are best friends. They eat lunch together while they tell each other about the joys and sorrows they have experienced since they last saw each other. Sam and David are also best friends. They relax as they play racquetball together on Saturday morning.

Recent research has focused on the nature of female friendships and whether or not female friendships differ in nature from male friendships (Wright, 1982; Caldwell and Peplau, 1982; Davidson and Duberman, 1982). Although there are great similarities between male friendships and female friendships, the scenarios described above reflect the sorts of differences that have been found. In general, women tend to emphasize talking and emotional sharing in their friendships, whereas men tend to emphasize activities and doing things together (Caldwell and Peplau, 1982). Topics of conversation between best friends also differ (Davidson and Duberman, 1982). Men are far more likely to talk about topical, external matters, such as current events, whereas women are more likely to spread the conversation out to include feelings and personal matters. For example, one man said:

> We are pretty open with each other, I guess. Mostly we talk about sex, horses, guns, and the Army. (Davidson and Duberman, 1982, p. 815)

Compare that with this report from a woman:

> We discuss everything with each other. From what we're doing, to how each of us might be feeling, or what's happening to us, to discussing what happens between the two of us. No matter how bad it is, I don't want to hide my feelings. (Davidson and Duberman, 1982, p. 814)

Research on friendship patterns in a group of women ranging in age from 14 to 80 indicates that friendship serves three important functions for women (Candy et al., 1981):

1. Intimacy and assistance — This involves disclosing personal feelings to the friend and helping the friend, points that are consistent with the findings on gender difference in friendship discussed above.
2. Status — This involves gaining status by having a particular person as a friend.
3. Power — This involves being able to influence the friend or give advice, or have the friend do the same to you.

Research also shows that women find their best friendships to be therapeutic (Davidson and Packard, 1981). This is true in a number of senses: best friends are reported to provide guidance, an opportunity to express feelings, feedback, the instillation of hope, and understanding.

In sum, it is clear that women's friendships in adulthood meet some important psychological functions. Men's and women's friendships are generally similar, but they also differ in some respects, with women emphasizing self-disclosure and emotional sharing and men emphasizing shared activities.

MIDDLE AGE

Most women move through adulthood and into middle age with their identity defined chiefly in terms of others — husband and children. In this context it is clear why middle age can be a difficult time for some women. Below we shall discuss the "empty nest" syndrome, one of the problems that may arise during this period.

The empty nest   During a woman's middle age her children may leave home — to go to work, to go away to college, to get married. For the middle-aged woman, a major source of identity — motherhood — has been taken away. The term *empty nest syndrome* has been used to describe the cases of depression in women at this time. Sociologist Pauline Bart (1971) has investigated the empty nest syndrome. Interestingly, her research indicates that it is the "supermothers," not those who chose nontraditional careers, who are most susceptible to this depression. The supermothers have invested so much of themselves in the mother role that they have the most to lose when it has ended. Confirming these results, a study of graduates of an Eastern women's college who had been out of college 35 years and were in their late fifties indicated that women employed full-time had significantly lower symptom scores than women not employed outside the home (Powell, 1977).

Sociologist Lillian B. Rubin (1979) has challenged many ideas about the empty nest syndrome. Her results are based on a study of 160 women, a cross section of white mothers aged 35 to 54, from the working, middle, and professional classes. To be included in the sample, they had to have given up work or careers after a minimum of three years and to have assumed the traditional role of housewife and mother for at least ten years after the birth of their first child. Therefore this group should be the most prone to the empty nest syndrome. Typically these women said, "My career was my child." Contrary to the empty nest, Rubin found that, although some women were momentarily sad, lonely, or frightened, they were not depressed in response to the departure or impending departure of their children. The predominant feeling of every woman except one was a feeling of relief. For mothers who have sacrificed so much for their children, such a reaction is probably not too surprising. Rather than experiencing an immobilizing depression, most of the women found new jobs and reorganized their daily lives. Rubin felt that the women's movement had helped many of the women by raising their sights to other careers and opportunities.

What should we conclude, then? Probably some women do experience empty nest depression, but not every woman does. Among those who do experience such depression, the experience may be brief. What is probably most important is the ability of the majority of women to adjust to the radical changes that occur in their lives and roles at this time.

Work   In an earlier section I noted the strains on women who work and have families in young adulthood. Then I noted fewer problems with depression among women who hold jobs outside the home. In the long run, is a woman better off psychologically to work or to have a career, or not?

Research on highly educated women now in their forties indicates that employed wives have higher self-esteem than women who are housewives exclusively (Birnbaum, 1975). These results contradict those found in women in their twenties: the family-oriented women possessed higher self-esteem, presumably because they were gaining satisfaction from having small children, while the career women experienced greater self-doubt during their struggle to establish a career. Other research indicates that work increases a woman's sense of well-being (Barnett and Baruch, 1979). It appears that the career role, while adding some conflicts particularly in early adulthood, may provide a rewarding payoff — a more positive sense of self-esteem in middle age.

THE ELDERLY WOMAN

Some have suggested that there is a "double standard of aging" (Sontag, 1972; Berman et al., 1981). That is, as a man reaches middle age and beyond, he may appear more distinguished, but a woman of the same age does not seem to become more beautiful. As we saw in a previous section, a woman's value in her youth is often judged by her appearance, which may decline with age. Here I shall examine some of the research on women in old age.

Widowhood There are far more widows than widowers. In the United States the ratio of widows to widowers is estimated to be about 4 to 1 (Berardo, 1968). Among adults over 65, 14 percent of men are widowed, compared with 52 percent of women (Marquis Academic Media, 1979). This is the result of two trends: the longer life expectancy of women, and the tendency of women to marry men older than themselves. Opportunities for remarriage are limited because there are so few men compared with women in this age group. Among all elderly persons (over age 65) in 1970, there were 722 men for every 1000 women. The Census Bureau predicts that by 1990 the ratio will be 675 men for every 1000 women (U.S. Bureau of Census, 1973). The average age of widowhood is 56 (Berardo, 1968; U.S. Department of Commerce, 1973). Therefore it is fairly frequent for women to face the last 15 years or so of their lives alone.

A number of psychological processes occur in the bereavement of women during the year following the death of a husband (Parkes, 1970). These occur in approximately the following order:

1. Shock or numbness — In the first few days after the death of a husband the usual reaction is not intense emotion, but rather a sense of numbness.
2. Yearning and intense mourning — There is intense preoccupation with thoughts of the dead husband, grieving is intense, and there is a great deal of crying.
3. Anger and protest — There may be anger or bitterness directed toward relatives, a doctor, clergy, or to the dead husband for leaving her alone.
4. Disorganization — Even by the end of the first year of bereavement, most widows expressed little interest in planning for the future.
5. Mitigation (reduction of the pain) — There are periods of time when grief is reduced, and the woman may discover ways to protect or defend herself from the pain she is experiencing.
6. Identification — The woman expresses identification with the dead spouse, perhaps behaving or thinking like him, perhaps expressing opinions he would have had.

Of course, there is variation from one woman to the next in how widowhood is experienced. Two factors that appear to be relevant are the woman's age, and whether the husband's death was quick and unexpected, or the result of a long illness and therefore expected. The very elderly woman seems psychologically better prepared for her husband's death.

It seems that the death of a spouse is harder on men than it is on women, as evidenced by low morale, mental disorders, and high death and suicide rates (Bock and Webber, 1972; Spreitzer et al., 1975; for an excellent review, see Stroebe and Stroebe, 1983). Put another way, women seem to cope better with widowhood. One reason for this appears to be that women are more likely to have deep friendships that they have developed over the years from which they can draw emotional support (Blau, 1973). In one study of people over 65, women had 38 percent more friends than men did (Fischer and Phillips, cited in Peplau et al., 1982). Although widowed men are significantly lonelier than married men, widowed women are no lonelier than married women (Perlman et al., 1978; for a review of loneliness, see Peplau et al., 1982).

Research indicates that, in modern American cities, roles and social support systems do not come automatically to widows as they might in a more traditional society (Lopata, 1979). In short, the widow has to be assertive in order to get the kinds of support and services she needs. Unfortunately, today's widows are from precisely that generation of women who were socialized not to be assertive. Lopata also found that women who are the most family-oriented and husband-dependent are the most devastated by widowhood. The consequences of the postponement of identity formation discussed earlier in this chapter can have serious consequences later in life.

Gender roles and androgyny Some scholars have suggested that gender roles become more relaxed or even reversed among the elderly. With the children grown, the woman is less restricted to the mother role. In some marriages, because the husband is older than the wife, he may have retired while she continues to hold a job. Thus he may do many of the household chores while she is the breadwinner.

This shifting of gender roles might suggest that the elderly are more androgynous than younger adults. To see whether this is true, subjects from age 13 to 85 were asked to complete the Bem Sex Role Inventory, discussed in Chapter 4 (Hyde and Phillis, 1979). Based on their scores, subjects were categorized as androgynous, feminine, masculine, or undiffer-

TABLE 7.2. **Percentages of males and females who are classified as androgynous in four age groups**

	Age			
Gender	13–20	21–40	41–60	61 and over
Females	26	31	11	7
Males	9	4	31	40

Source: Hyde and Phillis, 1979.

entiated. The results, shown in Table 7.2, indicate that older men are more androgynous than younger men, but that older women are less androgynous than younger women.[2] In fact, the percentage of feminine women increased in the oldest age categories. Perhaps this means that both men and women become more feminine with age, resulting in more androgynous men and more feminine women.

IN CONCLUSION

I have traced female development across the lifespan. Gender similarities seem to be the rule in infancy and childhood, with many gender differences not emerging until adolescence. The femininity-achievement incompatibility exerts an important force on female development. The postponement of identity formation, and forming an identity in terms of the wife-mother role are also important.

SUGGESTIONS FOR FURTHER READING

Bird, Caroline. (1979). *The two-paycheck marriage.* New York: Pocket Books. Caroline Bird, who is a professional journalist, did many interviews and amassed data from other sources to examine marriages in which both husband and wife hold paying jobs — how they deal with childcare, sex, and managing their careers, and the new kinds of families that are emerging.

Nieva, Veronica F., and Barbara A. Gutek. (1981). *Women and work: A psychological perspective.* New York: Praeger. This book offers an excellent summary of psychological research on all aspects of women and work.

Oakley, Ann. (1976). *Woman's work: The housewife, past and present.* New York: Vintage Books. This British sociologist's analysis of housewives and their work is fascinating reading.

Peterson, Nancy L. (1982). *The ever single woman.* New York: Quill. Based on interviews with 80 women, this book is a sensitive and highly readable account of the lives of single women.

---

[2] These data were cross-sectional (collected on many different people at different ages) and not longitudinal (collected on the same group of people repeatedly as they grew older). Therefore it is important to be cautious in concluding from them too much about actual developmental changes.

Abilities, Achievement, and Motivation

When Samuel Johnson was asked which is more intelligent, man or woman, he replied, "Which man, which woman?"

Part of the lore of the culture is that women are less intelligent than men. Put bluntly, they are dumb — witness the expression "dumb broad." An additional stereotype is that women's thought processes are less rational, more illogical than men's, more influenced by emotion. A familiar scene in movies and comics is the male shaking his head over his inability to understand the mind of his wife or girl friend. (This might in fact be evidence of inferior male intelligence or perceptiveness, but it never seems to be interpreted that way.)

Is there any scientific evidence to support the notion that women are less intellectually competent than men? In this chapter we shall explore empirical evidence regarding the intellectual and achievement characteristics of women, and whether these characteristics seem to differ from those of men.[1] It is important to remember that the finding of a gender difference does not say anything about what causes it, i.e., whether biological or environmental factors are responsible. We shall then examine motivational differences between females and males with the goal of better understanding the relationship between women's abilities and their achievements.

ABILITIES

General intelligence   There is no evidence to support the hypothesis that females are less intelligent than males. In fact, research has consistently shown that there are no gender differences in general intelligence. One of the most thorough studies of this sort was done in Scotland. All the children in the country who were born on February 1, May 1, August 1, and November 1 in 1926 were given the Stanford-Binet intelligence test. The average IQ for boys was 100.51, and for girls 99.7. This difference was not statistically significant, despite the large size of the sample (Scottish Council for Research in Education, 1939). Another extensive Scottish study showed boys four points higher on an individual IQ test, girls two points higher on a group IQ test (Scottish Council for Research in Education, 1949). Although these differences were statistically significant, the fact

---

[1] The reader who wishes to explore this subject in more detail may consult one of the excellent reviews available (Sherman, 1978; Maccoby and Jacklin, 1974).

that they were so small and in opposite directions once again indicates that neither gender is superior to the other in general intellectual performance.

These results need to be interpreted with some caution, because of the nature of IQ-test construction. It became clear to the early test constructors that, because of both biological and cultural factors, boys would do better on some kinds of tests, while girls would do better on others. They decided to balance these subtests so that there would be no gender differences in overall measured intelligence. Therefore, saying that there are no gender differences in overall tested intelligence essentially means that the test constructors succeeded in their goal of eliminating gender differences.

There is some evidence of gender differences in the development of intelligence, however. Girls tend to test somewhat higher than boys during the early school years, while boys surpass girls in high school. This might be due in part to higher drop-out rates among low-testing boys (Maccoby, 1966).

In conclusion, a multitude of studies in the past five decades fail to indicate any gender differences in general intelligence. Rather than looking at global assessments, it is more revealing to analyze patterns of specific abilities in males and in females.

Verbal ability   Females are superior to males in verbal ability (Sherman, 1978; Maccoby and Jacklin, 1974). Developmentally, girls appear to have a slight advantage at the beginning of language development, around the ages of two or three; but for the most part there are few gender differences during childhood. Gender differences in verbal ability increase in prominence beginning at about age 11, and the superiority of females continues through high school and possibly beyond. Girls do better not only at relatively simple verbal tasks such as spelling, but also at more complex tasks such as analogies and creative writing (Maccoby and Jacklin, 1974). In high school a smaller proportion of girls than of boys need remedial reading training. Further, Margaret Mead found girls to be more verbally precocious than boys in all the diverse cultures she has observed (Mead, 1958).

Spatial ability   Females show poorer spatial ability than males do. Tests of spatial ability generally involve testing the ability to visualize three-dimensional objects on the basis of a two-dimensional picture and to do mental rotations and other manipulations on them (see Figure 8.1).

Some researchers have speculated that gender differences in this ability might be due to different childhood experiences, boys playing with erector sets, girls with dolls (Sherman, 1967). However, the exact causes of the gender difference in spatial ability are not yet known. It is interesting to note, however, that gender differences in spatial ability do not appear until adolescence (Maccoby and Jacklin, 1974).

FIGURE 8.1

Sample item and solution from a test of spatial ability.

The test below is made up of pictures of blocks turned different ways. The block at the left is the reference block and the five blocks to the right are the answer blocks. One of these five blocks is the same as the reference block except that it has been turned and is seen from a different point of view. The other four blocks could not be obtained by turning the reference block. For example:

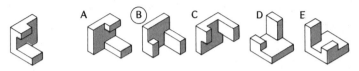

The illustration below shows that "B" is the correct answer.

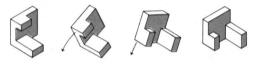

Source: From R. E. Stafford, *Identical Blocks*, form AA, 1962. Used with the permission of R. E. Stafford and Harold Gulliksen.

While many occupations do not rely heavily on spatial ability, there are some in which it is very important— for example, engineering, technical drawing, and mechanics (Smith, 1964). It might therefore be tempting to attribute the small number of women in these fields to women's relatively low spatial ability. However, the gender difference in spatial ability is not nearly large enough to account for the fact that only 1 percent of the engineers in the United States are women (Bird, 1968; Hyde, 1981).

Mathematical ability On numerical tests, boys do better, although here again the results are not simple. In early childhood, there seem to be no gender differences (Gesell, 1940). In fact, girls learn to count earlier (that wonderful resource, verbal ability?). The differences do not appear consistently in school until age 12–13 (Maccoby and Jacklin, 1974). This pattern of abilities persists through high school and into adulthood.

Reasoning ability Once again, there seems to be an absence of gender differences in reasoning ability until adolescence (Maccoby and Jacklin, 1974). Then, the observed gender differences depend on the content of the material. As we have already seen, boys excel on numerical tests. However, girls usually excel on tests of verbal reasoning such as analogies (Anastasi, 1958). There is therefore no support for the notion that women are less logical or less rational than men.

Perceptual speed The ability known as perceptual speed involves being able to perceive details quickly and accurately and to shift attention from one item to the next rapidly. Tests of perceptual speed are generally timed, and involve comparison of two strings of letters or numbers to see whether they are identical (see Figure 8.2). This seems to be the basic aptitude necessary for most forms of clerical work (Andrew and Patterson, 1959).

Women are consistently better than men on these tests. In one study, only about 18 percent of men scored equal to or above the median score for women. Even when only clerical workers were tested, only 21 percent of male clerical workers reached or exceeded the median for women clerical workers (Andrew and Patterson, 1959).

This gender difference appears very early — the youngest age group tested has been five-year-olds, and even here girls are superior to boys (Miele, 1958; Gainer, 1962); and the gender difference is consistent at intervening age levels (Schneidler and Patterson, 1942). It therefore seems

FIGURE 8.2

Sample items from a test of perceptual speed.

Instructions: Compare each line of the COPY at the bottom of the page with the corresponding line of the ORIGINAL at the top. Each *word* or *abbreviation* or *digit* in the copy that is not exactly the same as in the original is one error. In each line, mark every word or abbreviation or figure that is wrong. Then count the errors you have marked in the line and enter the total number in the column at the right. The first line has been done correctly to show you just how to mark and where to enter the total number of errors in the line. Work quickly and accurately.

ORIGINAL

Name	Address	Amount
Dr. Jane Frazier	Madison, Ind.	$7385.96
Mr. Michael Crane	Atlanta, Ga.	1435.64
Dr. Frank Thompson	Troy, N. Y.	2537.96
Miss Mary James	Washington, Conn.	4994.73

COPY

Name	Address	Amount	Number of Errors
Miss Jane Frazier	Madison, Wis.	$7385.96	5
Dr. Michael Crane	Atlanta, Ga.	1434.54	4
Dr. Frank Thompson	Troy, N.J.	2538.96	3
Mrs. Marie Jones	Washington, Conn.	4884.73	5

Source: From *General Clerical Test.* Reproduced by permission. Copyright 1944, renewed 1971, © 1969 by The Psychological Corporation, New York. All rights reserved.

improbable that gender differences are due to differential practice, since it is hard to believe that five-year-old girls have had more clerical experience than five-year-old boys. Training on perceptual speed problems does not erase gender differences unless only the males are given training (Long-staff, 1954) — that is, through training, males can be brought to the level of untrained females, but if males and females are given equal training, females remain superior in performance.

Motor skills   The traditional results from differential psychology indicate that boys surpass girls not only in muscular strength, but in speed and co-ordination of gross body movements. On the other hand, in finger dexterity and fine movements, females are generally superior (Maccoby and Jacklin, 1974; Anastasi, 1958).

Research in physical education indicates that, in general, large gender differences in motor performance do not appear until adolescence; there are correspondingly few physical differences between males and females until puberty with its onset of hormonal differences leading to larger height and musculature in the male (Singer, 1968). For example, Bayley's Scale of Motor Development (1936) does not differentiate the genders prior to five years of age. In general, developmental curves for physical performance (for example, speed in the 100-yard dash, grip strength) in males increase during childhood and show sharp increases during adolescence. The curves for girls are parallel to those for boys during childhood (girls being at only slightly lower levels), but during adolescence girls' performance levels off or even declines. Once again we see that in childhood, gender similarities are more the rule than gender differences; gender differences do not become prominent until adolescence. In physical performance, adolescent gender differences probably result from both actual physical differences and cultural factors (lack of training for girls, gender-inappropriateness of athletic competition for girls). As evidence of the importance of environmental factors such as nutrition and training, it has been noted that in the Olympic games, the first four places in the women's 100-meter dash in 1952 showed faster times than the winner in the 1896 men's event (Jokl, 1964).

The extent and importance of early gender differences in motor skills, and in particular their relevance to gender differences in adult abilities and occupations, might well be debated. Some authors argue that gender differences in childhood activities (with boys using large muscles in sports, girls using fine muscles in embroidery) are natural determiners of gender differences in adult roles, with men hunting and farming, women sewing and cooking. This is at least in part related to the issue of gender differences in motor activity (Chapter 6). My view is that prepubertal physical differences are not large, do not result in very great differentials in children's activity, and are probably not a good rationalization for differences in adult roles (D'Andrade, 1966).

How large are the differences? I have concluded that there are reliable gender differences in some — though certainly not all — abilities. Of the reliable differences, in verbal, mathematical, and spatial abilities and perceptual speed, how large are the differences between females and males? The answer is, not very large (Hyde, 1981; Sherman, 1978). In fact, they are not large enough to appear reliably in every study. I re-analyzed the statistics from the studies cited by Maccoby and Jacklin on verbal, mathematical, and spatial abilities (Hyde, 1981). I found that in those studies in which gender differences do appear, the difference between the means for males and females is generally small.[2] One implication is that the gender differences are so small as to be irrelevant in practical situations such as job counseling. It would be a great mistake, for example, to urge a high school girl against an engineering career because females on the average are lower than males in spatial ability. The gender difference is far too small to predict that an individual female will not have adequate spatial ability for such a career. A far better indicator would be her own score on a spatial ability test.

CHOOSING COURSES: HOW TO AVOID MATH

I hope that you didn't begin reading this section thinking that I would tell you how to avoid math courses, because that is not my intention at all. What I am going to tell you is that, beginning in high school, girls stop taking math courses — or they avoid math courses — and that the consequences are serious, keeping them out of many attractive careers.

I am convinced that the traditional approach of looking at gender differences in abilities (e.g., math ability) is not productive. Whether or not a significant gender difference is found, where does that approach get us, either in terms of better scientific understanding or in terms of helping women? Not very far. University of Michigan psychologist Jacquelynne Eccles-Parsons has broken ground with what I think is a much more productive approach — understanding why students choose or do not choose to take certain courses (e.g., Meece et al., 1982).

Eccles-Parsons points out that gender differences in math ability do not appear consistently until the tenth grade. That is just about the time when females become less likely than males to enroll in high school math courses. By the time women emerge from college, they have fewer mathematical skills than men, probably because they have not been taking math.

---

2 In statistical language, the difference between the means is about 0.25 SD (standard deviations) for verbal ability and 0.50 SD for spatial ability. The gender difference accounts for only about 1 percent of the variance in verbal ability and 4 percent of the variance in spatial ability (Hyde, 1981).

This in turn is significant because mathematical skills are important to success in many attractive occupations. Indeed, mathematics has been called the "critical filter" (Sherman, 1982) keeping women out of careers in engineering, computer science, the physical sciences, business, and finance. The point that should be investigated by researchers, then, is not whether females have less mathematical ability than males, but rather why it is that females stop taking math courses. If we understood the reasons behind this choice, it might be possible to help women to take more math courses, and perhaps to help them expand their career options.

Eccles-Parsons has proposed an elegant model to explain why students choose or avoid certain courses, such as math courses. A diagram of the model is shown in Figure 8.3. The final behavior Eccles-Parsons is trying to predict is achievement behavior — specifically, choosing a math course — and it is shown in the box on the far right in Figure 8.3. The multiple factors feeding into the choice of a course are shown in the other boxes in the diagram.

In overall terms, Eccles-Parsons has used an *expectation × value model* of achievement (course choice). That is, any particular achievement behavior is a product of the person's expectations and the person's values. Kim is a high school sophomore contemplating taking an optional course in geometry. The model says that she will sign up for geometry only if she has both positive expectations for success in the course (if she thinks she'll get an F, she won't sign up) and positive values with respect to the course (she thinks the course will be of value to her both now and in the future; but she may instead think that geometry will be of no value if she expects to spend the rest of her life as a housewife). The values part of the model is shown in the top half of Figure 8.3, and the expectancies part is shown in the bottom half.

Many factors shape Kim's values regarding math courses and her expectations for success in them. In the area of values are the following:

1. The cultural milieu — Kim probably perceives the division of labor by gender in the United States and notes that women are not found in math-related jobs. Further, math as a subject is stereotyped as a masculine domain. And success in an advanced math course may seem competitive to Kim, and competitiveness is not regarded as feminine.

2. Goals and self-schema — Kim has already formed a self-schema or self-concept and has some tentative occupational goals. If these involve being a housewife or a secretary, math courses will not be valued.

In the area of expectancies for success are the following factors:

1. Aptitudes and grades — Kim has some idea of her aptitude for math from a variety of sources, including her grades in past courses

FIGURE 8.3

Eccles-Parsons' model of academic course choice shows how girls' expectations and values may be shaped so that they do not take math courses in high school.

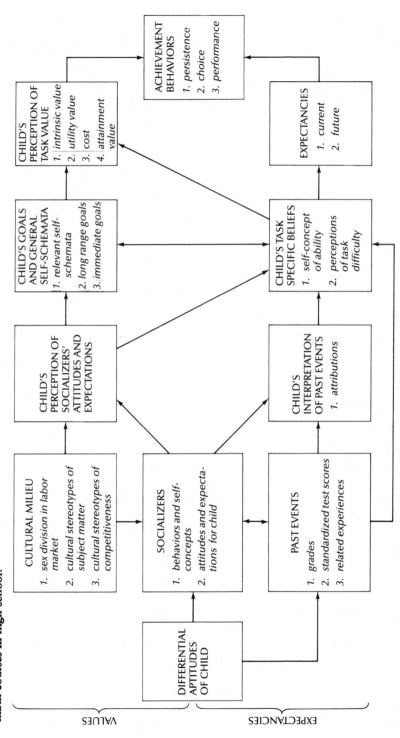

Source: From "Sex Differences in Math Achievement," 1982, *Psychological Bulletin,* 91. Copyright © 1982 by the American Psychological Association. Reprinted by permission of Judith L. Meece, Jacquelynne Eccles-Parsons et al. Also from J. E. Parsons et al. in *Perspectives on Achievement and Achievement Motivation* edited by J. T. Spence. W. H. Freeman and Company. Copyright © 1983.

and her scores on standardized achievement tests. It is strange that in elementary school and junior high girls' grades in math are as good as those of boys, yet in high school girls stop taking math courses and boys don't. This tendency is explained in part by the next factor.

2. Interpretations or attributions — Kim may have gotten B's in all her math courses, but may fail to attribute the good grades to her own abilities (see the section on attributions later in this chapter). She may think that the courses so far have just been easy. As a result, she has low expectations for success in future math courses.

Eccles-Parsons and her colleagues have done a number of studies testing various links in the model, and they have reviewed numerous pertinent studies done by others (Meece et al., 1982). Space does not permit me to review all of this research, but the model has generally been upheld. Although many links in it have been supported with data, a few have not. For example, one study showed that parents do not have lower expectations for their daughters' mathematical performance than they have for their sons', which is contrary to what the model would predict. On the other hand, research shows that, by junior high, boys have higher perceptions of their math ability than girls do, and self-concept of math ability is related to one's decisions to enroll in optional math courses. These findings support key points in the model. Like most models, this one isn't perfect, but I think it is good.

As an interesting exercise, you might want to trace through the model thinking of yourself, trying to see how it predicts why you did or did not continue taking math courses.

What are the practical implications of Eccles-Parsons' model? Suppose that our goal were to get more girls enrolled in math courses so as to expand their career options. How would we do that? We could work on the expectancies side of the model or on the values side or on both. On the expectancies side, we would try to get high school girls to have higher expectancies for success in math courses. This could be done in a number of ways: by stressing that there are no average gender differences in math ability prior to high school, by pointing to an individual girl's pattern of success in math courses, and by encouraging girls to attribute their previous good grades in math to their own abilities. On the values side, we would need to increase the value girls attach to math and math courses. They probably are not aware of the wide variety of careers that require math. Individual counseling sessions might examine each girl's anticipated career and the math required for it.

In sum, Eccles-Parsons has provided a detailed model for why girls choose or avoid math courses. In general, data support the model, although it needs to be tested further by independent researchers. It provides exciting avenues for intervening to get girls into math classes, which should have the beneficial result of expanding their career options.

COGNITIVE STYLE

Field dependence   Psychologist Herman Witkin and his colleagues (1954, 1964) have carried out a series of experiments from which they conclude that women have a field-dependent style, whereas men are field independent. This contrast has also been termed analytical versus global functioning — men are analytical, whereas women are global in their perceptions. Typical of the tests used in these studies is the rod-and-frame test (Figure 8.4). The subject is seated in a dark room facing a luminous rod inside a luminous frame. Both the rod and frame are tilted at an angle, and the subject's task is to adjust the rod to the true vertical. The tilt of the frame serves as a distraction in the task, so that people make errors from the true vertical in adjusting the rod. People who are very accurate in judging the true vertical are called field independent because they have been able to make their judgments independent of the misleading frame or field, whereas people who make errors are said to be field dependent. Because women make larger errors on the average than men do on this test, Witkin infers that women are field dependent, men field independent, in their cognitive styles. It should be noted that this may hold only in visual tests. In other tasks, performed with their eyes closed, women did as well as men.

FIGURE 8.4

The rod-and-frame apparatus is used to measure field dependence and field independence.

Error in judgment of the true vertical indicates field-dependence.

Accuracy in judgment of the true vertical indicates field-independence.

Source: After Witkin et al., 1954.

The interpretation Witkin places on his research is an interesting instance of the large leap of faith that is often made between results and interpretations, particularly when research confirms stereotyped expectations (Chapter 1). Some psychologists think that what is essentially a gender difference in susceptibility to an illusion has unjustifiably been interpreted to conform to gender-role stereotypes, namely that women are dependent and men independent. Consider this reinterpretation, which is equally consistent with the data: women are context-sensitive and men are context-insensitive.

On the basis of these criticisms, it is difficult to know what these results on cognitive style mean, except that women and men have different styles of perceiving and processing information, in this instance, when the field or context is misleading.

The Sherman hypothesis   Psychologist Julia Sherman (1967) hypothesized that many of the observed gender differences in abilities and cognitive style are simply due to gender differences in spatial ability. She believed that these spatial-ability differences were in turn due to different early experiences for boys and for girls — that boys' play experiences, for example, gave them a better education in spatial relations.

Where we observe many gender differences in abilities and cognitive style, there may be only one fundamental one. It is particularly likely that this is the case for field dependence-independence, because the content of the embedded-figures test (another test that, like the rod-and-frame test, is used to measure field dependence-independence) is so similar to that of many tests of spatial ability.

There is some evidence backing Sherman's hypothesis. Results indicate that, indeed, when differences in spatial ability are removed, no significant gender differences remain on the rod-and-frame test (Hyde, et al., 1975). Also, gender differences in a test of arithmetic reasoning are eliminated by removing differences in spatial ability.

To summarize, we have seen that there are no gender differences in general intelligence, but there are some differences in special abilities. Girls are superior on tests of verbal ability and perceptual speed, while boys are superior in spatial visualizing ability and mathematical ability, but these differences are all small. Males tend to be more accurate on the rod-and-frame test, a measure of cognitive style; this result has been used as evidence that males are more analytical than females, but the results are probably due simply to differences in spatial ability.

ACHIEVEMENT

School achievement   At all grade levels, girls consistently get better grades than boys, even in those areas in which boys score higher in ability tests.

Gender differences on standardized school achievement tests such as the Stanford Achievement Test closely parallel differences in tested abilities. Boys score higher in science, social studies, and arithmetic reasoning, whereas girls do better in spelling, language usage, and, less consistently, in arithmetic computation (Anastasi, 1958). The school progress of girls is also superior to that of boys. Girls less frequently have to repeat a grade, and are more frequently accelerated and promoted.

Vocational achievement   Stop for a moment and think of the name of a famous woman scientist. Write it down. Probably at least 90 percent of you wrote "Marie Curie," and the rest of you wrote nothing because you couldn't think of her name. Who else is there?

This illustrates how few women have achieved real eminence in science and how little recognition we give to those who have. (Other examples would have been Anna Freud, Jane Goodall, and Margaret Mead.) Standard biographical dictionaries generally show that less than 10 percent of the people who have achieved eminence have been women, and generally more than half of these are listed because they were sovereigns by birthright (Anastasi, 1958) or the wives or mistresses of famous men!

THE STORY OF A GIFTED WOMAN: BEATRIX POTTER

Beatrix Potter is best known as the author and illustrator of *The Tale of Peter Rabbit*. But her biography reveals a great deal about the struggles of a gifted woman trying to express her talent in the field of biology.

She was born in 1866, and by the age of eight, was already carefully drawing and labeling caterpillars. She became particularly interested in fungi, and through her teens and twenties she devoted as many hours as possible of every day to a search for new species she had not previously observed. She then painted each one that she saw.

By 1894, her studies of fungi and lichens were sufficiently advanced for her to take an interest in research from abroad suggesting that lichens result from symbiosis, a relationship between two organisms in which each is necessary for the other's survival. To test this hypothesis, she enlisted the help of her uncle, a distinguished chemist. On the basis of her research, Potter discovered the intimate interdependency between the fungus and alga which together formed the lichen.

It was through her uncle that she gained her first audience with the scientific establishment. He took her to the Royal Botanic Gardens to present her work. One after another of the scientists greeted her with apathy. The director dismissed her paintings of fungi as being too artistic to meet scientific criteria.

Although continually rebuffed by the scientific community, she continued her work on lichens, began work on spores, and started drafts of a paper describing her findings. As such, she was the first Britisher to explain the symbiotic relationship involved in a lichen and to begin to understand the germination of spores.

Her uncle became increasingly furious over her rejections by the scientific establishment and determined that her views would be heard. In 1897 a paper entitled "On the Germination of the Spores of Agaricineae" by Helen B. Potter was read to the Linnean Society of London. It was read by a friend; Beatrix Potter was not present because only men were allowed to attend the meetings.

But the prospects for her work to be appreciated remained nonexistent. Two years later she gave up her study of spores, finding the response of children to the books she wrote and illustrated to be much more satisfying. Her first book, complete with illustrations, was about a rabbit. Unable to get a publisher, she paid to have it printed. *The Tale of Peter Rabbit* has been on the list of children's bestsellers ever since its publication 70 years ago. Many of the psychological themes of Potter's own life are reflected in the characters, most notably frustration, a sense of being kept from a desired goal. For example, Peter Rabbit can't roam the garden at will because of the upraised rake of the pursuing gardener, MacGregor. Gifted in both science and art, Beatrix Potter finally found a socially acceptable, gender-appropriate way to express her creativity, by writing and illustrating children's books.

At the age of 47 she married, for the first time, a lawyer and spent her last 30 years living happily in the country. One wonders what great contributions she might have made to science had she not been so thwarted in her efforts.

Source: From Naomi Gilpatrick, "The Secret Life of Beatrix Potter." Used with permission from *Natural History* Vol. 81, No. 8. Copyright © the American Museum of Natural History, 1972.

An early statistical study of eminent women, collecting a total of 868 names representing 42 nations and extending from the seventh century B.C. to 1913, showed that the largest number (38 percent) had achieved eminence in literature. Women's high verbal ability has apparently been put to some use. However, the highest degree of eminence (as measured by the number of lines allotted in the biographical dictionaries) was obtained by sovereigns, political leaders, and mothers and mistresses of eminent men. Women achieved eminence in a number of other non-intellectual ways, such as tragic fate, beauty, and being immortalized in literature (Castle, 1913).

Even in fields traditionally assigned to women, the top-ranking, most prestigious positions are held by men. Professional interior decorating and clothing design are dominated by men. The world's great chefs are men.

In more recent years, there still remains a gap between the accomplishments of women and of men. In 1968, 3 percent of American lawyers were women, as were 7 percent of American doctors (Bird, 1968). In a

1965 sample from *Who's Who in America*, women comprised only 4.5 percent of the listings, down from 8.5 percent in 1925 (Chafetz, 1974, p. 132.) Women more frequently distinguished themselves in the arts, while men did so in business. Certainly a contemporary study like Castle's would have a host of interesting characters to add to the list — Indira Gandhi, Golda Meir, Eleanor Roosevelt, Jane Goodall, Margaret Mead, Margaret Thatcher, Isadora Duncan, and Coco Chanel, to name a few.

Studying the adult achievements of women labeled as gifted during the school years provides some insight into the "gap at the top" syndrome. The Stanford Gifted Child Study (Terman and Oden, 1947) is perhaps the most extensive research of its kind. More than 600 children with IQ's above 135 (which represents the upper 1 percent of the population) were identified in the California schools. Their progress was then followed into adulthood. The adult occupations of the women, whose childhood IQ's were in the same range as the men's, were on the whole undistinguished. Few became professionals. Although IQ showed a fairly close relationship to accomplishment among men, it showed essentially no relationship among women. In fact, two-thirds of the women with IQ's of 170 or above (certainly at the genius level) were housewives or office workers. One cannot help but be struck by the enormous waste of resources this represents.

In summary, in terms of achievement, girls surpass boys in school achievement in all areas, but in terms of professional achievement, females lag behind males. This deficit in achievement is particularly surprising in view of the high verbal abilities of females and their school successes; it is probably a result of a variety of forces including discrimination and gender-role socialization. In later sections of this chapter we shall explore various motivational factors that may also help to account for the lesser professional achievements of women.

MAKING IT IN A MAN'S WORLD

The exceptional woman   Despite the statistics noted above, some women have made it in a man's world. They are the exceptional women who have been highly successful in male-dominated occupations: professions such as law and medicine, business, and politics. What are these women like? (For a comprehensive review, see Lemkau, 1979; this review forms the basis for the conclusions that follow.)

In terms of personality, these exceptional women are high in certain traits related to competency that have been stereotyped as masculine: independence, assertiveness, and rationality. Interestingly, though, they do not differ from women in general when the feminine stereotyped traits of warmth and expressiveness are measured. In short, these women appear to have androgynous personalities.

Not surprisingly, given their occupations, these women do experience situational psychological stress. However, they tend to be emotionally healthy and have good coping skills, so that they are able to manage the stress levels with which they live.

In terms of family background characteristics, they very often are first-born children or only children. In fact, in one study of women presidents and vice-presidents of major American businesses, every single one was a first-born child (Hennig, 1973). These women also report a sense of having felt "special" since childhood. Having parents born outside the United States is common, and the parents tend to have high educational levels. These women's mothers tended to have a high rate of employment. For one sample of women receiving graduate degrees in medicine at Columbia University, three-quarters of their mothers were employed (Ginzberg et al., 1966). Perhaps more importantly, these successful women report that their mothers enjoyed their work. Thus the women had strong models for achievement in both their mothers and their fathers.

There are two possible theoretical frameworks from which to view these women who are successful in male-dominated occupations: the deviance perspective and the enrichment perspective (Almquist and Angrist, 1970). The *deviance perspective* views these women as unconventional people, the products of parental problems or poor peer relationships, who unnaturally reject feminine pursuits to strive after masculine goals. The *enrichment perspective*, in contrast, views these women as the products of unusual enrichment experiences that allow them to transcend the limitations of the traditional female role. The evidence seems to support the enrichment perspective (Lemkau, 1979). That is, these women seem to be products of unusual but positive experiences.

The Queen Bee syndrome   A very interesting phenomenon characteristic of some highly successful professional women has been documented: the "Queen Bee" syndrome (Staines et al., 1974). Some female antifeminists have the characteristics typical of people who resist social change: they are politically conservative, religious, less educated, and older. However there is another group of female antifeminists, the Queen Bees, with quite different characteristics: they are successful professionals in a man's world. They are the Uncle Toms of the women's movement, women who try to keep other women down, even though they are in a position to advance women's cause.

The Queen Bee rejects the feminist notion that many of women's problems are external in origin, the result of political and economic discrimination. Instead, she believes that the system is open and fair and that an individual succeeds on his or her own merits. If *she* can make it, then so can other women. Women who don't make it have no one but themselves to blame. Because of her belief in individual determinants of success, she also rejects the collective strategies of the women's movement for effecting social change.

The Queen Bee also generally is a "supermother," achieving not only in her career but also in the traditional feminine role of wife and mother. Her dedication to these traditional virtues is so strong as to appear almost defensive. Queen Bees are more likely, as compared with a control group of traditional women and another control group of feminists, to say that their husband's job has priority over theirs and to agree that children of working mothers tend to be maladjusted.

There are several possible explanations for this striking phenomenon. First, Queen Bees have been co-opted by the establishment. The first few members of minorities who are admitted to organizations are often co-opted. The system tolerates countermilitants most easily, and these few "tokens" are rewarded for not rocking the boat. Indeed, their success may almost be conditional on their countermilitancy. The Queen Bee's status and acceptance may be somewhat precarious, being dependent on her not adopting a militant stance. Second, the Queen Bee's antifeminism is a means of excluding the competition. Being the only successful woman around can be a lot of fun. Newer, younger women entering the ranks may take away her special, unique status. In addition, the Queen Bee may have had to overcome many obstacles to achieve her position, and therefore hates to see other women attain rank without the initiation rites. Hence, she has little interest in promoting the entry of women into her profession and indeed may make some efforts to keep them out. Finally, the Queen Bee is getting a lot of rewards from the system as it is. She is praised for being so feminine, yet thinking like a man. The status quo is comfortable for her, and she can be expected to have little animosity toward a system that rewards her so well.

In the context of the psychology of women, the Queen Bee syndrome is distressing yet not too surprising. Certainly it can at least in part be traced to the femininity-achievement double-bind. The Queen Bee has found one means for resolving this bind — or perhaps her solution represents no resolution at all. Staines et al. conclude on a hopeful note that the incidence of this syndrome may be decreasing and it is probably not very common to begin with. Certainly one hopes that as women begin to understand their own psychology better, such syndromes will be avoided.

ACHIEVEMENT MOTIVATION

A striking paradox has emerged in this chapter. Women start out life with good abilities, yet they end up in adulthood with lower status and less achievement than men. Little girls have better verbal ability than little boys, and in this age of rhetoric we should certainly appreciate the importance of verbal ability. Girls also have better fine motor coordination, and in a technological age, this is certainly more useful than brute strength. Girls also do better in school. Yet in adulthood we find them in unpaid occupations such as being housewives, or in unrewarding ones such as being clerks. Why?

There is currently a high consciousness about discrimination against women, and certainly discrimination is an important source of women's low achievement. (See Chapter 7 for a more complete discussion.)

However, psychologists believe that discrimination on the basis of gender is not the entire answer to "why women fail." Society has subtler ways of achieving its goals, in which women may internalize low drives to achieve, and may perpetuate this pattern in other women. Some of the personality factors that may act on women's achievements are achievement motivation, the motive to avoid success, and expectations about success. We shall examine these processes in women in this and the following sections.

The *achievement motive* is the desire to accomplish something of value or importance through one's own efforts, to meet standards of excellence in what one does. There are several methods for measuring it. The most commonly used is a projective technique in which subjects' stories in response to an ambiguous cue are scored for achievement imagery (McClelland et al., 1953). Subjects are shown a series of pictures and are asked to write a story about each picture after being told that this is a test of creative imagination. They are told to cover such questions as: What is happening? What has led up to this situation? What will happen? What is being thought? One of the pictures shows a young man standing on a sidewalk with a broom in his hand, looking off into the distance. Below are two stories written by different subjects about this picture:

> The boy works in the grocery store. He has just graduated from high school and hasn't enough money to go to college. He is standing there thinking about how long it will take him to save enough to get his education. He doesn't want to remain a store clerk all his life, and wants to make something of himself.

> It seems that this young man has been told by his father to clean up the sidewalk. This has prevented him from going off to the beach for the day with his pals. He is watching them go off in their car and is feeling left out and sore at his father.

The first story would be scored as indicating a high achievement motive, whereas the second indicates a low achievement motive.

Most of the classic literature on gender differences asserts that females have a lower level of achievement motivation than males (Tyler, 1965; Hoffman, 1972). These gender differences are of considerable interest because achievement motivation is related to achievement behaviors such as test performance and occupational choice. Thus, the lower achievement motivation of females might help to explain their lesser occupational achievement, and might therefore represent a kind of "internalized barrier to achievement." Theories were constructed to explain the developmental forces, such as socialization, that might lead females to have low achievement motivation (Hoffman, 1972). It was also believed that, although females were not motivated for achievement, they were motivated by social concerns, or by a *need for affiliation*. That is, females were thought to be motivated not by internalized standards of excellence (achievement motivation), but rather by a desire for approval from other people (Hoffman, 1972). Indeed, some authors even suggested that girls' achievement behavior (for example, school achievement) was not motivated by achievement motivation as it was for boys, but rather by a need for affiliation (the teacher's approval).

There is a need to reassess these results, however. From a review of available research, there actually appears to be little evidence for lower achievement motivation in females (Maccoby and Jacklin, 1974). The results are complex because achievement motivation may be tested under any of several conditions. In the simplest case (the "neutral" or "relaxed" condition), subjects are simply given the test. Under such conditions, females actually show higher achievement motivation than males. The test may also be given under "achievement arousal" conditions. For example, before taking the test of achievement motivation, subjects might be given an anagrams test that they are told measures not only intelligence, but also capacity to organize and to evaluate situations quickly and accurately, and to be a leader. Under these conditions, males' achievement motivation increases sharply, while females' does not. These results indicate that females generally have a high level of achievement motivation, but that certain situations — for example, competitive ones — do not arouse their achievement motivation as they do that of males. We shall return to this idea when we discuss the motive to avoid success in the next section. Gender differences in achievement motivation appear to depend on the situation in which the motive is measured.

Gender differences in achievement motivation also probably depend on age and stage of development. While females may generally have a high level of achievement motivation, at various periods of a woman's life achievement may become anxiety-provoking, so that she temporarily suppresses her achievement motivation (Bardwick, 1971). For instance, a girl who, because of a strong desire to go to medical school and become a doctor, has earned straight A's through her junior year in college, suddenly meets the man of her dreams. He has no plans for being married to a doctor, but rather wants a competent wife, housewife, and mother for his children. So she abandons all medical school plans. However, after her children are all in school, she may revive her educational goals and become a successful professional. Achievement may have been very anxiety-provoking to the young woman when she was of marriageable age, but having "accomplished" the female role, she may again express achievement motivation, and achievement can then become a source of satisfaction. Probably this relationship of achievement motivation to stage of development, as well as the failure of females to increase their achievement motivation under competitive situations, are results of the perceived incompatibility of femininity and achievement (see Chapter 7).

The belief in women's need for affiliation also needs reassessment (Maccoby and Jacklin, 1974; Stein and Bailey, 1973). This belief was based on the notion that females are more sensitive to interpersonal reinforcement; yet available research does not indicate that this is true. Much of what appears to be affiliative needs in females may actually be achievement needs expressed in a gender-appropriate fashion. Thus the traditional housewife may be highly motivated to be an outstanding cook and to throw fantastic dinner parties not because of her needs for social approval, but because this is a socially acceptable, gender-appropriate means of expressing her very real achievement strivings. She is displaying achievement that is gender-appropriate for women.

In summary, females appear to have high levels of achievement motivation on the average. This motivation, however, is not aroused by traditional achievement-arousal conditions, as is the case with males. Gender differences in achievement motivation appear to depend on the situation in which they are tested, as well as on the stage of development.

MOTIVE TO AVOID SUCCESS

In 1969 Matina Horner reported on the results of research on an anxiety about success called *motive to avoid success* or *fear of success*, among bright, high-achieving women.

In attempting to understand the basis of gender differences in achievement motivation, Horner first observed that achievement situations, such as test taking, are more anxiety-provoking for females than for males. In order to measure this phenomenon, Horner devised a projective test in which subjects were asked to complete a story that begins: "After first-term finals, Anne (John) finds herself (himself) at the top of her (his) medical-school class." Females wrote about Anne, males about John.

Males' stories generally indicated happiness and feelings of satisfaction over achievement. For example:

> John is a conscientious young man who worked hard. He is pleased with himself. John has always wanted to go into medicine and is very dedicated. . . . John continues working hard and eventually graduates at the top of his class.

Females' responses, on the other hand, were often bizarre:

> Anne starts proclaiming her surprise and joy. Her fellow classmates are so disgusted wtih her behavior that they jump on her in a body and beat her. She is maimed for life.

The negative imagery expressed by females generally fell into one of three categories — fear of social rejection, worries about maintaining woman-hood, and denial of the reality of success. For example:

Social rejection fears:

> Anne is an acne-faced bookworm. She runs to the bulletin board and finds she's at the top. As usual she smarts off. A chorus of groans is the rest of the class's reply . . .

Worries about womanhood:

> Unfortunately Anne no longer feels so certain that she really wants to be a doctor. She is worried about herself and wonders if perhaps she isn't normal . . . Anne decides not to continue with her medical work but to take courses that have a deeper personal meaning for her.

Denial of reality:

> Anne is a code name of a nonexistent person created by a group of medi-cal students. They take turns writing exams for Anne.

In her sample of undergraduates at the University of Michigan, Horner found that 65 percent of the females, as compared with less than 10 percent of the males, told stories that fell into one of these three cate-gories.

This motivational variable also seems to be related to performance (Horner, 1972; Karabenick and Marshall, 1974). When put in a competi-tive situation, females who did not show fear of success improved their scores over those they achieved when working individually, while females high in fear of success did worse in competition. The motive to avoid success, then, seems to be aroused in achieving, competitive situations. Attitudes of male peers are also important in evoking it (Horner, 1972). While all the females in the sample were intellectually talented, most of those high in fear of success were majoring in humanities and planned traditional careers such as housewife or teacher; those who were low in fear of success aspired to graduate degrees and careers in scientific areas like math and physics.

Presumably the motive to avoid success is related to the perceived conflict between achievement and femininity and the perceived connec-tion between achievement and aggressiveness, which is also gender-inap-propriate for females. Thus, for women, the rewards of achievement are contaminated by the accompanying anxiety.

Horner collected her original data in 1965 for her doctoral dissertation. The results were published in a 1969 *Psychology Today* article. They attracted quite a bit of attention, to put it mildly. The *New York Times* and other newspapers featured stories about the research. The article was reprinted a number of times and was required reading for many students. The research was — and is — appealing for a number of reasons. It appeared just at the time of rising interest in women and the women's movement. In particular, it seemed to offer a sensible explanation for why more women had not succeeded in high-status occupations — they simply feared success.

In the cold light of day some 15 years later, the research doesn't seem to provide the surefire answers it originally did. Horner's research has been criticized on a number of grounds (Tresemer, 1974; Shaver, 1976; Zuckerman and Wheeler, 1975): (1) Other studies using Horner's techniques often find men having fear-of-success imagery as much as or more than women. Therefore there is no reason to believe that the motive to avoid success is found only in women, or even that it is more frequent in women. If that is the case, then it cannot be used to explain the lesser occupational achievements of women.[3] (2) Anne's success was in a gender-inappropriate field, namely medical school. Therefore the research may not indicate a generalized fear of success, but rather a fear of being successful at something that is gender-inappropriate. Perhaps if Anne had been doing well in nursing school, she would not evoke much anxiety. One study has shown just that (Cherry and Deaux, 1978). (3) Women are responding to another woman, Anne, not themselves, in writing the stories. Perhaps they feel anxious about Anne's success, but would not feel anxious about their own success. (4) In technical language, Horner's technique confounds gender of subjects with the gender of the stimulus cue. That is, women write about Anne, men about John. From this, we cannot tell whether women are higher in fear of success than men, or whether successful women (cues) arouse more anxiety than successful men. Perhaps if men wrote about Anne, they too would indicate bizarre reactions to her. In fact, one study has shown that to be exactly what happens (Monahan et al., 1974). This suggests that Horner's techniques may simply be measuring cultural stereotypes about women rather than murky unconscious conflicts.

Where does this leave us? Is there a motive to avoid success that keeps some women from achieving, or that at least makes them miserable if they do? My intuitive feeling is that there probably is such a phenomenon, but I also must say that there is not much scientific evidence

---

[3] The failure to find gender differences in motive to avoid success in other studies cannot be explained by the fact that they occurred later, when gender-role standards became liberated. There appears to be no trend over time as to which studies show women having more fear of success and which don't (Zuckerman and Wheeler, 1975).

for it. In Chapter 1, I noted that one of the critical steps in psychological research is *measurement*. That is, when a researcher has some phenomenon to study, she or he must first devise a way to measure it. In Horner's case, she chose to measure the motive to avoid success by using a *projective test*. The idea is that subjects are given an ambiguous cue. Their stories about that cue presumably reflect a projection of their own unconscious motives. Most psychologists now consider projective tests to be poor methods of measurement, and might prefer some more direct method, perhaps a paper-and-pencil checklist (such as Bem used in measuring androgyny, as discussed in Chapter 4). My feeling is that the motive to avoid success probably exists, but no one has been able to measure it adequately as yet (Macdonald and Hyde, 1980), and it may affect both women and men.

ATTRIBUTIONS: WHEN A WOMAN SUCCEEDS, IS IT JUST LUCK?

Suppose a college woman gets an A on a calculus exam. When she thinks about her success, or when others think about it, what will they believe caused it? To what will they attribute her success? This is called the *attribution process*, and it has been studied in detail by social psychologists. Typically four kinds of causes have been studied: ability, effort, luck, and task ease. Applied to the example given here, people might think that the woman got an A because of her own high mathematical ability, because she studied hard (effort), simply because she was lucky, or because the exam was easy. These four kinds of causes can be further categorized into two groups, those attributing the event to *internal* sources (factors within the individual, that is, ability and effort) and those attributing the event to *external* sources (forces outside the individual, that is, luck and task ease).

Early research in this area tended to document gender differences in attribution patterns. Women were found to be more likely than men to attribute their own success to external sources, in particular, luck; men, in contrast, attributed their success to their own abilities (e.g., Simon and Feather, 1973). These results were also found when people explained the performance of another person; they thought that a woman succeeds because of luck, and that a man succeeds because of his skill or ability (Deaux and Emswiller, 1974). The early research also showed that, when people are explaining their failures, women are more likely than men to attribute failure to internal sources, namely to their own lack of abilities (McMahan, 1971, 1972).

Just as Maccoby and Jacklin (1974) felt a need to assess whether gender differences in abilities and behaviors really appeared consistently when all available studies were surveyed, so psychologist Irene Frieze and her colleagues (1982; see also Sohn, 1982) surveyed all available studies on attribution patterns to see whether gender differences appeared consistently. Their results indicated that the size of the gender differences described above is essentially zero. Once again, gender similarities in behavior are the reality.

Research may yet uncover important gender differences in causal attributions if the study designs become more complex, particularly if attention is given to situational factors such as the type of task that is used (McHugh et al., 1982). For example, if the task involves spatial ability problems or some kind of athletic performance, women might attribute their successes to luck, whereas if the task involves establishing a friendship with a new person or establishing a nurturant relationship with someone in need, then women might be more likely to attribute their successes to ability. But for now it must be said that we don't know whether there are gender differences in causal attributions.

At this stage of the research and theorizing, causal attributions are not going to be much help in explaining gender differences in achievements. What may be more helpful is a related result discussed in Chapter 6. It has been found that women have lower expectations for success than men do, for a wide variety of tasks and age groups (Crandall, 1969). Indeed, this gender difference has been discovered as early as the preschool years. Further, people with high expectations of success tend to do better. For example, when people are randomly assigned to high-expectancy and low-expectancy groups, the high-expectancy group tends to perform better (Tyler, 1958). Therefore, women may achieve less because they expect to achieve less. Expectations may be more important than attributions. Certainly this is another internalized source contributing to women's lack of achievement.

It is important to recognize the situational and social factors influencing these phenomena. As noted above, in competitive situations women have lower expectations for success than men do; however, in noncompetitive situations, women state expectancies similar to men's (House, 1974). These results parallel those for achievement motivation noted earlier in this chapter. Women's achievement motivation is as high or higher than men's in neutral situations, but men's becomes higher when competition is involved. Apparently women's gender-role concerns are more prominent when the situation involves competition.

IN CONCLUSION

In this chapter I reviewed evidence on gender differences in abilities, noting that females are superior in some areas (verbal ability, perceptual speed) and males are better in others (mathematical ability, spatial ability), but that these differences are small. Girls do better in school, yet men's adult achievements in the world of work exceed those of women's. There is a disparity, then, between the abilities and school achievement of females, on one hand, and their adult work achievements, on the other.

Two general classes of factors help to explain this discrepancy: external [4] barriers to achievement, and internal (or intrapsychic) barriers to achievement. External barriers are factors such as job discrimination and, as noted in Chapter 7, there is ample evidence that this exists, both in obvious and subtle forms. Internal barriers or intrapsychic factors — such as low achievement motivation in competitive situations and low expectations for success — and low value placed on some areas such as developing math skills — also seem to exist. Of course, the internal barriers may be caused by external forces; for example, a woman may have low expectations for success on her job because she has experienced job discrimination. Thus, a combination of external and internal factors is important in explaining the lesser achievements of women. It is also important to recognize both sets of factors when trying to bring about the social change necessary to allow women to achieve more.

SUGGESTION FOR FURTHER READING

Hyde, Janet S. (1981). How large are cognitive gender differences? A meta-analysis using ω^2 and d. *American Psychologist*, 36, 892–901. This article surveys gender differences in verbal, mathematical, and spatial abilities, assesses the size of those gender differences, and explores the implications of the gender differences.

---

[4] The use of *external* and *internal* here should not be confused with the language of external and internal used in discussing causal attributions earlier in this chapter.

9

Women and Language

Women are the decorative sex. They never have anything to say, but they say it charmingly.

OSCAR WILDE

Suppose that you found the following caption, torn from a cartoon: "That sunset is such a lovely shade of lavender, isn't it?" If you had to guess the gender of the speaker, what would you say? Most people would guess that the speaker was a woman. Most of us have ideas about what is "appropriate" speech for males and females, and "lovely" and "lavender" just don't sound like things that a man would (or should) say. In this chapter we shall explore the evidence on the difference between how women and men speak and communicate nonverbally, and on how women are treated in the English language.

GENDER DIFFERENCES IN LANGUAGE USE

Stereotypes   The example given above illustrates certain stereotypes about men's and women's speech — namely, that women use adjectives like "lovely" and "lavender" and men don't. Exactly what *are* the stereotypes concerning women's and men's speech?

Cheris Kramer (1974a, 1976) investigated this question by analyzing 156 cartoons containing adult human speech from 13 consecutive issues of *The New Yorker*. In addition, she had 25 female and 25 male students indicate, for each caption, whether they thought a man or a woman had said it. Kramer later expanded her study to include cartoons from *Ladies Home Journal, Playboy,* and *Cosmopolitan*. She found that male characters were more likely to swear, whereas female characters were more apt to use adjectives such as "nice" and "pretty." Generally men's speech was stronger than women's, with more exclamations and harsh words. Male speakers were more likely to be putting down someone, whereas when a woman spoke, it was likely that her words were themselves the joke. Students had no trouble identifying which lines had been spoken by males and which by females. Stereotyped identifications could be made in about 75 percent of the cases. Students of both genders stereotyped women's speech as stupid, vague, emotional, confused, and wordy. Men's speech was characterized as logical, concise, businesslike, and controlled.

With these stereotypes in mind, do they indicate "real" differences between men's and women's speech? What evidence exists on the actual speech patterns of women and men?

Correctness   There is some indication that women's speech tends to be more "correct" than men's (Thorne and Henley, 1975, p. 17). For example, in one study of the pronunciation of words ending in "-ing," males pronounced it "in'" 62 percent of the time, compared with only 29 percent for females (Shuy, 1969). Generally, it seems that females' speech is closer to the normative speech of their culture, while males' is more likely to contain errors or subcultural forms (Kramer, 1974b).

Tag questions   Linguist Robin Lakoff (1973) originally hypothesized that women use more tag questions than men. A tag question is a short phrase at the end of a declarative sentence that turns it into a question. An example would be "This is a great game, isn't it?"

More recently, data have been collected to see whether Lakoff's ideas are correct (McMillan et al., 1977). College students participated in a group problem-solving task in either same-gender or mixed-gender groups of five to seven people. The discussions, which involved solving a mystery and lasted thirty minutes, were tape recorded, and later were coded and analyzed by the experimenters. They found that the women used about twice as many tag questions as the men, a difference that was statistically significant.

Using the terminology of Chapter 1, we have a statistical result that women use significantly more tag questions than men do. How should that finding be interpreted? The standard interpretation has been that men's tendency not to use tag questions indicates the self-confidence and forcefulness of their speech. Women's tendency to use them is interpreted as indicating uncertainty or weak patterns of speech. As Lakoff put it,

> These sentence types provide a means whereby a speaker can avoid committing himself [sic], and thereby avoid coming into conflict with the addressee. The problem is that, by so doing, a speaker may also give the impression of not being really sure of himself, of looking to the addressee for confirmation, even of having no views of his own. (1975, pp. 16–17)

This interpretation implies that women's speech is somehow deficient, reflecting undesirable traits such as uncertainty. Are other interpretations possible? To interpret this difference in a way that would be more favorable to women, we might say that the tag question is intended to encourage communication, rather than to shut things off with a simple declarative statement. The tag question encourages the other person to express an opinion. Rather than reflecting uncertainty, women's greater use of tag questions may reflect greater interpersonal sensitivity and warmth (McMillan et al., 1977).

The researchers in the experiment discussed above attempted to determine which of these interpretations was more accurate (McMillan et al., 1977). They did this by comparing the use of tag questions in same-gender versus mixed-gender groups. They reasoned that, if tag questions reflect uncertainty, then women should use more tag questions when men are present (mixed-gender groups) than when only women are present (all-female groups). This hypothesis was confirmed by the data, thus supporting the "greater female uncertainty" interpretation. However, men also used more tag questions in mixed-gender groups than they did in all-male groups. The researchers had not hypothesized this, as it did not seem that men should be more uncertain when women were present. Thus the interpretation of this gender difference is still unclear, and more sophisticated experiments will be necessary before a definitive statement can be made. The more important point to keep in mind, however, is that often alternative interpretations, one favoring men, the other favoring women, can be made of the same statistical results.

Intonation   Say the phrase "Are you coming?" in a number of different ways. By varying the way you say it, you can convey a variety of feelings, from cheerful politeness to stern irritation. This is done by varying the intonation pattern, that is, the combination of high pitches plus low pitches.

Studies indicate that females and males tend to use somewhat different intonation patterns (Brend, 1971; McConnell-Ginet, 1978). Women are more likely to use intonation patterns of surprise, unexpectedness, cheerfulness, and politeness. Further, men have only three contrasting levels of pitch in their intonation, whereas women have four; the additional level that women have is the highest one. The distinctive intonation patterns used by women are probably advantageous in allowing them to express a wider range of emotions. However, they may also contribute to women's speech appearing overly emotional and high-pitched.

Interruptions   Researchers have repeatedly found that men interrupt women considerably more often than women interrupt men (McMillan et al., 1977; Zimmerman and West, 1975). To give an idea of the magnitude of the difference, some data from one study are shown in Table 9.1.

TABLE 9.1.   **Mean number of interruptions per half hour, according to gender of interrupter and gender of interruptee in mixed-gender groups**

Gender of Interruptee	Gender of Interrupter	
	Female	*Male*
Female	2.50	5.24
Male	0.93	2.36

Source: McMillan et al., 1977.

Notice that women interrupt women about as often as men interrupt men. However, women very seldom interrupt men, whereas men quite frequently interrupt women.

Once again, we have a statistical result that men interrupt women considerably more than women interrupt men. How should this gender difference be interpreted? The typical interpretation made by feminist social scientists involves the assumption that interruptions are an expression of *power* or *dominance*. That is, the interrupter gains control of a conversation, and that is a kind of interpersonal power. The gender difference, then, is interpreted as indicating that men are expressing power and dominance over women. This pattern may reflect the subtle persistence of traditional gender roles; it may also help to perpetuate traditional roles.

This power interpretation will also be discussed in the section on nonverbal communication later in this chapter. Such interpretations are central to feminist research and theory, as noted in Chapter 3.

Total talking time   The stereotype is that women talk a lot more than men. Women are reputedly always gabbing on the telephone or over the back fence. In the study of cartoon captions discussed at the beginning of this chapter, women's speech was characterized by students as being "wordy" (Kramer, 1974a, 1976).

What about the empirical data? Is this stereotype a real difference? In fact, there does seem to be a real difference, but it is just the opposite of the stereotype. In terms of total talking time, men talk more than women (Swacker, 1975; Argyle et al., 1968; Strodtbeck et al., 1957).

Other differences   Some other gender differences in speech have been documented. For example, males use more hostile verbs than females do (Gilley and Collier, 1970). Women say more supportive words, such as *mm hmm* (Hirschmann, 1974, cited in Thorne and Henley, 1975, p. 231; Fishman, 1978). Generally, the differences fall along the lines one would expect from gender-role stereotypes.

The gender differences in language use that we have discussed seem to be found rather consistently. Indeed, male-female differences in language are found in all cultures around the world (Bodine, 1975). Nonetheless, it is important not to overestimate the extent of the differences. In many ways, females and males use essentially the same vocabulary and grammar. Thus, while certain features of male and female language differ, it would be unwise to say that there are separate female and male languages. Gender similarities are the rule in language just as they are in other behaviors (Kramer et al., 1978).

BODY LANGUAGE:
NONVERBAL COMMUNICATION

The popularizers of the "body language" concept have pointed out the fact that we often communicate far more with our body than with the words we speak. For example, suppose you say the sentence "How nice to see you" while standing only six inches from another person or while actually brushing up against them. Then imagine, in contrast, that you say the sentence while standing three feet from the person. The sentence conveys a much different meaning in the two instances. In the first, it will probably convey warmth and possibly sexiness. In the second case, the meaning will seem formal and cold. As another example, a sentence coming from a smiling face conveys a much different meaning than the same sentence coming from a stern or frowning face.

Here I shall present what evidence there is on whether there are differences between women and men in nonverbal styles of communication, and what those differences mean (for a good, detailed discussion, see Mayo and Henley, 1981).

The politics of touch   Studies consistently show that men touch women considerably more frequently than women touch men (Henley, 1973; Jourard, 1966). Having demonstrated the existence of a gender difference, we must now proceed to an interpretation of its significance.

Feminist scientists have interpreted this particular gender difference as a reflection of dominance relations between men and women, with men expressing dominance by touching women, which in turn reinforces women's subordinate status (Henley, 1973, 1975). Below follows some of the theorizing and data that lead to and support that interpretation.

In his essay "The Nature of Deference and Demeanor," Erving Goffman (1967) argued that, between a superior and a subordinate, relations will be asymmetrical. That is, the superior will have the right to certain familiarities with the subordinate that the subordinate is not allowed to reciprocate. Goffman further argued that touch by one person to another operates in this way. As an example, he considered the status system in a hospital, where doctors (the superiors) touch patients (the subordinates), but the reverse would seem unreasonable and presumptuous. Certainly there are many other examples. The boss puts his hand on the secretary's shoulder while giving her instructions, but she scarcely puts her hand on his shoulder when she returns the typed letters. Age, too, is a status dimension, with adults having status over children. We see adults walk up to a baby and stroke its cheek or tickle its sides, liberties they would scarcely take with another adult.

Psychologist Nancy Henley (1973; see replication by Major and Williams, 1980, cited in Major, 1981) did the original research and theorizing suggesting that these principles apply to relations between women and men — namely, that touch is a means by which men express dominance over women. In her original study, an observer spent 60 hours recording instances of touching in places such as a shopping center, a bank, and a college campus. For each instance, the gender, age, and approximate socioeconomic status of the two persons involved were recorded. Of the 28 instances of touch between people of approximately equal age and socioeconomic status, 23 involved a man touching a woman, but only five involved a woman touching a man. Thus men do touch women considerably more than women touch men. To verify the dominance interpretation of this result, Henley examined the touch relationships along the other dimensions — both of which are status indicators — namely, socioeconomic status (SES) and age. Regarding SES, there were fourteen cases in which the toucher was of higher status than the person being touched, while there were only five cases in which the toucher was judged to be of lower

FIGURE 9.1

Men touch women more than the reverse, which may be an expression of power and dominance.

Source: Photo by Antonio Mendoza/The Picture Cube.

status. The results were similar for age. In 36 cases the toucher was judged to be at least ten years older than the person being touched, while there were only seven cases in which the toucher was at least ten years younger than the person being touched. From Henley's study it would be reasonable to conclude that (1) there is a gender difference in touching, with men touching women more than the reverse, and (2) higher-status, dominant individuals tend to touch lower-status, subordinate individuals more than the reverse.

A recent study provides further confirmation and elaboration of Henley's conclusions (Summerhayes and Suchner, 1978). Subjects were shown photographs of female-male interactions and were asked to rate the extent to which each person dominated the interaction. The photographs varied along two dimensions: the status differences between the two people as indicated by their age and dress (female higher, versus equal, versus male higher), and who was touching whom (female toucher, versus no touching, versus male toucher). They found that when either a man or a woman touches another person, the effect is to reduce the perceived dominance of the person being touched. They even found that lower-status women could reduce the status of higher-status men by touching them. Other studies also confirm the belief that touching conveys dominance (Forden, 1981).

Of course, a touch does not always convey the meaning of dominance. A touch can also convey feelings of sexuality or of solidarity and friendship, or love (Major, 1981). Which of these meanings is conveyed depends on the situation. Friendship tends to be conveyed if the touch is between persons of approximately the same status and the touch is reciprocal, such as a handshake or a mutual hug (the prior discussion has been concerned with *non*reciprocal touch, that is, one person touches another but the touch is not returned). While it is fairly easy for a man to convey dominance by a touch, it is probably more difficult for a woman to do so, and she is likely to have the touch interpreted as having a sexual meaning.

What are the practical implications of this research and theorizing? First, men who are concerned about establishing egalitarian relationships with women need to become aware of their use of touch. It can signal dominance and unequal roles even though one is not aware of doing so and does not intend to do so. Second, women who are concerned with trying to be more assertive and dominant in their interpersonal relations may want to consider increasing their use of touch. The risk in this approach is that the touch will be mistaken for a sexual message. One is therefore advised to aim for sexually neutral areas of the body, such as the shoulder or forearm.

Interpersonal distance   Generally it seems that in the United States, men prefer a greater distance between themselves and another person, while there tends to be a smaller distance between women and others. For example, women stand closer to other women in public exhibits than men do to men (Baxter, 1970). In a study of the initial speaking distance set by an approaching person, it was found that women were approached more closely than men (Willis, 1966). In another study, subjects seated themselves an average of 4.6 feet from a female stimulus person and an average of 8.5 feet from a male — i.e., they sat about twice as far from the male as from the female (Wittig and Skolnick, 1978). Thus it seems that interpersonal distance works much like touch — women are more likely to be touched and they are more likely to be approached closely.

These results can be interpreted in a manner similar to the interpretation of the results on touching. That is, it might be said that women essentially have their personal space or "territory" violated, and that this expresses dominance over them. On the other hand, an alternative interpretation would be that women have a small interpersonal distance as a result of, or in order to express, warmth or friendliness. More sophisticated research will be necessary to sort out these possibilities (see, for example, Wittig and Skolnick, 1978).

Smiling Women tend to smile more than men although, once again, it is not clear how this difference should be interpreted (Mehrabian, 1971; Ragan, 1982; LaFrance, 1981). Smiling has been called the female version of the "Uncle Tom shuffle" — that is, rather than indicating happiness or friendliness, it may serve as an appeasement gesture, communicating, in effect, "please don't hit me or be nasty." Smiling seems to be a part of the female role. Most women can remember having their faces feel stiff and sore from smiling at a party or some other public gathering at which they were expected to smile. The smile, of course, did not reflect happiness, but rather a belief that smiling was the appropriate thing to do. Women's smiles, then, do not necessarily reflect positive feelings, and may even be associated with negative feelings.

There is really very little research on smiling and its implications for women and gender roles. There is one interesting study, however, of smiling in interactions between parents and children (Bugental et al., 1971). When fathers were smiling they tended to make more positive statements to their children, compared with when they were not smiling. Mothers' statements, on the other hand, were no more positive when they were smiling than when they were not. Parents, and particularly mothers, smiled more when they thought they were being observed than when they thought they were not being observed. This suggests that smiling is indeed part of a role people play. Finally, it seemed that children had learned to sort out the contradictory messages (smile accompanied by a negative statement) they got from their mothers; they ignored the smile and responded to the negative statement.

FIGURE 9.2

Smiling is a part of the female role. Do women's smiles indicate happiness and friendliness, or are they forced because of role expectations?

Source: Ken Robert Buck / The Picture Cube.

HOW WOMEN ARE
TREATED IN LANGUAGE

To this point I have discussed women's communication styles, both verbal and nonverbal. The other aspect that needs to be covered in this discussion of women and language is how women and the concept of gender are treated in our language. Feminists have sensitized the public to the peculiar properties of terms like "chairman" and "man" used to refer to the entire species.[1] Here we shall discuss patterns that emerge in the way the English language treats women and concepts of gender.

Male as normative One of the clearest patterns in our language is the normativeness of the male, a concept discussed in Chapter 2. The male is regarded as the normative (standard) member of the species, and this is expressed in many ways in language. These ways include the use of "man" to refer to all human beings, and the use of "he" for a neutral pronoun (as in the sentence "The infant typically begins to sit up around six months

---

[1] Someone once commented cutely that feminists have a bad case of "pronoun envy." (Key, 1975)

of age; he may begin crawling at about the same time"). The male-as-normative principle in language can lead to some absolutely absurd statements. For example, there is a state law that reads "No person may require another person to perform, participate in, or undergo an abortion of pregnancy against his will" (Key, 1975).

Sometimes students in their essays mistakenly use the phrase "the male species" (the expression they really mean to use is "the male of the species"). But in a way they are expressing the principle well — the male is the species.

At the very least, the male-as-normative usage introduces ambiguity into our language (Beard, 1946). When someone uses the word "men," does *he* mean males, or does he mean people in general? When Dr. Karl Menninger writes a book entitled *Man Against Himself*, is it a book about people generally, or is it a book about the tensions experienced by males?

Some people excuse such usage by saying that terms like "man" are generic. Such an explanation, however, is not adequate. To illustrate how weak the "generic" logic is, consider the objections raised by some men who have recently joined the League of Women Voters. They have complained that the name of the organization should be changed, for it no longer adequately describes its members, some of whom are now men. Suppose in response to their objection they were told that by "woman," we mean "generic woman," which of course includes men. Do you think they would feel satisfied?

The male-as-normative principle is also reflected in the *female-as-the-exception* phenomenon. Recently a newspaper reported the results of the Bowling Green State University women's swimming team and men's swimming team in two articles close to each other. The headline reporting the men's results was "BG swimmers defeated." The one for the women was "BG women swimmers win." As another example, suppose a male doctor discovers a vaccine for cancer. The headline might read "Doctor discovers cancer vaccine." But if the doctor happens to be female, the headline would likely be "Woman doctor discovers cancer vaccine." The point is that we consider athletes and prestigious professionals to be normatively male. In cases where they are female it seems important to note this as an exception.

Parallel words   Another interesting phenomenon in our language is how parallel words for males and females often have quite different connotations (Lakoff, 1973; Key, 1975; Schulz, 1975). For example, consider the following list of parallel male and female words:

Male	*Female*
bachelor	spinster
dog	bitch
master	mistress

Note that the female forms of the words generally have negative connotations; a bachelor is viewed as a carefree, happy person, while a spinster is the object of pity. Also note that the negative connotation to the female words is often sexual in nature. For example, a man who is a master is good at what he does or is powerful, but a woman who is a mistress is someone who is financially supported in return for her sexual services. Another example would be the sentences "He's a professional" and "She's a professional." The former implies that the man is a doctor or lawyer or very good at what he does, while the latter suggests that the woman is a prostitute.

Of course, many of these parallel words originally had equivalent meanings for male and female. An example is *master* and *mistress*, terms originally used to refer to the male and female heads of the household. Over time, however, the female term took on negative connotations, a process known as *pejoration*. Linguist Muriel Schulz (1975) has argued that this process is caused simply by prejudice. That is, terms applied to women take on negative meanings because of prejudice against women (see also Allport, 1954).

Euphemisms   Generally when there are many euphemisms for a word, it is a reflection of the fact that people find the word and what it stands for to be distasteful or stressful (Schulz, 1975). For example, consider all the various terms we use instead of "bathroom" or "toilet." And then there is the great variety of terms such as "pass away" that we substitute for "die."

Feminist linguists have argued that we similarly have a strong tendency to use euphemisms for the word "woman" (Lakoff, 1973; Schulz, 1975). That is, people have a tendency to avoid using the word "woman," and instead substitute a variety of terms that seem more "polite" or less threatening, the most common euphemisms being "lady" and "girl." In contrast to the word "man," which is used quite frequently and comfortably, "woman" is used less frequently and apparently causes some discomfort or we wouldn't use euphemisms for it.

Infantilizing   A 25-year-old man wrote to an advice columnist, depressed because he wanted to get married but had never had a date. Part of the columnist's response was

> Just scan the society pages and look at the people who are getting married every day. Are the men all handsome? Are the girls all beautiful?

This is an illustration of the way in which people, rather than using "woman" as the parallel to "man," substitute "girl" instead. As we noted in the previous section, this in part reflects the use of a euphemism. But it is also true that "boy" refers to young males, "man" to adult males. Somehow "girl," which in a strict sense should refer only to young females, is used for adult women as well. Women are called by a term that seems to make them less mature than they are; women are thus *infantilized* in language. Just as the term "boy" became very offensive to black activists, so "girl" has become offensive to feminists.

There are many other illustrations of this infantilizing theme. When a ship sinks, it's "Women and children first," putting women and children in the same category. Other examples in language are expressions for women such as "baby," "babe," and "chick." The problem with these terms is that they carry a meaning of immaturity and perhaps irresponsibility.

How important is all of this?   Although many of the tenets of the women's movement — such as equal pay for equal work — have gained widespread acceptance, the importance of changing our language to eliminate sexism has not. Many people tend to regard these issues as silly or trivial. Just how important is the issue of sexism in language? (For a review, see Blaubergs, 1978.)

It is true that language reflects thought processes. This being the case, sexism in language may be the symptom, not the disease (Lakoff, 1973). That is, things like the generic use of "man" and "he" may simply reflect the fact that we do think of the male as the norm for the species. The practical conclusion from this is that what needs to be changed is our thought processes, and once they change, language will change with them.

On the other hand, one of the classic theories of psycholinguistics, the Whorfian hypothesis (Whorf, 1956), states that the specific language we learn influences our mental processes. If that is true, then things like the generic use of "man" make us think that the male is normative. This process might start with very young children when they are just beginning to learn the language. If such processes do occur, then social reformers need to pay careful attention to eliminate sexism in language because of its effect on our thought processes.

An important study demonstrated that, even when "he" and "his" are used in explicitly gender-neutral contexts, people tend to think of males (Moulton et al., 1978). College students were asked to make up stories creating a fictional character who would fit the theme of a stimulus sentence. The students were divided into six groups; for three of the groups, the stimulus sentence was

> In a large coeducational institution the average student will feel isolated in —— introductory courses.

One of the groups received *his* in the blank space, another received *their*, and the third received *his or her*. Another three groups received one of those alternative pronouns in the stimulus sentence:

> Most people are concerned with appearance. Each person knows when —— appearance is unattractive.

Averaging the responses of all groups, when the pronoun was "his," only 35 percent of the stories were about females; for "their," 46 percent were about females, and for "his or her" 56 percent were about females. Females were chosen as characters more often for the second stimulus sentence (concerned about appearance) than for the first. But the important point is that, even though a sentence referred to "the average student," when "his" was used most people thought of males. Though a linguist may say that "he" and "his" are gender-neutral, they are certainly not gender-neutral in a psychological sense. It seems likely that both processes — thought influencing language and language influencing thought — occur to some extent. Insofar as language does have the potential for influencing our thinking, sexism in language becomes a critical issue (e.g., Martyna, 1979; Moulton et al., 1978).

I became interested in a related question raised earlier — namely, the effect of sexist language on children — and so I began a series of studies to investigate the question (Hyde, 1984a). First, I generated an age-appropriate sentence like the one used by Moulton et al. and asked first-, third-, and fifth-grade children to tell stories in response to it:

When a kid goes to school, —— often feels excited on the first day.

As in the Moulton et al. study, one-third of the children received "he" for the blank, one-third received "they," and one-third received "he or she." The results were even more dramatic than those of Moulton et al. with college students. When the pronoun was "he," only 12 percent of the stories were about females. In fact, when the pronoun was "he," not a single elementary school boy told a story about a girl. It is clear, then, that when children hear "he" in a gender-neutral context, they think of a male. I also asked the children some questions to see if they understood the grammatical rule that "he" in certain contexts refers to everyone, both males and females. Few understood the rule; for example, only 28 percent of the first-graders gave answers showing that they knew the rule.

I also had the children fill in the blanks in some sentences such as the following:

If a kid likes candy, —— might eat too much.

The children overwhelmingly supplied "he" for the blank; even 72 percent of the first-graders did so.

Therefore, this research shows two things. First, the majority of elementary school children have learned to supply "he" in gender-neutral contexts (as evidenced by the fill-in task). Second, the majority of elementary school children do not know the rule that "he" in gender-neutral contexts refers to both males and females and have a strong tendency to think of males in creating stories from neutral "he" cues. For them, then, the chain of concepts is as follows: (1) the typical person is a "he"; (2) "he" refers only to males. Logically, then, might they not conclude that (3) the typical person is a male?

In previous chapters we have seen that girls have less self-confidence and lower expectations for success than boys do. I wonder whether part of that is due to language and the sort of thinking by children outlined above. Further research will be needed to test this speculation.

In a final task, I created a fictitious, gender-neutral occupation, wudge-maker.

> Few people have heard of a job in factories, being a wudgemaker. Wudges are made of plastic, oddly shaped, and are an important part of video games. The wudgemaker works from a plan or pattern posted at eye level as —— puts together the pieces at a table while —— is sitting down. Eleven plastic pieces must be snapped together. Some of the pieces are tiny, so that —— must have good coordination in —— fingers. Once all eleven pieces are put together, —— must test out the wudge to make sure that all of the moving pieces move properly. The wudgemaker is well paid, and must be a high school graduate, but —— does not have to have gone to college to get the job.

One-quarter of the subjects received "he" in all the blanks, one-quarter received "they," one-quarter received "he or she," and one quarter received "she." I then asked the children to rate how well a woman could do the job on a three-point scale: 3 for very well, 2 for just okay, and 1 for not very well. Next, I asked the children how well a man could do the job, giving ratings on the same scale. The results are shown in Figure 9.3. Which pronoun the children were given didn't seem to affect their ratings of men as wudgemakers, but the pronoun had a big effect on how women were rated as wudgemakers. Notice in the graph that when the pronoun "he" was used, women were rated at the middle of the scale, or just okay. The ratings of women rose for pronouns "they" and "he or she," and finally were close to the top of the scale when subjects heard the wudgemaker described as "she." These results, then, demonstrate that pronoun choice does have an effect on the concepts children form; in particular, children who heard "he" in the job description thought that women were significantly less competent at the job than children who heard other pronouns.

In answer to the original question of whether this pronoun business is really important, I think it is. We need to be concerned about the effects that sexist pronoun usage has on children; my research demonstrates that it can affect the concepts children form of occupations, and I think there is also reason for concern about its effect on broader issues such as girls' self-confidence.

One final bold experiment deserves discussion. In order to see what happens when pronoun usage changes away from the traditional sexist use of "he," a psychologist used "she" as the generic pronoun with two of her child development classes, and compared the student responses to those in a class in which she did not follow this practice (Adamsky, 1981).

FIGURE 9.3

Children's ratings of the competence of women and men as wudgemakers, as a function of the pronoun they heard repeatedly in the description of the wudge-maker. Women are rated as having only medium competence when the pronoun is "he," but their ratings rise for "they" and "he or she." When "she" is used in the description, women are rated near the top of the scale.

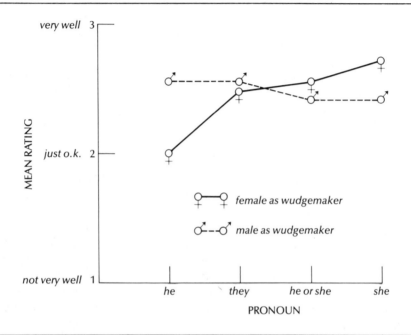

Source: Mean Rating Graph by Janet Hyde (in press). *Developmental Psychology.* Copyright 1984 by the American Psychological Association. Reprinted by permission of the author.

Strikingly, students in the experimental group started using the generic "she" in their written essays. Although many people think that the sexist usage of pronouns in English cannot be changed, this study demonstrates strikingly that it can be changed. Here are some student responses (all are from female students) to the use of generic "she"

> Once I started using the "she" I found it hard to stop. I liked using the generic "she" — it gave me a sense of equality — power even.
>
> I felt surprisingly proud when I used it.
>
> I could picture a female in roles so often pictured as strictly male. (Adam-sky, 1981, pp. 777–778)

You might try using "she" as the generic form for a day and try to analyze the reactions, both in yourself and in others. It's a wonderful conscious-ness-raising device.

SOME PRACTICAL SUGGESTIONS

Some people believe in theory that it would be a good idea to eliminate sexism from language, but in practice they find themselves having difficulty doing this in their speaking or writing. Here we shall discuss some practical suggestions for avoiding sexist language (for reviews, see Blaubergs, 1978; Miller and Swift, 1977) and for dealing with some other relevant situations.

Toward nonsexist language   The use of generic masculine forms is probably the most widespread and difficult problem of sexist language. The following are some ways to eliminate or avoid these usages.

One possibility is to switch from the singular to the plural, because plural pronouns do not signify gender. Therefore, the generic masculine in (1) can be modified as in (2):

1. When a doctor prescribes birth control pills, he should first inquire whether the patient has a history of blood clotting problems.
2. When doctors prescribe birth control pills, they should first inquire whether the patient has a history of blood clotting problems.

Another possibility is to reword the sentence so that there is no necessity for a pronoun, as in

3. A doctor prescribing birth control pills should first inquire whether the patient has a history of blood clotting problems.

One of the simplest solutions is to use "he or she" instead of the generic "he," "him or her" instead of "him," and so on. Therefore, the generic masculine in (1) can be modified to

4. When a doctor prescribes birth control pills, he or she should first inquire whether the patient has a history of blood clotting problems.

Many feminist scholars, however, believe that the order should be varied, so that "he or she" and "she or he" appear with equal frequency. If "he or she" is the only form that is used, women still end up second! One final possibility is the singular use of "they" and "their." For years people have been saying sentences like "Will everyone pick up their pencil?' and English teachers have been correcting them, saying that the correct form is "Will everyone pick up his pencil?" Since it is so natural to use the plural in this situation, and to do so eliminates the sexism, why not go ahead and do it?

With a little practice, these strategies can be used to eliminate the generic masculine.

Space does not permit a complete discussion of all possible practical problems that may arise in trying to avoid sexist language. Usually a little thought and imagination can solve most problems. For example, the salutation in a letter, "Dear Sir," can easily be changed to "Dear Madam or Sir," or "Dear Sir or Madam," or simply "To Whom It May Concern." The tendency to use euphemisms for "woman" can be changed by becoming sensitive to this tendency and making efforts to use the word "woman."

One other solution to the problem of generic masculine pronouns should also be mentioned — namely, the creation of some new singular pronouns that are gender-neutral. Unfortunately, at least ten alternatives for these new pronouns have been proposed, confusing the situation somewhat (Blaubergs, 1978). One set that has been proposed is "tey" for he or she, "tem" for him or her, and "ter" for his or her. Thus one might say, "The scientist pursues ter work; tey reads avidly and strives to overcome obstacles that beset tem." Entire books have been written with this usage (e.g., Sherman, 1978). Although in an ideal sense these new pronouns have a great deal of merit, they do not seem to be catching on. Probably they would need to be adopted by a number of respected, widely-circulated sources in order to find their way into the ordinary person's language. If the *New York Times*, the *Washington Post*, *Time*, *Newsweek*, Dan Rather, and the President all started using "ter," "tey," and "tem," they would probably have a chance. Such widespread adoption does not seem to be a very immediate possibility, however.

This brings us to the topic of institutional change in language use.

Institutional change   It is encouraging to note that a number of institutions have committed themselves to using and encouraging nonsexist language. For example, several textbook publishers have issued guidelines for nonsexist language and refuse to publish books that include sexisms (e.g., McGraw-Hill Book Company in 1974; Scott, Foresman and Company in 1972). The American Psychological Association has guidelines for the use of nonsexist language in articles in the journals it publishes (APA, 1975). These are all good sources for the reader wanting more detail on how to eliminate sexist language.

Many occupational titles, particularly in government agencies, have also changed. For those who worry about the linguistic properties of nonsexist language, it is worth noting that some of the changes introduce definite improvements. For example, "firemen" has been changed to "fire fighters." In addition to being nonsexist, the newer term makes more sense, since what the people do is fight fires, not start them, as one might infer from the older term.

Language, women, and careers   The discussion of gender differences in language use in the first part of the chapter raises an important practical question for women aspiring to careers in male-dominated occupations such as business. From the data presented in that part of the chapter, it seems reasonable to conclude, at least tentatively, that the average woman has some language characteristics that suggest that she is uncertain of herself or lacking in confidence. These are certainly not qualities that help one get ahead in the business world. Should women attempt to modify their language on the job, much as blacks speak standard English when the situation calls for it? And how should women modify their language?

One possibility is for women to become conscious of their "feminine" speech patterns, to eliminate them and substitute "masculine" ones. Women could stop using tag questions and high tones and start interrupting more. Although I have no data on the point, it is my opinion that this approach would probably not work very well, simply because many people feel threatened by "masculine" women. This approach also adopts male values and assumes that the male should be the norm.

As an alternative, I would suggest that women try to achieve androgynous speech — or perhaps a better term is nonstereotyped speech — that is, speech that has both the desirable qualities of "feminine" speech and the desirable qualities of "masculine" speech. Such speech would convey confidence and forcefulness together with a concern for the feelings of others. Such a combination of qualities should contribute to success in many careers.

SUGGESTION FOR FURTHER READING

Miller, Casey & Swift, Kate (1977). *Words and women: New language in new times.* New York: Doubleday (Anchor Books paperback). The authors, both professional journalists, have done an excellent job in this readable and thought-provoking review of the feminist critique of sexist language issues.

10
Biological Influences on Women's Behavior

GENES ◆

SEX HORMONES ◆

THE BRAIN ◆

> . . . *an extraordinarily important part of the brain necessary for spiritual life, the frontal convolutions and the temporal lobes are less well developed in women and this difference is inborn. . . . If we wish a woman to fulfill her task of motherhood fully, she cannot possess a masculine brain. If the feminine abilities were developed to the same degree as those of the male, her maternal organs would suffer, and we should have before us a repulsive and useless hybrid.*
>
> MOEBIUS, Concerning the Physiological
> Intellectual Feebleness of Women, 1907

Traditionally it was believed that psychological differences between females and males were created by biological differences. It was also popularly thought that biological influences were particularly potent forces on women's behavior. The turn-of-the-century psychologist quoted at the opening of this chapter believed that male and female brains differed and that the female brain was defective. Women are also thought to be the victims of their "raging hormones." In this chapter we shall examine the evidence on whether biological gender differences create psychological gender differences, and on whether women's behavior is controlled by biological forces.

The biological factors that may influence women and gender differences fall into three major categories: genetic factors, sex hormones, and brain differences.

GENES

Normal humans possess a set of 46 chromosomes. Because chromosomes occur in pairs, there are 23 pairs, classified as 22 pairs of autosomes (nonsex chromosomes) and one pair of sex chromosomes. The female has a sex chromosome pair denoted XX, while the male sex chromosome pair is XY. Therefore, there are no genetic differences between males and females except for the sex chromosomes.

Traits that are controlled by genes on the sex chromosomes are called *sex-linked traits* (for an excellent explanation of sex-linked genetic effects as related to the psychology of women, see Wittig, 1979). For such traits, the female will have a pair of genes controlling a particular sex-linked trait, but a male will have only one gene for that trait, because he has only one X chromosome. (The function of the Y chromosome and the functions of any genes on it are not yet well understood by geneticists; for our purposes, the Y chromosome can be considered genetically inert.) Sex linkage is a source of gender differences when one form of a gene (*allele*) is dominant or recessive to the other possible allele, as in the example of blue eyes (b) recessive to brown eyes (B). Normally, to manifest a recessive trait, both alleles must be recessive, while the dominant trait is manifested if both members of the pair are dominant, or one dominant and one recessive. However, for genes on the X chromosome, a male will have only one allele, and will therefore manifest the recessive if the one allele present is recessive. The female, of course, with two X's, needs two recessives to manifest the recessive trait. Thus if a trait is sex-linked recessive, it will be manifested more frequently by males than by females. A good example is color blindness.

This basic genetic gender difference is thought to be a source of the biological resiliency of the female compared with the male (for a popularized discussion, see Montagu, 1952). Women are known to be generally less susceptible to disease than men. Some sources of this difference are sex-linked recessive genetic diseases, such as hemophilia. Most diseases or other harmful genetic effects are recessive, while beneficial effects are generally dominant (the biological utility of this system is apparent). As stated above, it is easier for a man to manifest a sex-linked recessive trait, since he needs only one recessive gene, while a woman needs two recessives. Therefore, men are more likely than women to be affected by sex-linked recessive defects such as hemophilia and color blindness.

Except for color vision, there is no behavior for which there is good evidence of sex-linked genetic influence. There was some early evidence that spatial visualizing ability was influenced by an X-linked gene (Stafford, 1961; Hartlage, 1970; Bock and Kolakowski, 1973; Yen, 1975). However, later studies using larger samples failed to find evidence for this (Bouchard and McGee, 1977; DeFries et al., 1976).

One other important function of the sex chromosomes is to direct the course of prenatal gender differentiation. In doing this, they interact with hormones. This brings us to a second biological factor that may influence gender differences.

SEX HORMONES

Hormones are powerful chemical substances manufactured by the various endocrine glands of the body. Endocrine glands secrete hormones into the bloodstream so that they can have effects throughout the body, including effects on target organs far from the endocrine gland that secreted them. Among the endocrine glands are the gonads (ovaries and testes), pancreatic islets, pituitary, thyroid, and adrenal glands.

The "male" sex hormone is called *testosterone*. It is one of a group of "male" hormones called androgens, which are manufactured by the testes. The "female" sex hormones are *estrogen* and *progesterone*, which are manufactured by the ovaries. If these hormones influence behavior, then they may create gender differences.

Actually, it is a mistake to call testosterone the "male" sex hormone and estrogen and progesterone "female" hormones. Testosterone, for example, is found in females as well as males. The difference is in amount, not presence or absence. In women, testosterone is manufactured by the adrenal glands, and the level in women's blood is about one-sixth that in men's (Salhanick and Margulis, 1968).

The differences in levels of sex hormones may affect behavior at two major stages of development: prenatally (the time between conception and birth), and during and after puberty (adulthood). Endocrinologists refer to the effects that occur prenatally as *organizing effects* because they cause a relatively permanent effect in the organization of some structure, whether in the nervous system or the reproductive system. Hormone effects in adulthood are called *activating effects* because they activate or deactivate certain behaviors. In order to understand the prenatal effects, it will be helpful to discuss the process of prenatal gender differentiation first.

Prenatal gender differentiation At the moment of conception, there are gender differences. If the fertilized egg contains two X chromosomes, then the genetic gender of the individual is female; if it contains one X and one Y chromosome, the genetic gender is male. The single cell then divides repeatedly, becoming an embryo, then a fetus. Interestingly, during the first two months of human prenatal development, it appears that the only differences between females and males are in genetic gender. That is, anatomically and physiologically males and females develop identically during this period. Beginning approximately during the third month of pregnancy, and continuing through about the sixth month, the process of prenatal gender differentiation occurs (for an extended discussion, see Money and Ehrhardt, 1972). First, the sex chromosomes direct the differentiation of the primary sex characteristics, or gonads (see Figure 10.1). An XX chromosome complement directs the differentiation of ovaries; an XY complement produces testes. The gonads then have the important function of secreting sex hormones. Thus the fetal internal environment or physiology becomes different for females and males because of endocrine differences.

The sex hormones further affect the course of fetal differentiation. In particular, the male testes produce testosterone. The presence or absence of testosterone seems to be the critical factor determining the direction of further differentiation. If testosterone is present, the male penis forms. If testosterone is not present (or present only in small amounts), a clitoris and vagina differentiate. In addition to influencing the process of anatomical gender differentiation, the sex hormones also influence the developing brain. The structure most affected seems to be the hypothalamus. The importance of this differentiation will be discussed later in the chapter.

FIGURE 10.1

The sequences of prenatal differentiation of females and males.

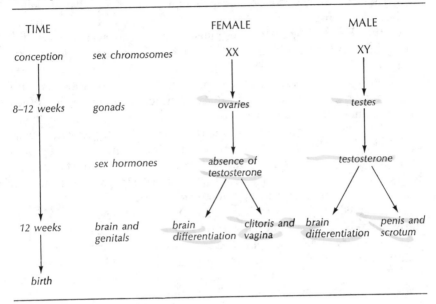

Prenatal sex hormone effects Male fetuses and female fetuses, then, live in different hormonal environments. Does this have any effect on their later behaviors?

Most of the evidence in this area is based on experiments done with animals. It may be that the effects on humans would not be the same. But let us consider the animal experiments, and then see what is known about similar processes in humans. (For a review, see Ehrhardt and Meyer-Bahlburg, 1981.)

Prenatal sex hormone exposure seems to affect mainly two behaviors: sexual behavior and aggressive behavior. The organizing effects of sex hormones on sexual behavior have been well documented. In a classic experiment, testosterone was administered to pregnant female guinea pigs (Phoenix et al., 1959). The female offspring that had been exposed to testosterone prenatally were, in adulthood, incapable of displaying female sexual behavior (in particular, lordosis, which is a sexual posturing involving arching of the back and raising the hindquarters so that the male can insert the penis). It is thought that this occurred because the testosterone "organized" the brain tissue (particularly the hypothalamus) in a male fashion. These female offspring were also born with masculinized genitals, and thus their reproductive systems had also been organized in the male direction. But the important point here is that the prenatal doses of testosterone had masculinized their sexual behavior. Similar results have been obtained in experiments with many other species as well.

In adulthood, these hormonally masculinized females displayed mounting behavior, a male sexual behavior. When they were given testosterone in adulthood, they showed about as much mounting behavior as males did. Thus the testosterone administered in adulthood *activated* male patterns of sexual behavior.

The analogous experiment on males would be castration at birth followed by administration of female sex hormones in adulthood. When this was done with rats, female sexual behavior resulted. These male rats responded to mating attempts from normal males the way females usually do (Harris and Levine, 1965). Apparently the brain tissue had been organized in a female direction during an early critical period when testosterone was absent, and the female behavior patterns were activated in adulthood by administration of ovarian hormones.

Similar effects have also been demonstrated for aggressive behavior. Early exposure to testosterone increases the fighting behavior of female mice (Edwards, 1969). Female rhesus monkeys given early exposure to testosterone show a higher incidence of rough-and-tumble play (Young et al., 1964). Thus it appears that early exposure to testosterone also organizes aggressive behavior in a "masculine" direction.

What relevance do these studies have for humans? (For a review, see Hines, 1982.) Generally, the trend is for hormones to have stronger effects on lower species, and less effect on humans (Beach, 1947). It would be unethical, of course, to do experiments like the ones mentioned above on human subjects. Nonetheless, a number of "accidental" experiments of this sort have occurred when pregnant women were given drugs containing hormones. The offspring of these women have been studied in detail by psychologist John Money and his colleagues. Money has concentrated particularly on the gender identity these individuals develop.

Biology and gender identity   Gender identity — the knowledge that one is a male or a female, and the integration of this fact into one's personal identity — is a very basic psychological characteristic. Is gender identity biologically determined (by chromosomes, by hormones, or by anatomical sex characteristics), or is it modifiable by environment?

On the basis of a long program of research, Money, Hampson, and Hampson conclude that the acquisition of gender role and of basic gender identity is dependent upon the environment (Money, 1961, 1970; Money and Ehrhardt, 1972; Hampson, 1965). Many of their data come from individuals with anatomical incongruities leading to contradictions among their various sexual characteristics.

In order to discuss gender identity, it is important first to understand the distinctions among the six variables of gender: (1) chromosomal gender (XX in the female versus XY in the male); (2) gonadal gender (ovaries versus testes); (3) hormonal gender (estrogen and progesterone versus testosterone); (4) internal accessory organs (uterus and vagina versus prostate and seminal vesicles); (5) external genital appearance (clitoris and vaginal opening versus penis and scrotum); and (6) assigned gender ("It's a girl!" or "It's a boy!") and gender role. Normally, of course, all of these variables are in agreement, apparently indicating that chromosomal gender determines gender identity. That is, normally the female's XX chromosome complement causes differentiation of the ovaries during fetal development (actually, it is not the presence of XX, but the absence of a Y chromosome that causes this), and the ovaries produce the appropriate female hormones, which cause further feminine differentiation of the internal accessory organs and external genitalia. The appearance of the external genitalia determines the gender assignment — the announcement "It's a girl!" — which then leads to rearing as a female.

However, a number of "accidents" during the course of development may result in the gender indicated by one or more of these variables disagreeing with the gender indicated by the others. In these cases, the gender of assignment and rearing may or may not correspond to the genetic gender, but the child seems to accept the assigned gender and to develop successfully in it. Hence, Money, Hampson, and Hampson (1955) conclude that gender identity is learned as a result of environmental factors.

One sort of individual they have studied is the *pseudohermaphrodite*, in whom there is a contradiction between external genital appearance and one of the other biological gender variables (genetic gender, gonads, hormones, or internal reproductive structures). In genetic females, this often results from a condition known as the *adrenogenital syndrome*. These females as fetuses develop ovaries normally, but during the course of prenatal development, the adrenal gland begins to function abnormally (as the result of a recessive genetic condition) and excess amounts of androgens are produced. Prenatal sexual differentiation does not follow the normal course. As a result, the external genitalia are partly or completely male in appearance — the labia are partly or totally fused, and the clitoris is enlarged to the size of a small penis. Hence, at birth, these genetic females are identified as being males.

Money and Ehrhardt (1972) cited one case of a matched pair of these individuals. Both were diagnosed as males at birth. One was from that time on reared as a male. He developed normally as a male, functioned normally in groups of boys, had outdoor, athletic, and sporting interests, and easily accepted the stereotype of the male role in marriage. The other child, because of further medical problems, returned for treatment and was at that time correctly rediagnosed as a female. Her external genitals were feminized surgically, and the internal reproductive structures were already feminine. She was reared as a female, and managed fairly successfully to adopt the female role, although she did have tendencies toward what Money calls "tomboyism." Despite identical genetic gender and geni-

FIGURE 10.2

A matched pair of individuals who are genetic females born with adrenogenital syndrome. The one on the right was reared as a female, with hormonal treatments and surgical treatment of her genitals. The one on the left was reared as a male, with hormonal treatments; no genital surgery was necessary. The one on the right has a female gender identity; the one on the left has a male gender identity.

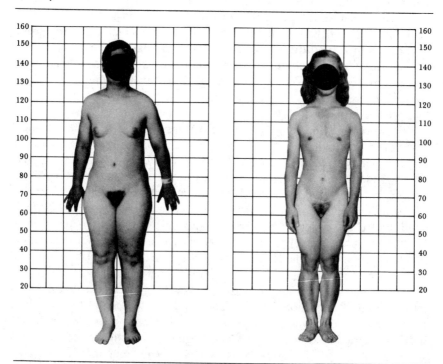

Source: Man & Woman, Boy & Girl by John Money & Anke A. Ehrhardt, Johns Hopkins University Press.

tals, these individuals could become either males or females, depending on the gender of the assignment and rearing.

Hampson says:

> Psychologic sex or gender role appears to be learned, that is to say, it is differentiated through learning during the course of the many experiences of growing up. In place of a theory of innate constitutional psychologic bisexuality we can substitute a concept of psychosexual neutrality in humans at birth. Such neutrality permits the development and perpetuation of many patterns of psychosexual orientation and functioning in accordance with the life experiences each individual may encounter and transact. (1965, p. 125)

The position of "psychosexual neutrality" argues that, from the time of gender assignment (in accordance with external genitalia), maleness or femaleness is continually reinforced. Gender identity may result solely from environmental contingencies, although certainly biological factors make some outcomes more likely.

An important related finding is that there appears to be a critical period for gender assignment and for the formation of gender identity. Up until the age of about 18 months, the child's gender may be almost arbitrarily reassigned, as in the case of the pseudohermaphrodite, and the child will accept the new gender and develop normally in it. Reassignment after that age can lead to serious conflicts in the child, and normal development in the new gender is unlikely. Note that this is in agreement with the view of cognitive-developmental theory (Chapter 3), which asserts that the formation of gender identity occurs at about the age of three years, and that this becomes a permanent lifelong concept.

The position espoused by Money and the Hampsons of psychosexual neutrality at birth and the immense importance of the environment in the formation of gender identity has not been accepted without challenge (e.g., Diamond, 1965, 1979; Rogers and Walsh, 1982). First, it should be noted that in almost all the cases given as evidence, sex reassignment was supplemented by appropriate surgical or hormonal therapy. That is, the individual's biological characteristics were modified to correspond to the assigned gender. Hence, it is not reasonable to say that gender could be assigned independent of biological gender characteristics. In fact, the very success of the reassignment often depends on the proper anatomical and hormonal modifications. Second, there are often traces of behaviors that are opposite to the behavior of gender of rearing. For example, born and raised as males, five patients showed interest during childhood only in activities typically characteristic of girls. A sixth patient, born and raised as a female, always showed masculine tendencies. All possessed genitalia normal to the assigned gender, and had no apparent physical defects, until adolescence, when they developed secondary sex characteristics normal for the opposite gender (Baker and Stoller, 1967). It appears that the pubertal cross-gender body change in effect agreed with their earlier gender wishes. One can therefore cite cases that contradict the rule that postnatal environmental forces determine gender identity. Finally, it is difficult to know how relevant the abnormal cases studied by Money are to understanding the normal process of acquiring a gender identity.

Nonetheless, Money's data do provide impressive evidence of the extent to which gender identity is a product of environmental forces.

Hormone effects in adulthood   The effects of sex hormones in adulthood that are of interest to us fall into two categories. First, sex hormone levels in women fluctuate over the menstrual cycle. This raises the question of whether these hormone fluctuations would cause fluctuations in mood or other psychological characteristics. This topic will be discussed in detail in Chapter 11. Second, levels of sex hormones differ in men and women. For example, as noted earlier, women have only about one-sixth the level of testosterone in the blood that men do. Could it be that these different levels of hormones "activate" different behaviors in men and women?

As noted above, studies done with animals indicate that sex hormones administered in adulthood may have effects on both aggressive behavior and sexual behavior. Once again, however, less information is available and the results are more mixed as to whether there are similar effects on humans (for a review, see Rubin et al., 1981). Several studies have shown increased sex drive in women as a result of the administration of testosterone (reviewed by Kane et al., 1969). A study of eighteen young men indicated that there was a significant correlation between testosterone production rate and a measure of hostility and aggression (Persky et al., 1971). Another recent study looked at testosterone levels existing in husbands and wives in relation to their sexual behavior (Persky et al., 1978). Intercourse frequency was not related to either partner's average testosterone levels, but it was related to wives' testosterone levels at their ovulatory peaks. The wives' self-rated sexual gratification also correlated significantly with their own plasma testosterone levels.

Probably sex hormone levels do have some effects on adult human behaviors, particularly aggressive and sexual behaviors. It is also likely that these effects are not so strong as they are in animals, and that they are more complex and interact more with environmental factors.

THE BRAIN

Although the quote at the beginning of this chapter may seem quaintly sexist, there are some differences between human male and female brains (MacLusky and Naftolin, 1981; Money and Ehrhardt, 1972). These differences are in two major areas: the hypothalamus, and the organization of the left and right hemispheres.

The hypothalamus Gender differences in the hypothalamus seem to be the result of differentiation of brain tissue in the course of fetal development, much as is the case for the reproductive organs (see Figure 10.1). Recall that the sequence of normal development consists of the sex chromosomes directing the differentiation of gonadal tissue into ovaries or testes. The gonads then secrete appropriate-gender hormones, which cause further reproductive-system differentiation. The fetal gonadal hormones also cause appropriate-gender differentiation of the hypothalamus.

Basically, then, brain differentiation in the fetus is a process much like reproductive-system differentiation. Earlier researchers believed that the embryo began with no differentiation on the basis of gender and therefore humans were inherently bisexual. It now appears to be more accurate to say that nature's primary impulse is to create a female. That is, if no additional forces intervene, female development occurs. The critical variable is the presence or absence of testosterone. If it is present, male characteristics develop; if absent, female characteristics. Thus it seems that, biologically, the female is normative! The male is a variant created by the addition of testosterone.

It appears that one of the most important organizing effects of prenatal sex hormones is the determination of the estrogen-sensitivity of certain cells in the hypothalamus (for a review, see Taleisnik et al., 1971). Once again, it is the presence or absence of testosterone that is critical. If testosterone is present during fetal development, certain specialized receptor cells in the hypothalamus become insensitive to estrogen; if no testosterone is present, these cells are highly sensitive to levels of estrogen in the bloodstream. This is important because of the hypothalamic-pituitary-gonadal regulating feedback loop (see Chapter 11). In this process, gonadal hormone output is regulated by the pituitary, which is in turn regulated by the hypothalamus. The hypothalamus responds to the level of gonadal hormones in the bloodstream. Male hypothalamic cells are relatively insensitive to estrogen levels, whereas female hypothalamic cells are highly sensitive to them. We also know that estrogen (and progesterone as well) lowers the threshold of central nervous system (CNS) excitability in adults. Hence, the estrogen-sensitivity effect in the female amounts to a much greater increase in CNS excitability in response to estrogen than in the male. The estrogen-sensitivity effect is a result of the organizing effect of hormones. Hormones administered in adulthood activate male and female nervous systems differentially depending on prenatal determination (organizing effects) of estrogen sensitivity.

What are the observable consequences of these gender differences in the hypothalamus? One consequence is the determination of a cyclic or acyclic pattern of pituitary release of hormones (e.g., Barraclough and Gorski, 1961). The hypothalamus directs pituitary hormone secretion. It appears that a hypothalamus that has undergone female differentiation will direct the pituitary to release hormones cyclically, creating a menstrual cycle, whereas a male hypothalamus directs a relatively steady production of pituitary hormones.

The gender differences in the hypothalamus may have some consequences for behavior, too, although these have not been well documented in humans (for a review, see Reinisch, 1974). As discussed earlier, the organization of the hypothalamus in a male or female direction may have some influence on both sexual and aggressive behavior.

Right hemisphere, left hemisphere   The brain is divided into two halves, a right hemisphere and a left hemisphere. It is thought that these two hemispheres carry out somewhat different functions. In particular, in right-handed, normal persons, the left hemisphere seems specialized for verbal tasks, and the right hemisphere for spatial tasks. The term *lateralization* usually refers to the extent to which a particular function, say verbal processing, is handled by one hemisphere rather than both. Thus, for example, if verbal processing in one person is handled entirely in the left hemisphere, we would say that that person is highly lateralized or completely lateralized. If another person processes verbal material using both hemispheres, we would say that that person is bilateral for verbal functioning.

Brain lateralization research is a very active, exciting area in psychological research at the moment. Because there are gender differences in both verbal ability and spatial ability (see Chapter 8), it is not surprising that various theories have been proposed using gender differences in brain lateralization to account for the observed differences in abilities. We shall review these theories and the evidence for them below (for a detailed review, see Sherman, 1978).

The *Buffery and Gray hypothesis* (1972) is that the left hemisphere becomes dominant for verbal functions earlier in girls, leading to less bilateral processing of spatial information. Buffery and Gray believe that bilateral representation of spatial information causes better spatial performance, and so they argue that the lesser bilaterality of females for spatial processing explains their poorer spatial performance.

The *Levy hypothesis* (Levy, 1972; Levy-Agresti and Sperry, 1968) is that females are like left-handed males in that they are more likely to be bilateral for verbal functions. She further hypothesized that the best spatial and verbal performance occurs with the most lateralization of these functions. The bilaterality of verbal functioning in females would impair spatial functioning, so that females, like left-handed males, would have poorer spatial ability.

Interestingly, the Buffery and Gray hypothesis and the Levy hypothesis contradict each other — one assumes that more bilaterality means better performance, while the other assumes that less bilaterality causes better performance.

The *Harshman and Remington hypothesis* (1976, cited in Sherman, 1978) is that, because females mature earlier than males, at young ages females are more lateralized than males; but when males are fully mature, they are more lateralized than females, both for verbal and spatial functions. Harshman and Remington believe that this greater lateralization of spatial function leads to better spatial performance in males.

One kind of experiment that psychologists use to test hypotheses such as these is the *tachistoscope study*. A tachistoscope is an instrument that contains a viewer through which the subject looks at slides as the experimenter presents them. If the subject keeps her or his eyes fixated on a center focus point, stimuli can be presented to the right half of the visual field or to the left half. Stimuli presented to the right half of the visual field are transmitted to the left hemisphere. Thus if a subject is better at recognizing verbal stimuli presented in the right visual field than in the left, that person would be said to be left-hemisphere dominant for verbal functions.

On the basis of studies of this kind and others, the Buffery and Gray hypothesis can be rejected (Sherman, 1978). There is little evidence to support it, and other evidence that contradicts it. The Levy theory can be rejected for the same reasons. The Harshman and Remington hypothesis also has little evidence backing it, but because the evidence is more ambiguous, judgment on it should probably not be made as yet (Sherman, 1978).

You may be somewhat dismayed by such an inconclusive statement after discussing these theories. Brain lateralization is a very active area of research, and there are often flashy newspaper or magazine articles on a scientist who has discovered *the* cause of gender differences in abilities based on right-hemisphere/left-hemisphere differences. It is worthwhile for you to know the kinds of theories that have been proposed and the fact that there is contradicting evidence. When the next theory comes along, you should know that it needs to be evaluated carefully, and how one could go about testing it, for example by using tachistoscope studies. Such theories are also sometimes evaluated using clinical studies of brain-damaged people.

From a feminist point of view, it is interesting to note that all of these theories were constructed to explain the female *deficit* in spatial ability. None of them tries to account for female *superiority* in verbal ability. Perhaps the theories will become more adequate when they do so.

One other hypothesis that has been advanced is the *bent-twig hypothesis* (Sherman, 1971, 1978). It states that because of earlier maturation of verbal abilities, females come to rely more on verbal processing and left-hemisphere processing than males do. Because of this differential experience, when faced with spatial problems, girls do not do as well as boys do. Thus a slight biological difference in maturation rates is magnified by later experiences. More data will be needed to test this hypothesis.

In sum, there do seem to be some gender differences in the use of the hemispheres of the brain. In particular, there is evidence that females use the left hemisphere for spatial functions more than males do (Sherman, 1978). However, the exact differences and the effect these have on gender differences in abilities have yet to be untangled by research.

IN CONCLUSION

We have considered three major classes of biological influences on gender differences and women's behavior: genes, hormones, and brain factors. Genes are not likely to be sources of gender differences, except when the genes are on the X chromosome, as for traits such as color blindness.

Hormones have effects prenatally as well as in adulthood, particularly on sexual and aggressive behaviors, and possibly on behaviors related to the menstrual cycle. Regarding brain factors, gender differentiation of the hypothalamus in a female direction controls the cyclic functioning of the menstrual cycle and may be related to both aggressive and sexual behavior. Finally, there may be some gender differences in the functioning of the hemispheres of the brain, but the exact nature of these differences is not yet well known.

SUGGESTION FOR FURTHER READING

Gersh, Eileen S. & Gersh, I. (1981). *Biology of women.* Baltimore: University Park Press. Written by two biologists, this book is an authoritative, detailed source on biological gender differences.

11
Psychology and Women's Health Issues

> [*There is*] *an imperative need for women everywhere to learn about our bodies in order to have control over them and over our lives. We seek to communicate our excitement about the power of shared information; to assert that in an age of professionals, we are the best experts on ourselves and our feelings; to continue the collective struggle for adequate health care.*
>
> FROM Our Bodies, Ourselves

One of the most important parts of the feminist movement of the last decade has been the women's health movement. It is based on the belief that women need to know more about their bodies in order to have more control over them. One of the best books to come out of that movement is *Our Bodies, Ourselves*, written by the Boston Women's Health Book Collective (1976).

In this chapter we shall consider some of the topics that are important in the women's health movement — menstruation, menopause, pregnancy and childbirth, abortion, and mastectomy. I will give brief information on the physical and medical aspects of each of these topics, and concentrate on the psychological research that has been done on them.

MENSTRUATION

Biology of the menstrual cycle It is estimated that the human female is born with approximately 500,000 primary follicles in both ovaries, each follicle containing an egg or ovum. ("Follicle" here refers to a group of cells in the ovary that encapsulates an egg and has nothing to do with the term "hair follicle.") A single menstrual cycle involves the release of one egg from a follicle, allowing it to move down the oviduct (fallopian tube) for possible fertilization and implantation in the uterus. Hence not more than 400 eggs are ovulated from puberty through menopause. The remaining follicles degenerate.

It is important to note that the menstrual cycle occurs only among primates (monkeys, apes, and humans), and not in lower species. Many people mistakenly compare the estrous cycle of the dog and other mammals, in which sexual receptivity and fertility occur at the time of slight bleeding during estrus or "heat," to the menstrual cycle. There are two major differences between the two types of cycles. First, the estrual female is sexually receptive only during the estrous phase of the estrous cycle, whereas menstrual females are continually capable of sexual behavior during the menstrual cycle. Second, menstruation occurs only for menstrual

FIGURE 11.1

Schematic cross section of the female pelvis, showing sexual and reproductive organs.

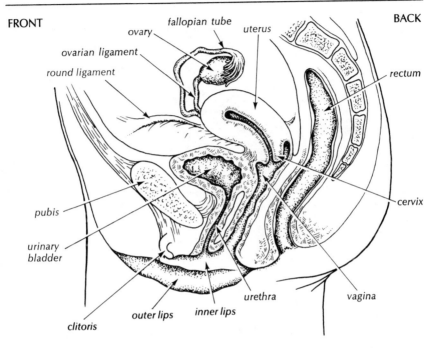

FRONT

fallopian tube   *uterus*

ovary

ovarian ligament

round ligament

BACK

rectum

pubis

urinary bladder

cervix

clitoris

outer lips   *inner lips*   *urethra*   *vagina*

Source: After McCary, 1973.

females, and not for estrual females (Turner and Bagnara, 1971). Thus the human female is continually sexually receptive and ovulates or is fertile about midway between periods of bleeding or menstruation.

A menstrual cycle can be separated into four phases, each describing the state of the follicles and ova within that phase (see Figure 11.2). It would be most convenient to call the period of menstruation the first phase, because it is easily identifiable, but physiologically it represents the last. The first phase, called the *follicular phase*, extends approximately from day 4 to day 14 after menstruation begins. (In counting days of the cycle, day 1 is the first day of menstruation.) During this phase, a follicle matures and swells. The termination of this phase is marked by the rupturing of the follicle and the release of the egg (*ovulatory phase*). During the next phase, the *luteal phase*, a group of reddish-yellow cells, called the corpus luteum, forms in the ruptured follicle. The final phase, marked by *menstruation*, represents a sloughing off of the inner lining (endometrium) of the uterus, which had built up in preparation for nourishing a fertilized egg.

FIGURE 11.2

Changes in hormone levels over the phases of the menstrual cycle.

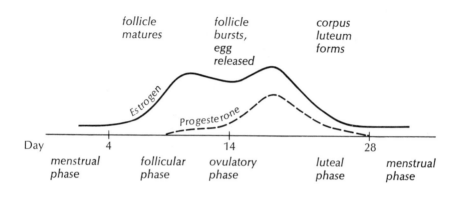

These cyclic phases are regulated by hormones that act in a negative feedback loop with each other (Figure 11.3), so that the production of a hormone increases to a high level, producing a desired physiological change. The level is then automatically reduced through the negative feedback loop. Here we are concerned with two basic groups of hormones — those produced by the ovaries, most importantly estrogen and progesterone, and those produced by the pituitary gland, most importantly follicle-stimulating hormone (FSH) and luteinizing hormone (LH). We also need to consider control of the activity of the pituitary by the hypothalamus, an important region of the brain on its lower side (Figure 11.3), by LH-releasing factor and FSH-releasing factor. The overall pattern of the negative feedback loop is that the activity of the ovary, including its production of estrogen and progesterone, is regulated by the pituitary, which in turn is regulated by the hypothalamus, which is sensitive to the levels of estrogen produced by the ovaries.

The regulation of the menstrual cycle involves interactions among the levels of these hormones. The follicular phase of the cycle is initiated by the pituitary gland sending out follicle-stimulating hormone (FSH), which signals the ovaries to increase production of estrogen and to bring several follicles to maturity. The resulting high level of estrogen, through the feedback loop, signals the pituitary to decrease production of FSH and to begin production of luteinizing hormone (LH), whose chief function is to induce ovulation. Temporarily, FSH and LH induce even more estrogen production, which further lowers the amount of FSH. At this

FIGURE 11.3

Schematic diagram illustrating the negative feedback loops controlling hormone levels during the menstrual cycle. FSH and LH are produced by the pituitary gland and influence production of estrogen and progesterone in the ovaries. The hypothalamus is sensitive to levels of these hormones and, in turn, regulates levels of FSH and LH. (See text for further explanation.)

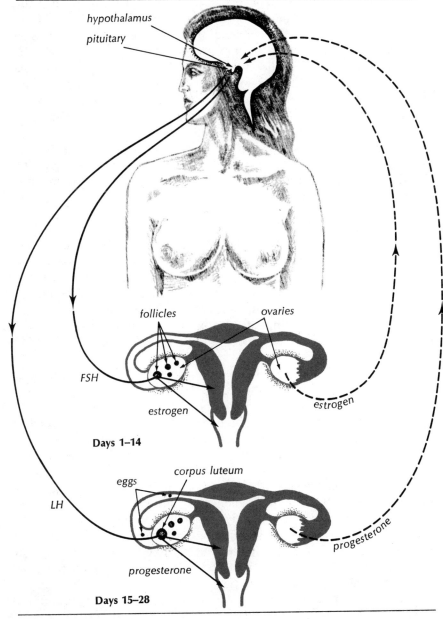

Source: After Appel, 1972.

point the LH becomes dominant, causing the follicle to rupture and release the egg. The corpus luteum then forms in the ruptured follicle. The corpus luteum is a major source of progesterone. When progesterone levels are sufficiently high, they will, through the negative feedback loop, inhibit production of LH, and simultaneously stimulate the production of FSH, beginning the cycle over again.

Estrogen has a number of functions and effects in the body. It maintains the lining of the vagina and uterus and provides the initial stimulation for breast growth. Its nonreproductive functions include increasing water content and thickness of skin and retarding growth rate. At the beginning and the end of the menstrual cycle, estrogen is at a low level. In between these two times, it reaches two peaks, one immediately prior to and during ovulation, the other in the middle of the luteal phase (Figure 11.2). It appears that mature ovarian follicles are the major producers of estrogen.

Progesterone is especially important in preparing the uterus for implantation of the fertilized ovum, maintaining pregnancy, and regulating the accessory organs during the reproductive cycle. The corpus luteum is a major source of progesterone. Hence progesterone level peaks during the luteal phase, and is otherwise low.

Menstrual problems: Cramps   Painful cramps during menstruation are called *dysmenorrhea*. Some women experience them regularly, some women experience them some of the time, and some women don't experience them. There are serious problems of understanding another person's experience here. It is very difficult for a man, or for a woman who does not experience severe dysmenorrhea, to understand precisely how those who do experience it feel, a point that is expressed poignantly in the selection included here.

Traditional medical remedies have not been completely successful in treating the problem. Over-the-counter drugs such as Midol help some people some of the time, but they do not help everyone. In fact, until a few years ago, it seemed that the best treatment was plain old aspirin. However, in the last several years there has been a major breakthrough in understanding the biology of cramps and corresponding advances in treating them.

Prostaglandins are currently thought to be the culprit responsible for cramps (Budoff, 1981). Prostaglandins are hormonelike substances produced by many tissues of the body, including the lining of the uterus. Prostaglandins cause smooth muscle to contract and can affect the size of blood vessels. Women with severe menstrual pain have unusually high levels of prostaglandins. The high levels cause intense uterine contractions, which are painful; these contractions in turn choke off some of the uterus's supply of oxygen-carrying blood, a painful process that resembles somewhat what occurs in a heart attack. Prostaglandins may also cause greater sensitivity in nerve endings. The combination of the uterine contractions, lack of oxygen, and heightened nerve sensitivity produces cramps.

As a result of this analysis of the causes of cramps, a new treatment is the use of *antiprostaglandin drugs*. The drug is mefanamic acid and is sold with brand names such as Ponstel. Other, similar drugs are Motrin and Anaprox. Interestingly, its application to menstrual cramps was discovered by a woman physician, Dr. Penny Wise Budoff (1981). In her research, 85 percent of the women tested reported significant relief from menstrual pain and symptoms such as nausea, vomiting, dizziness, and weakness. Not coincidentally, one of the traditional cures for cramps, aspirin, is a weak antiprostaglandin. The work on antiprostaglandin drugs looks promising enough to me that I would recommend that any women who has suffered severe problems with cramps and has not received satisfactory treatment consult a doctor about possibly receiving an antiprostaglandin drug (these drugs are available by prescription only).

In 1982 the Nobel Prize in medicine was awarded to the three scientists who pioneered prostaglandin research (*Time*, October 25, 1982). The news coverage focused on the physiology of prostaglandins and discussed applications in the treatment of ulcers, arthritis, and pain associated with heart attacks. Only fleeting mention was made of the application of prostaglandins to the treatment of menstrual pain. Millions of women who are sufferers might say that the priorities are wrong and that the menstrual-pain application is by far the most important.

A WOMAN DESCRIBES HER EXPERIENCES WITH MENSTRUAL CRAMPS

I started to menstruate when I was 12. The pain did not occur the first few times. The first time it happened I was in the kitchen getting tea for my mother. Suddenly, a terrible pain doubled me over, and I could hardly get my breath. I could not stand straight and when I reached my mother she told me to sit on my bed, and that it would pass. She was quite nice that time and told me that sometimes it had been bad for her, too. Later on, after a half-year had passed, she was fed up with me. She began to hate my crying and twisting in pain. . . . Finally, one day when I was thirteen she told me that if I didn't stop crying that instant, she would walk out on me and leave me alone. I sat there and shuddered, but I didn't make any more noise. My mother made it plain. I learned that I could not cry out or she and other people would withdraw from me.

When I got older, this lesson was reinforced. I could mention my problem once, maybe twice, but then the school nurses and personnel all turned a deaf ear. Teachers would not help me cope; they shook their heads at such absurdity, believing that I had suddenly turned into a goldbrick. . . . Past history also seemed to count for nothing. I always loved basketball and participated enthusiastically in gym. Once a month, however, I would incur the wrath of my gym teacher who decided that I suddenly just didn't want to improve my basketball skills. Her attitude cooled the attitudes of the girls in my class for me, also. Who would want to associate with such an unreliable person? . . .

When I was 18, I had a horseback-riding accident in which I broke my back in the middle. The first doctor who examined me failed to X-ray the middle back and said there was nothing wrong but some bruises. I seemed to have too much pain for bruises. . . . Two weeks later my father, who did not like the way I was moving, sent me to Knickerbocker Hospital for more X-rays. There they found out that my spine had been broken (in addition to my coccyx) and proceeded to put me in a wheel-chair and tell me that I must not take another step, which I thought was pretty funny (except for the pain) because for two weeks I had been walking, cleaning, living on my own, and even hiking in that condition. As you know, Knickerbocker is a busy New York City hospital, used to seeing plenty of the rougher side of life. Yet that night, the resident who had examined me and taken the X-rays stopped by my room to speak to me. He said, "I just wanted to see how the bravest girl I've ever met is getting along." His kindness surprised me, but so did the fact that he thought my talking calmly, normally, and not crying or fainting with the enormous pain I was in, was surprising. . . . The rest of the hospital staff also found my behavior very surprising. . . .

There was one thing they did not know, however, about my ability to take pain. It's not that I don't feel it; I have the same number of nerve endings per square foot as anyone else. The difference is that I had been in training for years to endure it. I was used to coping through a haze of nauseating pain, used to having a conversation when every nerve in me was screaming out, used to getting dressed and getting on a bus when I felt as though a red-hot iron was going to knock my stomach out. I got my training every month without fail, when my period came.

I, of course, developed such techniques as I could for enduring this experience, such as mentally talking myself through something, step by step. . . .

These great techniques were not much. Obviously they only helped me to endure what I had to endure anyway to live up to our society's conviction that this condition does not exist and need not be remedied.

Source: Penny Wise Budoff. *No More Menstrual Cramps and Other Good News.* New York: Penguin Books, 1981, pp. 35–37.

Is Sally blue? Psychological aspects of the menstrual cycle   The notion that women experience changes in personality or mood depending on the phase of the menstrual cycle is well known to the lay person (for example the Sally-is-blue advertisements) and scientist alike. In this section we shall examine the evidence on the nature and extent of these moods and behavior shifts, and their relationship to the hormone cycles occurring during the menstrual cycle.

In 1931, R. T. Frank gave the name "premenstrual tension" to the mood changes that occur during the three or four days immediately preceding menstruation (approximately days 23 to 26 or 28 of the cycle). This phase is characterized by negative feelings, including depression, anxiety, irritability, and low self-esteem. There is by now an extensive literature on this phenomenon, and the more general one of fluctuations in mood and behavior corresponding to the menstrual cycle (see Parlee, 1973, for a critical review).

Four types of studies have been used to document the existence of a premenstrual syndrome. First, attempts have been made to correlate observable behaviors with cycle phase. For example, it has been found that a large proportion of the criminal acts of violence and suicides committed by women occur during the four premenstrual and four menstrual days of the cycle (Dalton, 1964). Forty-five percent of the female industrial workers who call in sick, 46 percent of the women admitted to psychiatric care, and 52 percent of female accident-emergency admissions are in the eight premenstrual or menstrual days. In addition, 54 percent of the children brought to a clinic with minor colds were brought during their mothers' eight premenstrual and menstrual days, perhaps indicating an increase in mothers' anxiety at this time (Dalton, 1966). The premenstrual syndrome, then, may have rather important and far-reaching consequences. On the other hand, it is important to notice that the eight premenstrual and menstrual days do constitute 36 percent of the total days in a cycle. Hence a statistic like "49 percent of criminal acts committed by women are during this period," which appears impressive considered by itself, may not represent a substantial or meaningful increase over the 36 percent expected randomly. And even with these presumed hormone effects, it is important to note that women commit far fewer crimes than men do. Other studies attempting to demonstrate behavioral changes over the menstrual cycle have failed to find such fluctuations for intellectual performance (Sommer, 1972; Golub, 1976) and reaction time (Zimmerman and Parlee, 1973).

A second type of study used to document the premenstrual syndrome is based on questionnaires requesting that women report retrospectively their symptoms and moods at various phases of the cycle. Such studies are largely useless because retrospective accounts, particularly of such evanescent phenomena as moods in relation to menstrual cycle, are notoriously unreliable and have not been demonstrated to correlate with other indicators of premenstrual symptoms, that is, their validity is not established (Parlee, 1973).

A third type of study uses daily self-reports made by women throughout the cycle. Such studies generally find positive moods around the time of ovulation, and various symptoms, such as anxiety, irritability, depression, fatigue, and headaches, premenstrually (see summary by Parlee, 1973).

A fourth approach avoids direct questioning of subjects about symptoms and instead uses a kind of projective technique, in which subjects tell stories at regular intervals throughout the cycle. These stories are then subjected to a standardized scoring for themes manifested in them. An example is a study by Ivey and Bardwick (1968), who recorded the spontaneous stories of twenty-six college women at ovulation and premenstruation over two menstrual cycles and then scored them using Gottschalk and Gleser's Verbal Anxiety Scale. Their findings for these normal subjects were that anxiety about death, mutilation, and separation were highest premenstrually, while self-confidence and self-esteem were higher at ovulation. Ivey and Bardwick provided the following examples:

From one woman at ovulation:

> We took our skis and packed them on top of the car and then we took off for up north. We used to go for long walks in the snow, and it was just really great, really quiet and peaceful.

Mutilation anxiety from the same woman premenstrually:

> . . . came around a curve and did a double flip and landed upside down. I remember this car coming down on my hand and slicing it right open and all this blood was all over the place. Later they thought it was broken because every time I touched the finger, it felt like a nail was going through my hand.

From another woman at ovulation:

> Talk about my trip to Europe. It was just the greatest summer of my life. We met all kinds of terrific people everywhere we went, and just the most terrific things happened.

Hostility from this same woman premenstrually:

> . . . talk about my brother and his wife. I hated her. I just couldn't stand her . . . I used to do terrible things to separate them.

In summary, the results of the research using all of these approaches do seem to indicate that there are fluctuations in mood corresponding to the phases of the menstrual cycle.

It is tempting to speculate that these mood changes are related to, or perhaps even caused by, changes in hormone levels occurring during the cycle (Bardwick, 1971). In particular, it seems that high levels of estrogen (at ovulation) are associated with positive moods, while low levels of estrogen premenstrually are associated with negative moods.

However, such a conclusion has been severely criticized on a number of counts (Parlee, 1973). First, virtually all of the data (with some exceptions discussed below) presented to support this contention are correlational in nature; causal inferences are then made from these data, an unwise procedure at best. That is, the data simply demonstrate a correlation between cycle phase or hormone levels and mood. From this it is unwarranted to infer that hormones actually cause or influence mood.

From these data an equally tenable conclusion would be that the direction of causality is the reverse — that psychological factors affect hormone levels and menstrual-cycle phase. For example, gynecology texts state that stress may delay menstruation or precipitate its onset; many women in concentration camps during World War II ceased menstruating. Social factors may also have an influence; for example, females living together in a college dormitory came to have menstrual cycles more closely synchronized as the academic year progressed (McClintock, 1971). In sum, the inference that hormone level influences mood is not completely justifiable on the basis of the available data, although further data may yet substantiate this conclusion.

One study (Paige, 1971) that partially answers the objection about correlational data involved scoring the spoken stories of 102 married women four times during a single menstrual cycle: on days 4, 10, 16, and two days before the onset of menstruation. Other data were also collected to try to disguise the purpose of the study. The subjects fell into three groups: (1) those who were not taking oral contraceptives and never had; (2) those who were taking a combination pill (combination pills provide a steady high dose of both estrogen and progestin, a synthetic progesterone, for twenty or twenty-one days); and (3) those who were taking sequential-type pills (which provide fifteen days of estrogen, followed by five days of estrogen-progestin, similar to the natural cycle, but at higher levels). Nonpill women experienced statistically significant variation in their anxiety and hostility levels over the menstrual cycle as previous studies had shown. Women taking the sequential pill showed the same mood changes that nonpill women did, which agrees with the predicted outcome, since their artificial hormone cycle parallels the natural one. Combination-pill women showed *no* mood shifts corresponding to the menstrual cycle: their hostility and anxiety levels remained constant. Therefore it appears that the steady high level of both hormones leads to a steady level of mood. This study serves as a pseudo-experiment with respect to hormone levels, thereby answering, in part, the objections with regard to causal inferences on hormone-behavior relations.

A second criticism of this area of research is that the term "premenstrual syndrome" or "premenstrual tension syndrome" is only vaguely defined. For instance, some authors have defined it so broadly as to include "any combination of emotional or physical features which occur cyclically in a female before menstruation" (Sutherland and Stewart, 1965, p. 1182). While it would be worthwhile to know what percentage of the female population is afflicted with premenstrual symptoms, estimates of this percentage vary considerably from one study to another. In one study, premenstrual irritability was found in 69 percent of the sample, depression in 63 percent, and both symptoms together in 45 percent (Sutherland and Stewart, 1965). In another study, the responses of approximately 30 to 50 percent of 839 young married women to a questionnaire indicated mood cycles in irritability, tension, and depression (Moos, 1968). On the other hand, another investigator noted that 56 percent of the women in his sample did not report any significant premenstrual tension symptoms (Rees, 1953). In view of the vagueness of definition, it is not surprising that these estimates are not consistent, and until the "syndrome" is more clearly defined, we can have no really accurate estimate of its incidence. At least from these data it seems fair to conclude that the premenstrual syndrome is far from universal among women. It is possible that 50 percent of women have no premenstrual symptoms.

A third, and very real, problem with this area of research is the problem of subject expectations. Subjects may report more negative feelings premenstrually because such feelings are culturally prescribed — brainwashing through menstrual drug ads — or because they feel the experimenter expects them, since they must certainly be aware of the investigator's interest in their menstrual cycle.

Psychologist Diane Ruble (1977) did a clever experiment to determine whether subjects' expectations influence their reporting of premenstrual symptoms. College student subjects were tested on the sixth or seventh day before the onset of their next menstrual period. They were told that they would participate in a study on a new technique for predicting the expected date of menstruation using an electroencephalogram (EEG), a method that had already been successfully tested with older women. After the electroencephalogram had been run, the subject was informed of when her next period was to occur, depending on which of three experimental groups she had been assigned to: (1) the subject was told she was "premenstrual" and her period was due in 1 or 2 days; (2) the subject was told she was "intermenstrual" or "midcycle" and her period was not expected for at least a week to 10 days; or (3) she was given no information at all about the expected date of menstruation (control group). The women then completed a self-report menstrual distress questionnaire. The results indicated that subjects who had been led to believe they were in the premenstrual phase reported significantly more water retention, pain, and changes in eating habits, than did subjects who had been led to believe they were around midcycle. (In fact, subjects in these groups did not differ significantly in when their periods actually arrived.) There were no significant differences between the groups in ratings of negative moods, however. This study indicates that, probably because of learned beliefs, women overstate the changes in body states that occur over the menstrual cycle. When they think they are in the premenstrual phase, they report more problems than when they think they are at midcycle.

A subtle problem of interpretation exists in menstrual cycle research. A typical conclusion is that symptoms increase or that mood is negative premenstrually. Perhaps, however, the premenstrual state is the "usual" one, and what occurs is really a decrease in symptoms, or a positive mood shift, at ovulation. This is essentially a problem of establishing a baseline of behavior — and what should that be? Should it be the average for males? Or are males irrelevant to this research? This is a complex question needing further resolution.

Also noteworthy are the tremendous cultural influences on menstrual-cycle mood shifts. In many primitive societies and religions, the menstruating woman is seen as unclean, and many taboos arise to prevent her un-cleanness from spreading to others (Stephens, 1961). For example, she may not be permitted to cook while menstruating, or she may even be isolated from the rest of the community in a separate hut outside the village. Such superstitions become subtler in modern America, but they still persist. For example, many couples abstain from sexual intercourse during the woman's period. A survey of 960 California families showed that half the men and women had *never* had sex during menstruation (Paige, 1973). There is also considerable evidence of cultural influences on menstrual distress. For example, groups of married women were com-pared, according to their religious preference, on attitudes toward menstrua-tion and variations in anxiety during the cycle (Paige, 1973). Most of the Jews and Catholics said they would never have sex during menstruation, as compared with less than half the Protestants. Protestants did not ex-perience much fluctuation in anxiety level between the ovulation and premenstrual phase, while Catholics showed extreme fluctuations. These cultural variations in menstrual attitudes and symptoms may be related to religious teaching regarding menstruation (Paige, 1973). In any case, Protestant, Catholic, and Jewish women all have the same hormone cycles, but the correlated psychological cycles are different, so that the psychological cycles must surely be influenced by culture.

Finally, this area of research has seen too little attention devoted to coping mechanisms (Maccoby, 1972). Most women are simply not dis-solved in tears, reduced to a state of incompetency, for three to six days each month. Certainly women must develop mechanisms for coping with these mood shifts, particularly if they are so regular and predictable. In fact, it might be reasonable to expect that the women who experience the largest mood shifts would develop the best strategies for coping with them. Unfortunately, we have little empirical evidence on these points. My own interviews with undergraduates suggest that increased activity, "keeping busy," is the most common coping strategy. Another common coping mechanism is sleeping more than usual — a kind of escapism, but also a very practical means of dealing with feelings of fatigue. In addition, be-cause the premenstrual syndrome is so well known, it is easy to deal with accompanying symptoms such as depression — most women quickly spot that the depression is associated with the onset of menstruation and pro-ceed about their business, unconcerned that they are displaying serious psychological symptoms as they know that the symptoms will disappear in a few days.

Practical implications   In assessing the practical implications of research on mood shift and menstrual phase, some important considerations should be kept in mind. First, the *magnitude* of the mood shift depends very much on the individual woman. It is a function of her psychological adjustment, as well as her current experiences. Certainly in practical situations, the magnitude and content of the mood shift are most important. For instance, it is much more important to know that a particular woman experiences mood shifts so small as to be unnoticeable in her work and interpersonal relations, than to know that she experiences slight mood shifts detectable only by sensitive psychological tests. Hence the most important characteristics are individual ones, just as they are for men.

Second, in making practical decisions about hiring people, performance is certainly more important than mood. Most of the available research documents mood cycles. Few attempts have been made to demonstrate cycles in performance, such as intellectual or athletic performance, and most of these have demonstrated an absence of such cycles in females (Golub, 1976; Sommer, 1973). Thus there is no substantial evidence that the behaviors required in a work situation are influenced by menstrual-cycle phase.

In addition, it is possible that monthly hormonal cycles exist in men also (Parlee, 1978; Delaney et al., 1976; Ramey, 1972, Hersey, 1931), but until quite recently they have not been the subject of scientific investigation — probably because they produce no obvious signs like menstruation.

In summary, research suggests that menstrual-cycle changes in hormone levels may be related to corresponding changes in mood. Mood is generally positive at ovulation or mid-cycle, when estrogen levels are high, while it is negative, with feelings of depression, anxiety, and irritability, at the time of low estrogen levels premenstrually. The existing research has many problems: most of it is correlational in nature, and subject expectations complicate interpretations. Cultural factors may also contribute to mood shifts. In addition, probably a substantial proportion of women either do not experience such mood cycles, or their cyclic fluctuations are so small as to be undetectable.

Other menstrual cycle fluctuations   Research has demonstrated that there are menstrual-cycle fluctuations in the sensitivity of the senses: vision, smell, hearing, taste, and touch (Parlee, 1983). For example, sensitivity to the smell of certain compounds is greatest around the time of ovulation and is reduced during menstruation. In the search for psychological characteristics that are controlled by biological factors fluctuating over the menstrual cycle, these basic sensory processes may be a better place to look than more diffuse attributes such as moods, which are far more influenced by environment, socialization, and cognitions.

MENOPAUSE

Physical and psychological changes A number of physical as well as psychological changes occur during the climacteric. *Climacteric* refers to the gradual aging of the ovaries over the years, leading to a decline in their efficiency. Most importantly, estrogen production declines, leading to the most obvious symptom of the climacteric, menopause, which occurs on the average at age 47. Another effect is the atrophy of genital tissue and shrinking of the breasts.

A number of symptoms occur at this time: physical symptoms such as "hot flashes"; psychological symptoms such as depression, irritability, crying spells, and inability to concentrate; and what may be psychosomatic symptoms such as dizziness, headaches, and heart pounding.

Do all women experience these menopausal symptoms? In a survey of 638 women aged 45 to 55, conducted in London in 1964–1965, 30 to 50 percent of the women reported experiencing dizziness, palpitations, insomnia, depression, headache, or weight gain, and most of these women reported experiencing several of these symptoms rather than just one. About 50 percent of the women experienced hot flashes, and half of the 50 percent said the flashes were acutely uncomfortable (McKinlay and Jeffreys, 1974). It is generally estimated that only about 10 percent of all women suffer severe distress at menopause. Thus it might be concluded that at least as many as 50 percent (perhaps 80 to 90 percent) of all women suffer some of these uncomfortable menopausal symptoms, only about 10 percent are severely affected, and a sizeable proportion — at least 10 percent and perhaps as many as 50 percent — display none of these symptoms.

Psychological problems of menopause include depression, irritability, anxiety, nervousness, crying spells, inability to concentrate, and feelings of suffocation. In rare cases, the depression may be extremely severe (involutional melancholia) in a woman who has no previous history of mental problems. It is estimated that about 10 percent of women suffer from serious depression during menopause. Less severe depression during menopause is more common.

These psychological symptoms, however, involve a subtle problem of interpretation similar to the one mentioned in conjunction with the premenstrual tension syndrome. Women are said to have "more" problems during menopause. More than what? More than men? More than at other times in their own lives? Investigating the latter question, psychologists Bernice Neugarten and Ruth Kraines (1965) studied symptoms among women of different age groups. They found that adolescents and menopausal women reported the largest number of problematic symptoms. Postmenopausal women reported the smallest number of problematic symptoms. Apparently, menopause does not permanently "wreck" a woman. Among the adolescents, psychological symptoms were the most common (for example, tension), while among the menopausal women, physical symptoms such as hot flashes were most common. Menopausal women showed an increase in only five categories of psychological symptoms: headache, irritability, nervousness, feeling blue, and feelings of suffocation (the latter being associated with hot flashes). Thus menopause does not seem to be the worst time of a woman's life psychologically; probably it is not as bad as adolescence.

Biology or culture?   The difficulties associated with menopause are attributed to biology (in particular, to hormones) by some, and to culture and its expectations by others.

From the biological perspective, the symptoms of menopause appear to be due to the woman's hormonal state. In particular, the symptoms appear to be related either to low estrogen levels or to hormonal imbalance. The former hypothesis, called the *estrogen-deficiency theory*, has been the subject of the most research. Proponents of this theory argue that the physical symptoms, such as hot flashes, and the psychological symptoms, such as depression, are caused by declining amounts of estrogen in the body. It is also worth noting that, hormonally, this period is similar to the premenstrual period, with its declining estrogen levels, and that the psychological symptoms are also similar: depression and irritability.

The best evidence for the estrogen-deficiency theory comes from the success of estrogen-replacement therapy. Physicians may prescribe estrogen either in its natural form, Premarin, or in a synthetic form such as Stilbestrol, Progynon, or Meprane. Estrogen-replacement therapy is very successful in relieving low-estrogen menopausal symptoms like hot flashes, sweating, cold hands and feet, osteoporosis, and vaginal discharges. It may also relieve psychological symptoms such as irritability and depression (see Bardwick, 1971, for a review). The success of this therapy suggests that low estrogen levels cause menopausal symptoms and that increasing estrogen levels relieves the symptoms.[1]

On the other hand, advocates of the environmental point of view note the cultural forces that may act to produce psychological stress in women

---

[1] Any possible benefits of estrogen-replacement therapy should be weighed against the dangers, because there is increasing evidence linking it to cancer of the uterus (Mack et al., 1976; Marx, 1976; Weiss et al., 1976). On the other hand, estrogen replacement protects women from osteoporosis, or brittle bones, which may cause broken hips, which may in turn cause death. More women die annually from hip fractures than from endometrial cancer. Thus, on balance, not only may estrogen replacement be relatively safe, it may actually be relatively healthy (Budoff, 1981).

around the time of menopause. The aging process itself may be psychologically stressful in our youth-oriented culture. The menopausal years remind a woman forcefully that she is aging. Menopause also means that the woman can no longer bear children. For women who have a great psychological investment in motherhood, this can be a difficult realization. In Chapter 7 we reviewed research on the empty nest syndrome and found that some investigators question whether this is a time of depression among women. Further, I noted that menopausal symptoms do not occur in women in cultures in which women's status rises at this time (Bart, 1971).

We have a strong cultural bias toward expecting menopausal symptoms. Thus any quirk in a middle-aged woman's behavior is attributed to the "change." It simultaneously becomes the cause of, and explanation for, all the problems and complaints of the middle-aged woman. Given such expectations, it is not surprising that the average person perceives widespread evidence of menopausal symptoms. Ironically, idiosyncrasies in women of childbearing age are blamed on menstruation, while problems experienced by women who are past that age are blamed on the *lack* of it.

As a way of resolving this biology-culture controversy, it seems reasonable to conclude that the physical symptoms of menopause, such as hot flashes, are probably due to declining estrogen levels, and that the psychological symptoms, such as depression, are due to low estrogen levels or culturally imposed stresses, or a combination of both.

PREGNANCY AND CHILDBIRTH

Pregnancy is marked by radical hormone changes, in which both estrogen and progesterone levels are high. Early in pregnancy, the corpus luteum is responsible for this production, while later in pregnancy, the placenta is the major source of the two hormones.

Research on the exact emotional states of women during pregnancy has produced conflicting results and opinions (reviewed by Sherman, 1971), and the radiant contentment of the pregnant woman is far from a well-established fact. Benedek's view (1959) that pregnancy is a time of "vegetative calm" is countered by the view that pregnancy is a time of crisis (Bibring et al., 1961; Taylor, 1962). Some support for the former view comes from one study in which it was concluded that pregnancy was a time of unusual well-being (Hooke and Marks, 1962). Supporting the "crisis" view, pregnant Jewish women showed more depression as measured by the Rorschach inkblot test (though not by another personality test, the MMPI) than did a nonpregnant control group (Riffaterre, 1965). Negative attitudes and moods would not be surprising in view of the fact that some children are unwanted (Sherman, 1971, p. 170). For example, in a sample of Scottish women, 41 percent did not want the pregnancy, 18 percent did not mind, and 41 percent desired it (Scott et al., 1956). In another study, 80 percent of the women were happy about their first one or two children, but only 31 percent were happy about the fourth or more (Gordon, 1967). Further evidence of negative attitudes regarding pregnancy comes from data on the substantial number of induced abortions. In the sample of females in the Kinsey study, about 20 to 25 percent had had an induced abortion sometime in their lives (Gebhard et al., 1958).

Emotional state seems to be related to stage of pregnancy (Sherman, 1971, p. 177). During the first three months, depression and fatigue may occur. Women's emotions are generally most positive during the second trimester (months 4 to 6). The last trimester may be more stressful and anxious, as the woman begins to worry about how the delivery will go, whether the baby will be healthy, and so on. As Sherman concludes,

> So far as emotional state in pregnancy is concerned, the weight of the evidence suggests that it is not generally a period of unusual well-being. However, such feelings occur in some women during middle pregnancy, and there may be a decrease in psychotic reactions during pregnancy. Milder emotional disturbances, however, apparently increase, especially during the last six weeks. (1971, p. 179)

A recent, intensive study by Myra Leifer (1980) found generally similar results. Nineteen women, all pregnant for the first time, were interviewed once during each trimester of pregnancy, on the third day after giving birth, and at six to eight weeks postpartum; a questionnaire was also mailed to them at seven months postpartum. Leifer's general findings were that, rather than being a time of calm and bliss, pregnancy was, for most of the women in her sample, difficult and turbulent. She also found emotional changes during pregnancy and after giving birth were strongly related to the emotional support and help the woman received from her husband. The women tended to experience mood shifts and to be anxious. Specifically, in the first trimester, anxieties centered on the possibility of miscarriage. In the first trimester, only the four women for whom the pregnancy was unplanned expressed overall negative emotions. The other women were either positive or ambivalent during the first trimester. The second trimester was the high point psychologically — there was the most happiness and pride in pregnancy. Fears of miscarriage diminished as the women could feel the fetus moving, and there was an intense feeling of relief that the fetus was alive. In the third trimester, anxiety about the delivery and about possible deformity of the baby increased.

In sum, pregnant women are not all blissfully happy. The woman's psychological state depends on a number of factors: whether the baby was wanted, the stage of pregnancy, physical comfort or discomfort, and a variety of social factors such as support from the husband or friends.

Parturition, or childbirth, represents a major shock to the body. Estrogen and progesterone levels drop sharply, and it may take as long as several months for the levels to return to normal and for menstruation to resume. Psychologically, there is the well-known syndrome of *postpartum depression* ("baby blues") in which the woman, immediately after childbirth and perhaps for a week or more, feels depression. Suicide attempts are more frequent than usual. Estimates of the proportion of women experiencing some postpartum emotional disturbance or depression range from 25 to 67 percent (Sherman, 1971). Severe disturbance is rare; postpartum psychosis occurs in about one woman in every 400 (Gordon and Gordon, 1967).

Psychological and social influences on the symptoms of the pregnancy and postpartum periods should be noted. Our culture is full of lore on the psychological characteristics of pregnant women — the glow of radiant contentment, the desire for dill pickles and ice cream. Perhaps pregnant women display these symptoms as a result of learning rather than because of hormones. The proper behavior for pregnancy is learned through the process of gender-role socialization, and the behaviors are displayed when the time comes. Positive moods might be further related to a strong desire for a child. Negative moods might be related to not wanting the child, fear of the dangers of childbirth, or fear of responsibility for the child. Postpartum depression might be related to the sudden change that has occurred in one's life, not wanting the baby, fearing responsibility for it, or even such a simple factor as being in a hospital and being separated from one's husband and family. Separation from the baby, which is sometimes enforced for the first twelve to twenty-four hours in the hospital, may also contribute to depression (Klaus et al., 1972). It has been demonstrated that postpartum emotional reactions are influenced by both past and present stresses (Gordon et al., 1965). Thus depression symptoms could be as easily explained by psychological and social factors as by hormonal ones. Probably, in reality, postpartum depression is a result of a combination of biological factors (shock to the body, radically diminished hormone levels) and social-psychological factors.

CONTRACEPTION

Detailed information on the various methods of contraception is available elsewhere (e.g., Hyde, 1979). What I want to do here is concentrate on the psychological aspects of contraceptive use — or, more accurately, of nonuse.

In the United States in 1979 there were 1.25 million legal abortions; there is approximately one abortion for every three live births (*World Almanac*, 1983). In an era when highly effective contraceptives are readily available, why should so many unwanted pregnancies, leading to abortion, occur? The basic answer is that lots of women have sexual intercourse while using no contraceptive, even though they are single and don't want to get pregnant. For example, research in the 1970s indicated that 75 percent of sexually active single teenage girls used contraceptives not at all or only occasionally ("Teenage Sex," 1972). In a survey of a random sample of students on my own campus, Denison University, I asked the following question: "The last time you had sexual intercourse, what form of contraception was used?" The most frequent answer was "Nothing or don't know," the response of 32 percent of the men and 21 percent of the women. Similar statistics are reported at most universities.

Why? Why is there such widespread nonuse of contraceptives, and so many resulting abortions? There were two traditional theories to explain this phenomenon (for a summary, see Luker, 1975). One is the *contraceptive ignorance theory*. It holds that women fail to use contraceptives and have unwanted pregnancies because they lack knowledge about or access to contraceptives. The theory goes on to say that if women had more information about contraceptives, about their advantages, disadvantages, and so on, they would use them. That is probably true for some women, but not for the majority. In one study of women who were having abortions, more than half reported having previously used a prescription method of contraception (usually the pill), and the majority displayed some or considerable knowledge about birth control when interviewed (Luker, 1975).

A second theory is the *intrapsychic conflict theory*. It holds that women generally have adequate skills in contraception, but that they fail to use contraceptives because of internal psychological conflicts. According to this view, a woman might use an "accidental" pregnancy to trap a man into marrying her, or to get back at parents whom she feels have not given her enough love. This model portrays women as neurotic and manipulative. Stereotypes strike again!

Sociologist Kristin Luker (1975) has formulated an excellent alternative theory about why unwanted pregnancies occur in her book *Taking Chances: Abortion and the Decision Not to Contracept*. The cause of unwanted pregnancies, she argues, is *contraceptive risk taking*, which results from conscious decision-making processes about whether to use contraceptives in any given sexual encounter. She believes that the decision not to use contraceptives is analogous to the decision not to fasten one's seat belt when driving.

According to Luker's theory, the woman engages in an informal cost-benefit analysis (although she might not be able to articulate it) in which she weighs the costs and benefits of contraception against the costs and possible benefits of pregnancy. The woman must assess the risk or uncertainty (probability) of pregancy (which is actually unknown, even to scientists), and she generally decides that it is very low. Thus if there are many costs associated with contraception, the woman begins to engage in risk taking. Luker's model is based on data she collected at an abortion clinic in northern California, by analyzing the medical records of 500 women treated at the clinic and doing in-depth interviews with 50 women undergoing abortions at the clinic.

What are the costs of contraception? First, there are a number of social-psychological costs. Using, and planning to use, contraceptives involves acknowledging that one is a sexually active woman, and this is difficult for many women, even today. Using a contraceptive such as the pill signals that one is always sexually available, and this may be seen as decreasing the woman's right to say "no." Some methods, particularly foam and the diaphragm, decrease the spontaneity of sex, which is a psychological cost. Second, there are structurally created costs — women must call for an appointment with a physician for some methods, and they may be told that no appointments are available for several weeks. They are expected to have high motivation, and to use abstinence or to call repeatedly for appointments. Even the "drugstore" methods (foam or condoms) involve going into the store and openly acknowledging to the world — or at least to the people in the store — that one is sexually active. Third, there may be costs to the relationship — the woman may fear negative reactions from the man if she uses a contraceptive such as foam or a diaphragm, or rejection if she asks him to use a condom. Finally, there are biological-medical costs, particularly fears of side effects from the pill.

Luker also points out that the woman may anticipate benefits from pregnancy. Pregnancy is proof of womanhood, and this may be particularly important in a society with a fluctuating view of gender roles. Pregnancy may enhance one's feeling of self-worth, proving that one is a valuable person who can produce children. Unarguably, pregnancy is a proof of fertility, and some women may feel a need for this proof — fully two-thirds of the women interviewed by Luker said that their gynecologists had told them they would have trouble getting pregnant because of problems in their reproductive systems. Pregnancy can be a way of accomplishing something with a significant other, perhaps forcing a man to define the relationship more clearly or perhaps going from living together to marriage. Finally, the pure excitement of risk taking itself may be fun for some — the Evil Knievels of contraception.

Given all this, Luker argues, the woman weighs the costs and benefits and often decides to take the risk. The costs and benefits, of course, vary from one woman to the next and at different times in a woman's life. The costs of pregnancy to a single college student are probably far greater than they are to a married woman with two children who would rather have no more. Risk taking, if successful, may foster more risk taking: "I got away with it once, surely I can again." And so the cycle goes, eventually ending in an unwanted pregnancy. But the costs of this failure are no longer terribly high, with the legalization and availability of abortion. Accordingly, many women leave the abortion clinic with no plans to use an effective method in the future, and the risk taking begins again.

On a more hopeful note, Luker argues that as women become more aware of their own decision-making processes, they will become more effective in using contraceptives to achieve the goals they truly desire.

ABORTION

A number of methods of abortion are available (see Hyde, 1979, for a more complete discussion). The most commonly used method is vacuum curettage, also called dilation and evacuation (D and E), vacuum suction, and vacuum aspiration. It is done on an outpatient basis with a local anesthetic. The procedure itself takes only about ten minutes and the woman stays in the doctor's office, clinic, or hospital for a few hours. The woman is prepared as she would be for a pelvic exam, and an instrument is inserted into the vagina. The instrument dilates (stretches open) the opening in the cervix. A nonflexible tube is then inserted through the opening until one end is in the uterus. The other end is attached to a suction-producing machine, and the contents of the uterus, including the fetal tissue, are sucked out. Recent statistics indicate that D and E is the safest method of abortion, not only during the first trimester, but through the twentieth week of pregnancy (U. S. Public Health Service, 1976).

It is a common belief that making the decision to have an abortion and having one are times of extreme psychological stress, and that psychological problems may result. In fact, however, according to research that has been done on women who have had legal abortions, the experience is not traumatic (see review by Osofsky and Osofsky, 1972). Most women report feeling relieved and happy after the abortion. Fewer than 10 percent of women experience psychological problems afterward, and most of them had problems before the pregnancy and abortion.

Women generally appear to be well adjusted after having an abortion, but well adjusted compared with what? That is, what is the appropriate control or comparison group? One comparison group that has been studied is women who requested an abortion but were denied it. Women in this group have a much higher rate of disturbance than women who have had abortions. Another group that has been studied is children who were born because an abortion request was denied. They, too, show a high incidence of psychiatric disturbance (Forssman and Thuwe, 1966).

The highly publicized "Akron ordinance," passed by the voters of Akron, Ohio, requires that women requesting an abortion be told

> that abortion may leave essentially unaffected or may worsen any existing psychological problems she may have, and can result in severe emotional disturbances.

According to the research discussed above, the psychological "information" being given is not really true, at least as far as the scientific evidence shows

FIGURE 11.4

The procedures involved in a D and E (dilation and evacuation or vacuum curettage) abortion. A tube is inserted through the vagina and the cervix and into the uterus. The uterine contents are then suctioned out.

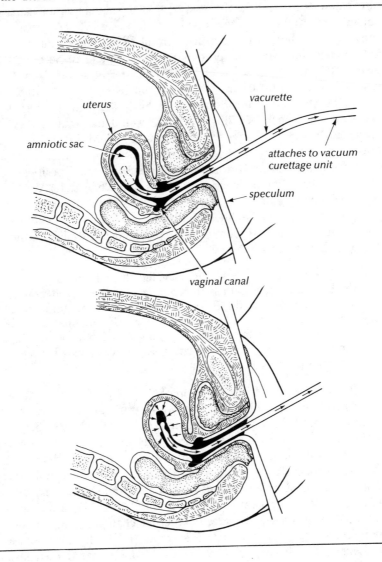

at this time. It seems unfortunate that people can vote to have incorrect information conveyed, particularly on such an important issue.

Somehow I don't think either of these views of the issue — the psychological research that shows it's no big thing or the pro-life scare tactic that abortion will make you go insane — truly captures the reality of the abortion experience for most women. I think that there are a number of methodological problems in most abortion research, which may lead to an overly optimistic conclusion. First, there is almost never any measurement of a woman's psychological adjustment *before* the abortion; in most studies she came to the attention of researchers when she had an unwanted pregnancy, and that is scarcely the time to get a measure of her normal state of adjustment. If there is no good measure of pre-abortion adjustment, how can we know how good the post-abortion adjustment is? Second, some of the research has involved mailing questionnaires; it seems likely that the response would be biased in that those who felt most comfortable about having the abortion would be the most likely to respond, whereas those for whom the experience was traumatic would not want to revive the trauma by filling out a questionnaire about it. Third, in studies involving interviews women may be grateful to an interviewer who is supportive and interested in them, so that they focus primarily on positive feelings. (Recall the discussion of experimenter effects in Chapter 1.) Women may also avoid talking about the negative effects of their abortions for fear of giving ammunition to pro-life activists.

A student of mine, having read the psychological studies on the effects of abortion, wrote this in an essay:

> After reviewing the literature and going through an abortion myself, I think the procedure and its aftermath are trivialized. Well-meaning counselors in an effort to dispel fear and pro-choice advocates in an effort to preserve the abortion option will often stress the routineness of abortion. This approach may do more harm than good. If a woman is told that an abortion is "no big deal," she will most likely suppress her fears, which could postpone the healing process.

I see two new approaches as being better ways of looking at the abortion experience. First, abortion involves a decision-making process. Little is known about this decision-making process, or about how to help women through it. In their essays, some of my students write, "As soon as I knew I was pregnant, I knew what I had to do and I did it. I had an abortion." They seem to go through the process with little thought and reflection. Others, in contrast, agonize about which course of action to choose, changing their minds several times. In one study of single black teenagers with unwanted pregnancies, 40 percent reported changing their minds about their decisions at least once (Bracken et al., 1978). By studying abortion decisions and their consequences, we may come to see the whole process of making a decision to have an abortion (or to have the baby and give it up for adoption, or to keep the baby) as fostering psychological development and growth, at least if handled well. Women may emerge from the process being more mature and having better-developed moral sensitivities (Gilligan, 1982b).

Second, the whole experience of having an unwanted pregnancy and deciding on an abortion can easily be conceptualized as a time of stress. We need to understand more precisely the nature of the stresses, how women cope with them, and how they can be helped to cope better. At least three kinds of stress are apparent. First, the decision-making process is stressful. Second, relationships with others are stressed. The relationship with the child's father is stressed. Studies show a high rate of the breaking up of relationships following abortions (Cvejic et al., 1977; Perez-Reyes et al., 1972). Relationships with the woman's parents are also likely to be strained. Third, the abortion procedure itself is somewhat stressful. In one study, 171 women were asked to rate how painful their abortions had been (Bracken et al., 1978). On a 7-point scale, with a 7 being extremely painful, the mean score was 4.8. A fourth kind of stress may occur after the abortion. Some therapists argue that mourning is necessary after an abortion because mourning is always necessary after any loss of life, even the loss of potential life. The problem is that women who have had an abortion are prevented from mourning (Mester, 1978). The woman herself may not realize that she is mourning or needs to mourn. In addition, the social structures of our society do not encourage post-abortion mourning in women. Thus, important grief work that needs to occur in order for psychological health to improve may not take place.

In sum, then, psychological research shows that women generally have good adjustment following abortions. However, I think that we need to know more about the complexities of the process — how the decision is made, what the stresses are, how women can be helped through it, and what the potentials for psychological growth are.

MASTECTOMY

Breast cancer is the most common form of cancer in women. It is rare in women under 25, and a woman's chances of developing it increase every year after that age. About 1 out of every 15 American women (7 percent) develops breast cancer at some time in her life (Lanson, 1975).

Because breast cancer is relatively common, every woman should do a breast self-exam monthly, around midcycle (*not* during one's period, when there may be natural lumps). Unfortunately, psychological factors such as fear prevent some women from doing the self-exam or, if they discover a lump, from seeing a doctor immediately. This is unfortunate because the more quickly breast cancer is discovered and treated, the better the chances of recovery.

In fact, not all breast lumps are cancerous. There are three kinds of breast lumps: cysts (fluid-filled sacs, also called fibrocystic disease or cystic mastitis), fibroadenomas, and malignant tumors. The important thing to realize is that 80 percent of breast lumps are cysts or fibroadenomas and are therefore benign, that is, not dangerous. Techniques for diagnosis of breast cancer are controversial. Most physicians feel that the most definitive method is the excisional biopsy, in which a small slit is made in the breast, the lump removed, and a pathologist determines whether it is cancerous. Other diagnostic techniques include needle aspiration, thermography, mammography, and xeroradiography.

If a malignancy is confirmed, what is the best treatment? This is also controversial. The treatment usually is some form of mastectomy, that is, surgical removal of the breast. In *radical mastectomy*, the most serious form of surgery, the entire breast, as well as the lymph nodes and underlying muscles are removed. Advocates of this procedure argue that it is best to be as thorough as possible, and that the muscle and lymph nodes should be removed in case the cancer has spread to them. In *modified radical mastectomy*, the entire breast and lymph nodes, but not the muscles, are moved. In *simple mastectomy*, only the breast, and possibly a few lymph nodes are removed. In partial mastectomy or *lumpectomy*, only the lump and some surrounding tissue are removed. Unfortunately, the data do not provide definite evidence of which procedure leads to a higher survival rate (Lanson, 1975). What is clear is that radical mastectomy has no higher survival rates than those after the less radical procedures, and, because it causes serious problems after surgery, it should generally be an operation of the past (Budoff, 1981). Simple mastectomy and lumpectomy are to be preferred. Some experts believe that survival rates are as good with lumpectomy combined with radiation therapy after surgery as they are with other methods; they therefore advocate the lumpectomy plus radiation method (Budoff, 1981).

Breast cancer and mastectomy are topics with important psychological consequences. The psychological impact of a mastectomy can be enormous (Asken, 1975). Severe depression as well as suicides following mastectomy have been reported (Ervin, 1973). Our culture is very breast-oriented. For a woman whose identity has been defined in terms of her beauty and her voluptuous figure, mastectomy may be perceived as a destruction of her womanhood and a blow to her sense of identity. There may be effects on her sexual expression, and she may feel that no man would want her in such a disfigured condition.

A systematic study of 41 women who had mastectomies indicated that 60 percent judged their postmastectomy emotional adjustment to be excellent or very good, but 10 percent judged it not very good, poor, or very poor (Jamison et al., 1978). About one-fourth of the women reported having suicidal thoughts following the mastectomy. About 15 percent sought professional help for their emotional problems related to the mastectomy. Interestingly, however, it was not the postmastectomy period that was rated as most difficult psychologically; rather, the period immediately following discovery of the lump was reported as being the worst. About three-quarters of the women reported that their sexual satisfaction in marriage had not changed or was better, but one-quarter reported a change for the worse. In sum, this study provides evidence of successful coping by the majority of mastectomy patients, but it also indicates that a substantial minority of women suffer considerable psychological stress. It is extremely important for mastectomy patients and their husbands to have counseling available. The American Cancer Society has organized support groups for mastectomy patients in many towns.

IN CONCLUSION

In this chapter we have discussed the psychological aspects of some topics considered important by the women's health movement. We considered the evidence on whether women experience menstrual-cycle fluctuations in mood and whether these shifts are caused by fluctuating hormone levels. Although there is a great deal of research in this area, there are fundamental problems with the research itself which make it difficult to draw firm conclusions. My conclusion is that some, though not all, women experience menstrual-cycle fluctuations in mood. There is evidence of both hormonal and cultural influences on the fluctuations; it seems likely that cultural forces act to increase the woman's perception of relatively small body changes.

The conclusions about menopause were similar. Some, though not all, women experience psychological symptoms such as depression and irritability. Once again, the perception of a body change is magnified by cultural factors — expectations that there should be menopausal depression, loss of role and the empty nest, and so on.

Research on the psychological aspects of pregnancy indicates that a woman's psychological state depends on the stage of pregnancy she is in; negative moods are more common in the first and third trimesters, and positive moods are more common in the second. Once again, environmental factors probably influence the woman's perception of her body changes.

Research on the psychological consequences of having an abortion indicate that it is generally not a traumatic experience, but more complex research is needed on this topic.

Finally, I emphasized the psychological aspects of mastectomy, something physicians often fail to recognize.

In all these cases, I feel that as women inform themselves more about the functioning of their bodies, they should inform themselves about the *psychological* aspects of these processes.

SUGGESTIONS FOR FURTHER READING

Arms, Suzanne (1975). *Immaculate deception: A new look at women and child-birth in America.* Boston: Houghton Mifflin. A provocative, critical analysis of modern childbirth practices in the United States.

12
Female Sexuality

Clitoral stimulation is more intensive and produces a more violent reaction. . . . Vaginal stimulation is much more relaxing and much less intense. I like it. I love clitoral stimulation . . . vaginal stimulation is soothing and produces a rhythmical rocking and rotating of the pelvis. . . . It is never intense as clitoral stimulation, yet feels extremely good in its own way. The best analogy I can contrive is the difference between someone lightly and caressingly stroking your bare back or arm or face and being violently, exhaustingly tickled. The former resembles vaginal, the latter clitoral stimulation. Vaginal stimulation soothes me and produces an involuntary contented hum deep in my throat. The vaginal stimulation of intercourse produces a closeness, a coordination, a sense of oneness unmatched by any other sexual activity.

A woman respondent quoted in S. FISHER,
Understanding the Female Orgasm

It is not coincidental that the liberation of women and the sexual revolution are taking place simultaneously. Historically, sex for women has always meant pregnancy, which has meant babies, and which, in turn, has meant a life devoted to motherhood. For the first time in the history of any species, we are now able to separate sex from reproduction, both in theory and in practice.

As a result, women are now free to be sexy without making a twenty-year commitment to motherhood. And so, perhaps, we may begin to consider the real nature of female sexuality, uncomplicated by reproductive functions (and fears).

PHYSIOLOGY

Only recently has female sexual physiology been the subject of scientific investigation. Most of our contemporary knowledge in this area is due to the important work of William Masters and Virginia Johnson (1966). Here I will give only a summary of their results, concentrating on the female response. Readers who wish more detail should consult the original technical reports (Masters and Johnson, 1966, 1970), or one of the analyses of their results intended for the lay person (Brecher and Brecher, 1966; Belliveau and Richter, 1970).

Masters and Johnson distinguish four phases in sexual response, although these stages actually flow together. The first phase is *excitement*. In the female, the primary response is *vasocongestion* or engorgement of

FIGURE 12.1

Female sexual and reproductive anatomy.

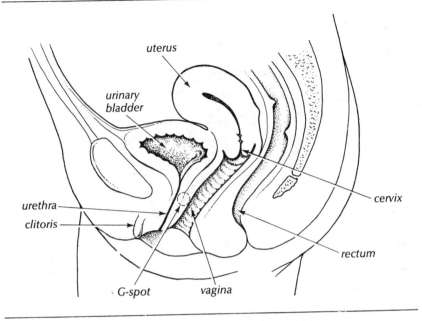

Source: After Belliveau and Richter, 1970.

the tissues surrounding the vagina. This simply means that a great deal of blood accumulates in the blood vessels of the pelvic region. A secondary response is the contraction of various muscle fibers (termed *myotonia*), which results, among other things, in erection of the nipples.

Perhaps the most noticeable response in the excitement phase is the moistening of the vagina with a lubricating fluid. This seems quite different from the most noticeable response in males, erection of the penis. In fact, Masters and Johnson have discovered that the underlying physiological mechanisms are the same, namely vasocongestion or engorgement. It is fairly common knowledge that engorgement causes erection in the male. Masters and Johnson believe that the droplets of moisture that appear on the walls of the vagina during sexual excitation are fluids that have seeped out of congested blood vessels in the surrounding region. Hence the physiological underpinnings are the same in males and in females, although the observable response seems different.

Lubrication marks only the beginning of female sexual response, however. In the excitement phase, a number of other changes take place, most notably in the clitoris. The clitoris, located just in front of the vagina (see Figure 12.2), is, like the penis, a shaft with a bulb or "glans" at the tip. The glans is densely packed with highly sensitive nerve endings. Hence

FIGURE 12.2

The vulva, or external genitals, of the human female.

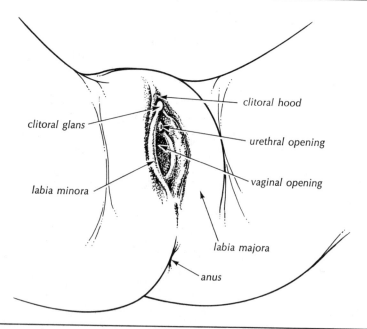

clitoral hood

clitoral glans

urethral opening

labia minora

vaginal opening

labia majora

anus

Source: After Belliveau and Richter, 1970.

clitoral stimulation contributes greatly to female sexual response. In sexual intercourse, the clitoris is stimulated both by direct clitoral-area friction, and by movement of the penis through the labia minor (inner lips), which causes the "hood" or prepuce of the clitoris to move back and forth across the glans of the clitoris, resulting in stimulation of this organ. Hence the clitoris gets some stimulation even in intercourse.

In response to further arousal, the clitoral glans swells, and the shaft increases in diameter probably also due to engorgement. This may be in response to the stimulation described above, to stimulation in another area of the body, such as the breasts, or to purely psychological stimulation, such as an erotic train of thought.

The vagina also responds in the excitement phase. Think of the vagina as a barrel in the resting state, divided into an outer third (or lower third, in a woman standing upright) and an inner two-thirds (or upper two-thirds). During the successive stages of sexual response, the inner and outer portions react in very different ways. In the latter part of the excitement phase, the inner two-thirds of the vagina undergoes a dramatic expansion or ballooning. This produces a tenting or pulling apart of the vaginal walls surrounding the cervix (see Figure 12.3).

FIGURE 12.3

Female sexual and reproductive organs during the plateau phase of sexual response. Notice the ballooning of the upper part of the vagina, the elevation of the uterus, and the formation of the orgasmic platform.

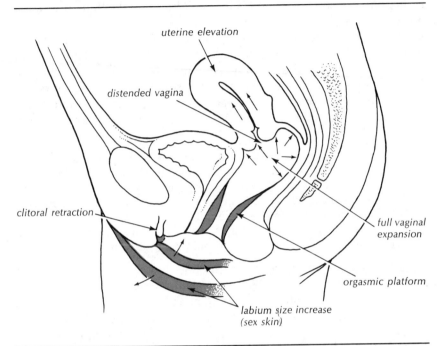

uterine elevation

distended vagina

clitoral retraction

full vaginal expansion

orgasmic platform

labium size increase
(sex skin)

Source: After Belliveau and Richter, 1970.

In the second phase of the woman's sexual response, the *plateau phase*, the major change is the appearance of the "orgasmic platform" (Masters and Johnson, 1966). This refers to the outer third of the vagina when it swells and is engorged with blood, with its diameter reduced by as much as 50 percent (see Figure 12.3). Hence while the upper portion of the vagina expands during excitement, the lower or outer portion narrows during the plateau phase. The orgasmic platform therefore grips the penis (if there happens to be a penis in the vagina at that point), resulting in a noticeable increase in the erotic stimulation experienced by the male.

The other major change occurring during the plateau phase is the elevation of the clitoris. The clitoris retracts and draws away from the vaginal entrance, but continues to respond to stimulation. A number of autonomic responses also occur, including an increase in pulse rate, and a rise in blood pressure and in rate of breathing.

Once again, these complex changes seem to be the result of two basic physiological processes, vasocongestion (the blood vessels becoming engorged with blood) and increased muscular tension, which occur similarly in both men and women. Readiness for orgasm occurs when these two processes have reached adequate levels. As Masters and Johnson describe it, in the plateau phase "the female gathers psychological and physiological strength from the stockpile of mounting sexual tension, until she can direct all her physical and mental forces toward a leap into the third or orgasmic phase of sexual tension expression."

The female *orgasm*, the third phase of sexual response, consists of a series of rhythmic muscular contractions of the orgasmic platform. Generally there is a series of three to twelve contractions, at intervals of slightly less than a second. The onset of the subjective experience of orgasm is an initial spasm of the orgasmic platform preceding the rhythmic contractions.

The sensations of orgasm in the female have been described as follows:

> In the female, orgasm starts with a feeling of momentary suspension followed by a peak of intense sensation in the clitoris, which then spreads through the pelvis. This stage varies in intensity and may also involve sensations of "falling," "opening up," or even emitting fluid. Some women compare this stage of orgasm to mild labor pains. It is followed by a suffusion of warmth spreading from the pelvis through the rest of the body. The experience culminates in characteristic throbbing sensations in the pelvis. (Katchadourian and Lunde, 1972, p. 58)

Contrary to popular belief, orgasm does not signal the end of sexual response. In the fourth or *resolution phase* of sexual response, the major physiological changes are a release of muscular tensions throughout the body and a release of blood from the engorged blood vessels. In the female, the breasts, which were formerly enlarged with nipples erect, return to the normal state. The clitoris returns to its normal, unretracted position and shrinks to normal size. The orgasmic platform relaxes, and the ballooned upper portion of the vagina shrinks. The return of the female to the unstimulated state may require as long as a half-hour following orgasm. If the woman reaches the plateau phase without having an orgasm, the restoration process takes longer, often as much as an hour. Indeed, prostitutes who habitually experience arousal without orgasm may experience cumulative physiological effects, resulting in chronic engorgement of the vaginal tissues (Masters and Johnson, 1966).

COMMON FALLACIES

Because sexuality has been so often the subject of superstition and so seldom the subject of scientific research, even modern American culture is filled with distorted ideas about it. A discussion of several misconceptions about female sexuality and the results of relevant scientific research follow.

Clitoral and vaginal orgasm   Freud believed that women can experience two different kinds of orgasm — clitoral and vaginal. According to his view, little girls learn to achieve masturbatory orgasm through stimulation of the clitoris. However in adulthood, they have to learn to transfer the focus of their sexual response from the clitoris to the vagina, and to orgasm from intercourse. Because some women fail to make this transfer, they can only experience clitoral orgasm, and are therefore "vaginally frigid." Freud thought that the only mature female orgasm was vaginal.

Masters and Johnson have dispelled this myth by showing convincingly that, physiologically, there is only one kind of orgasm. The major response is the contraction of the orgasmic platform. That is, physiologically an orgasm is the same, whether it results from clitoral stimulation or from vaginal stimulation. Indeed some women are even able to have orgasms through breast stimulation — and the physiological response is identical to that occurring from vaginal intercourse (Masters and Johnson, 1966). Moreover, even in vaginal intercourse, the clitoris is stimulated as described previously.

While it is well established that orgasms resulting primarily from vaginal and clitoral stimulation are physiologically the same, psychologically they may be experienced differently. The sensations arising from heterosexual intercourse and clitoral masturbation, for example, may be quite different. Physiologically, the orgasm is the same, but attending conditions (presence of the male and contact with his body) may lead to quite different perceptions of the sensation.

Recent research indicates that women who prefer vaginal stimulation to clitoral stimulation have high levels of anxiety as compared with women who prefer clitoral stimulation or both. This provides further evidence against Freud's belief that vaginal orgasm represents more maturity or better adjustment than clitoral orgasm (Fisher, 1973).

The single, satiating orgasm   It has been thought that women, like men, experience only one orgasm, followed by a "refractory period" of minutes or even hours when they are not capable of arousal and orgasm. Research shows that this is not true and that, in fact, women can have multiple orgasms. Kinsey and his colleagues (1953) discovered this, reporting that 14 percent of the women he interviewed experienced multiple orgasms. The scientific establishment dismissed these reports as unreliable, however.

Observations from the Masters and Johnson laboratory have provided convincing evidence that women do indeed experience multiple orgasms within a short time period. Moreover, these multiple orgasms do not differ from single ones in any significant way except that there are several. They are not minor experiences. In fact, the second and third orgasms are usually experienced subjectively as more satisfying than the first.

Physiologically, after an orgasm, the vaginal region loses its engorgement of blood. However, in the female, but not in the male, this process is immediately reversible. That is, under continued or renewed erotic stimulation the region again becomes engorged, the orgasmic platform appears, and another orgasm is initiated. This is the physiological mechanism that makes multiple orgasms possible in females. In some women, this process may continue to the point of exhaustion.

Most frequently, multiple orgasms are attained through masturbation rather than vaginal intercourse, since it is difficult for a male to postpone his orgasm for such long periods, and his stimulation would be necessary for the orgasms to continue.

Sex during pregnancy   Until recently, most physicians as well as the general public have believed that having intercourse during the last stages of pregnancy or too soon after giving birth was dangerous because of possible infection or discomfort to the woman. Women were often forbidden by their doctors from having intercourse from the sixth month of pregnancy through three months postpartum, a total of six months, probably creating some marital strains. This long prohibition appears not to be necessary except in unusual cases. In fact, during the second trimester of pregnancy, there is an increased sexual responsiveness in women (Masters and Johnson, 1966).

Ordinarily, intercourse may continue safely until four weeks before the baby is due, although this is clearly an individual matter. Usually by the third week postpartum, the woman is physically sufficiently recovered for coitus, and her sexual responsiveness also generally returns at this time. Hence it appears that the prohibition need be only slightly less than two months, except in cases of medical complications.

Sexuality and the elderly   It is a popular belief that a woman's sexual responsiveness is virtually gone by the time she is 60 or so, and perhaps even ceases at menopause. Some people believe that sexual activity is a drain on their health and physical resources, and deliberately stop all sexual activity in middle age in order to prevent or postpone aging. Once again, Masters and Johnson have exploded these myths.

As they conclude, "There is no time limit drawn by the advancing years to female sexuality." For the male, also, under conditions of good health and emotional adjustment, there is "a capacity for sexual performance that frequently may extend beyond the eighty-year age level." One important factor in maintaining sexual responsiveness is a regularity of sexual expression. Inactivity cannot prolong one's sex life.

It is true that certain physiological changes occur in the woman in her later years that influence her sexual activity. The ovaries sharply reduce their production of estrogen at menopause, causing the vagina to lose much of its resiliency, the amount of lubrication becoming substantially reduced. However, it is common for women to be given hormone-replacement therapy after menopause, which minimizes these changes. Application of lubricants is also helpful. Sexual performance depends much more on the opportunity for regular active sexual expression and physical and mental health than it does on hormone imbalance (Masters and Johnson, 1966).

THE G-SPOT

There has been a great deal of recent publicity given to a new discovery in sex research: the G-spot. The G-spot (short for Gräfenberg spot, named for a German obstetrician-gynecologist who discovered it originally in 1944, although his work was overlooked) is a small organ located on the top or front side of the vagina, about halfway between the pubic bone and the cervix (see Figure 12.1). It is thought to be an anatomical structure rather like the prostate in the male.

There are two reasons why the G-spot is thought to be important. First, the researchers who have been investigating it believe that it is the source of *female ejaculation* (Perry and Whipple, 1981; Addiego et al., 1981; Belzer, 1981; Ladas et al., 1982). Traditionally, it was thought that men ejaculate and women don't. However, sex researchers John Perry and Beverly Whipple (1981) have discovered fluid spurting out of the urethra of some women during orgasm. According to one study, the fluid is chemically similar to the seminal fluid of men, but contains no sperm. Perry and Whipple estimate that 10 to 20 percent of women ejaculate during orgasm. This is an important discovery because, given the old wisdom that women don't ejaculate, many women who did ejaculate suffered extreme embarrassment and anxiety, thinking that they were urinating during sex. Now that female ejaculation is recognized, their response can be seen as a normal part of female sexual response.

There is a second reason why the G-spot might be important. Based on its discovery, Perry and Whipple have theorized that there is a *uterine orgasm*. They believe that there are two kinds of orgasm: vulvar orgasm (the kind studied by Masters and Johnson, produced by clitoral stimulation, and named for the vulva, or external genitals, of the female) and uterine orgasm (felt more deeply and produced by stimulation of the G-spot). This sounds like the old argument about clitoral versus vaginal orgasm, and certainly we should withhold judgment on Perry and Whipple's work until there can be independent replication by other scientists.

The report of a discovery of female ejaculation is fascinating. It is an unexpected testimony to a recurrent theme in this book — gender similarities. Even in an era of changing gender roles, we thought we could count on at least one thing: men ejaculate and women don't. Even that rule may not hold firm. Once again, our notions of gender differences are challenged, and gender similarities turn out to be the rule.

In one study designed to test Perry and Whipple's hypotheses, two female gynecologists examined eleven women, six of whom claimed to be ejaculators. The gynecologists found an area like the G-spot in four of the eleven women, but not in the rest, and the G-spot was not found more frequently among the ejaculators. Analysis of the ejaculate indicated that it was chemically like urine, not like semen (Goldberg et al., 1983). Thus the G-spot research must be regarded as tentative and not definitive.

PSYCHOLOGICAL ASPECTS

Gender differences in sexuality   It is a stereotype in our culture that female sexuality and male sexuality are quite different. Women are reputed to be uninterested in sex and slow to arouse. Men, in contrast, are supposed to be constantly aroused. What is the scientific evidence on gender differences in sexuality?[1] There is evidence of differences in two areas: orgasm consistency and masturbation. Evidence is more mixed in two other areas: desire for sex and motives for having intercourse, and arousal to erotic materials. These will all be discussed below.

There is some evidence that males and females differ in the consistency with which they have orgasms during heterosexual intercourse. Women, on the average, seem to be less consistent at having orgasms — at least during coitus — than men are. Investigators have repeatedly found that about 30 percent of married women never have orgasms, or do so only occasionally, during intercourse with their husbands (for example, Kinsey et al., 1953; Terman, 1951). Kinsey estimated that the average married female in his sample had orgasms about 75 percent of the time during intercourse with her husband (Kinsey et al., 1953, p. 375). Kinsey believed that males have orgasms 100 percent of the time, or so close to it that he did not bother to tabulate comparable statistics for them. He also found that about 36 percent of the women in his sample had never had an orgasm before marrying. These data generally reflect the phenomenon that it is harder for females to have orgasms. In fact, one book on female sexuality contains a chapter entitled "The Struggle for Orgasm" (Kronhausen and Kronhausen, 1964), and it expresses how some women feel — as if they have to struggle to have an orgasm.

More recent surveys seem to indicate a trend toward women having orgasms with greater consistency during marital sex. In the Hunt survey (1974), only about 10 to 15 percent of the women reported having orgasms seldom or never. This increased consistency of orgasm might be related to

---

[1] Some of the evidence to be cited comes from the Kinsey report, which was based on interviews with over 11,000 subjects (Kinsey et al., 1948, 1953). There are two main criticisms of it: (1) the sample is not a random or representative sample of the United States population, and this might lead to mistaken statistics; and (2) it is based on people's self-reports of their sexual behavior, which may not be accurate (Hyde, 1979). The survey by Hunt (1974) is more up-to-date, but subject to the same two criticisms.

a number of factors, including the increased variety of techniques — such as cunnilingus — that are used in marital sex at the present time. The trend generally seems to be in the direction of diminishing what formerly was a large gender difference in orgasm consistency.

One striking gender difference that emerged in the Kinsey studies was in masturbation. In that sample, 92 percent of the males had masturbated to orgasm at least once in their lives, as compared with 58 percent of the females (Kinsey et al., 1953). Not only did fewer women masturbate, but also, in general, those who did masturbate had begun at a later age than the males. Virtually all males said they had masturbated before age 20 (most began between ages 13 and 15), but substantial numbers of women reported masturbating for the first time at age 25, 30, or 35.

Unlike some other gender differences in sexuality — which were present in the older Kinsey study but which seem to have evaporated by the time of the more recent Hunt study — gender differences in masturbation still seem to be a very real phenomenon. Hunt (1974) found that 94 percent of the males and 63 percent of the females in his sample had masturbated to orgasm at least once, percentages that are very close to those found by Kinsey a generation before. Hunt found that both boys and girls in his sample appeared to have begun masturbating earlier than those in Kinsey's study, but girls still began later than boys.

One question we must ask, however, is whether this is a real gender difference or just an inaccuracy induced by using self-reports. In our culture, particularly in previous decades, more restrictions have been placed on female sexuality than on male sexuality. It might be that these restrictions have discouraged females from ever masturbating. On the other hand, they might simply lead females to not report masturbating. That is, perhaps women do masturbate but are simply more reticent to report it than men are.

There are, of course, no data to answer that question directly. However, a comparison of the Kinsey data and the Hunt data can provide a clue. In the time intervening between these two studies, presumably restrictions against female sexuality lessened to some extent. A likely consequence of this change is that women began to feel freer to admit that they engaged in various forms of sexual behavior; for example, many more women report that they engage in premarital sex and in oral-genital sex now than at the time of the Kinsey study. Yet the percentage of women who say they masturbate has remained relatively constant (58 percent in the Kinsey study, 63 percent in the Hunt study). This suggests that the women in Hunt's study would have felt free to say that they masturbated if they really did; after all, they were willing to say that they engaged in premarital sex and oral-genital sex. Thus we can conclude that those who said they did not masturbate were being honest. In the absence of direct evidence, however, this reasoning is purely speculative.

The data suggest, then, that there is a substantial gender difference in the incidence of masturbation — virtually all males masturbate to orgasm, whereas about one-third of all women never do.

Another area in which there is some evidence of a gender difference is desire for sex and motives for having intercourse. In a 1920 survey, two-thirds of the wives reported that they desired intercourse less frequently than their husbands did (cited by R. R. Bell, 1966, p. 137). Though Kinsey provided no direct data on this point, he noted that early in marriage, many husbands desired intercourse more frequently than their wives did, although the pattern was often reversed in middle age (Kinsey et al., 1953, p. 353). Traditionally then, there appeared to be a gender difference in desire for intercourse, with men wanting it more frequently than women did.

In the Hunt survey, however, fewer than 5 percent of the wives said they wished marital intercourse was less frequent (Hunt, 1974). Thus it seems that the "I have a headache" syndrome in women is mostly a thing of the past. In fact, in a *Redbook* survey, one-third of the wives said that they wished they had intercourse *more* frequently than they did (Levin and Levin, 1975).

There is a stereotype that men and women differ in their motives for having sex. Men — at least according to the stereotype — are more interested in the physical aspects of sex and have a "love 'em and leave 'em" attitude. Women, on the other hand, are thought to be most interested in love and romance and to be concerned with the interpersonal more than the physical aspects of the relationship. To investigate this stereotype, Jan Carroll, Kari Volk, and I surveyed a random sample of students at Denison University (Carroll et al., 1984). The results generally tended to confirm the stereotype as being a real difference between women and men. In one open-ended question, we asked, "What would be your motives for having sexual intercourse?" These were some typical answers from women:

> emotional feelings that were shared, wonderful way to express LOVE!!
>
> my motives for sexual intercourse would all be due to the love and commitment I feel for my partner
>
> to show my love for my partner and to feel loved and needed
>
> wanting to share myself with someone I love, needing to be needed
>
> love, to feel loved, to express love to someone

These responses clearly indicate the importance most women attach to love and a close relationship as part of their sexual expression. Contrast those quotations with these typical responses from men:

> need it
>
> to gratify myself
>
> for the pleasure or the love
>
> to satisfy my needs
>
> when I'm tired of masturbation

These responses reflect the greater importance men — at least in this college-aged group — attach to physical gratification from sex.

Of course, not every respondent gave typical responses. For example, a response to that same question from one woman was "to enjoy myself physically, for experimentation, exercise, fun, and to get to know someone better." And this atypical answer came from a male: "Intercourse makes me happy, and people enjoy doing things that make them happy. I express myself oftentimes better physically. I have lots of love to give, and it's one way that is a better avenue of expressing my feelings for others."

We also found decided differences when we asked the respondents how they would feel about sex in a "one-night stand." The results are shown in Table 12.1. Notice that virtually all of the women said they would

TABLE 12.1. Percentages of males and females giving different responses to the question "How would you feel about sex in a 'one-night stand'?"

	Guilty	Anxious	Comfortable/ Relaxed	Satisfied
Males	28	22	22	28
Females	68	23	6	3

Source: Carroll et al., 1984.

feel either guilty or anxious, whereas about half of the men said they would feel comfortable, relaxed, or satisfied. Thus the results of our study indicate that men and women do differ in their motives for sexual intercourse and in the quality of the emotional relationship they see as a prerequisite for engaging in intercourse.

Another stereotype is that a gender difference exists in arousal to erotic materials, men being much more responsive to them than women are. Is there any scientific evidence that this is true?

The females in the Kinsey sample were considerably less likely to report responses to erotic materials than the males. For example, about half of the males reported having been aroused at some time by erotic stories; although almost all the women had heard such stories, only 14 percent had been aroused by them. These data are often cited as evidence that women are not as easily aroused as men.[2]

Studies done in the last decade, however, have provided little evidence that males and females differ in their arousal to erotic materials. For

---

[2] Actually, however, the Kinsey data were not that simple. Kinsey noted wide variability in women's responses and speculated that perhaps one-third of all women are as erotically responsive as the average male. Further, there were no gender differences in certain behaviors; for example, about the same number of females as males reported having been aroused by erotic literary materials.

example, in one study the responses of 128 male and 128 female university students to erotic slides and movies were studied (Schmidt and Sigusch, 1970). The slides and movies showed petting and coitus. In several tests for gender differences, either there were no differences, or the differences were small, with about 40 percent of the females reporting a stronger arousal response than the average male. All the females and almost all the males reported genital responses to the slides and movies. And women, not men, showed an increase in petting and coitus in the 24 hours after seeing the erotic stimuli. Therefore, there seems to be little basis for saying that women are not erotically responsive to such materials.

An interesting study by psychologist Julia Heiman (1975) provides a good deal of insight into the responses of males and females to erotic materials. Her subjects were sexually experienced university students, and she studied their responses as they listened to tape recordings of erotic stories. Not only did Heiman obtain subjects' self-ratings of their arousal, as other investigators had done, but she also got objective measures of their physiological levels of arousal. To do this, she used two instruments: a penile strain gauge and a photoplethysmograph. The penile strain gauge is used to get a physiological measure of arousal in the male; it is a flexible loop that fits around the base of the penis. The photoplethysmograph measures physiological arousal in the female; it is an acrylic cylinder that is placed just inside the entrance to the vagina. Both instruments measure vasocongestion in the genitals, which is the major physiological response during sexual arousal. These physiological measures are a great advance since they are not subject to the errors or distortions that may occur when subjects simply rate their own arousal.

Subjects heard one of four kinds of tapes. There is a stereotype that women are more turned on by romance, while men are more aroused by "raw sex." The tapes varied according to which of these kinds of content they contained. The first group of tapes was *erotic*; they included excerpts from pornographic material and popular novels giving explicit descriptions of heterosexual sex. The second group of tapes was *romantic*; a couple were heard expressing affection for each other, but they did not actually engage in sex. The third group of tapes was *erotic-romantic*; they included erotic elements of explicit sex and also romantic elements. Finally, the fourth group of tapes served as a *control*; a couple were heard engaging in conversation but nothing else. The plots of the tapes also varied according to whether the male or the female initiated the activity and whether the description centered on the female's physical and psychological responses or on the male's. Thus the tapes were male-initiated or female-initiated and female-centered or male-centered. Three important results emerged from the study:

1. Explicit sex (the erotic and erotic-romantic tapes) was most arousing, both for women and for men. The great majority of both

males and females responded most, both physiologically and in self-ratings, to the erotic and erotic-romantic tapes. Women, in fact, rated the erotic tapes as more arousing than men did. Neither men nor women responded — either physiologically or in self-reports — to the romantic tapes or to the control tapes.
2. Both males and females found the female-initiated, female-centered tape to be the most arousing.
3. Women were sometimes not aware of their own physiological arousal. Generally there was a high correlation between self-ratings of arousal and objective physiological measures of arousal, both for men and for women. When men were physically aroused, they never made an error in reporting this in their self-ratings — it's pretty hard to miss an erection. But when the women were physically aroused, about half of them failed to report it in their self-ratings. (One might assume that women who were sophisticated enough to volunteer for an experiment of this sort and who were willing to insert a photoplethysmograph into their vagina would not suddenly become bashful about reporting their arousal; that is, it seems likely that these women honestly did not know when they were aroused.)

In sum, then, Heiman's study indicates that females and males are quite similar in their responses to erotic materials, but that women can sometimes be unaware of their own physical arousal. This study, however, dealt only with the preliminary stages of arousal; perhaps women vary in the point at which they recognize their arousal.

Development of ideas about sexuality   The earliest sexual experiences many people have are in masturbation. But as we have seen, the data indicate that substantial numbers of females never masturbate, and many of those who do, do so later in life than males do. This may have important consequences in other areas of sexuality as well.

Childhood and adolescent experiences with masturbation are important early sources of learning about sexuality. Through these experiences we learn how our bodies respond to sexual stimulation and what the most effective techniques for stimulating our own bodies are. This learning is important to our experience of adult, two-person sex. Perhaps the women who do not masturbate, and who are thus deprived of this early learning experience, are the same ones who do not have orgasms in sexual intercourse. This is exactly what Kinsey's data suggested — that women who masturbate to orgasm before marriage are more likely to have orgasms in intercourse with their husbands. For example, 31 percent of the women who had never masturbated to orgasm before marriage had not had an orgasm by the end of their first year of marriage, compared with only 13 to 16 percent of the women who had masturbated (Kinsey et al., 1953,

p. 407). There seems to be a possibility, then, that women's lack of experience with masturbation in adolescence is related to their problems with having orgasms during intercourse.

It is interesting to note from the Kinsey data that boys and girls seem to learn about masturbation in different ways. Most males reported having heard about it before trying it themselves, and a substantial number had observed others doing it. Most females, on the other hand, learned to masturbate by accidental discovery of the possibility. Apparently communication about sexual behavior is not so free among girls as it is among boys, or perhaps girls are not so eager to pursue this information. At any rate, it appears that most males have learned to associate the genital organs with pleasure by the time of puberty, while many females have not.

Not only may women's relative inexperience with masturbation lead to a lack of sexual learning, but it may also create a kind of "erotic dependency" on men. Typically, boys' earliest sexual experiences are with masturbation. They learn that they can produce their own sexual pleasure. Girls typically have their earliest sexual experiences in heterosexual petting. They therefore learn about sex from boys, and they learn that their sexual pleasure is produced by the male. As sex researcher John Gagnon commented:

> Young women may know of masturbation, but not know *how* to masturbate — how to produce pleasure, or even what the pleasures of orgasm might be. . . . Some young women report that they learned how to masturbate after they had orgasm from intercourse and petting, and decided they could do it for themselves. (1977, p. 152)

An illustration of the way in which masturbation can expand female sexuality is given by what one young woman student wrote in an essay:

> At twelve years old, I discovered masturbation. . . . I was almost relieved to have, quite by accident, discovered this practice. This actually was one of the nicest discoveries that I've ever made. I feel totally comfortable with this and have actually discussed it with some of my friends. One of my favorite theories centers around this. When men have asked me to have intercourse with them and I felt that I was basically going to only serve the purpose of being an instrument to produce their orgasm, I usually tell them that I'm sure that they'd "have a better time by themselves." Masturbation does produce a better, more controlled, orgasm for me. I've read in Shere Hite's study on male sexuality that the same is true for men. I'm not saying that it's better than sexual contact with a man for me but I do think it's more satisfying than waking up next to someone I don't care about and feel comfortable with. I'm surprised that according to Kinsey, only 58 percent of women masturbate at some time in their lives. I thought everyone did. It's very creative for me. I've tried several techniques and it certainly helps me in my sexual experiences. I know a great deal about my sexual responses and I think that in knowing about myself, some of it relates to men and their sexual responses.

Experiences with masturbation — or lack of such experiences — then, may be very important in shaping female sexuality and making it different from male sexuality.

Of course, socialization forces on the female's developing sexuality are also important. Our culture has traditionally placed tighter restrictions on women's sexuality than it has on men's, and vestiges of these restrictions linger today. It seems likely that these restrictions have acted as a damper on female sexuality, and thus they may help to explain why some women do not masturbate or do not have orgasms. In an essay one woman student recalled one of her childhood socialization experiences as follows:

> A big part of my childhood was Catholic grammar school. The principal and teachers were nuns of the old school. . . . I remember one day the principal called all of the girls (third grade to eighth) to the auditorium. "I can't blame the boys for lifting your skirts to see your underwear," she scolded, "you girls wear your skirts so short it is temptation beyond their control." I had no idea what she was talking about, but throughout school the length of our skirts was of utmost importance. Nice girls did not show their legs.

One of the clearest examples of the differences in restrictions on female and male sexuality is the *double standard*. The double standard says, essentially, that the same sexual behavior is evaluated differently, depending on whether a male or a female engages in it. An example is premarital sex. Traditionally in our culture, premarital intercourse has been more acceptable for males than for females. Indeed, premarital sexual activity might be considered a status symbol for a male but a sign of cheapness for a female.

These different standards have been reflected in behavior. For example, the Kinsey data, collected in the 1940s, indicated that over twice as many males (71 percent) as females (33 percent) had premarital sex. Apparently, society's message got through to young women of that era. Most of them managed to keep themselves chaste before marriage, while their male contemporaries tended to get the experience that was expected of them.

Generally, there seems to be less of a double standard today than there was in former times. For example, people now approve of premarital sex for females about as much as they do for males. In Hunt's sample, 82 percent of the men felt that premarital sex was acceptable for males when the couple is in love, and 77 percent felt that it was acceptable for females under the same circumstances (Hunt, 1974).

This change in attitude is reflected in behavior. A much higher percentage of women report having engaged in premarital intercourse now than in Kinsey's time. In the Hunt sample, among respondents aged 18 to 24, 95 percent of the males and 81 percent of the females had had premarital intercourse. Thus there is much less of a difference between females and males now than there was a generation ago.

As I noted in Chapter 7, *ambivalence* is an important theme in the psychology of women. In that chapter I discussed ambivalence about achievement and femininity. Sexuality is another area of ambivalence for women. Doubtless this ambivalence results from the kind of mixed message that females get from society. Beginning in adolescence, they are told that popularity is important for them, and being sexy increases one's popularity. But actually engaging in premarital intercourse can lead to a loss of status. The ambivalence-producing message is "Be sexy but don't be sexual."

Ambivalence toward sexual relations is reflected in the large number of unwanted pregnancies among unmarried women who were well informed about contraception (Stiller, 1960). For example, research in the 1970s indicated that of sexually active single girls, 75 percent said they used contraceptives not at all, or only occasionally ("Teen-Age Sex," 1972). The evidence shows that they failed to use contraceptives. Why? Taking a birth-control pill every day indicates that the woman thinks intercourse is a real possibility. For unmarried women, particularly those not involved in a long-term relationship, this is a difficult admission to make. Constantly being ready for sexual relations still suggests cheapness. In fact, the antipathy toward taking a daily measure against conception is apparently so great that it outweighs the undesirability of pregnancy, as discussed in Chapter 11. The woman would much prefer to believe that she was "swept off her feet," rather than the implied alternative, that she was expecting to have sex.

Research on the development of sexuality suggests that discussing gender differences in sexuality is too simple an approach. It is the developmental process of sexuality that differs for males and females (Kaplan and Sager, 1971). In a sense, males and females appear to move through the stages of sexual development in adolescence and adulthood in opposite orders. For males, adolescent sexuality is genitally focused with strong orgasmic needs — four to eight orgasms per day are not unusual. But by the time a man reaches fifty, emphasis has shifted away from genitally centered sensations to a more generalized, sensuously diffuse experience, and two orgasms per week are considered satisfactory. For the female, adolescent sexuality is diffuse and not genitally focused, with little emphasis on orgasm. Genital sexuality and orgasmic potential develop later, not reaching a peak until the thirties and forties. Orgasmic response in women is faster and more consistent in the forties than it is in the teens or twenties. It appears, then, that early male sexuality is genital and gradually evolves to a more complex, diffuse sensuous experience, whereas female sexuality begins as a complex, diffuse experience, and only later develops the genital component.

Fantasies The psychoanalytic school has traditionally considered fantasies during intercourse as a sign of pathology. Some women further resist fantasies because they seem to be a sign of disloyalty to their partners. Hence, these fantasies have been considered rare, and have received little attention in research.

A questionnaire study of 141 adult women volunteers indicated that 65 percent fantasized during intercourse with their husbands (Hariton, 1973). An additional 28 percent reported occasional thoughts during intercourse that might be counted as fantasies, leaving only 7 percent of the sample indicating no fantasies at all. Statistically, then, it seems that it is the woman who does *not* fantasize who is abnormal!

The following are the ten most common fantasies listed in order of frequency:

1. Thoughts of an imaginary lover enter my mind.
2. I imagine that I am being overpowered or forced to surrender.
3. I enjoy pretending that I am doing something sick or forbidden.
4. I am in a different place like a car, motel, beach, woods, etc.
5. I relive a previous sexual experience.
6. I imagine myself delighting many men.
7. I imagine that I am observing myself or others having sex.
8. I pretend that I am another irresistibly sexy female.
9. I pretend that I struggle and resist before being aroused to surrender.
10. I daydream that I am being made love to by more than one man at a time. (Hariton, 1973)

The two most common themes are being with another man, and being overpowered. It should be noted that males and females share fantasies of common content; for example, fantasies of both may involve being dominated by a member of the other gender (Hunt, 1974).

Women who have fantasies during coitus are generally independent, impulsive, and nonconformist — all personality characteristics typical of creative people. Their fantasies do not appear to be signs of poor marital adjustment; on the contrary, they seemed to have better sexual relations than the nonfantasizers. This latter group, in contrast, were generally conciliatory, unassuming, nurturing, and affiliative (Hariton, 1973).

In previous sections, I have emphasized the need for interpersonal relationships as an important aspect of female sexuality. Here is the other side of the coin, the woman's experience of her own, individual, creative sexuality.

Sex and androgyny Chapter 4 included a discussion of androgyny — integrating masculine and feminine traits into one's personality and behaviors — and some of the advantages it might have. Is androgyny advantageous to one's sexuality? Are androgynous people more sexually liberated? Are they more sexually satisfied? It might be expected that androgynous people would have the most flexible and satisfying sexuality, insofar as they can combine both masculine elements of sexuality (e.g., initiating sex, being easily aroused) and feminine elements of sexuality (integrating love and emotion with sex, communicating). What is the evidence?

In one study, androgynous females were more comfortable with sex than feminine females were, and androgynous males were more comfortable with sex than masculine males were (Walfish and Myerson, 1980). In another study, androgynous women reported having orgasms more frequently than feminine women did (Radlove, 1983). In a third study, college student subjects viewed slides of couples having intercourse either in the traditional man-above position or in the woman-above position (Allgeier and Fogel, 1978). They then rated their attitudes toward the individuals in the slides. Females were more negative about the woman-above position than were males. The subjects' gender-typing (androgynous versus stereotyped) was *unrelated* to their attitudes about the woman-above position. Thus, of these three studies, two indicate that androgynous people are more liberated and satisfied in their sexuality, whereas the third does not show that. Androgyny is probably related to some good things in sexuality, but we shouldn't expect it to be the surefire solution to everything.

As an interesting aside, another study found a relationship between sexual satisfaction and feminism among women who were married or cohabiting (Kirkpatrick, 1980). That is, the more feminist a woman was in her attitudes, the greater was her sexual satisfaction in her relationship.

SEXUAL DYSFUNCTION AND THERAPY

The term *sexual dysfunction* refers to various disturbances or impairments of sexual functioning, such as inability to have an orgasm (orgasmic dysfunction), or premature ejaculation. Once again, we have Masters and Johnson to thank for investigating this field and pioneering in therapy for these problems (Masters and Johnson, 1970; for a critique, see Zilbergeld and Evans, 1980).

The Masters and Johnson approach   Most authorities agree that the majority of cases of sexual dysfunction are psychogenic rather than organic (physical) in nature. But Masters and Johnson have rejected most of the traditional notions about the psychological sources of the problem. They say

> Sociocultural deprivation and ignorance of sexual physiology, rather than psychiatric or medical illness, constitute the etiologic background for most sexual dysfunction. (1970, p. 21)

That is, sexual problems may not be symptoms of deep psychiatric disturbance, but may have simpler sources, such as educational deprivation. Their theoretical orientation, then, is learning theory rather than psychoanalytic theory. Therefore, Masters and Johnson have adopted a rapid treatment program, two weeks in duration, which has attained remarkable success.

Their treatment program has a number of unusual features. One is that it requires that both husband and wife participate in the therapy. Masters and Johnson maintain that there is no such thing as an uninvolved partner in cases of sexual dysfunction, even if only one person displays overt symptoms. For instance, a wife who does not experience orgasm is anxious and wonders whether there is anything wrong with her, or whether she is unattractive to her husband. The husband, on the other hand, while performing adequately, may wonder why he is failing to stimulate his wife to orgasm. Hence both partners are deeply involved. Realizing the reciprocal nature of sexual gratification, Masters and Johnson employ the practice of having both partners participate.

The major objective in their therapy is abolishing goal-directed sexual performance. Most people think that certain things should be *achieved* during sexual activity — for example, that the female should achieve or attain an orgasm. This emphasis on achieving leads to a fear of failure, which spells disaster for sexual enjoyment. Masters and Johnson therefore try to remove the individual from a spectator role in sex — observing her or his own actions, evaluating their success. Instead, the emphasis is on the enjoyment of all sensual pleasures. Patients use a series of "sensate focus" exercises, in which they learn to touch and to respond to touch. Patients are also taught to express sexual needs to their partners, which people generally are reluctant to do. For instance, the woman is taught to tell her husband in which regions of her body she enjoys being touched most, and how firm or light the touch should be. Beyond this basic instruction, which includes lessons in sexual anatomy and physiology, Masters and Johnson simply allow natural sexual response to emerge. Sexual pleasure is natural, sexual response is natural. After removing artificial impediments to sexual response, they find that people quickly begin joyful, "successful" participation in sex.

Masters and Johnson have evaluated the success of their therapy, both during the two-week therapy session, and in follow-up studies five years after couples leave the clinic. Their research indicates that therapy is successful in approximately 75 percent of the cases (although their results have been disputed — see Zilbergeld and Evans, 1980).

Let us now look at some specific examples of sexual dysfunction in females.

Orgasmic dysfunction In *primary orgasmic dysfunction* the woman has had intercourse but has never experienced an orgasm (for a review, see

Anderson, 1983). Masters and Johnson do not use the term "frigidity" because it has a variety of imprecise, negative connotations. Examples of some of the causes of orgasmic dysfunction in a woman are: (1) strong religious prohibitions that treat sex as dirty and sinful; (2) inability to identify with her partner — she generally dislikes one or several of his characteristics; and (3) marriage to a sexually inadequate man (Masters and Johnson, 1970). In this last case, it is obvious how primary dysfunction in one partner can bring about dysfunction in the other partner — that is, the relationship is critical.

Masters and Johnson's assertion that the above factors cause orgasmic dysfunction has been challenged, however. In multiple samples of women, Fisher (1973) found repeatedly that orgasm consistency was unrelated to the following factors: the woman's psychological stability; her amount of "practice" with sex, or her husband's attitudes; her degree of femininity, or her hostility and dominance; her degree of religiosity; or her parents' attitudes toward sex. That is, the factors Masters and Johnson suggest promote orgasmic dysfunction do not in the Fisher study appear to be related to the consistency with which women do have orgasms. For example, the suggestion that orgasmic dysfunction is related to a family and religious background that treated sex as dirty is not borne out by the lack of correlation between orgasm consistency and parents' attitudes toward sex or strength of religious ties. The two factors that do emerge as related to orgasm capacity are fears of separation or loss in personal relationships, and father's lack of interest during childhood (Fisher, 1973).

In *situational orgasmic dysfunction*, according to Masters and Johnson, the woman has orgasms in some situations, but not in others. Clearly in this case, there is no organic impairment of orgasm, since the woman is capable of experiencing it. The systematic nature of the situations in which the woman can and cannot experience orgasm often leads to an understanding of the psychogenic nature of the problem (Masters and Johnson, 1970). Sometimes a woman who has frequently experienced orgasm in intercourse with her husband is no longer capable of it. This may be related to a change in her identification with him. For instance, in one case a woman who strongly desired an increase in the family's social and economic status became sexually dysfunctional after her husband lost several jobs. Apparently she realized he would not accomplish what she wanted, and her disillusionment was channeled into her sexual response, or lack of it. A strong homosexual orientation can also be a source of situational orgasmic dysfunction. If a woman has had a long and significant homosexual relationship, particularly when she is young, she may be capable of experiencing orgasm in homosexual relations, but not in heterosexual ones. Another kind of situational dysfunction is masturbatory orgasmic inadequacy, in which the woman cannot masturbate to orgasm (the reverse is much more common — women who can masturbate to orgasm, but cannot experience orgasm in heterosexual intercourse). This syndrome is frequently associated with guilt over masturbation.

The basic therapy technique Masters and Johnson use with these patients involves teaching them how to be sexual creatures in an appropriate psychosocial context. Because of the societal "double standard" that prohibits women from being honorable sexual beings, many women feel they need special permission for sex, or that it is only a duty to their husband. Naturally, this will inhibit their response. Therefore, Masters and Johnson see the overcoming of these inhibitions as their major task.

Vaginismus Vaginismus involves a tightening or spasm of the outer third of the vagina, possibly to such an extent that the opening of the vagina is closed and intercourse becomes impossible. Factors in the woman's history that seem to cause this condition include marriage to an impotent man, family background in which sex was considered dirty and sinful, a previous physical assault, and long experience of painful intercourse due to a physical problem (Masters and Johnson, 1970).

In therapy, Masters and Johnson find it important to demonstrate to both husband and wife the reality and nature of the vaginal spasm, of which they are frequently unaware. The treatment consists mainly of using vaginal dilators of progressive size to enlarge the opening. In cases where physical problems seem to be the source, treatment of these problems often seems to help the emotional problems.

Painful intercourse Painful intercourse or *dyspareunia* may be organic or psychogenic in origin. Too often, the woman's complaints of pain are dismissed, particularly if the physician cannot find an obvious physical problem. However, this is a serious condition, and should be treated as such. When pain is felt in the vagina, it may be due to failure to lubricate, to infection, to special sensitivity of the vagina (such as to the contraceptives being used), or to changes in the vagina due to age. Pain may also be felt in the region of the vaginal outlet and clitoris, or deep in the pelvis. In this latter case, the causes may be infection or tearing of the ligaments supporting the uterus, particularly following childbirth.

Disorders of sexual desire In the late 1970s and early 1980s, sex therapists began seeing a new kind of sexual dysfunction, and cases of it quickly became more common than cases of any of the preceding kinds. This new category was termed *disorders of sexual desire* (H. Kaplan, 1979; LoPiccolo, 1980). It should be stressed that, contrary to stereotypes, this problem is found in both women and men.

Sexual desire, or libido, refers to a set of feelings that lead the individual to seek out sexual activity or to be pleasurably receptive to it. When sexual desire is inhibited, so that the individual is not interested in sexual activity, the dysfunction is termed low sexual desire or a disorder of sexual desire. People with inhibited sexual desire typically manage to avoid situations that will evoke sexual feelings. If, despite their best efforts, they find themselves in an arousing situation, they experience a rapid "turn-off" of their feelings. The turn-off may be so intense that some people report negative, unpleasant feelings; others simply report sexual anesthesia, that is, no sexual feeling at all, even though they may respond to the point of orgasm.

A survey of a "normal" (nonpatient) population indicated that 35 percent of the women and 16 percent of the men complained of disinterest in sex (Frank et al., 1978).

As with other dysfunctions, with disorders of sexual desire, there are complex problems of definition. There are many circumstances when it is perfectly normal for a person's desire to be inhibited. For example, one cannot be expected to find every potential partner attractive. Sex therapist Helen Singer Kaplan (1979) recounts an example of a couple consisting of a shy, petite woman and an extremely obese (350 pounds, 5 feet 3 inches tall), unkempt man. He complained of her lack of desire, but one can understand her inhibition and would certainly hesitate to classify her as having a sexual dysfunction. One cannot expect to respond sexually at all times, in all places, and with all persons.

It is also true that an individual's absolute level of sexual desire is often not the problem — rather, the problem is a *discrepancy* between the partners' levels (Zilbergeld and Ellison, 1980). That is, if one partner wants sex less frequently than the other partner wants it, there is a conflict.

Because recognition of this dysfunction is relatively recent, there is little agreement in the field about its definition or diagnosis. However, it seems unlikely that low sexual desire will turn out to be a single category (LoPiccolo, 1980). Rather, it probably represents a single symptom that can be caused by many factors. The following have been implicated as determinants of low sexual desire: hormones, psychological factors (particularly anxiety and/ depression), and cognitive factors (not having learned to perceive one's arousal accurately or having limited expectations for one's own ability to be aroused) (LoPiccolo, 1980).

New therapies for women's sexual dysfunctions   The incidence of women who have problems having orgasms, particularly in intercourse, is so high that it seems that this pattern is well within the range of normal female sexual response. It is questionable whether it should be called a dysfunction, except insofar as it causes unhappiness for the woman. With the growing awareness of the frequency of this problem have come a number of self-help sex therapy books for women, one of the best being Lonnie Garfield Barbach's *For Yourself: The Fulfillment of Female Sexuality* (1975; see also Heiman et al., 1976). Reading and working through the exercises in these self-help books actually has a fancy name — bibliotherapy — and it has been demonstrated to produce significant gains in women's frequency of orgasm during sexual intercourse (Dodge et al., 1982).

A common recommendation of Barbach and other therapists (e.g., LoPiccolo and Lobitz, 1972) is that pre-orgasmic women practice masturbation in order to increase their capacity for orgasm. The idea is that women must first explore their own bodies and learn how to bring themselves to orgasm before they can expect to have orgasms in heterosexual intercourse. As noted earlier in this chapter, many women have not had this kind of practice, and sex therapists recommend that they get it.

Another exercise that is recommended is the *Kegel exercises* or *pubococcygeal muscle exercises* (Kegel, 1952). The pubococcygeal (PC) muscle runs along the sides of the entrance of the vagina. Exercising this muscle seems to increase women's sexual pleasure by increasing the sensitivity of the vaginal area. This exercise is particularly helpful to women who have had the PC muscle stretched in childbirth or who simply have poor tone in it. The woman is instructed first to find the PC muscle by sitting on a toilet with her legs spread apart, urinating, and stopping the flow of urine voluntarily. The muscle that stops the flow is the PC. After that, the woman is told to contract the muscle 10 times during each of six sessions per day. Gradually she can work up to more.

GENDER SIMILARITIES

In previous chapters I have stressed gender similarities in psychological processes. There are also great gender similarities in sexuality. A few decades ago, at the time of the Kinsey research, there were marked gender differences in several aspects of sexuality. However, more recent research shows that these differences are greatly decreased, or even absent now.

For example, according to Kinsey's data collected in the 1940s, 71 percent of males, but only 33 percent of females had premarital intercourse by age 25 (Kinsey et al., 1953). There was, at that time, a marked gender difference in premarital sexual activity. However, data on the youngest (18 to 24) age group in the Hunt survey (1974) indicate that 95 percent of males and 81 percent of females had had premarital intercourse. The data, then, indicate that in the future nearly everyone, both female and male, will engage in premarital intercourse. Thus the general trend seems to be toward gender similarities in sexuality. Even ejaculation, which used to be seen as an exclusively male prerogative, has now been found in some women.

SUGGESTIONS FOR FURTHER READING

Barbach, Lonnie G. (1975). *For yourself: The fulfillment of female sexuality*. Garden City, NY: Anchor Press/Doubleday. This is the classic self-help book on female sexuality and, I think, still the best one around.

Hyde, Janet S. (1982). *Understanding human sexuality* (2nd ed.). New York: McGraw-Hill. Obviously, I have a prejudice in favor of this book, but I would like to recommend it if you want more information on sexuality than I could provide in one brief chapter here.

13
Lesbianism and Bisexuality

Between man and woman love is an act; each torn from self becomes other: what fills the woman in love with wonder is that the languorous passivity of her flesh should be reflected in the male's impetuosity; the narcissistic woman, however, recognizes her enticements but dimly in the man's erected flesh. Between women love is contemplative; caresses are intended less to gain possession of the other than gradually to re-create the self through her; separateness is abolished, there is no struggle, no victory, no defeat; in exact reciprocity each is at once subject and object; sovereign and slave; duality becomes mutuality.

SIMONE DE BEAUVOIR, The Second Sex

With the sexual revolution and the feminist movement has also come the rise of gay liberation. The gay liberation movement can probably be counted as dating from June 1969, when, in response to police harassment, homosexuals rioted in Greenwich Village in New York. Lesbians have sometimes been united with the women's movement and sometimes in conflict with it. Radical lesbians argue that to be truly liberated, women must become separatists, that is, they must stay separate from men. Among other things, this would argue *against* heterosexuality and *for* lesbianism. More moderate lesbians join in working for the moderate goals of the women's movement, such as an end to job discrimination. It is clear that a discussion of women today would be incomplete without a discussion of lesbianism.

THE LESBIAN EXPERIENCE

I shall try in the following section to describe the lesbian experience, how lesbians think and feel. Historically, there was little written information on this topic (For a discussion of lesbianism through history, see Faderman, 1981). With the recent liberalization of attitudes toward homosexuality, some lesbians have stepped forward to openly acknowledge, indeed proclaim, their sexual preferences. Accompanying this trend toward openness are a number of published accounts of the lesbian experience (see, for example, Martin and Lyon, 1972).

We must keep in mind that describing lesbians as a group engenders the same error that occurs when we collectively describe any group. That is, lesbians are as varied and differ as much among themselves as do heterosexual women or men. In addition, it is likely that the lesbians about whom the most is known from research are those who seek psychotherapy in order to stabilize their adjustment. Therefore they may provide a distorted view of lesbianism.

Discrimination and stereotypes   Certainly society's discrimination against homosexuals is a part of the experience of lesbians. There are numerous documented cases of women being fired from their jobs or dishonorably discharged from the armed forces upon disclosure of their sexual preferences (Martin and Lyon, 1972). Court cases have repeatedly upheld the right of employers to fire persons on the basis of sexual preference. The lesbian must live with the knowledge that this might also be her fate if her lifestyle becomes known. The alternative is to publicly deny her lifestyle. She must then role-play a denial of that which is so important to her.

A subtler result of social discrimination is the prohibition against lesbians rearing children. In most states it is illegal for lesbians to adopt children, and lesbianism may be grounds for a father to regain custody from a lesbian mother of children they had when married. Yet many lesbians desire children, and these restrictions may be a great source of sadness to them. There is currently a move in several states to modify some of this discrimination against lesbians, which will help to ease at least one strain.

The forms of discrimination discussed to this point are institutional, most often encoded in our legal system. Other forms of discrimination are more subtle and psychological, involving the stereotyping of lesbians. They are expected to be unfeminine or even mannish, and certainly to be man-haters. In one study, subjects were exposed to written and tape-recorded descriptions of one of the following women: a feminine woman (described as feminine, emotional, warm toward others, and kind) or masculine woman (described as masculine, competitive, active, feeling superior) with heterosexual or homosexual feelings (Storms et al., 1981). Afterwards, subjects rated their perceptions of the woman described to them. The woman who was described as homosexual was rated as being more masculine than the heterosexual woman. The woman who was described as feminine and homosexual was perceived as having a confused, unstable sexual identity. This sort of stereotyping is another unpleasant fact of life for lesbian women.

In considering this stereotype of the lesbian as masculine, it is important to make a distinction between gender identification and choice of sexual partner. Most lesbians have a female identification — that is, they are quite definitely women; they dress and behave like women; but they simply choose to direct emotional, sexual love toward other women. Indeed, a large proportion of them have had heterosexual relations, and many are or have been heterosexually married. According to the Kinsey data, about 13 percent of all females have had at least one homosexual experience leading to orgasm, but less than 1 percent of all females are exclusively homosexual throughout their lives.

Lesbian relationships   Psychologist Anne Peplau and her colleagues (1978) have studied the nature of lesbian relationships based on lengthy questionnaires administered to 127 lesbians recruited through feminist and gay organizations in Los Angeles. They found a number of interesting results, and concluded that two fundamental values were related to the nature of lesbian relationships: attachment to the partner and personal autonomy. That is, lesbians vary in the extent to which they want a strong attachment to the partner, emphasizing emotional closeness, love, and security, and the extent to which they want personal independence. These two values are related to the kind of relationship that is formed. The feminist lesbians tended to emphasize the personal autonomy value.

The length of the longest lesbian relationship these women had had ranged from one month to 25 years, with a median of 2.5 years. In describing their current relationship, most of the women reported it as being close and loving. About 75 percent reported that they and their current partner were "in love." There was a high degree of satisfaction with the relationship (mean of 7.1 on a 9-point scale). There was also a great deal of satisfaction with the sexual aspects of the relationship. Over 70 percent of the women said that they almost always experienced orgasm when having sex with their partner. In regard to power in the relationship, the majority said that they and their partner shared equally in power. Peplau and her colleagues concluded that lesbians can and do form committed, satisfying relationships.

One stereotype is that lesbians play "butch" and "femme" roles in their relationships, that is, that they mimic the male and female roles found in traditional marriages. Research shows this stereotype to be false (Peplau, 1982). Only a small minority of lesbian couples play such roles. In contrast, the majority of lesbian couples stress flexibility and taking turns — that is, equality — in their relationships. One gay woman said,

> I don't like role-playing because it copies the traditional male/female relationship. I'm proud I'm a woman. And I love women, not pseudo-men. (Jay and Young, 1979, p. 320)

Coping   Lesbians' lives are filled with stresses, some resulting from the kinds of discrimination discussed previously, some from the kinds of stresses that everyone, heterosexual and homosexual alike, must deal with. How do lesbians cope? Far more research is needed in this area, but at least one study provides information. (See also Brooks, 1981.)

In this study, 79 lesbians, all working women, responded to a mailed questionnaire (Shachar and Gilbert, 1983). They were questioned about various conflicts they experienced and how they coped with them. Of the interrole conflicts (conflicts between two different roles the woman must fulfill), the one most frequently mentioned was that between the lover and worker roles (mentioned by 41 percent of the women). As one woman commented,

> My lover wants the security of staying in one area and spending much time with me; I am very busy with my career . . . and I must move frequently to gain experience/opportunities. (Shachar and Gilbert, 1983, p. 249)

Other interrole conflicts mentioned with less frequency were conflicts between the roles of worker and political activist (13 percent), lover and daughter (7 percent), and lover and political activist (6 percent). Interestingly, certain other potential conflicts — e.g., mother versus lover — were reported by no more than one respondent. On the other hand, those conflicts were rated as very stressful.

Intrarole conflicts are internal conflicts within a single role. As an area of intrarole conflict, work was mentioned most frequently (33 percent). One woman said,

> Expectations of co-workers and boss (all male) that I be heterosexual (dress, act, and have evidence of so being) when I really wish I could just be who I am at work. I cannot, usually, because I am afraid of what'd result. (Shachar and Gilbert, 1983, p. 250)

On the other hand, it is worth noting that the fact that one-third of the lesbian respondents reported intrarole conflicts at work implies that two-thirds do not experience such conflicts.

Coping mechanisms for dealing with role conflicts can be placed in three categories (Shachar and Gilbert, 1983):

1. Structural role redefinition — The individual deals directly with those people who communicate role demands and negotiates a change that is mutually acceptable.
2. Personal role redefinition — The individual changes her own perceptions of roles and role demands rather than changing the external environment.
3. Reactive behavior — The individual assumes that role demands are unchangeable and denies or tries to meet all role demands.

Generally, Type 1 or Type 2 coping is more successful, resulting in less stress and greater satisfaction with coping. In dealing with interrole conflicts, 82 percent of the lesbian respondents reported using Type 1 or Type 2 strategies. Further, those who used one of those two strategies had significantly higher self-esteem than those who used the Type 3 strategy. In general, then, the majority of lesbians use healthy strategies for coping with their stresses.

LESBIANISM: NORMAL
OR ABNORMAL?

The majority of Americans disapprove of homosexuality and view it as abnormal. In a 1970 study conducted by the Institute for Sex Research, two-thirds of the respondents regarded homosexuality as "very obscene and vulgar" (Weinberg and Williams, 1974). In a 1969 Harris poll, 63 percent of Americans considered homosexuals harmful to American life. What scientific evidence is there regarding whether homosexuality is abnormal?

To answer this question, I must first define what is meant by "abnormal." A variety of definitions are possible (Hyde, 1979). The one that seems most appropriate here is that a sexual behavior is abnormal if it is associated with poor psychological adjustment and the person is unhappy about it.

The massive research of Kinsey and his colleagues (Kinsey et al., 1948, 1953) contributed to destroying simplistic classifications of sexual behaviors as normal or abnormal. Many behaviors that were thought to be rare perversions turned out in reality to be fairly common. A good example is male homosexuality, long thought to be a deviant form of behavior; in fact, it is engaged in by substantial proportions of males. Kinsey found that about 60 percent of all males had some form of homosexual experience before adulthood; about 37 percent of all males had at least one adult homosexual experience leading to orgasm. Indeed, many men who engage in homosexual activities are respectable, middle-class citizens, and many are married (Humphreys, 1970). In view of such statistics it is difficult to view the behavior as deviant.

Empirical research also supports the view that lesbianism is not a deviant form of behavior (see review by Rosen, 1974). First, it is important to note that much of the early research on lesbian adjustment used lesbians who were patients in psychotherapy as subjects. The use of such a subject pool was not surprising, since they were easy to recruit, and, with the assumption that lesbianism was an abnormal form of adjustment, the researcher could rationalize the sampling techniques by saying that the "typical" lesbian would be in therapy.

In view of the subjects, it is not surprising that some of these early research efforts did find abnormal personality characteristics in lesbians. However, a major breakthrough occurred with the advent of research on *nonpatient* lesbians, recruited through homophile organizations or newspaper ads. Such studies have generally found that lesbians do not differ psychologically from control groups of heterosexual women in any consistent ways, with the one exception of their choice of sex partner. For example, lesbians could not be distinguished from heterosexual women on the basis of projective test performance, although there was some evidence that the lesbians were more likely to have a hostile-fearful conception of the female role (Armon, 1960). While the results of one study indicated that a nonclinical group of lesbians were higher in neuroticism than a comparison group of heterosexuals (Kenyon, 1968), another study indicated that lesbians and heterosexuals did not differ in neuroticism (Hopkins, 1969). Similar results, in which lesbians and heterosexuals did not differ, were obtained in several other studies (Freedman, 1968; Saghir and Robins, 1971; Siegelman, 1972). While Saghir and Robins found that depression, suicide attempts, and alcohol abuse were more common among nonpatient lesbians than among heterosexuals, such differences were not found in another study (Asimos and Rosen, unpublished, reported in Rosen, 1974). No differences in adjustment as measured by the MMPI were found between a group of single homosexual women and a group of single heterosexual women (Oberstone and Sukoneck, 1976). And in another study, lesbians had significantly higher self-esteem than college women (Spence and Helmreich, 1978).

Thus the assumption that lesbianism is an inadequate form of adjustment is not supported by the available data and, as Rosen concludes, "The only difference between the lesbian and other women is the choice of love object" (1974, p. 65). The comparative absence of psychological disturbance among lesbians is even more remarkable in view of the social pressures to which they are subject. The notion that lesbianism, and homosexuality more generally, is an adequate form of adjustment is reflected in the 1973 decision of the American Psychiatric Association to remove the term "homosexual" from its official list of diagnostic categories.

In a recent study the gender-role identities of lesbians were examined, using the categories of androgynous, feminine, masculine, and undifferentiated discussed in Chapter 4 (Spence and Helmreich, 1978). The results, in comparison with college women, are shown in Table 13.1. It is true that a relatively low percentage of lesbians fall into the feminine category. We also find corresponding increases in the androgynous and masculine categories, and a slight increase in the undifferentiated category. The largest group of lesbians fall into the androgynous category. Given the earlier

TABLE 13.1. Percentages of lesbians and unselected female college students in the four gender-role categories (discussed in Chapter 4)

	Gender-Role Category			
	Androgynous	*Feminine*	*Masculine*	*Undifferentiated*
Lesbians	33	13	22	32
College women	27	32	14	28

Source: Spence and Helmreich, 1978, pp. 53, 67.

conclusions about androgyny being mentally healthy, this is a further indication that lesbianism is a healthy form of adjustment.

In another study, lesbian mothers and heterosexual mothers rated their concept of the ideal child using the Bem Sex Role Inventory, which measures androgyny (Kweskin and Cook, 1982). There were no significant differences between the lesbian and heterosexual women in their rating of the ideal child. This evidence indicates that lesbians are not "abnormal" mothers, and that they have views similar to those of heterosexual women concerning what children should be like.

THEORETICAL VIEWS

The psychoanalytic view   Sigmund Freud was one of the first medical therapists to attempt the treatment of a homosexual woman, publishing his insights in a paper, "The Psychogenesis of a Case of Homosexuality in a Woman" in 1920.

Freud considered human beings to be bisexual in nature. In this assertion, he recognized that all humans are capable of homosexual behavior. According to Freud, the sources of sexual pleasure in the young are many and diffuse.

At about age three, the boy encounters the Oedipal complex. In the positive component of the complex, the mother is a love object for the boy and the father is the object of ambivalence. In resolving the Oedipal complex, the boy comes to identify with his father. A *negative Oedipal complex* occurs when the shift to identification with the father is not made, and the boy continues his initial identification with the mother, wanting (like her) to be loved by the father. According to Freud, people never really completely shed themselves of this negative component, but homosexual people remain fixated on it.

Freud initially viewed these psychological mechanics as highly similar for boys and for girls. It was some years before the gap between the logic of the theory and the realities of female development disposed Freud to a revised version of sexual development in women. He finally recognized that the boy's Oedipal development was far simpler than the girl's. The boy retains his original love object (mother), merely substituting another female for the original. For the girl, the mother is also naturally the original love object, but the father must become the object. Thus presumably the negative Oedipal situation for the girl — in which she continues to love the same gender parent, the mother — may well be more intense, last longer, and not be resolved. The lesbian alternative, according to Freud, occurs when the negative Oedipal component persists, so that mother and later other women are the object of love. The masculine component of the woman's personality is retained and the object choice is homosexual.

FIGURE 13.1

Lesbians can and do form satisfying, long-term relationships.

Source: Photo by Eric A. Roth, © 1978 / The Picture Cube.

Freud speculated that the basis for homosexuality in men and in women may well be a matter of self-love or *narcissism*. The outcome, then, is to love the self, and to seek a same-gender person, who resembles the self, for a sex partner. From this perspective we may be seeing a positive aspect of lesbian development. A problem with "normal" female development is that many women end up with low self-confidence and low regard for other women. Lesbian development may be an alternative in which the self and the female can be loved and valued.

A psychoanalytic variant   In her book *Love Between Women* (1971), Charlotte Wolff provides a variant of the psychoanalytic model based on her research with nonpatient lesbians. Her theory of gender-role development in women emphasizes the normal, intense attachment of the young girl for her mother, where the mother is seen as all-powerful and godlike. It is not long before the developing female realizes that the mother values males more highly than females in a man-valuing society, and that her chances of getting her mother's love are less than her father and brother have. This perception that the mother values her own gender less leads the developing girl to be insecure about her own value.

In a sense, then, the mother gives a second-rate status to the young girl. At this point the girl may choose to pursue one of two strategies for dealing with this situation: she may strive to be a very feminine female, ingratiating herself to the mother (the heterosexual course); or she may seek to become like the superior gender, becoming masculine and competitive(the lesbian course). More commonly, she chooses the first course of action, becoming like the mother and emulating those many aspects of femininity that the mother models.

The homosexual woman, on the other hand, has chosen a different strategy and therefore need not play such games. She fights for equality with men in order to be worthy of her mother's love. "Emotional incest with the mother is indeed the very essence of lesbianism" (p. 72). Further, there is a suggestion that males are basically alien to the lesbian. Wolff found that many of the lesbians she studied had a history of a father who was absent for a substantial period during their childhood — for example, during the war. Such girls grow up in a basically feminine world in which males are strange and alien. Thus, according to Wolff's view, lesbianism arises from the girl taking a masculine, competitive strategy to deal with the insufficiency of her mother's love.

Wolff's theory rests on the somewhat tenuous assumption that the mother is the girl's only real love object, that she continues to seek the mother's love throughout life, and that males are loved or manipulated only as a substitute. Further, Wolff commits an error similar to Freud's in confusing gender identity with choice of sexual partner — that is, she assumes that lesbian development leads to masculinity. Yet empirical research shows that lesbians generally have a feminine identification, and that they may be aggressive and competitive, or passive and shy, just as may heterosexual women. Wolff assumes that all lesbians enter into direct competition with males — again, that they are masculine. Nonetheless, her theory and research give some insights into the emotional and love aspects of lesbianism.

Learning theory   Learning theory (for example Bermant, 1972; Ford and Beach, 1951) emphasizes the point that all animals, including humans, display or are capable of homosexual activities. Thus, animals appear to be bisexual, and the environment may have a great influence on whether one or another choice of sex partner is made. In some primitive cultures, a male may be the appropriate sex partner for a young male, whereas in his adulthood the accepted partner may be a female (Mead, 1961).

Therefore humans may have no inborn preference for the opposite gender as an appropriate sex partner, but the nature of conditioning and socialization channels this disposition. That is, cultural pressures channel a generalized drive in a culturally prescribed direction. Ford and Beach (1951) in their classic work on sexual behavior in humans and animals give detailed evidence of the bisexual inheritance of humans that tends to confirm the above notion. One might conclude that heterosexual behavior is an acquired, that is, a learned, state of being. Learning theory points out that heterosexual development is actually far more chancey than most people realize. We should ask not only "Why do homosexuals and lesbians develop?" but also "Why do heterosexuals develop?"

The learning theory view, then, is that humans have a general pool of sex drives that may, depending on experience and circumstance, be conditioned in one direction or another, into heterosexuality or into homosexuality. One problem with this view is that it assumes that male homosexual and female homosexual development are similar. This would seem unlikely in view of the different experiences and status of men and women in our culture, a point more adequately acknowledged in the psychoanalytic theories. On the other hand, the learning theory model readily accommodates lesbianism as a normal form of behavior in contrast to the psychoanalytic theories, which treat it as deviant or compensatory.

The feminist and sociological perspectives   Feminists and modern sociologists have rather similar things to say about lesbianism, so I have grouped them together here. One of the main points of the feminist perspective is that, when trying to understand the behavior of a woman, the emphasis should be shifted away from *internal factors* (her personality, adjustment, early childhood) to *external factors* (institutions, laws, interactions with others). (See Chapter 3.) Sociological theories share this emphasis on external factors. They agree with the feminist perspective in criticizing previous theories for focusing too much on internal factors, such as disturbances in early childhood. They hold instead that researchers should focus on external forces acting on women: institutions and laws discriminating against lesbians, and stereotypes that produce unpleasant interactions with others.

Sociologists also focus on *norms*, rules for behavior that are understood by the people in a culture and that guide their behavior. Feminists point out that heterosexuality is a strong — indeed, a coercive — norm in our society. The term *compulsory heterosexuality* has been used to describe this norm (Rich, 1980). Thus lesbians can be understood as norm-violators, much as women who achieve are also norm-violators.

Both sociologists and feminists, then, view lesbians as a minority group (Brooks, 1981). As such, they are denied civil rights, much as blacks traditionally were. They are also prevented from contributing to various social institutions that affect their lives — it is doubtful, for example, that an out-of-the-closet lesbian could be elected to most state legislatures. Lesbian women, then, can be seen as occupying two minority statuses.

When lesbians have sought psychotherapy, traditional psychologists have assumed that the sexual orientation itself was the pathology. In contrast, feminists and sociologists see the problems of lesbian women as resulting from the stress that falls on them because they are a minority group (Brooks, 1981). The emphasis in therapy, then, would not be on changing the woman's sexual preference, but on helping her develop skills for coping with the stresses she experiences. Research shows that three resources help lesbians cope with stress: positive identification as a lesbian, having higher socioeconomic status, and "coming out of the closet," or self-disclosing one's sexual orientation (Brooks, 1981).

Existentialism and lesbianism   Existential philosophy maintains that anyone can change one's self-view and view of the world at any time, and can thus profoundly alter the course of one's life — that humans are always free to reappraise their own condition and to take some action to alter it. People need not rely forever on the "crutches" of morals, social expectations, and past habits, but can in their own lives think for themselves and disavow all those things that they have been in the past. The only dictum is that humans should be authentic, and *authenticity* demands that one accept full responsibility for one's actions.

The existentialist who has commented most on lesbianism is Simone de Beauvoir (1952). Exemplifying the existentialist theme, she insists that: "The truth is that homosexuality [lesbianism] is no more perversion deliberately indulged in than it is a curse of fate. It is an attitude *chosen in a certain situation* — that is at once motivated and freely adopted" (p. 398, italics the author). She views female homosexuality not as a compensatory condition of life, but as an instance of self-reappraisal and choice. Further, de Beauvoir is in accord with the modified psychoanalytic position of Wolff (1971, p. 74) that all women have a natural homosexual component. Thus, lesbianism from this viewpoint is merely the reflection of conscious choice and a willingness to accept the responsibilities for such a choice.

A woman who enters upon heterosexual relations enters upon a social contract society expects and reinforces. It appears to require much greater, not less, emotional strength and conviction (authenticity) for a woman to enter upon a homosexual relationship, risking social rejection. So, according to the existentialists, in some sense it requires a much more integrated woman to make the choice to be a lesbian.

The language of existentialism remains at the level of "conscious choice" and "authenticity," words difficult to define precisely. It is a language unsatisfying to the psychologist because it gives little insight into the development or meaning of lesbianism; indeed, the existentialist rejects the notion that a homosexual choice of sex partners is rooted in previous experiences, insisting instead that it is simply a matter of free choice. On the other hand, the existentialist position does treat lesbianism as a legitimate, normal form of behavior.

Some final thoughts about the theoretical perspectives   Psychoanalysts, learning theorists, feminists, sociologists, and existentialists all have rather different things to say about lesbianism. Psychoanalysts and learning theorists focus on what causes lesbianism to develop. Feminists, sociologists, and existentialists reject the search for causes. Instead, they focus on understanding the lesbian's current experiences. Increasingly — though there are exceptions — that is the trend in research, to investigate the experiences of lesbians, in trying to build strong romantic relationships, in trying to deal with co-workers, or in trying to balance love, work, and children. Research on the lesbian experience was reviewed in an earlier section of the chapter. Below I review some of the empirical research on the causes of lesbianism.

RESEARCH ON THE GENESIS OF LESBIANISM

Having tried to understand the nature of lesbian development through both experiential and theoretical approaches, I must next bring these ideas to the test by comparing them with the available empirical data on the life histories and family backgrounds of lesbians to see what factors appear to predispose a woman to choose another woman as her sexual and love partner.

One study of lesbians and their developmental histories, typical of the psychoanalytic approach, is that of the psychiatrist Charlotte Wolff (1971). She studied more than a hundred nonpatient lesbians, comparing them with a control group of heterosexual women matched for family background, profession, and social class. Her results suggest that the relationship with the mother has a strong influence on the sexuality of the developing young girl. Mothers of lesbians were significantly higher on destructive maternal attitudes; they tended to be either indifferent or neglectful. Additionally, the mothers of lesbians more frequently had an avowed preference for the girl's brother. In contrast, the family life of the control subjects was characterized as sound, caring, and protective. There were more stepfathers present in the families of lesbians, which often gave rise to traumatic experiences that further drove the subject to rejection of male figures. The sibling structure of the family is also of interest, lesbians more often being only children or first-born children. The majority of lesbians had wished to be a boy when they were young, and tomboyism was widespread among the homosexual girls in contrast with the controls. However, as adults lesbians did not wish to be men, suggesting a basic female identification. They manifested a willingness or desire to accept the homosexual role, implying comfort in that role, rather than to imitate the role of heterosexual relationships. It is not surprising that many lesbians were hostile to males, and specifically to their younger brothers whom they envied and had to care for while growing up.

In sum, then, Wolff concluded from her research that the family is important in the development of lesbianism, and that the rejecting or indifferent mother may be particularly important. However, it should be emphasized that while such factors may be statistically more common in the families of lesbians than in the families of controls, they may be far from typical for lesbians. For example, while mothers of lesbians were more frequently indifferent or negligent, indifference was characteristic of only 27 percent of the mothers of lesbians (as compared with 10 percent of mothers of controls), and negligence was characteristic of only 10 percent of the mothers of lesbians (with 0 percent for controls) (Wolff, 1971, p. 273). Thus, maternal indifference or negligence is more common among lesbians than among controls, but was experienced by only a minority of lesbians.

Saghir and Robins (1973) in similar research found that as children lesbians had more frequently been tomboys and wished they could be boys. The gender ratio of their siblings showed an unusually high proportion of males. I question Saghir and Robins' suggestion that tomboyism is a precursor of lesbianism, however (Hyde et al., 1977). This view attempts to reinforce the stereotype that the lesbian is masculine or boyish, which confuses the concepts of gender identity and choice of sexual partner. In my own samples of the general population, I have found that tomboyism is quite typical of girls — in several samples, the percentages of women claiming to have been tomboys in childhood range from 51 to 78 percent. Thus, tomboyism appears to be typical in female development, not just in pre-lesbian development.

There have been numerous other speculations as to the factors causing lesbianism (Romm, 1965; Wilbur, 1965; Martin and Lyon, 1972). As Rosen summarizes them, they include

> fear of growing up and assuming adult responsibilities; fear of dominance and destruction; fear of rejection; fear of the opposite sex; fear of castration and of the penis; the desire to conquer and possess the mother;

neurotic dependency; heterosexual trauma (including rape); seduction in adolescence by an older female; first sexual experience with someone of the same sex and finding it pleasurable; tomboy behavior in early childhood; prolonged absence of the mother; masturbation with a resulting clitoral fixation; social factors (such as heterosexual taboos and unisexual, all female, groups); and physical factors (genetic, constitutional, and endocrine abnormalities). (1974, p. 8)

With regard to the last possibility, that of physical factors, research has consistently failed to find anatomical or genetic differences between lesbians and comparison groups of heterosexual women (Wolff, 1971; Marmor, 1965). While there have been numerous attempts to document hormonal differences between male homosexuals and heterosexuals — and the attempts have generally been unsuccessful or not replicatable — I know of only one similar attempt to document such differences between lesbians and heterosexual women. There was some suggestion of hormonal imbalance among lesbians who had higher testosterone and lower estrogen levels than a comparison group of heterosexual women (Loraine et al., 1971; see also Dörner, 1969). These results should be viewed cautiously, however, until they are replicated. Given the available research, it would seem dangerous to conclude that lesbianism is a result of simple biological determinants.

To be blunt, the state of the research is that no one really knows what causes lesbianism to develop. In a recent highly publicized study of the development of sexual preferences, Kinsey Institute researchers Alan Bell, Martin Weinberg, and Sue Hammersmith (1981) reported on interviews with 979 homosexual and 477 heterosexual women and men living in the San Francisco area. The questions used in each interview covered a wide variety of topics, including early home life and previous sexual experiences, designed to test some of the theories proposed to account for the development of homosexuality. Their results showed *no* evidence for the following common explanations: (1) The psychoanalytic view is that homosexuality results from a disturbed early family experience, including dominant mothers or weak or detached fathers. There was little or no difference in family experiences between homosexuals and heterosexuals. (2) The learning theory view is that homosexuality results from conditioning, either in early unpleasant heterosexual experiences or in early pleasant homosexual experiences. Homosexuals were no more likely than heterosexuals to have had negative experiences such as rape or parental punishment for early heterosexual sex play with children of the opposite gender; nor were they more likely to have been seduced by an older person.

This same study has been widely cited in the press for its conclusion that homosexuality is biologically determined. However, if one reads the study critically, one notes that the researchers collected no biological data, such as measuring hormone levels. They speculated about biological causes only because all of the standard environmental explanations failed the test of their data. The best conclusion, then, is that the cause of homosexuality remains unknown.

Perhaps the failure of research to uncover a consistent single "cause" of lesbianism is a result of the fact that there is no single cause, just as there is no single "lesbian personality." Variability among lesbians is great, and they come in all sizes, shapes, and personality types, just as do heterosexuals. "Lesbian" is not a homogeneous category, although we have been misled into thinking it is because of the superficial similarity that all lesbians prefer women as lovers. Because the category is nonhomogeneous, a single cause would not be expected. Throughout this chapter I referred to "lesbianism," using a single label with the understanding that it refers to a collectivity of behaviors, experiences, and developmental processes. Indeed, it has been recommended that we stop using the term "homosexuality" and substitute "homosexualities" (Bell, 1974), in order to recognize more adequately the diversity and heterogeneity of the category. Such a view helps to make sense out of the finding that factors such as maternal neglect and indifference are more common among lesbians than among controls, but that they are still relatively rare for lesbians — maternal indifference and neglect may contribute in the development of lesbianism in some cases, but not in others.

DIFFERENCES BETWEEN LESBIANS AND GAY MEN

Theorists frequently refer to homosexuality as if there were no difference between male and female homosexuality (or else as if male homosexuality were the only phenomenon of interest or concern). The interesting question arises as to whether these two phenomena are in fact different.

There do appear to be some differences between male and female homosexuality. First, the lesbian appears to place more emphasis on the emotional intimacy of her relationship than does the male homosexual (Peplau, 1983). Second, male homosexuals frequently have many different sex partners, while lesbians more often form long-term relationships (Loney, 1972). In one study of female and male homosexuals, the males reported a median (average) of 75 different partners, contrasted with a median of 5 for the females; 56 percent of the men had had 50 or more partners, but only 5 percent of the women had had that number (Schafer, 1977). In another study, 64 of the 65 gay women interviewed said they preferred a stable, long-term relationship (Hedblom, 1972). Third, bisexuality is more characteristic of lesbians and exclusive homosexuality less common than among male homosexuals. According to Kinsey data, by age 45 about 13 percent of all women and about 37 percent of all men have had a homosexual experience to orgasm; lesbianism is therefore less frequent than male homosexuality. But exclusive homosexuality is even less common among women. Kinsey estimated that only about 1 to 3 percent of all women are exclusively homosexual, as compared with about 3 to 16 percent of all men. Most lesbians, then, have had at least some heterosexual experience, while a substantial proportion of male homosexuals are exclusively homosexual (Kinsey et al., 1953, pp. 487–488).

Psychologist Michael Storms (1981; see also Bermant, 1972) has constructed a theory of the development of erotic orientation that neatly explains some of these statistics, particularly that more men than women have had homosexual experiences. According to this theory, most people develop the sex drive in early adolescence, around the ages of 12 to 15. It is at that time that certain stimuli (e.g., a member of the same or the opposite gender) become conditioned to be arousing or erotic. If one examines the social patterns of pre-adolescents and adolescents, it is clear that homosocial patterns (same-gender friendships and groups) predominate in pre-adolescence, reaching a peak at around age 12. Heterosexual interactions begin to emerge after that time, and most people have engaged in heterosexual dating by age 15. According to Storms, homosexuality results when individuals have an early maturing sex drive, at about age 12, when they are still in homosocial groupings, so that erotic conditioning is more likely to focus on members of their own gender, since heterosexuality has not yet emerged as an alternative.

Supporting Storms's theory, data show that homosexual women are earlier sexual maturers than heterosexual women, as measured by age of beginning to masturbate, age of earliest feelings of sexual arousal, and age of first sexual fantasizing (Goode and Haber, 1977; Saghir and Robins, 1973). This theory therefore explains why there are more men than women who have experienced homosexual activity and who are exclusively homosexual: the sex drive in males emerges earlier, as evidenced by the more frequent and earlier appearance of masturbation, a point discussed in the previous chapter. Females are more likely to experience the emergence of their sex drive later, after heterosexuality has become the norm in their lives. In addition, it could be argued that the models girls are taught to emulate from their early years are more explicitly bound up with heterosexuality (wife, mother) than are the models boys are taught to emulate (involving careers or sports). The theory is a recent one, so it should not yet be accepted as definitive, but it does provide some intriguing ideas.

In sum, male and female homosexuality appear to be similar only in a superficial sense. The differences between the two are logical consequences of psychological differences between the genders and differences in their developmental experiences. Indeed, although it has been found that one's gender is a fairly good predictor of a number of psychological characteristics, one's homosexual status is not (Bell, 1974). Therefore, a lesbian is probably more like a heterosexual woman than she is like a homosexual man. Her identity is first as a woman and only second as a homosexual.

BISEXUAL WOMEN

Bisexuality has become rather chic in recent years, particularly on the East and West coasts, and many large cities now have "bi" bars and discos. Because the topic and research on it are new — although the behavior certainly is not — my discussion will be relatively brief.

Bisexuality refers to having sexual relations with both males and females. As noted earlier, using this definition, bisexuality is actually more common than is exclusive homosexuality. For example, Kinsey found the following percentages of women to have had more than incidental homo-sexual experience: 6 to 14 percent of unmarried women, 2 to 5 percent of married women, and 8 to 10 percent of previously married women (Kinsey et al., 1953). The comparable statistics for exclusive homosexuality were 2 to 6 percent, 1 percent, and 1 to 6 percent, respectively.

In the absence of more systematic psychological research, the case of Joan, a bisexual woman, is offered to illustrate the life experience of a bisexual woman. One interesting fact that emerges from such cases is that women often become bisexual after a long history of exclusive hetero-sexuality or exclusive homosexuality, at relatively late ages (Blumstein and Schwartz, 1976).

Sociologists Philip Blumstein and Pepper Schwartz (1976) have con-ducted interviews with bisexual women. On the basis of these interviews, they concluded that a number of factors contributed to a woman with a lesbian history moving toward bisexuality. Most lesbians — probably 50 to 80 percent (Hedblom, 1972; Saghir and Robins, 1973) — have had at least some heterosexual experience, including intercourse. When these are re-called as pleasurable it is reasonable to return to them later in life. Another factor is all of the social rewards in our society that go with a heterosexual lifestyle, including having a husband and children. Bisexuality can be a way of avoiding the social ostracism that lesbians must often face, while still engaging in some lesbian activity. On the other hand, some forces discourage the movement from lesbianism to bisexuality. Many lesbians receive their major emotional support in a lesbian community, and they stand to lose this if they adopt bisexuality. Some lesbians view bisexual women with suspicion or downright hostility.

Blumstein and Schwartz feel that a number of factors contribute to heterosexual women moving in a bisexual direction. They believe that women learn, as part of learning how to compete with women in being attractive to men, what is attractive in other women. They thereby become aware of erotic qualities in other women. Further, women are more permit-ted to be emotionally and physically expressive toward each other in our society, once again making a move towards bisexuality easier. As part of the more liberated sexual standards in recent years, some people experiment with having sex in groups of more than two persons at once, allowing an

JOAN, A BISEXUAL WOMAN

Joan, a professional woman in her middle thirties, considered herself exclusively heterosexual until about four years ago. Until that time she had never had homosexual fantasies or feelings, but she had been generally liberal about "sexual alternatives" and believed in equal rights for homosexuals. Four years ago, however, Joan became active in the women's liberation movement and developed closer friendships with some of the women with whom she worked. None of these relationships was sexualized, but her curiosity was aroused by sexual possibilities with women. Her approach to her own potential homosexual behavior was at this time still more intellectual than emotional and was not accompanied by graphic fantasies or feelings of attraction to other women whom she might meet or see in public.

During this period, Joan met another woman in her profession whom she found both intellectually and socially attractive. Vivian was also heterosexual, but she had had a few homosexual experiences. The relationship between the two women became closer, and during an exchange of confidences Joan learned that Vivian had had sexual experiences with women. At this point, Joan began to have sexual fantasies involving Vivian and began to be more overtly physical toward her, but she never crossed the bounds of female heterosexual friendship. The relationship intensified, and intimate discussions about sexuality turned to the possibility of sex between the two women. After about six months of such discussions, they slept together, first having overcome their initial worries concerning the effect that any guilt feelings about their "experimentation" might have on their friendship.

After the first successful sexual experience, Joan and Vivian repeated it approximately once every month for over a year. Vivian, however, continued to think of herself as a heterosexual, while Joan began to feel that she was in love with her friend and to want a more committed relationship. Joan stopped sleeping with Vivian when she realized that Vivian did not agree with her terms for the relationship. The two remained close friends, but Joan looked for someone else who might wish to share a committed relationship. She eventually fell in love with another woman, and an intense romantic and sexual relationship continued for two years. At the present, Joan is unsure of what sexual label to apply to herself, but she prefers "bisexual." At the time of her interview, she had both a male and a female lover.

Source: Philip W. Blumstein and Pepper Schwartz. "Bisexual Women." In J. P. Wiseman, ed., *The Social Psychology of Sex* (New York: Harper & Row, 1976), pp. 156–157.

opportunity to experiment with lesbianism. Finally, the women's movement has created an environment that is relatively supportive of lesbianism, and some heterosexual women decide to experiment with lesbianism, and thereby become bisexuals, out of feminist convictions.

IN CONCLUSION

This chapter has been based on the assumption — supported by the available data — that lesbianism is a normal form of behavior. The accounts of the lesbian experience emphasize the discrimination she experiences, and the satisfaction of her relationships and how she copes with stress. Theoretical views of the nature of lesbianism are varied. Psychoanalytic theory sees it as an outcome of a persisting negative Oedipal complex, so that the woman continues to love her mother, and later other women, throughout her life. Wolff's neoanalytic theory sees lesbianism as a continued competition with males for the mother's love, which the lesbian was deprived of as a child. Learning theory stresses that sex drive is a generalized drive that is channeled toward one or another object through experience and circumstance; thus both heterosexuality and homosexuality are learned. Sociologists are more concerned with the impact on lesbian women of institutions and norms. Existentialism does not concern itself with the developmental origins of lesbianism, but instead treats it simply as a free and legitimate choice. Research on the development of lesbianism suggests that there is probably no one single causal factor. Finally, male and female homosexuality are different in nature as a logical consequence of psychological and developmental differences between females and males.

Research on lesbianism is in its infancy, and the conclusions we draw must be tentative. Certainly the nature of research on lesbianism is changing as we shed the assumption that it is a form of pathology. We now no longer seek to find what disturbances in development would create such a perversion; instead, we ask what developmental factors would lead a woman to choose heterosexuality or homosexuality or bisexuality. And just as surely, with society's increasing acceptance of lesbianism, the nature of lesbianism will change, presumably as many of the tensions are removed from it. Indeed, in the future we may even come to consider lesbianism preferable to heterosexuality. As Szasz provocatively suggests:

> We might even advocate homosexuality over heterosexuality: this choice could be supported as a contraceptive technique, especially for women intellectually or artistically gifted, for whom the value of traditional feminine heterosexuality is a barrier to achievement. (1965, p. 137)

SUGGESTION FOR FURTHER READING

Brown, Rita Mae (1977). *Rubyfruit jungle.* New York: Bantam Books (paperback). This semi-autobiographical novel gives a view of lesbianism that is both insightful and hilarious. It is delightful reading.

14

Problems of Adjustment and Psychotherapy

I was eighteen when I started therapy for the second time. I went to a woman for two years, twice a week. She was constantly trying to get me to admit that what I really wanted was to get married and have babies and lead a "secure" life; she was very preoccupied with how I dressed, and just like my mother, would scold me if my clothes were not clean, or if I wore my hair down; told me that it would be a really good sign if I started to wear makeup and get my hair done in a beauty parlor (like her, dyed blond and sprayed); when I told her that I like to wear pants she told me that I had a confusion of sex roles . . . I originally went to her when my friends started to experiment with sex, and I felt that I couldn't make it, and that my woman friends with whom I had been close had rejected me for a good lay. . . .

FROM *Women and Madness*

Stories such as the one told by this woman are all too common among women who have been patients in psychotherapy. What is known about the experiences of such women? In this chapter we shall explore some of the adjustment problems women have, the evidence on whether there is sexism in traditional psychotherapy, and newly emerging therapies for women.

GENDER RATIOS AND MENTAL ILLNESS

Studies consistently show that more women than men are patients in psychotherapy (Gove and Tudor, 1973; Chesler, 1972). One British study found the lopsided ratio of 35 women for every one man in psychotherapy (cited by Chesler, 1972). This is probably an overestimate of the differential. Based on a survey of many studies, it seems likely that there are about two women in psychotherapy for every one man (Gove and Tudor, 1973).

How should this differential be interpreted? One possibility is that it simply means that more women than men are mentally ill. This may be a result of the stresses or unhealthiness of the female role (Gove and Tudor, 1973). Another possibility is that women in fact have no more adjustment problems than men do, but women are just more willing to admit their problems and seek psychotherapy (Phillips and Segal, 1969).

It is not possible at this time to say which of these interpretations is correct. Possibly they are both correct to some extent.

It is also true that the diagnoses given to women differ substantially from those applied to men. Women are more frequently diagnosed as depressed, hysterical,[1] neurotically anxious, and phobic. Men, on the other hand, are termed alcoholic, organic (referring to psychological disorders caused by organic or physical problems such as brain damage), and anti-social (Gove and Tudor, 1973; Howard and Howard, 1974).

Space does not permit a discussion of all possible problems of adjustment in women. Below I shall consider three that are of special interest: depression, alcoholism and drug abuse, and the eating disorders (anorexia and bulimia).

DEPRESSION

The symptoms of depression include (1) emotional aspects — a dejected mood, apathy; (2) cognitive aspects — a low self-evaluation and negative expectations about the future; (3) motivational aspects — motivation is low and there is an inability to mobilize oneself to action; and (4) behavioral aspects — appetite loss, sleep disturbance, loss of interest in sex, and tiredness (Beck and Greenberg, 1974).

Among persons with serious depression requiring hospitalization, the ratio of women to men is about two to one (Gove and Tudor, 1973; Weissman and Klerman, 1979). It has been estimated that the incidence of depression may be as high as 8 percent among women, compared with 4 percent among men (Roth, 1959). Even in large-scale surveys of the general American population, women have reported more symptoms of depression than men do (Radloff, 1975; Weissman and Klerman, 1979). It seems reasonable to conclude that there is more depression among women than among men.

Some have argued that these higher rates of depression in women are not cause for concern, because the gender difference in depression is an "artifact," not a true difference. That is, it is possible that in actuality, men and women suffer equally from depression, but women are overrepresented in the statistics, perhaps because they are more willing to admit mood symptoms, or perhaps because they are more willing to seek help (therapy) for their problems. However, a detailed review of available research led to the conclusion that the gender difference in depression is a true difference, not an artifact (Weissman and Klerman, 1979). That is, the

---

[1] For many centuries, hysteria was thought to be a problem caused by a wandering uterus! Now the term is used to refer to someone who overreacts to situations, responding in a histrionic or melodramatic way (adjectives like "coquettish" or "seductive" may be used). In extreme cases, the person converts the high levels of anxiety into a physical symptom, such as blindness.

evidence is that women report more depression because they actually experience more depression.

Why do women have more problems with depression? There are a variety of factors associated with depression in women, including the empty nest syndrome, postpartum factors, and organic (physical) factors. There is even some evidence that sex-linked genetic factors are related to manic-depressions (Winokur et al., 1969).

Freud believed that overly dependent people are prone to depression. When they experience a loss, such as the death of a loved one, or a symbolic loss, such as perceived rejection by someone close to them, they become depressed. Further, Freud viewed women as naturally more dependent than men. Therefore, his theory would account for the greater occurrence of depression in women based on their greater dependency.

Learning theorists believe that depression occurs when the reinforcements one is accustomed to — for example, a satisfying job or a congenial spouse — are suddenly withdrawn. The person responds by reducing activities. If there is not some reinforcement for the person's remaining efforts, he or she sinks further into depression. The pattern of inactivity itself may be rewarded if the person gets special attention for being "sick." Following these notions, a behaviorist might explain the greater occurrence of depression in women as being a result of women not receiving sufficient reinforcements for their actions (an assumption that is not too difficult to make); or as a result of women being especially likely to find themselves in situations in which their customary reinforcements are withdrawn (for example, having to leave one's friends and job and move to follow a husband's career, or having the children leave home when they grow up).

Two other factors are relevant in discussing the causes of depression in women: women's roles and learned helplessness.

A large-scale survey of 2,829 women in the general population investigated the relationship between *women's roles* and reported symptoms of depression (Radloff, 1975). There was some evidence that the marital role for women contributes to depression. Married women have higher depression scores than married men and never-married women. The housewife role has also been proposed as a source of women's depression. Many of the tasks of a housewife are unchallenging, repetitive, and lacking in a sense of accomplishment, as, for example, making beds that will just be unmade that evening and made again the next day. In this study, full-time housewives were more depressed than married men, but so were working wives. Therefore, it doesn't seem that getting a job, by itself, is the cure for women's depression. It is also possible that part of the problem is that women continue all of their (depressing) housewife responsibilities even though they take jobs outside the home.

Gender roles are also involved in the ways in which females and males cope with depression. In one large-scale survey of strategies for coping with depression, females were most likely to report crying, eating, becoming irritable, and confronting their feelings (Kleinke et al., 1982). Males, in contrast, were more likely to become aggressive or to engage in sexual behavior. People apparently don't escape from stereotypes even when depressed.

Following in the behaviorist tradition, psychologist Martin Seligman's (1975) theory of *learned helplessness* as a cause of depression may be helpful in explaining depression in women (Radloff, 1975; Radloff and Monroe, 1978; Radloff, 1980). Seligman believes that depressives have a history of learning that they are incapable of successful mastery and control over their lives. In short, they have learned to regard themselves as helpless. When confronted with a difficult situation, they feel that they cannot deal with it successfully, and depression results. The sense of helplessness and lack of control Seligman talks about sound very much like the powerlessness that feminists say is characteristic of women. If women in our society do indeed lack power — in everything from interpersonal relationships to national politics — this may contribute to a sense of helplessness and thus to depression. Further, traits that women are socialized for, such as passivity, may contribute to helplessness. An observational study in nursery schools found that girls received fewer reactions from adults for all behaviors (Serbin et al., 1973). Perhaps even at an early age girls learn that their behaviors do not produce results.

One large-scale study attempted to determine which of these factors — women's roles or women's powerlessness and learned helplessness — contributed more to psychological problems (Horwitz, 1982). The results provided some support for both factors, but indicated that powerlessness was particularly important in producing psychological distress.

How can one deal with this situation? First, it is probably possible to apply some "preventive medicine" based on the learned helplessness theory. Child-rearing practices and other factors should be examined to see whether they encourage helplessness in females, and if they do, they should be changed. As two authorities commented,

> . . . young women will do well to concentrate on preventing future depressions by cultivating habits of self-respect and self-reliance and by leading a balanced life, participating in a variety of activities rather than depending on family ties alone for emotional and intellectual sustenance. (Beck and Greenberg, 1974, p. 130)

But psychological changes in women alone will probably not be enough. As long as the society around them is unresponsive to their actions, problems will still result. As the same authors commented,

> A woman can learn to be aware of what she wants, to take direct action to get it, and to take credit for her successes. But to avoid helplessness, her environment must cooperate. (1974, p. 130)

ALCOHOLISM AND
DRUG ABUSE

Just as depression has been a "feminine" problem, alcoholism has been a "masculine" problem. In the Victorian era, drinking was viewed as a male-only activity, and the prohibition movement was led by women. However, the percentage of women who drink has risen steadily. The proportion of college women who drink socially rose from 61 percent in 1950 to 75 percent in 1977; the comparable figures for college men are 79 percent and 80 percent (Engs, 1977). However, while there is now tolerance of social drinking for women, there is little tolerance for drunken women, and the drunk woman is viewed with more scorn and disgust than the drunk man (Gomberg, 1974).

In Europe and America, the ratio of male alcoholics to female alcoholics is about 4 to 1 (Willis, 1973; Gomberg, 1979). However, such statistics are based on patients seen in therapy. It may be that there are actually as many women alcoholics as men alcoholics (Block, 1962), but that the women are just less likely to be noticed. For example, no one notices the drunken housewife, but the drunk man who must show up at work on Monday morning and fails to do so is much more conspicuous.

What is known psychologically about alcoholic women? Traumatic events — in particular, loss of a parent during childhood, psychiatric illness in the family, or alcoholism in the family — are all more likely among women alcoholics than among women in the general population (Gomberg, 1974; 1979). There is actually one longitudinal study available, although the sample is small (Jones, 1971). The Oakland Growth Study was a longitudinal study begun in the 1920s, with continuing followups. When the women in the study were in their late forties, they were categorized as to whether they were abstainers, light, moderate or heavy drinkers, or problem drinkers. It was then possible to examine the data collected on them when they were younger to see what characterized the problem drinker as compared with others. For the future problem drinker, adolescence was a crisis. According to the researcher, the following is characteristic of the future problem drinker (pp. 67–68):

> At fifteen, life is full of adolescent self-doubt and confusion. She fears and rejects life, is distrustful of people, follows a religion which accentuates judgment and punishment. She escapes into ultrafemininity.

The composite picture, then, is a history of emotional deprivation, with a submissive, passively resentful girl undergoing a stressful adolescence, fearful of dependency relationships and trying to solve her problems with superfemininity (Gomberg, 1974). In a 20-year followup study of college drinking, the two variables in college women most predictive of later drinking problems were "some degree of intoxication" and "psychological dependence" (Fillmore, 1974, 1975). That is, women with eventual drinking problems already showed drunkenness in college, as well as being dependent and perhaps overly responsive to peer pressure.

There appears to be a strong relationship between depression and drinking problems in women (Schuckit et al., 1969; Schuckit, 1972). There is also a rather high rate of alcoholism among husbands of alcoholic women. The evidence suggests that alcoholism may begin with the husband and be transmitted to the wife, although the reverse rarely occurs (Gomberg, 1974).

While the alcoholic woman is superfeminine on the surface, the evidence also suggests that she is ambivalent and in conflict about her femininity, with her aggressive and assertive tendencies barely pushed beneath the surface (Gomberg, 1974). That is, she is overidentified with the female role (Wilsnack, 1973), but also ambivalent about it.

In summary, a number of factors seem to contribute to alcoholism in women: an emotionally deprived childhood, a stormy adolescence, low self-esteem, peer pressure to drink, drinking to escape from problems, alcoholism in an important family member such as the husband, and immediate precipitating factors such as divorce or illness (Gomberg, 1979). Alcoholism is particularly likely if a combination of two or more of these occur.

There are also important variations among alcoholic women. At least two basic types emerge (Gomberg, 1979). One group consists of women with an early onset of alcoholism in their teens or twenties; they are likely to have trouble with controlling their impulses and are very similar to women who become delinquents. The other group consists of women with a later onset of alcoholism in their thirties or forties. Earlier in life they showed better coping skills, but they gradually began to use alcohol to cope with feelings of depression, and its use then accelerated.

Although men and women alcoholics have much in common, some gender differences are found (Gomberg, 1979). Women have their first drink and their first episode of intoxication at a later age than men do. In addition, women alcoholics are more likely to drink at home or alone, whereas men alcoholics are more likely to do their drinking in gregarious social settings.

The data on drug addiction also indicate a male to female ratio of about 5 to 1 (Willis, 1973). These statistics are for addiction to illicit drugs such as morphine and heroin, however. Data also show that large numbers of women are hooked on legal prescription drugs such as tranquilizers and diet pills. Physicians simply seem to be more willing to suggest drugs as cures for women's problems. For example, female depressives receive more drugs, and stronger ones, than males with the same symptoms (Stein et al., 1976). In another study, women accounted for 58 percent of the frequent users of major tranquilizers, 70 percent of the minor tranquilizer users, and 66 percent of the sedative users (Cooperstock, 1971). In a study of repeat prescriptions of drugs, more women (5 percent) than men (3.3 percent) received ten or more prescriptions within a year (Cooperstock, 1976). Thus dependence on or addiction to legal prescription drugs is a serious problem for some women and, once again, gender roles seem to play a part.

EATING DISORDERS

Have you ever heard the saying "A woman can never be too rich or too thin?" I'm not sure about the rich part, but I am sure about the thin part. A woman *can* be too thin. The condition is anorexia nervosa, and it can kill. Experts estimate that it is fatal in 10 to 15 percent of the cases (Minuchin et al., 1978).

Anorexia nervosa: symptoms and diagnosis   Anorexia nervosa is a disorder in which a person essentially starves herself. A typical definition is "over-control of eating for weight reduction" (Levenkron, 1982, p. 2). "Herself" is used intentionally here because the disorder is present disproportionately among females — 90 to 95 percent of anorexics are females, and the great majority are adolescents, the usual age of onset being between 13 and 22 (Levenkron, 1982). Anorexia is currently estimated to afflict 1 in 250 adolescent girls (Levenkron, 1982). It has most frequently been found among the upper-middle and upper class, although recent statistics indicate that it is spreading to other social classes (Garfinkel and Garner, 1982).

Although there is some disagreement among experts, the following are generally the criteria for diagnosis of anorexia (Minuchin et al., 1978; Garfinkel and Garner, 1982; Levenkron, 1982):

1. Loss of 20 percent or more of body weight — the person is emaciated.
2. Amenorrhea, or the absence of a menstrual period.
3. Thinning hair.
4. Dry, flaking skin.
5. Constipation.
6. Lanugo — this is a growth of downy hair on the body, probably part of the body's effort to keep warm when few calories are coming in.
7. Lowered body temperature — often 95–97° F. The anorexic may be found wearing four sweaters in the winter to keep herself warm.

The extreme weight loss results from the anorexic's compulsive dieting. Although she may begin with normal dieting, the dieting soon gets out of control. She limits herself to perhaps 600–800 calories per day (Garfinkel and Garner, 1982). Her thoughts become obsessively focused on food and eating, and rituals surrounding eating develop. She may limit herself to only a few low-calorie foods, perhaps existing solely on cottage cheese

FIGURE 14.1

The anorexic becomes emaciated because of compulsive, extreme dieting.

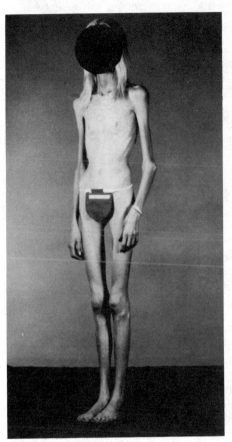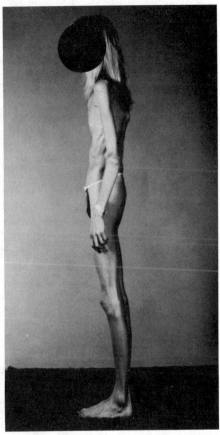

and apples. She eats in private and generally becomes a loner. One anorexic described her ritualistic behavior to me: At work after her co-workers had eaten their lunches, she looked for opportunities when they were out of the office and then searched through the trash can for the waxed paper wrappings from their lunches. She would finger the wrappings and sniff them for odors of food, then quickly return them to the trash can before she was discovered.

The compulsive dieting is a result of a phobia of gaining any weight and a corresponding drive toward thinness. But the anorexic's body image is often distorted, so that she believes herself to be fat even though she is emaciated, 25 percent under normal body weight. Despite the low intake of calories, the anorexic typically has abundant energy, to the point of

AN ANOREXIC TELLS HER STORY

At age 27 I am a recovered anorexic. I am 6 feet tall and weigh 140 pounds, which is just right for me. But things were not always that way.

At age 3 I was already fat. My mother loved to cook and I loved to eat. She was 5 feet 2 inches tall and weighed 180 pounds herself. When I got to school, I found that the other kids rejected me because I was fat. I quickly learned that the only way to get attention and have people like me was to cater to them, doing what they wanted, giving them things, never thinking of myself. When I was 14, my mother dieted down to 120 pounds. When my sister was 15 and I was 18, she became anorexic. I swore that would never happen to me.

At age 23 I weighed 187 pounds and had never had a date. One day a co-worker casually commented to me, "We both need to lose some weight." The comment instantly triggered something in me, and I started dieting. Within a few months, I was down to 140 pounds. I was asked on my first date. People said, "You look great, don't lose any more." I found that good things happen when you diet.

At that point, things were going so well that I decided, just to be on the safe side, that I should take off a few more pounds. I cut out sweets entirely. In the next three months, I went from 140 to 113 pounds. My menstrual period stopped.

When I reached 113 pounds, I decided to set 100 pounds as my goal. Dieting became an obsession. It was everything to me. I bought calorie counters, including seven copies of one of them. I cut out almost all foods. Typically I consumed 500 calories per day maximum. Breakfast would be a slice of toast with a dab of peanut butter (I couldn't give up peanut butter). I skipped lunch. I ate dinner "out" so my family wouldn't know what I was doing. Usually it would be one bowl of chili, which has 280 calories. I drank lots of tea and chewed on ice so I could chew on something with no calories. Sometimes I also skipped breakfast, but got up early, before the rest of my family, and banged around the kitchen, pretending to fix breakfast but eating nothing. When I did eat, I always ate alone, never with others. I baked for my family, but then ate none of it. Everything was ritual and compulsion. I thought of nothing but food. Life with my family was a constant battle. The more they told me they wanted me to eat, the less I wanted to eat. When they asked me what I had for supper, I said, "I ordered a hamburger, french fries, and a milkshake." And I did. I ordered them at a fast food place, picked them up at the drive-through window, and then threw all of it in the trash can without eating any of it.

I never did make it to 100 pounds. The lowest I reached was 110. At that point, I missed work (I work as a dental assistant) and didn't care. I was perpetually cold and had my electric blanket on "high" in the middle of the summer. In the winter I would typically dress in panty hose, thermal underwear, two pairs of slacks, and several sweaters, and still be cold. Despite the small number of calories I consumed, my energy level was high. I sometimes woke up in the middle of the night and did sit-ups. I exercised while my co-workers were out at lunch.

Then I started having dizzy spells. That scared me. I got glasses, thinking my eyes were the problem and that glasses would help me. Needless to say, they didn't. Then I went to a physician. He told me to start eating. I didn't.

Soon after that I read a magazine article on anorexia. It triggered a rather dull click in my head. Some of the things that woman did sounded like me. The article contained the address of a national agency that made referrals for help.* I wrote to the address. They referred me to a nearby support group for anorexics. I went to it only twice. I didn't want to be with all of those thin people when I was so fat, as I saw myself.

The support group leader told me that I couldn't continue in the support group. unless I also went for individual psychotherapy. Obedient person that I was, catering to her wishes as I always did to everyone's, I went to a therapist at a nearby community mental health clinic. I didn't want to go. At the first session I told him I didn't know why I was there. The first session converted me. Therapy was wonderful. Dr. G didn't tell me I had to eat or that I had to gain weight, as everyone else in my life was doing. He said, "We won't talk about weight. We'll talk about you." He helped me find out what my own wants were, a first for me because I had spent my life catering to others. After that first session, there was no doubt in my mind — I definitely wanted to continue therapy. In later sessions I learned to be assertive, doing something about my own wants. I learned how I had had no control of things in my life, and so chose to control one thing within my power — my weight. I came to realize that I had had chronically low self-esteem, and I learned that I was a worthy human being. Previously I had been afraid to be anything but an angel with other people. With Dr. G, I could be myself, and our relationship was still okay. I learned to take that out to the rest of the world. I made new friends and started dating. In sessions with Dr. G, I had his undivided attention.

In all, I was in intensive therapy for about seven months, once per week. I still go in for a session occasionally if I feel particularly stressed or feel like I need a "booster shot." After the first session, I decided that eating was safe. I ate, and it was the first thing I'd ever done for myself. I added one thing a day to my eating. After three months I was still eating only small amounts, but it was progress and I had gained 7 pounds. My eating habits were still rigid, though. Then I got up to 127 pounds and stayed there for a year. I was less of a loner and had more of a social life. After that I got up to 140 pounds, and I have been there ever since.

I'm confident that I will never be anorexic again. Occasionally, if I am under great stress, I stop eating. But I instantly recognize the signs, I remember how horrible it was to be anorexic, and I start eating again.

Source: Based on an interview conducted by the author.

* One such organization is the National Anorexic Aid Society, P.O. Box 29461, Columbus, OH 43229. They make referrals to therapists, support groups, and hospitals, as well as offering many other services.

being hyperactive. She often undertakes strenuous exercise programs to try to burn off further calories.

The title of one excellent novel about anorexia, which was made into a television special, is *The Best Little Girl in the World* (Levenkron, 1978). The title refers to the fact that most anorexics are good little girls, obedient and high-achieving at school. Despite this, they typically have feelings of inferiority about their intelligence and appearance. Depression and anxiety are also common, the anxiety being relieved only by weight loss and fasting. The anorexic is also typically distinterested in sexuality. Finally, the anorexic typically engages in denial: she firmly maintains that she has no problem and that she is not underweight, and she resists undergoing psychotherapy.

Bulimia   Bulimia (also called bulimarexia) is a variation on anorexia in which the weight loss is achieved in another way. It is sometimes called the bingeing-and-purging syndrome because the woman gorges herself by overeating, then, before the calories enter her body, purges herself of the food either by forcing herself to vomit or by abusive use of laxatives (Boskind-Lodahl and Sirlin, 1977; Garfinkel and Garner, 1982). The bulimic may have an intake of 4,000 to 5,000 calories per day, yet continue to lose weight (Garfinkel and Garner, 1982). In one case, a bulimic spent six hours every evening eating, yet weighed 62 pounds (Levenkron, 1982).

Surveys of college populations indicate that 4 to 7 percent of the women have engaged in bulimic behaviors including binge eating followed by vomiting (Hawkins and Clement, 1980; Garfinkel and Garner, 1982). Thus this problem is not a rare one, and there is some evidence that it is on the increase.

The prevalance of this disorder is disturbing, particularly because it has some serious health consequences. Some of those are the results of starvation and will be discussed in the next section. In addition, the bulimic may suffer serious damage to her teeth, due to the acidity of the repeated vomiting.

Theories and therapies   Many theories as to the causes of anorexia have been proposed, leading to correspondingly different forms of therapy. All seem to agree, though, that therapy is slow and difficult — two to five years of therapy are common (Levenkron, 1982).

It has been proposed that anorexia is a result of *biological causes* (reviewed by Garfinkel and Garner, 1982). Anorexics do have many disturbances of their biological functioning. But the problem is that physicians never see these people until they are already anorexic. At that point, it is not clear whether the physiological problems are the cause of the anorexia or the result of starvation. Research indicates that, most likely, the problematic conditions are the result of starvation because most of them reverse themselves and return to normal as the person gains weight (Garfinkel and Garner, 1982). The functioning of the hypothalamus in the anorexic is disturbed. The levels of the hormones LH and FSH are at very low levels, comparable to those of a girl before puberty. Electrolytes are important for the proper functioning of the nervous system, and electrolyte levels (e.g., potassium) are disturbed in anorexics. Low potassium levels are a particular problem in bulimics, resulting from the vomiting and misuse of laxatives. Convulsions, low blood pressure, low heart rates, and irregular heart beats are other results of the starvation. It seems, though, that all of these biological abnormalities are results, rather than causes of the anorexia.

Psychoanalytic theory has viewed anorexia as resulting from a fear of oral impregnation (see reviews by Minuchin et al., 1978; Garfinkel and Garner, 1982). That is, the anorexic sees food taken in through the mouth as causing pregnancy. Not eating prevents pregnancy. Simultaneously, the starvation produces amenorrhea, which further reduces pregnancy fears. And the weight loss erases the curves of the adult female body, returning the anorexic to the straight body of a girl — a kind of regression. These problems are traced to disturbed parent-child relationships. Disturbed family relationships are common among anorexics, but once again, it is not clear whether the disturbed family is cause or effect — that is, does the disturbed family cause the anorexia, or does having an anorexic in the family create disturbances?

In a variation of the psychoanalytic approach, Levenkron (1982) recommends *nurturant-authoritative therapy* for the anorexic. Levenkron believes that the origins are laid in early childhood, when the girl is forced to become independent and to take on responsibility too early, perhaps by a mother pleading her own incompetence and forcing her daughter to take charge of things. Accordingly, the daughter becomes the "best little girl in the world." Then, in adolescence, when there is real pressure to separate from one's parents and become an adult, the pathology surfaces. Levenkron argues that therapy must include nurturance to compensate for that which was missing from parents in early childhood. Therapy must also include an authoritative approach, in which the therapist actively directs the patient in specific steps to take to overcome the disorder; because anorexics are highly resistant to therapy, they will not improve unless the therapist is highly directive.

A *behavior therapy* approach, based on learning theory, treats anorexia as an eating phobia (e.g., Brady and Rieger, 1975). The idea is that, for an anorexic, eating causes anxiety. Therefore, fasting causes anxiety reduction, which is a powerful reinforcer. An understanding of these principles can be useful in the hospital treatment of anorexics, the goal being to get them to eat. This may be an extremely important short-term goal because, as noted previously, there is some risk of death due to starvation. Behavior therapy can be used to reduce the anxiety that the patient associates with eating. Simultaneously, the patient may be taught to associate positive reinforcers with eating (reviewed by Garfinkel and Garner, 1982). Unfortunately, when patients treated this way return to their old home environment, they often revert to their previous anorexic behavior patterns.

Bulimia might seem difficult to explain using learning theory. Vomiting is so inherently aversive, why would anyone do it repeatedly? The answer, once again, lies in anxiety. The bulimic wants to lose weight; therefore an eating binge creates a high level of anxiety. Vomiting reduces the anxiety, and thus actually becomes a positive reinforcer.

Systems theory and *family therapy* represent yet another approach to anorexia. Systems theory regards the anorexic not as an isolated, disturbed individual, but rather as a person embedded in a complex system that includes her family and society at large (Minuchin et al., 1978). Her parents may have done things in her early childhood to predispose the girl to anorexia. Family interaction and communication patterns trigger and then perpetuate the problem in adolescence. But the girl's problem behavior also has disastrous effects on the functioning of the family. Her pathology becomes the focus of the family, and if she were to get well, a whole new family organization would be required. The predominantly upper-middle-class families of anorexic girls tend to emphasize or place importance on beauty (and therefore thinness) and externally visible signs of success, such as good grades. The girl thus learns to subordinate herself. As one team of researchers commented,

> Her expectation from a goal-directed activity, such as studying or learning a skill, is therefore not competence, but approval. The reward is not knowledge, but love. (Minuchin et al., 1978, p. 59)

Dieting produces external, tangible signs of "success," and simultaneously allows the girl to gain a sense of control.

In following the systems theory approach, family therapy is necessary. Therapy for the girl alone will not work, because she remains embedded in the family that maintains her illness. Thus both the family and the anorexic must participate in therapy.

The *feminist perspective* emphasizes not the pathology of the individual, but rather the socialization practices and messages of our society (e.g., Boskind-Lodahl, 1976). The anorexic shows an extreme reaction to the socialization messages that all women in American society hear while growing up. The emphasis is on thinness — as the saying quoted earlier put it, "a woman can never be too thin." High-fashion models, *Playboy* centerfolds, and Miss America contestants provide images of slimness that are difficult to live up to. Just as wealthy Chinese for centuries bound the feet of their daughters to achieve a culturally defined standard of beauty, so a particular standard of appearance of thinness is enforced in American society, not through physical methods but rather by socialization (Garfinkel and Garner, 1982). In one survey, 70 percent of American high school girls were dissatisfied with their bodies and wanted to lose weight (Huenemann et al., 1966). In another survey, 80 percent of female high school seniors wanted to weigh less; 30 percent were actively dieting, and 60 percent had dieted at some time in their senior year (Dwyer et al., 1969). In contrast, only 20 percent of male high school seniors wanted to weigh less, and only 6 percent of the men were currently dieting. Anorexia and the anorexic look have even been glorified, with *Playgirl* magazine titling an article on anorexia "The Golden Girl Disease" (June, 1975). All of these facts testify to the widespread stimuli for anorexia that are present in our culture.

Feminist therapists also note that anorexia is often precipitated by breaking up with a boyfriend or some other perceived rejection by a male (Boskind-Lodahl, 1976). The problem here is that the anorexic has given males the power to define her life and control her self-esteem.

Where does this vast array of possible explanations leave us? Garfinkel and Garner (1982) have proposed what I think is a useful way of organizing and understanding why anorexia develops, incorporating most of the foregoing ideas (see Figure 14.2). First, there are a number of *predisposing factors*, to anorexia: a disturbed family, cultural pressures for thinness, a distorted body image, and so on. Compulsive dieting may be started when someone who is characterized by many of the predisposing factors is then exposed to a *precipitating factor*, such as the loss of a boyfriend or a demand from a boyfriend for the beginning of sexual activity. Once excessive dieting begins, several *sustaining factors* keep it going — starving and vomiting cause anxiety reduction, and there may be secondary gains when the anorexia attracts attention. Thus many factors play their parts, and all must be understood and addressed if therapy is to be successful.

SEXISM AND PSYCHOTHERAPY

With the rise of the women's movement in the late 1960s, psychotherapists and the institution of psychotherapy became the object of sharp attacks for sexism (e.g., Chesler, 1972). What evidence is there that sexism in psychotherapy is a problem?

The Broverman study By far the most frequently cited study used as evidence of sexism in psychotherapy is one done by psychologist Inge Broverman and her colleagues (1970). They investigated the judgments of clinicians (psychiatrists, clinical psychologists, and social workers) on criteria of mental health for males and females. The clinicians in the sample were given a personality questionnaire with a series of bipolar rating scales of gender-typed personality characteristics, for example:

very *aggressive*		*not at all* *aggressive*
∣_____∣		

One-third of the clinicians were instructed to indicate on each item the pole to which a mature, healthy, socially competent *male* would be closer. Another third were told to do this for a *female*, and the remaining third were told to do so for an *adult*. Three interesting results emerged. First, while there were no significant differences between the standards for males and for adults, there were differences between the standards for females and for adults. This is a good example of the male-as-normative principle in psychology. The standards for human mental health are for males, and females are a deviation from them — or, as one feminist put it, the Broverman results show that "a normal, average, healthy woman is a crazy human being." A second result was that socially desirable personality characteristics tended to be assigned to males, undesirable ones to females. For example, a mature, healthy, socially competent woman is supposed to be more submissive, more excitable in minor crises, have her feelings more easily hurt, and be more conceited about her appearance than a mature, healthy, socially competent man. A third result was that there was no difference in the results depending on whether the clinician-rater was a man or a woman (more than one-third of the clinicians were females). Apparently female clinicians are no more exempt than males from these views of "healthy" womanhood.

On the basis of this study, it appears that the same double-bind situations that bring women to therapy may be present in the therapy situation. Basically the woman has two alternatives: she can adjust to female norms, in which case she will have a number of undesirable personality characteristics (for example, excitable in minor crises); or she can develop certain desirable human traits such as independence and assertiveness, in which case she may be accused of rejecting her femininity, and therefore of being abnormal. Of course, not every clinician is guilty of such situations, and there has been some dispute over the Broverman results (Fabrikant, 1974), but the general trends discovered in this study are disturbing.

As evidence of sexism in psychotherapy, there are some problems with the Broverman study. The basic problem is that it does not provide a direct measure of what we are concerned with: whether therapists, in their treatment of patients, act in a sexist manner. This study does not measure what therapists actually do in therapy, but rather what their attitudes are, based on their responses to a paper-and-pencil questionnaire. What we need are data on therapists' actual treatment of patients (Stricker, 1977), but these are in short supply. I shall review those that are available in a later section. Another problem with the Broverman study is that it is now about 15 years old. It is possible that therapists have changed their attitudes substantially in the last 15 years, in response to changing attitudes about gender roles in our culture.

APA: Defining sexism in psychotherapy   In 1974, the American Psychological Association appointed a task force to investigate sexist bias and

FIGURE 14.2

A model proposed for understanding the causes of anorexia.

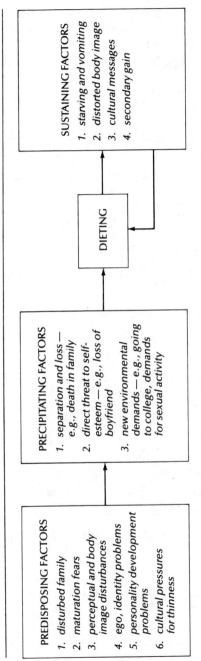

PREDISPOSING FACTORS

1. *disturbed family*
2. *maturation fears*
3. *perceptual and body image disturbances*
4. *ego, identity problems*
5. *personality development problems*
6. *cultural pressures for thinness*

PRECIPITATING FACTORS

1. *separation and loss — e.g., death in family*
2. *direct threat to self-esteem — e.g., loss of boyfriend*
3. *new environmental demands — e.g., going to college, demands for sexual activity*

DIETING

SUSTAINING FACTORS

1. *starving and vomiting*
2. *distorted body image*
3. *cultural messages*
4. *secondary gain*

Source: After Garfinkel and Garner, 1982

sex-role stereotyping in psychotherapeutic practice. In an initial report, they attempted to catalogue the kinds of practices that can reasonably be considered to indicate sexist bias in psychotherapy (APA, 1975b). These ideas were based on a preliminary survey of women psychotherapist members of APA.

The report identified four general areas in which sexist bias and sex-role stereotyping occur. These are listed below.

1. Fostering of traditional gender roles.

   Example:
   The therapist assumes that the woman's problems will be solved by marriage or being a better wife.

   > My therapist suggested that my identity problems would be solved by my marrying and having children; I was 19 at the time and in no way ready for marriage.

2. Bias in expectations and devaluation of women.

   Example:
   The therapist denies self-actualization or assertiveness for female clients and instead fosters concepts of women as passive and dependent.

   > Whenever a female becomes active, assertive, and aggressive in group situations the label "castrating bitch" is applied to her.

3. Sexist use of psychoanalytic concepts.

   Examples:
   a. The therapist maintains that vaginal orgasm is a prerequisite for emotional maturity and thus a goal of therapy.
   b. The therapist labels assertiveness and ambition with the Freudian concept of "penis envy."

4. Responding to women as sex objects including seduction of female clients.

Regarding the point about seducing clients, the 1978 revision of the American Psychological Association's ethical code states: "Sexual intimacies between therapist and client are unethical." A survey investigated the sexual activities of a sample of licensed Ph.D. psychologists with their patients (Holroyd and Brodsky, 1977); 5.5 percent of the male and 0.6 percent of the female psychologists returning the questionnaire admitted having engaged in sexual intercourse with a patient during the time the patient was in therapy, and an additional 2.6 percent of male and 0.3 percent of female therapists had intercourse with patients within three months of termination of therapy. These are probably best regarded as minimum figures, because they are based on the self-reports of the therapists and some might not be willing to admit such activity, even though the questionnaire was anonymous. Of those therapists who had intercourse with patients, 80 percent repeated the activity with other patients.

The Task Force report is helpful in providing a cataloguing of the kinds of practices in therapy that may be sexist or sex-biased. Nonetheless, the information is based on self-reports. There is still a lack of data, based on direct observations of therapy sessions, that would tell us more accurately the nature and extent of sexist bias. In addition, it could be that there are some very subtle sexist practices that neither patient nor therapist is aware of, which could be discovered only by analysis of direct observations of therapy sessions. For example, it could be that therapists give more verbal reinforcements (e.g., *"mm hmm"*) when female clients are talking about being mothers than when they are talking about their careers.

Other evidence   As noted above, the Broverman study provides some evidence of stereotyped attitudes on the part of therapists, but by itself it does not provide very direct evidence of sexist bias in therapy. A number of other studies have been done to try to provide better evidence. These are called *analog studies* because they investigate a situation that is analogous to the therapy situation rather than the therapy situation itself. Space does not allow a review of all of them here, so instead I shall consider in detail one analog study that is fairly typical.

Beverly Gomes and Stephen I. Abramowitz (1976) mailed a case history to a sample of psychotherapists. The therapists were asked to rate the patient whose history they read on a number of scales such as emotional maturity (very inadequate to very adequate) and mental disorder (extremely disturbed to mildly disturbed). The case history a particular therapist received was actually one of four case histories prepared by the investigators. All four were identical, except that half said the person was male, and half said she was female; they also differed in the concluding paragraph. In half the cases, it described the person with a number of "feminine" adjectives such as warm and dependent. In the other half, the person was described as having "masculine" characteristics such as ambitious and cold. Therefore the case history a therapist received might be about a feminine woman, a masculine woman, a feminine man, or a masculine man. In all other respects, however, all the case histories were identical.

On the ratings of mental disorder, there were no significant differences in the ratings given to male compared with female patients, nor to masculine versus feminine patients. Neither was there any difference between the ratings of male and female therapists. The absence of difference between ratings of males and of females suggests that there may not be as much sexist bias among therapists as one would think from the Broverman study. As the authors concluded,

The overall failure to detect prejudice against women or sex-role non-conformists among any therapist subgroup would tentatively appear to exonerate clinicians of the charges of unwitting antifemale sentiment and norm-enforcement. (Gomes and Abramowitz, 1976, pp. 10–11)

This study is interesting, then, because of its failure to find sexist bias.

Other studies using a similar technique have found that liberal female clients receive lower adjustment ratings from politically conservative therapists (Abramowitz et al., 1973) and that female clients receive a *better* prognosis — prediction for successful cure — than male clients (Abramowitz et al., 1976).

The problem with analog studies such as the one by Gomes and Abramowitz is that they still do not look at the actual therapy session. Further, the subjects (therapists) may have guessed the purpose of the study and tailored their responses to look respectable— that is, unbiased. Other investigators have used a confederate posing as a client who told the therapist a standard story, and the therapist's responses were measured (e.g., Shapiro, 1977).

In an attempt to overcome some of these problems of previous research, Teresa Buczek (1981) played tape-recordings of an initial counseling session to counselors. The client in each tape (half of the counselors heard a man, and half heard a woman, but otherwise the tapes were identical) mentioned a number of concerns about social relationships, about vocational issues, and about general issues. Afterwards, the counselors were asked to do two things: write down as many of the things the client said as they could, and write a list of further questions they would like to ask the client in order to plan treatment. The study is clever because it apparently has nothing to do with stereotyping and sexism in therapy, and thus counselor-subjects are not alerted to tailor their responses to be socially acceptable. Also, you can't cheat on a memory test! If sexism were a problem in psychotherapy, it might be expected that counselors would not be able to remember as many of the vocational, career-related remarks made by the woman client as they would of those made by the man client; conversely, they might remember more of the social facts stated by the woman client. The results were mixed, but did show some interesting effects. First, contrary to the charges of sexism, counselors remembered as many vocational concerns from the female client as from the male client. However, looking at the total number of concerns recalled, counselors recalled fewer overall concerns of the female client — she just wasn't remembered as well. The results also showed that female counselors remembered more facts about the clients than male counselors did. Finally, male counselors wanted to ask the female client significantly more follow-up questions on social concerns than they did the male client. This study, then, found evidence of more subtle kinds of sexism that may operate in psychotherapy, with counselors perhaps using gender schemas to process the information they receive from clients.

A few investigators have studied actual therapist-client behaviors, such as length of time the patient is kept, or remains, in therapy or in the hospital (e.g., Chesler, 1972). The problem with these "real life" measures is that it is possible that female patients are harder to cure than male patients, something that can't be controlled in real life studies, but can be controlled in studies like the one by Gomes and Abramowitz.

Conclusion   Where does all of this leave us? Is sexism a problem in psychotherapy? Probably three conclusions are reasonable at this point. First, the scientific evidence is not very good for the existence or non-existence of sexism in psychotherapy (Hare-Mustin, 1983; Sherman, 1980). Many of the studies have problems or contradicting results. However, it seems unlikely that there would be so many tales of sexism around — such as those found by the APA Task Force — if there were no sexism. It probably does exist, and one hopes that future research will document exactly where and what it is. Second, it is probably true that some therapists are sexists, but that not every therapist is a sexist. This may account for the failure of most studies to find overall evidence of sexist bias. But if only one therapist in ten is a sexist and you get that therapist, you may have a very unpleasant experience. It is probably wise, therefore, to become sensitized to problems of sexist bias so that you can spot them. Whether a therapist is a sexist probably depends on a number of factors, such as his or her political beliefs, personality, and individual reactions to a particular client. Third, from the research it would appear to be inaccurate to say that male therapists are biased and female therapists are not. Many studies find no differences between male and female therapists in their bias. Probably more important than the therapist's gender is her or his attitudes about gender roles.

HOW TRADITIONAL THERAPIES APPLY TO WOMEN

One of the most important factors influencing a woman's experience in therapy is the theoretical orientation of the therapist and the corresponding type of therapy she or he uses. Below we shall consider three kinds of therapy to see how they relate to women and whether they are likely to be biased.

Psychoanalysis   Psychoanalysis is a system of therapy based on Freud's theory (see Chapter 3). Both Freudian theory and psychoanalysis have received sharp criticisms from feminists. Some feminists feel that psychoanalysis is inherently, or at least very likely to be, sex-biased (e.g., American Psychological Association, 1976). Others, however, feel that it can be applied in an unbiased way, and even speak of feminist psychoanalysis (e.g., Shainess, 1977; Eichenbaum and Orbach, 1983).

The problem with psychoanalysis is that some of its central concepts *are* sex-biased. For example, women's achievement strivings may be interpreted as penis envy. Women who enjoy orgasm from masturbation may be regarded as immature and thus be urged to strive for the more mature, vaginal orgasm. The evidence indicates that women in psychoanalysis have sometimes been convinced that they are inferior, masochistic, and so on (American Psychological Association, 1976).

Therefore, although feminist or nonsexist psychoanalysis may be a possibility, clients should be sensitized to the potential sexism of psychoanalysis.

Behavior therapy Behavioral therapy (behavior mod) is a set of therapies based on principles of classical conditioning (usually associated with Pavlov) and operant conditioning (usually associated with Skinner). In contrast to psychoanalysis, behavior therapy attempts no in-depth analysis of the patient's personality or unconscious motives. Instead, the focus is on problematic behavior and how it can be modified by learning principles, such as rewarding desired behaviors or punishing undesired ones (for a detailed discussion of behavior therapy and its implications for women, see Blechman, 1980).

A number of specific therapy techniques may be used. One is *systematic desensitization*, which is used in the treatment of phobias. The patient and therapist make a list of events that arouse the patient's anxiety, and these are listed in a "hierarchy" from least anxiety-provoking to most anxiety-provoking (see Table 14.1). The patient is then trained in deep muscle relaxation. Next, the patient relaxes and, while relaxed, is asked to imagine the least anxiety-provoking item on the hierarchy; if there is any tension, the patient goes back to concentrating on relaxation. Once the

TABLE 14.1.   A client's hierarchy for systematic desensitization

most anxiety-arousing	1. An argument she raises in a discussion is ignored by the group.
	2. She is not recognized by a person she has briefly met three times.
	3. Her mother says she is selfish because she is not helping in the house (studying instead).
	4. She is not recognized by a person she has briefly met twice.
	5. Her mother calls her lazy.
least anxiety-arousing	6. She is not recognized by a person she has briefly met once.

Source: Adapted from Joseph Wolpe and A. A. Lazarus *Behavior Therapy Techniques: A Guide for the Treatment of Neuroses,* 1966, Pergamon Press. Used by permission.

patient is relaxed while imagining that situation, the therapist moves on to the next situation on the hierarchy, and so on, until the patient is relaxed while imagining the most anxiety-provoking situation. Once patients feel relaxed imagining these events, they are often able to feel relaxed and confident when actually confronting them.

Another therapy technique that is practiced is *positive reinforcement,* in which desired behaviors are rewarded. *Observation* and *imitation* can also be used, such as assertiveness training for women, which we will discuss later in this chapter. Finally, *aversive learning procedures* — in which some unpleasant stimulus functions to eliminate an undesired behavior — may be another technique applied. For example, the drug antabuse may be given to alcoholics; if they drink, the drug causes unpleasant body reactions such as nausea and vomiting. Such therapy is called *aversive counterconditioning.*

There is no inherent sexism in the concepts of behavior therapy (Lazarus, 1974). It does not assume that there should be gender differences, or that only women should engage in certain behaviors. Certainly behavior therapy does contain value judgments, but these should be applied equally to females and males. For example, assertiveness is valued by behavior therapists, but it should be valued both for males and for females. Of course, it would be possible for an individual behavior therapist to be sex-biased, but there is nothing in the theoretical system itself that is biased.

As an example of the treatment of a particularly common problem for women, the behavior therapist would attack depression by trying to increase the level of positive reinforcement the woman receives in her environment (Beck and Greenberg, 1974). For example, it might be that her husband is unresponsive, or even that he responds negatively, to her attempts at conversation or her work around the house, or to discussion of her own job. Her husband might be trained to be more responsive to her, thus providing more positive reinforcement. Or she may receive little positive reinforcement in her job, in which case she might be encouraged to alter her work or find a different job that would provide more positive reinforcement.

Gestalt therapy Gestalt therapy is a system of psychotherapy formulated by Fritz and Laura Perls in the 1940s. It is one of a group of therapies known as humanistic therapy because of their emphasis on treating the whole person (Perls, 1969; for reviews of Gestalt applied to women, see Brien and Sheldon, 1977; Polster, 1974). The basic aim of Gestalt therapy is to help people develop more intelligent behavior. This is done by helping them realize that alternatives or choices are open to them, which they often did not realize. With an awareness of choices, there is a greater range of action available. With the realization of these alternatives, though, comes responsibility. That is, the patient is encouraged to take responsibility for his or her life. It is no longer sufficient to blame one's unhappiness on forces around oneself (husband, job, etc.). With the realization of alternatives comes the responsibility for molding one's own life in an exciting way. This philosophy is helpful to women who often have the unpleasant feeling of being "stuck" in a lifestyle they don't seem to want. Gestalt therapy should help them to realize they have other alternatives open to them, and should give them the energy to move into those alternatives.

The following case illustrates the way Gestalt therapy worked for one woman's problems.

> One depressed woman named Polly felt she was "sick." Home alone with the children all day, she was very lonely and isolated. Her husband wanted to be her only adult contact. As her depression continued, her ex-therapist and her husband felt she should be hospitalized. Gradually, she saw that she had been accepting her husband's idea of a suitable lifestyle for her. She realized two things she wanted: adult companionship and self-understanding. At this point, depressed, frightened, yet resolute, she came into Gestalt therapy.
>
> Directing Polly away from focusing on what was *wrong* with her led her to open many new avenues. In addition to meeting new friends, she took a trip to India with an anthropology class and rekindled an old interest in flying planes. More important than these specific changes, however, was her realization that her depression was the result of turning her energies inward. Laura Perls recently said in a workshop in San Francisco that "depression is the opposite of expression." This was certainly the case with Polly. (Brien and Sheldon, 1977, p. 123)

As in behavior therapy, there is nothing inherent in the theory of Gestalt therapy that makes it sex-biased, although of course it would still be possible for an individual therapist to be biased.

NEW THERAPIES
FOR WOMEN

With the critiques of traditional therapies, particularly psychoanalysis, has come the suggestion that there is a need for feminist therapy or nonsexist therapy, or therapies especially tailored to the needs of women. In this section we shall discuss some of these alternatives.

Feminist therapy and nonsexist therapy   Feminist and nonsexist therapies may be characterized as allowing

> clients to determine their own destinies without the construction of culturally prescribed sex-role stereotypes based upon assumed biological differences. Both approaches attempt to facilitate equality (in personal power) between females and males. (Rawlings and Carter, 1977, p. 50)

Clinical psychologists Edna Rawlings and Dianne Carter (1977) distinguish between nonsexist therapy and feminist therapy. Feminist therapy, in particular, includes an advocacy of positions of the women's movement. They state that *nonsexist therapy* has the following particular values and assumptions:

1. The therapist should be aware of her or his own values.
2. There are no prescribed gender-role behaviors.
3. Gender-role reversals (e.g., female breadwinner, male at home) are not labeled pathological.
4. Marriage is not regarded as any better an outcome of therapy for a female than for a male.
5. Females are expected to be as autonomous and assertive as males; males are expected to be as expressive and tender as females.
6. Theories of behavior based on anatomical differences (e.g., Freud, Erikson) are rejected.

The assumptions of *feminist therapy* are as follows (Gilbert, 1980; Rawlings and Carter, 1977):

1. The inferior status of women is due to their having less political and economic power than men. Power analysis is central to feminist thought (see, for example, Chapter 3) and to feminist therapy.
2. The primary source of women's pathology is social, not personal; external, not internal.
3. The focus on environmental stress as a major source of pathology is not used as an avenue of escape from individual responsibility.
4. Feminist therapy is opposed to personal adjustment to social conditions; the goal is social and political change.
5. The therapist-client relationship is viewed as egalitarian.
6. Clients are encouraged to express anger and then deal with it.
7. Women must be economically and psychologically autonomous.
8. Relationships of friendship, love, and marriage should be equal in personal power.
9. Major differences between "appropriate" gender-role behaviors must disappear.

Terminology in this area is not standardized, however, so some therapists might refer to themselves as feminist therapists when in fact their assumptions correspond to what I have here called nonsexist therapy.

Perhaps the two points that are most central to feminist therapy, and that most distinguish it from traditional psychotherapy, are points 2 and 4 above. Regarding point 2, traditional therapies have viewed people's problems as being internal (within the individual) and have correspondingly prescribed personal changes to achieve better adjustment. Feminist therapists, in contrast, view women's problems as being external in origin, caused by oppression in the society around them. From this follows point 4: if the problems are external in origin, then the goal should be to change society, not oneself.

Assertiveness training   Assertiveness training — a technique of behavior therapy — has become popular among women, and it can take place as a part of formal psychotherapy, in informal self-help groups, or in classes. (For more detailed discussions, see Jakubowski-Spector, 1973; Jakubowski, 1977.) First, some terms need to be defined.

Assertion or assertiveness involves standing up for one's basic interpersonal rights in such a way that the rights of another person are not violated. Assertion should be a direct, honest, and appropriate expression of one's feelings. *Aggression,* in this context, involves standing up for one's rights in such a way that the rights of the other person are violated. It involves dominating, humiliating, or putting down the other person. *Nonassertion* is failing to stand up for one's rights and, consequently, permitting one's rights to be violated by others (Jakubowski-Spector, 1973).

Women tend to have more problems with being assertive than men do. In part it is because assertiveness is confused with aggressiveness, and aggressiveness is definitely not part of the feminine role — but then neither is assertiveness. Passivity and many of the other traits females are socialized for are contrary to assertiveness. Women are often concerned with maintaining harmonious relationships with others, and they may fear that being assertive will cause friction. The problem is that there is a cost in always swallowing one's feelings — a sense of frustration, ineffectiveness, or hurt. Some therapists believe that depression can result from lack of assertion (Jakubowski, 1977). Because assertiveness is a valuable human quality, many women are taking assertiveness training.

Assertiveness training often consists of role playing, in which students respond to people who are being aggressive or infringing on their rights, the idea being that assertiveness is learned through practice and through seeing models of assertive behavior. The following is an example of how high-quality assertion can be used to resolve a conflict.

> A graduate professor often continued evening class ten minutes or more beyond the normal class period. Although many students were irked by this behavior, one student was assertive and approached the professor after class one evening.
>
> *Student:*   I recognize that sometimes we get so involved in the discussion that you may not realize that the class is running overtime. I'd appreciate your ending the class on time because I have several commitments which I need to keep immediately after this class.
>
> *Professor:*   I don't really think that I've been late so often.
>
> *Student:*   I guess that you haven't noticed but the last three classes have been ten or fifteen minutes late. Is there any way I could help you end it on time?
>
> *Professor:*   As a matter of fact there is. I'm often so interested in the class that I don't look at my watch. It'd help me if you'd raise your

hand five minutes before the end of the class period. If I don't stop in five minutes, signal me again.

> *Student*: I'd be happy to do that. (Jakubowski, 1977, pp. 157–158)

Notice that the student was assertive, expressing her feelings directly, but in a way that showed regard for the professor. She did not show aggression (for example, "You're so damned inconsiderate of us, making us stay late all the time.") Neither was she nonassertive (in this case, doing nothing and continuing to suffer). The situation proceeded to a satisfactory resolution.

Consciousness-raising groups as therapy for women   With the rise of the feminist movement and consciousness-raising groups, and corresponding criticism of traditional psychotherapy, has come the suggestion that consciousness-raising groups may serve as a form of therapy for women (for reviews, see Kravetz, 1980; Brodsky, 1977; Kirsh, 1974).

A consciousness-raising group is usually a group of eight or so women. Consistent with beliefs of the women's movement, there is no leader; rather, all members are considered equal. The groups usually meet on a regular basis, such as for two hours one evening every week, lasting anywhere from a few weeks to a year or more. The participants talk about themselves, about their feelings, their experiences, and problems they are having. Beyond this, there is an analysis of how society's gender-role stereotypes and the lesser status and power of women create many of these problems. Many positive results may come from this process. The women often realize that they have many problems in common, which can relieve the feeling of abnormality resulting from the sense of being the "only one" with a problem. The sense of competition with other women may decrease and real bonds between women may develop. Other women become role models of effectiveness. The major goal, however, is a heightened awareness of themselves as women.

Therapy is not the goal of consciousness-raising groups, although the groups may be therapeutic. Feminists are careful to point out the difference in ideology between C-R groups and psychotherapy:

> The basic difference in the structures is that the patient-therapist relationship is unequal and hierarchical, contrasted with the peer equality among women in consciousness-raising groups. The basic difference in the ideologies is that traditional psychotherapy stresses adjusting the inner workings of individuals to fit society; consciousness-raising groups emphasize the need to change society by showing individuals that their "person" problems are rooted in socio-cultural phenomena. (Kirsh, 1974, pp. 336–337.)

Note that this is quite similar to the principles of feminist therapy discussed earlier. Because consciousness-raising groups are not specifically designed to be therapy, women with serious problems are generally referred to a feminist therapist.

FIGURE 14.3

Some have argued that consciousness-raising groups are better for women than psychotherapy.

Source: Photo by Owen Franken / Stock Boston.

There has been some research into the psychological effects of participating in a C-R group, although the research has been rather unsystematic,
in part because some C-R groups are suspicious of the motives of professional researchers. Some of the changes that have been reported include:
increased autonomy, activity, and self-esteem; an increased sense of control
and decreased depression; expanded jobs and career orientation; desire for
more egalitarian relationships with men; a new understanding of the concept of "mother"; "finding one's anger"; and more positive feelings about
other women (Kravetz, 1980; Weitz, 1982; Kirsh, 1974; Kincaid, 1977).
These, of course, would all be considered positive outcomes, whether from
a C-R group or from psychotherapy. More research in this area is needed.

ANDROGYNY AS A MODEL
OF MENTAL HEALTH

To this point we have discussed studies that are critical of setting traditional standards of masculinity and femininity as criteria of mental health
(e.g., Broverman et al., 1970). These studies argue that it makes little
sense to call traits such as passivity and submissiveness healthy for women.

Now that we know what women shouldn't be like, what should they be? Is it possible to state in some positive way what characteristics a healthy, well-adjusted woman should have?

One suggestion that has been raised is that androgyny should be the new model of mental health for women, and for men as well (Kaplan, 1976). The idea is that assertiveness and self-confidence ("masculine" traits) and interpersonal sensitivity and emotional expressiveness ("feminine" traits) are all desirable, so why not put them all together in one individual? The result would be the androgyn. The research reviewed in Chapter 4 indicates that the androgynous person tends to be more healthy than the gender-typed individual, because androgynous people have higher self-esteem and seem to function more effectively in a wider variety of situations. Thus there is also some scientific evidence to support androgyny as a model of mental health. Perhaps if the young women of today become more androgynous than the women of previous generations, women will have fewer problems of adjustment such as depression. It will be interesting to see if this actually occurs.

However, one should not expect that androgyny will be the perfect medicine for all of women's psychological problems. Some psychologists have pointed out problems with androgyny as a model of mental health (e.g., A. Kaplan, 1979). One of the basic problems seems to be that a person may have an androgynous combination of personality characteristics, but may apply them in the wrong situations. For example, a woman might be assertive and demanding to her husband when he needs her nurturance, and then become soft and nurturant when it would be better for her to be firm and assertive. Thus, having androgynous personality characteristics does not ensure that they will be used in the most adaptive way.

Androgyny holds a great deal of promise as a vision of mental health free from gender-role stereotypes, but it will require a great deal of societal change and more sophisticated scientific understanding before that vision is realized.

SUGGESTIONS FOR FURTHER READING

Boskind-Lodahl, Marlene, & Sirlin, Joyce (1977, March). The gorging-purging syndrome. *Psychology Today*, p. 50. This article provides a good introduction to bulimia.

Chernin, Kim (1981). *The obsession: Reflections on the tyranny of slenderness*. New York: Harper (Colophone paperback). This moving book documents our society's demand that women be thin, and what the consequences of that demand can be.

Federation of Organizations for Professional Women. *Women and Psychotherapy: A Consumer Handbook*. Available for $3.75 from the Federation of Organizations for Professional Women, 1825 Connecticut Avenue, N.W., Suite 403, Washington, DC 20009. This is an excellent source for women considering psychotherapy.

15
The Victimization
of Women

Rape is a crime against the person, not against the hymen.
DEENA METZGER, The Rape Victim

Rape has been one of the most important topics in the women's liberation debate. Feminists assert that rape is one of the ways that men exercise power and control over women (e.g., Brownmiller, 1975). With feminist attention to the topic, rape has "come out of the closet"; in the span of a decade, it has gone from being the secret that no woman would tell, to being the topic of television specials. More recently, attention has been drawn to the plight of battered wives and girls who are incest victims, and to the issue of sexual harassment. These topics have also moved from being something a woman felt she should hide to being a topic of public debate.

This chapter is about the victimization of women as seen in rape, wife-beating, sexual harassment, and incest. A discussion of all aspects of these problems (e.g., legal, self-defense) is beyond the scope of this book. Here I will concentrate on the psychological aspects.

RAPE

Theoretical views of rape   To provide a perspective for the discussion that follows, we can distinguish among three major theoretical views of the nature of rape (Albin, 1977):

1. Victim-precipitated — This view holds that a rape is always caused by a woman "asking for it." Rape, then, is basically the woman's fault. This view represents the tendency to "blame the victim."
2. Psychopathology of rapists — This theoretical view holds that rape is an act committed by a psychologically disturbed man. His deviance is responsible for the crime occurring.
3. Feminist — Feminist theorists view rapists as the standard (normal) product of gender-role socialization in our culture. They de-emphasize the sexual aspects of rape and instead view rape as an expression of power and dominance by men over women.

You personally may subscribe to one or the other of these views. It is also true that researchers in this area have generally based their work on one of these theoretical models, and this may influence their research. You should keep these things in mind as you continue to read the rest of this chapter.

Attitudes toward rape Psychologist Hubert Feild (1978) investigated attitudes toward rape among police, rapists, rape-crisis counselors, and citizens from the general population. He began his research by constructing a paper-and-pencil questionnaire that would measure people's attitudes toward rape on a number of different dimensions. Items were ranked on a scale from 1 (strongly agree) to 6 (strongly disagree) and consisted of statements such as "A woman should be responsible for preventing her own rape." Once Feild had developed this attitude scale, he administered it to people from the groups listed above. He obtained a number of interesting results.

In general, there was strong agreement with the following statements: "A woman can be raped against her will," and "A woman should feel guilty following a rape." There was strong disagreement with "A raped woman is a less desirable woman"; "If a woman is going to be raped, she might as well relax and enjoy it"; "Most women secretly desire to be raped"; "It would do some women some good to get raped"; " 'Nice' women do not get raped"; and "Rape serves as a way to put or keep women in their 'place.' " On the other hand, people on the average were fairly neutral (ratings around 3.5) on items such as "Women provoke rape by their appearance or behavior" and "The reason most rapists commit rape is for sex."

There were a number of gender differences in attitudes toward rape, as might be expected. Men indicated to a significantly greater extent that it was a woman's responsibility to prevent rape, that punishment for rape should be harsh, that victims precipitate rape through their appearance or behavior, that rapists are mentally normal, that rapists are not motivated by a need for power over women, that a woman is less attractive as a result of being raped, and that women should not resist during rape. It was also true that attitudes toward rape were correlated with attitudes toward women.

Comfortingly, there was a significant difference between rapists and rape-crisis counselors in their attitudes toward rape. Convicted rapists were more likely to endorse the following views: rape prevention is primarily a woman's responsibility; rape is motivated by a desire for sex; victims are likely to precipitate rape through their appearance or behavior; and rapists are not mentally normal.

Distressingly, however, police officers' views of rape were more similar to the rapists' than they were to the counselors'. No significant differences were found between police and rapists on most dimensions. It was also true that citizens from the general population had attitudes more like those of rapists than those of counselors. The citizens generally seemed to hold a negative view of rape victims.

Psychological responses of the rape victim[1]   A major program of research on rape victims has been done at Boston City Hospital by Ann Wolbert Burgess, a nurse, and Lynda Holmstrom, a sociologist (Burgess and Holmstrom, 1974a, 1974b). They have found that rape is a time of crisis for a woman and the effects on her adjustment may last for six months or more. Based on a study of 92 victims of forcible rape, Burgess and Holmstrom documented the existence of a *rape trauma syndrome*, which refers to the emotional changes that a woman undergoes following a rape or an attempted rape.

The rape trauma syndrome progresses in two phases: an acute phase and a long-term reorganization phase. The *acute phase* begins immediately after the rape and generally lasts for several weeks. During the first few hours following the rape, women have a wide variety of emotional reactions that may be classified into two basic categories: an expressive reaction, in which the woman cries and expresses fear, anger, anxiety, and tension; and a controlled reaction, in which the woman apparently masks her feelings and appears calm and composed or subdued.

The women studied by Burgess and Holmstrom reported many physical reactions during the acute phase. Some of these were direct results of the bruises and cuts they had received during the scuffle. Some women were forced to have oral sex and suffered irritation or damage to the throat. Rectal bleeding and pain were reported by the women who had been forced to have anal intercourse. Various irritations of the genitals were also common, as were symptoms of tension such as headaches, sleeplessness, and a feeling of jumpiness. Women also reported stomach pains and nausea.

Emotional reactions varied widely, ranging from fear, humiliation, and embarrassment to anger and a desire for revenge. Two feelings were especially prominent: fear and self-blame. Many women reported an overwhelming fear of physical violence and said that they had believed they would be murdered during the attack. These feelings of fear sometimes persisted long after the rape had taken place. Self-blame also occurred, with the woman spending hours agonizing over what she had done to bring on the rape or what she might have done to prevent it: "If I hadn't worn that tight sweater, . . ." "If I hadn't worn that short skirt, . . ." "If I hadn't been stupid enough to walk on that dark street, . . ." "If I hadn't been dumb enough to trust that guy, . . ." This is an example of a tendency, on the part of both the victim and others, to "blame the victim."[2]

---

[1] Portions of the material that follows on rape are adapted from *Understanding Human Sexuality* by Janet S. Hyde. © 1979 by McGraw-Hill Book Co. Used with permission of McGraw-Hill Book Co.

[2] In fact, however, in 71 percent of the cases, the rapist planned the rape ahead of time (Amir, 1971); it is therefore difficult to believe that it was the victim's fault.

The acute phase is followed by a *long-term reorganization phase*. The rape creates a major disruption in the woman's life. For example, some women are unable to return to work after being raped, particularly if the rape occurred at work (Brodsky, 1976). They may quit their jobs and remain unemployed for some time. Many of the women studied by Burgess and Holmstrom moved during the long-term reorganization phase, sometimes several times; many also changed their telephone number, and some got an unlisted number. These actions seemed to result from a fear that the rapist would find them and attack them again. Some women who had been raped indoors developed fears of being indoors, and some who had been raped outdoors developed fears of being outdoors. Sexual phobias were also common. The women's normal sexual lifestyles were often severely disrupted for long periods. For example, one woman reported, five months after being raped, "There are times I get hysterical with my boyfriend. I don't want him near me; I get panicked" (Burgess and Holmstrom, 1974a, p. 984).

If a woman reports the rape and decides to press charges, the police investigation and the trial itself may be further crises for her. She must recall the traumatic experience in detail. The police and the courts have a history of callous or even abusive treatment of rape victims. The woman may be offered little sympathy, and the police may adopt a cynical attitude, suggesting that she agreed to have sex but then changed her mind afterward. The attitudes of the police are not too surprising, growing up as they did in a culture that abounds with stereotypes about women, including the one that says that rape is only a situation in which a woman changed her mind. Of course, not all police officers have been guilty of such cynicism, but too many victims report treatment like this:

> They finally told me they thought I was lying. They said I'd probably been having sex with my boyfriend and probably was afraid I was pregnant. They also theorized that my boyfriend had set me up for it. They wanted to know if he'd ever asked me to have relations with his friends. (Brownmiller, 1975, p. 366)

Or this:

> I went to the police station and said, "I want to report a rape." They said, "Whose?" and I said, "Mine." The cop looked at me and said, "Aw, who'd want to rape you?" (Brownmiller, 1975, p. 364)

Beyond these anecdotal reports, we have more solid scientific evidence of negative attitudes of the police in the study by Feild discussed earlier in this chapter.

The defense lawyer, in attempting to defend the rapist, may try to make it look as if the victim was actually the criminal — that she seduced him and later decided to call it rape, that she is a slut and therefore cannot be raped, and so on. She may be questioned about her prior sexual experiences, the idea being that if she has had premarital or extramarital sex, she is promiscuous and cannot be raped. As one woman expressed it:

> They trotted out my whole past life, made me go through all these charges, while he just sat at the defendant's table, mute, surrounded by his lawyers. Of course that was his right by law, but it looked like I was the one who was on trial. (Brownmiller, 1975, p. 372)

Recently some states have passed "reform" evidence laws, which do not permit the woman's previous sexual experience (except with the alleged rapist) to be a topic during a trial for rape.

Recently, perhaps partly as a result of several excellent television programs dramatizing the plight of the woman who has been raped, many police departments have tried to change their handling of rape victims. Some have special "rape squads" composed of women police officers who record the woman's story and investigate the case; this spares the woman the embarrassment of describing the incident to a man.

It also appears that the victim's sense of guilt over the crime contributes to the trauma she experiences. According to a specialist in criminal psychiatry, "The victim who is beaten into almost senselessness may suffer far less emotional trauma than the woman who submits to rape when her life is threatened" (Brussel, 1971, p. 30). That is, emotional non-involvement between the victim and the criminal helps the victim adjust better afterward. The woman who is beaten unconscious is much less likely than the woman who escapes with only minor scratches to have others imply (or to think in her own mind) that she brought on the attack or that she cooperated or enjoyed it.

To say the least, then, rape is an extremely traumatic experience for many women. In view of this, Burgess and Holmstrom emphasize the need for counseling for rape victims. The counselor provides support and encourages the victim to vent her feelings. The counselor should be with the victim during the hospital stay and while the police are questioning her, and then should provide follow-up counseling; the counselor should also be with the woman during the court procedures since, as has been noted, they can be extremely traumatic.

Carefully conducted research indicates that rape victims are significantly more depressed than nonvictims, but research also indicates that the adjustment of victims has typically stabilized by four months after the rape (Atkeson et al., 1982; Resick et al., 1981). Thus, while it is important to understand the psychological trauma of rape, it is also important to appreciate the coping strengths of women in recovering from it. Most women do not allow themselves to remain permanent victims (see also Gruber et al., 1982).

Burgess and Holmstrom (1974a) have also documented the existence of a phenomenon they call the *silent rape reaction*. Probably the majority of rapes (experts say 80 percent) are not reported. Not only do some women fail to report the rape to the police, but they also do not tell anyone about it. They, of course, experience the same problems of adjustment that other rape victims do, but they have no way of expressing or venting these feelings. People who do counseling or psychotherapy should be aware of this syndrome. For example, a woman may come for counseling complaining of quite different problems — perhaps inability to have orgasms or anxiety and depression — when her real problem is that she has been raped but is unable to talk about it. Symptoms of this silent rape reaction are similar to those associated with the rape trauma syndrome, described above. Such women should be gently helped to begin to talk about the experience so that they can start to deal with it.

The rapist What is the profile of the typical rapist? The basic answer to that question is that there is no typical rapist. Rapists vary tremendously from one to the next in occupation, education, marital status, previous criminal record, and motivation for committing the rape. To deal with this diversity, some scientists have attempted to develop typologies of rapists (ways of classifying them). These will be discussed below.

A few generalizations can be made about rapists. Most are young. According to the FBI *Uniform Crime Reports*, 61 percent are under 25. Many have a tendency to repeat their offense (Cohen et al., 1971). It is also true that most rapists are not murderers (Selkin, 1975). Probably only about one rape in 500 is accompanied by a murder (Brownmiller, 1975).[3] This statistic is important for women who wonder how best to react in a rape situation. Statistically, although the rapist may threaten the woman with violence or murder, he is unlikely to carry through on this and is only using the threat to get her to submit. This may encourage women to resist the attacker rather than to submit to him.

In an attempt to deal with the diversity of personalities and approaches among rapists, some researchers have developed typologies, or schemes for categorizing them. According to one such typology, rapists vary according to whether their aim is primarily aggressive, primarily sexual, or a mixture of the two (Cohen et al., 1971). The trouble with research of this kind is that it is based on reported rapes only, and typically investigates rapists who have been arrested, convicted, and sent to jail. It seems likely that these rapists are more deviant than those who escape being reported. Thus the research ignores the more common, "normal" rapist, such as the date rapist or the boss who rapes his secretary.

The date rape Though often not categorized as rape, some acts of coitus on dates involve a great deal of force and could at least be called *sex aggression*.

---

[3] If anything, this is probably an overestimate of the number of rapes that end in murder, since rape-murders are invariably discovered, whereas the rape in which the woman escapes with minor scratches is likely to go unreported.

Incidents of this type were investigated by Eugene J. Kanin (1969; see also Kanin and Parcell, 1977). He began by contacting a random sample of unmarried male university students; 95 percent cooperated. Of those who responded, 25 percent reported having performed at least one act of sex aggression, defined as making a forceful attempt at coitus to the point of being disagreeable and offensive to the woman, with the woman responding by fighting or crying, for example. The 87 males who had engaged in such acts reported 181 episodes with 142 females.

The incidents of sex aggression were not confined to cases of casual bar pick-ups. They occurred in every degree of involvement, from pick-ups and first dates to couples who dated regularly or were pinned.

In some cases, the sex aggression appeared to result from female-male miscommunication. There is a saying among males that "When she says 'no,' she really means 'yes.'" How, then, is a woman supposed to say "no" when she really means it? Such confused communication patterns between men and women can contribute to the date rape, as described in the following example:

> I picked up M and she suggests we go and park and "talk." Talk shifts to "old times." I move over and kiss her. One thing leads to another and I am petting her breasts. M begins to complain about her girdle and removes it. The pace increases to the point where I try to lay her down on the front seat of the car. She resists and I keep going until she suddenly starts fighting and screaming at me. I finally told her to shut up and took her home. She was really sore. (Kanin, 1969)

In this case, the man doubtless interpreted the woman's taking off her girdle as an invitation to intercourse, while she probably in fact took it off because it felt very uncomfortable.

In some cases, miscommunication and misunderstanding are so great as to be nearly unbelievable. For example, some rapists have been reported to ask, after the rape, whether the victim had an orgasm (see, for example, the case reported by Anonymous, 1975).

In other cases, the rape appears to be a way for the man to exert social control over the woman. For example, sex aggression was apparently used by some men to punish women whom they perceived as being "teases" or "gold diggers."

In a more recent survey of a representative sample of university students, similar results were obtained (Koss and Oros, 1982). In response to the question "Have you ever been raped?" 6 percent of the women replied "yes." But when the question was broadened to include other kinds of sexual behaviors, the percentage of affirmative replies went up substantially. In response to "Have you ever been in a situation where a man used some degree of physical force (twisting your arm, holding you down, etc.) to try to make you engage in kissing or petting when you didn't want to?" 30 percent of the women said "yes." And 21 percent of the women said that they had had sexual intercourse with a man when they didn't really want to because they felt pressured by his continual arguments.

The point of both of these studies is that incidents of sex aggression were not found to be rare, but rather fairly common, even in "normal" populations.

Marital rape   The possibility that a man could rape his wife was brought to public attention when Greta Rideout brought suit against her husband for marital rape. Defining marital rape is complicated by the fact that, in many states, rape laws exclude the possibility of marital rape; the assumption seems to be that sex in marriage is always the husband's "right."

How common is marital rape? In a random sample of San Francisco women, 12 percent of the married women reported that they had experienced some form of forced sex in marriage (Russell, 1982).

One phenomenon that emerges in research on marital rape is an association between it and marital violence — that is, the man who batters his wife is also likely to rape her. For example, in a study of 137 women who had reported being physically assaulted by their husbands, 34 percent reported being raped by their husbands (Frieze, 1983). The fact that some women are unwilling to define certain acts as marital rape is evident from the 43 percent of that sample (more than the number who reported being raped) who said that sex was unpleasant because it was forced upon them by their husbands. Asked why they had been raped, 78 percent felt that the cause was the husband's belief that the act would prove his manhood. An additional 14 percent attributed the rapes to the husband's drinking. The psychological consequences of marital rape were studied in this research, much as they have been in other rape research. The response of the majority of the women was anger toward the husband. However, women who had been frequently raped by their husbands began to experience self-blame. Marital rape also appeared to have consequences for the marriage: The raped women were more likely to say that their marriages had been getting worse over time.

Thus, research shows that marital rape is a real phenomenon, that it is associated with wife-battering, and that it has negative consequences, both for the woman and for the marriage.

Sex and aggression   Psychologists Seymour Feshbach and Neal Malamuth (1978) have done a series of studies on the link between sex and aggression. These studies may provide us with some clues about how forces in our society encourage rapists, and what might be done to remedy this situation.

In one of their typical experiments, they exposed subjects (college students) to an erotic film or written story. Afterward, they gave the subjects an opportunity to act aggressively by allowing them to shock a "subject" (really a confederate of the experimenters) for making errors in a guessing game. The amount of shock the subject administered was used as an index of aggression. The results indicated that subjects who were sexually aroused from seeing a film showed significantly more aggression than a control group who had seen a neutral film.

In explaining this phenomenon, Feshbach and Malamuth believe that it is not a simple link between sex and aggression, with sexual arousal causing increased aggression. Instead, they believe the link is in the fact that our society has taboos on both sexual and aggressive behavior. When the taboo on one is lifted, it tends to lift the taboo on the other. As the researchers commented, "By showing the erotic film, we communicated the unspoken message that 'taboo behavior like sex is okay.' "

Other studies have also shown that the effect can work in the reverse direction — that is, by giving subjects permission to be aggressive, they can become more sexually aroused (Feshbach and Malamuth, 1978). However, aggressive behavior that is stronger and more deviant can interfere with sexual feelings. Generally, reading about a rape inhibited the sexual responses of both men and women. However, there was some variation depending on the content of the passage, in particular whether the victim was described as being in pain and whether she finally succumbed and enjoyed the act. For women, strong pain cues inhibited sexual arousal, regardless of whether the woman finally gave in. For men, however, the theme of the woman getting aroused in the end, despite the pain and violence of the rape, led them to increased arousal. Indeed, there was some evidence that men identify with the rapist and consider his behavior within their own potential range. When asked how likely they would be to behave as this man did under the same circumstances, 51 percent responded that they might do it if they were assured that they would not be caught.

Although not opposed to pornography *per se*, Feshbach and Malamuth argue strongly that sadomasochistic pornography, in which violence and sexual arousal are shown together, can be harmful. In particular, it may help to form a conditioned association between sexual arousal and violent responses. In an analysis of five years of pictures and cartoons in *Playboy* and *Penthouse*, they found that the amount of sexual violence increased each year. There is cause for concern about this because, if they are correct, combining sex and aggression and showing it to men may lift some of their inhibitions against rape.

Gender-role socialization and rape   How do men become rapists and women become victims of rape? In this section we will discuss the notion that many of the qualities for which females are socialized make them vulnerable to rape and many of the qualities for which men are socialized contribute to the creation of rapists (Russell, 1975; Weis and Borges, 1973).

According to gender-role stereotypes, weakness is feminine, while strength is masculine. The stereotype of weakness is compounded by the lack of athletic training that females generally receive, compared with males. As a result, many women think of themselves as being physically weak, and, because they lack training and do not exercise, they may actually be weak. This weakness is symbolized in many ways, as when men open doors for women or carry heavy bundles for them. To expect a person who needs such assistance to fight off a 220-pound attacker would be silly. Thus, the weakness and passivity for which females are socialized contribute to making them rape victims.

Females are also socialized for nurturance (taking care of others) and altruism (paying attention to the needs of others rather than one's own needs). The woman who has been socialized to be nurturant and who spends her days expressing her gentleness toward her children can scarcely be expected to attempt to gouge out a man's eyes with her fingernails, as some self-defense experts advise. Female altruism has an ironic effect in the rape situation. Some women report the rape but then choose not to press charges because they say they are afraid that the rapist might have to go to jail for a long time[4] or that his reputation will be ruined. Thus, the victim may adopt a nurturant, altruistic attitude toward her attacker, considering his needs and feelings first.

The feelings of altruism that lead to nonreporting are magnified by the fact that, in nearly half the cases, the victim knows her attacker at least casually. Statistics indicate that in 53 percent of all cases, the attacker is a total stranger. However, in 30 percent of all cases, the woman and the rapist are slightly acquainted; in 7 percent, they are relatives (father and daughter, brother and sister, uncle and niece, etc.); and in 3 percent, they are not related but have had a previous close association (Mulvihill et al., 1969).

Females are also socialized for a group of qualities that might be called collectively "being ladylike." Ladies, for example, do not make scenes. To fight off a rapist, of course, one needs to make a scene, but many women may be inhibited from screaming or engaging in a rough scuffle because that is not ladylike behavior. Ladies are also neat and clean and pretty. Some women, immediately after a rape, go home to shower, wash their hair, and change their clothes; then they proceed to the police station. While their emotional need to get themselves clean is understandable, they have destroyed most of the evidence of the crime, and the skeptical reaction of the police is not surprising. If you look neat and clean and pretty, it is hard to believe that you have just been raped.

Female adolescents are taught to fear sex crimes (Burt and Estep,

---

[4] Those who worry about condemning a man to a long jail sentence may be interested to know that the average convicted rapist spends less than four years in jail for the offense (Brownmiller, 1975).

1981). They are told never to accept rides with strange men or to take candy from them. Yet the exact nature of the potential danger remains unknown, and so the girl may build up an exceedingly great dread of a mysterious crime, perhaps thinking that it would be the worst thing that could ever happen to her. Thus, when she is attacked, she may be immobilized with fear. She freezes and is unable to wage an effective counterattack.

The reader can probably think of other examples of qualities that females are socialized for that contribute to making them rape victims. However, the important point is that conformity to traditional standards of femininity makes women more vulnerable to rape, at least when they are in a situation in which a man intends to rape them (Russell, 1975).

The parallel argument to the one above is that males are socialized for characteristics that contribute to making them rapists (Russell, 1975; Weis and Borges, 1973).

Aggression, dominance, power, and strength are considered to be manly. Having been socialized to be aggressive, it is not surprising that men commit the aggressive crime of rape. Further, rapists may themselves be victims of our culture's confusion of sex and aggression. For example, we often refer to the male as playing the "aggressive" role in sex, suggesting that sex is supposed to have an aggressive component. As noted above, sex and aggresssion are also combined in the sadomasochistic pornography that is so common. The rapist's confusion of sex and aggression reflects a confusion existing in our society.

It may be, then, that rape is a means of proving masculinity for the male who is insecure in his role. For this reason, the statistics on the youthfulness of rapists make sense; youthful rapists may simply be young men who are trying to adopt the adult male role, who feel insecure about doing it, and who therefore commit a rape as proof of their manhood. Further, heterosexuality is an important part of manliness. Raping a woman is a flagrant way to prove that one is heterosexual. Interestingly, some rapists have a history of passivity, heterosexual inadequacy, and being called "queers" or "pansies" by their peers in adolescence. Rape may seem to them to be a way of establishing their heterosexual manliness.

Further support for this viewpoint comes from the fact that, in one study, 43 percent of rapes were committed by pairs or groups of men (Amir, 1971). Often in such cases the men or boys appear to be vying to prove their masculinity (Blanchard, 1959), and rape appears to them to be a way of accomplishing that.

The wider impact of rape   To this point, the discussion has centered on rapists and the impact of rape on the victim. But rape has much broader ramifications in our society, and it affects many people besides the victim. Most women perform a number of behaviors that stem basically from rape fears. For example, a single woman is not supposed to list her full first name in the telephone book, because that is a giveaway that she is

FIGURE 15.1

Karate demonstration at International Women's Day, March, 1973. Many experts feel that women should learn self-defense skills as a way of combating rape.

Source: Photo by Elizabeth Hamlin / Stock Boston.

alone. Rather, she should list a first initial or a man's name. Many women, when getting into their car at night, almost reflexively check the back seat to make sure that no one is hiding there. Most college women avoid walking alone through dark parts of the campus at night. At least once in their lives, most women have been afraid of spending the night alone. If you are a woman, you can probably extend the list from your own experience. However, the point is that most women experience the fear of rape, if not rape itself (Burt and Estep, 1981).[5] In addition, this fear restricts their activities.

There are also bad consequences for society at large. Surely it is not pleasant for the average man to be viewed by a woman as a potential rapist. Further, there are probably effects on husbands of raped women, although these have yet to be studied.

---

[5] Actually, statistics indicate that the chances of being raped are higher than you might think. Statistical analysis of a well-sampled survey in the San Francisco area indicated that there is a 26 percent chance that a woman in that area will be the victim of a completed rape at some time in her life (Russell and Howell, 1983). The rape rate in San Francisco, of course, is higher than rape rates in some other areas of the country, but the statistic is nonetheless disturbing.

BATTERED WIVES [6]

One solution that some people propose to the rape problem is for women simply to stay home, off the streets. However, the data indicate that a woman may actually be less safe in her own home than on the street. The following statistics give some indication of the extent of the problem (Martin, 1976):

— In Atlanta, Georgia, 60 percent of all police calls on the night shift are domestic disputes.

— In 1974, Boston police responded to 11,081 family disturbance calls, most of which involved physical violence.

— Women are the ones who need help most of the time in these disturbances. About 75 to 95 percent of the complaints in domestic disturbances are filed by women.

— In order to get a control group for his study *The Violent Home*, Richard Gelles (1974) interviewed 40 neighbors of known violent families. Of these supposedly "nonviolent" families, 37 percent had experienced at least one incident of violence, and for 12 percent, the violence was a regular occurrence.

— About one-third of female murder victims in California in 1971 were killed by their husbands.

It is only recently that the topic of battered wives has been brought to the attention of the public, and thus it is a topic that has received less research than rape. In fact, wife-beating has a long history, and at many times has been considered a legitimate form of behavior, a logical extension of the roles of men and women. For example, in the sixteenth century in France, the Abbé de Brantôme, although reluctant to speak against the teachings of the Church, felt compelled to ask, "But however great the authority of the husband may be, what *sense* is there for him to be allowed to kill his wife?" (Davis, 1971, p. 261). In Russia during the reign of Ivan the Terrible, the state church supported such practices by issuing a Household Ordinance that detailed how a man might most effectively beat his wife (Mandel, 1975, p. 12). Probably the first contemporary book exposing the topic was *Scream Quietly or the Neighbors Will Hear*, by Erin Pizzey (1974), who has opened a shelter for battered women in England.

---

[6] Battering can occur in situations other than marriage; examples are a divorced or separated couple in which the husband returns to beat the woman, or couples who are simply living together. To simplify the terminology, I shall refer to "battered wives." It is also true that in some cases it is the wife who beats the husband. However, when the violence is physical but not homicidal, the greater physical strength of the male means that far greater damage is done in wife-beating than in husband-beating (Steinmetz, 1977). The focus here will be on wife-beating rather than on husband-beating.

FIGURE 15.2
Battered women's shelters are a necessary part of aid to battered wives.

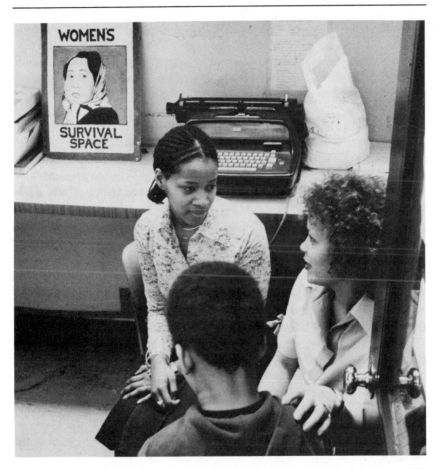

Source: © Bettye Lane

Although the family in America is romanticized as a haven of peace and safety, current estimates are that the incidence of family violence is high. In the largest and best study on the topic, sociologist Murray Straus (1980) analyzed a probability sample of over 2,000 families. The data indicated that 16 percent of the couples experienced some violence between themselves (ranging from slapping to actual beating) within the last year. Over the duration of a marriage, that would mean that about 28 percent would be involved in violence between spouses. Straus estimates that in about 5 percent of marriages the wife is actually beaten at some time during the marriage. The average frequency of beating is 2.4 times per year. It should be recognized, though, that these statistics doubtless represent an underestimate because many people are unwilling to admit that beating occurs.

Attitudes toward marital violence   Several surveys indicate that a surprisingly large number of Americans approve of some violence in marriage, and that acceptance of such practices is actually stronger in the middle class than the lower class. In one sample of American adults, 25 percent approved of husband-wife battles. Among grade-school graduates, 17 percent approved, but 32 percent of college graduates approved (cited in Martin, 1976, p. 19). A Harris poll done in 1968, based on interviews with a representative national sample of 1176 adults, showed that one-fifth approved of slapping one's spouse on "appropriate" occasions (Stark and McEvoy, 1970). It would be interesting to know how the respondents construed the term "slap," and whether they would have answered differently had the term been "beat" or "hit."

Insofar as there is social approval of marital violence, the abused woman's situation worsens. It is difficult for her to complain about her crisis if people do not view it as such.

The batterer: Psychological aspects   What kind of man beats his wife? As with the rapist, I can give no profile of the "typical" wife-beater. Such men are found in all social classes and in a wide variety of occupations. Contrary to stereotypes, the wife-batterer is not always an unemployed man in the lower class (Martin, 1976). One woman, whose physician husband beat her, said that he was "a general practitioner and while at medical school was an amateur boxer, so he had plenty of brawn as well as brain, plus enough money to keep him well-supplied with as much whiskey as he wanted" (Martin, 1976, p. 45).

Within this diversity, a few factors do emerge as common among wife-batterers. Drugs, particularly alcohol, are common problems among wife-beaters, and they are often being used at the time of violent incidents. In one study of women seeking help from an abused women's crisis center, 85 percent reported that their violent husbands had either alcohol or other drug problems (Roy, 1977b). Of the men who drank occasionally, 80 percent beat their wives only while under the influence of alcohol. Some authorities, however, feel that the effects of alcohol in family violence have been exaggerated (Martin, 1976). In our society, we believe that people do things that are "out-of-character" while they are drunk, and thus drunkenness can become a kind of excuse for the batterer and his victim, disguising what is really happening.

It does appear that wife-batterers come from violent families. In one study, 81 percent of wife-beaters had either been abused as children or had witnessed their father beating their mother (Roy, 1977b). Thus violence in families perpetuates itself from one generation to the next.

In an attempt to describe the diversity of types of men who seriously assault their wives, one study of men who had been arrested for such assaults found that there were five different personality types among these men (Faulk, 1974):

1. Dependent and suspicious — The husband is extremely jealous and the violence arises from this.
2. Violent and bullying — These men use violence to solve problems in many areas of their lives including their marriage.
3. Dominating — These men have a great need to be dominant over their wives, and apparent insubordination could lead to violence.
4. Dependent and passive — In this case the wife appears to dominate the relationship, and violence occurs after prolonged poor treatment from her.
5. Stable and affectionate — In this group, the men appear to have a long-term, affectionate relationship with their wives, and violence occurred during an episode of psychological disturbance, typically depression.

It is worth noting that these descriptions could be applied to many married men.

The violent episode is often preceded by an argument. According to one study, the following are the four most common areas of disagreement when wife-beating occurs: arguments over money, jealousy, sexual problems, and alcohol and other drugs (Roy, 1977b).

The battered woman: Psychological aspects   Battered women, just like their husbands, are a diverse group, varying in social class, education, and occupation. Compared with the 81 percent of wife-beaters who came from violent homes, however, only 33 percent of battered women were abused as children or witnessed their father beating their mother (Roy, 1977b). This suggests that characteristics of the husband are more critical than characteristics of the wife in leading to battering.

One of the most interesting questions to ask about battered women is, why do they stay? Many of these women endure years of repeated beating. Often to the frustration of crisis counselors, a battered woman who has left her husband may return to him. The following were the five most common reasons given for staying by battered wives, listed in order from most to least frequent: (1) hope that the husband would reform; (2) having no other place to go; (3) fear that there would be reprisals from the husband; (4) concern about the children (they need a father, can't support them herself, etc.); and (5) economic dependence (can't support herself) (Roy, 1977b). Although a psychoanalyst might think that these women are masochistic, the reasons listed above more often reflect stark practical and economic factors, such as not being able to support oneself and having no place else to live.

Beyond this, there is little research available on the psychological characteristics of the battered woman. The letter from a battered woman is offered here as an example that provides more psychological insights than scientific research has yet achieved.

The children   In addition to the effects on the battered woman, it is also important to consider the effects on the children. These effects fall into two categories. First, the man who beats his wife is likely to abuse his children. In one study of battered wives, 45 percent reported that the husband also assaulted the children (Roy, 1977b). In a study of battered women in England, 54 percent said that their husband also committed acts of violence against the children (Gayford, 1975). Second, even if the man does not abuse the children, one must consider the effects on the children of watching their father beat their mother. Those effects have not been precisely documented, but, as noted earlier, wife-beaters frequently come from such families.

Theories of the causes of wife-battering   A number of theoretical perspectives are available for understanding why wife-beating occurs (for reviews of these, see Walker, 1980; Straus, 1980). These perspectives in some ways parallel the different theoretical views of the nature of rape described earlier in this chapter.

Several different *psychological theories* are possible. One is that the man who batters his wife is simply a rare, psychologically disturbed individual, perhaps a psychopath. This view does not seem acceptable given the high incidence of wife-beating documented by research. A second approach is to say that battering occurs because of the psychopathology of the wife. In this view, the woman is seen as a disturbed individual who brings on the attack and self-destructively stays with the man who batters her. The psychoanalyst might call her masochistic. Note that this view blames the victim.

A third psychological approach is a *learned helplessness theory* of battering proposed by Lenore Walker, a psychologist who has done extensive research with battered women (Walker, 1980). This explanation rests on the same learned helplessness theory that was used in explaining depression in women in Chapter 14. It is based in learning theory. According to this view, the battered woman has a history of childhood gender-role socialization to passivity and helplessness. In adulthood, the experience of being battered reinforces her helplessness. This theory explains the depression experienced by battered women. It also neatly explains why battered women stay with their husbands or return to them after having tried to escape. Their conditioning to helplessness is so complete that they cannot act to save themselves.

Sociological theory presents yet another view (Straus, 1980). It focuses on norms and attitudes in our society that condone violence within families, particularly violence by husbands to wives. Some statistics supporting this view were given earlier in the chapter (e.g., Martin, 1976; Stark and McEvoy, 1970). Sociologists also call attention to the process of gender-role socialization in childhood, in which girls are expected to be passive and boys are expected to be aggressive.

The *feminist perspective* holds that wife-beating is both cause and effect of the inequality of power between men and women in our society (Walker, 1980). The inequality of power causes wife-beating because it serves as a rationale for a man to "discipline" his wife, much as a parent may discipline a child. But inequality of power is also affected by wife-beating, because battering serves to perpetuate the dominance of men over women. Feminists also note both the historical and contemporary approval of wife-beating. Finally, feminists have focused public attention on both the police-court system and psychotherapy as institutions in which the battered woman is often blamed for the beating and is seldom helped.

What can be done? The problems of battered women are complex, and no single measure is likely to solve them. If violence in American society could be reduced in general, that would probably help to a certain degree. Some of the problems of battered women, however, are special and require special solutions. One solution is providing refuge houses. These houses provide the woman with a safe place to go (one of her most immediate needs), with emotional support from those around her, and possibly with job counseling and legal advice. These shelters have sprung up like mushrooms in the last decade in the United States. Interestingly, it appears that these shelters and the paraprofessional and peer counseling they provide are the most successful treament for battered women (Walker, 1980).

Community social services are also needed to deal with the problem of wife-beating. Crisis hotlines are important so that the woman can get immediate help. In addition, counseling services for the batterer, the victim, and the children are needed. Feminist therapy (see Chapter 14) should be particularly helpful to the battered woman.

Self-defense training for battered women has been recommended by some experts (e.g., Martin, 1976). The woman who is an expert in karate or some other system can offset the greater strength of her husband and assertively discourage his attacks.

Legal and police reform are also important (e.g., Roy, 1977a; Martin, 1976). One problem is that the American legal system has considered the family and home to be sacred, and has been loath to interfere with them in any way. Somehow the police officer who intervenes in a "family" fight is viewed as violating the sanctity of the family. Police officers are often unwilling to arrest a husband for assault unless the officer has actually witnessed the attack, which is rare since the police are usually called after the fact. A simple solution is for the woman to make a citizen's arrest, but women are often not aware that they can do so, and the police neglect to inform them of this option.

At least some of the blame must also rest with traditional gender roles and socialization. Wife-beating, after all, is a way of being dominant and thereby of fulfilling the male role. And staying with such a husband is consistent with the submissiveness for which women are socialized. Reforms in gender roles, socialization, and education, therefore, might be expected to help remedy this situation.

A LETTER FROM A BATTERED WIFE

I am in my thirties and so is my husband. I have a high school diploma and am presently attending a local college, trying to obtain the additional education I need. My husband is a college graduate and a professional in his field. We are both attractive and, for the most part, respected and well-liked. We have four children and live in a middle-class home with all the comforts we could possibly want.

I have everything, except life without fear.

For most of my married life I have been periodically beaten by my husband. What do I mean by "beaten"? I mean that parts of my body have been hit violently and repeatedly, and that painful bruises, swelling, bleeding wounds, unconsciousness, and combinations of these things have resulted. . . .

I have had glasses thrown at me. I have been kicked in the abdomen when I was visibly pregnant. I have been kicked off the bed and hit while lying on the floor — again, while I was pregnant. I have been whipped, kicked and thrown, picked up again and thrown down again. I have been punched and kicked in the head, chest, face, and abdomen more times than I can count.

I have been slapped for saying something about politics, for having a different view about religion, for swearing, for crying, for wanting to have intercourse.

I have been threatened when I wouldn't do something he told me to do. I have been threatened when he's had a bad day and when he's had a good day. . . .

Few people have ever seen my black and blue face or swollen lips because I have always stayed indoors afterwards, feeling ashamed. I was never able to drive following one of these beatings, so I could not get myself to a hospital for care. I could never have left my young children alone, even if I could have driven a car.

Hysteria inevitably sets in after a beating. This hysteria — the shaking and crying and mumbling — is not accepted by anyone, so there has never been anyone to call.

My husband on a few occasions did phone a day or so later so we could agree on the excuse I would use for returning to work, the grocery store, the dentist appointment, and so on. I used the excuses — a car accident, oral surgery, things like that.

Now, the first response to this story, which I myself think of, will be "Why didn't you seek help?"

I did. Early in our marriage I went to a clergyman who, after a few visits, told me that my husband meant no real harm, that he was just confused and felt insecure. I was encouraged to be more tolerant and understanding. Most important, I was told to forgive him the beatings just as Christ had forgiven me from the cross. I did that, too.

Things continued. Next time I turned to a doctor. I was given little pills to relax me and told to take things a little easier. I was just too nervous.

I turned to a friend, and when her husband found out, he accused me of either making things up or exaggerating the situation. She was told to stay away from me. She didn't, but she could no longer really help me.

I turned to a professional family guidance agency. I was told there that my husband needed help and that I should find a way to control the incidents. I couldn't control the beatings — that was the whole point of my seeking help. At the agency I found I had to defend myself against the suspicion that I wanted to be hit, that I invited the beatings. Good God! Did the Jews invite themselves to be slaughtered in Germany? . . .

I called the police one time. They not only did not respond to the call, they called several hours later to ask if things had "settled down." I could have been dead by then!

I have nowhere to go if it happens again. No one wants to take in a woman with four children. Even if there were someone kind enough to care, no one wants to become involved in what is commonly referred to as a "domestic situation." . . .

No one has to "provoke" a wife-beater. He will strike out when he's ready and for whatever reason he has at the moment.

I may be his excuse, but I have never been the reason. . . .

I have suffered physical and emotional battering and spiritual rape because the social structure of my world says I cannot do anything about a man who wants to beat me. . . . But staying with my husband means that my children must be subjected to the emotional battering caused when they see their mother's face or hear her screams in the middle of the night.

I know that I have to get out. But when you have nowhere to go, you know that you must go on your own and expect no support. I have to be ready for that. I have to be ready to support myself and the children completely, and still provide a decent environment for them. I pray that I can do that before I am murdered in my own home. . . .

It must be pointed out that while a husband can beat, slap, or threaten his wife, there are "good days." These days tend to wear away the effects of the beating. They tend to cause the wife to put aside the traumas and look to the good — first, because there is nothing else to do; second, because there is nowhere and no one to turn to; and third, because the defeat is the beating and the hope is that it will not happen again. A loving woman like myself always hopes that it will not happen again. When it does, she simply hopes again, until it becomes obvious after a third beating that there is no hope. That is when she turns outward for help to find an answer. When that help is denied, she either resigns herself to the situation she is in or pulls herself together and starts making plans for a future life that includes only herself and her children.

For many the third beating may be too late. . . .

What determines who is lucky and who isn't? I could have been dead a long time ago had I been hit the wrong way. My baby could have been killed or deformed had I been kicked the wrong way. What saved me?

I don't know. I only know that it has happened and that each night I dread the final blow that will kill me and leave my children motherless. I hope I can hang on until I complete my education, get a good job, and become self-sufficient enough to care for my children on my own.

Source: Excerpted from *Battered Wives.* Copyright © 1976 by Del Martin. All rights reserved. Published by Glide Publications, Inc., 330 Ellis Street, San Francisco, CA 94102 ($7.95). Used with permission.

SEXUAL HARASSMENT

The sexual victimization of women is not limited to cases of out-and-out rape. Most women have experienced incidents of varying degrees of sexual harassment, what one author called "the little rapes" (Offir, 1982).

Because incidents of sexual harassment differ in the degree of offensiveness and coercion, they are rather difficult to define, both in a legal or scholarly sense and in a personal sense. Stanford Law School Professor Catharine MacKinnon has proposed this definition: "Sexual harassment, most broadly defined, refers to the unwanted imposition of sexual requirements in the context of a relationship of unequal power" (1979, p. 1). Examples include

verbal sexual suggestions or jokes, constant leering or ogling, brushing against your body "accidentally," a friendly pat, squeeze or pinch or arm against you, catching you alone for a quick kiss, the indecent proposition backed by the threat of losing your job, and forced sexual relations. (MacKinnon, 1979, p. 2)

Sexual harassment can occur in a variety of settings — at work, in education, in psychotherapy, on the street.

Sexual harassment at work   Sexual harassment at work may take a number of different forms. A prospective employer may make it clear that sexual activity is a prerequisite to being hired. Stories of such incidents are rampant among actresses. On the job, sexual activity may be made a condition for continued employment, for a promotion, or for other benefits, such as a raise. Here is one case:

> June, a waitress in Arkansas, was serving a customer when he reached up her skirt. When she asked her manager for future protection against such incidents, she was harassed by him instead. "They put me on probation," she recalled, "as if I was the guilty one. Then things went from bad to worse. I got lousy tables and bad hours." (Phillips, 1977)

Such an incident is a clear case showing how the man uses his position of power to punish the woman for her noncompliance with sexual requests.

More than 9000 working women responded to a *Redbook* survey on sexual harassment at work (Safran, 1976). Almost 90 percent of them experienced some form of sexual harassment at work. The typical experi-

FIGURE 15.3
Sexual harassment at work may be blatant, such as making it clear that sexual activity is a prerequisite to being hired; or it may be more subtle, as is the case in this photograph. The woman cannot avoid physical contact. Yet, if the man is her boss, she may feel too intimidated to complain.

Source: © Frank Siteman, 1983.

ence was described as being degrading and humiliating, with the woman feeling a sense of helplessness similar to that reported by rape victims.

In 1981 *Redbook* and the *Harvard Business Review* surveyed nearly 2000 business executives about sexual harassment (Safran, 1981). They found that women in top management positions had considerably different perceptions of this problem than did men in similar positions. Two-thirds of the men believed that the scope of the problem "is greatly exaggerated," whereas only one-third of the women agreed with that statement. Approximately three-quarters of both males and females, though, favored the issuing a statement from management to all employees, expressing disapproval of sexual harassment.

Sexual harassment at work is more than just an annoyance. It can mean the difference between a career advancement or none. For the working-class woman who supports her family, being fired for sexual non-compliance is a catastrophe. The potential for coercing her is enormous.

Sexual harassment in education   The scene is also set for sexual harassment in an educational setting: the male teacher or professor wields power over the female student. A survey of psychologists indicated that 17 percent of the women, but only 3 percent of the men, had experienced sexual contact with their professors while they were in graduate school (Pope et al., 1979). "Sexual contact" included intercourse or genital stimulation, but excluded such things as derogatory comments. Defining terms is tricky in this area and doubtless some of the sexual activity reported in that survey was by mutual consent and was not "unwanted" by the student. On the other hand, many instances of sexual harassment are clear-cut. One woman wrote of her experience in a political science course in a large state university:

> This professor made sexist and derogatory comments about the women in the class, women in public life, women in general:
>
> "You women are going to waste your education raising babies."
>
> "There is no future for women in political science. I don't believe in women in government at all."
>
> "Now if Justice Marshall had been a woman he would have sat down and cried, which is the reason — and a good one — we don't have a woman on the Supreme Court."
>
> Any husband who is foolish enough to listen to what his wife says politically deserves anything he gets."
>
> I discussed with him the fact that his remarks were at first irritating and then progressively more offensive. I said that some of the women in the class felt intimidated and put down. The point is that if I, with all kinds of positive reinforcement from women professors and feminist friends, was brought down in spirit by this man, then surely so are other women students. (Williams, 1983, pp. 366–367)

The problem, once again, is unequal power. Women students in such a situation hardly have the power to protest, because the professor holds the power of having their grades in his hands. In the cases in graduate school noted above, the professor controls critical evaluations and recommendations that affect the course of the woman's career.

(For a detailed analyses of sexual harassment in education, see Dziech and Weiner's *The Lecherous Professor,* 1983).

Legal aspects   Currently, there are no laws that define sexual harassment or make it illegal. Catharine MacKinnon (1979) has been active on this issue, arguing that sexual harassment at work should be illegal. Her argument rests on considering harassment a form of sex discrimination at work, which is illegal under Title VII of the Civil Rights Act. When women have gone to court on this basis, they have sometimes been upheld and sometimes not. In the cases that were lost, even if the sexual harassment was proven, it was considered to be a "personal" matter and not an instance of sex discrimination.

In 1977, women students sued Yale University, complaining of sexual harassment. This important case, *Alexander v. Yale,* recognized sexual harassment of women in education as a possible violation of Title IX of the Civil Rights Act.

Feminist analysis   Feminists make several points about sexual harassment. First, traditional thinking often blames the victim, suggesting that the woman behaves provocatively or explicitly initiates sexual activity in the hope of getting a promotion, getting a good grade, etc. In contrast, the feminist perspective is that such activity is usually initiated by the male in the powerful position. Second, feminist analysis emphasizes issues of power and control. It is precisely because men are so often in positions of greater power — whether at work or in education — that sexual harassment becomes a possibility. Further, the woman who is the victim of sexual harassment experiences a lack of control over her own life, perhaps much like that of a rape victim. Research on the psychological aspects of sexual harassment is lacking and sorely needed.

INCEST

Incest is another topic that has come out of the closet in recent years. A decade ago it was considered unmentionable and rare. Today one can flip on the television at 10 a.m. and watch incest victim Katherine Brady talk openly on the *Phil Donahue Show.*

Incest is typically defined as sexual relations between blood relatives, although the definition is often extended to include sex between non-blood relatives, for example, stepfather and stepdaughter (Maisch, 1972; Sagarin, 1977).

Incidence of incest Traditionally, it was thought that incest was a rare and bizarre occurrence. Early research confirmed this notion, indicating that the incidence of incest prosecuted through the police and courts in the United States was only about one or two people per million per year (Weinberg, 1955). The catch, though, is that the overwhelming majority of cases go unreported and unprosecuted. To get a better idea of the true incidence of incest, it is necessary to survey the general population. In one such survey, 7 percent of the sample had had sexual intercourse with a relative (Hunt, 1974). In a general survey of undergraduates, 15 percent of the females and 10 percent of the males said they had had a sexual experience with a brother or sister (Finkelhor, 1980). In most cases, the activity was limited to fondling and exhibiting the genitals. Intercourse occurred in only 5 percent of the incidents where the respondent was under age 8 and 18 percent of the incidents where the respondent was over age 13. The point is that incest, particularly if it is defined to include sexual contact other than intercourse, is not at all rare.

Of father-daughter incest and brother-sister, or sibling incest, which is more common? In a study of *reported* incest (reported to the police or other authorities), father-daughter cases were by far the most common: father-daughter cases constituted 78 percent of the sample, 18 percent were brother-sister, 1 percent were mother-son, and the remaining 3 percent were multiple incestuous relationships (Weinberg, 1955). However, in surveys of the *general* population, brother-sister incest is far more common, outnumbering father-daughter incest by about five to one (Gebhard et al., 1965). Thus it appears that brother-sister incest is actually the most common form, but it is far less likely to be reported to the police than father-daughter incest is. However, most research has been done on reported cases, that is, on father-daughter incest.

Father-daughter incest What kind of man commits incest with his daughter? The stereotype is that such men are cases of extreme psychopathology. However, extensive reviews of the research literature on incest show that this stereotype is not true (Meiselman, 1978; Herman, 1981). Rather, the man who commits incest appears to be a classical patriarch within his family (Herman, 1981). He is a good provider, but he rules the family. The division of roles in the family in which father-daughter incest occurs is traditional, and the mother is typically a full-time housewife. She also seems somewhat isolated within the family, often because her health is poor. Given these family dynamics, the daughter-victim seems to take on the role of holding the family together and develops a "special" relationship with her father, within which the incest occurs.

The sexual activity with his daughter appears to fulfill several needs for the father (Herman, 1981). He often has feelings of dependency and a need for nurturance, which he receives in the relationship with his daughter (Justice and Justice, 1979). Doubtless he experiences a sense of power in the act, for he can control it exactly as he wishes and need not fear a rejection of his techniques, such as he might receive from a mature woman (Herman, 1981). The excitement coming from the secrecy may be pleasurable. Finally, it has been suggested that the daughter's unhappiness with the sexual activity may contribute to pleasure in the father who is basically expressing hostility.

One of the best accounts of the internal dynamics of father-daughter incest is Katherine Brady's autobiography, *Father's Day* (1979).

Psychological impact on the victim Many therapists who are experienced with cases of incest feel that the effects of father-daughter incest on the victim are serious and long-lasting, despite the fact that the incidents were not reported and seem to have been repressed (Herman, 1981). Consider the following case:

> A twenty-five-year-old office worker was seen in the emergency room with an acute anxiety attack. She was pacing, agitated, unable to eat or sleep, and had a feeling of impending doom. She related a vivid fantasy of being pursued by a man with a knife. The previous day she had been cornered in the office by her boss, who aggressively propositioned her. She needed the job badly and did not want to lose it, but she dreaded the thought of returning to work. It later emerged in psychotherapy that this episode of sexual harassment had reawakened previously repressed memories of sexual assaults by her father. From the age of six until mid-adolescence, her father had repeatedly exhibited himself to her and insisted that she masturbate him. The experience of being trapped at work had recalled her childhood feelings of helplessness and fear. (Herman, 1981, p. 8)

Unfortunately, research in this area has not yet yielded any definitive conclusions about the effects on the victim, in part because this aspect of the issue has received attention only recently so little research has yet been done, and in part because there are some inherent methodological difficulties in doing such research. Most of the research has been on reported or prosecuted cases, in which father-daughter incest is overrepresented, and in which police and court proceedings may have done as much damage to the victim as the incest itself did, a situation that is also found with rape victims. Thus most research gives little information on sibling incest and its effects, on the less traumatic cases that are not reported to the police or do not result in the woman's seeking psychotherapy.

Two studies are worthy of attention. One of these is the general survey of undergraduates cited earlier, in which 15 percent of the females and 10 percent of the males said they had had a sexual experience with a sibling (Finkelhor, 1980). Among those who had been involved in sibling incest, there was an almost even division between those who felt the experience had been positive for them and those who felt it had been negative. There seemed to be some long-term effects on sexuality. Women who had had sexual experiences with a sibling had substantially higher levels of current (college-age) sexual activity than did women who had not experienced sibling incest. In addition, those who had had experiences with a much older sibling before the age of nine suffered lowered sexual self-esteem, but those who had had positive experiences after the age of nine had heightened sexual self-esteem.

In a second, well-designed study, newspaper advertisements were used to recruit women falling into these three categories: women who were victims of childhood molestation and were seeking therapy for the result- ing problems (called the clinical group); women who were victims of childhood molestation but felt well-adjusted and not in need of therapy (nonclinical group); and a group of women who were not victims of childhood molestation (control group) (Tsai et al., 1979). It turned out that 73 percent of the clinical group and 63 percent of the nonclinical group had been molested by their fathers, stepfathers, or grandfathers, so the study essentially became an investigation of father-daughter incest. The results showed that the clinical and nonclinical groups differed in a number of ways (see Table 15.1). The molestation went on for nearly five years, on the average, for the clinical group, whereas it lasted only about half that long for the nonclinical group. Also, the molestation continued to older ages for the girls in the clinical group. Attempted intercourse was more common in the clinical group. And, finally, women in the clinical group were significantly less satisfied with their current, adult sexual relation- ships than were women in the nonclinical group, indicating the existence of long-term consequences of being a victim of incest during one's child- hood. This study is particularly interesting because it shows some of the factors — long duration of molestation, molestation at older ages, attempted intercourse — that seem to be related to long-term psychological damage in women who are incest victims.

Given the statistics cited previously showing a high frequency of sibling incest, it may seem peculiar that the study by Tsai et al. found father-daughter and similar forms of incest to account for the great major- ity of cases. I think that the answer lies in the fact that the newspaper ad recruiting participants in this study used the term "molestation." An adult woman who was the victim of an incestuous relationship with her step- father probably realizes that she was the victim of molestation. But sibling incest, particularly between a brother and sister close in age, may not seem to be "molestation," and therefore women who had experienced it would be relatively unlikely to respond to newspaper advertisements using that term.

What, then, are the psychological consequences of incest for the victim? Basically, I think there is too little research to be able to answer

TABLE 15.1. Summary of differences between two groups of molestation victims, a clinical group (women who felt in need of therapy) and a nonclinical group (women who felt well-adjusted and not in need of therapy)

	Clinical (n = 30)	Nonclinical (n = 30)
Age at which last molestation occurred	12.4 years	9.2 years
Duration of molestation	4.7 years	2.5 years
Intercourse attempted	70 percent	40 percent
Intercourse completed	20 percent	17 percent
Feelings of satisfaction in current sexual relationship (7-point scale, 7 = very satisfied)	3.80	5.67

this fully. But I think the following conclusion is warranted: in some cases incest is highly damaging to the victim psychologically, but it is probably not damaging in every case. Many factors are probably involved in whether or not it is damaging: whether it is father-daughter or brother-sister incest (father-daughter being the more damaging form), the age at which the victim experiences the incest, the age difference between the victim and her brother if it is sibling incest, the extent to which coercion is used, how often the activity is repeated, and the extent to which the family is disrupted by the activity. In short, it depends.

Feminist analysis Having brought rape and wife-battering to public attention, feminists have more recently focused on incest. Feminists make several points about incest. First, they warn against blaming the victim — that is, suggesting that a daughter initiates incest with her father by her seductive behavior and that he therefore cannot be held responsible. The evidence indicates that it is usually the father who is the initiator; even if the daughter were the initiator, the father, because of his age and position of responsibility in the family, must certainly refuse her. The most common pattern is for the incest to begin when the daughter is eight or nine years old (Herman, 1981), scarcely an age at which she can be held responsible. Second, feminists point out that this is another instance in which men exercise power and control over women — in this case a father uses his power in the family to coerce his daughter into sexual activity. Third, feminists want to alert the public to the frequency of incest and the psychological damage it can do to women. Feminist therapists report that women come to them with complaints apparently unrelated to incest, but that, in the course of therapy, a history of incest, which had been repressed, surfaces (Herman, 1981; Leidig, 1982).

There is a conflict of points of view here — feminists are alarmed by the psychological damage done by incest, whereas sex researchers, looking at studies such as the one by Finkelhor, conclude that incest is not always damaging. I feel a need to resolve this difference particularly because I count myself a member of both of those groups. I think that the resolution lies in the fact that the two groups are looking at different kinds of incest. Sex researchers, alert to issues of sampling the general population, realize that sibling incest is the most common form and, studying it, find generally less serious consequences. Feminists focus on father-daughter incest, because it represents a clear-cut case of male abuse of power, and they have found the consequences to be serious. Once again, the conclusion about the psychological impact of incest on the victim must be that it depends on many factors.

IN CONCLUSION

In this chapter we have considered four situations in which women are victimized: rape, wife-battering, sexual harassment, and incest. All have in common the reticence of the victims to report the occurrences and a corresponding difficulty in helping the unknown victims. In all four, the victim traditionally was blamed. Feminists emphasize the basic ways in which rape, wife-battering, sexual harassment, and incest represent male expressions of power and dominance over women.

We need to recognize the victimization of women. But we also need to move beyond that recognition. For example, contrast these two terms: *rape victim* and *rape survivor*. The woman who has been raped, yet manages to return to a productive life, is a survivor, not a victim; she is strong, not weak. Even tragic situations in which women are made powerless can be a means for women to begin to discover and regain their strength and power, both at the individual level and at the level of the larger society.

SUGGESTION FOR FURTHER READING

Brady, Katherine (1979). *Father's days.* New York: Dell (paperback). This autobiography of an incest victim is both moving and insightful.

Black Women and Women as a Minority Group

Sometimes I dream a dream in which I am . . . on a TV program. . . . In real life I am a large, big-boned woman with rough, man-working hands. In the winter I wear flannel nightgowns to bed and overalls during the day. I can kill and clean a hog as mercilessly as a man. My fat keeps me hot in zero weather. I can work outside all day, breaking ice to get water for washing. . . . One winter I knocked a bull calf straight in the brain between the eyes with a sledge hammer and had the meat hung up to chill before nightfall. But of course all this does not show on television. I am the way my daughter would want me to be: a hundred pounds lighter, my skin like an uncooked barley pancake.

From ALICE WALKER, *In Love and Trouble: Stories of Black Women*

We must confront a serious problem: much of what I have referred to as "the psychology of women" is, in reality, a psychology of white, middle-class, American women. But is the femininity-achievement double-bind, or low expectation for success, a phenomenon inherently part of womanhood? When we consider other groups of women, in particular black women, it becomes immediately apparent that the complex social forces acting on them are so different that their psychology is probably also different. Among these forces are poverty, discrimination, variations in family structure (the extended family, more frequently absent fathers), more frequent necessity for them to hold a job, evaluation of their appearance by white standards of beauty, and identification with the black power movement. What impact do all these forces have on the psychology of black women?

While it is interesting to explore subcultural variation in the psychology of women, I do not wish to treat the psychology of black women as being of interest only insofar as it represents a deviation from white norms. It has an intrinsic interest and integrity of its own. Indeed, some writers have suggested that black culture has progressed further than white culture and that the trend may be for whites to become more like blacks. Thus the psychology of black women may have important implications for the psychology of women in general, and particularly for the psychology of women in the future.

Parenthetically I should note that I originally intended this to be a chapter on minority-group women, including Hispanics, Asian-Americans, and native Americans. In researching the chapter, it quickly became apparent that there simply was not sufficient research available to be able to make any conclusions about the psychology of minority-group women other than blacks. Certainly here is a large area of potential research sorely in need of attention. In addition, the amount of research on black women is not large; the reader should keep in mind that many of the conclusions I draw in this chapter are based on only a limited amount of data and therefore should be accepted only tentatively, awaiting further research.

A fundamental problem in much of the research to be cited is the confounding of race and social class. Because blacks tend to be overrepresented in the lower class and whites in the middle class, it is generally not clear whether differences between blacks and whites should be attributed to race differences or to social-class differences. Research techniques generally have not been powerful enough to conquer this ambiguity. The reader should keep in mind that much of what are called race differences may actually be due to social-class differences.

BLACK WOMEN

Gender roles A singularly important input into the gender identity of any woman comes from the gender roles prescribed for her by her culture or subculture. So we begin our discussion of the psychology of black women by looking at these roles. The constellation of gender roles for black women seems to differ in important ways from that for white women. Gender role for black women involves multiple roles — worker, head of household, mother, lover. Most notably, the traditional white middle-class feminine gender role — that of full-time housewife and mother, with an attending definition of one's identity almost exclusively in terms of these gender roles — has been denied to the black woman because of economic necessity. Allowing women to be economically unproductive is a luxury of the modern middle class. Because black women have not been permitted this luxury, they have taken on other gender roles and found alternative definitions of womanhood. This was expressed with a brilliant clarity by Sojourner Truth at a Women's Rights Convention in the 1800s:

> Dat man ober dar say dat women needs to be helped into carriages, and lifted ober ditches, and to have de best place every whar. Nobody ever help me into carriages, or ober mud puddles, or gives me any best places . . . and ar'nt I a woman? Look at me! Look at my arm! . . . I have plowed and planted, and gathered into barns, and no man could head me — and ar'nt I a woman? I could work as much and eat as much as a man (when I could get it), and bear de lash as well — and arn't I a woman? I have borne thirteen children and I seen 'em mos' all sold off into slavery, and when I cried out with a woman's grief, none but Jesus heard — and ar'nt I a woman? (*Abolitionist*, 1831)

Black women have had to define their identity, including their gender identity, in terms of roles other than housewife-mother. Although motherhood is still a prime gender-role definer, they have taken on additional roles, such as worker and head of household. Black women generally expect that they must hold paying jobs as adults (Kuvlesky and Obordo, 1972; Turner and McCaffrey, 1974), and this has important consequences for their educational and occupational attainments, as we shall see in later sections.

The role of the black woman as head of household has received a great deal of publicity under the name of *black matriarchy,* suggesting that the black female has greater power than the male in the black family and culture. The high frequency with which black households, as compared with white households, are headed by females is usually given as evidence for this phenomenon. In 1974, 34 percent of all black households were headed by females, compared with 10 percent of white households (Clay, 1975). This in turn seems to be the result of three factors: the obstacles black men have encountered in seeking and maintaining jobs necessary to support their families; the rules of the welfare system, which make it financially desirable for the man to live separately from his family; and the greatly disproportionate gender ratio (number of males to number of females) among blacks. While there are more white women than men (about 98 adult males to 100 women), the ratio is even more imbalanced for blacks (in 1970, about 91 men to 100 women), so that there are just not enough men to go around (Jackson, 1973; Malina, 1973). On the other hand, the emphasis on matriarchal domination of black society ignores the fact that if 34 percent of black households are headed by females, then surely 66 percent must be headed by males or by males and females jointly. Thus, the female head of household, while more frequent in black than in white society, is far from typical for blacks.

Other studies have not looked at the simple notion of head of household in determining matriarchy or patriarchy, but rather have tried to assess more subtle patterns, of *spouse dominance* by looking at the ways in which couples solve problems (such as childcare and purchasing). The emerging conclusions from this research are that there are no race differences in spouse domination patterns — the equalitarian pattern is by far the most common one for both blacks and whites (see review by Jackson, 1973). Interestingly, husbands tend to be more dominant when the wife works, a parallel also noted for white working women (Hartley, 1960). Also, matriarchy and patriarchy seem to be more common among the lower class, although even here, equalitarianism is probably quite common. There are also regional variations: In the South, lower-class, intact black families are more frequently patriarchal than whites, while in the North, the reverse pattern seems to hold.

Because black women seem to assume "male" roles with some frequency — worker and head of household — the question arises as to whether their status in the black community might be higher than the status of white women in the white community. In fact, the term "black matriarchy" seems to imply that the black woman enjoys higher status than the black man. However, some simple income figures will correct this notion. Statistics from the Women's Bureau of the United States Department of Labor show that in 1982 black women had the lowest average wage of any of the race-gender groups (U.S. Department of Labor, 1982):

White males	$21,160
Black males	$15,119
White females	$12,287
Black females	$11,312

(Notice that black males still make more than white females.) Hence the most accurate statement seems to be that black women enjoy higher status within their community than white women do in theirs, but it is questionable whether their status is higher than that of black men (Jackson, 1973).

Indeed, some scholars (such as Ladner, 1971) argue that the extent of black matriarchy, with attending psychological castration of the black male, has been magnified out of all proportion in the writings of social scientists. The strengths of black women, standing in sharp contrast to the passivity of white women, have been misinterpreted as being dominance. In addition, the importance to the black woman of the emotional and financial support of "boyfriends" has generally been ignored. Certainly problems arise in research in this area as a result of evaluating black behavior by white standards. At the very least, the term "black matriarchy" oversimplifies the complex relationships between black men and women.

In terms of development, black girls appear to assume the adult female role much earlier than do white girls (Ladner, 1971). The white middle-class luxury of a protected, carefree childhood is generally not available to poor black girls, who may move into womanhood in early adolescence. They learn to relate to boys as sexual persons at an earlier age than do white girls (Broderick, 1965; Ladner, 1971). Adolescent black girls may have a baby in order to define themselves as responsible adults — that is, in order to define their womanhood — although premarital pregnancies are generally avoided by the upwardly mobile black girl. It appears, then, that womanhood is defined, and the role assumed, much earlier for black girls than for white girls.

The roles assumed by an aging black woman also seem to differ somewhat from those for aging white women. The sense of uselessness and lack of role suffered by many aging whites does not seem so common among blacks. The extended-family structure characteristics of blacks provides a secure position and role for the elderly. The "granny" role is a meaningful and valued role for the elderly black woman (Bart, 1971) — helping to care for young grandchildren, giving advice based on experience. It seems that old age can be assumed with dignity by the black woman.

Gender roles, then, are defined somewhat differently for black Americans than for white Americans. Gender-role definition for blacks may not be exclusively a result of the experience of slavery and subsequent racial oppression, but actually may have earlier roots in the African heritage (Ladner, 1971; Dobert, 1975). Two characteristics of the African female role were perpetuated in slavery: (1) an important economic function; and (2) a strong bond between mother and child. African women have traditionally been economically independent, functioning in the market place and as traders. Black women continue to play this important economic function in the family to the present day. Mother-child bonds also continue to be extremely important in the structure of black society.

The black woman as mother   The black woman's role as mother certainly occurs in the context of, and is influenced by, the structure of the black family. We have already noted that black women are more frequently heads of households. It appears that the mother role among blacks has correspondingly adapted to this difference in family structure, and further, that this adaptation has been successful (Rhodes, 1971).

Talcott Parsons has made the distinction between male roles as being *instrumental* and female (mother) roles as being *expressive* (Parsons, 1942; Parsons and Bales, 1955). It has been noted, however, that lower-class black mothers seem to play dual instrumental-expressive roles to their teenage sons (Nobers, 1968). These women appeared to provide adequate role models for their sons, making up for the absence of their fathers. White mothers in the same sample, on the other hand, were more exclusively feminine-expressive in their role orientations. Further, the absence of fathers for preschool black boys may not be as much a problem as the literature suggests it is for white boys (Williams, 1969), probably because the black woman is capable of being both mother (expressive) and father (instrumental) to her sons. Black mothers without husbands appear to function much more effectively than do white mothers with absent husbands (Hartnagel, 1970).

In a study much like the one on lesbians' strategies for coping with interrole stress (Chapter 13), married and single employed black mothers were questioned about their methods for coping with conflicts between the mother role and the worker role (Harrison and Minor, 1982). Recall that there are three types of coping strategies: Type 1, in which the woman negotiates with the role sender in order to change the demands of the role to mutually acceptable ones; Type 2, in which the woman changes her own understanding of the role demands, perhaps overlooking certain things or partitioning the demands; and Type 3, in which the woman accepts all of the demands and just tries to work harder to satisfy them all. Recall also that Type 3 is supposed to be the least successful strategy, leading to the least satisfaction. The results showed that the majority of the married working mothers used Type 2 strategies for coping, that is, changed their own understandings and perceptions. These women expressed satisfaction with the mother role, and 50 percent of those who used Type 2 coping strategies simply gave priority to the mother role. In contrast, the majority of the single working mothers used Type 3 coping strategies; that is, they simply worked harder to satisfy all of the many demands on them — what might be called the "supermother strategy." These women, too, expressed high satisfaction with their performance in the mother role.

One interesting finding of this study is that apparently none of the women used Type 1 strategies, such as negotiating with the role sender — a boss, for example. From the point of view of a feminist analysis of power in this situation, a black, nonprofessional (all of the women in the sample were nonprofessionals) woman probably does not have the power to negotiate with a boss, for example, to ask that she be allowed to leave at 3 p.m. in order to be home when her children return from school. A professional woman is much more likely to be able to do that kind of negotiating.

Self-concept and identity The traditional psychological literature indicates that blacks, like white women (presumably as a result of similar patterns of oppression and its psychological consequences), have negative self-concepts, or a low sense of self-esteem. Experiments several decades ago showed that black children rejected dolls with dark skin in favor of those with light skin, presumably indicating a corresponding self-rejection (Clark and Clark, 1947; for more recent reviews, see Banks, 1976; Williams and Moreland, 1979). The implication is that blacks had introjected the negative valuation of themselves held by the dominant white culture. However, it seems quite possible that the complex of social changes in the last decades, particularly the black power movement, with its emphasis on black pride and "black is beautiful" has made real improvements in black self-concept. Hence, although many of the studies I cite may appear to be contradictory, in reality they represent a change over time in the self-esteem of black people.

For black women, physical appearance and beauty may have been particular sources of low esteem. American standards of beauty, which emphasize light skin, straight hair, and shapely legs, apparently were assimilated by blacks so that the black woman was in the position of valuing a kind of beauty she would never have (Grier and Cobbs, 1968).

For example, Americans (including, for many years, black Americans) valued light-colored skin highly. Black women, then, on the average, must be less attractive than white women, and very black women must be very ugly. It is hard for many whites to grasp the intensity of the value blacks attached to skin shade. Perhaps these quotes taken from an autobiography written by a black woman will convey some of this intensity. After explaining that both of her parents and her twin brother had much lighter skin than she, she wrote:

> People were always haunting me about the color of my skin. It wasn't enough that the white people would reject me because of it. I had to be rejected by my own people as well. People were always making bets on . . . my skin color. When I was in elementary school one teacher bet another teacher (right in front of my face) that I wasn't as good-looking as my twin brother. The two teachers had found out from one of the students in the class that Don and I were twins. Obviously they found this so hard to believe that they were going to actually let the class vote on who looked the best Don or Donna. Luckily for me, my pride wasn't shattered because the other teacher looked into my eyes and saw how hurt I felt and he then refused to accept the bet . . . As a child I was made aware that black is bad and I grew to hate myself for not being born with a lighter skin shade. The lighter you were the more you were accepted.[1]

The eagerness with which many black women have endeavored to bleach their facial skin, sometimes leading to burns and serious disfiguration, also attests to the high value placed on light skin and the low value placed on natural appearance.

Weight has also been a problem for black women (but not so much so for black men). While black girls from six to ten years old are more frequently thin than white girls, by the age of fourteen to eighteen, twice as many black as white girls were classified as obese (Rauh et al., 1967).

The "black is beautiful" motto was well-chosen for black women, and presumably it is bringing about a more positive sense of self as it replaces the culturally conditioned low valuation of the black woman's natural physical appearance. The black power movement has placed an emphasis on getting more black women in television commercials, on stage, and working as models. This points up the possibility that problems relating to beauty for black women may have resulted not only from devaluation of black characteristics, but also from an absence of attractive gender-role models. That is, the rejection by blacks of white standards of beauty as normative is not sufficient — blacks must develop their own sense of what it means to be beautiful — and certainly black actresses and models will be instrumental in conveying these standards and aspirations to other black women.

Recent years have seen an increase in systematic psychological studies on gender and race differences in self-esteem (for reviews, see Baughman, 1971; Christmas, 1973). Traditional research would have led one to expect that blacks — and particularly black women, because of the "double jeopardy" situation (Beal, 1970) of being both black and female — would have lower self-esteem than whites. However, research findings have been quite contradictory. Black children in essentially segregated schools had

---

[1] From a student essay for a psychology of women course, paraphrased and with names changed.

higher self-esteem than whites, and females were higher than males, so that the order, from highest to lowest self-esteem, was: black girls, black boys, white girls, white boys (Wendland, 1967). Race differences appeared to be of larger magnitude than gender differences. On the other hand, other investigators have found boys and whites having higher self-esteem, so that black girls had the lowest self-esteem of any race-gender group (Bridgette, 1970); Carpenter and Busse, 1969). Yet another investigator found no gender differences in self-concept among Southern rural black high school students (Blair, 1972). In the midst of social changes aimed at improving the self-concept of blacks in general, and of women in particular, it is not too surprising that these studies, over time and in different geographical locations and in the midst of desegregation, should obtain different results. At any rate, it is not at all clear from the empirical data whether the low self-esteem thought to be characteristic of black women actually exists. If anything, the recent data indicate that black females maintain high self-esteem (Samuel and Laird, 1974).

Strength and adaptation   The apparent tragedy of the black woman — poverty, the victim of both racial and sexual oppression, welfare mother, managing a fatherless household, former slave — has often led to romanticizing her plight. While this is certainly one aspect of the black woman's condition, it leads one to ignore the immense strengths and coping abilities black women have cultivated so well. Historically, black women have frequently exerted leadership roles in resisting poor treatment from whites and were experts at waging psychological warfare. Lerner (1972) recounts an amusing example that illustrates this point well:

> Not long ago I heard some Negro women talking of old times over their sewing. One said . . . "I couldn't read, but my uncle could . . . I was waiting-maid, an' used to help missis to dress in the morning. If massa wanted to tell her something he didn't want me to know, he used to spell it out. I could remember the letters, an' as soon as I got away I ran to uncle an' spelled them over to him, an' he told me what they meant."
>
> I was attracted by this, and asked if she could do this now.
>
> "Try me, missis; try me an' see!" she exclaimed. So I spelled a long sentence as rapidly as possible, without stopping between the words. She immediately repeated it after me, without missing a letter.
>
> The children of this woman were amongst the first to enter a freedman's school during the war. They took to books as ducks take to water.[2]

This black woman, while feigning ignorance, was actually managing to get a great deal of information from the whites through her own clever-

---

[2] From E. Botume, *First Days Among the Contrabands* (Boston: Lee & Shepard, 1893), pp. 29–30.

ness, a quality she cultivated in her children as soon as opportunities were available.

While acknowledging that many blacks may have experienced feelings of inadequacy as a result of judging themselves on the basis of white standards, it is possible then, that the results have not been as psychologically devastating as some have suggested. Black women have developed mechanisms for coping with their situation (as noted in the previous section). For example, in interviews with adolescent black girls in a housing project, when asked what it meant to be a poor black girl, some replies were

> I feel good as a Negro. I think that we have special rights as everyone else because you know Thomas Jefferson said every man was created equal and I think that just being a Negro doesn't mean we can't have the finer things of life just as the white person does.

> I'm very fond of being a Negro because Negroes have much talent. . . . I was kind of glad to see that we have one Negro in the White House working and they can sing and dance, and do things just as well as white people can. I don't mind being poor . . . because I'm getting along and it doesn't matter to me . . . I think my friends feel the same because I never hear any of them say anything like "I wish I was white." . . . To me a Negro knows how to have fun. (Ladner, 1971, pp. 88–89)

Instead of feelings of low self-esteem and inadequacy, there appears to be a remarkable feeling of pride and adjustment. Ladner concludes "Thus, there was no evidence of low self-esteem and severely damaged psyches among these young ladies" (1971, p. 91). Black women, then, have developed surprisingly adaptive psychological resources and coping mechanisms to deal with their situations, beginning in the days of slavery and continuing to the present.

Further evidence of the strengths of the black woman comes from research showing that black mothers without husbands function much more effectively in rearing their children than do white mothers experiencing father absence (Hartnagel, 1970). This seems related to the observation mentioned in an earlier section that black women are capable of playing dual instrumental-expressive roles for their children. Apparently the stresses placed on black women have effectively functioned to yield adaptive psychological results.

Abilities, achievement, and motivation   If decades of deprivation have resulted in successful adaptations to the social system, in what ways, if any, is this reflected in the abilities, school achievements, and motivation of black females? Once again, the strengths of black women are striking.

The best information on this point is Baughman and Dahlstrom's (1968) massive study of gender and race differences. They found a small gender difference among blacks in general intelligence (IQ) favoring females. But on the basis of the size of the difference and of comparison with other studies, they concluded that there are no gender differences among blacks in general intelligence (Baughman, 1971). The result, then, is similar to that for whites (Chapter 8). On the other hand, there do seem to be some gender differences among blacks on special abilities as measured by the Primary Mental Abilities Test (PMA). Black girls do better than black boys at all age levels except age ten on both Verbal Meaning and Number Facility. Interestingly, the well-documented, consistent gender differences in spatial ability (Chapter 8) do not appear to hold for blacks. The spatial relations subtest of the PMA showed no gender differences at any age level for blacks.

In terms of school achievement, research seems to show that black girls consistently achieve more than black boys at every age level (Baughman and Dahlstrom, 1968; Smith, 1982). In fact, the gap between the performance of black girls and white boys, particularly at upper-age levels, is small — black girls actually do better than white boys on spelling. To this point, the developmental parallels in achievement and abilities for black girls and white girls are apparent.

In the absence of gender differences in general intelligence, Baughman and Dahlstrom attributed the observed gender differences in scholastic achievement to higher motivation on the part of black females. In fact, the consistent findings from a large body of research literature are that black females have higher aspirations, more achievement motivation, and greater plans and expectations (that are more likely to be carried out) than do both black males and white females (Kirkpatrick, 1973; Smith, 1982). A survey administered to students in North Carolina indicated that black girls aspired to professional or technical occupations more frequently than did white girls (Thorpe, 1969). Nonetheless, black women's career aspirations appear to be constrained by gender roles; as professionals, they are found mainly in feminine areas such as teaching, social work, and nursing (Murray and Mednick, 1977).

In explaining the high aspirations and motivation of black women, one set of investigators concluded ". . . intellectual mastery is not threatening and professional achievement may in fact not lead to rejection by the [black] male" (Weston and Mednick, 1970, p. 290). This suggests that the structure of black society is such that achievement is not in conflict with femininity and therefore does not threaten female gender identity; indeed the structure of black society may actually encourage women to achieve.

In Chapter 8 I discussed results on patterns of casual attributions and expectations for success. There is some evidence that black women have a pattern different from white women (Murray and Mednick, 1977). Black women tend to attribute their successes both to their effort and to their ability, in a manner similar to men (Weiner and Kukla, 1970; Kukla 1972). Once again, this might be explained by achievement being more gender-appropriate for black women than it is for white women.

Black professional women By virtue of school achievement and motivation, the black woman should be well equipped to enter high-status, professional occupations. And, indeed, she has, to an impressive extent. For example, in 1983 of the 418 white members of the United States House of Representatives, 19, or 5 percent, were women; but of the 17 black Representatives, 2, or 12 percent, were women. In 1979, 42 percent of white professional-technical workers were women, compared with 58 percent of black professional-technical workers (teachers and nurses are counted as professionals, which explains the high percentages of women in these categories). Similarly, 24 percent of white administrative-managerial workers were women, compared with 34 percent of black administrative-managerial workers (U.S. Department of Labor, 1980).

Black women, then, have contributed much more at high occupational levels than would be predicted on the basis of their race and gender. One rationale advanced to explain their success is the "farmer's daughter effect" — black women have had greater access to the upper echelons of the white world than have black men because they were less feared sexually and less threatening occupationally (Bock, 1969). In addition, it is thought that black families have often given preferential treatment and made more sacrifices for their daughters', rather than their sons', education (Lerner, 1972). However, the actual data provide no evidence that black daughters are given preferential treatment over black sons in socialization for high educational and career aspirations (Smith, 1982; see also Jackson, 1972).

Epstein (1973b) has conducted perhaps the most intensive psychological–sociological research on black women professionals, using a sample of 31 black female professionals in New York. Several common biographical themes emerged among these highly successful black women. A large proportion (over one-third) of the women in the sample were of West Indian extraction. They seem to have been reared according to the Protestant ethic of American immigrants, with middle-class values (if not standard of living) and strong emphasis on "getting ahead." All 31 of these black women uniformly reported that their families had supported them in their striving for education. In contrast to the white women professionals, the black women never considered dropping their career ambitions once they had begun. And finally, they generally seem to have had mothers who were good models of instrumental behavior. Only four of the thirty-one subjects reported that their mothers had not held jobs outside the home. Apparently they learned an image of woman as "doer," capable of coping with the outside world — and they continued this image themselves.

The psychological characteristics of these women were also interesting, particularly in their contrast to those of white women professionals. In general, the black professional women seemed to show much less self-hatred and more self-confidence than their white counterparts. In addition,

the black women had a higher regard for other female professionals —
some white women indicated doubts about their female colleagues'
competence.

In general, these black female professionals showed much less ambivalence about combining the worker and mother roles. Blacks do not
assume that marriage will lead to a woman's withdrawal from the labor
force, and most black women hold jobs outside the home. Hence blacks
do not perceive marriage and motherhood as incompatible with work as
many whites do (Murray and Mednick, 1977), and black women are not
forced into a double-bind, ambivalent situation. Black women professionals
seemed much less anxious about their children than whites were. The
black female professional benefits from the tradition of the extended
family, so that she has relatives to help with care of her children while
she pursues her career, unlike the white female professional, who must
generally bear this burden alone.

The marital patterns of these women are also interesting. The general
pattern among white women professionals of being married to another
professional in the same field is unlikely for blacks, because there are fewer
black male than black female professionals and the chance of finding one
in the same field is even slimmer. Therefore a substantial number of the
women in this sample were unmarried, or were married to men lower in
occupational status than themselves. This seemed to create some marital
tensions. On the other hand, black women were also less likely to slip
into the white professional woman's pattern of seeing her own career as
subordinate to her husband's. In addition, the black women were not
subject to the constant demoralizing temptation to quit work and let their
husbands support them, because they generally could not maintain middle-
class standards of living on their husband's earnings alone. The women
in Epstein's sample also had a very low fertility rate, as is true of upper-
class blacks in general.

Epstein's explanation of the apparent paradox of the black female
professional, subject to double prejudice, being more successful than either
her race or gender would predict, is similar to some of the reasoning
outlined above. Some of the women she interviewed said they believed
they had succeeded where black men had failed because they faced less
discrimination. About a third of her subjects subscribed to the notion
that black men were a threat to white men. Black women, comparatively,
are less threatening, and therefore have more access to and less discrimination in the white world. Epstein (1973a) has also suggested that positive effects may result from a doubly negative (black/female) status. For
example, two statuses in combination may form a new status category
that has no established "price" because it is unique. An employer may
know how he pays blacks and how he pays women, but what does he do
when confronted with a black woman? Because her status is unique, she
may be in a better bargaining position to set her own value. Further, her

unique position may encourage her to experiment with alternative life-styles.

The double-bind theme   I have suggested that one of the chief factors in female personality is the double-bind, in which femininity and achievement are perceived as being incompatible. The discussion above would seem to indicate that black women are less likely to encounter this double-bind, that achievement seems quite compatible with gender-role expectations for them. However, the black woman is not completely free from double-binds, and here we will discuss some of them.

It is striking that black women have generally shown a lack of interest in the women's movement. Presumably this is because black women feel racial oppression much more keenly than they do sexual oppression, and therefore identify with the black power movement more than the women's movement. Oddly, though, a large-scale national poll showed that black women were twice as likely as white women to approve of the women's liberation movement and its goals (Harris poll, cited in Torrey, 1979). It seems quite possible that the black woman is being put in a double-bind situation here. Certainly if the oppression of women is not attacked, the abolition of racial oppression alone will not lead black women to utopia. And yet many males in the black power movement suggest that black women who identify with the women's movement are betraying their race — a double-bind, indeed. Militant black women have recently recognized this problem — that striving for middle-class status for blacks may not be totally satisfactory:

> A woman who stays at home, caring for children and the house, leads an extremely sterile existence. . . . Black women were never afforded such phony luxuries.
>
> It must also be pointed out at this time, that black women are not resentful of the rise to power of black men. We welcome it. We see in it the eventual liberation of all black people from this oppressive system of capitalism. Nevertheless, this does not mean that you have to negate one for the other. This kind of thinking is a product of miseducation; that it's either X or it's Y. It is fallacious reasoning that in order for the black man to be strong, the black woman has to be weak.
>
> Those who are exerting their "manhood" by telling black women to step back into a submissive role are assuming a counterrevolutionary position.
> (Beal, 1970, pp. 341–344)

It does seem that black women are in a double-bind in that their search for rights as women is perceived to be in conflict with their search for rights as blacks; the two, of course, need not be antagonistic, but could well be complementary (Torrey, 1979), as could achievement and femininity for white women.

In a sense, the lesser participation of black women in the women's

FIGURE 16.1
Black women have achieved more in the professions than either their race or their gender would predict.

Source: Photo by Constantine Manos / Magnum.

movement highlights a more general source of ambivalence for the black woman, the conflict between white standards and black standards, the conflict between the values of the dominant culture and her own culture (Ladner, 1971). The issues raised by the women's movement do not seem relevant because they are problems in white culture, and other problems are much more salient to blacks. The "battle of the sexes" may seem a rather luxurious pastime to the black woman by comparison with the stark realities of unemployment and poverty.

One fascinating study investigated how some black women professionals manage to resolve these conflicts — specifically, conflicts between their (white-defined) professionalism and their commitment to activist work in the black community (Gilkes, 1982). Some of the women had accomplished their family responsibilities early in life and had then gone back to college to get their professional credentials, with the goal of using them to help the black community. For example, one woman got a degree in education, although she never intended to teach, in order to give herself more credibility with teachers and black parents.

> Parents had always had the feeling, and I was under the same impression until I became involved with the teachers, that teachers were always right because we (black people) always have this great respect for education. . . . Parents were afraid that since they were less educated they should not go and talk to the teacher. (Gilkes, 1982, p. 293)

She used her credentials to organize the parents and improve the schools.

Other women got their education and established themselves in their profession early, and then also wanted to work for black community needs. Early in their careers they witnessed abuses of professionalism. Most of them had become heads of agencies and, as a result of their past experiences, structured their agencies so as not to include the abuses they saw in white-run bureaucracies. Gilkes called these women "rebellious professionals." They had managed to get to a position of power in which they were their own bosses and could structure things the way they wanted to, to serve the black community. Thus they exemplify the black community's goal of self-government. As Nikki Giovanni put it in her poem "my House" 1972),

> . . . it's my house
> and i plan to live in it
> . . . cause i run the kitchen
> and i can stand the heat

These women, then, have managed to transcend the double-bind between issues of freedom as women and of working for the black community. What dazzling role models they are!

Another seeming double-bind for black women is in the area of sexuality and reproduction. Black leaders have for some time opposed the use of modern methods of birth control and abortion, saying that it represents genocide, a way for whites to decimate blacks by preventing their reproduction. However, one cannot help but wonder whether this is not so much the position of blacks as it is of black males. Black women must ultimately bear and rear the children, and surely must have some feelings on the issue. Research shows that modern black women do not value large families (Bernard, 1966). Mothers of kindergarten-age children were asked whether they had been pleased when they discovered they were pregnant with the child. Of the black mothers, 59 percent replied no, as compared with 23 percent among the white mothers (Baughman and Dahlstrom, 1968). Once again, the black woman seems to be in a double-bind in which birth control, which may seem desirable to her as an individual and as a woman, is seen as being incompatible with her racial loyalties.

The ambivalence of black women toward sexuality and reproduction also seems to be conveyed to their daughters. Black mothers seem to offer information on reproduction to their daughters less frequently than do whites. In one study it was found that 63 percent of black girls aged eleven to eighteen had been prepared for menstruation, as compared with 76 percent of white girls, and that very few of the black girls had been informed by their mothers (Henton, 1961). Many black adolescent girls who have become pregnant appear to have done so because contraceptive information was unavailable to them (Furstenberg, 1971). Apparently black mothers hide contraceptive information from their daughters, hoping to prevent their sexual activity. Unfortunately, instead of preventing sexual activity, it seems to promote pregnancy. Once again, this seems to be a manifestation of the black mother's ambivalence to sexuality, another instance of a double-bind for her.

These ambivalences are clearly expressed in the following excerpt from an autobiography by a black woman:

> Recently it dawned on me that the reason a former boyfriend and I had to call it quits was because he felt intimidated by the fact that I am a college student whereas he works in the steel mill six days a week. Anytime I used a word not in his vocabulary he would ask me to "break down that college term." I sincerely doubt that my vocabulary had increased so noticeably in a few quarters. Actually I had been talking the same all the time but we were on the same educational level before. Here is an example where I felt that my identity was more important than playing a sex determined role in which I would watch that I only used five letter words so that I could humor his male ego.
>
> Humoring an ego is not the same as helping a person discover that he has one. Here is the dilemma the black woman finds herself in. Where does she draw the line between denying herself and helping her man? . . . My sexual identity I believe is typical of other black educated women who discovered that there is such a thing as a sexual identity and struggle with themselves trying to define one. The black woman doesn't want to be used yet she doesn't want to use anyone of the opposite sex. She realizes that her strong, overbearing matriarchal nature must step

> aside so that the black man can find and utilize himself. Yet she knows she cannot step behind him because she wants to maintain her identity as a person, also. So, the black woman desires to walk beside her man and it is a truly difficult task especially for an educated black woman.[3]

Therefore, it seems reasonable to conclude that, although the femininity-achievement double-bind is salient for white women, black women have their own version of the double-bind, in the areas of sexuality, reproduction, and racial versus gender identity.

WOMEN AS A MINORITY GROUP

In 1951, sociologist Helen Hacker pointed out a number of striking sociological and psychological parallels between blacks and women. These are summarized in Table 16.1. There is good reason to think that women have many of the sociological and psychological characteristics of a minority group. Because of obvious physical characteristics, neither blacks nor women can hide the respective facts of their race or gender. Stereotypes and discrimination against both have relegated them to inferior job status. And so the list goes.

We are most interested here in the psychological parallels, the commonalities between minority-group psychology and the psychology of women. First, there are certain parallels in ascribed psychological characteristics — that is, in stereotyped notions of the ways blacks and females behave. Both groups are believed to have inferior intelligence and to be incapable of producing outstanding persons; both groups are supposed to have little control of their impulses (immature superego!); and both groups are seen as sexually threatening.

One of the items on Hacker's list that has always fascinated me is the conflict experienced by minorities between achieved and ascribed status (last item in Table 16.1). An achieved status is what a person has actually achieved; an ascribed status is what people ascribe to the person, or think the person has achieved, judging from that person's being a black or woman. When I taught at Bowling Green State University, we lived in a small town nearby. One man I knew asked one day if I were getting close to finishing my degree at Bowling Green. For him, my ascribed status was student, and it apparently made much more sense to him for a woman to be a student than for her to be a professor. I politely corrected him. Interestingly, though, he made the same error two more times within the next year. High-achieving blacks often experience this conflict between achieved and ascribed status. A black physician once told me about some-

---

[3] From a student essay for a psychology of women course, paraphrased.

TABLE 16.1.   **Some parallels between blacks and women**

1. High social visibility
    a. skin color; secondary sex characteristics
    b. clothing — "flashy" clothes; dresses
2. Ascribed psychological characteristics
    a. inferior intelligence; few geniuses
    b. more free in instinctual gratifications; emotional, childlike
    c. threatening sexuality — virility of black male; woman as temptress
    d. general stereotype of inferiority
3. Behaviors used to "cope"
    a. deferential manner
    b. apparent need for directions — fake shows of ignorance; pretended help-lessness
    c. sensitivity to methods of outwitting dominant group; dominant groups' susceptibility
4. Rationalization of status
    a. are all right in their place
    b. myth of contented black; contented housewife
5. Discriminations
    a. limitations on education
    b. jobs — confined to traditional jobs; barred from being supervisors; their competition feared; no family precedents (role models) for higher education
    c. little political power
6. Resulting psychological problems
    a. roles not clearly defined; roles conflicting
    b. conflict between achieved and ascribed status

Source: After Hacker, 1951.

thing that occurred one day when he was working on a flower bed in his front yard. A man drove up to the house, clearly assumed he was the hired gardener, and asked if he could see Dr. ———. As a thought-provoking exercise, try to determine how Bem's gender schema theory (Chapter 3) would explain these instances of conflict between achieved and ascribed status.

There are also parallels in the true, not ascribed, psychological characteristics that blacks and women share, which may be seen as common products of similar relegation to inferior status. Perhaps most striking of these is the low self-esteem that has long been a common characteristic of minority groups (Adelson, 1958, pp. 486–489; Allport, 1954; Simpson and Yinger, 1965, pp. 227–229; Lewin, 1941). In Chapter 8 we looked at the experiment by Goldberg (1968) which showed that females value the work of a female less than that of a male. Women devalue the work of other women and, by implication, devalue themselves.

It would appear that both blacks and women, then, hold members of their own race or gender and by implication themselves, in low esteem.

On the other hand, I noted in the discussion of black women that much of the low self-esteem of blacks may be changing as a result of black pride, the emphasis on "black is beautiful," and so forth. White women are not nearly so far along in their own personal advancement.

Attacking the psychological handicap of low self-esteem is clearly essential in any attempts at improving the status of women or minority groups. Perhaps the most important achievement of the women's movement has been the establishment of consciousness-raising groups in which this very problem is attacked and in which women attempt to improve their attitudes toward and relations with other women and with themselves.

Simone de Beauvoir (1952) has expressed many of the underlying parallels between minorities and women in her concept "the Other." Men see themselves as the Subject, the One — women then become the Other.

> Thus it is that no group ever sets itself up as the One without at once setting up the Other over against itself . . . In small-town eyes all persons not belonging to the village are "strangers" and suspect; to the native of a country all who inhabit other countries are "foreigners"; Jews are "different" for the anti-Semite, Negroes are "inferior" for American racists, aborigines are "natives" for colonists, proletarians are the "lower class" for the privileged. (de Beauvoir, 1952, p. xviii)

And so both blacks and women are an out-group, perceived as "the Other" by whites and by men.

There is one notable flaw in the parallel between women and other minority groups. Most minority groups are "colonized" — that is, they live together with others of their group apart from the larger society, as in a ghetto. Women, however, are not colonized, because they live intermingled with men. Colonization has both positive and negative aspects. Among the negative, it results in various forms of environmental disadvantage such as inadequate housing. Women, on the other hand, share the life-style of their husbands. But a positive aspect of colonization is that it promotes the cohesion and identity of the group, which is certainly important as a first step in raising the group's status and self-esteem. Probably because of their lack of colonization, women have only recently come to identify themselves as an oppressed group; even now the identification is far from complete.

SOME CONCLUSIONS — IN THE MIDST OF SOCIAL CHANGE

So often in this chapter I have been forced to reconcile apparently contradictory results from two different pieces of research by saying that social change accounted for the differences. That is, two contradictory studies may both be accurate descriptions of reality — only one describes reality before a complex of social changes including the black power movement, the other during or after it. On the other hand, there have been few studies demonstrating that such changes have indeed occurred. This has introduced a certain awkwardness into my descriptions of the psychology of black women, because of the necessity of describing some "traditional" phenomena, and their "new" versions. On a more positive note, one cannot help but be impressed with the apparent potential for improving the psychological state of a group by means of social change.

There seems to be a great potential for the emerging disciplines of black psychology and psychology of women to be complementary, that is, mutually beneficial to each other. The psychology of women may take several cues from black psychology, especially from the psychology of black women. First, women might follow the example of blacks in attacking the problem of low self-confidence directly. Emphasis needs to be put on female as good and worthwhile and valuable. The women's movement has stressed the importance of women having rights equal to those of men, but an equally important drive should be to emphasize that women's roles, such as motherhood, are valuable. Otherwise the low self-confidence of the housewife may simply be compounded. A second cue women may take from blacks is that role redefinition actually seems to be feasible. Blacks have demonstrated, for example, that family organization can adapt to women working, and that in fact actual psychological benefits may result for the woman. Blacks have demonstrated that occupational achievement need not be incompatible with femininity.

Conversely, black psychology may benefit from some of the insights of the psychology of women, which is now largely a psychology of middle-class white women. In particular, blacks seem in imminent danger of having among them a lot of middle-class women. While this may represent great improvements economically and socially, it also carries with it the danger that black women, in becoming middle class, will develop the psychological problems of their white sisters — low self-confidence, motive to avoid success, depression, to name a few. Indeed, it almost seems that black leaders advocate the advent of these phenomena. For example, the first sentence in Grier and Cobb's chapter, "Achieving Womanhood," in their book *Black Rage* is: "In the world of woman an abundance of feminine narcissism is not only a cheerful attribute but a vital necessity to emotional well-being" (1968, p. 32). While surely a certain amount of narcissism is an improvement over the feelings of the self as ugly, which black women may have traditionally endured, emphasis on narcissism can lead to an overvaluation of the external self and little cultivation of one's own inner resources. At a time when many women feel that Freud's description of women as narcissistic is an insult, Grier and Cobbs' opening sentence seems strange indeed. Black women and blacks in general may want to guard against the black power movement achieving better jobs for black men and only more cosmetics for black women. The potential for negative psychological change is indicated by a study that found that the motive to avoid success is frequent among black college women who endorse black militant attitudes (Puryear and Mednick, 1974). On the other hand, a study by Weston and Mednick (1970) suggests that black women in the middle class may not assume some of its psychological pitfalls such as the motive to avoid success.

One tempting game of speculation to play is "who's got it worse" — black women, or white women? Certainly in terms of the cold realities of life, one could well make the argument that black women have it much worse — poverty, inadequate housing, the necessity for raising children without the help of an adult male. Yet, one could also make the argument that, in a psychological sense, it is white women who are disadvantaged. Black females seem in some ways better equipped to take advantage of the opportunities arising from drives for equal opportunity, not having the handicap of the femininity-achievement incompatibility. In fact, some authors (such as Jackson, 1973) have suggested that black family structure is actually *ahead* of white family structure — perhaps by as much as 100 years — in adapting to existing social conditions. Statistics on marital status and illegitimacy rates indicate that whites are becoming more like blacks. White women in growing numbers are having children out of wedlock, and premarital sex is on the rise among whites (both trends of whites behaving more like blacks) (Ladner, 1971). A social structure that permits women to achieve occupationally and to still hold a wife-mother role would seem very attractive, indeed necessary, in view of apparent current social trends. Perhaps blacks have pioneered in creating such a structure.

Some data bearing on this point come from a study that found that black males and black females did not differ significantly in their conception of the "ideal woman," whereas there were significant differences between white males and white females (Steinman and Fox, 1970; see also Crovitz and Steinmann, 1980). Black males and females preferred a balancing of self-actualizing and family orientations for women. White males shared this view, but white females *expected* white males to demand nearly exclusive family orientation from them. Black males and females also showed greater similarity in their expectations about gender roles in marriage and child rearing than did white males and females. Apparently blacks have managed a greater harmony among the various roles demanded of women. Certainly this is a direction in which one hopes whites can also move.

SUGGESTION FOR FURTHER READING

Epstein, Cynthia F. (1973, August). Black and female: The double whammy. *Psychology Today*, p. 57. This is an interesting article on black professional women.

17
Retrospect and Prospect

Standing on the ground of common sense and the constitution of the human mind, I deny that anyone knows, or can know, the nature of the two sexes, so long as they have only been seen in their present relation to one another . . . What is now called the nature of woman is an eminently artificial thing — the result of forced repression in some directions, unnatural stimulation in others.

JOHN STUART MILL

The great philosopher and feminist John Stuart Mill, quoted at the opening of the chapter, lived in an era in which there was no science of psychology. He believed that no one could understand the true nature of women and men. Over 100 years — and a great deal of psychological research — later, how can one respond to Mill?

Certainly scientists would not claim to know the "true nature" of woman any more than Mill did. But I would argue that that is not the right question. Rather than trying to establish the "true nature" of woman, we would do better to try to understand how women function psychologically now in our culture, how they function in some other cultures and other times, and what their potential for the future is.

This book has focused particularly on trying to understand how women function psychologically in our contemporay culture. To do this, I have reviewed the existing scientific theories and research. Often I was not able to provide definitive answers, but at least was able to provide some reasonable ideas that further research will continue to refine.

Several important themes have cropped up repeatedly in this book. One is gender similarities, the notion that women and men are more similar to each other than they are different. Another theme has been ambivalence, as seen in the conflict between achievement and femininity, between motherhood and career, and in ambivalence about sexuality. Finally, androgyny has emerged as an important mode of psychological functioning that may represent the ideal of the psychologically healthy individual of the future.

FUTURE RESEARCH

In 1974, in writing the first edition of this book, I commented that research on the psychology of women was in its infancy. However, coming away from the most recent (1983) convention of the American Psychological Association, I found that real progress had been made, and that research and theory were becoming increasingly sophisticated. There are now tests available to measure androgyny, and research is progressing in the investigation of exactly what the psychological consequences of being androgynous are. There are some fairly well-documented differences in the verbal and nonverbal communication styles of females and males, and research is proceeding to determine exactly what these differences mean. Feminist therapy is more than a twinkle in some feminist's eye, and is now widely practiced. Major revisions of male-dominated theories, such as Carol Gilligan's feminist reconstruction of moral development theory, provide exciting new insights. And so the list goes.

Of course, this does not mean that we know everything there is to know about women. Far from it. There is much information that we do not yet have. The reader may want to spend some time thinking about what the most important questions for future research are. I will suggest a few that I think are important.

In this time of social change, we are all curious about child-rearing practices, and what sort of socialization procedures might be used to shape desirable characteristics in females. Much of the research that would be most appealing in this area would involve experimental manipulation of child-rearing procedures; such research would, unfortunately, generally be unethical. However, there are dozens of naturalistic experiments occurring now — communes, groups experimenting with alternative life styles — which all may be zealously performing the child-rearing practices that might be designed in an experiment. Certainly it would be fruitful to follow the development of children reared under such radically different conditions. The studies on children in the kibbutz are perhaps the best example (Maccoby and Feldman, 1972).

A great deal of research on the psychology of women has focused on high-achieving women, looking at their personality characteristics, common biographical themes, and so on. Such an approach has merit if one's goal is to improve women's achievements; studying high-achieving women may give suggestions as to how one "creates" a high-achieving female through child-rearing practices or other factors. The problem is that we concentrate 90 percent of the research on 1 percent of the population, and compound the problem by calling it the psychology of women, implying all women. While we need research on high-achieving women, we also need to redirect our efforts toward understanding the psychology of housewives, the psychology of secretaries, the psychology of mentally retarded women, the psychology of handicapped women, and many others. I am not suggesting that all studies must involve random sampling, but that groups other than high achievers, who are also of importance or interest, be defined. Of course, the study of all these groups of women is as important a task for psychology in general as it is for psychology of women.

We need more research on adjustment problems in women, particularly depression, alcoholism, and the eating disorders because they are all so frequent. We need to know what causes depression and what can be done to prevent it (e.g., changing child-rearing practices, school policy, or family roles). Along with this, we need more work on psychotherapy for women's problems, and research on the effectiveness of these therapies. Related research should be directed toward the psychological aspects of women's health issues such as abortion and mastectomy.

We need to know more scientifically about feminism. What happens to women psychologically when they become feminists? How do other people react to women who are feminists? What impact does feminism have on men? Two recent studies provide examples of the sorts of research that can be done in this area. Psychologist Arnold Kahn (1981) studied the differences between profeminist men and antifeminist men in their reactions to a woman who assertively disagreed with them. For half of the men, the woman had relevant expertise to the topic under discussion, whereas the other half of the men interacted with a woman whose expertise was irrelevant. In half of the cases, the topic was traditionally masculine (the military), and in half of the cases, the topic was traditionally feminine (childcare). As it turned out, the profeminist and antifeminist men did not differ from one another in their actual behavior toward the woman. However, as might be predicted, the profeminist and antifeminist men did differ in their ratings of their liking of the women. The profeminist men liked the woman who was assertive on the masculine topic, whereas the antifeminist men liked the woman who was assertive on the feminine topic.

Another study evaluated the impact of a women's studies course on students' gender-role attitudes (Steiger, 1981). The attitudes of the students in the women's studies course became significantly more liberal, compared with those of a group of students in introductory sociology, which did not change over the term. In the women's studies course, the attitudes of both men and women changed, although the women's attitudes changed more than the men's did. The author concluded that it was the consciousness-raising component of the course that changed people's attitudes. Further, he speculated that the consciousness-raising component of the women's movement is having a significant impact on people.

We need to know what impact recent advances in sex-related technology will have on women's lives. Some have argued that the greatest single stimulus to the current liberation of women was the development of the birth control pill. If a single technological advance of that sort can have such far-reaching consequences, what will be the impact of other technologies? What will be the effect of test-tube babies, surrogate mothering, sex-choice technologies? Regarding the latter, it may be possible within a few decades to choose the gender of one's offspring. In a sense, that is possible now; a woman could have amniocentesis, find out the gender of her child, and have an abortion if it were the "wrong" one. Personally, I would hate to see women abort fetuses on the basis of gender, and I think very few women would do so. But more sophisticated methods of gender choice will be available soon. One study investigated the impact of gender-choice technology by surveying 710 undergraduates (Fidell et al., 1979). As previous surveys have shown, people have an overwhelming preference for a boy as the first child; 85 percent express that preference. Having the second child be a girl was preferred by 73 percent. Given the preference people express as to the size of families, more boys (55 percent) would be born than girls. And given previous findings on differences between first-borns and second-borns, psychological gender differences would probably be magnified. Much more research of this sort is needed.

As I have discussed in previous chapters, feminist scholars stress the importance of power relations between women and men. More psychological research is needed in this area. We need to know how men express power over women, and how women might more effectively begin to express power themselves. Psychologists Wendy McKenna and Florence Denmark (1979) did an interesting study that shows some of the possibilities for future research in this area. They attempted to find out whether women really could improve their perceived status by adopting some of the nonverbal communication patterns typical of males and high-status individuals. To do this, they made videotapes of a short skit involving two people who were described as working for the same company. One person asked for a favor, and the other at first refused but then complied. In all possible combinations of men and women in the two roles, the researchers had one person exhibit high-status nonverbal behaviors (e.g., smiling infrequently, touching the person they are dealing with) and the other, low-status nonverbal behaviors. College students rated the job level of each of the videotaped men and women. Overall, the subjects thought that the person who showed high-status behaviors held the high-level job, regardless of the person's gender. Therefore, it seems that if women convey their competence nonverbally, they will be recognized as being competent and of high status. That is an encouraging finding. Unfortunately, there was also a suggestion that a man who showed low-status behaviors in the presence of a woman showing high-status behaviors was judged as having a lower-level job than when his partner was a man showing high-status behaviors. Therefore, men may lose prestige by working for high-status women, and male resentment may ensue. It is exactly this kind of information — about the positive and negative consequences of new patterns of behavior — that we need.

FEMINISM REVISITED

In Chapter 1 a short definition of feminism was given: "a feminist is a person who favors political, economic, and social equality of women and men, and therefore favors the legal and social changes that will be necessary to achieve that equality." Your understanding of feminism is now much more complex than that. I hope that your view of feminism has been transformed in reading this book. Feminists are not a bunch of ugly women burning their bras; nor are they a group of screaming picketers protesting discrimination. Feminism, or the feminist perspective, or the feminist paradigm, whichever term you prefer, offers a substantially different view of the world, and specifically of psychology, than traditional science has (see the selection on paradigms). The feminist paradigm says that the focus of psychology should be on women as much as on men. Issues of

PARADIGMS, SCIENCE, AND FEMINISM

Thomas Kuhn's *The Structure of Scientific Revolutions* (1970) has become a modern classic in the philosophy of science. A consideration of Kuhn's analysis of science will help us to understand science, and specifically how feminism fits into science.

The general public tends to view science as advancing continually in small steps by accumulating facts. One of Kuhn's fundamental points is that, if we look at the history of science, that is not at all the way it works. His analysis indicates that science instead proceeds in occasional revolutionary leaps that disrupt calm periods of data collection. Essential to his conceptualization is the term *paradigm*. As he defines it, a paradigm refers to the set of beliefs, underlying assumptions, values, and techniques shared by a particular community of scientists. In a sense a paradigm is a "world view," or at least a view of the piece of the world that is the focus of the particular scientific specialty. A new paradigm is usually drastically different from the paradigm that preceded it in its given field, but it gains followers because it solves some problems that the old paradigm could not handle; a radical revolution occurs as the science shifts from the old paradigm to the new. A paradigm is also sufficiently open-ended that it creates within its context a whole new set of questions that scientists can busy themselves with answering.

A specific example that may clarify these concepts is Copernicus and the Copernican revolution in astronomy. In Europe at the beginning of the fifteenth century, everyone, scientists included, believed that the earth was the center of the universe and that the sun revolved around the earth, a view known as the geocentric (earth-centered) or Ptolemaic view. Copernicus (1473–1543) came up with a new view, or paradigm — namely, that the sun was the center (heliocentric view) around which the earth rotated yearly, while the earth spun on its own axis daily. The Copernican view solved some problems that existed with the old, geocentric view. One of these was that, in order for geocentrism to be correct, the other planets must be traveling at irregular speeds around the earth, darting ahead and then slowing down. Using the Copernican view, the planets could be seen as moving at constant speed, while the earth (with the astronomer on it) moved simultaneously. Copernicus's ideas were opposed by the Church as erroneous and possibly heretical, which is often the case with new scientific paradigms. But eventually his ideas were widely accepted by astronomers, who then used them as the basis for their research. Kuhn's point is clear: science proceeds in occasional revolutionary leaps as new paradigms, representing radically different ideas, arise.

The general public, as well as many scientists, tends to view science as fundamentally objective. Kuhn also disputes this notion. He believes that there is no such thing as a pure fact in science; rather, there are only facts that exist within the context of a particular paradigm. Once a new paradigm has taken over, the old "facts" will seem wrong or downright stupid. For example, if we had lived before the time of Copernicus, we would naturally have observed the "fact" that the sun rises in the east every morning and sets in the west every evening. We would further have taken this as ample evidence of the "fact" that the sun is revolving around the earth. From our modern, post-Copernican perspective, these do not seem to be facts at all. This illustrates Kuhn's argument that there are no objective facts in science; facts exist only from the point of view of a particular paradigm.

How does all of this relate to psychology? Psychology has had several paradigms, the actual number depending on how broad or narrow one wants to be in identifying paradigms. Certainly *learning theory* has been a dominant paradigm in psychology. Rosnow (1981) has traced the history of *experimentalism* as a dominant paradigm in social psychology. The belief in social psychology has been that the tightly controlled laboratory experiment is the best, perhaps the only, way to get good "facts" on people's social behavior. Rosnow also documents a crisis that experimentalism faces. Experimenter effects and observer effects (discussed in Chapter 1) mean that scientists may get poor data from their experiments, or only data that conform to their own biases. And serious questions about the ethics of experimentalism have arisen, particularly in the wake of Milgram's famous experiment that demonstrated the obedience of subjects to an authority who directed them to administer terribly high levels of shock to another person. Because of this crisis, experimentalism may be abandoned and a new paradigm may arise to take its place.

Feminists point out that the paradigms of psychology have been *androcentric*, that is, focusing on males and coming from a male perspective.

In the context of Kuhn's arguments, feminism can be seen as an emerging new paradigm in the science of psychology. Feminism fits the definition of a paradigm in that it comprises a set of beliefs, values, and techniques (explained in other chapters of this book) that are shared by a community of scientists, namely, feminist psychologists. Feminism provides a new world view. Traditional psychology could be viewed as seeing the world revolving around men (androcentrism), just as the pre-Copernicans saw the sun revolving around the earth. Feminists do not want to shift to viewing the world as revolving around women. Rather, the feminist desire is to view the world revolving around men and women jointly.

Another characteristic of a paradigm, according to Kuhn, is that it provides answers to a set of problems that could not be solved by the old paradigm and were creating a crisis. There are a number of such problems that have not been solved by traditional psychology. One of these is the nature of masculinity and femininity (Pleck, 1981). Traditional psychology has viewed masculinity-femininity as an essential personality dimension (see Chapter 4 for an extended discussion). Further, gender-typing was supposed to be essential to mental health. That is, the highly masculine male and the highly feminine female were supposed to be the most well-adjusted, according to that paradigm. Actual research, however, shows that this is not true. For example, highly masculine males are actually less well-adjusted than less masculine males (e.g., Mussen, 1961, 1962). Traditional psychology's paradigm cannot handle that result. Feminism provides a framework that answers that difficulty. It suggests the possibility that people can be androgynous, and that, in fact, it would be the androgynous person who would be most healthy psychologically.

Paradigms, according to Kuhn, also create a whole new set of research questions because they present a different way of looking at the world. And so the feminist paradigm has created a new set of research topics that had not come to light in traditional psychology: androgyny, rape, wife battering, sexual harassment of women at work, and sexism in psychotherapy, to name a few.

Feminist psychology, then, fits nicely into Kuhn's definition of a paradigm. One final comment is in order, however. It is sometimes argued that feminism has no place in scientific psychology because feminism consists merely of a set of political biases and these biases do not permit objective research. Concerning this point, it is well to remember Kuhn's argument that science is not truly objective and that facts are facts only in the context of a particular paradigm. Thus feminist psychology is neither more nor less objective than other paradigms in psychology. What it does is provide a set of "facts" that make sense in the feminist context.

Sources: Kuhn, 1970. Rosnow, 1981. Pleck, 1981. Masterman, 1970.

concern to women — rape, battering, menstruation — should be given research attention. Scientists must be careful in interpreting outcomes: for example, when they investigate rape, they must not automatically blame it on the victim, the woman. People need to be aware of the power of gender roles in their lives. And so the list goes. The point is that feminism provides a new view in psychology, a new set of questions, a fresh set of hypotheses. I find that exciting, and I hope you do, also.

FUTURE ROLES
FOR WOMEN

How will the female role emerge in the United States from the present upheaval in gender roles? I shall structure our discussion of this question around two further questions that, while superficially similar, have quite different answers in my view: (1) How would males and females behave (what would be the nature of gender roles) in the absence of all forces demanding gender differences, whether in child-rearing practices or in social pressures, legal, economic, or otherwise? That is, if males and females were treated identically, would they behave identically, or would differences still emerge? If differences emerged, what would they be? (2) How would males and females behave if all social forces were directed toward making them behave identically — that is, if we systematically shaped males and females to behave as similarly as possible? (Note that this second hypothetical condition, unlike the first, might include differential treatment of females and males in order to bring about the desired similarity in behavior, such as encouraging aggressive behavior in girls while discouraging it in boys in order to bring both to some intermediate level of aggressive behavior, neither too aggressive nor too passive.)

My feeling is that, under condition (1), there would be gender differences, and that under condition (2) there wouldn't be. Although I have argued for the prevalence of gender similarities, I also believe that there are some gender differences that would emerge under condition (1); yet I am equally convinced that human beings are so malleable that even these differences could be eliminated by appropriate environmental manipulations.

What evidence do I have for these assertions? My belief that gender differences would emerge in the absence of efforts at shaping them (condition 1) arises from two sources — the cross-cultural data and the biological data. The universality of the existence of gender roles cross-culturally is a strong argument that if things started from a state where no roles were expected, it would not be long until they reached an equilibrium in which there were differences, although the content of the differences might be quite different from those that now hold in the United States. Humans seem to have a universal tendency to create gender roles, although the precise content of the roles may vary. The biological data further persuade me that biological gender differences do create some psychological gender differences. Gender differences in physical strength surely will have some consequences, as will sex hormones, probably most importantly on aggressive behaviors. Biologically determined experiences, most notably pregnancy and breastfeeding, probably have consequences, particularly when the pregnancy/breastfeeding functions become generalized to include child-rearing.

On the other hand, the cross-cultural data also persuade me that such differences could be eliminated under appropriate environmental manipulations (condition 2). For example, among the Mundugumor observed by Margaret Mead, females can be just as aggressive as males, because the culture shapes them to be so. Certainly males could be assigned an equal role in care of infants, particularly when bottle feeding is so common, and the assignment would be a successful one. The hallmark of the human species is malleability, the ability to adapt, whether to diverse climatic conditions or to changes in gender roles.

Which course of action to take is ultimately not a scientific question, but rather a question of values — what we as a culture believe females and males should be like. Margaret Mead (1949) made an elegant analogy in this decision-making process to differences between people with good eyesight and people with poor eyesight. Certainly there are biological differences between them, one group being physiologically capable of seeing better than the other. But society holds that those with the inferior physiology should not be handicapped in their status in society, and so we provide them with eyeglasses to remedy their physiological deficiency, allowing them to function equally with those who have good vision. Does our value system also hold that females should function equally with males? If so, certainly technology is adequate to overcome biological gender differences (for example, the use of machines to perform heavy lifting for females with inadequate physical strength, or the use of bottles to feed babies for males with inadequate mammary endowment), just as it is in the case of giving glasses to those with poor vision.

The question remains, what course of action will we, as a society, take? Will it be condition (1) or condition (2), or some alternative such as a modified version of the status quo? I, of course, am not a seer, and so I shall not make a prediction as to what course will be taken. What I do wish to do is to stimulate the reader to explore the consequences of the various alternatives.

In many ways, ours may be an optimal time for gender-role change for women. The de-emphasis on fertility and child-rearing may be critical. The nature of the female role is intimately tied to whether or not a society wants to reproduce at a high rate. With a strong emphasis on reproduction, maternal aspects of the female role are stressed. With the current de-emphasis on fertility, careers for women are much more viable alternatives than they formerly were. Indeed, childlessness is becoming an option for women, freeing them for substantially different roles than housewife/mother (Hoffman, 1974b).

On the other hand, we must recognize the emergence of a political movement known as the New Right (for a feminist analysis of the New Right, see Eisenstein, 1982). The New Right abhors recent social change. It claims that its stance is "pro-family," but it narrowly defines the family as a married heterosexual couple with children, with the husband working in the labor force and the wife staying home full-time. The New Right rues the demise of patriarchy and the loss of the father's authority within the family. To say the least, the forces of the New Right act in opposition to the forces of feminism. It remains to be seen which will win out. Interestingly, the New Right has been losing some key legislative battles; in 1983 it lost a critical Senate vote attempting to put into law a constitutional amendment that would have prohibited abortion. (On the other hand, the ERA also went down to defeat.)

One problem to be faced is that we really have no adequate measure of social change. There has been a tendency to equate work outside the home with progress for women. Yet, working outside the home is the opposite of progress if it must be done in addition to all the housewife and mother tasks. The work of women, whether inside the home or outside the home, must be evaluated in terms of its contributions to society in general and to the growth of the individual (Dahlstrom, 1971). A much more complex and adequate measure of social change would result.

We need, then, to expand our notion of the meaning of equality — it means more than just women holding jobs outside the home, for example. Part of the expansion must include changes in the male role (Palme, 1972). Equality requires modification of the male role, not only to make possible change in the female role, but because the male role itself is in need of revision.

But I must add one note of caution, and this is in regard to the values attached to gender roles. Cross-culturally (at least currently) it is a universal phenomenon that the male role is always more powerful and the female role is always valued less. This devaluing of the female role surely has many consequences, among them psychological ones such as the higher frequency of psychiatric problems found in women. In my opinion it is imperative that, whatever the reallocation or modification of gender roles, the result be that the male role and the female role be valued equally.

Although I am emphasizing the need for a higher valuing of the female role, it is also true that this higher valuing must come not only from without, but also from within. That is, institutional change aimed at raising the value of the female role — for example, treating child-rearing as a profession — and changing male attitudes are not enough. Women must also value themselves. This is an important goal of the many consciousness-raising groups formed by women across the country.

Whatever the reallocation of gender roles in the future, it is most important that equal respect and value be attached to both roles. In part, I am suggesting that gender roles in some form will probably continue, and that, rather than trying to eliminate them, we might more profitably concentrate on improving the valuation attached to the female role. Much as blacks have shifted from an emphasis on integration and assimilation into white culture to a proclamation that black is beautiful, so I hope women will come to believe that female is good. As Christabel Pankhurst, a turn-of-the-century British suffragette said,

> Remember the dignity
> of your womanhood.
> Do not appeal,
> do not beg,
> do not grovel.
> Take courage,
> join hands,
> stand beside us.

Appendix: Psychology of Women Resource Directory

Below are listed various organizations that may provide services useful to you. All have focuses on issues related to the psychology of women.

I. GENERAL

National Women's Studies
  Association
University of Maryland
203 Behavioral and Social Sciences
  Bldg.
College Park, MD 20742

This organization is devoted to women's studies in all disciplines, including psychology. It sponsors a yearly women's studies conference that includes many excellent activities.

American Psychological Association
1200 Seventeenth St. N.W.
Washington, DC 20036

This is the major organization of psychologists in the United States. Division 35 of the APA is Psychology of Women. APA has a Women's Program Officer (in 1984, Dr. Nancy Russo). Numerous useful publications can be obtained from APA, e.g., *Graduate Faculty Interested in the Psychology of Women*, and *Understanding the Manuscript Review Process: Increasing the Participation of Women*.

National Organization for Women
425 13th Street, N.W., Suite 723
Washington, DC 20004
(202) 347-2279

NOW seeks to take action to bring women into full participation in the mainstream of American society now, so that they will exercise all the privileges and responsibilities thereof in truly equal partnership with men.

Women's Bureau
U.S. Department of Labor
Washington, DC 20210

This agency publishes information on women and work (such as *20 Facts About Women Workers*), including career options, legal information, and program models; it also proposes policies and programs to the government.

413

PEER: Project on Equal
  Education Rights
1413 K St., N.W., 9th Floor
Washington, DC 20005

PEER offers information on Title IX
and its banning of sex discrimination in
education.

Federation of Organizations for
  Professional Women
1825 Connecticut Avenue, N.W.,
  Suite 403
Washington, DC 20009
(202) 328-1415

This organization provides a number of
excellent publications, including *Sexual
Harassment Kit, National Women's
Resource Register,* and *Women &
Psychotherapy.*

Association for Women in
  Psychology
c/o Judi Sprei
8321 Snowden Oaks Place
Laurel, MD 20811

This is a political action group of
women psychologists.

The Feminist Press
P.O. Box 334
Old Westbury, NY 11568

This organization publishes books with
a feminist perspective in a wide variety
of disciplines.

II. HEALTH ISSUES: CONTRACEPTION, ABORTION, SEXUALITY

Planned Parenthood of America,
  Inc.
810 Seventh Avenue
New York, NY 10019
(212) 541-7800

PPFA is the nation's largest family
planning agency. Through local clinics
(check your telephone directory) it
offers birth control instruction and prescriptions, pregnancy testing, infertility
care, voluntary sterilization for men and
women, prenatal care, early abortions,
testing for sexually transmissible diseases,
screening for sickle cell anemia, cancer,
DES exposure, and diabetes, blood and
urine tests, and pelvic and breast exams.

National Abortion Rights Action
  League
1424 K St., N.W.
Washington, DC 20005
(202) 347-7774

This is a political action organization
working at both state and national levels
and dedicated to preserving a woman's
right to legal abortion and to teaching
its members effective use of the political
process to ensure abortion rights.

National Women's Health Network
224 Seventh Street, S.E.
Washington, DC 20003

This feminist group is concerned with
women's health issues; it provides a
newsletter, news alerts, information
clearinghouse, health resource guides,
speakers bureau, and educational con-
ferences.

VD National Hotline
260 Sheridan Avenue
Palo Alto, CA 94306
(800) 227-8922 (national number)
(800) 982-5883 (California
  number)

This organization provides these toll-free
numbers for telephone information on
sexually transmitted diseases; it also
provides referrals to free or low-cost
clinics or private physicians.

National Women's Health
Organization
110 East 59th Street, Suite 1011
New York, NY 10022

This organization operates ten facilities throughout the country, which provide abortion and gynecological services.

National Gay Task Force
80 Fifth Avenue, Suite 1601
New York, NY 10011
(22) 741-5800

This group offers information and support to gay women and men and distributes educational pamphlets, such as *About Coming Out*. It has a toll-free crisis line for reports of anti-gay violence and information and referral on AIDS (acquired immune deficiency syndrome): (800) 221-7044 (national); (212) 807-6016 (in New York).

National Anorexic Aid Society
P.O. Box 29461
Columbus, OH 43229

This organization offers information and support groups on anorexia.

III. VICTIMIZATION ISSUES: RAPE, BATTERING, HARASSMENT

Working Women's Institute
593 Park Avenue
New York, NY 10021

This organization builds public awareness of sexual harassment on the job and builds systematic protection against it, through consultation and training with a variety of institutions and through policy analysis.

National Center for the Prevention
and Control of Rape
National Institute of Mental Health
5600 Fishers Lane, Room 6C-12
Rockville, MD 20857

The NCPCR is the focal point in the National Institute of Mental Health for research, training, and public education activities in the area of rape and sexual assault of children and adults.

National Center for Women and
Family Law
Room 402, 799 Broadway
New York, NY 10003
(212) 674-8200

This is a legal services back-up center, providing assistance on legal issues affecting women and families, such as battering, rape, marital rape, divorce, and child-snatching.

Center for Women Policy Studies
2000 P Street, N.W., Suite 508
Washington, DC 20036

This organization publishes a newsletter on domestic violence, *Response to Violence in the Family*, and offers a two-day training package on working with men who batter.

Bibliography

Abramowitz, S. I., et al. (1976). Sex bias in psychotherapy: A failure to confirm. *American Journal of Psychiatry, 133,* 706–709.

Abramowitz, S. I., Abramowitz, C. V., & Gomes, B. (1973). The politics of clinical judgment: What nonliberal examiners infer about women who do not stifle themselves. *Journal of Consulting and Clinical Psychology, 41,* 385–391.

Abramson, P. R., et al. (1977). The talking platypus phenomenon as a function of sex and professional status. *Psychology of Women Quarterly, 2,* 114–117.

Abu-Laban, Sharon M. (1981). Women and aging. A futurist perspective. *Psychology of Women Quarterly, 6,* 85–98.

Adams, Kathryn A., & Landers, Audrey D. (1978). Sex difference in dominance behavior. *Sex Roles, 4,* 215–224.

Adamsky, Catherine (1981). Changes in pronomial usage in a classroom situation. *Psychology of Women Quarterly, 5,* 773–779.

Addiego, F., et al. (1981). Female ejaculation: A case study. *Journal of Sex Research, 17,* 13–21.

Adelson, J. (1958). A study of minority group authoritarianism. In M. Sklare (Ed.), *The Jews: Social patterns of an American group.* Glencoe, IL: Free Press.

Alba, Joseph W., & Hasher, Lynn (1983). Is memory schematic? *Psychological Bulletin, 93,* 203–231.

Albee, G. W. (1977). The Protestant ethic, sex, and psychotherapy. *American Psychologist, 32,* 150–161.

Albin, Rochelle S. (1977). Psychological studies of rape. *Signs, 3,* 423–435.

Allgeier, Elizabeth R., & Fogel, A. (1978). Coital position and sex roles: Responses to cross-sex behavior in bed. *Journal of Consulting and Clinical Psychology, 46,* 588–589.

Allport, G. (1937). *Personality.* New York: Holt, Rinehart & Winston.

In the bibliography I have followed the style of spelling out first names of female authors. I do this not to discriminate against men but to help readers become aware of the scientific contributions made by women.

————— (1954). *The nature of prejudice.* Reading, MA: Addison-Wesley.

Almquist, Elizabeth (1977). Women in the labor force. *Signs, 2,* 843–853.

Almquist, E. M., & Angrist, S. (1970). Career salience and atypicality of occupational choice among college women. *Journal of Marriage and the Family, 32,* 242–249.

American Psychological Association (1975a). Task force on issues of sexual bias in graduate education. Guidelines for nonsexist use of language. *American Psychologist, 30,* 682–684.

————— (1975b). Report of the task force on sex bias and sex-role stereotyping in psychotherapeutic practice. *American Psychologist, 30,* 1169–1175.

Amir, M. (1971). *Patterns in forcible rape.* Chicago: University of Chicago Press.

Anastasi, Anne (1958). *Differential psychology* (3rd ed.). New York: Macmillan.

————— (1970). On the formation of psychological traits. *American Psychologist, 25,* 899–910.

Anderson, Barbara L. (1983). Primary orgasmic dysfunction: Diagnostic considerations and review of treatment. *Psychological Bulletin, 93,* 105–136.

Andrew, D. M., & Patterson, D. G. (1959). *Minnesota clerical test.* New York: Psychological Corporation.

Andrews, Eva, & Cappon, D. (1957). Autism and schizophrenia in a child guidance clinic. *Canadian Psychiatric Association Journal, 2,* 1–25.

Angrist, Shirley S. (1969). The study of sex roles. *Journal of Social Issues, 25,* 215–232.

Angrist, Shirley S., Lefton, M., Dinitz, S., & Pasamanick, B. (1968). *Women after treatment: A study of former mental patients and their normal neighbors.* New York: Irvington.

Anonymous (1974). Life in the military. In J. Pleck and R. Sawyer (Eds.), *Men and masculinity.* Englewood Cliffs, NJ: Prentice-Hall.

————— (1975). When a woman is attacked. In L. G. Schultz (Ed.), *Rape victimology.* Springfield, IL: Charles C Thomas.

Ardrey, R. (1967). *African genesis.* New York: Dell.

Argyle, Michael, et al. (1968). The effects of visibility on interaction in a dyad. *Human Relations, 21,* 3–17.

Arkin, W. & Dobrofsky, Lynne R. (1978). Military socialization and masculinity. *Journal of Social Issues, 34*(1), 151–168.

Armon, Virginia (1960). Some personality variables in overt female homosexuality. *Journal of Projective Technique in Personality Assessment, 24,* 292–309.

Asch, S. E. (1956). Studies of independence and conformity: I. A minority of one against an unanimous majority. *Psychological Monographs, 70*(9), whole no. 416.

Asher, S. R., & Gottman, J. M. (1973). Sex of teacher and student reading achievement. *Journal of Educational Psychology, 65,* 168–171.

Asken, Michael J. (1975). Psychoemotional aspects of mastectomy: A review of recent literature. *American Journal of Psychiatry, 132,* 56–59.

Astin, Helen S., & Bayer, A. E. (1972). Sex discrimination in academe. *Educational Record, 53,* 101–118.

Atkeson, Beverly M., et al. (1982). Victims of rape: Repeated assessment of depressive symptoms. *Journal of Consulting and Clinical Psychology, 50,* 96–102.

Bailyn, Lotte (1970). Career and family orientation of husbands and wives in relation to marital happiness. *Human Relations, 23,* 97–113.

Bakan, D. (1966). *The duality of human existence.* Chicago: Rand McNally.

Baker, H. J., & Stoller, R. J. (1967). Biological forces postulated as having role in gender identity. *Roche Reports: Frontiers of Hospital Psychiatry, 4,* 3.

Baldwin, A. L. (1967). *Theories of child development.* New York: John Wiley.

Balswick, Jack O., & Peek, C. W. (1971). The inexpressive male: A tragedy of American society. *Family Coordinator, 20,* 363–368.

Bamberger, Joan (1974). The myth of matriarchy: Why men rule in primitive society. In M. Z. Rosaldo and L. Lamphere (Eds.), *Woman, culture and society.* Stanford: Stanford University Press.

Bandura, A. (1965). Influence of model's reinforcement contingencies on the acquisition of imitative responses. *Journal of Personality and Social Psychology, 1,* 589–595.

Bandura, A., & Walters, R. H. (1963). *Social learning and personality development.* New York: Holt, Rinehart & Winston.

Banks, W. Curtis (1976). White preference in blacks: A paradigm in search of a phenomenon. *Psychological Bulletin, 83,* 1179–1186.

Banton, Michael (1979). Black and white: Male and female. *New Society, 48,* 704–706.

Barash, David P. (1982). *Sociobiology and behavior* (2nd ed.). New York: Elsevier.

Barbach, Lonnie G. (1975). *For yourself: The fulfillment of female sexuality.* Garden City, NY: Anchor Press/Doubleday.

Barclay, A., & Cusumano, D. R. (1967). Father absence, cross-sex identity, and field-dependent behavior in male adolescents. *Child Development, 38,* 243–250.

Bardwick, Judith M. (1971). *Psychology of women: A study of biocultural conflicts.* New York: Harper & Row.

——— (ed.) (1972a). *Readings on the psychology of women.* New York: Harper & Row.

——— (1972b, February). Her body, the battleground, *Psychology Today, 5,* 50–54.

Barnett, Rosalind C., & Baruch, Grace (1978). *The competent woman: Perspectives on development.* New York: Wiley.

——— (1979). Career competence and well-being of adult women. In B. Gutek (Ed.), *New directions for education, work, and careers: Enhancing women's career development.* San Francisco: Jossey-Bass.

Barraclough, C. A., & Gorski, R. A. (1961). Evidence that the hypothalamus is responsible for androgen-induced sterility in the female rat. *Endocrinology, 68,* 68–79.

Barry, H., Bacon, Margaret K. & Child, I. L. (1957). A cross-cultural survey of some sex differences in socialization. *Journal of Abnormal and Social Psychology, 55,* 327–332.

Bart, Pauline B. (1971). Depression in middle-aged women. In V. G. Gornick and B. K. Moran (Eds.), *Women in sexist society.* New York: Basic Books.

Baruch, Grace K. (1975). Sex-role stereotyping, the motive to avoid success, and parental identification. *Sex Roles, 1,* 303–309.

Baruch, Rhoda (1967). The achievement motive in women: Implications for career development. *Journal of Personality and Social Psychology, 5,* 260–267.

Baucom, Donald H. (1983). Sex role identity and the decision to regain control among women: A learned helplessness investigation. *Journal of Personality and Social Psychology, 44,* 334–343.

Baughman, E. E. (1971). *Black Americans: A psychological analysis.* New York: Academic Press.

Baughman, E. E., Dahlstrom, W. G. (1968). *Negro and white children: A psychological study in the rural south.* New York: Academic Press.

Baxter, J. C. (1970). Interpersonal spacing in natural settings. *Sociometry, 33,* 444–456.

Bayley, Nancy (1936). *The California infant scale of motor development.* Berkeley: University of California Press.

Beach, F. A. (1947). Evolutionary changes in the physiological control of mating behavior in mammals. *Psychological Review, 54,* 5.

Beal, Frances M. (1970). Double jeopardy: To be black and female. In R. Morgan (Ed.), *Sisterhood is powerful.* New York: Random House.

Beard, Mary (1946). *Woman as a force in history.* New York: Macmillan.

Beauvoir, Simone de (1952). *The second sex.* New York: Knopf.

Beck, A. T., & Greenberg, Ruth L. (1974). Cognitive therapy with depressed women. In V. Franks and V. Burtle (Eds.), *Women in therapy.* New York: Brunner/Mazel.

Beckman, Linda J. (1978). The relative rewards and costs of parenthood and employment for employed women. *Psychology of Women Quarterly, 2,* 215–234.

Beckman, Linda J., & Houser, Betsy B. (1979). The more you have, the more you do: The relationships between wife's employment, sex-role attitudes, and household behavior. *Psychology of Women Quarterly, 4,* 160–174.

Bell, A. P. (1974). Homosexualities: Their range and character. In *Nebraska symposium on motivation 1973.* Lincoln: University of Nebraska Press.

Bell, A. P., Weinberg, M. S., & Hammersmith, Sue K. (1981). *Sexual preference: Its development in men and women.* Bloomington, IN: Indiana University Press.

Bell, R. Q. (1960). Relations between behavior manifestations in the human neonate. *Child Development, 31,* 463–477.

Bell, R. Q., Weller, G. M., & Waldrop, M. F. (1971). Newborn and pre-schooler: Organization of behavior and relations between periods.

Monographs of the Society for Research in Child Development, 36(1–2) (serial no. 142).

Bell, Robert R. (1966). *Premarital sex in a changing society.* Englewood Cliffs, NJ: Prentice-Hall.

Belliveau, F., & Richter, Lyn (1970). *Understanding human sexual inadequacy.* New York: Bantam Books.

Belzer, E. G. (1981). Orgasmic expulsions of women: A review and heuristic inquiry. *Journal of Sex Research, 17,* 1–12.

Bem, Sandra L. (1974). The measurement of psychological androgyny. *Journal of Consulting and Clinical Psychology, 42,* 155–162.

———— (1975). Sex-role adaptability: One consequence of psychological androgyny. *Journal of Personality and Social Psychology, 31,* 634–643.

———— (1977). On the utility of alternative procedures for assessing psychological androgyny. *Journal of Consulting and Clinical Psychology, 45,* 196–205.

———— (1981). Gender schema theory: A cognitive account of sex-typing. *Psychological Review, 88,* 354–364.

———— (1983). Gender schema theory and its implications for child development: Raising gender-aschematic children in a gender-schematic society. *Signs, 8,* 598–616.

Bem, Sandra L., & Bem, D. J. (1970). Case study of nonconscious ideology: Training the woman to know her place. In D. J. Bem (Ed.), *Beliefs, attitudes, and human affairs.* Belmont, CA: Brooks/Cole.

Bem, Sandra, L., & Lenney, Ellen (1976). Sex-typing and the avoidance of cross-sex behavior. *Journal of Personality and Social Psychology, 33,* 48–54.

Bem, Sandra L., Martyna, W., & Watson, C. (1976). Sex typing and androgyny: Further explorations of the expressive domain. *Journal of Personality and Social Psychology, 34,* 1016–1023.

Benedek, Therese F. (1959). Sexual functions in women and their disturbance. In S. Arieti, *American Handbook of Psychiatry.* New York: Basic Books.

Benedek, Therese, & Rubenstein, B. B. (1942). The sexual cycle in women: The relation between ovarian function and psychodynamic processes. *Psychonomic Medicine Monographs, 3,* 1–307.

Bentzen, F. (1963). Sex ratios in learning and behavior disorders. *American Journal of Orthopsychiatry, 33,* 92–98.

Berardo, F. (1968). Widowhood status in the United States: Perspective on a neglected aspect of the family life-cycle. *Family Coordinator, 17,* 191–203.

Berg, Phyllis, & Hyde, Janet S. (1976, September). *Gender and race differences in causal attributions.* Paper presented at American Psychological Association Meetings.

Berman, Ellen, Sacks, Sylvia, & Lief, H. (1975). The two-professional marriage: A new conflict syndrome. *Journal of Marital and Sex Therapy, 1,* 242–253.

Berman, Phyllis W., O'Nan, Barbara A., & Floyd, W. (1981). The double standard of aging and the social situation. *Sex Roles, 7*, 87–96.

Bermant, G. (1972). Behavior therapy approaches to modification of sexual preferences: Biological perspective and critique. Paper presented at the California State Psychological Association. Reprinted in J. Bardwick (Ed.), *Readings on the psychology of women.* New York: Harper & Row.

Bernard, Jesse (1966). *Marriage and family among Negroes.* New York: Prentice-Hall.

Berscheid, Ellen, et al. (1971). Physical attractiveness and dating choice: A test of the matching hypothesis. *Journal of Experimental Social Psychology, 7,* 173–189.

Bettelheim, B. (1962). *Symbolic wounds.* New York: Collier Books.

Bibring, Grete L., Dwyer, T. F., Huntington, D. S., & Valenstein, A. F. (1961). A study of the psychological processes in pregnancy and of the earliest mother-child relationship. In *The Psychoanalytic Study of the Child, 16.* New York: International Universities Press.

Biller, H. B. (1971). *Father, child, and the sex role.* Lexington, MA: D. C. Heath.

————— (1974). *Paternal deprivation: Family, school, sexuality and society.* Lexington, MA: D.C. Heath.

Biller, H. B., & Bahm, R. M. (1971). Father absence, perceived maternal behavior, and masculinity of self-concept among junior high school boys. *Developmental Psychology, 4,* 178–181.

Bird, Caroline (1968). *Born female.* New York: David McKay.

Birnbaum, Judith A. (1975). Life patterns and self-esteem in gifted family oriented and career committed women. In M. Mednick, L. W. Hoffman, & S. Tangri (Eds.), *Women and achievement: Social and motivational analyses.* New York: Halsted Press.

Blair, G. E. (1972). The relationship of selected ego functions and academic achievement of Negro students. *Dissertation Abstracts, 28,* 3031A.

Blanchard, W. H. (1959). The group process in gang rape. *Journal of Social Psychology, 49,* 259–266.

Blau, Zena Smith (1973). *Old age in a changing society.* New York: New Viewpoints.

Blaubergs, Maija S. (1978). Changing the sexist language: The theory behind the practice. *Psychology of Women Quarterly, 2,* 244–261.

Bleckman, Elaine A. (1980). Behavior therapies. In A. M. Brodsky and R. Hare-Mustin (Eds.), *Women and psychotherapy.* New York: Guilford.

Block, Jeanne H. (1973). Conceptions of sex role: Some cross-cultural and longitudinal perspectives. *American Psychologist, 28,* 512–526.

————— (1976). Issues, problems and pitfalls in assessing sex differences. *Merrill-Palmer Quarterly, 22,* 283–308.

————— (1978). Another look at sex differentiation in the socialization behaviors of mothers and fathers. In J. Sherman & F. Denmark (Eds.),

Psychology of women: Future directions of research. New York: Psych Dimensions.

Block, M. A. (1962). *Alcoholism: Its facets and phases.* London: Oxford University Press.

Blumstein, P. W., & Schwartz, Pepper (1976). Bisexual women. In J. P. Wiseman (Ed.), *The social psychology of sex.* New York: Harper & Row.

Bock, E. W. (1969). Farmer's daughter effect: the case of the Negro female professionals. *Phylon, 30,* 17–26.

Bock, E. W., & Webber, I. (1972). Suicide among the elderly: Isolating widowhood and mitigating alternatives. *Journal of Marriage and the Family, 34,* 24–31.

Bock, R. D., & Kolakowski, D. (1973). Further evidence of sex-linked major-gene influence on human spatial visualizing ability. *American Journal of Human Genetics, 25,* 1–14.

Bodine, Ann (1975). Sex differentiation in language. In B. Thorne and N. Henley (Eds.), *Language and sex: Difference and dominance.* Rowley, MA: Newbury House.

Bohannon, P. (Ed.) (1970). *Divorce and after.* Garden City, NY: Doubleday.

Bonaparte, Marie (1953) *Female sexuality.* New York: International Universities Press. (Reprinted 1965. New York: Grove Press.)

Booth, A. (1977). Wives' employment and husbands' stress: A replication and refutation. *Journal of Marriage and the Family, 39,* 645–650.

Boskind-Lodahl, Marlene (1976). Cinderella's stepsisters: A feminist perspective on anorexia nervosa and bulimia. *Signs, 2,* 120–146.

Boskind-Lodahl, Marlene, & Sirlin, Joyce (1977). The gorging-purging syndrome. *Psychology Today,* March, *10*(10), 50.

Bosselman, Beulah C. (1960). Castration anxiety and phallus envy: A reformulation. *Psychiatric Quarterly, 34,* 252–259.

Boston Women's Health Book Collective (1976). *Our bodies, ourselves.* New York: Simon & Shuster.

Bouchard, T. J., & McGee, M. G. (1977). Sex differences in human spatial ability: Not an X-linked recessive gene effect. *Social Biology, 24,* 332–335.

Brackbill, Yvonne, & Schroder, Kerri (1980). Circumcision, gender differences, and neonatal behavior: An update. *Developmental Psychobiology, 13,* 607–614.

Bracken, M., Klerman, L., & Bracken, M. (1978). Abortion, adoption, and motherhood: An empirical study of decision-making during pregnancy. *American Journal of Obstetrics and Gynecology, 130*(3), 251–262.

Bradburn, W., & Caplovitz, D. (1965). *Reports on happiness.* Chicago: Aldine.

Brady, J. P., & Rieger, W. (1975). Behavioral treatment in anorexia nervosa. In T. Thompson and W. Dockens (Eds.), *Applications of behavior modification.* New York: Academic Press.

Brannon, R., & David, D. S. (1976). The male sex role: Our culture's blueprint of manhood, and what it's done for us lately. In D. S. David and R. Brannon (Eds.), *The forty-nine percent majority*. Reading, MA: Addison-Wesley.

Brecher, Ruth, & Brecher, E. (1966). *An analysis of human sexual response.* Boston: Little, Brown.

Brend, Ruth M. (1971). Male-female intonation patterns in American English. *Proceedings of the 7th International Congress of Phonetic Sciences*, 866–869. The Hague: Mouton. (Reprinted in B. Thorne and N. Henley (Eds.), *Language and sex: Difference and dominance*. Rowley, MA: Newbury House, 1975.)

Bridgette, R. E. (1970). Self-esteem in Negro and white southern adolescents. Unpublished Ph.D. dissertation, University of North Carolina at Chapel Hill.

Brien, Lois, & Sheldon, Cynthia (1977). Gestalt therapy and women. In E. I. Rawlings and D. K. Carter (Eds.), *Psychotherapy for women*. Springfield, IL: Charles C Thomas.

Briffault, R. (1927). *The mothers*. New York: Macmillan.

Brim, O. J. (1957). The parent-child relation as a social system: 1. Parent and child roles. *Child Development, 28*, 343–364.

——— (1958). Family structure and sex role learning in children: A further analysis of Helen Koch's data. *Sociometry, 21*, 1–16.

——— (1960). Personality development as role learning. In I. Iscoe and H. Stevenson (Eds.), *Personality development in children*. Austin: University of Texas Press.

——— (1976). Theories of the male mid-life crisis. *Counseling Psychologist, 6*(1), 2–9.

Broderick, C. (1965). Social heterosexual development among urban Negroes and whites. *Journal of Marriage and the Family, 27*, 200–203.

Brodsky, Annette (1977). Therapeutic aspects of consciousness-raising groups. In E. I. Rawlings and D. K. Carter (Eds.), *Psychotherapy for women*. Springfield, IL: Charles C Thomas.

——— (1978). A decade of feminist influence on psychotherapy. Presidential address to Division 35 of the American Psychological Association, Toronto.

Brodsky, Carroll M. (1976). Rape at work. In M. J. Walker and S. L. Brodsky (Eds.), *Sexual assault: The victim and the rapist*. Lexington, MA: D. C. Heath.

Bronfenbrenner, U. (1970). *Two worlds of childhood*. New York: Sage.

Brooks, Virginia R. (1981). *Minority stress and lesbian women*. Lexington, MA: Lexington Books.

Broverman, Inge K., Broverman, D. M., Clarkson, F. E., Rosenkrantz, P. S., & Vogel, S. R. (1970). Sex role stereotypes and clinical judgments of mental health. *Journal of Consulting and Clinical Psychology, 34*, 1–7.

Broverman, Inge K., Vogel, Susan R., Broverman, D. M., Clarkson, F. E. & Rosenkrantz, P. S. (1972). Sex role stereotypes: A current appraisal. *Journal of Social Issues, 28*, 59–78.

Brown, C. A., Feldberg, R., Fox, E. M., & Kohen, J. (1976). Divorce: Chance of a new lifetime. *Journal of Social Issues, 32*(1), 119–133.

Brown, D. R. (1968). *Role and status of women in the Soviet Union.* New York: Teachers College Press.

Brown, R. (1965). *Social Psychology.* New York: Free Press.

Brownmiller, Susan (1975). *Against our will: Men, women, and rape.* New York: Simon & Schuster.

Brussel, J. A. (1971). Comment following Menachem Amir. Forcible rape. *Sexual Behavior, 1,* 8.

Buczek, Teresa A. (1981). Sex biases in counseling: Counselor retention of the concerns of a female and male client. *Journal of Counseling Psychology, 28,* 13–21.

Budoff, Penny W. (1981). *No more menstrual cramps and other good news.* New York: Penguin Books.

Buffery, A. W. H., & Gray, J. A. (1972). Sex differences in the development of spatial and linguistic skills. In C. Ounsted and D. C. Taylor (Eds.), *Gender differences: Their ontogeny and significance.* Baltimore, MD: Williams & Wilkins.

Bugental, Daphne E., Love, Leonore R., Gianetto, Robert M. (1971). Perfidious feminine faces. *Journal of Personality and Social Psychology, 17,* 314–318.

Burgess, Ann W., Holmstrom, Lynda L. (1974a). Rape trauma syndrome. *American Journal of Psychiatry, 131,* 981–986.

——— (1974b). *Rape: Victims of crisis.* Bowie, MD: Robert J. Brady Company.

Burt, Martha R., & Estep, Rhoda E. (1981). Apprehension and fear: Learning a sense of sexual vulnerability. *Sex Roles, 7,* 511–522.

Bussey, Kay, & Maughan, Betty (1982). Gender differences in moral reasoning. *Journal of Personality and Social Psychology, 42,* 701–706.

Cade, Toni (ed.) (1970). *The black woman.* New York: New American Library.

Calahan, D., Cislin, I. H., Crossley, H. M. (1969). *American drinking practices: A national study of drinking behavior and attitudes.* New Haven, CT: College and University Press.

Caldie, Roberta W. (1981). *Dominance and language: A new perspective on sexism.* Washington: University Press of America.

Caldwell, Mayta A., Peplau, Letitia Anne (1982). Sex differences in same-sex friendship. *Sex Roles, 8,* 721–732.

Campbell, A., Converse, P. E., & Rodgers, W. L. (1975). *The quality of American life.* Ann Arbor, MI: ISR Social Science Archive.

Candy, Sandra G., Troll, Lillian E., & Levy, S. G. (1981). A developmental exploration of friendship functions in women. *Psychology of Women Quarterly, 5,* 456–472.

Caplan, G. (1960). Emotional implications of pregnancy and influences on family relationships. In H. C. Stuart and D. G. Prugh (Eds.), *The healthy child.* Cambridge, MA: Harvard University Press.

Carlson, Rae (1971a). Where is the person in personality research? *Psychological Bulletin, 75*, 203–219.

———— (1971b). Sex differences in ego functioning. *Journal of Consulting and Clinical Psychology, 37*, 267–277.

———— (1972). Understanding women: Implications for personality theory and research. *Journal of Social Issues, 28*(2), 17–32.

Carpenter, T. R., & Busse, T. V. (1969). Development of self-concept in Negro and white welfare children. *Child Development, 40*, 935–939.

Carroll, Janell, Volk, Kari, & Hyde, Janet S. (1984). Differences between males and females in motives for engaging in sexual intercourse. *Archives of Sexual Behavior*, in press.

Castle, C. S. (1913). A statistical study of eminent women. *Archives of Psychology, 27*.

Cazenave, Noel A. (1979). Middle-income black fathers: An analysis of the provider role. *Family Coordinator*, 583–593.

Chafetz, Janet S. (1974). *Masculine/feminine or human? An overview of the sociology of sex roles.* Itasca, IL: F. E. Peacock.

Cherry, Frances, & Deaux, Kay (1978). Fear of success versus fear of gender-inappropriate behavior. *Sex Roles, 4*, 97–102.

Chesler, Phyllis (1972). *Women and madness.* Garden City, NY: Doubleday.

———— (1978). *About men.* New York: Simon & Schuster.

Chess, S. (1960). Diagnosis and treatment of hyperkinetic children. *New York State Journal of Medicine, 60*, 2379.

Chisholm, Shirley (1971). Race, revolution and women. *The Black Scholar*, December.

Chodorow, Nancy (1974). Family structure and feminine personality. In M. Z. Rosaldo & L. Lamphere (Eds.), *Woman, culture, and society.* Stanford: Stanford University Press.

———— (1978). *The reproduction of mothering.* Berkeley: University of California Press.

Christmas, June J. (1973). Self-concept and attitudes. In K. S. Miller & R. M. Dreger (Eds.), *Comparative studies of blacks and whites in the United States.* New York: Academic Press.

Clark, K. B., & Clark, Mamie P. (1947). Racial identification and preferences in Negro children. In T. M. Newcomb and E. L. Hartley (Eds.), *Readings in social psychology.* New York: Holt, Rinehart & Winston.

Clay, W. L. (1975). The socio-economic status of blacks. *Ebony*, September, 29.

Cobb, Nancy J., et al. (1982). The influence of televised models on toy preference in children. *Sex Roles, 8*, 1075–1080.

Cohen, L. J., & Campos, J. J. (1974). Father, mother and strangers as elicitors of attachment behaviors in infancy. *Developmental Psychology, 10*, 146–154.

Cohen, M. L., Garofalo, R., Boucher, R., & Seghorn, T. (1971). The psychology of rapists. *Seminars in Psychiatry, 3,* 311.

Colby, Ann, Kohlberg, L., et al. (1983). A longitudinal study of moral development. *Monographs of the Society for Research in Child Development,* 48(200).

Coleman, J. (1976). Athletics in high school. In D. S. David and R. Brannon (Eds.), *The forty-nine percent majority: The male sex role.* Reading, MA: Addison-Wesley.

Constantinople, Anne (1973). Masculinity-femininity. An exception to a famous dictum. *Psychological Bulletin, 80,* 389–407.

Cooperstock, R. (1971). Sex differences in the use of mood-modifying drugs: An explanatory model. *Journal of Health and Social Behavior, 12,* 238–244.

———— (1976). Women and psychotropic drugs. In A. MacLennan (Ed.), *Women: Their use of alcohol and other legal drugs.* Toronto, Canada: Addiction Research Foundation of Ontario.

Cordaro, L., & Ison, J. R. (1963). Psychology of the scientist: X. Observer bias in classical conditioning of the planarian. *Psychological Reports, 13,* 787–789.

Cosentino, F., & Heilbrun, A. B. (1964). Anxiety correlates of sex-role identity in college students. *Psychological Reports, 14,* 729–730.

Costrich, N., et al. (1975). When stereotypes hurt: Three studies of penalties for sex-role reversals. *Journal of Experimental Social Psychology, 11,* 520–530.

Crandall, Virginia C. (1967). Achievement behavior in young children. In W. W. Hartup & Nancy L. Smothergill (Eds.), *The young child: Reviews of research.* Washington, DC: National Association for the Education of Young Children.

———— (1969). Sex differences in expectancy of intellectual and academic reinforcement. In C. P. Smith (Ed.), *Achievement-related motives in children.* New York: Russell Sage Foundation.

———— (1978). Expecting sex differences and sex differences in expectancies: A developmental analysis. Paper presented at American Psychological Association Meetings, Toronto, August.

Crovitz, Elaine, & Steinman, Anne (1980). A decade later: Black-white attitudes toward women's familial role. *Psychology of Women Quarterly,* 5, 170–176.

Cvejic, H., et al. (1977). Follow-up of 50 adolescent girls two years after abortion. *Canadian Medical Association Journal, 116,* 44–46.

Dahlstrom, E. (Ed.) (1971). *The changing roles of men and women.* Boston: Beacon Press.

Dalton, Katharina (1964). *The premenstrual syndrome.* Springfield, IL: Charles C Thomas.

———— (1966). The influence of mother's menstruation on her child. *Proceedings of the Royal Society for Medicine, 59,* 1014.

Dan, A. J., Beekman, S. (1972). Male versus female representation in psychological research. *American Psychologist, 27,* 1078.

D'Andrade, R. G. (1966). Sex differences and cultural institutions. In E. E. Maccoby (Ed.), *The development of sex differences.* Stanford: Stanford University Press.

Daneal, J. (1975). A definition of fatherhood as expressed by black fathers. Unpublished doctoral dissertation, University of Pittsburgh.

Davidson, Lynne R., & Duberman, Lucile (1982). Friendship: Communication and interactional patterns in same-sex dyads. *Sex Roles, 8,* 809–822.

Davidson, S., & Packard, T. (1981). The therapeutic value of friendship between women. *Psychology of Women Quarterly, 5,* 495–510.

Davis, Elizabeth Gould (1971). *The first sex.* New York: G. P. Putnam's Sons.

Davis, K. E. (1971). Sex on campus. Is there a revolution? *Medical Aspects of Human Sexuality,* January, 128–142.

Deaux, Kay (1976). *The behavior of women and men.* Monterey, CA: Brooks/Cole.

Deaux, Kay, & Emswiller, T. (1974). Explanations of successful performance on sex-linked tasks: What is skill for the male is luck for the female. *Journal of Personality and Social Psychology, 29,* 80–85.

Deaux, Kay, & Taynor, Janet (1973). Evaluation of male and female ability: Bias works two ways. *Psychological Reports, 32,* 261–262.

de Castillejo, Irene C. (1973). *Knowing woman: A feminine psychology.* New York: G. P. Putnam's Sons.

Deckard, Barbara S. (1983). *The women's movement* (3rd ed.). New York: Harper & Row.

DeFries, J. C., et al. (1976). Parent-offspring resemblance for specific cognitive abilities in two ethnic groups. *Nature, 261,* 131–133.

Delaney, Janice, Lupton, Mary Jane, & Toth, Emily (1976). *The curse: A cultural history of menstruation.* New York: E. P. Dutton.

Dellas, M., & Gaier, E. L. (1975). The self and adolescent identity in women: Options and implications. *Adolescence, 10,* 399–407.

Denmark, Florence L., & Goodfield, Helen M. (1978). A second look at adolescence theories. *Sex Roles, 4,* 375–380.

Deutsch, Helen (1924). The psychology of woman in relation to the functions of reproduction. *International Journal of Psychoanalysis, 6.*

——— (1944). *The psychology of women.* New York: Grune & Stratton.

Diamond, M. (1965). A critical evaluation of the ontogeny of human sexual behavior. *Quarterly Review of Biology, 40,* 147–175.

——— (1979). Sexual identity and sex roles. In V. Bullough (Ed.), *The frontiers of sex research.* Buffalo, NY: Prometheus Books.

Diner, Helen (1930). *Mothers and Amazons: The first feminine history of culture.* (Originally in German; U.S. edition in 1965. New York: Julian Press.)

Dobert, Margarete (1975). Tradition, modernity and woman power in Africa. In M. S. Mednick, L. W. Hoffman, & S. S. Tangri (Eds.), *Women:*

psychological perspectives on achievement. Washington, DC: Hemisphere.

Dodge, Laura J. T. et al. (1982). Bibliotherapy in the treatment of female orgasmic dysfunction. *Journal of Consulting and Clinical Psychology, 50,* 442–443.

Donelson, Elaine (1977). Becoming a single woman. In E. Donelson and J. Gullahorn (Eds.), *Women: A psychological perspective.* New York: John Wiley.

Dornbusch, S. M. (1966). Afterword. In E. E. Maccoby (Ed.), *The development of sex differences.* Stanford: Stanford University Press.

Dörner, G. (1969). Prophylaxie und therapie angeborener sexualdeviatonen. *Deutsche Medizinische Wochenschrift-Sonderdruck,* February 2.

Douvan, Elizabeth (1970). New sources of conflicts in females at adolescence and early adulthood. In J. Bardwick, E. Douvan, M. Horner, & D. Gutman (Eds.), *Feminine personality and conflict.* Belmont, CA: Brooks/Cole.

Douvan, Elizabeth, & Adelson, J. (1966). *The adolescent experience.* New York: John Wiley.

Dowty, Nancy (1972). To be a woman in Israel. *School Review, 80,* 319–332.

Doyle, James A. (1983). *The male experience.* Dubuque, IA: William C. Brown.

Dreger, Ralph M., et al. (1964). Behavioral classification project. *Journal of Consulting Psychology, 28,* 1–13.

Dweck, Carol S., & Reppucci, N. D., (1973). Learned helplessness and reinforcement responsibility in children. *Journal of Personality and Social Psychology, 25,* 109–116.

Dworkin, Andrea (1981). *Pornography: Men possessing women.* New York: Putnam.

Dworkin, Rosalind J. (1981). Prestige ranking of the housewife occupation. *Sex Roles, 7,* 59–64.

Dwyer, J. T., et al. (1969). Body image in adolescents: Attitudes toward weight and perception of appearance. *American Journal of Clinical Nutrition, 20,* 1045–1056.

Dziech, Billie W., & Weiner, Linda (1983). *The lecherous professor: Sexual harassment.* Boston: Beacon.

Eagly, Alice H. (1978). Sex differences in influenceability. *Psychological Bulletin, 85,* 86–116.

Eagly, Alice H., & Carli, Linda L. (1981). Sex of researchers and sex-typed communications as determinants of sex differences in influenceability: A meta-analysis of social influence studies. *Psychological Bulletin, 90,* 1–20.

Edwards, D. A. (1969). Early androgen stimulation and aggressive behavior in male and female mice. *Physiology and Behavior, 4,* 333–338.

Ehrhardt, Anke A., & Meyer-Bahlburg, Heino (1981). Effects of prenatal sex hormones on gender-related behavior. *Science, 211,* 1312–1318.

Eichenbaum, Luise, & Orbach, Susie (1983). *Understanding women: A feminist psychoanalytic approach.* New York: Basic Books.

Eisenberg, Nancy, & Lennon, Randy (1983). Sex differences in empathy and related capacities. *Psychological Bulletin, 94,* 100–131.

Eisenstein, Zilla R. (1982). The sexual politics of the New Right: Understanding the "Crisis of Liberalism" for the 1980s. In N. O. Keohane et al. (Eds.), *Feminist theory.* Chicago: University of Chicago Press.

Elder, Glenn H. (1969). Appearance and education in marriage mobility. *American Sociological Review, 34,* 519–533.

Engs, R. C. (1977). Drinking patterns and drinking problems of college students. *Journal of Studies on Alcohol, 38,* 2144–2156.

Epstein, Cynthia F. (1970). *Woman's place: Options and limits in professional careers.* Berkeley: University of California Press.

——— (1973a). Positive effects of the multiple negative. *American Journal of Sociology, 78,* 912–935.

——— (1973b, August). Black and female: The double whammy. *Psychology Today, 7*(3), 57.

Erikson, E. H. (1950). *Childhood and society.* New York: Norton.

——— (1959). Identity and the life cycle. *Psychological Issues, 1*(1).

——— (1964). Inner and outer space: Reflections on womanhood. In R. J. Lifton (Ed.), *The woman in America.* Boston: Beacon.

Eron, Leonard, et al. (1974). The convergence of laboratory and field studies of the development of aggression. In J. de Wit & W. W. Hartup (Eds.), *Determinants and origins of aggressive behavior.* The Hague: Mouton.

Ervin, C. V. (1973). Psychologic adjustment in mastectomy. *Medical Aspects of Human Sexuality,* February, 7(2), 42–45.

Fabrikant, B. (1974). The psychotherapist and the female patient: Perceptions, misconceptions and change. In V. Franks & V. Burtle (Eds.), *Women in therapy.* New York: Brunner/Mazel.

Faderman, Lillian (1981). *Surpassing the love of men: Romantic friendship and love between women from the Renaissance to the present.* New York: William Morrow.

Fagot, Beverly, & Patterson, G. (1969). An *in vivo* analysis of reinforcing contingencies for sex-role behaviors in the preschool child. *Developmental Psychology, 1,* 563–568.

Falbo, Toni (1982). PAQ types and power strategies used in intimate relationships. *Psychology of Women Quarterly, 6,* 399–405.

Fasteau, M. F. (1974). *The male machine.* New York: McGraw-Hill.

Faulk, M. (1974). Men who assault their wives. *Medicine, Science, and Law, 14,* 180–183. (Reprinted 1977 in M. Roy (Ed.), *Battered women.* New York: Van Nostrand.)

Feather, N. T. (1969). Attribution of responsibility and valence of success and failure in relation to initial confidence and perceived locus of control. *Journal of Personality and Social Psychology, 13,* 129–144.

Feild, Hubert S. (1978). Attitudes toward rape: A comparative analysis of police, rapists, crisis counselors, and citizens. *Journal of Personality and Social Psychology, 36,* 156–179.

Feinman, S. (1981). The limits of masculinity: Male identity and women's liberation. *Sex Roles, 7,* 577–579.

Feshbach, S. and Malamuth, N. (1978, November). Sex and aggression: Proving the link. *Psychology Today, 12*(6), 110.

Fidell, L. S. (1970). Empirical verification of sex discrimination in hiring practices in psychology. *American Psychologist, 25,* 1094–1098.

Fidell, Linda, Hoffman, Donnie, & Keith-Spiegel, Patti (1979). Some social implications of sex-choice technology. *Psychology of Women Quarterly, 4,* 32–42.

Fillmore, K. M. (1974). Drinking and problem drinking in early adulthood and middle age: An exploratory 20-year follow-up study. *Quarterly Journal of Studies on Alcohol, 35,* 819–840.

—— (1975). Relationships between specific drinking problems in early adulthood and middle age. *Quarterly Journal of Studies on Alcohol, 36,* 882–907.

Finkelhor, D. (1980). Sex among siblings: A survey on prevalence, variety and effects. *Archives of Sexual Behavior, 9,* 171–194.

Firestone, S. (1970). *The dialectic of sex.* New York. Bantam,

Fisher, S. (1973). *Understanding the female orgasm.* New York: Basic Books.

Fisher, S., & Osofsky, H. (1967). Sexual responsiveness in women: Psychological correlates. *Archives of General Psychiatry, 17,* 214–226.

Fishman, Pamela M. (1978). Interaction: The work women do. *Social Problems, 25,* 397–405.

Fling, S., & Mamosevitz, M. (1972). Sex typing in nursery school children's play interests. *Developmental Psychology, 7,* 146–152.

Fogarty, M. P., Rapoport, Rhona, & Rapoport, R. (1971). *Sex, career, and family.* Beverly Hills, CA: Sage Publications.

Ford, C. S., & Beach, F. A. (1951). *Patterns of sexual behavior.* New York: Harper & Row.

Forden, Carie (1981). The influence of sex-role expectations on the perception of touch. *Sex Roles, 7,* 889–894.

Forssman, H., & Thuwe, I. (1966). One hundred and twenty children born after application for therapeutic abortion refused. *Acta Psychiatrica Scandinavica, 43,* 71–88.

Franck, Kate, & Rosen, L. (1949), A projective test of masculinity and femininity. *Journal of Consulting Psychology, 13,* 247–256.

Frank, E., et al. (1978). Frequency of sexual dysfunction in "normal" couples. *New England Journal of Medicine, 299*(3), 111–115.

Frank, R. T. (1931). The hormonal causes of premenstrual tension. *Archives of Neurological Psychiatry, 26,* 1053.

Franks, Violet, & Burtle, V. (1974). *Women in therapy.* New York: Brunner/Mazel.

Freedman, J. L., Carlsmith, J. M., & Sears, D. O. (1970). *Social psychology.* Englewood Cliffs, NJ: Prentice-Hall.

Freedman, M. J. (1968). Homosexuality among women and psychological adjustment. *Ladder, 12,* 2–3.

French, E. G. (1964). Some characteristics of the achievement motive in women. *Journal of Abnormal and Social Psychology, 68,* 119–128.

Freud, S. (1933). *New introductory lectures in psychoanalysis.* New York: W. W. Norton.

———— (1948). Some psychical consequences of the anatomical distinction between the sexes. In J. Riviere (trans.), *Collected papers,* Vol. V, pp. 186–197. London: Hogarth Press.

———— (1955). *The interpretation of dreams.* J. Strachey, (trans.). New York: Basic Books.

Friedman, M., & Rosenman, R. H. (1974). *Type A behavior and your heart.* New York: Fawcett Books.

Frieze, Irene H. (1983). Causes and consequences of marital rape. *Signs, 8,* 532–553.

Frieze, Irene H., & Ramsey, S. J. (1976). Nonverbal maintenance of traditional sex roles. *Journal of Social Issues, 32*(3), 133–141.

Frieze, Irene H., Parsons, Jacquelynne E., Johnson, Paula B., Ruble, Diane N., & Zellman, Gail L. (1978). *Women and sex roles: A social psychological perspective.* New York: W. W. Norton.

Frieze, Irene H., et al. (1982). Assessing the theoretical models for sex differences in causal attributions for success and failure. *Sex Roles, 8,* 333–334.

Frodi, Ann, Macauley, Jacqueline, & Thome, Pauline R. (1977). Are women always less aggressive than men? A review of the experimental literature. *Psychological Bulletin, 84,* 634–660.

Furstenberg, F. (1971). Birth control experience among pregnant adolescents: The process of planned parenthood. *Social Problems, 19,* 192–203.

Gagnon, John H. (1977). *Human sexualities.* Glenview, IL: Scott, Foresman.

Gainer, W. L. (1962). Ability of the WISC subtests to discriminate between boys and girls of average intelligence. *California Journal of Educational Research, 13,* 9–16.

Gall, M. D. (1969). The relationship between masculinity-femininity and manifest anxiety. *Journal of Clinical Psychology, 25,* 294–295.

Garfinkel, Paul E., & Garner, D. M. (1982). *Anorexia nervosa: A multidimensional perspective.* New York: Brunner/Mazel.

Gayford, J. S. (1975). Wife battering: A preliminary survey of 100 cases. *British Medical Journal,* January 25, 196.

Gebhard, P. H., Gagnon, J. H., Pomeroy, W. B., & Christenson, C. V. (1965). *Sex offenders: An analysis of types.* New York: Harper & Row.

Gebhard, P. H., Pomeroy, W. B., Martin, C. E., & Christenson, Cornelia V. (1958). *Pregnancy: Birth and abortion.* New York: John Wiley.

Gelles, Richard (1974). *The violent home: A study of physical aggression between husbands and wives.* New York: Sage Publications.

Gerson, Mary-Joan (1980). The lure of motherhood. *Psychology of Women Quarterly, 5,* 207–218.

Gesell, A. (1940). *The first five years of life.* New York: Harper.

Gigy, Lynn L. (1980). Self-concept of single women. *Psychology of Women Quarterly, 5,* 321–340.

Gilbert, Lucia A. (1980). Feminist therapy. In A. Brodsky & R. Hare-Mustin (Eds.), *Women and psychotherapy.* New York: Guilford.

Gilkes, Cheryl T. (1982). Successful rebellious professionals: The black woman's professional identity and community commitment. *Psychology of Women Quarterly, 6,* 289–311.

Gilley, H. M., & Collier, S. S. (1970). Sex differences in the use of hostile verbs. *Journal of Psychology, 76,* 33–37.

Gilligan, Carol (1982b). *In a different voice: Psychological theory and women's development.* Cambridge, MA: Harvard University Press.

Ginzberg, E., et al. (1966). *Life styles of educated women.* New York: Columbia University Press.

Goble, F. C., & Konopka, E. A. (1973). Sex as a factor in infectious disease. *Transactions of the New York Academy of Science, 35,* 325.

Goffman, E. (1967). *Interaction ritual: Essays on face-to-face behavior.* Garden City, NY: Anchor Books.

————— (1977). Genderisms. *Psychology Today, 11*(3), 60.

Gold, Delores, & Reis, Myrna (1982). Male teacher effects on young children: A theoretical and empirical consideration. *Sex Roles, 8,* 493–514.

Goldberg, Daniel C., et al. (1983). The Grafenberg spot and female ejaculation: A review of initial hypotheses. *Journal of Sex and Marital Therapy, 9,* 27–37.

Goldberg, P. (1968). Are some women prejudiced against women? *Transaction,* April, *5,* 28–30.

Goldberg, Susan, & Lewis, M. (1969). Play behavior in the year-old infant: Early sex differences. *Child Development, 40,* 21–31.

Goldstein, Alvin G., & Jeffords, Judy (1981). Status and touching behavior. *Bulletin of the Psychonomic Society, 17,* 79–81.

Goleman, Daniel (1976). Jason and Medea's love story. *Psychology Today, 9*(11), 84.

————— (1978). Special abilities of the sexes: Do they begin in the brain? *Psychology Today, 12*(6), 48.

Golub, Sharon (1976). The effect of premenstrual anxiety and depression on cognitive function. *Journal of Personality and Social Psychology, 34,* 99–104.

Gomberg, Edith S. (1974). Women and alcoholism. In V. Franks and V. Burtle (Eds.), *Women in therapy.* New York: Brunner/Mazel.

————— (1979). Problems with alcohol and other drugs. In E. S. Gomberg & V. Franks (Eds.), *Gender and disordered behavior.* New York: Brunner/Mazel.

Gomberg, Edith, & Franks, Violet (1979). *Gender and disordered behavior.* New York: Brunner/Mazel.

Gomes, Beverly, & Abramowitz, S. I. (1976). Sex-related patient and therapist effects on clinical judgment. *Sex Roles, 2,* 1–14.

Goode, E., & Haber, L. (1977). Sexual correlates of homosexual experience: An exploratory study of college women. *Journal of Sex Research, 13,* 12–21.

Gordon, E. M. (1967). Acceptance of pregnancy before and since oral contraception. *Obstetrics and Gynecology, 29,* 144–146.

Gordon, R. E., & Gordon, Katherine K. (1967). Factors in postpartum emotional adjustment. *American Journal of Orthopsychiatry, 37,* 359–360.

Gordon, R. E., Kapostins, E. E., & Gordon, Katherine K. (1965). Factors in postpartum emotional adjustment. *Obstetrics and Gynecology, 25,* 158–166.

Gottschalk, L. A., Gleser, Goldine D., & Winget, Carolyn M. (1962). Variations in magnitude of emotion: A method applied to anxiety and hostility during phases of the menstrual cycle. *Psychosomatic Medicine, 24,* 300–311.

Gough, H. G. (1952). Identifying psychological femininity. *Educational and Psychological Measurement, 12,* 427–439.

——— (1957). *Manual for the California psychological inventory.* Palo Alto, CA: Consulting Psychologists Press. (Rev. ed., 1964.)

——— (1966). A cross-cultural analysis of the CPI femininity scale. *Journal of Consulting Psychology, 30,* 136–141.

Gove, W. R., & Tudor, Jeannette F. (1973). Adult sex roles and mental illness. *American Journal of Sociology, 78,* 812–835.

Grady, Kathleen E. (1981). Sex bias in research design. *Psychology of Women Quarterly, 5,* 628–636.

Gray, S. W. (1957). Masculinity-femininity in relation to anxiety and social acceptance. *Child Development, 28,* 203–214.

Green, R. (1975). Adults who want to change sex; adolescents who cross-dress; and children called "sissy" and "tomboy." In R. Green (Ed.), *Human sexuality: A health practitioner's text.* Baltimore: Williams & Wilkins.

Greenblatt, R. (1955). Metabolic and psychosomatic disorders in menopausal women. *Geriatrics, 10,* 165.

Greenglass, Esther R., & Devins, Reva (1982). Factors related to marriage and career plans in unmarried women. *Sex Roles, 8,* 57–72.

Grier, W. H., & Cobbs, P. M. (1968). *Black rage.* New York: Basic Books.

Gross, Alan E. (1978). The male role and heterosexual behavior. *Journal of Social Issues, 34*(1), 87–107.

Gruber, Kenneth J., Jones, R. J., & Freeman, M. H. (1982). Youth reactions to sexual assault. *Adolescence, 17,* 541–551.

Gurin, G., Veroff, J., & Feld S. (1960). *Americans view their mental health.* New York: Basic Books.

Gurin, Patricia (1981). Labor market experiences and expectancies. *Sex Roles, 7,* 1079–1092.

Guttman, D. (1976). Individual adaptation in the middle years: Development issues in the masculine mid-life crisis. *Journal of Geriatric Psychology, 9*(1), 41–59.

Haan, Norma (1975). Hypothetical and actual moral reasoning in a situation of civil disobedience. *Journal of Personality and Social Psychology, 32,* 255–270.

Haavio-Mannila, Elina (1967). Sex differentiation in role expectations and performance. *Journal of Marriage and the Family, 29,* 568–578.

Hacker, Helen M. (1951). Women as a minority group, *Social Forces, 30,* 60–69.

Hall, C. S., & Lindzey, G. (1970). *Theories of personality* (2nd ed.). New York: John Wiley.

Hall, Judith A. (1978). Gender effects in decoding nonverbal cues. *Psychological Bulletin, 85,* 845–857.

———— (1979). Gender, gender roles, and nonverbal communication skills. In R. Rosenthal (Ed.), *Skill in nonverbal communication.* Cambridge, MA: Oelgeschlager, Gunn & Hain.

Hall, Nor. (1980). *The moon and the virgin.* New York: Harper & Row.

Hamilton, Eleanor (1955). Emotional aspects of pregnancy: An intensive study of fourteen normal primiparae. Unpublished doctoral dissertation, Columbia University.

Hampson, J. L. (1965). Determinants of psychosexual orientation. In F. A. Beach (Ed.), *Sex and behavior.* New York: John Wiley.

Hampson, J. L., & Hampson, J. G. (1961). The ontogenesis of sexual behavior in man. In W. C. Young (Ed.), *Sex and internal secretions,* Vol. II. Baltimore: Williams & Wilkins.

Harding, M. Esther (1971). *Woman's mysteries ancient and modern: A psychological interpretation of the feminine principle as portrayed in myth, story, and dreams.* New York: G.P. Putnam's Sons.

Hare-Mustin, Rachel T. (1983). An appraisal of the relationship between women and psychotherapy: 80 years after the case of Dora. *American Psychologist, 38,* 593–601.

Harford, T. C., Willis, C. H., & Deabler, H. L. (1967). Personality correlates of masculinity-femininity. *Psychological Reports, 21,* 881–884.

Hariton, E. Barbara (1973, March). The sexual fantasies of women. *Psychology Today, 6,* 39–44.

Harris, Gloria G., & Osborn, Susan M. (1974). *Assertiveness training for women.* Springfield, IL: Charles C Thomas.

Harris, G. W., & Levine, S. (1965). Sexual differentiation of the brain and its experimental control. *Journal of Physiology, 181,* 379–400.

Harris, S. (1971). Influence of subject and experimenter sex in psychological research. *Journal of Consulting and Clinical Psychology, 37,* 291–294.

Harrison, Algea O., & Minor, JoAnne H. (1982). Interrole conflict, coping strategies, and role satisfaction among single and married employed black mothers. *Psychology of Women Quarterly, 6,* 354–360.

Harrison, J. (1978). Warning: The male sex role may be dangerous to your health. *Journal of Social Issues, 34*(1), 65–86.

Harry, J. (1976). Evolving sources of happiness for men over the life cycle: A structural analysis. *Journal of Marriage and the Family, 38,* 289–296.

Hartlage, L. (1970). Sex-linked inheritance of spatial ability. *Perceptual and Motor Skills, 31,* 610.

Hartley, Ruth E. (1959). Sex role pressures and socialization of the male child. *Psychological Reports, 5,* 457–468.

———— (1959–1960). Children's concepts of male and female roles. *Merrill-Palmer Quarterly, 6,* 83–91.

———— (1960). Some implications of current changes in sex role patterns. *Merrill-Palmer Quarterly, 3,* 153–164.

Hartnagel, T. F. (1970). Father absence and self-conception among lower class white and Negro boys. *Social Problems 18,* 152–163.

Havens, Elizabeth (1973). Women, work and wedlock: A note on female marital patterns in the United States. *American Journal of Sociology, 78,* 975–981.

Hawkins, R. C., & Clement, P. F. (1980). Development and construct validation of a self-report measure of binge eating tendencies. *Addictive Behaviors, 5,* 219–226.

Haynes, S. G., et al. (1978). The relationship of psychosocial factors to coronary heart disease in the Framingham Study. II. Prevalence of coronary heart disease. *American Journal of Epidemiology, 107,* 384–402.

Hays, H. R. (1964). *The dangerous sex: The myth of feminine evil.* New York: G. P. Putnam's Sons.

Hedblom, J. H. (1972). The female homosexual: Social and attitudinal dimensions. In J. A. McCaffrey (Ed.), *The homosexual dialectic.* Englewood Cliffs, NJ: Prentice-Hall.

Heilbrun, A. B. (1976) Measurement of masculine and feminine sex role identities as independent dimensions. *Journal of Consulting and Clinical Psychology, 44,* 183–190.

Heiman, Julia R. (1975). The physiology of erotica: Women's sexual arousal. *Psychology Today, 8*(11), 90–94.

Heiman, Julia, LoPiccolo, Leslie, & LoPiccolo J. (1976). *Becoming orgasmic: A sexual growth program for women.* Englewood Cliffs, NJ: Prentice-Hall.

Helmreich, R. L., et al. (1980). Making it in academic psychology: Demographic and personality correlates of attainment. *Journal of Personality and Social Psychology, 39,* 896–908.

Helson, Ravenna (1966). Personality of women with imaginative and artistic interests. The role of masculinity, originality, and other characteristics in their creativity. *Journal of Personality, 34,* 1–25.

———— (1967). Sex differences in creative style. *Journal of Personality, 35,* 214–233.

————. (1971). Women mathematicians and the creative personality. *Journal of Consulting and Clinical Psychology, 36,* 210–220.

Hemmer, Joan D., & Kleiber, D. A. (1981). Tomboys and sissies: Androgynous children? *Sex Roles, 1,* 1205–1212.

Henley, Nancy (1973). Status and sex: Some touching observations. *Bulletin of the Psychonomic Society, 2,* 92–93.

—— (1975). Power, sex, and nonverbal communication. In B. Thorne & N. Henley (Eds.), *Language and sex: Difference and dominance.* Rowley, MA: Newbury House.

Henley, Nancy, & Freeman, Jo (1975). The sexual politics of interpersonal behavior. In J. Freeman (Ed.), *Women: A feminist perspective.* Palo Alto, CA: Mayfield.

Hennig, M. (1973). Family dynamics and the successful woman executive. In R. Knudsin (Ed.), *Women and success.* New York: Morrow.

Henton, C. L. (1961). The effect of socioeconomic and emotional factors on the onset of menarche among Negro and white girls. *Journal of Genetic Psychology, 98,* 255–264.

Herman, Judith L. (1981). *Father-daughter incest.* Cambridge, MA: Harvard University Press.

Hersey, R. B. (1931). Emotional cycles in man. *Journal of Mental Science, 77,* 151–169.

Hines, Melissa (1982). Prenatal gonadal hormones and sex differences in human behavior. *Psychological Bulletin, 92,* 56–80.

Hodgson, J. W., & Fischer, Judith L. (1981). Pathways of identity development in college women. *Sex Roles, 7,* 681–690.

Hoffman, Lois W. (1972). Early childhood experiences and women's achievement motives. *Journal of Social Issues, 28*(2), 129–155.

—— (1974a). Effects of maternal employment on the child: A review of the research. *Developmental Psychology, 10,* 204–228.

—— (1974b). The employment of women, education and fertility. *Merrill-Palmer Quarterly, 20,* 99–119.

Hoffman, M. L. (1977). Sex differences in empathy and related behaviors. *Psychological Bulletin, 84,* 712–722.

Holahan, C. K., & Gilbert, L. A. (1979). Interrole conflict for working women: Career versus jobs. *Journal of Applied Psychology, 64,* 86–90.

Holmstrom, Lynda (1972). *The two-career family.* Cambridge, MA: Schenkman.

Holroyd, Jean C., & Brodsky, Annette M. (1977). Psychologists' attitudes and practices regarding erotic and nonerotic physical contact with patients. *American Psychologist, 34,* 843–849.

Holstein, Constance (1976). Development of moral judgment: A longitudinal study of males and females. *Child Development, 47,* 51–61.

Holter, Harriet (1970). *Sex roles and social structure.* Oslo: Universitet-forlaget.

—— (1971). Sex roles and social change. *Acta Sociologica, 14,* 2–12.

Hooke, J. F., & Marks, P. A. (1962). MMPI characteristics of pregnancy. *Journal of Clinical Psychology, 18,* 316–317.

Hopkins, J. H. (1969). The lesbian personality. *British Journal of Psychiatry, 115,* 1433–1436.

Horner, Matina S. (1969). Fail: Bright women. *Psychology Today, 3*(6), 36.

—— (1970a). Femininity and achievement: A basic inconsistency. In J. Bardwick, E. Douvan, M. Horner, & D. Gutman (Eds.), *Feminine personality and conflict*. Belmont, CA: Brooks/Cole.

—— (1970b). The motive to avoid success and changing aspirations of college women. In *Women on campus: 1970, a symposium*. Ann Arbor, MI: Center for the Continuing Education of Women.

—— (1972). Toward an understanding of achievement-related conflicts in women. *Journal of Social Issues, 28*(2), 157–175.

Horney, Karen (1924). On the genesis of the castration complex in women. *International Journal of Psychoanalysis, 5*, 50–65.

—— (1926). The flight from womanhood. *International Journal of Psychoanalysis, 7*, 324–339.

Horwitz, A. V. (1982). Sex-role expectations, power, and psychological distress. *Sex Roles, 8*, 607–624.

House, W. C. (1974). Actual and perceived differences in male and female expectancies and minimal goal levels as a function of competition. *Journal of Personality, 42*, 493–509.

Houseknecht, Sharon K. (1977). Reference group support for voluntary childlessness: Evidence for conformity. *Journal of Marriage and the Family, 39*, 285–292.

—— (1979). Timing of the decision to remain voluntarily childless: Evidence for continuous socialization. *Psychology of Women Quarterly, 4*, 81–96.

Howard, E. M., & Howard, Joyce L. (1974). Women in institutions: Treatment in prisons and mental hospitals. In V. Franks & V. Burtle (Eds.). *Women in therapy*. New York: Brunner/Mazel.

Hrdy, Sarah B. (1981). *The woman that never evolved*. Cambridge: Harvard University Press.

Huang, Lucy J. (1963, May). A re-evaluation of the primary role of the Communist Chinese woman: The homemaker or the worker. *Marriage and Family Living*, pp. 162–168.

Huenemann, R. L., et al. (1966). A longitudinal study of gross body composition and body conformation and their association with food and activity in a teenage population. *American Journal of Clinical Nutrition, 18*, 325–338.

Humphreys, L. (1970). *Tearoom trade: Impersonal sex in public places*. Chicago: Aldine.

Hunt, M. (1974). *Sexual behavior in the 1970s*. Chicago: Playboy Press.

Huston-Stein, Aletha, & Higgins-Trenk, Ann (1978). The development of females from childhood through adulthood: Career and feminine role orientations. In P. B. Baltes (Ed.), *Lifespan development and behavior*, Vol. I. New York: Academic Press.

Hyde, Janet S. (1979). *Understanding human sexuality*. New York: McGraw-Hill.

—— (1981). How large are cognitive gender differences? A meta-analysis using ω^2 and d. *American Psychologist, 36*, 892–901.

————— (1982). *Understanding human sexuality.* (2d ed.). New York: McGraw-Hill.

————— (1984a). Children's understanding of sexist language. *Developmental Psychology 20,* 697–706.

————— (1984b). How large are gender differences in aggression? A developmental meta-analysis. *Developmental Psychology, 20,* 722–736.

Hyde, Janet S., Geiringer, Eva R., & Yen, Wendy M. (1975). On the empirical relation between spatial ability and sex differences in other aspects of cognitive performance. *Multivariate Behavioral Research, 10,* 289–310.

Hyde, Janet S., & Phillis, Diane E. (1979). Androgyny across the lifespan. *Developmental Psychology, 15,* 334–336.

Hyde, Janet S. & Rosenberg, B. G. (1976). *Half the human experience: The pychology of women.* 1st ed. Lexington, MA: D.C. Heath.

Hyde, Janet S., Rosenberg, B. G., & Behrman, JoAnn (1977). Tomboyism. *Psychology of Women Quarterly, 2,* 73–75.

Hyde, Janet S., & Schuck, J. R. (1977). The development of sex differences in aggression. Paper presented at American Psychological Association Meetings, San Francisco.

Hyman, H. H., & Reed, J. S. (1969). Black matriarchy reconsidered: Evidence from secondary analysis of sample survey. *Public Opinion Quarterly, 33,* 346–354.

Instone, Debra, Major, Brenda, & Bunker, Barbara B. (1983). Gender, self-confidence, and social influence strategies: An organizational simulation. *Journal of Personality and Social Psychology, 44,* 322–333.

Intons-Peterson, M. J., & Samuels, Arlene K. (1978). The cultural halo effect: Black and white women rate black and white men. *Bulletin of the Psychonomic Society, 11,* 309–312.

Isaacs, Marla Beth (1981). Sex role stereotyping and the evaluation of the performance of women: Changing trends. *Psychology of Women Quarterly, 6,* 187–203.

Ivey, M. E., & Bardwick, Judith M. (1968). Patterns of affective fluctuation in the menstrual cycle. *Psychosomatic Medicine, 30,* 336–345.

Jacklin, Carol N., Maccoby, Eleanor E., & Dick, A. E. (1973). Barrier behavior and toy preference: Sex differences and their absence in the year-old child. *Child Development, 44,* 196–200.

Jackson, Jacquelyne J. (1972). Black women in racist society. In B. Brown, B. Kramer, & C. Willie (Eds.), *Racism and mental health.* Pittsburgh: University of Pittsburgh Press.

————— (1973). Family organization and technology. In K. S. Miller & R. M. Dreger (Eds.), *Comparative studies of blacks and whites in the United States.* New York: Seminar Press.

Jaggar, Alison M. (1977). Political philosophies of women's liberation. In M. Vetterling-Braggin et al. (Eds.), *Feminism and philosophy.* Totowa, NJ: Littlefield, Adams.

Jaggar, Alison M., & Struhl, Paula R. (1978). *Feminist frameworks.* New York: McGraw-Hill.

Jakubowski, Patricia A. (1977). Assertive behavior and clinical problems of women. In E. I. Rawlings and D. K. Carter (Eds.), *Psychotherapy for women*. Springfield, IL: Charles C Thomas.

Jakubowski-Spector, Patricia (1973). Facilitating the growth of women through assertive training. *The Counseling Psychologist, 4,* 75.

Jamison, Kay R., Wellisch, D. K., & Pasnau, R. O. (1978). Psychosocial aspects of mastectomy: I. The woman's perspective. *American Journal of Psychiatry, 135,* 432–436.

Janowsky, D. S., et al. (1969). Premenstrual-menstrual increases in psychiatric hospital admission rates. *American Journal of Obstetrics and Gynecology, 103,* 189–192.

Janowsky, D. S., Fann, W. E., & Davis, J. M. (1971). Monoamines and ovarian hormone linked sexual and emotional changes: A review. *Archives of Sexual Behavior, 1,* 205–218.

Janson-Smith, Deirdre (1980). Sociobiology: So what? In Brighton Women & Science Group, *Alice through the microscope*. London: Virago.

Jay, Karla, & Young, Allen (1979). *The gay report*. New York: Summit Books.

Jokl, E. (1964). *Medical sociology and cultural anthropology of sport and physical education*. Springfield, IL: Charles C Thomas.

Jones, E. E., Kanouse, D. E., Kelley, H. H., Nisbett, R. E., Valins, S., & Weiner, B. (1971). *Attribution: Perceiving the causes of behavior*. Morristown, NJ: General Learning Press.

Jones, Mary C. (1971). Personality antecedents and correlates of drinking patterns in women. *Journal of Consulting and Clinical Psychology, 36,* 61–69.

Jourard, Sidney M. (1966). An exploratory study of body-accessibility. *British Journal of Social and Clinical Psychology, 5,* 221–231.

Jung, C. G. (Ed.) (1964). *Man and his symbols*. Garden City, NY: Doubleday.

Juni, Samuel, & Bremon, Robert (1981). Interpersonal touching as a function of status and sex. *Journal of Social Psychology, 114,* 135–136.

Kagan, J. (1971) *Understanding children*. New York: Harcourt Brace Jovanovich.

Kagan, J., & Moss, H. A. (1962). *Birth to maturity*. New York: John Wiley.

Kahn, Arnold (1981). Reactions of profeminist and antifeminist men to an expert woman. *Sex Roles, 7,* 857–866.

Kane, F. J., Lipton, M.A., & Ewing, J. A. (1969). Hormonal influences in female sexual response. *Archives of General Psychiatry, 20,* 202–209.

Kanin, Eugene J. (1969). Selected dyadic aspects of male sex aggression. *Journal of Sex Research, 5,* 12–28.

Kanin, Eugene J., & Parcell, S. R. (1977). Sexual aggression: A second look at the offended female. *Archives of Sexual Behavior, 6,* 67–76.

Kanner, A. D. (1976). Femininity and masculinity: Their relationships to creativity in male architects and their independence from each other. *Journal of Consulting and Clinical Psychology, 44,* 802–805.

Kanter, Rosabeth Moss (1977). Women in organizations: Sex roles, group dynamics, and change strategies. In A. Sargent (Ed.), *Beyond sex roles.* St. Paul, MN: West.

Kantor, H. I., Michael, Carmen M., Boulas, S. H., Shore, H., & Ludvigson, H. W. (1966, June). The administration of estrogens to older women: A psychometric evaluation. Seventh International Congress of Gerontology Proceedings.

Kaplan, Alexandra G. (1976). Androgyny as a model of mental health for women: From theory to therapy. In A. G. Kaplan & J. P. Bean (Eds.), *Beyond sex-role stereotypes: Readings toward a psychology of androgyny.* Boston: Little, Brown.

———— (1979). Clarifying the concept of androgyny: Implications for therapy. *Psychology of Women Quarterly, 3,* 223–230.

Kaplan, Helen Singer (1979). *Disorders of sexual desire.* New York: Simon & Schuster.

Kaplan, Helen S., & Sager, C. J. (1971). Sexual patterns at different ages. *Medical Aspects of Human Sexuality,* 10–23.

Karabenick, S. A., & Marshall, Joan M. (1974). Performance of females as a function of fear of success, fear of failure, type of opponent, and performance-contingent feedback. *Journal of Personality, 42,* 220–237.

Katchadourian, H. A., & Lunde, D. D. (1972). *Fundamentals of human sexuality.* New York: Holt, Rinehart & Winston.

Kegel, A. H. (1952). Sexual functions of the pubococcygeus muscle. *Western Journal of Surgery, 60,* 521–524.

Keith, Patricia M., & Brubaker, Timothy H. (1979). Male household roles in later life: A look at masculinity and marital relationships. *Family Coordinator, 28,* 497–502.

Kenny, T. J., et al. (1971). Characteristics of children referred because of hyperactivity. *Journal of Pediatrics, 79,* 618–622.

Kenyon, F. E. (1968). Studies in female homosexuality — Psychological test results. *Journal of Consulting and Clinical Psychology, 32,* 510–513.

Keohane, Nannerl O., Rosaldo, Michelle, & Gelpi, Barbara C. (1981). *Feminist theory.* Chicago: University of Chicago Press.

Key, Mary Ritchie (1975). *Male/female language.* Metuchen, NJ: Scarecrow Press.

Kincaid, Marylou B. (1977). Changes in sex-role attitudes and self-actualization of adult women following a consciousness-raising group. *Sex Roles, 3,* 329–336.

Kinsey, A. C., Pomeroy, W. B., & Martin, C. E. (1948). *Sexual behavior in the human male.* Philadelphia: Saunders.

Kinsey, A. C., Pomeroy, W. B., Martin, C. E., & Gebhard, P. H. (1953). *Sexual behavior in the human female.* Philadelphia: Saunders.

Kinsey, Barry A. (1966). *The female alcoholic: A social psychological study.* Springfield, IL: Charles C Thomas.

Kirkpatrick, Carole S. (1980). Sex roles and sexual satisfaction in women. *Psychology of Women Quarterly, 4,* 444–459.

Kirkpatrick, J. J. (1973). Occupational aspirations, opportunities, and barriers. In K. S. Miller & R. M. Dreger (Eds.), *Comparative studies of blacks and whites in the United States.* New York: Seminar Press.

Kirsh, Barbara (1974). Consciousness-raising groups as therapy for women. In V. Franks and V. Burtle (Eds.), *Women in therapy.* New York: Brunner/Mazel.

Klaus, M. A., et al. (1972). Maternal attachment: Importance of the first postpartum days. *New England Journal of Medicine, 286,* 460–463.

Kleinke, Chris L., et al. (1982). Sex differences in coping with depression. *Sex Roles, 8,* 877–890.

Knop, C. A. (1946). The dynamics of newly born babies. *Journal of Pediatrics, 29,* 721–728.

Koch, Helen L. (1956). Sissiness and tomboyishness in relation to sibling characteristics. *Journal of Genetic Psychology, 88,* 231–244.

Kohlberg, Lawrence (1966). A cognitive-developmental analysis of children's sex-role concepts and attitudes. In E. E. Maccoby (Ed.), *The development of sex differences.* Stanford: Stanford University Press.

—— (1969). Stage and sequence: The cognitive-developmental approach to socialization. In D. A. Goslin (Ed.), *Handbook of socialization theory and research.* Chicago: Rand McNally.

Komarovsky, Mirra (1946). Cultural contradictions and sex roles. *American Journal of Sociology, 52,* 184–189.

—— (1973). Cultural contradictions and sex roles: The masculine case. *American Journal of Sociology, 78,* 873–884.

—— (1982). Female freshmen view their future: Career salience and its correlates. *Sex Roles 8,* 299–314.

Konopka, Gisela (1975). *Young girls: A portrait of adolescence.* Englewood Cliffs, NJ: Spectrum Books.

Koss, Mary P., & Oros, Cheryl J. (1982). Sexual experiences survey: A research instrument investigating sexual aggression and victimization. *Journal of Consulting and Clinical Psychology, 50,* 455–457.

Kramer, Cheris (1974a, June). Folk-linguistics: Wishy-washy mommy talk. *Psychology Today,* 82–89.

—— (1974b). Women's speech: Separate but unequal. *Quarterly Journal of Speech,* February, 14–24.

—— (1976). Stereotypes of women's speech: The word from cartoons. *Journal of Popular Culture.*

Kramer, Cheris, Thorne, Barrie, & Henley, Nancy (1978). Perspectives on language and communication. *Signs, 3,* 638–651.

Kravetz, Diane (1980). Consciousness-raising and self-help. In A. Brodsky & R. Hare-Mustin (Eds.), *Women and psychotherapy.* New York: Guilford.

Kronhausen, Phyllis, & Kronhausen, E. (1964). *The sexually responsive woman.* New York: Grove Press.

Kuhn, D. (1976). Short-term longitudinal evidence for the sequentiality of Kohlberg's early stage of moral development. *Developmental Psychology, 12,* 162–166.

Kuhn, Thomas S. (1970). *The structure of scientific revolutions.* Chicago: University of Chicago Press.

Kukla, A. (1972). Attributional determinants of achievement-related behavior. *Journal of Personality and Social Psychology, 21,* 166–174.

Kuvlesky, W., & Obordo, A. (1972, February). A racial comparison of teenage girls' projection for marriage and procreation. *Journal of Marriage and the Family, 34,* 75–84.

Kweskin, Sally L., & Cook, Alicia S. (1982). Heterosexual and homosexual mothers' self-described sex-role behavior and ideal sex-role behavior in children. *Sex Roles, 8,* 967–976.

Ladas, Alice K., Whipple, Beverly, & Perry, J. D. (1982). *The G-spot.* New York: Holt, Rinehart & Winston.

Ladner, Joyce A. (1971). *Tomorrow's tomorrow: The black woman.* Garden City, NY: Doubleday.

LaFrance, Marianne (1981). Gender gestures: sex, sex-role, and nonverbal communication. In C. Mayo and N. Henley (Eds.), *Gender and nonverbal behavior.* New York: Springer-Verlag.

Lakoff, Robin (1973). Language and woman's place. *Language and Society, 2,* 45–79. (Reprinted 1975 in paperback. New York: Harper & Row.)

Lamb, Michael E. (1976). *The role of the father in child development.* New York: John Wiley.

——— (1979). Paternal influences and the father's role. *American Psychologist, 34,* 938–943.

Lansky, L. M. (1967). The family structure also affects the model: Sex-role attitudes in parents of preschool children. *Merrill-Palmer Quarterly, 13,* 139–150.

Lanson, Lucienne (1975). *From woman to woman.* New York: Knopf.

Laws, Judith L., & Schwartz, Pepper (1977). *Sexual scripts: The social construction of female sexuality.* Hinsdale, IL: Dryden Press.

Lazarus, Arnold A. (1974). Women in behavior therapy. In V. Franks and V. Burtle (Eds.), *Women in therapy.* New York: Brunner/Mazel.

Lear, M. W. (1973). Is there a male menopause? *New York Times Magazine,* January 28.

Lederer, W. (1968). *The fear of women.* New York: Harcourt Brace Jovanovich.

Leidig, Marjorie W. (1982, April). Incest. Colloquium presented at Denison University.

Leifer, Myra (1980). *Psychological effects of motherhood: A study of first pregnancy.* New York: Praeger.

Lemkau, Jeanne P. (1979). Personality and background characteristics of women in male-dominated occupations: A review. *Psychology of Women Quarterly, 4,* 221–240.

Lenney, Ellen (1977). Women's self-confidence in achievement settings. *Psychological Bulletin, 84,* 1–13.

—— (1981). What's fine for the gander isn't always good for the goose: Sex differences in self-confidence as a function of ability area and comparison with others. *Sex Roles, 7,* 905–924.

Lerner, Gerda (1972). *Black women in white America: A documentary history.* New York: Pantheon.

Levenkron, Steven (1982). *Treating and overcoming anorexia nervosa.* New York: Charles Scribner's.

Levin, Robert J., & Levin, Amy (1975, September). Sexual pleasure: The surprising preferences of 100,000 women. *Redbook, 145*(5), 51. (See also the *Redbook* report on premarital and extramarital sex, October 1975, *145*(6), 38.)

Levinson, Daniel J. (1978). *The seasons of a man's life.* New York: Ballantine.

Levinson, Daniel J., et al. (1976). Periods in the adult development of men: Ages 18–45. *Counseling Psychologist, 6*(1), 21–25.

Levy, Jere (1972). Lateral specialization of the human brain: Behavioral manifestation and possible evolutionary basis. In J. A. Giger (Ed.), *The biology of behavior.* Corvallis, OR: Oregon University Press.

Levy-Agresti, Jere, & Sperry, R. W. (1968). Differential perceptual capacities in major and minor hemispheres. *Proceedings of the National Academy of Science, 61,* 1151.

Lewin, K. (1941). Self-hatred among Jews. *Contemporary Jewish Record, 4,* 219–232.

Lewis, M. (1972). State as an infant-environment interaction: Analysis of mother-infant interaction as a function of sex. *Merrill-Palmer Quarterly, 18,* 95–121.

Lewis, M., Meyers, W., Kagan, J., & Grossberg, R. (1963). Attention to visual patterns in infants. Paper presented at the Symposium on Studies of Attention in Infants, American Psychological Association, Philadelphia.

Lipman-Blumen, Jean (1972). How ideology shapes women's lives. *Scientific American, 226*(1), 34–42.

Ljung, B. (1965). The adolescent spurt in mental growth. *Stockholm Studies in Educational Psychology, 8.*

Loewenstein, Sophie F., et al. (1981). A study of satisfactions and stresses of single women in midlife. *Sex Roles, 7,* 1127–1141.

Loney, J. (1972). Background factors, sexual experiences and attitudes toward treatment in two "normal" homosexual samples. *Journal of Consulting and Clinical Psychology, 38,* 57–65.

Longstaff, H. P. (1954). Practice effects on the Minnesota Vocational Test for clerical workers. *Journal of Applied Psychology, 38,* 18–20.

Lopata, Helen Z. (1973). Social relations of black and white widowed women in a northern metropolis. *American Journal of Sociology, 78,* 1003–1010.

—— (1979). *Women as Widows.* New York: Elsevier.

LoPiccolo, Joseph, & Lobitz, C. (1972). The role of masturbation in the treatment of sexual dysfunction. *Archives of Sexual Behavior, 2,* 163–171.

LoPiccolo, Leslie (1980). Low sexual desire. In S. R. Leiblum and L. A. Pervin (Eds.), *Principles and practice of sex therapy*. New York: Guilford Press.

Loraine, J. A., Adampopoulos, D. A., Kirkhan, K. E., Ismail, A. A., & Dove, G. A. (1971). Patterns of hormone excretion in male and female homosexuals. *Nature, 234*, 552–554.

Lott, Bernice (1978). Behavioral concordance with sex role ideology related to play areas, creativity, and parental sex typing of children. *Journal of Personality and Social Psychology, 36*, 1087–1100.

———— (1981). A feminist critique of androgyny: Toward the elimination of gender attributions for learned behavior. In C. Mayo & N. Henley (Eds.), *Gender and nonverbal behavior*. New York: Springer-Verlag.

Lowenthal, M. F., et al. (1975). *Four stages of life: A comparative study of women and men facing transitions*. San Francisco: Jossey-Bass.

Luker, Kristin (1975). *Taking chances: Abortion and the decision not to contracept*. Berkeley: University of California Press.

Luria, Zella (1974). Recent women college graduates: A study of rising expectations. *American Journal of Orthopsychiatry, 44*, 312–326.

Lynn, David B. (1974). *The father: His role in child development*. Monterey, CA: Brooks/Cole.

Maccoby, Eleanor E. (1966). Sex differences in intellectual functioning. In E. E. Maccoby (Ed.), *The development of sex differences*. Stanford: Stanford University Press.

———— (1972). The meaning of being female. *Contemporary Psychology, 17*, 369–372.

Maccoby, Eleanor E., & Feldman, S. Shirley (1972). Mother-attachment and stranger reactions in the third year of life. *Monographs of the Society for Research in Child Development, 37*(1), 1–86.

Maccoby, Eleanor E., & Jacklin, Carol N. (1973). Stress, activity and proximity seeking: Sex differences in the year-old child. *Child Development, 44*, 34–42.

———— (1974). *The psychology of sex differences*. Stanford: Stanford University Press.

Macdonald, Nancy E., & Hyde, Janet S. (1980). Fear of success, need achievement, and fear of failure: A factor-analytic study. *Sex Roles, 6*, 695–712.

Machotka, P., & Ferber, A. S. (1967). Delineation of family roles. *American Journal of Orthopsychiatry, 37*, 409–410.

Mack, Thomas M., et al. (1976). Estrogens and endometrial cancer in a retirement community. *New England Journal of Medicine, 294*, 1262–1267.

MacKinnon, Catherine A. (1979). *Sexual harassment of working women*. New Haven: Yale University Press.

———— (1982). Feminism, Marxism, method, and the state: An agenda for theory. In N. O. Keohane et al. (Eds.), *Feminist theory*. Chicago: University of Chicago Press.

MacKinnon, D. W. (1962). The nature and nurture of creative talent. *American Psychologist, 17*, 484–495.

MacLusky, Neil J., & Naftolin, F. (1981). Sexual differentiation of the central nervous system. *Science, 211,* 1294–1303.

Madigan, F. C. (1957). Are sex mortality differentials biologically caused? *Milbank Memorial Fund Quarterly, 35,* 203–223.

Maisch, H. (1972). *Incest.* New York: Stein and Day.

Major, Brenda (1981). Gender patterns in touching behavior. In C. Mayo & N. Henley (Eds.), *Gender and nonverbal behavior.* New York: Springer-Verlag.

Malamuth, Neil M., & Check, V. P. (1983). Sexual arousal to rape depictions: Individual differences. *Journal of Abnormal Psychology, 92,* 55–67.

Malina, R. M. (1973). Biological substrata. In K. S. Miller & R. M. Dreger (Eds.), *Comparative studies of blacks and whites in the United States.* New York: Seminar Press.

Mamay, Patricia D., & Simpson, R. L. (1981). Three female roles in television commercials. *Sex Roles, 7,* 1223–1232.

Mandel, William (1975). *Soviet women.* Garden City, NY: Anchor.

Marcus, Dale E., & Overton, W. F. (1978). The development of cognitive gender constancy and sex preferences. *Child Development, 49,* 434–444.

Marini, Margaret M. (1978). Sex differences in the determination of adolescent aspirations: A review of research. *Sex Roles, 4,* 723–754.

Markus, Hazel, et al. (1982). Self-schemas and gender. *Journal of Personality and Social Psychology, 42,* 38–50.

Marmor, J. (Ed.) (1965). *Sexual inversion: The multiple roots of homosexuality.* New York: Basic Books.

Marquis Academic Media (1979). *Sourcebook on aging* (2nd ed.). Chicago: Marquis Who's Who.

Martin, Carol L., & Halverson, C. F. (1983). The effects of sex-typing schemas on young children's memory. *Child Development, 54,* 563–574.

Martin, Del (1976). *Battered wives.* San Francisco: Glide Publications.

Martin, Del & Lyon, Phyllis (1972). *Lesbian/Woman.* San Francisco: Glide Publications.

Martyna, Wendy (1980). Beyond the he/man approach: The case for nonsexist language. *Signs, 5,* 482–493.

Marx, Jean L. (1976). Estrogen drugs: Do they increase the risk of cancer? *Science, 191,* 838.

Masters, W. H., & Johnson, Virginia E. (1966). *Human sexual response.* Boston: Little Brown.

—— (1970). *Human sexual inadequacy.* Boston: Little Brown.

Matthews, Karen A. (1982). Psychological perspectives on the Type A behavior pattern. *Psychological Bulletin, 91,* 293–323.

Matthews, Sara H. (1979). *The social world of old women: Management of self-identity.* Beverly Hills, CA: Sage.

Mayo, Clara, & Henley, Nancy M. (Eds.) (1981). *Gender and nonverbal behavior.* New York: Springer-Verlag.

Mayo, Peter (1976). Sex differences and psychopathology. In B. Lloyd and J. Archer (Eds.), *Exploring sex differences*. New York: Academic Press.

McArthur, Leslie & Eisen, S. (1976a). Achievement of, male and female story-book characters as determinants of achievement behavior by boys and girls. *Journal of Personality and Social Psychology, 33,* 467–473.

——— (1976b). Television and sex-role stereotyping. *Journal of Applied Social Psychology, 6,* 329–351.

McArthur, Leslie, & Resko, Beth G. (1975). The portrayal of men and women in American television commercials. *Journal of Social Psychology, 97,* 209–220.

McCary, J. L. (1973). *Human sexuality* (2nd ed.). New York: Van Nostrand.

McClelland, D. C., Atkinson, J. W., Clark, R. A., & Lowell, F. L. (1953). *The achievement motive*. New York: Appleton-Century-Crofts.

McClintock, M. K. (1971). Menstrual synchrony and suppression. *Nature, 229,* 244–245.

McConnell-Ginet, Sally (1978). Intonation in a woman's world. *Signs, 3,* 541–559.

McGinnis, M. (1974). *Single: The woman's view*. Old Tappan, NJ: Fleming H. Revell.

McGraw-Hill Book Company (1974). *Guidelines for equal treatment of the sexes in McGraw-Hill Book Company publications*. New York: McGraw-Hill.

McHugh, Maureen C., Frieze, Irene H., & Hanusa, Barbara H. (1982). Attributions and sex differences in achievement: Problems and new perspectives. *Sex Roles, 8,* 467–479.

McKay, R. (1978). One child families and atypical sex ratios in an elite black community. In R. Staples (Ed.), *The black family*. Belmont, CA: Wadsworth.

McKenna, Wendy, & Denmark, Florence L. Gender and nonverbal behavior as cues to status and power. *Annals of the New York Academy of Sciences*, in press.

McKenna, Wendy, & Kessler, Suzanne J. (1977). Experimental design as a source of sex bias in social psychology. *Sex Roles, 3,* 117–128.

McKinlay, Sonja M., & Jeffreys, Margot (1974). The menopausal syndrome. *British Journal of Preventive and Social Medicine, 28*(2), 108.

McMahan, Ian D. (1971, April). Sex differences in causal attributions following success and failure. Paper presented at Eastern Psychological Association Meetings.

——— (1972, April). Sex differences in expectancy of success as a function of task. Paper presented at Eastern Psychological Association Meetings.

——— (1982). Expectancy of success on sex-linked tasks. *Sex Roles, 8,* 949–958.

McMillan, Julie R., et al. (1977). Women's language: Uncertainty or interpersonal sensitivity and emotionality? *Sex Roles, 3,* 545–560.

Mead, Margaret (1935). *Sex and temperament in three primitive societies*. New York: William Morrow.

——— (1949). *Male and female.* New York: William Morrow.

——— (1958). In J. M. Tanner and B. Inhelder (Eds.), *Discussions on child development,* New York: International Universities Press.

——— (1961). Cultural determinants of sexual behavior. In W. C. Young (Ed.), *Sex and internal secretions,* vol. II. Baltimore: Williams & Wilkins.

——— (1969). *Culture and commitment: A study of the generation gap.* Garden City, NY: Doubleday.

Mead, Margaret, & Kaplan, Frances B. (Eds.) (1965). *American women: The report of the President's Commission on the Status of Women.* New York: Charles Scribner's.

Mednick, Martha T. S. (1975). Social change and sex-role inertia: The case of the kibbutz. In M. T. S. Mednick, S. G. Tangri, & L. L. Hoffman. (Eds), *Women and achievement: Social and motivational analyses.* New York: Halsted Press.

Meece, Judith L., Eccles-Parsons, Jacquelynne et al. (1982). Sex differences in math achievement: Toward a model of academic choice. *Psychological Bulletin, 91,* 324–448.

Meeker, B. F., & Weitzel-O'Neill, P. A. (1977). Sex roles and interpersonal behavior in task-oriented groups. *American Sociological Review, 42,* 91–104.

Mehrabian, Albert (1971). Verbal and nonverbal interaction of strangers in a waiting situation. *Journal of Experimental Research in Personality, 5,* 127–138.

Meiselman, Karin (1978). *Incest.* San Francisco: Jossey-Bass.

Mendes, Helen A. (1976). Single fathers. *The Family Coordinator, 25,* 439.

Messer, S. B., & Lewis, M. (1972). Social class and sex differences in the attachment and play behaviors of the year-old infant. *Merrill-Palmer Quarterly, 18,* 295–306.

Mester, R. (1978). Induced abortion and psychotherapy. *Psychotherapy and Psychosomatics, 30*(2), 98–104.

Meyer, J. W. & Sobieszek, Barbara I. (1972). Effects of a child's sex on adult interpretations of its behavior. *Developmental Psychology, 6,* 42–48.

Miele, J. (1958). Sex differences in intelligence: The relationship of sex to intelligence as measured by the Wechsler Adult Intelligence Scale and the Wechsler Intelligence Scale for Children. *Dissertation Abstracts, 18,* 22213.

Mill, J. S. (1869). The subjection of women. (Reprinted in *Three essays by J. S. Mill.* London: Oxford University Press, 1966.)

Miller, Casey, & Swift, Kate (1976). *Words and women.* Garden City, NY: Anchor Press/Doubleday.

Millett, Kate (1969). *Sexual politics.* Garden City, NY: Doubleday.

Minuchin, S., Rosman, Bernice L., & Baker, L. (1978). *Psychosomatic families: Anorexia nervosa in context.* Cambridge, MA: Harvard University Press.

Mischel, W. (1966). A social-learning view of sex differences in behavior. In E. E. Maccoby (Ed.), *The development of sex differences*. Stanford: Stanford University Press.

Monahan, Lynn, Kuhn, Deanna, & Shaver, P. (1974). Intrapsychic versus cultural explanations of the "fear of success" motive. *Journal of Personality and Social Psychology, 29*, 60–64.

Money, J. (1961). Sex hormones and other variables in human eroticism. In W. C. Young (Ed.), *Sex and internal secretions*, Vol. 2. Baltimore: Williams & Wilkins.

———— (1970). Sexual dimorphism and homosexual gender identity. *Psychological Bulletin, 73*, 425–440.

Money, J., & Ehrhardt, Anke (1968). Prenatal hormonal exposure: Possible effects on behavior in man. In R. P. Michael (Ed.), *Endrocrinology and human behavior*. London: Oxford University Press.

———— (1972). *Man & woman, boy & girl*. Baltimore: Johns Hopkins University Press.

Money, J., Hampson, J. L. & Hampson, J. G. (1955). An examination of some basic sexual concepts: The evidence of human hermaphroditism. *Bulletin of John Hopkins Hospital, 97*, 301–319.

Montagu, A. (1964). *The natural superiority of women*. New York: P.F. Collier. (First published 1952.)

Moos, R. (1968). Psychological aspects of oral contraceptives. *Archives of General Psychiatry, 30*, 853–867.

Moss, H. A. (1967). Sex, age and state as determinants of mother-infant interaction. *Merrill-Palmer Quarterly, 13*, 19–36.

Moulton, Janice R., Robinson, G. M., & Elias, Cherin (1978). Psychology in action: Sex bias in language use: "Neutral" pronouns that aren't. *American Psychologist, 33*, 1032–1036.

Mulvihill, D. J., et al. (1969). *Crimes of violence, a staff report to the National Commission on the Causes and Prevention of Violence*, Vol. II. Washington, DC: U.S. Government Printing Office.

Murdock, G. P. (1937). Comparative data on the division of labor by sex. *Social Forces, 15*, 4.

Murray, Saundra R., & Mednick, Martha T. S. (1977). Black women's achievement orientation: Motivational and cognitive factors. *Psychology of Women Quarterly, 1*, 247–259.

Murty, Lakshmi (1978). Transition for whom? Adolescence theories with androcentric bias. *Sex Roles, 4*, 369–374.

Mussen, P. H. (1961). Some antecedents and consequents of masculine sex-typing in adolescent boys. *Psychological Monographs, 75*(2), 1–24.

———— (1962). Long-term consequents of masculinity of interests in adolescence. *Journal of Consulting Psychology, 26*, 435–444.

Neugarten, Bernice L. (1973). A new look at menopause. In C. Tavris (Ed.), *The female experience*. Del Mar, CA: CRM.

Neugarten, Bernice L., & Kraines, Ruth J. (1965). Menopausal symptoms in women of various ages. *Psychosomatic Medicine, 27*, 266.

Newton, Niles (1973). Interrelationships between various aspects of female reproductive behavior: A review. In J. Zubin & J. Money (Eds.), *Contemporary sexual behavior: Critical issues in the 1970s.* Baltimore: Johns
Hopkins University Press.

Nieva, Veronica F., & Gutek, Barbara A. (1981). *Women and work: A psychological perspective.* New York: Praeger.

Nobers, D. R. (1968). The effects of father absence and mother's characteristics
on the identification of adolescent white and Negro males. *Dissertation
Abstracts,* 1508-B-1509-B.

Oakes, Merilee (1970). Pills, periods, and personality. Unpublished doctoral
dissertation, University of Michigan.

Oakley, Anne (1974). *The sociology of housework.* Bath, England: Pitman.

Oberstone, Andrea K., & Sukoneck Harriet (1976). Psychological adjustment
and life style of single lesbians and single heterosexual women. *Psychology of Women Quarterly, 1,* 172–188.

Offir, Carole W. (1982). *Human sexuality.* New York: Harcourt, Brace, Jovanovich.

O'Keefe, Eileen S. C., & Hyde, Janet S. (1983). The development of occupational sex-role stereotypes: The effects of gender stability and age. *Sex
Roles, 9,* 481–492.

O'Leary, Virginia E. (1977). *Toward understanding women.* Monterey, CA:
Brooks/Cole.

O'Leary, Virginia E., & Donaghue, J. M. (1978). Latitudes of masculinity: Reactions to sex-role deviance in men. *Journal of Social Issues, 34*(1),
17–28.

O'Neil, James M. (1981). Male sex role conflicts, sexism, and masculinity: Psychological implications for men, women, and the counseling psychologist.
Counseling Psychologist, 9, 61–80.

Orloff, Kossia (1978). The trap of "androgyny." *Regionalism and the Female
Imagination, 4*(ii), 1–3.

Osofsky, Joy D., & Osofsky, Howard J. (1972). The psychological reactions of
patients to legalized abortions. *American Journal of Orthopsychiatry, 42,*
48–60.

Paige, Karen E. (1971). Effects of oral contraceptives on affective fluctuations
associated with the menstrual cycle. *Psychosomatic Medicine, 33,* 515–
537.

———— (1973, September). Women learn to sing the menstrual blues. *Psychology Today, 7*(4), 41.

Palme, O. (1972). The emancipation of men. *Journal of Social Issues, 28*(2),
237–246.

Paloma, Margaret M., & Garland, T. N. (1971). The married professional
woman: A study in the tolerance of domestication. *Journal of Marriage
and the Family, 33,* 531–540.

Papanek, Hanna (1973). Men, women and work: Reflections on the two-
person career. *American Journal of Sociology, 78,* 852–872.

Parke, Ross D. (1979). Perspectives in father-infant interaction. In J. D. Osofsky (Ed.), *Handbook of infant development.* New York: Wiley.

Parke, Ross D., & O'Leary, S. E. (1976). Father-mother-infant interaction in the newborn period. In K. Riegel & J. Meacham (Eds.), *The developing individual in a changing world*, Vol. 2. The Hague: Mouton.

Parkes, C. M. (1970). The first year of bereavement. *Psychiatry, 33*(4), 444–467.

Parlee, Mary B. (1973). The premenstrual syndrome. *Psychological Bulletin, 80*, 454–465.

———— (1978). The rhythms in men's lives. *Psychology Today*, 82–91.

———— (1981). Appropriate control groups in feminist research. *Psychology of Women Quarterly, 5*, 637–644.

———— (1983). Menstrual rhythms in sensory processes: A review of fluctuations in vision, olfaction, audition, taste, and touch. *Psychological Bulletin, 93*, 539–548.

Parsons, T. (1942). Age and sex in the social structure in the United States. *American Sociological Review, 7*, 604–606.

Parsons, T., & Bales, R. F. (1955). *Family, socialization and interaction process.* Glencoe, IL: The Free Press.

Peplau, Letitia Anne. (1982). Research on homosexual couples: An overview. *Journal of Homosexuality, 8*(2), 3–8.

Peplau, Letitia Anne, Cochran, Susan, Rook, Karen & Padesky, Christine (1978). Loving women: Attachment and autonomy in lesbian relationships. *Journal of Social Issues, 34*(3), 7–27.

Peplau, L. A., et al. (1982). Being old and living alone. In L. A. Peplau & D. Perlman (Eds.), *Loneliness.* New York: Wiley.

Perez-Reyes, M., et al. (1972). Follow-up after therapeutic abortion in early adolescence. *Archives of General Psychiatry, 28*(1), 120–126.

Perlman, D., et al. (1978). Loneliness among senior citizens: An empirical report. *Essence, 2*(4), 239–248.

Perls, Fritz S. (1969). *Gestalt therapy verbatim.* Moab, UT: Real People Press.

Perry, J. D. & Whipple, Beverly (1981). Pelvic muscle strength of female ejaculators: Evidence in support of a new theory of orgasm. *Journal of Sex Research, 17*, 22–39.

Persky, H., Smith, K. D., & Basu, G. K. (1971). Relation of psychologic measures of aggression and hostility to testosterone production in man. *Psychosomatic Medicine, 33*, 265–277.

Persky, Harold, et al. (1978). Plasma testosterone level and sexual behavior of couples. *Archives of Sexual Behavior, 1*, 157–173.

Perun, Pamela J., & Bielby, Denise (1981). Toward a model of female occupational behavior: A human development approach. *Psychology of Women Quarterly, 6*, 234–252.

Peterson, Rolf A. (1983). Attitudes toward the childless spouse. *Sex Roles, 9*, 321–332.

Pettigrew, T. (1964). *A profile of the Negro American*. Princeton, NJ: Van Nostrand.

Pheterson, G. I., Kiesler, S. B. & Goldberg, P. A. (1971). Evaluation of the performance of women as a function of their sex, achievement, and personal history. *Journal of Personality and Social Psychology, 19*, 114–118.

Phillips, Derek, & Segal, B. (1969). Sexual status and psychiatric symptoms. *American Sociological Review, 34*, 58–72.

Phillips, Leslie (1977). For women, sexual harassment is an occupational hazard. *Boston Globe*, September 9.

Phoenix, C. H., Goy, R. W., Gerall, A. A. & Young, W. C. (1959). Organizing action of prenatally administered testosterone propionate on the tissues mediating mating behavior in the female guinea pig. *Endocrinology, 65*, 369–382.

Piaget, J. (1954). *The construction of reality in the child*. New York: Basic Books.

Pizzey, Erin (1974). *Scream quietly or the neighbors will hear*. London: If Books.

Planned Parenthood (1977). *Planned births, the future of the family and the quality of American life*. New York: Alan Guttmacher Institute.

Pleck, Joseph H. (1975). Masculinity-femininity: Current and alternate paradigms. *Sex Roles, 1*, 161–178.

———— (1981). *The myth of masculinity*. Cambridge, MA: MIT Press.

———— (1983). Husbands' paid work and family roles: Current research issues. In H. Lopata & J. Pleck (Eds.), *Research in the interweave of social roles*, Vol. 3: *Families and Jobs*. Greenwich, CT: JAI Press.

Polster, Miriam (1974). Women in therapy: A Gestalt therapist's view. In V. Franks & V. Burtle (Eds.), *Women in therapy*. New York: Brunner/ Mazel.

Ponzo, Zander, & Strowig, R. Wray (1973). Relations among sex-role identity and selected intellectual and non-intellectual factors for high school freshman and seniors. *Journal of Educational Research, 67*, 137–141.

Pope, Kenneth S., Levenson, H. & Schover, L. R. (1979). Sexual intimacy in psychology training: Results and implications of a national survey. *American Psychologist, 34*, 682–689.

Porter, Natalie P., Geis, Florence L., & Walstedt, Joyce J. (1978). Are women invisible as leaders? Paper presented at American Psychological Association Meetings, Toronto, August.

Powell, Barbara (1977). The empty nest, employment, and psychiatric symptoms in college-educated women. *Psychology of Women Quarterly, 2*, 35–43.

Psathas, G. (1968). Toward a theory of occupational choice for women. *Sociology and Social Research, 52*, 253–265.

Puryear, G. R., & Mednick, Martha S. (1974). Black militancy, affective attachment, and fear of success in black college women. *Journal of Consulting and Clinical Psychology, 42*, 263–266.

Rabin, A. I. (1970). The sexes: Ideology and reality in the Israeli kibbutz. In G. H. Seward & R. C. Williamson (Eds.), *Sex roles in changing society.* New York: Random House.

Radloff, Lenore (1975). Sex differences in depression: The effects of occupation and marital status. *Sex Roles, 1,* 249–265.

——— (1980). Risk factors for depression: What do we learn from them? In M. Guttentag et al. (Eds.), *The mental health of women.* New York: Academic Press.

Radloff, Lenore G., & Monroe, Megan K. (1978). Sex differences in helplessness —with implication for depression. In L. S. Hansen and R. S. Rapoza (Eds.), *Career development and counseling of women.* Springfield, IL: Charles C Thomas.

Radlove, Shirley (1983). Sexual response and gender roles. In E. R. Allgeier & N. B. McCormick (Eds.), *Changing boundaries: Gender roles and sexual behavior.* Palo Alto, CA: Mayfield.

Ragan, Janet H. (1982). Gender displays in photographs. *Sex Roles, 8,* 33–44.

Ramey, Estelle (1972). Men's cycles. *Ms.,* Spring, 8–14.

Rauh, J. L., Schumsky, D. A. & Witt, M. T. (1967). Heights, weights, and obesity in urban school children. *Child Development, 38,* 515–530.

Rawlings, Edna T., & Carter, Dianne K. (1977). Feminist and nonsexist psychotherapy. In E. I. Rawlings & D. Carter (Eds.), *Psychotherapy for women.* Springfield, IL: Charles C Thomas.

Rebecca, Meda, Hefner, Robert & Oleshansky, Barbara (1976). A model of sex-role transcendence. *Journal of Social Issues, 32*(3), 197–206.

Rebelsky, Freda, & Hanks, C. (1971). Fathers' verbal interaction with infants in the first three months of life. *Child Development, 42,* 63–68.

Rees, L. (1953). Psychosomatic aspects of the premenstrual tension syndrome. *Journal of Mental Science, 99,* 62–73.

Reinisch, June M. (1974). Fetal hormones, the brain, and human sex differences: A heuristic, integrative review of the literature. *Archives of Sexual Behavior, 3,* 51–90.

Reiss, I. L. (1963). Sociological studies of sexual standards. In G. Winokur (Ed.), *Determinants of human sexual behavior.* Springfield, IL: Charles C Thomas.

Resick, Patricia, et al. (1981). Social adjustment of victims of sexual assault. *Journal of Consulting and Clinical Psychology, 49,* 705–712.

Rhodes, Barbara (1971). The changing role of the black woman. In R. Staples (Ed.), *The black family.* Belmont, CA: Wadsworth Publishing Co.

Rich, Adrienne (1980). Compulsory heterosexuality and lesbian existence. *Signs, 5,* 631–660.

Riffaterre, Brigitte B. (1965). Determination of pregnancy depression and its relation to marital status and group affiliation in a single ethnic group. *Dissertation Abstracts, 25,* 53–90.

Riger, Stephanie, & Galligan, P. (1980). Women in management: An exploration of competing paradigms. *American Psychologist, 35,* 902–910.

Rogers, Lesley, & Walsh, Joan (1982). Shortcomings of the psychomedical research of John Money and co-workers into sex differences in behavior. *Sex Roles, 8,* 269–282.

Romm, M. E. (1965). Sexuality and homosexuality in women. In J. Marmor (Ed.), *Sexual inversion: The multiple roots of homosexuality.* New York: Basic Books.

Rooks, E., and King R. (1973). A study of the marriage role expectations of black adolescents. *Adolescence, 8,* 317–324.

Rosaldo, Michelle Z. (1974). Women, culture, and society: A theoretical overview. In M. Z. Rosaldo & Lamphere L. (Eds.), *Woman, culture, and society.* Stanford: Stanford University Press.

Rosaldo, Michelle Z., & Lamphere, Louise (1974). *Woman, culture, and society.* Stanford: Stanford University Press.

Rosen, D. H. (1974). *Lesbianism: A study of female homosexuality.* Springfield, IL: Charles C Thomas.

Rosenbaum, Alan, & O'Leary, K. D. (1981). Marital violence: Characteristics of abusive couples. *Journal of Consulting and Clinical Psychology, 49,* 63–71.

Rosenberg, B. G. (1971). Social roles and social control: Changing concepts of masculinity-feminity. In J. P. Scott & S. F. Scott (Eds.), *Social control and social change.* Chicago: University of Chicago Press.

Rosenberg, B. G., & Sutton-Smith, B. (1964). Ordinal position and sex-role identification. *Genetic Psychology Monographs, 70,* 297–328.

——— (1968). Family interaction effects on masculinity-femininity. *Journal of Personality and Social Psychology, 8,* 117–120.

——— (1972). *Sex and identity.* New York: Holt, Rinehart & Winston.

——— (1974). Family structure and sex role variations. In *Nebraska Symposium on Motivation, 1973.* Lincoln: University of Nebraska Press.

Rosenberg, Florence R., & Simmons, Roberta G. (1975). Sex differences in the self-concept in adolescence. *Sex Roles, 1,* 147–159.

Rosenberg, Morris (1965). *Society and the adolescent self-image.* Princeton, NJ: Princeton University Press.

Rosenblatt, Paul C., & Cunningham, M. R. (1976). Sex differences in cross-cultural perspective. In B. Lloyd and J. Archer (Eds.), *Exploring sex differences.* New York: Academic Press.

Rosenkrantz, P. S., et al. (1968). Sex-role stereotypes and self-concepts in college students. *Journal of Consulting and Clinical Psychology, 32,* 287–295.

Rosenthal, R. (1966). *Experimenter effects in behavioral research.* New York: Appleton-Century-Crofts.

Rosner, M. (1967). Women in the kibbutz: Changing status and concepts. *Asian and African Studies, 3,* 35–68.

Rosnow, Ralph L. (1981). *Paradigms in transition: The methodology of social inquiry.* New York: Oxford University Press.

Rossi, Alice S. (1965). Women in science: Why so few? *Science, 148,* 1196–1202.

Roth, M. (1959). The phenomenology of depressive states. *Canadian Psychiatric Association Journal, 4* (Supplement), 532–554.

Roy, Maria (Ed.) (1977a). *Battered women.* New York: Van Nostrand.

———— (1977b) A current survey of 150 cases. In M. Roy (Ed.), *Battered women.* New York: Van Nostrand.

Rubin, Lillian (1979). *Women of a certain age.* New York: Harper & Row.

Rubin, Robert T., Reinisch, J. M. & Haskett, R. F. (1981). Postnatal gonadal steroid effects on human behavior. *Science, 211,* 1318–1324.

Ruble, Diane N. (1977). Premenstrual symptoms: A reinterpretation. *Science, 197,* 291–292.

Ruble, Thomas L. (1983). Sex stereotypes: Issues of change in the 1970s. *Sex Roles, 9,* 397–402.

Rumenick, Donna K., Capasso, Deborah R., & Hendrick, C. (1977). Experimenter sex effects in behavioral research. *Psychological Bulletin, 84,* 852–887.

Russell, Diana (1975). *The politics of rape: The victim's perspective.* New York: Stein and Day.

———— (1982). *Rape in marriage.* New York: Macmillan.

Russell, Diana E. H., & Howell, Nancy (1983). The prevalence of rape in the United States revisited. *Signs, 8,* 688–695.

Russo, Nancy F. (1979). Overview: Sex roles, fertility, and the motherhood mandate. *Psychology of Women Quarterly, 4,* 7–15.

Safran, C. (1976, November). What men do to women on the job: A shocking look at sexual harassment. *Redbook,* p. 148.

———— (1981, March). Sexual harassment: The view from the top. *Redbook.*

Sagarin, E. (1977). Incest: Problems of definition and frequency. *Journal of Sex Research, 13,* 126–135.

Saghir, M., & Robins, E. (1971). Male and female homosexuality: Natural history. *Comprehensive Psychiatry, 12,* 503–510.

———— (1973). *Male and female homosexuality.* Baltimore: Williams & Wilkins.

Salhanick, H. A., & Margulis, R. H. (1968). Hormonal physiology of the ovary. In J. J. Gold (Ed.), *Textbook of gynecologic endocrinology.* New York: Harper & Row.

Samuel, N., & Laird, D. S. (1974). The self-concepts of two groups of black female college students. *Journal of Negro Education, 43,* 228–233.

Sayers, Dorothy (1946). *Unpopular opinions.* London: Victor Gollancz.

Scanzoni, Letha, & Scanzoni, J. (1976). *Men, women, and change.* New York: McGraw-Hill.

Schafer, Siegrid (1977). Sociosexual behavior in male and female homosexuals: A study in sex differences. *Archives of Sexual Behavior, 6,* 355–364.

Schmidt, G., & Sigusch, V. (1970). Sex differences in responses to psychosexual stimulation by films and slides. *Journal of Sex Research, 6,* 268–283.

Schneidler, Gwendolyn G., & Patterson, D. G. (1942). Sex differences in clerical aptitude. *Journal of Educational Psychology, 33,* 303–309.

Schuckit, M. (1972). The woman alcoholic: A literature review. *Psychiatry in Medicine, 3*, 37–44.

Schuckit, M., et al. (1969). Alcoholism I.: Two types of alcoholism in women. *Archives of Environmental Health, 18*, 301–306.

Schultz, Ardelle P. (1977). Radical feminism: A treatment modality for addicted women. In E. I. Rawlings & D. K. Carter (Eds.), *Psychotherapy for women*. Springfield, IL: Charles C Thomas.

Schulz, Murial R. (1975). The semantic derogation of woman. In B. Thorne & N. Henley (Eds.), *Language and sex: Differences and dominance*. Rowley, MA: Newbury House.

Sclare, A. B. (1970). The female alcoholic. *British Journal of Addictions, 65*, 99–107.

Scott, Eileen, Illsley, R., & Biles, M. E. (1956). A psychological investigation of primigravidae, III. Some aspects of maternal behavior. *Journal of Obstetrics and Gynaecology of the British Empire, 63*, 494.

Scott, Foresman and Company (1972). *Guidelines for improving the image of women in textbooks*. Glenview, IL: Scott, Foresman.

Scottish Council for Research in Education (1939). *The intelligence of a representative group of Scottish children*. London: University of London Press.

———— (1949). *The trend of Scottish intelligence*. London: University of London Press.

Sears, R. R. (1965). Development of gender role. In F. A. Beach (Ed.), *Sex and behavior*. New York: John Wiley.

———— (1970). Relation of early socialization experiences to self-concepts and gender role in middle childhood. *Child Development, 40*, 267–289.

———— (1977). Sources of life satisfaction of the Terman gifted men. *American Psychologist, 32*, 119–128.

Seavy, Carol A., Katz, Phyllis A. & Zalk, Sue R. (1975). Baby X: The effects of gender labels on adult responses to infants. *Sex Roles, 1*, 103–110.

Seligman, Martin E. P. (1975). *Helplessness: On depression, development and death*. San Francisco: Freeman.

Selkin, J. (1975). Rape. *Psychology Today, 8*(8), 70.

Serbin, Lisa A., et al. (1973). A comparison of teacher response to the pre-academic and problem behavior of boys and girls. *Child Development, 44*, 796–804.

Serbin, Lisa A., Connor, Jane M., & Iler, Iris (1979). Sex-stereotyped and non-stereotyped introductions of new toys in the preschool classroom: An observational study of teacher behavior and its effects. *Psychology of Women Quarterly, 4*, 261–265.

Seyfried, B., & Hendrick, C. (1973). When do opposites attract? When they are opposite in sex and sex-role attitudes. *Journal of Personality and Social Psychology, 25*, 15–20.

Shachar, Sandra A., & Gilbert, Lucia A. (1983). Working lesbians: Role conflicts and coping strategies. *Psychology of Women Quarterly, 7*, 244–256.

Shainess, Natalie (1977). The equitable therapy of women in psychoanalysis. In E. I. Rawlings & D. K. Carter (Eds.), *Psychotherapy for women.* Springfield, IL: Charles C Thomas.

Shanor, Karen (1978). *The sexual sensitivity of the American male.* New York: Ballantine.

Shapiro, Johanna (1977). Socialization of sex roles in the counseling setting: Differential counselor behavioral and attitudinal responses to typical and atypical female sex roles. *Sex Roles, 3,* 173–184.

Shaver, Phillip (1976). Questions concerning fear of success and its conceptual relatives. *Sex Roles, 2,* 305–320.

Sherfey, Mary Jane (1966). The evolution and nature of female sexuality in relation to psychoanalytic theory. *Journal of the American Psychoanalytic Association, 14,* 28–128.

Sherman, Julia A. (1967). Problem of sex differences in space perception and aspects of intellectual functioning. *Psychological Review, 74,* 290–299.

——— (1971). *On the psychology of women: A survey of empirical studies.* Springfield, IL: Charles C Thomas.

——— (1978). *Sex-related cognitive differences.* Springfield, IL: Charles C Thomas.

——— (1980). Therapist attitudes and sex-role stereotyping. In A. M. Brodsky & R. Hare-Mustin (Eds.), *Women and psychotherapy.* New York: Guilford Press.

——— (1982). Mathematics, the critical filter: A look at some residues. *Psychology of Women Quarterly, 6,* 428–444.

Shields, Stephanie A., & Cooper, Pamela E. (1983). Stereotypes of traditional and nontraditional childbearing roles. *Sex Roles, 9,* 363–376.

Shope, David F. (1975). *Interpersonal sexuality.* Philadelphia: Saunders.

Shusterman, Lisa R. (1976). The psychosocial factors of the abortion experience: A critical review. *Psychology of Women Quarterly, 1,* 79–106.

Shuttleworth, Margaret (1959). A biosocial and developmental theory of male and female sexuality. *Marriage and Family Living, 22,* 163–170.

Shuy, Roger W. (1969). Sex as a factor in sociolinguistic research. Paper presented at the Anthropological Society of Washington. (Available from Educational Resources Information Clearinghouse, no. ED027522.)

Siegel, A., Stolz, L., Hitchcock, E., & Adamson, J. (1963). Dependence and independence in children. In F. Nye & L. Hoffman (Eds.), *The employed mother in America.* Chicago: Rand McNally.

Siegel, J. S. (1978). *Prospective trends in the size and structure of the elderly population, impact of mortality trends, and some implications.* U.S. Bureau of the Census, Current Population Reports (Special Studies Series P-23, no. 59, 2nd printing, rev.). Washington: U.S. Government Printing Office.

Siegelman, M. (1972) Adjustment of homosexual and heterosexual women. *British Journal of Psychiatry, 120,* 477–481.

Simon, J. G., & Feather, N. T. (1973). Causal attributions for success and failure at university examinations. *Journal of Educational Psychology, 64,* 45–56.

Simon, Rita J., Clark, Shirley M., & Galway, Kathleen (1967). The woman Ph.D.: A recent profile. *Social Problems, 15,* 221–236.

Simpson, G. E., & Yinger, J. M. (1965). *Racial and cultural minorities* (3rd ed). New York: Harper & Row.

Singer, R. N. (1968). *Motor learning and human performance.* New York: Macmillan.

Skin, Peter J., & Hoffman, S. (1978). Sports and male role strain. *Journal of Social Issues, 34*(1), 136–150.

Skord, K. G., & Schumacher, B. (1982). Masculinity as a handicapping condition. *Rehabilitation Literature, 43,* 284–289.

Slater, P. (1961). Parental role differentiation. *American Journal of Sociology, 67,* 296–311.

Slater, P. E. (1973, December). Sexual adequacy in America. *Intellectual Digest,* 132–135.

Smith, Elsie J. (1982). The black female adolescent: A review of the educational, career, and psychological literature. *Psychology of Women Quarterly, 6,* 261–288.

Smith, Howard L., & Grenier, Mary (1982). Sources of organizational power for women: Overcoming structural obstacles. *Sex Roles, 8,* 733–746.

Smith, I. M. (1964). *Spatial ability: Its educational and social significance.* San Diego: R. R. Knap.

Snow, Margaret E., Jacklin, Carol N., & Maccoby, Eleanor E. (1983). Sex-of-child differences in father-child interaction at one year of age. *Child Development, 54,* 227–232.

Snyder, Douglas K., & Fruchtmann, Lisa A. (1981). Differential patterns of wife abuse: A data-based typology. *Journal of Consulting and Clinical Psychology, 49,* 878–885.

Sohn, David (1982). Sex differences in achievement self-attributions: An effect-size analysis. *Sex Roles, 8,* 345–357.

Sommer, Barbara (1972). Menstrual cycle changes and intellectual performance. *Psychosomatic Medicine, 34,* 263–269.

——— (1973). The effect of menstruation on cognitive and perceptual motor behavior: A review. *Psychosomatic Medicine, 35,* 515–535.

Sontag, Susan (1972). The double standard of aging. *Saturday Review,* October, *55*(39), 29–38.

Spence, Janet T., & Helmreich, Robert L. (1978). *Masculinity and femininity.* Austin: University of Texas Press.

——— (1980). Masculine instrumentality and feminine expressiveness: Their relationships with sex-role attitudes and behaviors. *Psychology of Women Quarterly, 5,* 147–163.

——— (1981). Androgyny versus gender schema: A comment on Bem's gender schema theory. *Psychological Review, 88,* 365–368.

Spence, Janet T., Helmreich, R. L., & Stapp, J. (1975). Ratings of self and peers on sex-role attributes and their relations to self-esteem. *Journal of Personality and Social Psychology.*

Spiro, M. E. (1956). *Kibbutz: Venture in Utopia.* Cambridge, MA: Harvard University Press.

Spivack, G., & Spotts, J. (1965). The Devereux Child Behavior Scale: Symptoms behaviors in latency age children. *American Journal of Mental Retardation, 67,* 839–853.

Spreitzer, Elmer, & Riley, Lawrence (1974). Factors associated with singlehood. *Journal of Marriage and the Family, 36,* 533–542.

Spreitzer, Elmer, Snyder, Eldon E., & Larson, D. (1975). Age, marital status, and labor force participation as related to life satisfaction. *Sex Roles, 1,* 235–247.

Stafford, R. (1961). Sex differences in spatial visualization as evidence of sex-linked inheritance. *Perceptual and Motor Skills, 13,* 428.

Staines, Graham L. (1978). Wives' employment status and marital adjustment: Yet another look. *Psychology of Women Quarterly, 3,* 90–120.

Staines, G. L., Tavris, Carol & Jayaratne, Toby E. (1974, January). The Queen Bee Syndrome. *Psychology Today, 7*(8), 55.

Staples, Robert (1978). Masculinity and race: The dual dilemma of black men. *Journal of Social Issues, 34*(1), 169–183.

Stark, Rodney, & McEvoy, James (1970). Middle-class violence. *Psychology Today,* November, *30,* 52.

Steiger, John C. (1981). The influence of the feminist subculture in changing sex-role attitudes. *Sex Roles, 7,* 627–634.

Stein, Aletha H. (1969). The influence of social reinforcement in the achievement behavior of fourth-grade boys and girls. *Child Development, 40,* 727–736.

Stein, Aletha H., & Bailey, Margaret M. (1973). The socialization of achievement orientation in females. *Psychological Bulletin, 80,* 345–366.

Stein, L. S., et al. (1976). A comparison of female and male neurotic depressives. *Journal of Clinical Psychology, 32,* 19–21.

Stein, P. J., & Hoffman, Steven. (1978). Sports and male role strain. *Journal of Social Issues, 34*(1), 136–150.

Steinman, Ann, & Fox, P. J. (1970). Attitudes towards women's family role among black and white undergraduates. *The Family Coordinator, 19,* 363–367.

Steinmetz, Suzanne K. (1977). Wifebeating, husband beating — A comparison of the use of physical violence between spouses to resolve marital rights. In M. Roy (Ed.), *Battered Women.* New York: Van Nostrand.

Stephens, W. N. (1961). A cross-cultural study of menstrual taboos. *Genetic Psychology Monographs, 64,* 385–416.

Stericker, Anne (1981). Does this "he or she" business really make a difference? The effects of masculine pronouns as generics on job attitudes. *Sex Roles, 7,* 627–642.

Stevens, Barbara (1974). The sexually oppressed male. *Psychotherapy: Theory, Research and Practice, 11,* 16–21.

Stevenson, A. C. (1966). Sex chromatin and the sex ratio in man. In K. L. Moore (Ed.), *The sex chromatin*. Philadelphia: Saunders.

Stewart, M., Pitts, F., Craig, A., & Dieruf, W. (1966). The hyperactive child syndrome. *American Journal of Orthopsychiatry, 36,* 861.

Stiller, R. (1966). Why girls get pregnant. *Sexology,* October, 162–165.

St. John-Parsons, Donald (1978). Continuous dual-career families: A case study. *Psychology of Women Quarterly, 3,* 30–42.

Storms, Michael D. (1981). A theory of erotic orientation development. *Psychological Review, 88,* 340–353.

Storms, Michael D., et al. (1981). Sexual scripts for women. *Sex Roles, 7,* 699–708.

St. Peter, Shirley (1979). Jack went up the hill . . . but where was Jill? *Psychology of Women Quarterly, 4,* 256–260.

Straus, M. A. (1980). Wife beating: How common and why? In M. A. Straus and G. T. Hotaling (Eds.), *The Social Causes of Husband-Wife Violence*. Minneapolis: University of Minnesota Press.

Stricker, G. (1977). Implications of research for psychotherapeutic treatment of women. *American Psychologist, 32,* 14–22.

Strodtbeck, F. L., & Mann, R. D. (1956). Sex differentiation in jury deliberation. *Sociometry, 19,* 3–11.

Strodtbeck, F. L., James, Rita M., & Hawkins, C. (1957). Social status in jury deliberations. *American Sociological Review, 22,* 713–719.

Stroebe, Margaret S., & Stroebe, W. (1983). Who suffers more? Sex differences in health risks of the widowed. *Psychological Bulletin, 93,* 279–301.

Summerhayes, Diana L., & Suchner, R. W. (1978). Power implications of touch in male-female relationships. *Sex Roles, 4,* 103–110.

Sutherland, H., & Stewart, I. (1965). A critical analysis of the premenstrual syndrome. *Lancet, 1,* 1180–1183.

Sutton-Smith, B., & Rosenberg, B. G. (1970). *The sibling.* New York: Holt, Rinehart & Winston.

Swacker, Marjorie (1975). The sex of the speaker as a sociolinguistic variable. In B. Thorne & N. Henley (Eds.), *Language and sex: Difference and dominance.* Rowley, MA: Newbury House.

Szasz, T. S. (1965). Legal and moral aspects of homosexuality. In J. Marmor (Ed.), *Sexual inversion: The multiple roots of homosexuality.* New York: Basic Books.

Taleisnik, S., Caligaris, L., & Astrada, J. J. (1971). Sex differences in hypothalamo-hypophysial functions. In C. H. Sawyer and R. A. Gorski (Eds.), *Steroid hormones and brain function.* Berkeley: University of California Press.

Tamir, Lois M. (1982). *Men in their forties: The transition to middle age.* New York: Springer.

Tavris, Carol (1977, January). Masculinity. *Psychology Today, 19*(8), 34.

Taylor, H. P. (1962). Nausea and vomiting of pregnancy: Hyperemesis gravidarum. In W. S. Kroger (Ed.), *Psychosomatic Obstetrics, Gynecology, and Endocrinology.* Springfield, IL: Charles C Thomas.

———— (1972). Teen-age sex: Letting the pendulum swing. *Time*, August 21, 34–38.

Taylor, Marylee C., & Hall, Judith A. (1982). Psychological androgyny: Theories, methods, and conclusions. *Psychological Bulletin, 92,* 347–366.

Taylor, R. (1976). Psychosocial development of black youth. *Journal of Black Studies, 6,* 353–372.

Teen-age sex: Letting the pendulum swing. *Time,* August 21, 1972, 34–38.

Terman, L. M. (1951). Correlates of orgasm adequacy in a group of 556 wives. *Journal of Psychology, 32,* 115–172.

Terman, L. M., & Oden, Melita H. (1947). *The gifted child grows up.* Stanford University Press.

Terman, L., & Miles, C. (1936). *Sex and personality.* New York: McGraw-Hill.

Thorne, Barrie, & Henley, Nancy (1975). Difference and dominance: An overview of language, gender, and society. In B. Thorne & N. Henley (Eds.), *Language and sex: Difference and dominance.* Rowley, MA: Newbury House.

Thorpe, C. B. (1969). Status, race, and aspiration: A study of the desire of high-school students to enter a professional or a technical occupation. *Dissertation Abstracts, 29,* 10-A, 3672.

Torrey, Jane W. (1979). Racism and feminism: Is women's liberation for whites only? *Psychology of Women Quarterly, 4,* 281–293.

Tresemer, D. (1974). Fear of success: Popular, but unproven. *Psychology Today, 7*(10), 82.

Trivers, R. L. (1972). Parental investment and sexual selection. In B. Campbell (Ed.), *Sexual selection and the descent of man.* Chicago: Aldine.

Tsai, Mavis, & Wagner, N. (1978). Therapy groups for women sexually molested as children. *Archives of Sexual Behavior, 7,* 417–428.

Tsai, Mavis, Feldman-Summers, S., & Edgar, M. (1979). Childhood molestation: Variables related to differential impacts on psychological functioning in adult women. *Journal of Abnormal Psychology, 88,* 407–417.

Turner, Barbara F. (1982). Sex-related differences in aging. In B. B. Wolman (Ed.), *Handbook of developmental psychology.* Englewood Cliffs, NJ: Prentice-Hall.

Turner, B. F., & McCaffrey, J. H. (1974). Socialization and career orientation among black and white college women. *Journal of Vocational Behavior, 55,* 307–319.

Turner, C. D., & Bagnara, J. T. (1971). *General endocrinology* (5th ed.). Philadelphia: Saunders.

Tyler, B. B. (1958). Expectancy for eventual success as a factor in problem-solving behavior. *Journal of Educational Psychology, 49,* 166–172.

Tyler, Leona E. (1965). *The psychology of human differences.* New York: Appleton-Century-Crofts.

Ullian, Dorothy Z. (1976). The development of conceptions of masculinity and femininity. In B. Lloyd and J. Archer (Eds.), *Exploring sex differences.* New York: Academic Press.

Unger, Rhoda (1979). The rediscovery of gender. *American Psychologist.*

U.S. Bureau of the Census (1972). *Current Population Reports, 20*(r39), 5.
———— (1973). *We the American elderly.*
———— (1981). *Statistical Abstract of the U.S.: 1981* (102d ed.), Washington, DC.

U.S. Department of Commerce (1973). *Some demographic aspects of aging in the U.S. growth of the population 65 years and over.* Washington, DC: U.S. Government Printing Office.

U.S. Department of Labor (1978). *20 facts on women workers.* Washington, DC: U.S. Department of Labor.
———— (1980). *Perspectives on working women: A data book.* Washington, DC: U.S. Government Printing Office.
———— (1982). *20 facts on women workers.* Washington, D.C: U.S. Department of Labor.

U.S. Public Health Service, Center for Disease Control (1976). Comparative risks of three methods of midtrimester abortion. *Morbidity and Mortality Weekly Report,* November 26, 370.

von Franz, M.-L. (1964). The process of individuation. In C. G. Jung (Ed.), *Man and his symbols.* New York: G. P. Putnam's Sons.

Waber, Deborah P. (1977). Biological substrates of field dependence: Implications of the sex difference. *Psychological Bulletin, 84,* 1076–1087.

Waldron, J. (1976). Why do women live longer than men? *Social Science and Medicine, 10,* 349–362.

Waldron, J., & Johnston, S. (1976). Why do women live longer than men? *Journal of Human Stress, 2,* 19–29.

Walfish, S., & Myerson, Marilyn (1980). Sex role identity and attitudes toward sexuality. *Archives of Sexual Behavior, 9,* 199–204.

Walker, Lenore E. (1980). Battered women. In A. Brodsky & R. Hare-Mustin (Eds.), *Women and psychotherapy.* New York: Guilford.

Wallston, Barbara S. (1981). What are the questions in psychology of women? A feminist approach to research. *Psychology of Women Quarterly, 5,* 597–617.

Walters, Cathryn, Shurley, J. T., & Parsons, O. A. (1962). Differences in male and female responses to underwater sensory deprivation: An exploratory study. *Journal of Nervous and Mental Diseases, 135,* 302–310.

Ward, Russell A. (1979). The never-married in later life. *Journal of Gerontology, 34,* 861–869.

Warr, P., & Parry, G. (1982). Paid employment and women's psychological well-being. *Psychological Bulletin, 91,* 498–516.

Webb, A. P. (1963). Sex-role preferences and adjustment in early adolescents. *Child Development, 34,* 609–618.

Weideger, Paula (1976). *Menstruation and menopause.* New York: Knopf.

Weil, M. W. (1961). An analysis of the factors influencing married women's actual or planned work participation. *American Sociological Review, 26,* 91–96.

Weinberg, Martin S., & Williams, Colin (1974). *Male homosexuals: Their problems and adaptations.* New York: Oxford University Press.

Weinberg, S. K. (1955). *Incest behavior.* New York: Citadel Press.

Weiner, B., & Kukla, A. (1970). An attributional analysis of achievement motivation. *Journal of Personality and Social Psychology, 15,* 1–20.

Weingarten, Kathy (1978). The employment pattern of professional couples and their distribution of involvement in the family. *Psychology of Women Quarterly, 3,* 43–52.

Weis, Kurt, & Borges, Sandra S. (1973). Victimology and rape: The case of the legitimate victim. *Issues in Criminology, 8(2),* 71–115.

Weiss, Noel S., et al. (1976). Increasing incidence of endometrial cancer in the United States. *New England Journal of Medicine, 294,* 1259–1261.

Weiss, R. S. (1976). The emotional impact of marital separation. *Journal of Social Issues, 32(1),* 135–145.

Weissman, Myrna M., & Klerman, G. L. (1979). Sex differences and the epidemiology of depression. In E. S. Gomberg & V. Franks (Eds.), *Gender and disordered behavior.* New York: Brunner/Mazel. (Originally in *Archives of General Psychiatry,* 1977, *34,* 98–111.)

Weissman, Myrna M., & Paykel, E. S. (1974). *The depressed woman.* Chicago: University of Chicago Press.

Weisstein, Naomi (1971). Psychology constructs the female, or the fantasy life of the male psychologist. In M. H. Garskof (Ed.), *Roles women play: Readings toward women's liberation.* Belmont, CA: Brooks/Cole.

————— (1982). Tired of arguing about biological inferiority? *Ms.,* November, 41–46.

Weitz, Rose (1982). Feminist consciousness raising, self-concept, and depression. *Sex Roles, 8,* 231–242.

Weitz, Shirley (1976). Sex differences in nonverbal communication. *Sex Roles, 2,* 175–184.

Weitzman, Lenore J., Eifles, Deborah, Hodaka, Elizabeth, & Ross, Catherine (1972). Sex role socialization in picture books for pre-school children. *American Journal of Sociology, 72,* 1125–1150.

Wendland, M. M. (1967). Self-concept in southern Negro and white adolescents as related to rural-urban residence. Unpublished Ph.D. dissertation, University of North Carolina at Chapel Hill.

Werry, J. S., & Quay, H. C. (1971). The prevalence of behavior symptoms in younger elementary school children. *American Journal of Orthopsychiatry, 41,* 136–143.

Weston, P. J. & Mednick, Martha T. (1970). Race, social class, and the motive to avoid success in women. *Journal of Cross-Cultural Psychology, 1,* 285–291.

White, M. S. (1970). Psychological and social barriers to women in science. *Science, 170,* 413–416.

Whorf, B. L. (1956). *Language, thought, and reality.* Cambridge, MA: MIT Press.

Wilbur, C. B. (1965). Clinical aspects of female homosexuality. In J. Marmor (Ed.), *Sexual inversion: The multiple roots of homosexuality*. New York: Basic Books.

Wiley, Mary G., & Eskilson, Arlene (1982). Coping in the corporation: Sex-role constraints. *Journal of Applied Social Psychology, 12,* 1–11.

Williams, D. E. (1969). Self-concept and verbal mental ability in Negro preschool children. *Dissertation Abstracts, 29,* 3475-B.

Williams, John E., & Morland, J. Kenneth (1979). Comment on Banks's white preference in blacks: A paradigm in search of a phenomenon. *Psychological Bulletin, 86,* 28–32.

Williams, Juanita H. (1983). *Psychology of women* (2nd ed.). New York: Norton.

Willis, Frank N. (1966). Initial speaking distance as a function of the speaker's relationship. *Psychonomic Science, 5,* 221–222.

Willis, J. (1973). Addicts: *Drugs and alcohol re-examined.* London: Pitman.

Wilsnack, Sharon C. (1973a, April). Femininity by the bottle. *Psychology Today, 6*(11), 39.

———— (1973b). Sex role identity in female alcoholism. *Journal of Abnormal Psychology, 82,* 253–261.

Wilson, Edward O. (1975). *Sociobiology: The new synthesis.* Cambridge, MA: Harvard University Press.

———— (1978). *On human nature.* Cambridge, MA: Harvard University Press.

Winokur, G., Clayton, P. J., & Reich, T. (1969). *Manic depressive illness.* St. Louis: C. V. Mosby.

Winter, David, Stewart, A., & McClelland, D. (1977). Husband's motives and wife's career level. *Journal of Personality and Social Psychology, 35,* 159–166.

Witkin, H. A. (1964). Origins of cognitive style. In C. Sheerer (Ed.), *Cognition: Theory, research, promise.* New York: Harper & Row.

Witkin, H. A., Lewis, H. B., Hertzman, M., Machover, K., Meissner, P. B., & Wapner, S. (1954). *Personality through perception.* New York: Harper & Row.

Wittig, Michele A. (1979). Genetic influences on sex-related differences in intellectual performance: Theoretical and methodological issues. In M. A. Wittig & A. C. Peterson (Eds.), *Sex-related differences in cognitive functioning: Developmental issues.* New York: Academic Press.

———— (1983). Values, goals, and methods for a feminist psychology of gender. Paper presented at American Psychological Association Meetings, August, Los Angeles.

———— (1984). Value-fact-intervention dilemmas in the psychology of gender: A feminist perspective. *American Psychologist* (in press).

Wittig, Michele A., & Skolnick, Paul (1978). Status versus warmth as determinants of sex differences in personal space. *Sex Roles, 4,* 493–503.

Wohlford, Paul, et al. (1971). Older brothers' influence on sex-typed, aggressive, and dependent behavior in father-absent children. *Developmental Psychology, 4,* 124–134.

Wolff, Charlotte (1971). *Love between women.* New York: Harper & Row.

Wolfish, Steven & Myerson, Marilyn (1980). Sex role identity and attitudes toward sexuality. *Archives of Sexual Behavior, 9,* 199–204.

Wolpe, Joseph, & Lazarus, A. A. (1966). *Behavior therapy techniques: A guide to the treatment of neuroses.* New York: Pergammon Press.

Women on Words and Images (1972). *Dick and Jane as victims: Sex stereotyping in children's readers.* Princeton, NJ: Women on Words and Images.

Wong, M. R., Davey, J. & Conroe, R. M. (1976). Expanding masculinity: Counseling male in transition. *Counseling Psychologist, 6,* 58–61.

Woudenberg, Roger A. (1977). The relationship of sexual attitudes, attitudes toward women, and racial attitudes in white males. *Sex Roles, 3,* 101–110.

Wright, Logan, Schaefer, Arlene B., & Solomons, G. (1979). *Encyclopedia of pedriatric psychology.* Baltimore: University Park Press.

Wright, Paul H. (1982). Men's friendships, women's friendships, and the alleged inferiority of the latter. *Sex Roles, 8,* 1–20.

Yen, Wendy M. (1975). Sex-linked major-gene influences on selected types of spatial performance. *Behavior Genetics, 5,* 281–298.

Yogev, Sara (1982). Happiness in dual-career couples: Changing research, changing values. *Sex Roles, 8,* 593–606.

Young, W. C., Goy, R., & Phoenix, C. (1964). Hormones and sexual behavior. *Science, 143,* 212–218.

Zelditch, M. (1955). Role differentiation in the nuclear family. A comparative study. In T. Parsons & R. F. Bales (Eds.), *Family, socialization and interaction process.* Glencoe: IL: Free Press.

Zilbergeld, Bernie (1978). *Male sexuality.* Boston: Little, Brown.

Zilbergeld, Bernie & Ellison, Carol R. (1980). Desire discrepancies and arousal problems in sex therapy. In S. R. Leiblum & L. A. Pervin (Eds.), *Principles and practice of sex therapy.* New York: Guilford Press.

Zilbergeld, Bernie, & Evans, M. (1980, August). The inadequacy of Masters and Johnson. *Psychology Today, 14*(3), 28–43.

Zimbardo, P. G., & Meadow, Wendy (1974). Sexism springs eternal — In *The Reader's Digest.* Paper presented at Western Psychological Association Meetings, April.

Zimmerman, Don H., & West, Candace (1975). Sex roles, interruptions and silences in conversation. In B. Thorne & N. Henley (Eds.), *Language and sex: Difference and dominance.* Rowley, MA: Newbury House.

Zimmerman, E., & Parlee, Mary B. (1973). Behavioral changes associated with the menstrual cycle: An experimental investigation. *Journal of Applied Social Psychology, 3,* 335–344.

Zuckerman, M., & Wheeler, L. (1975). To dispel fantasies about the fantasy-based measure of fear of success. *Psychological Bulletin, 82,* 932–946.

Index

Gelles, R., 362
Gender
  definition of term, 3
  distinctions among variables of, 236–237
  feminist perspective on, 80–81
  power and, 81
  society and, 2
  as status, 80–81
  technology for choice of, 405
Gender constancy, 67–68
Gender differences, 137–152
  achievement and, 196–197
  achievement motivation and, 202–204
  activity and, 148–149, 155–156
  aggressiveness and, 143–147, 158
  alcoholism and, 326
  anxiety and, 150
  attitudes toward rape and, 351
  attribution of success and, 207–208
  biological and environmental factors in,
    140
  brain hemisphere use and, 243
  in childhood, 158
  communication styles and, 403
  developmental theory on, 4–5
  definition, 3
  depression rates and, 321–322
  dominance and, 146–147
  drug abuse and, 325–326
  empathy and, 150–151
  field dependence and, 196
  future roles for women and, 409–411
  gender-role stereotypes and, 138–139
  genes and, 233
  hypothalamus and, 240, 241
  individual differences versus, 140–141
  infancy and, 155–156
  influenceability and, 149–150
  intelligence and, 186–187, 388–389
  language use and, 212–215
  Maccoby and Jacklin studies on, 141–143
  mathematical ability and, 188
  in moral development, 71
  motor skills and, 190, 202
  perceptual speed and, 189–190
  prenatal, and hormones, 234–235
  real difference and, 139
  reasoning ability and, 188
  school adjustment and, 159
  self-confidence and, 147–148, 174
  self-esteem and, 386–387
  sex reassignment and, 239
  sexuality and, 282–287
  sociability and, 151
  social learning theory on, 62, 65, 66
  sociobiology on sexual selection and,
    59–60
  spatial ability and, 187–188, 196
  touch and, 155–156, 216–218
  toy and game preference and, 158
  verbal ability and, 187, 201
Gender identity
  androgyny and, 100
  biological influences on, 236–239
  childrearing and assignment of, 237–238
  cognitive development and, 67
  Erikson's developmental theory on, 53
  lesbians and, 305–306
  male sex-role identity (MSRI) paradigm
    with, 110–114

psychoanalytic theory on, 45
Genderism, and advertising, 40
Gender role, 237
  acquisition of, 86
  black women and, 381–384
  cognitive developmental model on, 67–68
  college women and, 7
  depression and, 322–323
  elderly women and, 182–183
  female, see Female role
  feminist perspective on, 82
  gender schema theory on, 77
  male, see Male role
  masculinity-femininity tests and, 94
  rape and socialization to, 358–360
  research questions and stereotypes in, 10
  sex role-strain (SRS) paradigm and, 114–
    115
  socialization and, 82, 158–159
  social learning theory on, 63–65
  stages of, 102–104
  story content of magazines and, 39
  study of psychology of women and, 6–7
  women's studies courses on, 404
Gender-role stereotypes, 138–139
  adults' treatment of infants and, 157
  anxiety in women and, 150
  choice of subjects in research and, 10
  empathy in women and, 150–151
  femininity-achievement incompatibility and,
    161–162
  gender-role development and, 103
  language use and, 212
  leadership role for women and, 174
  lesbianism and, 301–302
  men and, 106–107
  rape and, 359
  research on, 5, 10
  schools and, 158
  talking time and, 215
  women and work and, 170–172
Gender schema theory, 75–79, 85
Gender similarities, 16
  adults' treatment of infants and, 156–157
  in infancy, 115, 155
  language use and, 215
  psychology of women and, 5
  sexuality and, 297
Genesis (Bible), 30, 34
Genghis Khan, 37
Gestalt therapy, 341–342
Gigy, L., 178
Gilbert, L., 302, 303, 343
Gilkes, C., 394
Gilley, H., 215
Gilligan, Carol, 71–75, 268, 403
Ginzberg, E., 200
Goble, F., 127
Goddesses, 27, 29, 30, 33
Goffman, Erving, 40, 216
Gold, D., 113
Goldberg, D., 172, 397
Goleman, Daniel, 38, 39
Golub, S., 253, 258
Gomberg, E., 324, 325
Gomes, Beverly, 337–338, 339
Good provider role for men, 119–120
Goode, E., 315
Goodfield, H., 165
Gordon, E., 262

Marriage (cont.)
  Judaic tradition on, 33
  lesbians and, 301, 302, 316
  provider role for men in, 119–120
  rape in, 357
  sex before, 289–290
  violence in, see Battered wives
Marshall, J., 205
Martin, D., 77, 78, 300, 301, 312, 364, 367
Martyna, W., 224
Marxist feminism, 84
Mary, 30, 36
Mary Tyler Moore Show (television show),
  177
Masculine behavior, 10
Masculinity complex, 52
Masculinity-femininity (M-F) concept, 90–94
  androgyny and, 96
  bipolarity of, 92, 93–94
  M-F continuum in, 91–92
  M-F typology in, 90–91
Masochism, 10, 46–47
Mastectomy, 269–271
Masterman, 408
Masters, William, 5, 128, 130, 274–281,
  292–295
Masturbation, 280, 282, 283–284, 287–288,
  294, 340
Mathematical ability, and gender differences,
  188, 191–192
Mathematics courses, and girls, 191–194
Matriarchal societies, 36–38, 382–383
Matthews, K., 127
Maughan, B., 75
Mayo, C., 216
McArthur, L., 111, 158
McCaffrey, J., 382
McClelland, D., 10, 202
McClintock, M., 255
McConnel-Ginet, S., 214
McEvoy, J., 364, 367
McGee, M., 233
McGinnis, M., 178
McGraw-Hill Book Co., 228
McHugh, M., 208
McKay, R., 134, 172
McKenna, W., 10, 405
McKinlay, S., 259
McMahan, Ian, 147, 207
McMillan, J., 213, 214
Mead, Margaret, 82, 170, 187, 309, 409–410
Meadow, W., 38
Medea, 38–39
Mednick, M., 389, 391, 400
Meece, J., 191, 194
Meeker, B., 80
Mehrabian, A., 219
Meiselman, K., 374
Men
  anxieties about female sexuality in, 28–29
  death of spouse and, 182
  experience of women different from experi-
    ence of, 6–7
  fear of success among, 206
  feminine evil belief and, 26
  friendship patterns among, 178
  hormone cycles in, 258
  as normative, 30–31, 220–221, 334
  parenting and, 55–56
  psychology of, see Psychology of men

  study of psychology of women by, 7
Menninger, Karl, 221
Menopause, 259–261
  biological factors in, 260–261
  environmental and cultural factors in,
    260–261
Menstruation, 246–259
  biology of, 246–250
  cramps in, 250–252
  criticism of research on, 254–257
  derivation of word, 29
  estrus cycle of animals compared with,
    246–247
  hormones and, 239, 248–250
  implications of research on, 258
  male anxieties in mythology about, 28
  moon and, 29
  phases of, 247
  psychological aspects of, 252–258
  research on, 10, 258
  sensory fluctuations with, 258–259
Mental illness
  diagnosis differences for men and, 321
  gender ratios in, 320–321
Mester, R., 269
Meyer, J., 12
Meyer-Bahlburg, H., 235
Middle age, 179–180
Middle Ages, 26, 28
Miele, J., 189
Miles, C., 108
Military
  black men in, 134
  male role and, 120–121
  women in, 121
Mill, John Stuart, 402
Miller, C., 227
Millett, Kate, 28, 81
Minor, J., 384
Minority group
  lesbians as, 310
  women as, 396–398
  see also Black men; Black women
Minuchin, S., 326, 332
Mischel, W., 62
Modeling, and gender role identity, 111
Models in psychological research, 8–10
Monahan, L., 206
Money, John, 234, 236–239, 240
Monroe, M., 323
Montagu, A., 233
Montezuma, 37
Moon, in mythology, 29–30
Moos, R., 256
Moral development, 69–75
Moreland, J. K., 385
Mortality rates, and men, 126–128
Moss, H., 155
Motherhood
  black women and, 381–382, 384–385, 391,
    400
  Chodorow's theory of, 54–56
  female role and, 168
  gender-role identity of son and, 112–113
  lesbians and, 301, 306, 316
  New Right on, 410
  role of mother in, 164, 166–169
  supermother in, 201
  women's psychological development and, 52

Motherhood mandate, 168
Motivation
  achievement and, 201–204, 208
  black women and, 388–389
Motor skills, and gender differences, 190,
  202
Moulton, J., 223, 224
Mulvihill, D., 359
Murray, S., 389, 391
Mussen, P., 100, 111, 112
Myerson, M., 292
Mythology, 20–40
  castrating vagina symbol in, 27–28
  creation myths in, 30, 34, 37
  feminine evil theme in, 25–27, 33–35, 39
  fertility goddess/earth mother in, 27
  Judeo-Christian tradition and, 31–36
  Jungian psychology on, 25
  male anxiety about female sexuality in,
    28–29
  male as normative in, 30–31
  male sexuality and, 129–131
  matriarchal societies and, 36–38
  nonconscious ideologies and, 38–40
  psychoanalytic theory similarities with, 50
  women as sexual beings and, 27–29

Naftolin, F., 240
Narcissism
  homosexuality and, 307
  psychoanalytic theory on, 46–47
National Council of Churches, 41
National Organization of Women (NOW),
  84
Natural selection in evolution, 56–57, 62
Near Eastern mythology, 29, 32, 34
Neugarten, Bernice, 259
Neuroticism, 100
New Right, 85, 140
New Testament, 36, 41–42
New Yorker, The, 212
Nieva, V., 170, 173
Nonconscious ideologies, 38–40
Nonsexist therapy, 342–344
Nurturant-authoritative therapy, 331

Oakland Growth Study, 324
Oakley, Ann, 166–167
Oberstone, A., 305
Obordo, A., 382
Observation, in therapy, 341
Observational learning, 62, 64, 66
Observer effects in research, 11–12
Occupation, see Work
Oden, M., 199
Oedipal complex, 45, 46, 48, 51, 306
Offir, C., 370
O'Keefe, Eileen, 68, 102, 103–104
Old Testament, 32, 33, 34–35
O'Leary, V., 109, 110, 122, 176
Operant conditioning, 340
Oral contraceptives, 255
Oral stage of development, 45
Orbach, S., 340
Orgasm, female, 128, 278
  clitoral, 278–279
  consistency in, 282–283
  development of women's ideas about, 287–
    288

  dysfunction with, 293–295
  Freud's theory on, 44, 50
  G-spot in, 281–282
  lesbian relationships with, 301–302
  single, satiating, 279–280
  uterine, 281
  vaginal, 278–279
  vulvar, 281
Orgasm, male, 128–129, 131, 132
Orloff, K., 101
Osofsky, J. and H., 266
Oros, C., 356
Our Bodies, Ourselves (Boston Women's
  Health Collective), 246
Overton, W., 68

Packard, T., 179
Paige, K., 255, 257
Paloma, M., 175
Palme, O., 411
Pandora, 26
Pankhurst, Christabel, 411
Papanek, H., 166
Parcell, S., 356
Parenthood
  Chodorow's theory of, 54–56, 57
  dual-career couples and, 176
  father in childrearing and, 123
  femininity-achievement incompatibility
    and, 160–161
  gender identity and assignment and, 237–
    238
  lesbians and, 301, 316
  mathematical skills and expectations in,
    194
  research needs in, 403
  smiling in, 219
  sociobiology on, 57–59
  treatment of infants in, 156–157
  working mothers and, 175
  see also Fatherhood; Motherhood
Parke, R., 122
Parkes, C., 181
Parlee, M., 14, 253, 254, 258
Parsons, Talcott, 384
Parthogenesis, 37
Passivity, in psychoanalytic theory, 46–47
Patriarchal societies, 32–33, 36–37, 410
Patterson, D., 189
Patterson, C., 116
Paul, St., 32, 36
Penis envy, 10, 44, 46, 49–50, 55, 340
Peplau, Anne, 178, 182, 302, 314
Perceptual speed abilities, 189–190
Perez-Reyes, M., 269
Performance
  fear of success and, 205
  menstruation and, 258
Perls, Fritz and Laura, 341
Perry, John, 281
Persky, H., 240
Personal identity, 163–164
Personality
  androgyny and, 100
  batterer in marital violence and, 365
  exceptional women and, 199–200
  Freud's theory on, 45, 46, 48
  Jung's theory on, 22–24
  masculinity-femininity of, 94
Peterson, R., 168

police attitudes toward, 351, 353
psychological responses of victims in, 352–355
rapist profile in, 355
sex and aggression and, 357–358
silent rape reactions in, 354–355
theoretical views of, 350–351
wider impact of, 360–361, 378
women's behavior and fear of, 360–361
Rape-crisis counselors, 351
Rape trauma syndrome, 352
Rauh, J., 386
Rawlings, E., 342, 343
Reasoning ability, and gender differences, 188
Rebecca, M., 102
Rebelsky, F., 123
Rees, L., 256
Reinforcement, and social learning theory, 62, 63, 66
Reinisch, J., 241
Reis, M., 113
Religion
feminism and, 40–42
inclusive language used in, 41–42
leadership in, 40
menstruation and teachings of, 257
ordination of women in, 40
see also Mythology
Research
choice of subjects in, 10
double-blind method in, 12
experimenter effects in, 11
feminist alternatives to, 14–15
future needs in, 402–405
gender-fair, 14, 15
interpretation bias in, 12–13
observer effects in, 11–12
publishing results in, 13
sexist bias in, 6, 7–15
theoretical model bias in, 8–10
Resick, P., 354
Resko, B., 158
Reuther, Rosemary Radford, 41
Reverse sexism, 3
Revised Standard Version (Bible), 41–42
Rich, Adrienne, 310
Richter, L., 274
Rieger, W., 331
Riffaterre, B., 261
Riley, L., 178
Robins, E., 305, 312, 315, 316
Rogers, L., 239
Role playing, in assertiveness training, 344
Roles, see Female role; Gender role; Male role
Roman Catholic Church
feminine evil belief in, 26
women's issues in, 41
Roman Empire, 35
Romm, M., 312
Rooks, E., 134
Rosaldo, M., 82
Rosen, D., 304, 305
Rosenberg, B., 10, 90, 159
Rosenberg, F., 162
Rosenman, R., 127
Rosenkrantz, P., 106, 138–139
Rosenthal, R., 11
Rosnow, R., 407, 408
Roy, M., 364–366

Roth, M., 32
Rubin, Lillian B., 179–180, 240
Ruble, Diane, 138–139, 256
Rumenik, D., 11
Russell, D., 357, 358, 360
Russo, N., 168

Sadomasochistic pornography, 358
Safran, C., 371–372
Sager, C., 290
Saghir, M., 312, 315
Salhanick, H., 234
Samuel, N., 387
Sayers, D., 35
Scanzoni, L. and J., 176
Schafer, S., 314
Schema, concept of, 76
Schmidt, G., 286
Schneidler, G., 189
Schuck, J., 144, 146
Schuckit, M., 325
Schwartz, P., 316
Schulz, Muriel, 222
Scottish Council for Research in Education, 186
Sears, R., 100, 111
Seavy, C., 156
Segal, B., 320
Self-concept
black men and, 132–133, 385–387
femininity-achievement incompatibility and, 162
gender schema theory on, 77
Self-confidence
gender differences and, 147–148, 174
supervisory role for women and, 174
Self-esteem
androgyny and, 99–100
black women and, 385–387
gender differences in, 386–387
women as minority group and, 397–398
women in middle age and, 180
Self-examination for breast cancer, 269
Self-socialization, 68–69
Selkin, J., 355
Sensitivity, and gender differences, 155–156
Separation distress, and gender differences, 155
Serbin, L., 144, 323
Sex aggression in rape, 355–357
Sex differences, 3
brain and, 232
mental illness and, 320–321
psychoanalytic theory on, 45
psychology of, 141–143
Sexism, 3–4
behavior therapy with, 341
gender as status and, 80–81
language and, 223–229
psychological research and, 6, 7–15
psychotherapy and, 333–339
Sex-linked traits, 232–233
Sex reassignment, 239
Sex-role identity paradigm, 134
Sex-role strain (SRS) paradigm, 114–115, 118, 135
Sexual dysfunction, 292–297
disorders of sexual desire in, 295–296
Kegel exercises in, 297
Masters and Johnson approach to, 292–293

0 1 2 3 4 5 6 7 8 9